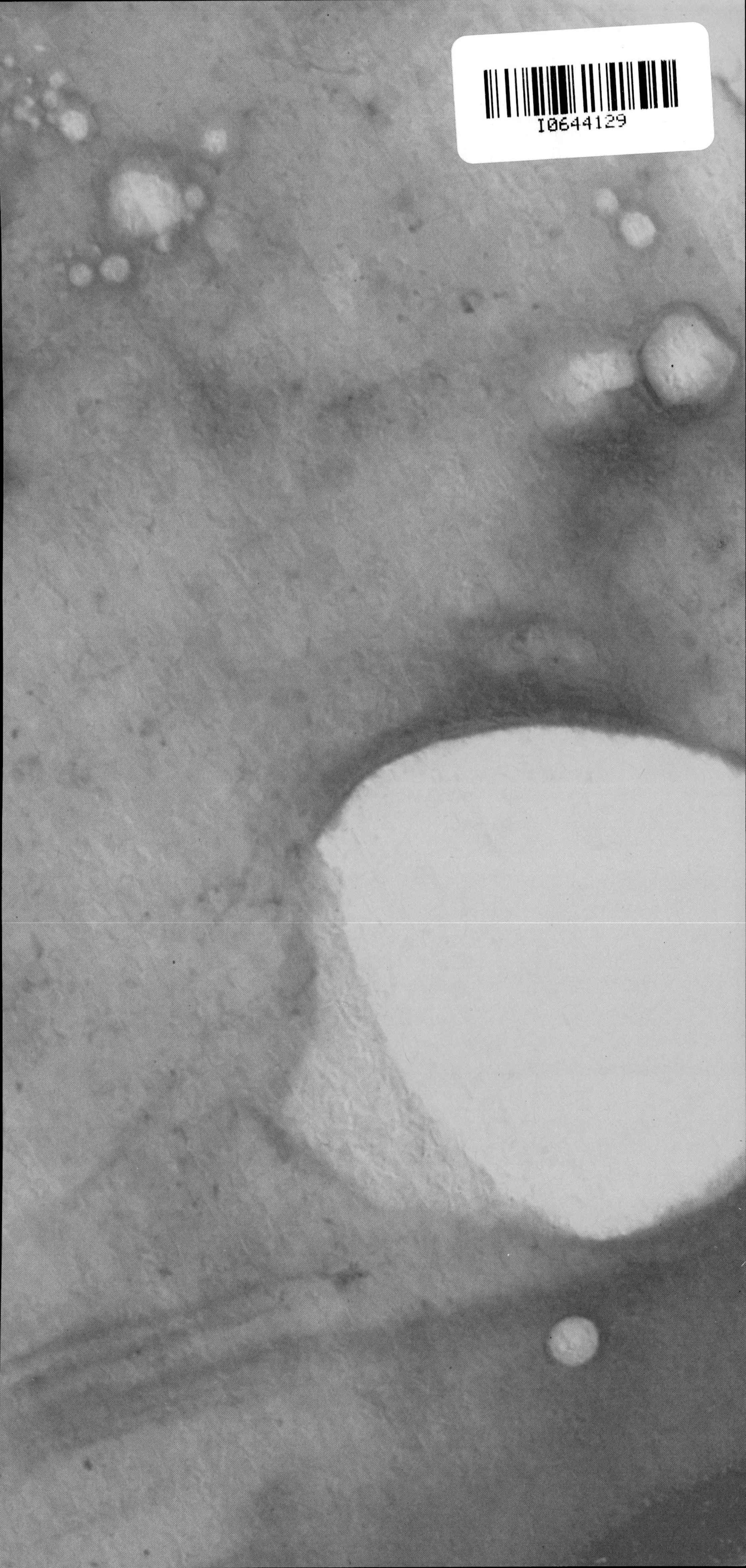

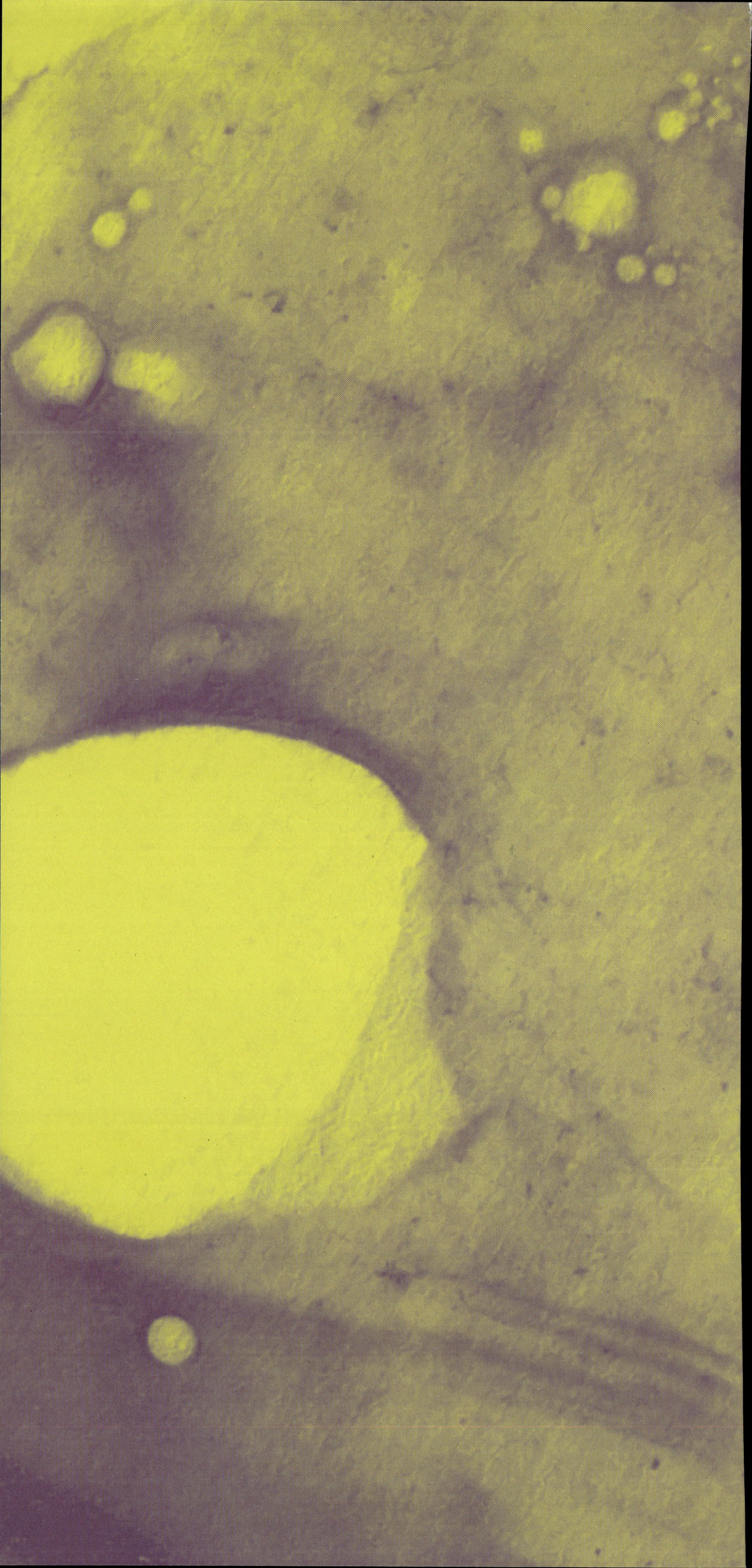

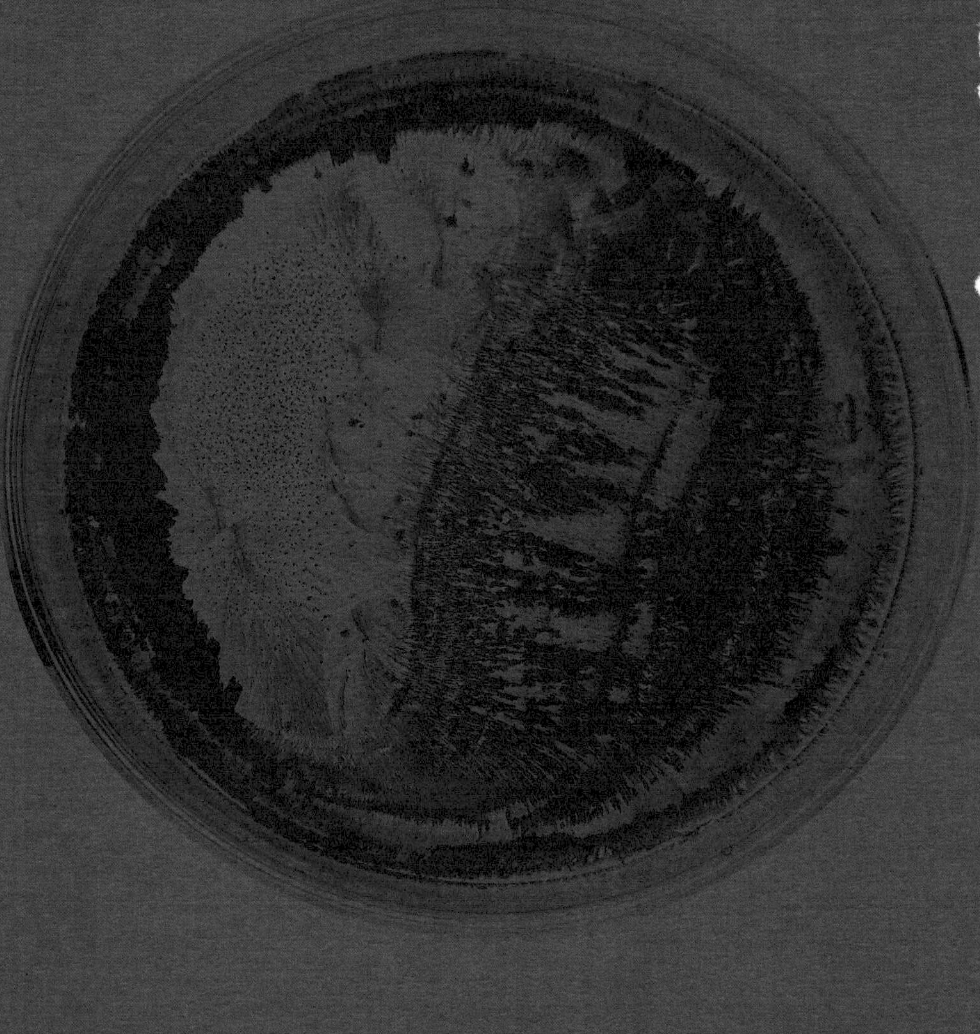

Edition Angewandte – Book series of
the University of Applied Arts Vienna
Edited by Ulrike Kuch, Rector

edition:'angewandte
Universität für angewandte Kunst Wien
University of Applied Arts Vienna

Choreo-ethical Assemblages – Embodied Research as Cosmopoietic Œkology

By Mariella Greil

DE GRUYTER

Table of Contents

Poetic Distillates
– A Short Guide to Reading the Blue Pages

Throughout this book, poetic condensations emerge as tangible afterimages – bare, fragmentary, and ethically entangled, interrupting the flow and tone of the scholarly text.

The poetry changes the pace of reading and also invites the reader to navigate the text choreographically.

These poems are spread throughout the book, embedded particles that act as interval signals. They appear in associative proximity to passages where thematic resonances or conceptual connections emerge, functioning as affective residues. They could be seen as extensive, speculative footnotes, or maybe even as sensuous narrations countering the argument of the book.

Collection of Poetic Distillates – Overview

Prelude

Barbara Putz-Plecko

Resonating with the Beats of a Bold Heart

Mariella Greil's practice of artistic and conceptual theory construction is rooted in her particularly refined, subtle capacity for perception, expression, and reflection, her extensive expertise and great openness towards the still unknown, and her genuine interest in 'others' (in human beings and everything that constitutes worlds, including that which goes beyond the human-centric view). For more than ten years, she has made a significant contribution to exploring the potentials of performance and its implementation as a highly relevant and extremely multifaceted field of contemporary artistic practice in the academic landscape. Through her artistic research – which always takes ethical, philosophical, and biopolitical perspectives into account and is embedded within vibrant transdisciplinary networks – she is in continuous dialogue with distinguished colleagues in the arts, humanities, and various scientific fields.

As former head of the Department of Art and Communication Practices and Vice-Rector for Research at the University of Applied Arts Vienna, I am deeply grateful to Mariella: by advocating for situated, embodied, and choreographic practices as 'world-making' (as described in this publication), and in her understanding of performance as an assertion, activation, and negotiation of caring coexistence, she has lived, shared, and expanded our understanding of the arts as communicative and relational practices. She does this by emphasising dialogue and supporting the 'we' as a 'performative collectivity' – as a generative capacity that acts collectively.

Communicating means building relationships, and Mariella achieves this in her own distinctive manner: with the utmost openness and a courageous heart, trusting her body as an instrument. As a choreographer and researcher, as she says herself, she is particularly attracted to 'embodied' communication and its micro-phenomenological density and richness, including the intensity of perception in performance. Presence and resonance are essential elements of embodied communication. In Mariella's artistic work and in her research and teaching, we can compellingly experience both. *Presence* is identified by Otto Scharmer, action researcher at MIT, as 'the core capacity needed to access the field of the future' and described as 'deep listening, [...] being open beyond one's preconceptions and historical ways of making sense'.[i]

German sociologist Hartmut Rosa, on the other hand, posits that *resonance* describes a meaningful relationship with the world as a counterweight to continuous acceleration and alienation, referring to a mutual emotional interaction that allows

i. See C. Otto Scharmer et al., *Presence: Exploring Profound Change in People, Organisations, and Society* (Doubleday, 2004).

us to experience the world as something breathing, responsive, connected, and as something that touches and changes us.[ii]

Writing this, I recall two recent performance sequences by the artist that made me feel the exceptional intensity of such a process and left a lasting impression on me: first, Mariella cowering on the lava field of a volcano, absorbing the inner movement of the mountain, breathing with it, exposed, and at the same time embedded within an archaic landscape that appeared both beautiful and eerie;[iii] second, Mariella, holding a bare heart in her outstretched hands, entirely turned towards it, feeling it, sensing it, absorbing it with all her senses… and finally preparing it and offering it to the witnessing audience.[iv]

I see this huge ability for bold resonance that enables Mariella to achieve what she describes as her motivation, effort, and aim: to reveal the tangible dimensions of presence in all its various manifestations; to allow oneself to be fragile and vulnerable; to unwaveringly advocate for the value of encounters, relationships, and solidarity (even more so at a time when these values are being eroded); to explore in practice how ethical responsibility and social organisation can be embodied (beyond mere reflection); to negotiate complex phenomenological relationships with the world as mediated by our senses; to experiment with new aesthetic practices and views on biospheric contexts and biotic communities; and to thereby sense other potential realities.[v]

Mariella does not see any dichotomy between theory and practice, subjectivity and objectivity, or artistic and scientific approaches; rather, she trusts in the innovative potential of intertwining these notions in each case. In this sense, this publication once again conveys how artistic research can open, deconstruct, and expand our perception and understanding of the world, with all its vivid, experimental, sensory, and media-diverse practices – practices that are equal parts reflexive and conceptual. If we engage with the artist, her body, her bare body, a body that becomes an ethical agent, one that restores an ethic of encounter, one that enables us to cultivate alternative collectivities – that body returns our gaze. And what does this gaze that bounces back on us fall upon? What does it touch? What does it provoke? What does it challenge? How bold is *our* heart?

ii. See Hartmut Rosa, *Resonanz: Eine Soziologie der Weltbeziehung* (Suhrkamp, 2016).

iii. See 'Shaken Grounds. Seismography of Precarious Presences', accessed 10 March 2026, https://shaken-grounds.org.

iv. Mariella Greil, *Opening Up the Choreographic: Presence 3*, Angewandte Performance Laboratory (APL), University of Applied Arts Vienna, 2020.

v. See Mariella Greil, 'Choreo-ethische Experimente', in Barbara Putz-Plecko, ed., *Heterotopien des Künstlerischen: Lehren als künstlerische Praxis* (Edition Angewandte, De Gruyter, 2025), 344–55.

Preface

Alexander Damianisch

In my foreword to this generous offering, I am delighted to express my fascination with the notion of *cosmopoiesis*. I myself once introduced the concept of *heteropoiesis*, which describes how a formative force opens up in relation to alternatives: if something is the way it is here, how might it unfold in a project that does not merely attempt to approach the other as a context and instead situates itself within the cosmic? The relations are different, that is clear – with more, one is less alone. Mariella Greil's book is equally rich, and I will frequently return to the flow of relations she offers us there – always in dialogue with the other, with others.

What I am particularly interested in is something already embedded in the word *dialogue* itself: the prefix *dia*. In Greek, this refers to a movement of passing-through; *dia* denotes a thoroughfare, a passage, a mediation, an event that does not remain at the surface but unfolds between, through, and across something. It carries within it the idea of transition, transparency, permeability – a reminder that meaning is not based on the singular but on the relational fabric that emerges in the act of passing-through.

Thus, it is not the singular characteristics that are compelling but the relations that emerge. This is why Mariella Greil has woven conversations directly into her text, demonstrating how relational her work is – in her artistic practice, in her research practice, in the way she connects the two, and in what she does beyond them, for which we still need concepts, which we may find through her work. How beautiful it is that the book begins by invoking a 'Mariella Greil Museum' – with its etymological echo of a place of study, a school of art or poetry, and simultaneously a temple or shrine of the Muses, yet entirely secular, a repository and place to display objects relating to art, literature, or science. What we hold in our hands is a book, and our readings are attempts to engage with the in-between that is offered to us. It is a challenge, and what a wonderful challenge it is.

Alongside these passages, it is also the introductions that are of interest. And here I return to the image of the river: we always step into the relation, the flow afresh, but one might also say that the body itself flows as it enters the river. I am not the one who began the sentence. A deep understanding is inscribed into Mariella Greil's work – one that embraces this very engagement. I consider this to be the very willingness to undertake an ongoing introduction. The book also demonstrates a rigorous openness to and readiness for encounter, both sensory and intellectual. One senses how deeply Mariella Greil commits herself to contexts that extend beyond her while also acknowledging that they have shaped her. In this I see an expression of artistic integrity.

With each page, each chapter, one feels as if one is looking in a new direction, and Mariella Greil willingly shares what is to be taken along. She exceeds expectations with great detail and brings us with her. It is well worth taking the time for this. Again and again, it becomes clear that behind the contexts she names lie extremely dynamic experiential spaces. We come to know not only concepts but also the contexts of her practice.

I hope that reading this book will allow all readers more becoming-in-between, more relations, and more of what could be called cosmopoietic resonances. Perhaps *diapoesy* could be an apt term to describe what Mariella Greil offers here – something that enables us to encounter each other differently. Once again, artistic research opens up to us a precise space of experience that would otherwise remain sensorially inaccessible – dynamic, unconstrained, and open in all directions.

All of this is only possible through, on the one hand, institutional support and, on the other, targeted funding, such as that provided by the FWF through its programmes for the development and advancement of the arts and artistic research. My thanks therefore go to the FWF for creating and maintaining such a context, but above all to the author and all her collaborators. Without them, this expansion of our horizon of understanding would not have been possible.

I warmly invite you to enter this poetic cosmos and assure you that you will leave it transformed – with a deeper understanding, especially of your own transformation.

What is salient to an organism through perception and in regard to action depends on its body, its emotions, its history, its long- and short-term projects, and an overarching enculturation process. Such contextualized agents will act differently depending on their situation and bring forth perceptual experiences highly dependent on that situation. Cognition, from the most basic to the most advanced, happens in the dynamic unfolding of interactions with affordances in the material environment.

Christian Kronsted and Shaun Gallagher, 'Dances and Affordances: The Relationship between Dance Training and Conceptual Problem-Solving', *Journal of Aesthetic Education* 55, no. 1 (2021): 38.

What is also needed is a cultivated, patient, sensory attentiveness to nonhuman forces operating outside and inside the human body.

Jane Bennett, *Vibrant Matter: A Political Ecology of Things* (Duke University Press, 2010), 14.

Assemblages #1

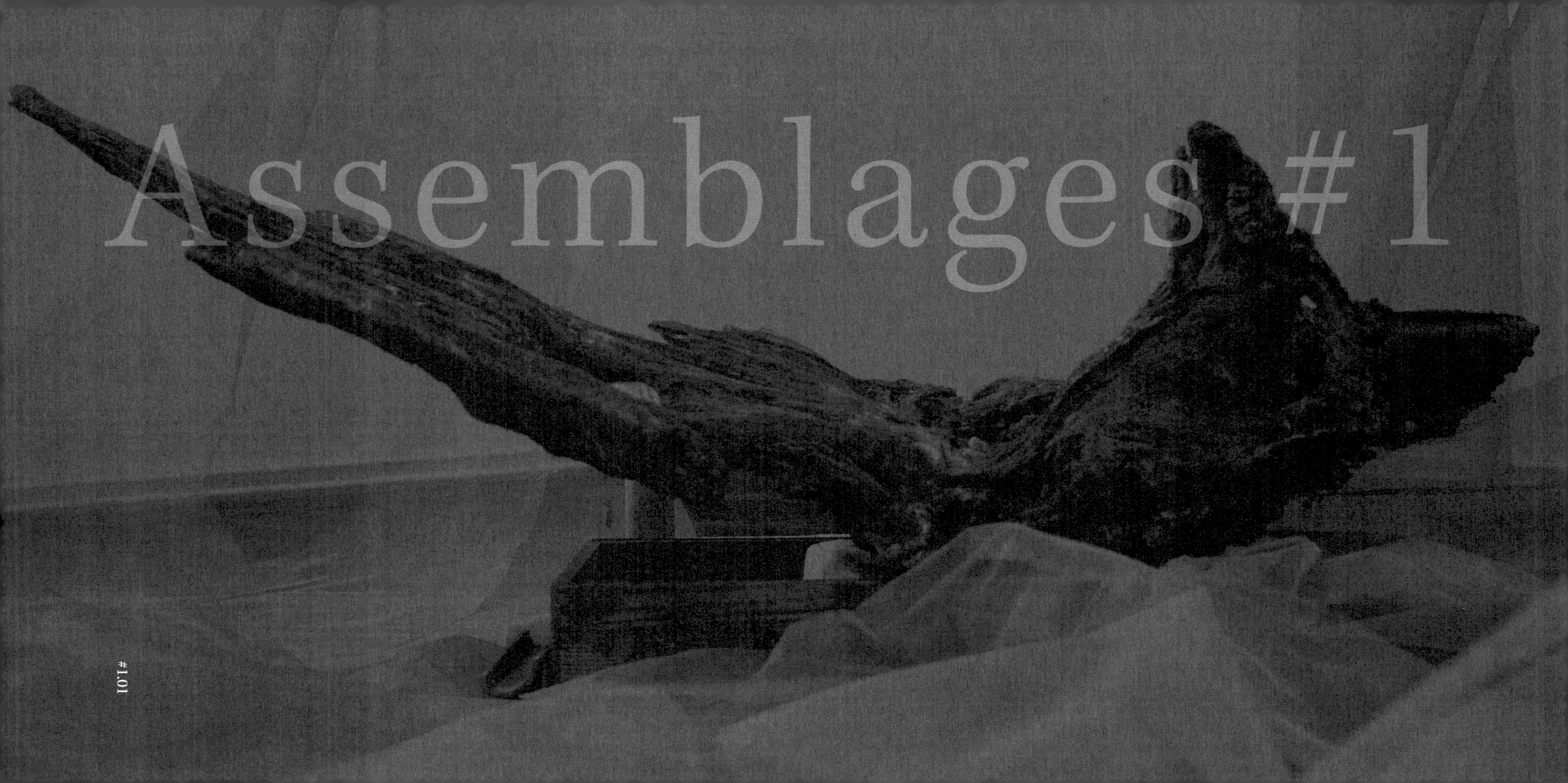

#1.01

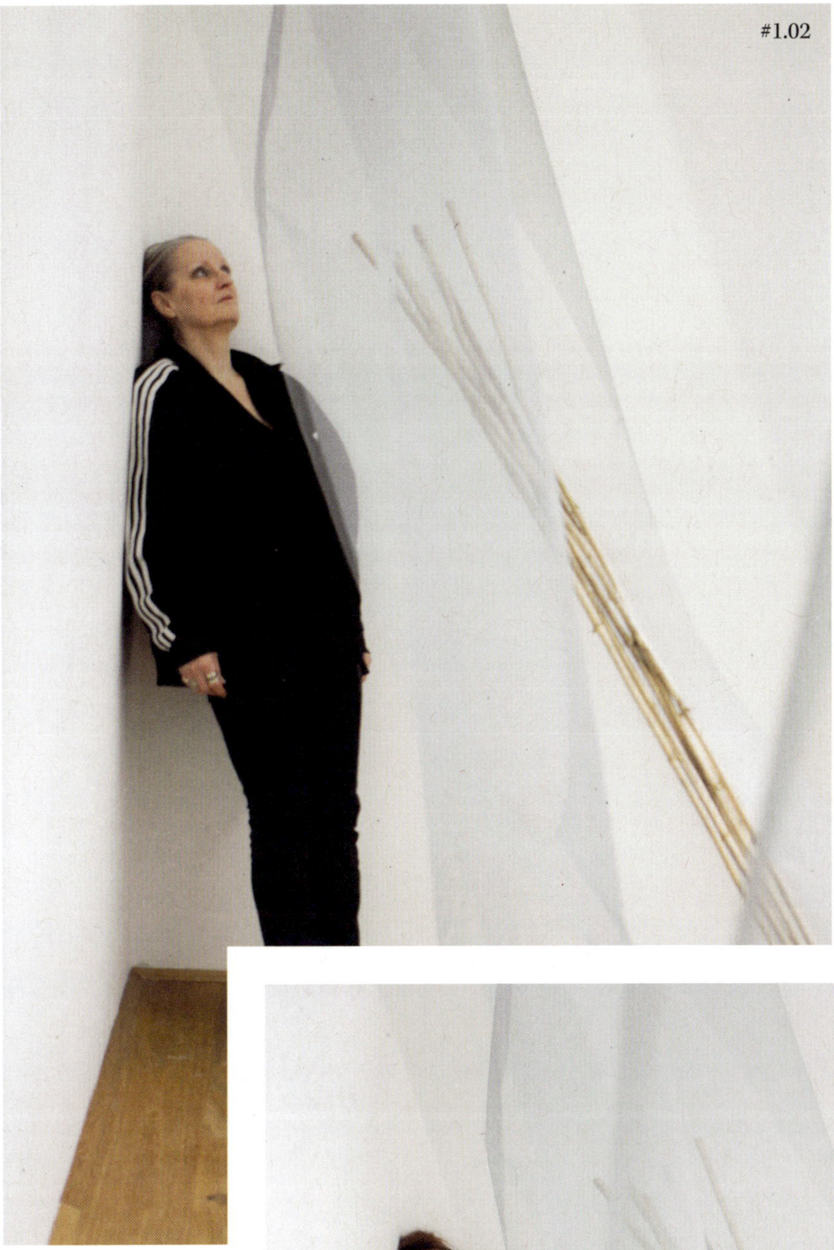
#1.02

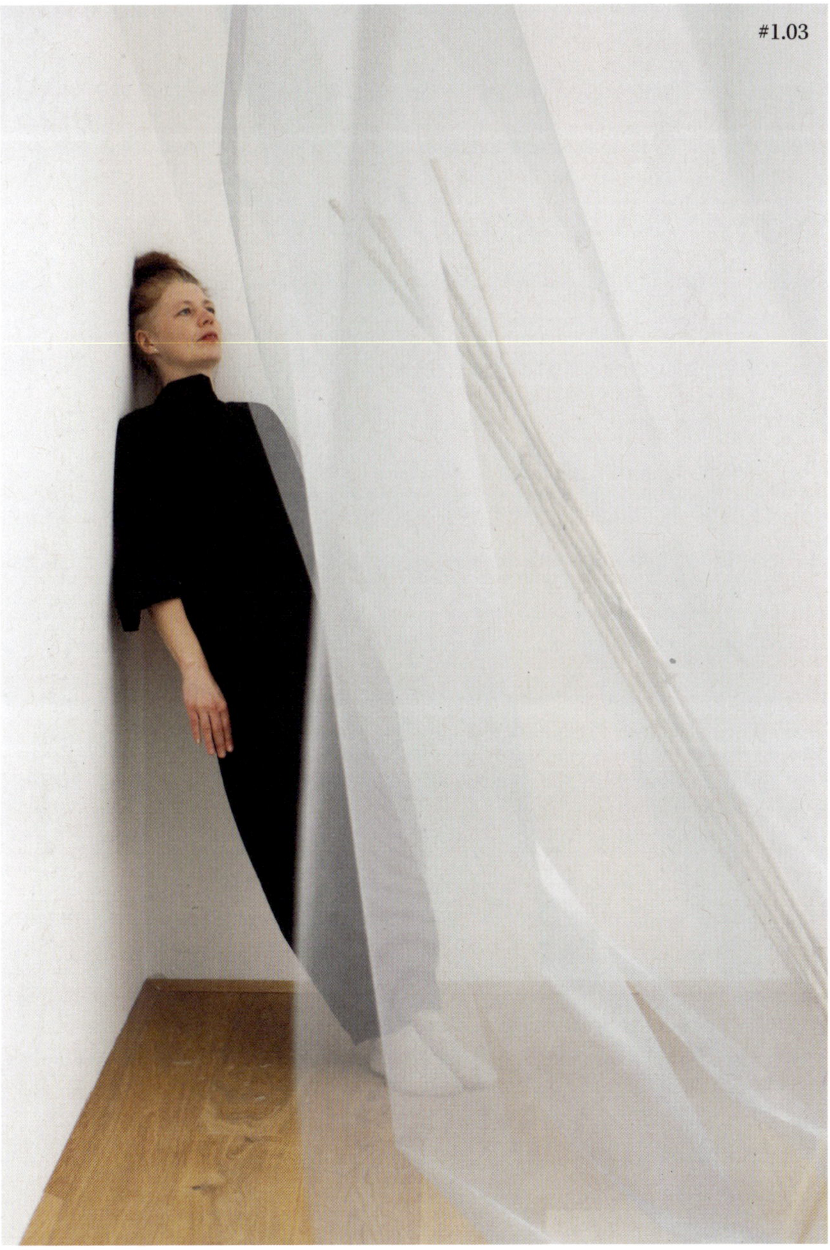
#1.03

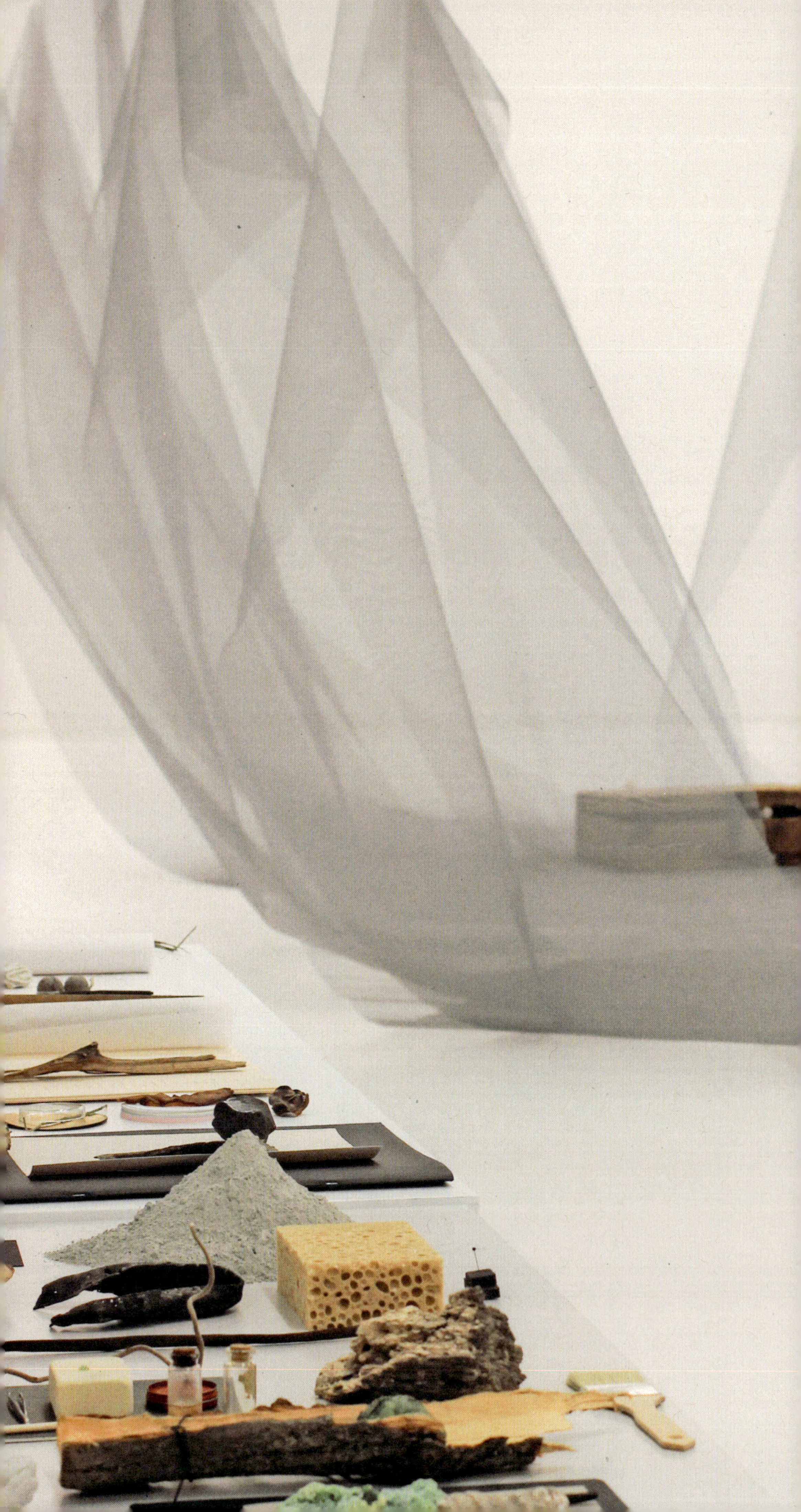

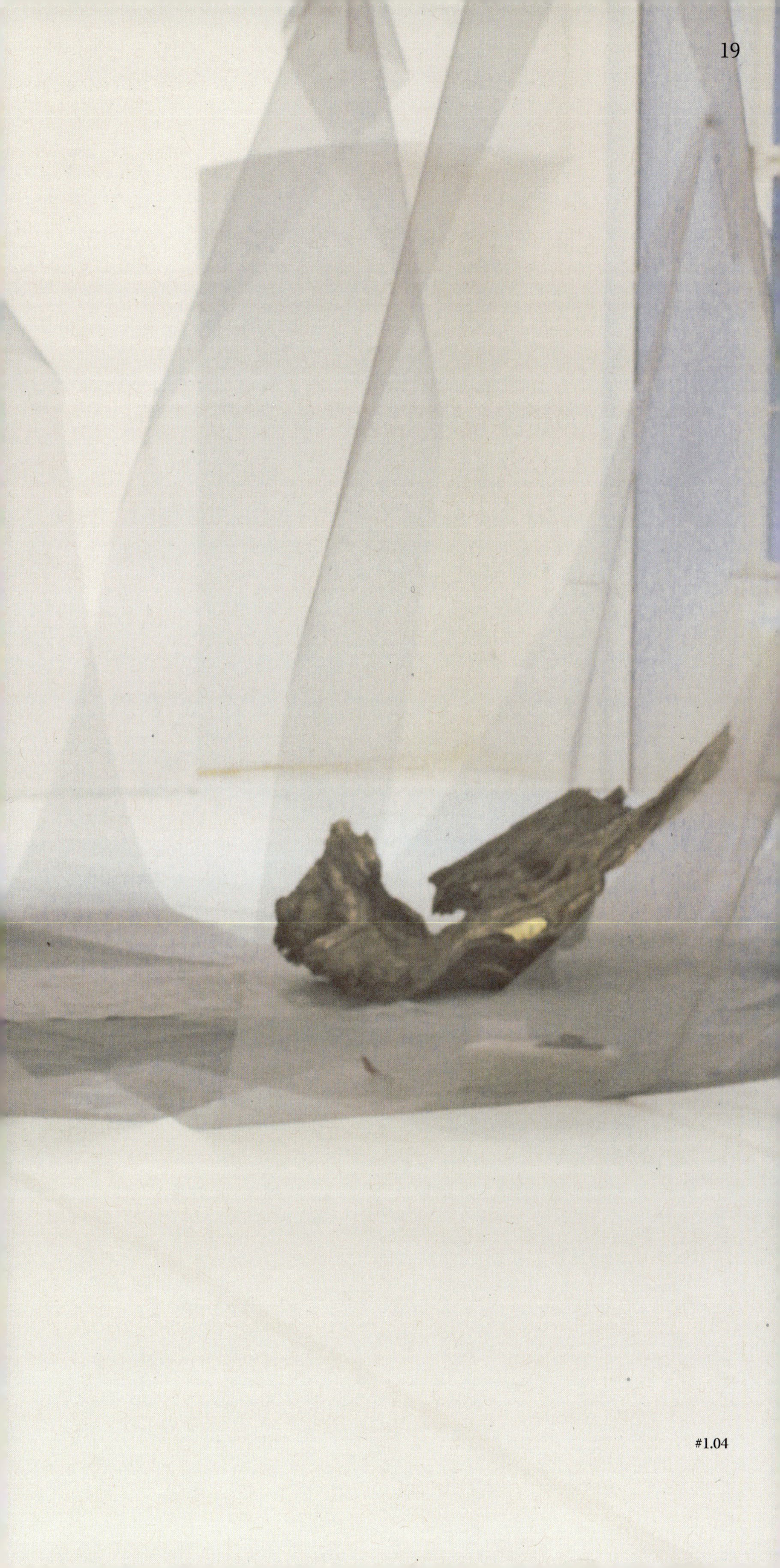

#1.04

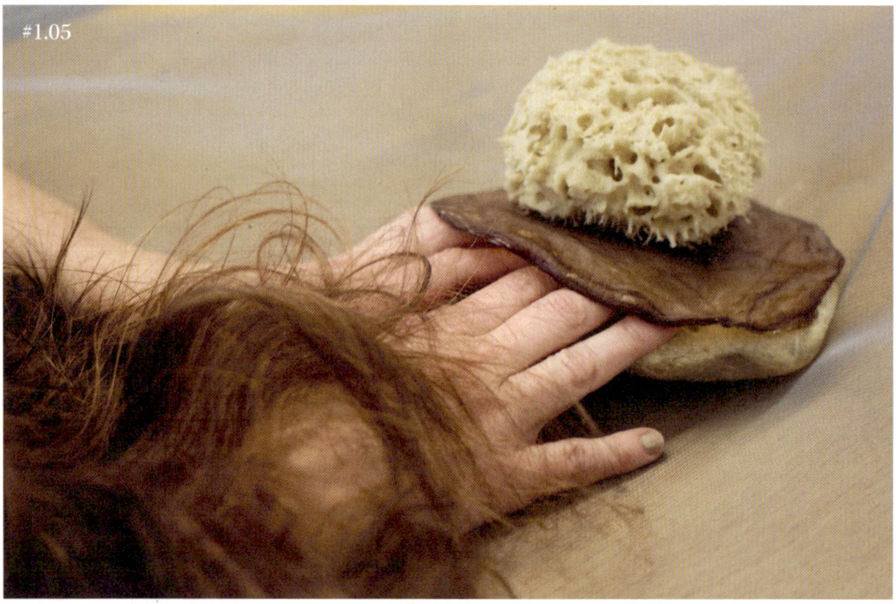

#1.05

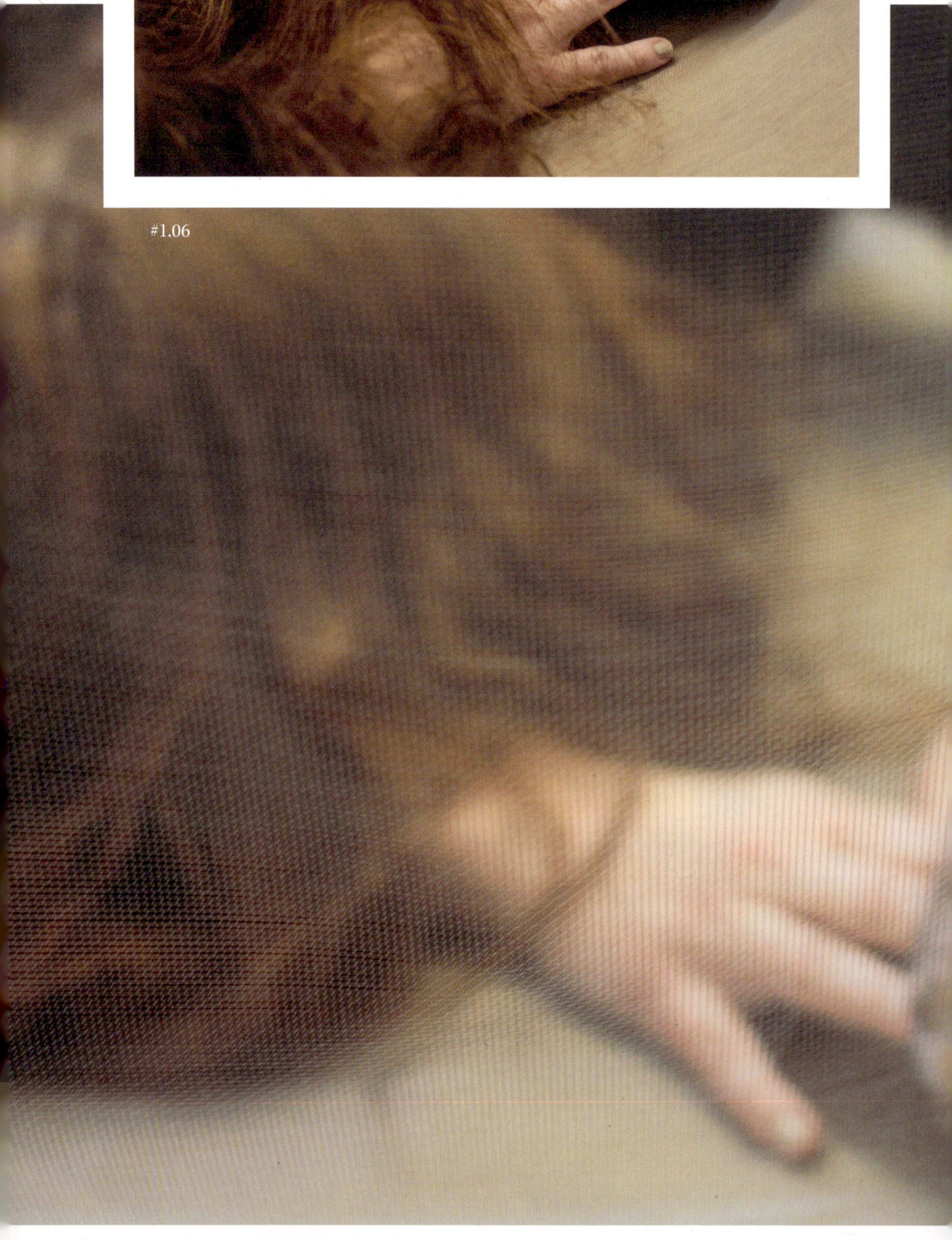

#1.06

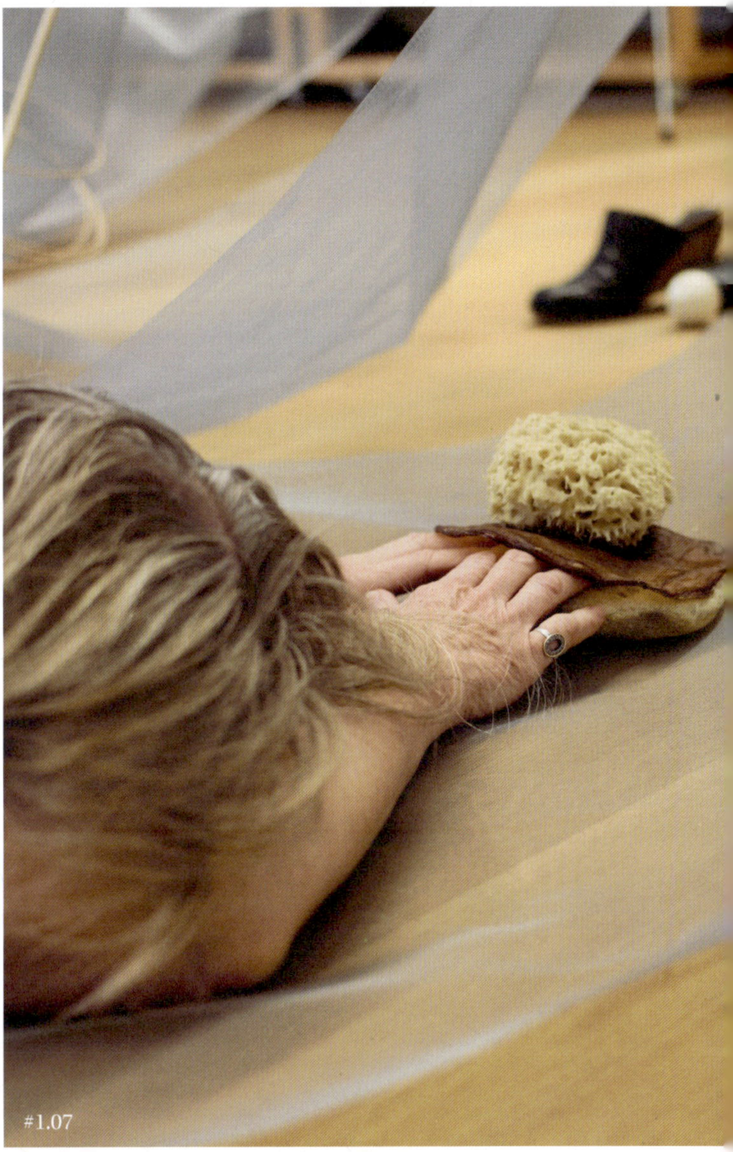

#1.07

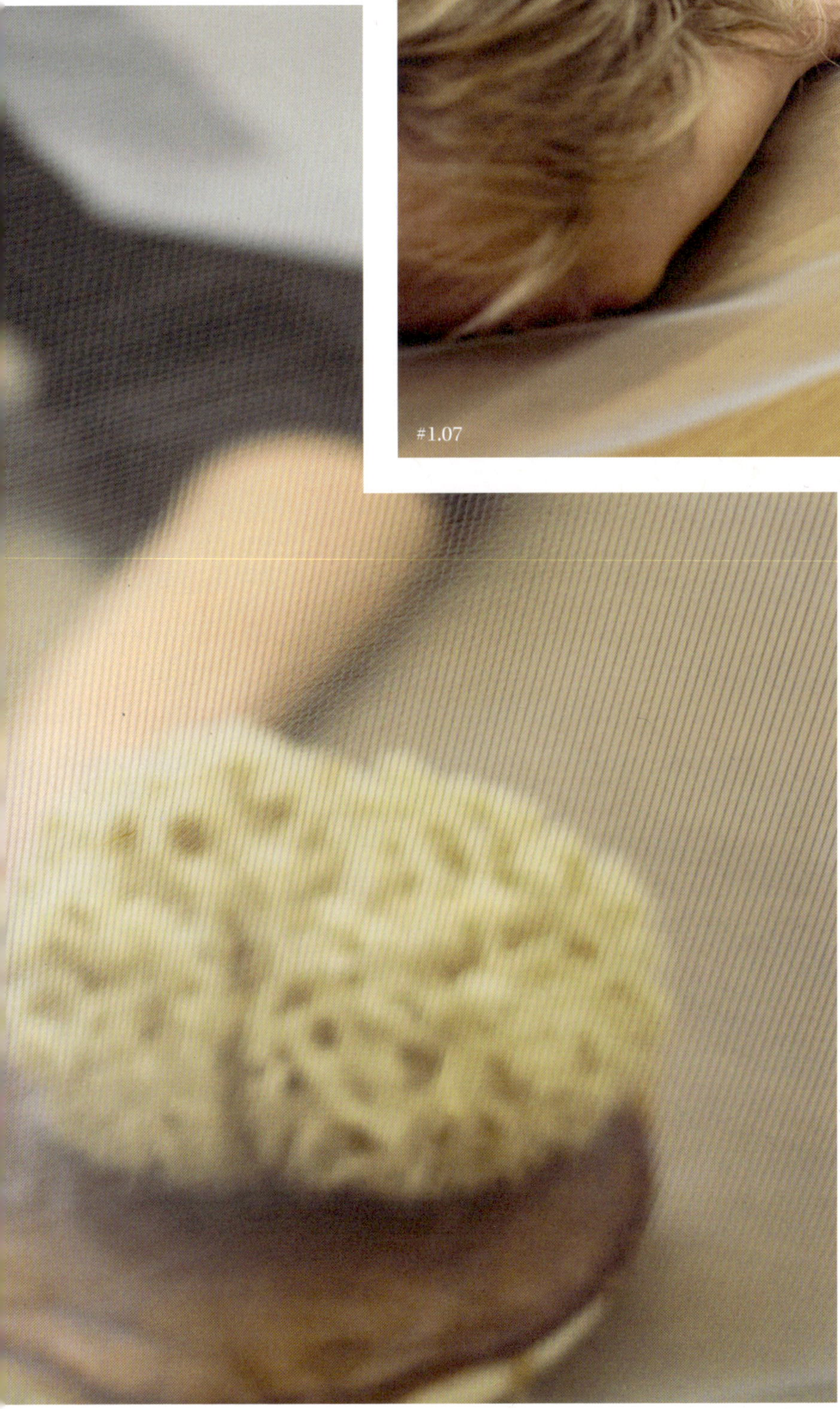

#1.08

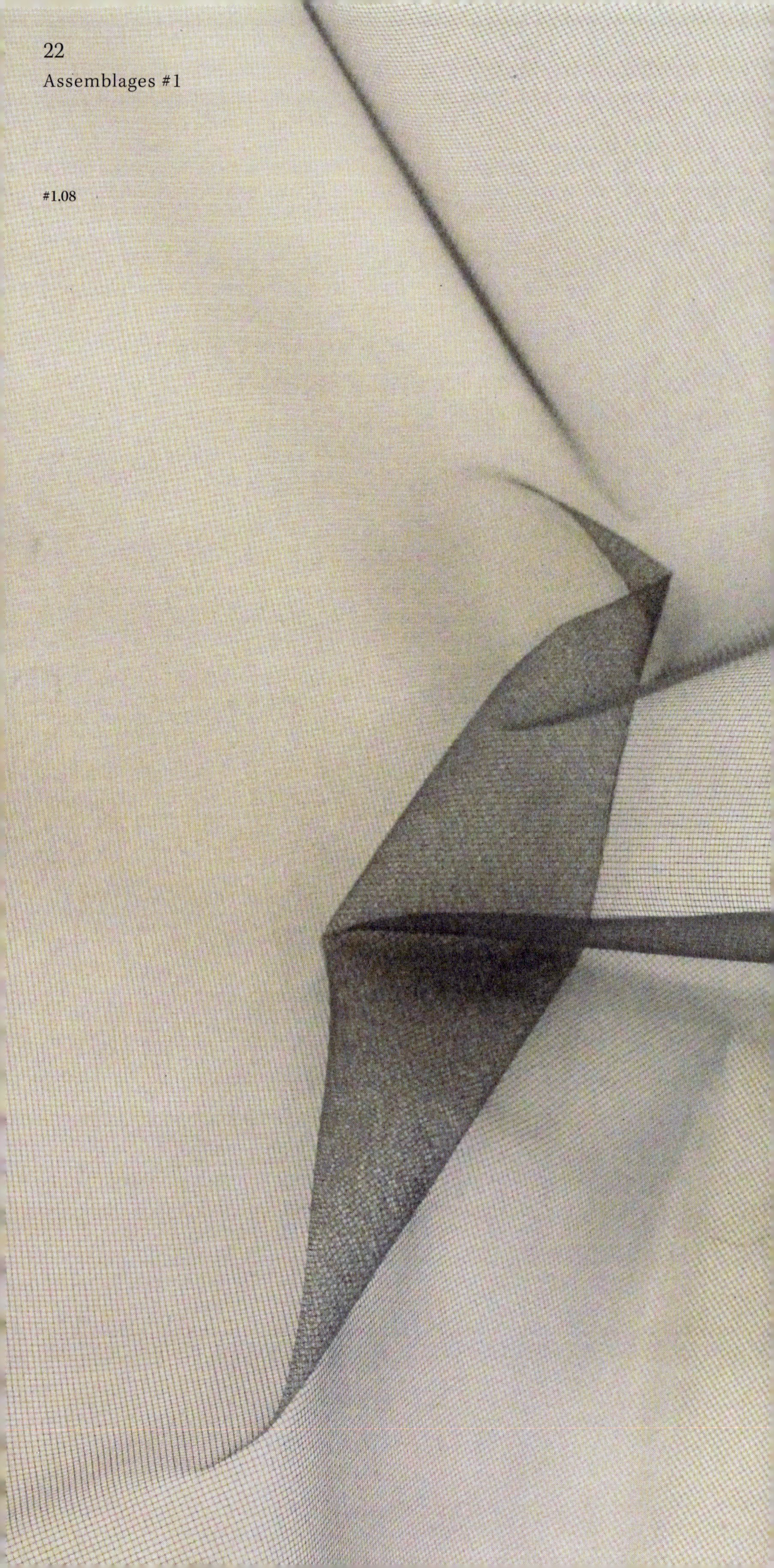

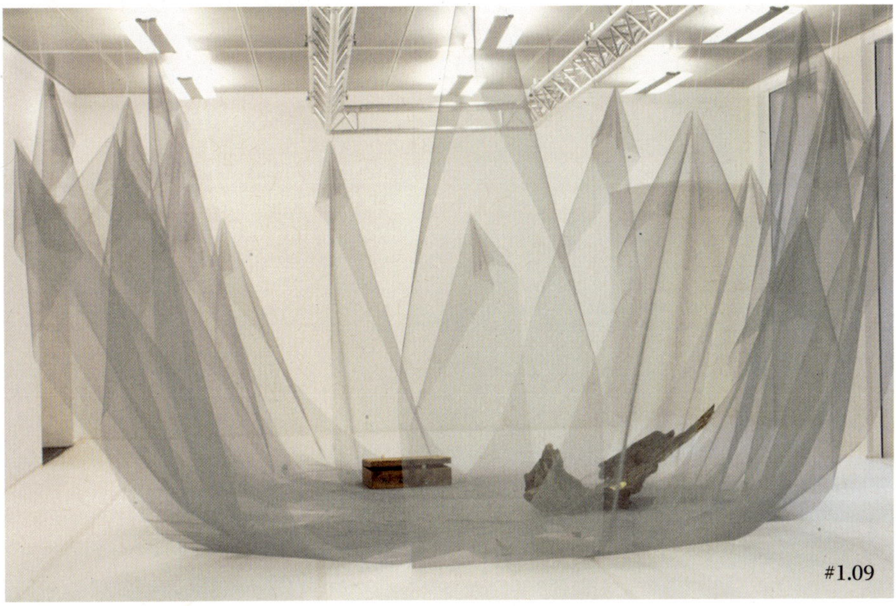

#1.09

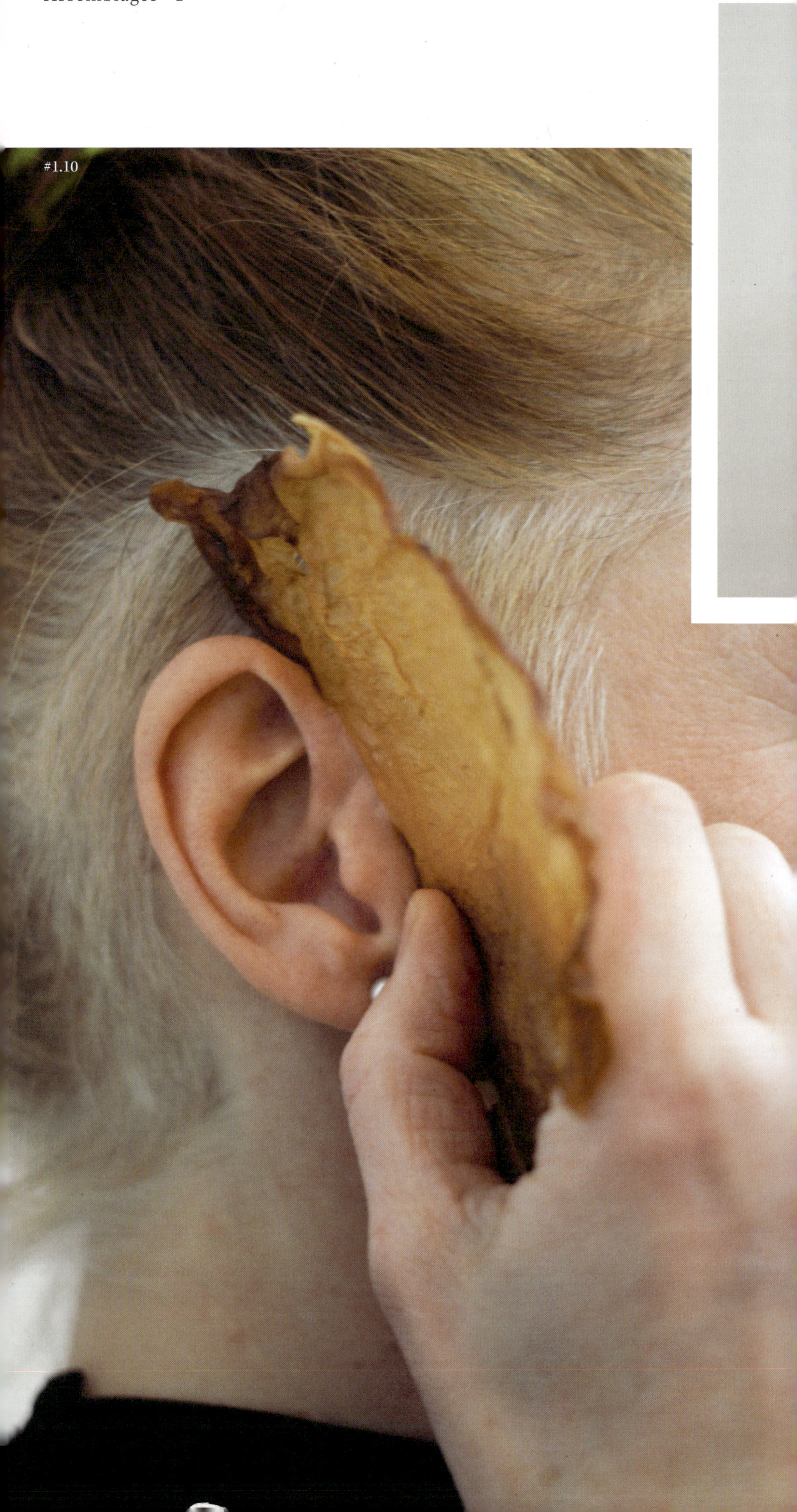
#1.10

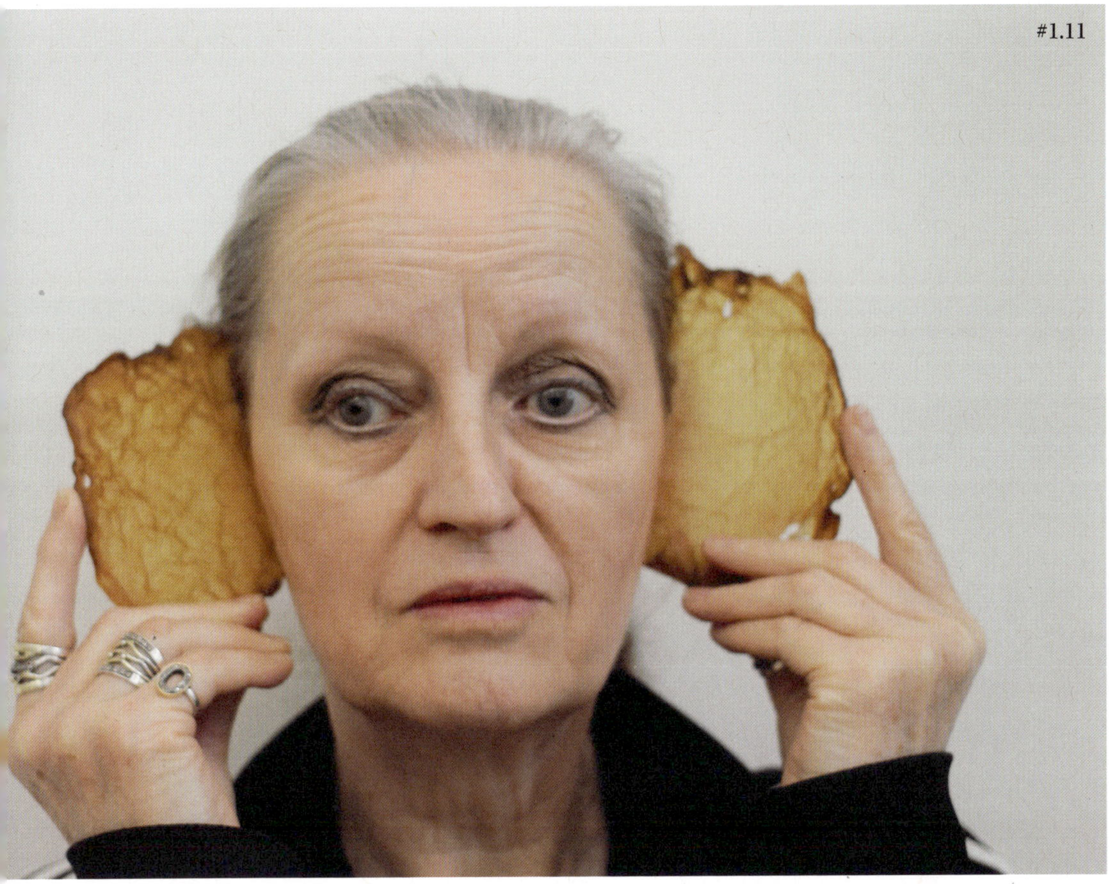

#1.11

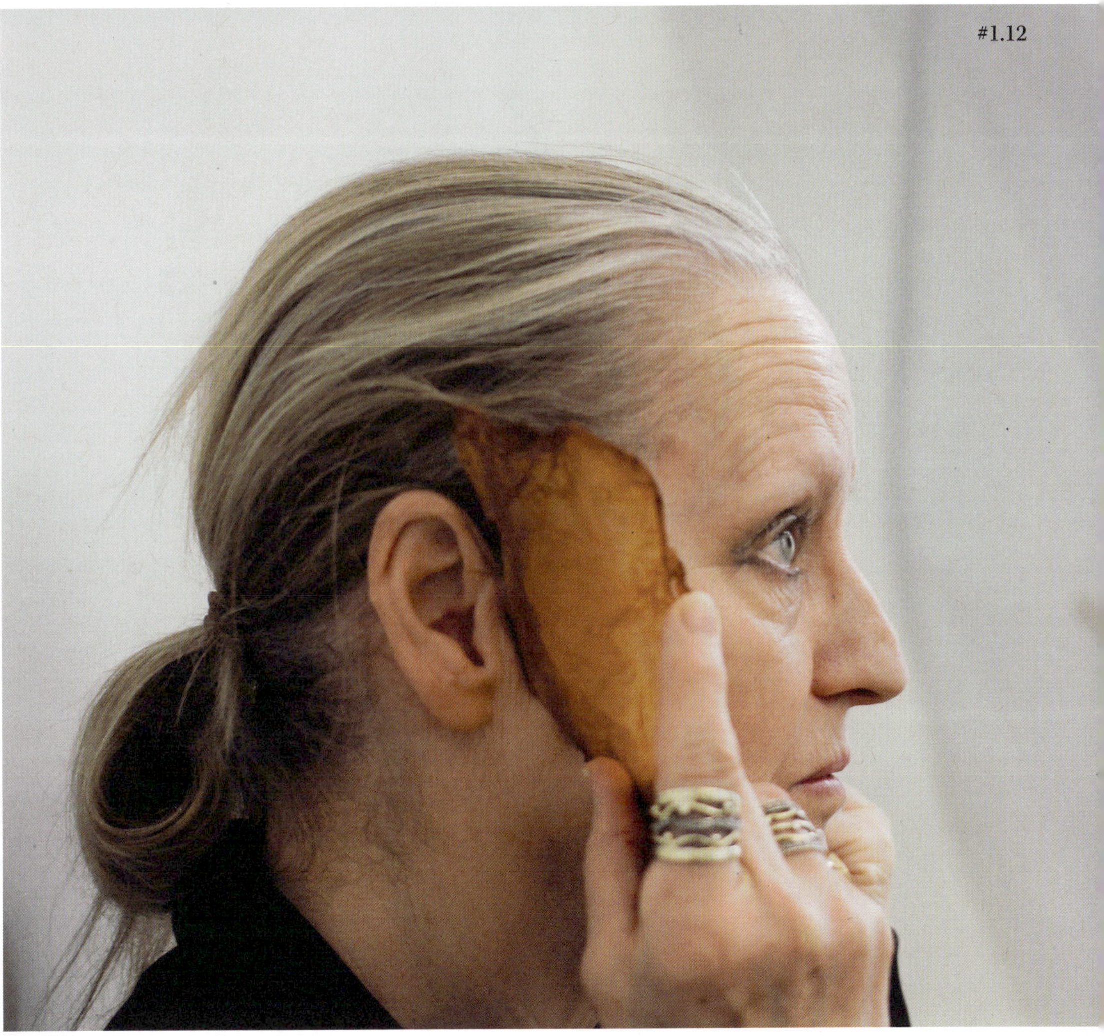

#1.12

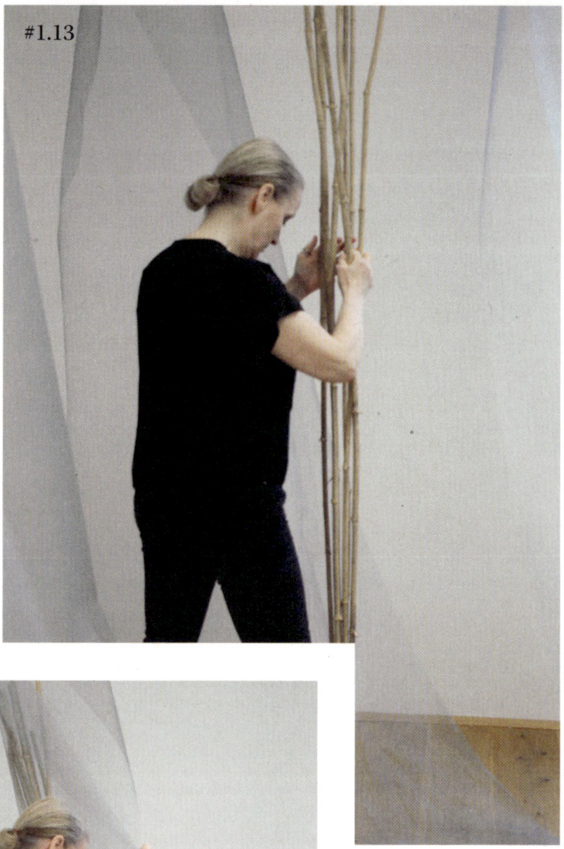
#1.13

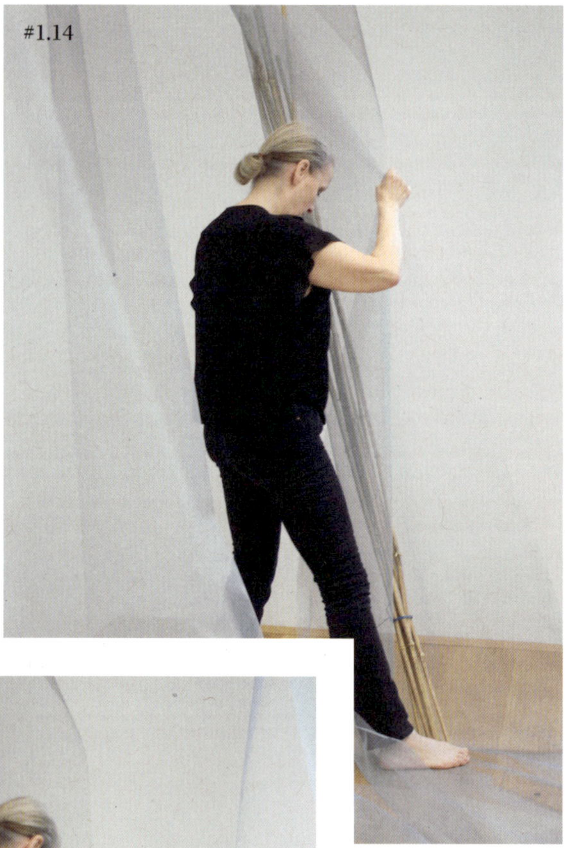
#1.14

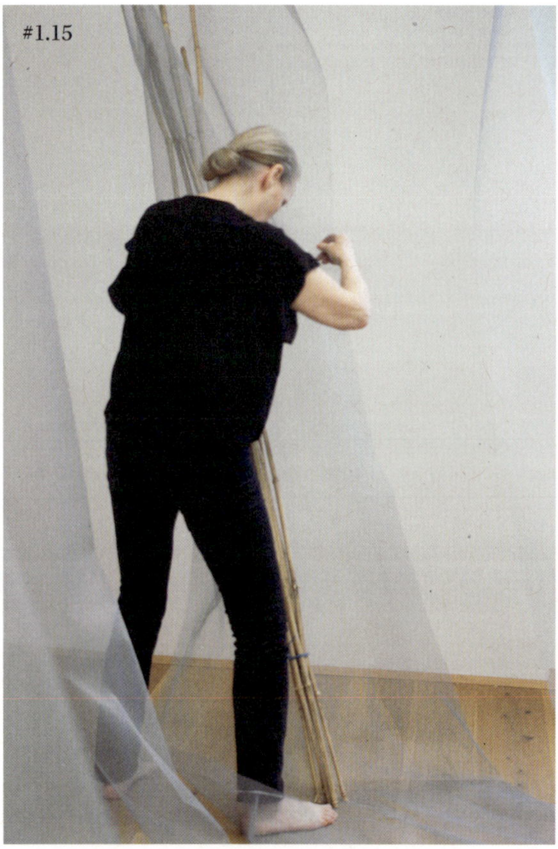
#1.15

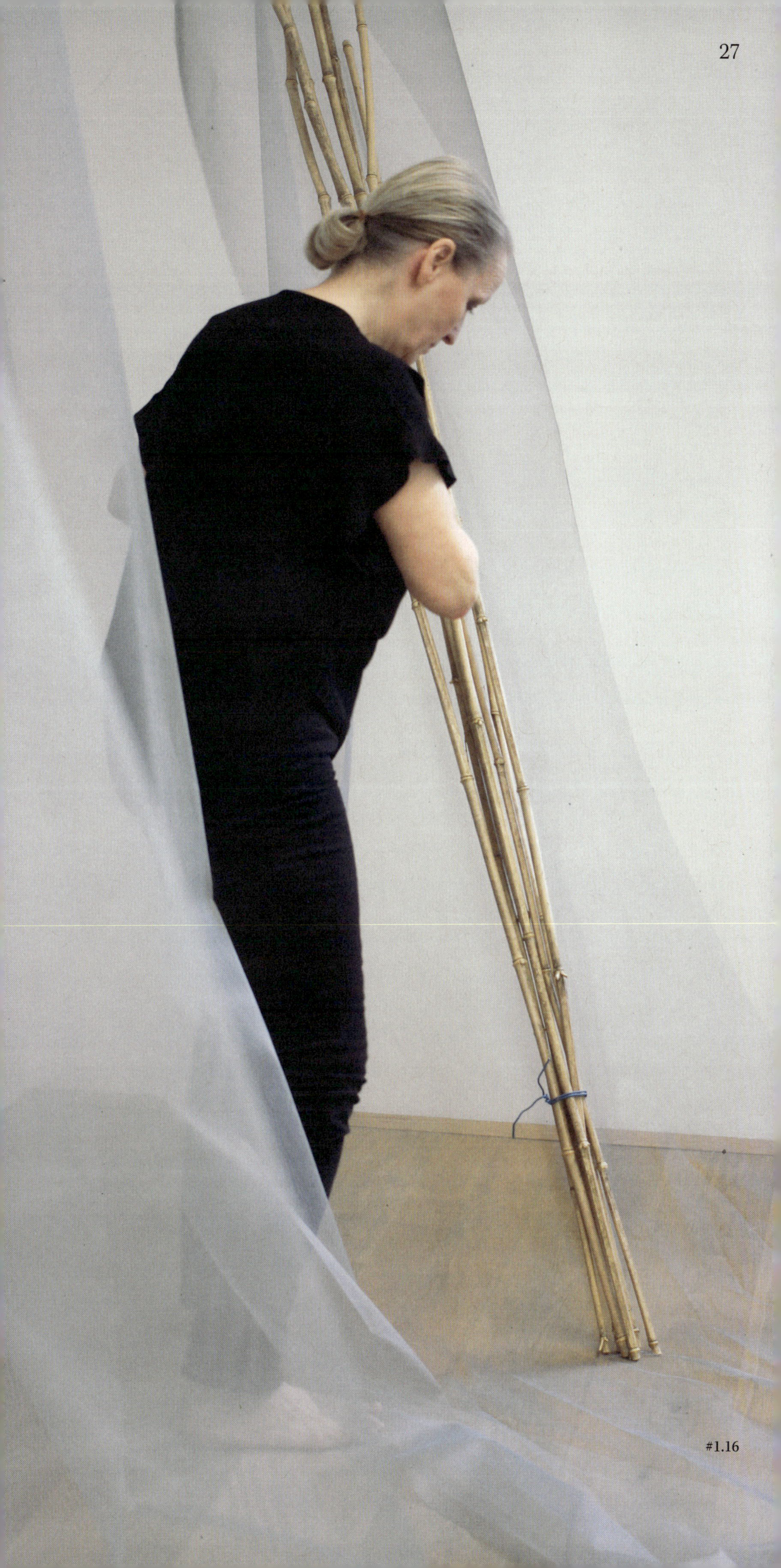

#1.16

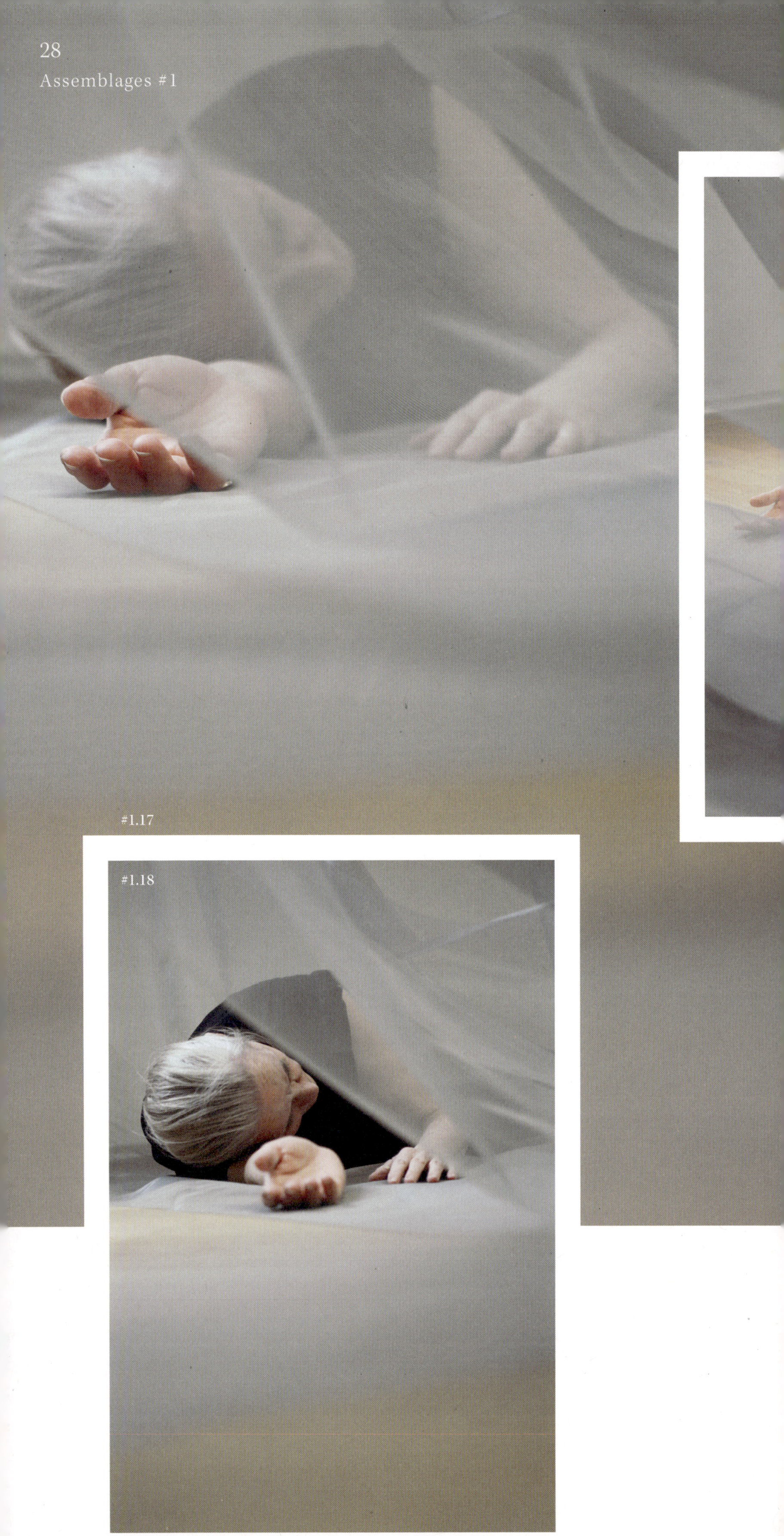

#1.17

#1.18

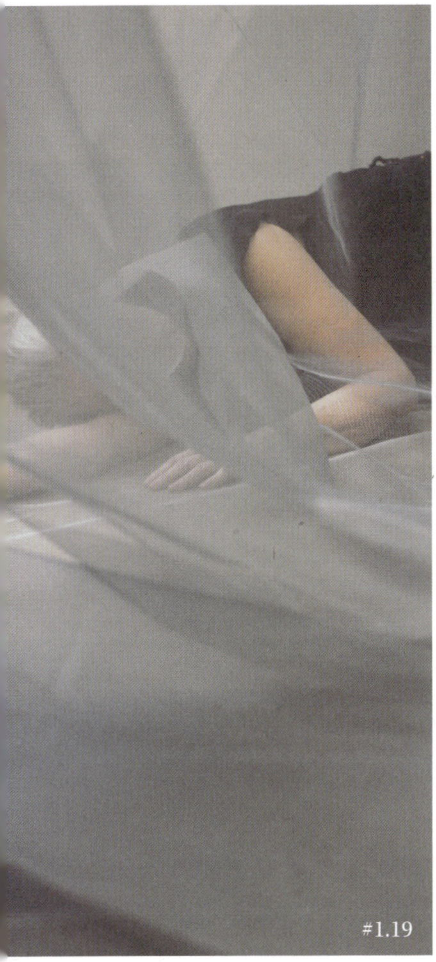

#1.19

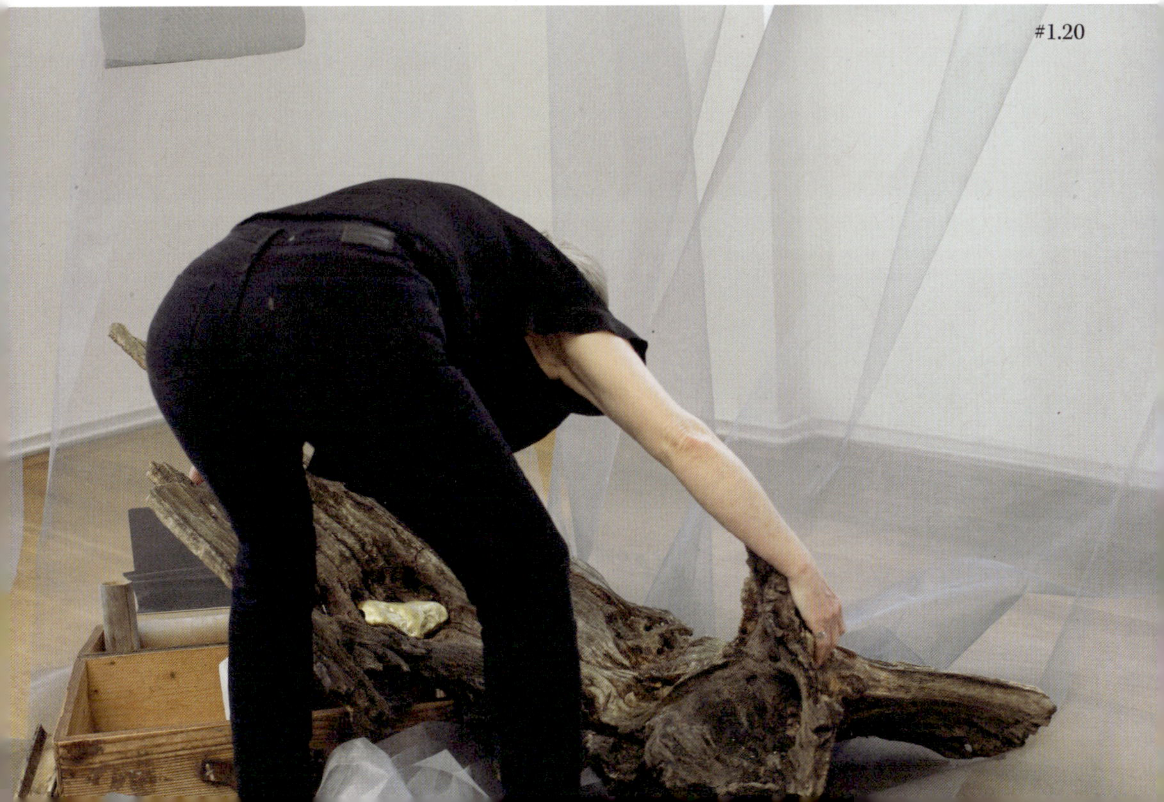

#1.20

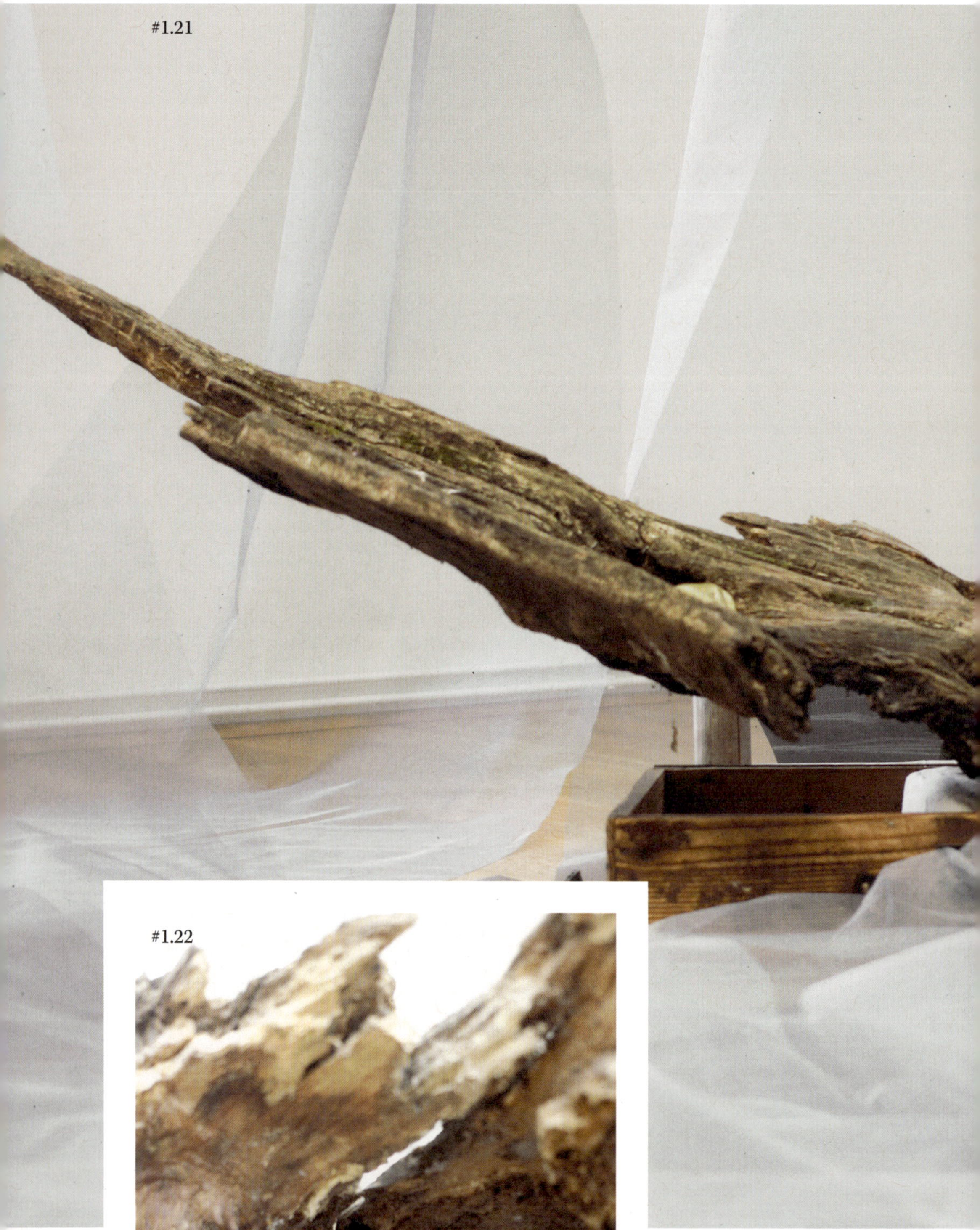

#1.21

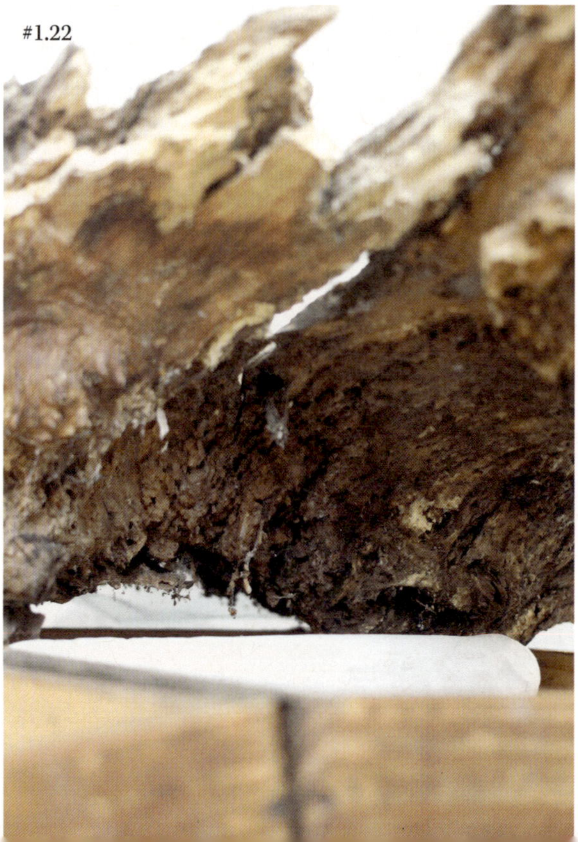

#1.22

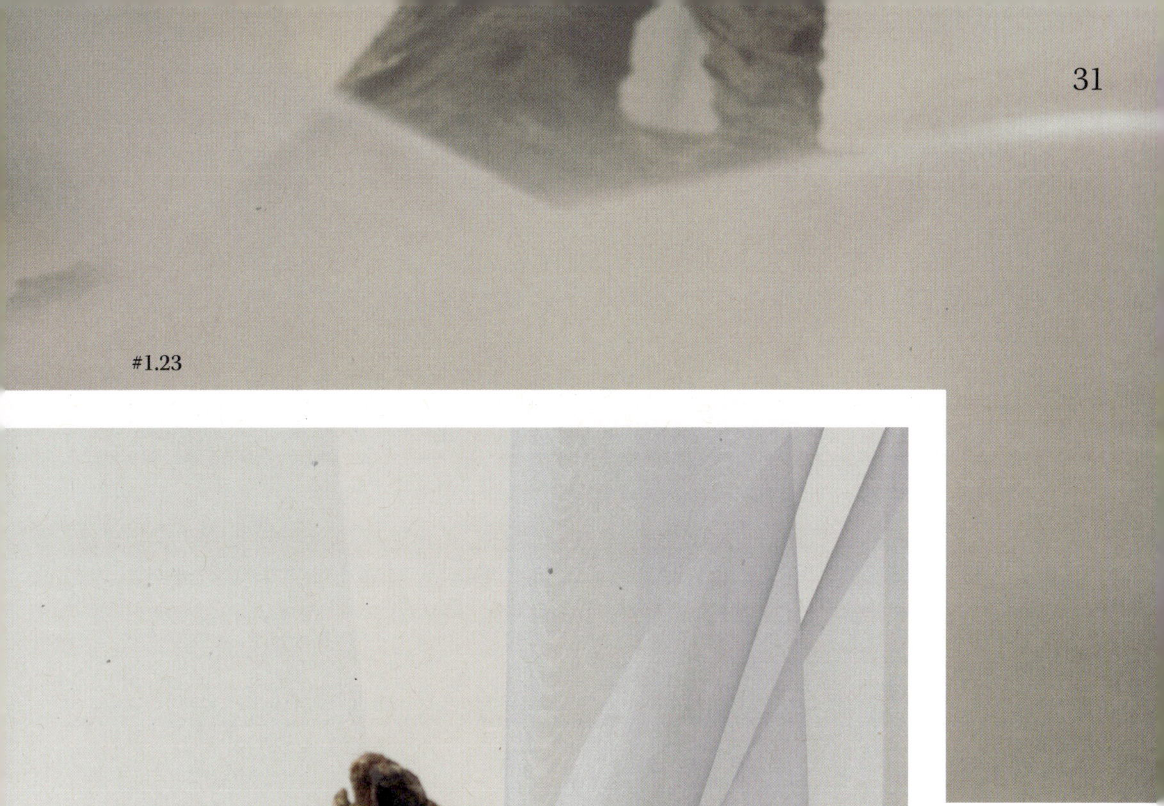

#1.23

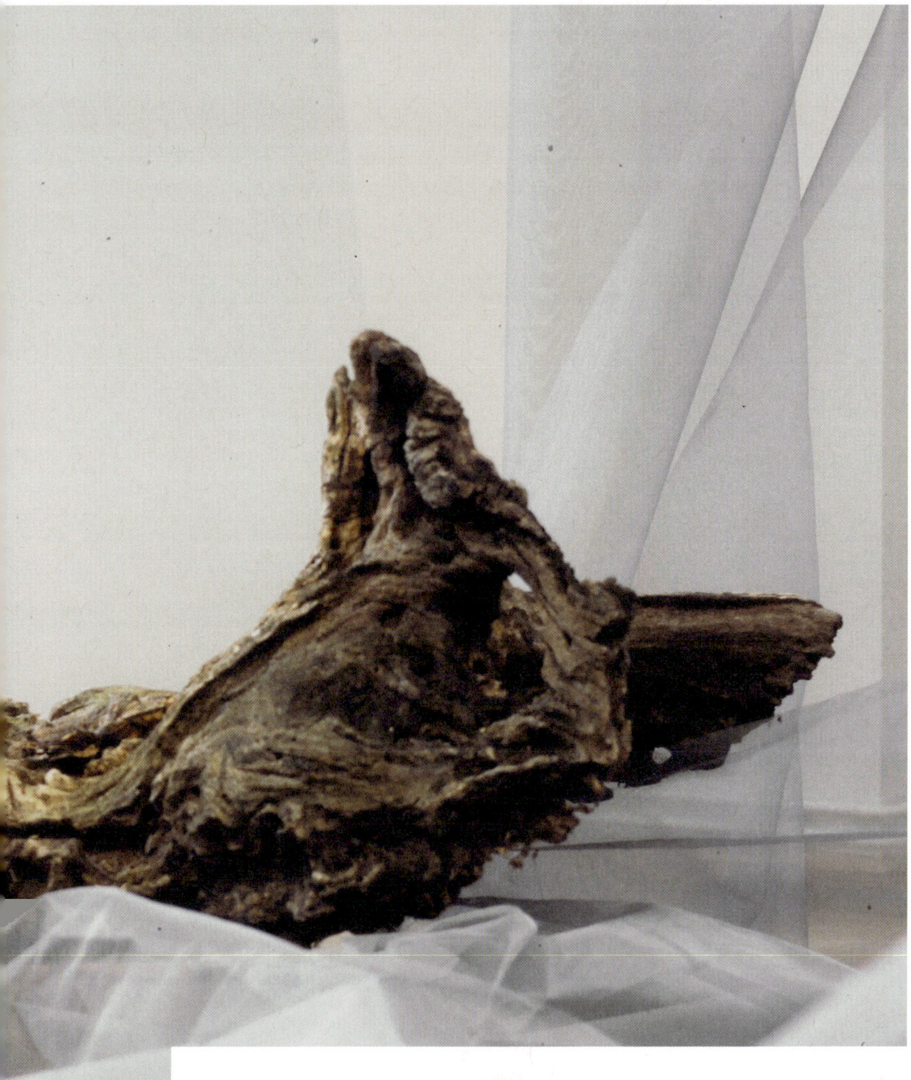

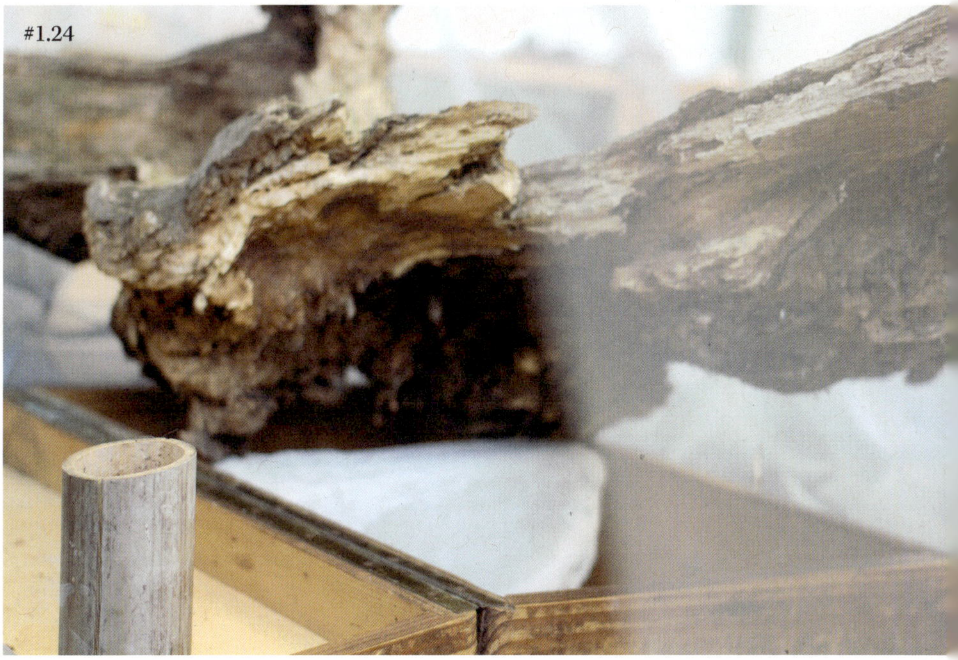

#1.24

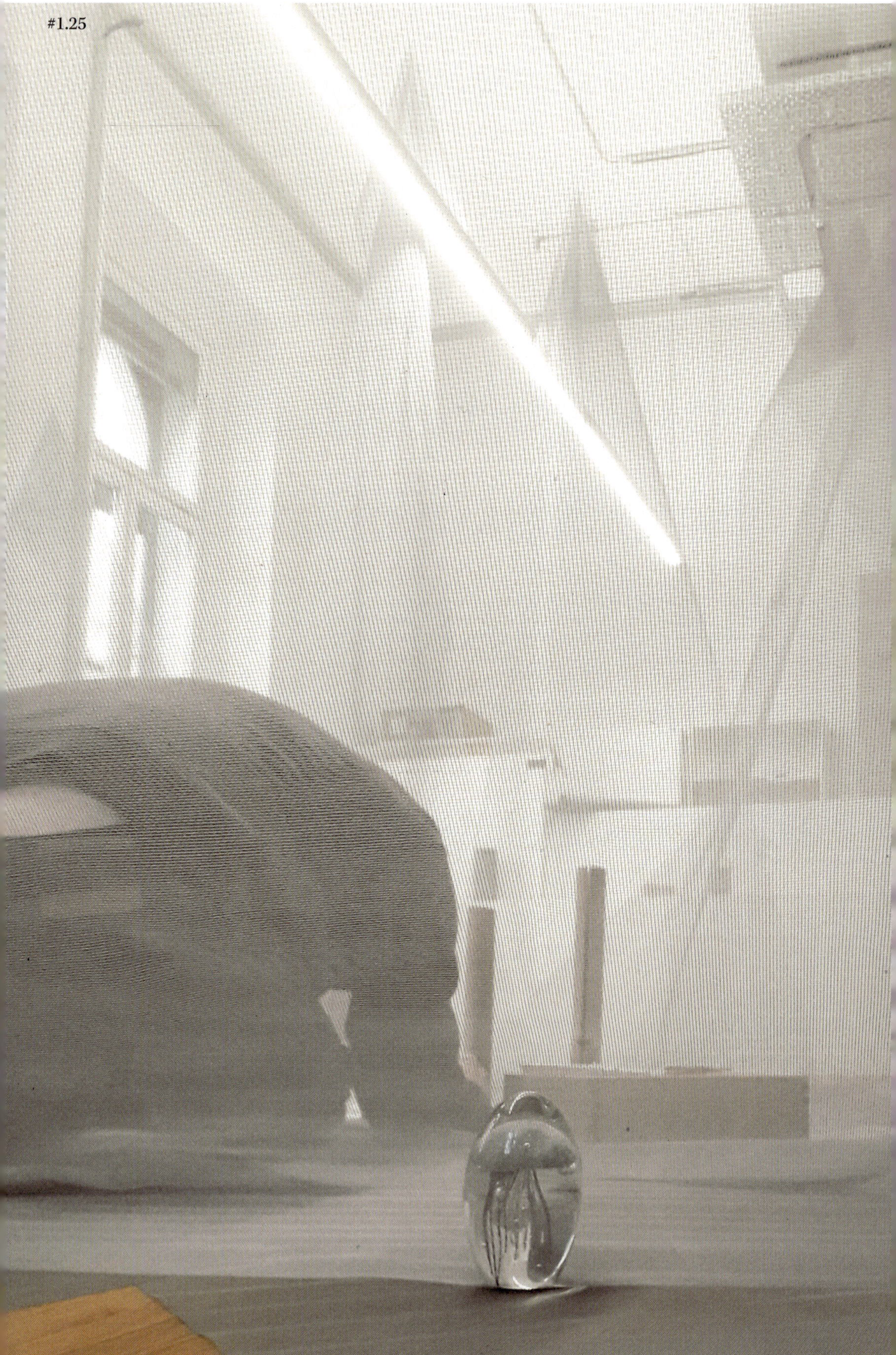
#1.25

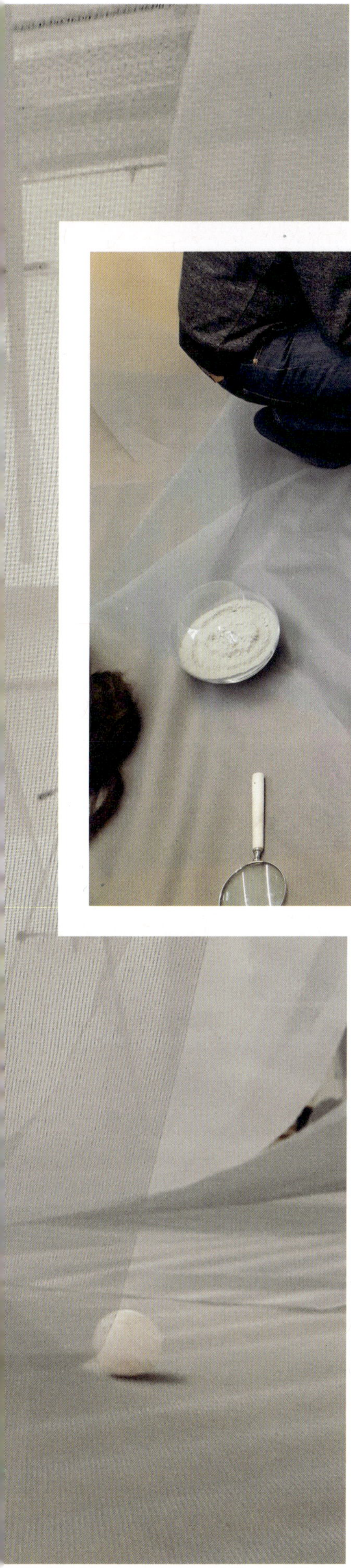

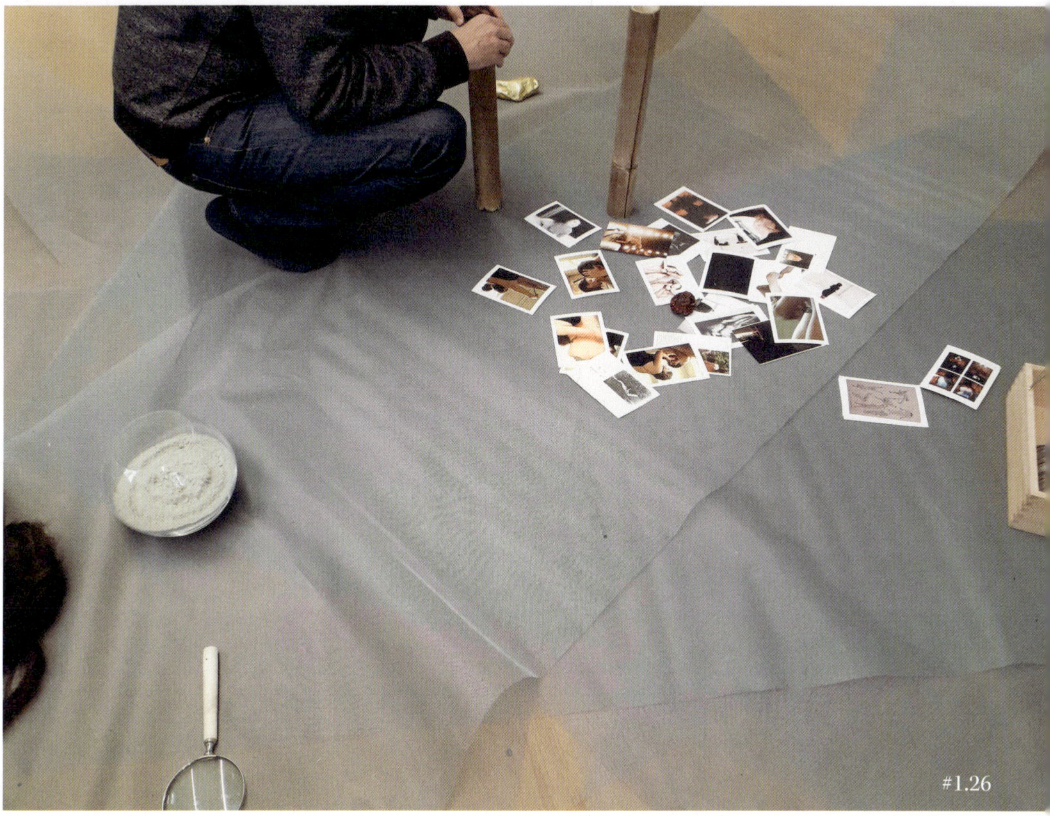

#1.26

#1.27

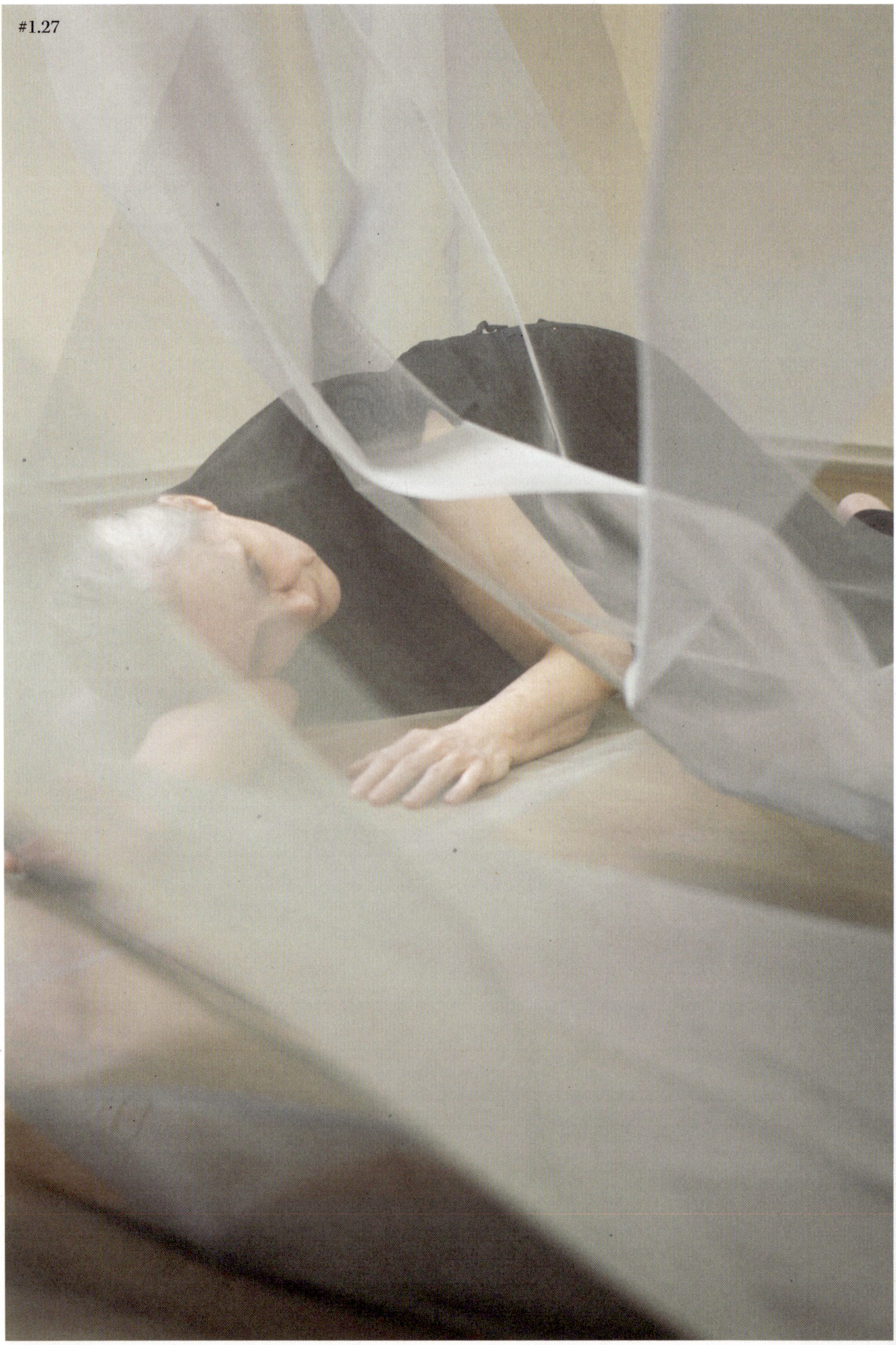

#1.01: *Choreographic Environment*, 2022, © Mariella Greil, Walter Lauterer and Simona Koch.

#1.02: *Choreo-ethical Assemblages*, 2023, © photo: Mariella Greil, performance: Efva Lilja.

#1.03: *Choreo-ethical Assemblages*, 2023, © photo: Evfa Lilja, performance: Mariella Greil.

#1.04: *Choreographic Environment*, 2022, © Mariella Greil and Walter Lauterer.

#1.05: *Choreo-ethical Assemblages*, 2023, © photo: Evfa Lilja, performance: Mariella Greil.

#1.06: *Choreo-ethical Assemblages*, 2023, © photo: Evfa Lilja, performance: Mariella Greil.

#1.07: *Choreo-ethical Assemblages*, 2023, © photo: Mariella Greil, performance: Efva Lilja.

#1.08–#1.09: *Choreographic Environment*, 2022, © Mariella Greil and Walter Lauterer.

#1.10: *Choreo-ethical Assemblages*, 2023, © photo: Evfa Lilja, performance: Mariella Greil.

#1.11–#1.20: *Choreo-ethical Assemblages*, 2023, © photo: Mariella Greil, performance: Efva Lilja.

#1.21–#1.24: *Choreographic Environment*, 2023, © Mariella Greil and Walter Lauterer.

#1.25–#1.26: *Choreo-ethical Assemblages*, 2023, © photo: Mariella Greil, performance: Werner Moebius.

#1.27: *Choreo-ethical Assemblages*, 2023, © photo: Mariella Greil, performance: Efva Lilja.

Ouverture in Two Acts: Introductions in the Plural

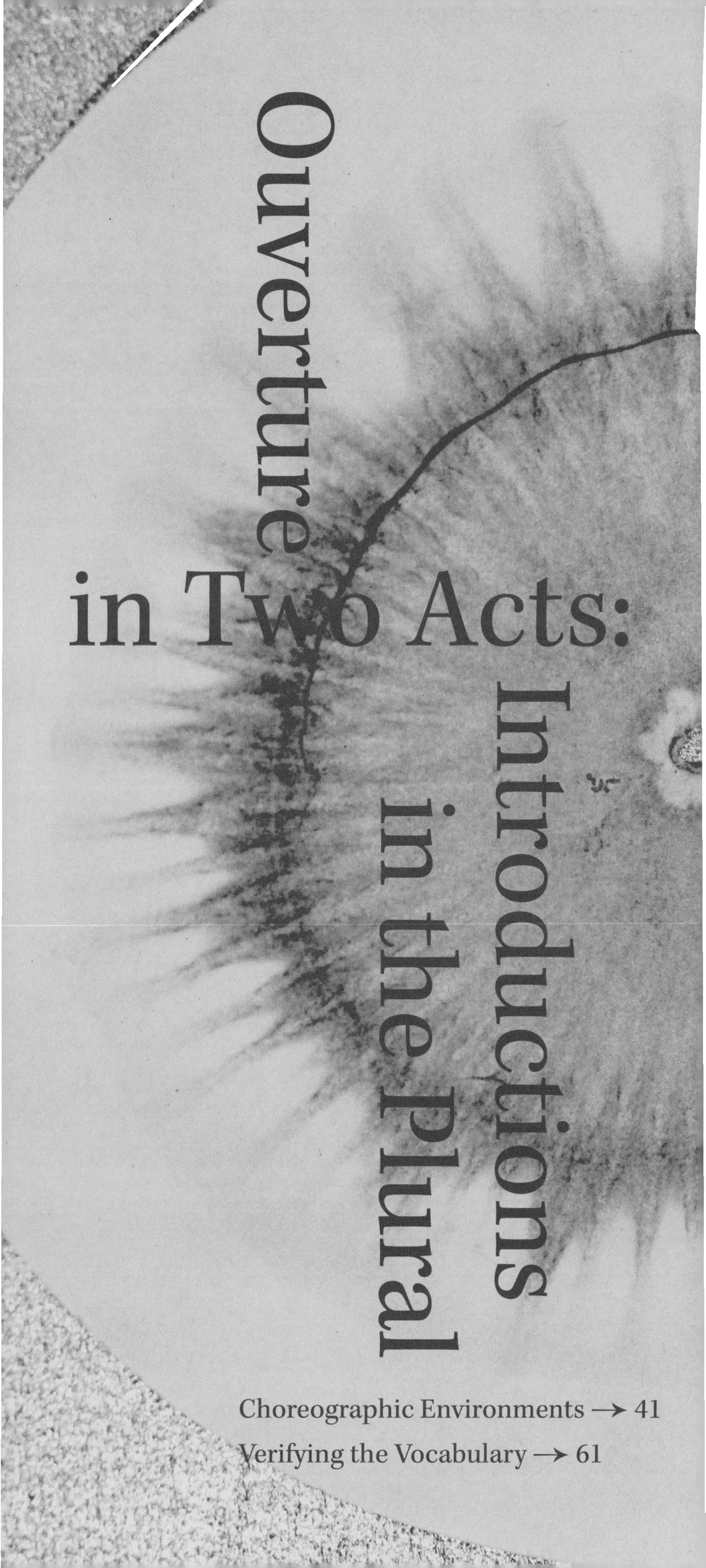

Embodiment – thoroughly erotic – is also the impossibility of escaping oneself, that is, running away from one's responsibilities. Thereby the illusionary character of the rupture with submission is seen.[1]
Emmanuel Levinas

This Levinasian provocation places embodiment at the threshold of ethics: not as a retreat into interiority but as an exposure to alterity that insists upon responsibility. To inhabit a body is never neutral – it is to be addressable, accountable, and implicated in networks of relation that exceed inner life. This erotic register – understood as the excess of relational intensity rather than mere libidinal concatenation – reveals embodiment as an ethical aperture for choreo-ethical thinking: a practice that situates movement and stillness, gesture and perception, within a field where responsibility is never simply chosen but always already given. Movement is more than aesthetic form; it is a modality of accountability that uncovers others, environments, and conditions of cohabitation. The book *Choreo-Ethical Assemblages – Embodied Research as Cosmopoietic Œkology* has evolved in close connection with the research project *Choreo-ethical Assemblages – Narrations of Bare Bodies* and proposes to conceive of choreography not exclusively as the design of forms in space and time but as an epistemic and ethical practice that configures environments of sensibility and relation, and reframes it as a tool for composing worlds. To choreograph means to create the conditions for co-appearance, to situate bodies – human and other-than-human – within assemblages where their modes of being are tested, altered, and reconfigured.

Such an approach foregrounds choreography as something *cosmopoietic*: a process that makes worlds through the interlacing of corporeal, affective, and material forces. At stake here is not only an ecology of bodies but an *œkology* – a term that recalls the ancient Greek οἶκος (*oikos*), the 'household', the 'site of dwelling', and extends it out towards an ethics of inhabitation that is simultaneously existential and planetary. This project had just begun, when the Covid-19 pandemic hit the world and profoundly changed how we inhabit our households as well as the world. This also led to a renegotiation of the relations between the *oikos* and the *cosmos*. This book is an account of that process, a scrutinizing of the interactions and communications between environments and bodies through cosmopoietic practices and diffractive dialogues.

Embodied research, from this perspective, becomes a mode of inquiry that cannot separate epistemology from ontology or aesthetics from ethics. The distinction between an epistemology and assumptions about the (objective or constructed) existence of facts and objects has become obsolete and invalid, insofar as the traditional separation between *how* we know things (epistemology) and the question of *what* exists (ontology) are collapsed in embodied research, as the body both *knows* and *exists*. The body's knowledge is performed through its existence. The body does not function as an object of study but as a generative matrix, a site where knowledge

1. Emmanuel Levinas, *Humanism of the Other*, trans. Nidra Poller (University of Illinois Press, 2006), 74n18.

emerges through encounter, vulnerability, and attention. Assemblage-thinking, as articulated by Gilles Deleuze and Félix Guattari, proves fruitful here: choreography is less an authored composition than a provisional constellation of forces, intensities, and agencies. These assemblages are fragile yet resilient, contingent yet structuring. They operate choreo-ethically insofar as they demand responsiveness – an awareness of how movement participates in the shaping of shared worlds. Worlds in the plural are produced by diverse, pluralised bodies that truly are a generative matrix rather than objectified instruments. The practice of writing an introduction must therefore reflect that generativity. The decision to write *introductions* in the plural is not rhetorical excess but methodological necessity: each opening stages a different mode of attention, a distinct entry into the dense field of choreoethical inquiry. In particular, the chapter Purposeful Polysemy discusses *poly*morphic approaches. *Poly-*, when mobilised as a method, designates more than multiplicity; it denotes a strategic practice of divergence and convergence, holding together heterogeneous registers – narrative, sensory, performative, temporal, and logical – in a way that resists univocal coherence while remaining accountable to the cosmopoietic œkology of choreographic research.

Through sustained engagement with polymorphous narrations, I will interrogate how narrative form – fragmentary, braided, contrapuntal – can resist authorial closure and attend instead to distributed authorship across bodies, archives, and nonhuman agencies. Polysensory encounters are developed in this book as methodological protocols: they are not just ornamental multimodality but elaborate practices of attunement that reconfigure perception, enact synaesthetic scorings, and render visible micromovements and the otherwise marginal flows of air, heat, smell, and tactility that constitute a given environment. In my ongoing practice, I analyse polyvalent performances as situated devices whose meanings are multiply invested – simultaneously epistemic experiments, civic interventions, and affective infrastructures – making performance a test bed for ethical consequences rather than solely a site of aesthetic singularity. Reading these assemblages as polymodern, this research refuses linear historicism and instead maps overlapping chronologies – Indigenous temporalities, colonial registers, techno-accelerations – to show how choreographic practices mediate and are mediated by asynchronous modernities. Finally, I will propose the Polylogic Lab as an experimental milieu where theory and practice co-produce protocols: iterative, accountable, and formally plural methods that combine sensory ethnography, score-making, critical fabulation, and speculative prototyping with an explicit ethics of accountability.

This book positions choreographic practice as a mode of cosmopoietic œkology precisely because it insists upon the inseparability of ethics, aesthetics, and environmentality. To move together is to be implicated in the conditions of each other's existence; to choreograph is to modulate those conditions and make them perceptible. The cosmopoietic dimension indicates that embodied research does not merely describe environments but participates in their composition, contributing to the ongoing negotiation of cohabitation on a fragile planet.

To ground this argument, the subsequent section turns to the notion of *choreographic environments as conditions.* Here, 'condition'[2] must be understood in a twofold sense: as both the given milieu within which embodied research takes place and as the generative force through which possibilities are enabled, constrained, or transformed. By shifting from choreography as a product to choreography as environmental conditioning, I hope to open up a conceptual and experiential field where movement articulates not only patterns of kinaesthesia but also ethical and cosmological orientations. This approach situates choreographic practice at the threshold of an œkological thinking that takes responsibility for the relational textures of existence.

Talk with Werner Moebius
Excerpt, edited transcript
20 October 2020

Mariella Greil: You just mentioned the room sound as a lived space and also that it's good that the textile panels here kind of interact with the acoustics...

Werner Moebius: ... yes, I would say that they break up the reverb in the room a little bit. Just as the panels themselves create a visual break in the room structure, they, too, are, so to speak, an equivalent, an acoustic break.

Mariella: ... a refraction on the sound level...

Werner: ... yes, in the sound wave range. That's what absorbs or interrupts.

Mariella: And before that, you talked about the *Handapparat** with the collection of images, which has been very clearly selected, so that the room generally appears very 'designed' due to my choice of materials.

Werner: Yes, the space has been created by your materials. And of course, there is already a bit of personal context. So, that means these are individual things that people associate with you and your artistic work. Because I know you well, I recognise you and your performative artwork very clearly in them. But I think that the way it's staged has an impact, where someone who doesn't know you so well might assume that it's a very personal setting because the objects themselves – a wig, the *Handapparat*, the old suitcase – carry stories within them. There's something about it that makes you think that it doesn't come from anywhere, but that might not be true at all. Perhaps the dialogue partner will think that you have staged other people there. That could also be the case. But the composition of these things naturally results in the revealing of a personality structure, I would say, that one can imagine.

Mariella: So, you don't see it as a spatial structure but read it as a personality structure.

Werner: Yes, when I think of a museum and I go inside; in this case, I see what is essentially a Mariella Greil Museum. It is actually an archive. Or would you call it an anarchive? Yes, that's what comes to mind when I think of a museum. It would be completely different if there was a sofa inside, an old carpet, and personal photos on the wall. Then the things inside would constitute something in the space, and one might think that someone could have lived there. So, in this case, it's alive. What emerges from the materials is performative, it's constantly being negotiated. But of course, it also has something to do with the past. So, you're actually producing the past, right now, I would say, on site. My impression is definitely something historical, which perhaps has to do with memory as well. With things that were used in performances, perhaps selected materials. There are a few materials that stand on their own, where you don't know exactly, but where you might think that you have used them before. The clay block, for example, is more neutral to me than the wig. There are materials that specify these qualities – the neutral or the personal. A photo with an image already creates a narrative, while a block of clay waiting to be worked on is still more open as a material.

Mariella: Yes, although the block of clay is no longer so easy to work with because it has already dried out.

Werner: In any case, it's material that isn't so precisely defined yet; it leaves open what you can do with it. So, a block of clay gives me the feeling that I can create something with it.

2. In this context, Martin Heidegger formulates a tongue-twister: 'For the condition of being a thing, which conditions the thing as a thing, cannot itself again be a thing, i.e., something conditioned. The thingness must be something un-conditioned (*un-bedingtes*).' Martin Heidegger, *What is a Thing?* (H. Regnery Co., 1967), 8–9.

I can make a collage with the photo or something, but it's difficult to really intervene in the image. I would say that they differ in terms of form and also in terms of their inviting nature and call to action.

Mariella: Well, you can rearrange the cards with the images.

Werner: Yes, that is exactly the possibility. And I can play the handpan, I can put on the wig, I can open the suitcase and see what's inside...

Mariella: Yes, for me, on the sound level, it's also about unearthing the haptic quality, about sound as a material that binds acoustic substance and also opens up a space of possibility.

Werner: And when the material is released, it becomes even more exciting when it is actually there as material. That's what I meant. If you scratch something into a vinyl record, for example, then of course that also produces rhythms and similar artefacts. So, the question is how freely you can then work with the materials. On the one hand, a record, for instance, naturally captures the sounds you put on it, but it is also a material in its own right. The same question probably applies to other materials: can you cut up a photograph? So, if I really have the freedom to act within it, then perhaps it ultimately becomes an ethical question of how respectfully I treat the materials.

Mariella: That's a central question for me, one that I want to explore with the choreo-ethical assemblages.

* The *Handapparat* is a collection of 365 cards filed in a wooden box. One card per day was created over the duration of a year. The rigour of the daily commitment ensured an accumulation and, in the process, a certain thickness in the surveying process. The cards display photos, drawings, cut-ups, cut-outs, and collages related to bare bodies, encounters, and exposure in contemporary performance. They exist as a tangible deck and a physical object, that is, a small wooden box with a lid. The *Handapparat* is a mapping device for dis- and re-organising the movements of my thought. The apparatus made it possible to flip through memories and experiences of performances, which I either created or wit(h)nessed.

Choreographic Environments

Outlining plurality as an active practice means resisting the temptation of the singular[3] that consolidates meaning into a stable, authoritative point of departure. The singular introduction, the univocal voice, the monologic gesture all carry with them the sedimented weight of Western metaphysics, which privileges unity, coherence, and closure over multiplicity, relationality, and emergence. In contrast, the practice of writing *introductions in the plural* is not a rhetorical flourish but a methodological commitment. It acknowledges that the subject matter at hand – *choreo-ethical assemblages as cosmopoietic œkology* – cannot be adequately approached from a single trajectory. Instead, it requires an active, pluralising practice: a proliferation of openings that remain porous, responsive, and ethically attuned to the conditions that they themselves engender.

Plurality for me does not denote the mere presence of many; it articulates a quality of relation that emerges when thought, practice, and environment are allowed to resonate within their heterogeneity without being reduced to a common denominator. My proposition here – to think-feel-act in the plural – is to cultivate a mode of attention that is at once distributive and differential, one that affirms divergence while simultaneously attending to the convergences through which meaning is co-generated. In this sense, plurality is not the antithesis of singularity but its necessary complication: the recognition that every singular carries within itself traces of the multiple – that every ground is already fissured, layered, and inhabited by others.

3. Jean-Luc Nancy, *Being Singular Plural* (Stanford University Press, 2022).

Active pluralising, then, denotes a practice: a continual process of unsettling and scrutinising the closure[4] of the form through multiplying perspectives, holding open the possibility that what is articulated could always have been otherwise. In choreographic research, such gestures of pluralisation manifest in the proliferation of scores, acts, voices, and registers of sensibility. They materialise in the simultaneity of verbal and non-verbal articulations, in the layering of sensory registers – kinaesthetic, tactile, auditory, visual – that refuse hierarchy. The pluralising gesture aims at resonance rather than synthesis; it does not seek to overcome difference but to inhabit it.

Philosophically, this commitment resonates with philosopher Emmanuel Levinas insistence that the ethical arises not from the autonomy of the self but from its exposure to alterity. Responsibility, he argues, precedes choice; it is the condition of embodiment itself that is the basis for encountering the Other. To pluralise is to honour this ethical imperative: to recognise that one's practice is always already implicated in the lives, gestures, and environments of others. Similarly, Donna Haraway reminds us that '"getting on together" with less denial and more experimental justice' is a crucial part of 'staying with the trouble'. She writes that 'Response-ability is about both absence and presence, killing and nurturing, living and dying – and remembering who lives and who dies and how in the string figures of naturalcultural history.'[5] This close-to-life insistence on cultivating *response-ability* anchors plurality as not just a celebration of multiplicity in the abstract but an embodied commitment to situated relationality.

For choreographic practice, plurality operates on multiple levels. It unfolds in the creation of environments where different bodies co-appear and negotiate shared space. It informs the compositional strategies that invite multiple readings, and it guides the epistemological orientation of embodied research that refuses reductive categorisation. It cannot be overemphasised that plurality here is not moral relativism or universalism, but actually intends to instigate the critical discussion, especially given that the notion of being a relativist[6] has lately been warped and turned into a pejorative. This does not mean falling into relativism, where all interpretations are equally valid – on the contrary, it requires a heightened sense of responsibility, for to work in the plural is to recognise that every gesture reverberates differently across bodies, environments, and temporalities. In my view, a pluralising practice demands accountability to those differences.

4. In the artistic research project *Choreo-graphic Figures: Deviations from the Line* (2014–17), we developed the 'Figure of Temporary Closing' as part of the *Elemental Figures* in relation to the arc of creative exploration. Nikolaus Gansterer, Emma Cocker, and Mariella Greil, 'Elemental Figures', *Choreo-graphic Figures: Deviations from the Line*, ed. Nikolaus Gansterer, Emma Cocker, and Mariella Greil (Edition Angewandte, De Gruyter, 2017), 100–10. In 'Prologue – Cutting Across, Passing Through', we wrote, 'We used the term *figuring* for referring to those small yet transformative energies and experiential shifts within the artistic process that are often hard to discern, but which ultimately shape or steer the evolving action, whilst *figure* describes the point at which awareness of "something happening" (*figuring*) becomes recognisable, communicable' (ibid., 14). In *Choreo-ethical Assemblages*, the closure itself is scrutinised.

5. Donna J. Haraway, *Staying with the Trouble: Making Kin in the Chthulucene* (Duke University Press, 2016), 28.

6. Philosophers Benedict de Spinoza and, in particular, David Hume – who is considered the father of moral relativism as he famously suggested that the universe remains indifferent to our preferences and our troubles –claimed that nothing is inherently good or evil.

This insistence on plurality is also a response to the historical and disciplinary specificity of choreography. While dance histories have often been narrated through the singular 'genius' of choreographers or the canonical coherence of styles, an alternative historiography foregrounds multiplicity: the collective practices, the intercorporeal transmissions, the improvisational proliferations that resist capture. Choreographic research today must actively pluralise in order to counteract the homogenising tendencies of institutionalisation and canonisation. To write, think, and practice in the plural is to allow the manifold genealogies and futurities of movement to co-exist without foreclosure.

From an epistemological perspective, the plural is essential because embodied research unfolds through a polyphonic process. No singular method suffices; rather, methods must be layered, juxtaposed, and continually reconfigured in response to the situation. One could say that plurality itself is the method – a poly-methodology that integrates narrative, sensory, performative, temporal, and logical registers without collapsing them into a unified system. Knowledge, understanding, and wisdom emerge in the interplay of heterogeneous modes, each of them partial, situated, and indispensable.

In the research practice developed within the framework of the project *Choreo-ethical Assemblages – Narrations of Bare Bodies* (2019–26), and summarised, presented, and reflected upon in this book, one of the methods that I used consistently was conversation. As an artistic practice, it exceeds the exchange of information. Etymologically, *conversatio* derives from *conversari*: 'to dwell', 'to live with', 'to turn together', 'to keep company'.[7] Conversation, then, cannot be reduced to an exchange of words; rather, it designates a shared turning, a being-with that unfolds through linguistic, gestural, sonic, and affective registers. To converse is to orient oneself towards another while being simultaneously reoriented by them. This turning-together is always pluralising: it resists the closure of monologue and opens up the possibility of co-generative sense-making. To converse is thus to co-inhabit a field of attention, to shape a shared temporality through gestures, pauses, sounds, and words. In the context of my research, this is an embodied practice of co-presence,[8] where meaning arises not from what is said alone but from the weaving together of silences, rhythms, and relational attunements. Therefore, in my artistic research, conversation functions as an artistic modality, as a method of embodied inquiry, where, rather than being transmitted, knowledge emerges dialogically through gestures, interruptions, and resonances. Conversation becomes a choreographic device, structuring attention and distributing agency.

Dialogical practice cannot be reduced to dialogue-as-discourse; rather, it signals a mode of practice in which the *in-between* – what philosopher Martin Buber calls the *Zwischen* – becomes the locus of generativity. Rather than focusing

7. 'Origin and history of conversation', etymonline, accessed 10 February 2025, https://www.etymonline.com/word/conversation.

8. Shortly after the kick-off event of *Choreo-ethical Assemblages – Narrations of Bare Bodies*, which made a contribution to the exhibition *Understanding Art and Research* at the MAK – Museum of Applied Arts, Vienna, the Covid-19 pandemic caused social, economic, and, of course, also scholarly disruptions. The Polylogic Labs had to be reorganised several times or were cancelled due to lockdowns. I am therefore deeply indebted to everyone who continued to contribute their conversations once it was safe to have them.

on individual voices asserting positions, it emphasises the relational dynamics that emerge in their interplay. Physicist David Bohm identifies the crucial difference between dialogue[9] and discussion, arguing that dialogical practice values responsiveness over assertion, resonance over conclusion. Since 2019, I have been developing a 'Diffractive Dialogue Score' (→ Scores, 387) that cultivates an attentiveness to how meaning shifts as it passes between bodies, materials, and atmospheres.

In my embodied research, material conversation and diffractive dialogue function as parallel yet interwoven practices. Material conversation emphasises dwelling-with, the lived quality of cohabitation, while the practice of diffractive dialogue emphasises the generativity of the in-between. It is drawn into focus and amplified through the micro-phenomenological interview technique.[10] Together, they articulate an œkological mode of relation: one that acknowledges the intertwining of physical, relational, and environmental practices as embodied processes. To converse through materials and to engage dialogically is to participate in the co-constitution of a conversational ground that is an emergent space of shared responsibility.

This perspective reframes conversation from being merely a tool of verbal articulation to itself becoming a choreographic gesture – an embodied, rhythmic, and responsive practice of relation. Diffractive dialogue practice extends this, insisting that the space between interlocutors, between bodies, between gestures, is not void but vibrant, a co-generative field of possibility (for which psychoanalyst Henri Maldiney has coined the term *transpossibilité*, as I discuss in → Aesthetics and Ethics are Twins, 271). Choreo-ethical assemblages enact plurality, cultivate responsibility, and render perceptible the œkological intertwinement of selves and worlds.

It is also an œkological practice in the sense that it intertwines the physical (voices, gestures, bodies), the relational (attention, reciprocity, response), and the environmental (the acoustic space, the material conditions, the atmospheres that enable or constrain dialogue). Thus, conversation exemplifies the œkological dimension of embodied research: knowledge emerges not from isolated cognition but from entangled, situated, and material processes of co-presence. Conversation as an artistic practice highlights the œkological entwinement of the physical, relational, and environmental. When dancers converse through movement, when performers and audiences converse through shared atmospheres, when words and silences converse in the space of writing, what is at stake is not communication as transmission but co-habitation as world-making. For me, engaging in conversation is acknowledging that meaning is always plural, provisional, and co-generated. It is to practice œkology in the sense of cultivating conditions for dwelling-with, for sustaining relational intensity, and for attending to the material and environmental forces that shape dialogue.

9. David Bohm, *On Dialogue* (Routledge Great Minds, 2014).

10. I learned the technique of conducting micro-phenolomenological interviews from phenomenologist Claire Petitmengin. Micro-phenomenology was born from the idea of creating a rigorous method to study human experience, advocated by neurobiologist Francisco Varela. The *entretien d'explicitation*, an interview method initially established by Pierre Vermersch, was further developed and elaborated by Claire Petitmengin into the micro-phenomenological interview tool. The development of this 'psychological microscope' opens up vast fields of investigation in the clinical and therapeutic, educational, technological, contemplative – and in my case artistic – domains. See 'Micro-Phenomenology', accessed 14 March 2025, https://www.microphenomenology.com.

Foregrounding

A rhythm of narration
stepping forward, stepping back,
a pulse that refuses background.
Even what comes to the fore lingers
perforce at the rear side of things,
guarded by traces,
protected by legacies.

Counterpoints composed in the margins
withering slowly, deliberately,
paving the way for acts of civil courage,
evidence threaded across agencies,
materialities, and aeons.

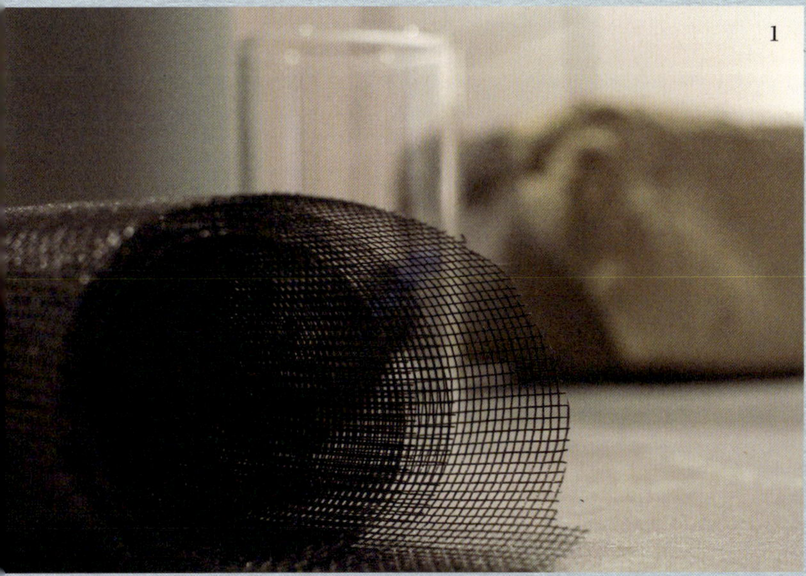

1

Timely dialogues with and through matter,
its hardness and hardships,
through softness insisting on touch,
warmth, delight.
Permeability reacts to opacity,
transparency folds into shadow,
they intertwine and radiate both:
absorbing darkness and luminous light,
leaking bright consequences.

Conductivity listens.
Porosity exhales.
Openness generates urgency.
Together they come to the fore:
sculptural, malleable, vivid.

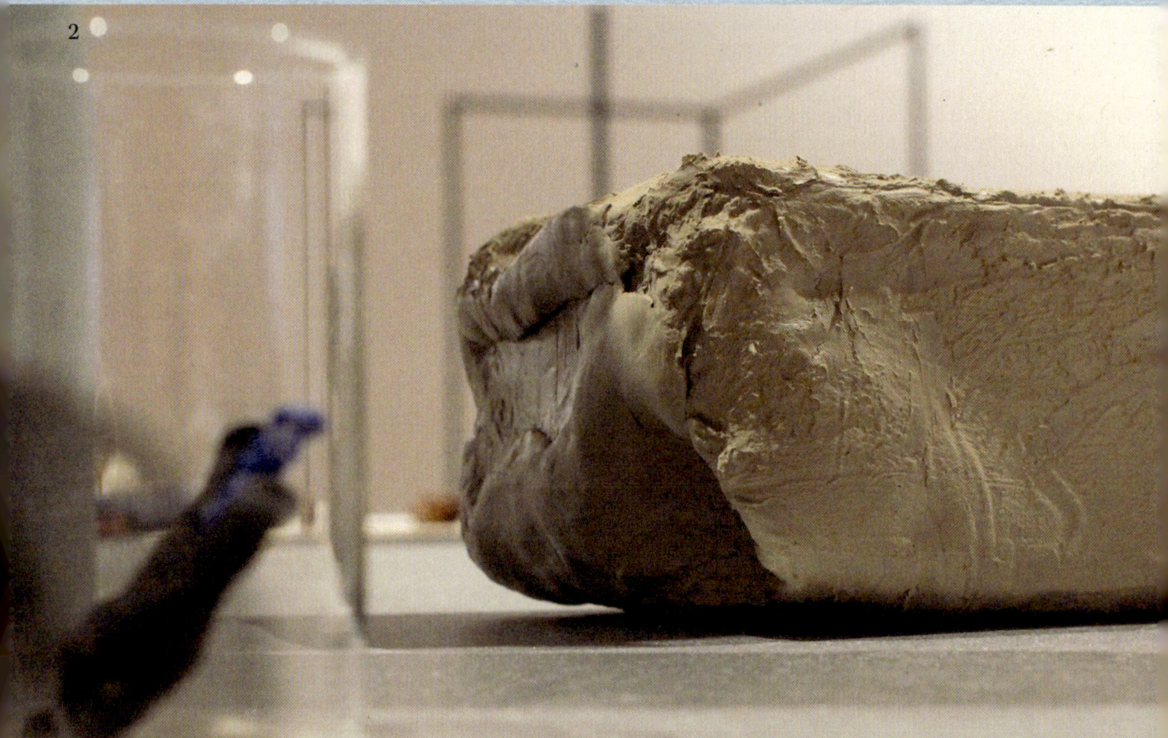

2

This habitat is not a backdrop,
it is a ground of survival,
a resource for evolution,
an œkological niche for oneself and
significant others
amidst multispecies assemblages.

Bodies become intertidal zones of
coming together,
drifting along or sometimes staying apart,
meeting, resisting.
Alien communities affect presence
and absence,
futures are postponed.
Their intensity couples with our life forces,
erotic, complex, colourful,
still defending themselves,
warding off enemies and scarcity.

There is abundance in attention,
love for microworlds,
for minuscule creatures
suspended in gum-like time
and endangered environments
where they cannot breed generations to come.
Stickiness becomes a palm-caresser,
then fingertips remember the yielding
before mass resisted.
First it was soft,
then harder to penetrate.

A rolled-up black grid waited impatiently
to come out,
ducking away while ready to show
everything it had.
It quietly queered the architecture,
lightness and levity lay dormant
in the spaces between the dark fibres.
Interspaces of potential and elation,
potential hums when it arrives.

Foreground and background trade
places again,
maybe misreading the material tides.
Attention condenses, dilutes,
becomes a method of substantiation.

The metre of the narration is not telling
but holds open
a practice of staying
with unfinished matter.

In this last coming-forward,
time bends sideways,
history exhales,
future spores scatter.

What is foregrounded
waits to be changed again.
No more domination,
instead eventually listening,
sheltering in the cracks.

Here, right at the thresholds,
slow insistence emerges,
foregrounding becomes ethical:
to notice,
to respond,
to remain porous,
when brittle disappearance asks
to be seen.

It is in this sense that → *Purposeful Polysemy*, 157, becomes a crucial linchpin in my argument. Rather than celebrating multiplicity for its own sake, this section interrogates how plurality can be cultivated with purpose and care. Polymorphous narrations challenge the hegemony of linear storytelling, making space for fragmented, braided, and contrapuntal forms that reflect the multiplicity of lived experience. Polysensory encounters expand the field of attention, integrating sight, sound, touch, and proprioception into research practices that honour the body's distributed intelligence. Polyvalent performances refuse singular interpretation, allowing works to function simultaneously as aesthetic events, epistemic experiments, and civic interventions. Polymodern times have disrupted linear temporality, foregrounding the coexistence of asynchronous rhythms and heterogeneous historicities. Finally, Polylogic Labs instantiate environments where theory and practice co-generate, where multiple logics – artistic, therapeutic, philosophical – are allowed to resonate with and inform one another. Purposeful polysemy insists that plurality be practiced with attentiveness, accountability, and rigor. It requires criteria – ethical, aesthetic, methodological – that guide when and how multiplicity is generative. It demands that pluralising practices remain responsive to the conditions they create and the communities they implicate. Thus, plurality as an active practice is not a *de*scriptive category but a *pre*scriptive orientation. It calls for the cultivation of environments where differences are sustained rather than erased, where multiplicity is foundational rather than ornamental, where responsibility is distributed rather than centralised. It takes the position that choreographic research, in its embodied and expanded forms, must become plural to remain ethical, œkological, and cosmopoietic.

Plurality, then, is both a method and an ethic, both a condition and a practice. Therefore, to write introductions in the plural is to enact this orientation from the outset: to acknowledge that no single entry suffices, that every beginning is already one of many. A pluralising practice presupposes a ground, a condition from which the manifold can emerge and remain intelligible. This ground, however, is not to be mistaken for a static foundation or inert substrate. Rather, it is co-generative: a universal singular that gathers without totalising, that enables the emergence of situations while itself coming into being through those very situations. It is universal insofar as it affords a shared locus of emergence, singular insofar as it cannot be duplicated, and generative insofar as it continually produces conditions for relational unfolding. The co-generative ground is thus less a site than an event of attunement. It resonates with philosopher and biologist Humberto Maturana and neuroscientist and biologist Francisco Varela's insights into autopoietic systems, which sustain themselves only through ongoing relational processes. Likewise, the ground here is enacted through embodied practices – dancing, sounding, writing, pausing, sculpting – that weave together physical, affective, and environmental registers. The ground is never external to the situation but is produced within and through it by the choreographic environment, while intercorporeal gestures, atmospheric shifts, and material resonances settle into a shared field of sense-making.

This orientation calls for an œkological vocabulary. Etymologically rooted in *oikos* – 'dwelling', 'household' – œkology here extends beyond the naturalist domain of ecosystems to designate a choreo-ethical process of dwelling-in. It is a descriptive category as well as a performative one: œkology articulates how physical, relational, and environmental practices are inextricably intertwined as embodied processes and phenomena. In the œkological sense, one does not merely inhabit an environment but participates in its continual re-constitution. Breath, gesture, material density, and social resonance all co-compose the space as a space of appearance. A space is not just an empty container but is actively shaped by breathing bodies, their movements, the material environment, and the shared social atmosphere – all of which together create a place where people can appear to and with one another. Such œkology is inseparable from responsibility. Levinas reminder that embodiment is 'the impossibility of escaping oneself'[11] suggests that every embodied action situates the subject within an irreducible ethical relationship. To breathe together, to move in proximity, to shape a gesture that impinges on others – these are œkological acts, where responsibility is more than an afterthought – it is constitutive of the very possibility of dwelling. The co-generative ground thus functions as an œkological matrix: instead of providing a neutral backdrop, it constitutes an ethically charged milieu of becoming, where relational intensities exceed any single agent yet bind all participants in shared accountability.

My contention is that artistic embodied research practice makes this co-generativity palpable. Improvisational scores, site-sensitive (micro-)choreographies, conversational material exchanges, and diffractive dialogues do not merely unfold *upon* a pre-given ground; rather, they bring the ground into being, bring the choreographic environment to life. In such moments, the œkological intertwining of the physical, relational, and environmental becomes perceptible: a rustle of fabric, the refraction of light, the temporality of a pause – all acquire agency in shaping the situation. The universal singular is not just *there*; it emerges as a lived matrix or an embodied ground sustaining vital multiplicity by allowing difference to resonate rather than demanding resolution. In this sense, œkology as an embodied process is both descriptive and prescriptive. It describes the interdependence of corporeal, relational, and environmental practices, and prescribes an ethical-aesthetic orientation that insists on attentiveness to these interdependencies. It is here that the co-generative ground and the œkological process converge: both articulate the condition through which choreo-ethical assemblages take shape, and both insist that this condition is itself an emergent, embodied practice. Thus, the universal singular does not oppose plurality but is its very enabler, and œkology is the articulation of this enmeshment, rendering visible and sensitive the relational forces through which bodies, environments, and practices co-constitute a world. In their intertwinement, œkology and the co-generative ground establish the conditions of choreo-ethical assemblaging: the art of dwelling together in plurality, attuned to the generative responsibilities that embodiment entails. If the universal singular and its œkological processes establish a generative ground, then the question arises: who or what participates in this co-composition? To speak of *selves* in the plural is to move cautiously from the outset, for the self cannot be reduced to

11. Levinas, *Humanism of the Other*, 74n18.

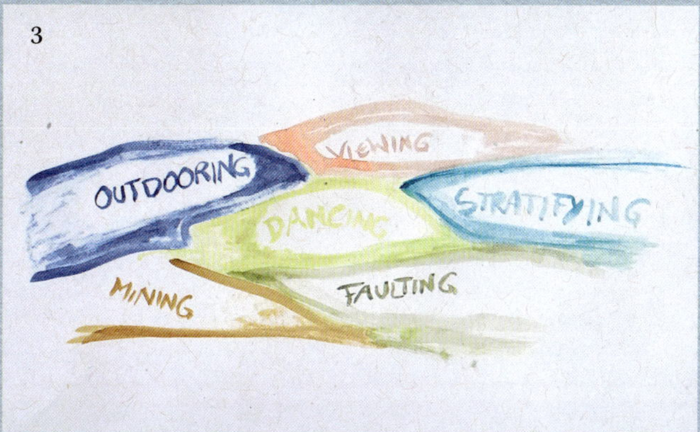

Stratification

Walking-running-starting my way.
Folding beautiful resistance,
reading the soul,
resting the heart.
Dancing, going lower, surrendering.

Pressing my hand against my mouth,
not in order to silence,
– I wasn't speaking anyway –
but to feel how my lips push against my hand
from inside, sensing the threshold.

Wild desperations,
tamed addictions pass,
fears and hopes turn up in circular community,
then I suddenly lift my head and realise the weight
of a chest held high.

Can we get lower?
Get down, make love, yes, Freddy.
Coming from an island, rising to be a star,
dying from AIDS.
Archipelago enchantments.

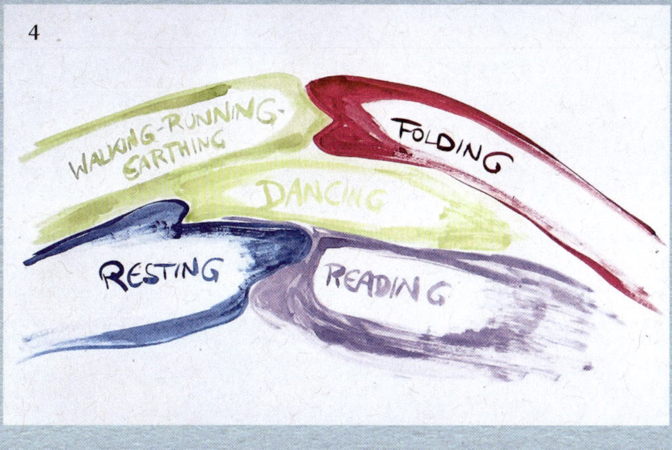

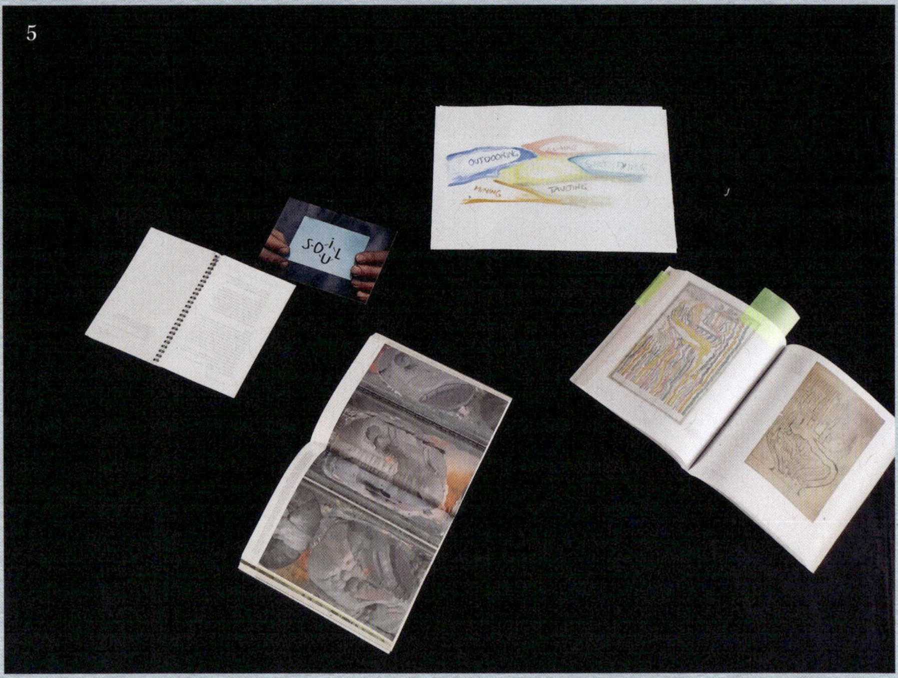

Finally get down, get lower, get down below.
Low energy, low expectations, low bodies,
their pressure is a rich physical sensation,
understanding weight and yielding,
then relinquishing to earthly dances.

Holding the space open,
fostering blessed relationships –
no, clearly no more emotional exploitation.
There are rituals of releasing,
identifications trained –
yes, time is always a gift.

Stratifying the practice,
viewing power asymmetries,
outdooring the studio.
Faulting the soil,
mining the soul,
Dancing ideas.

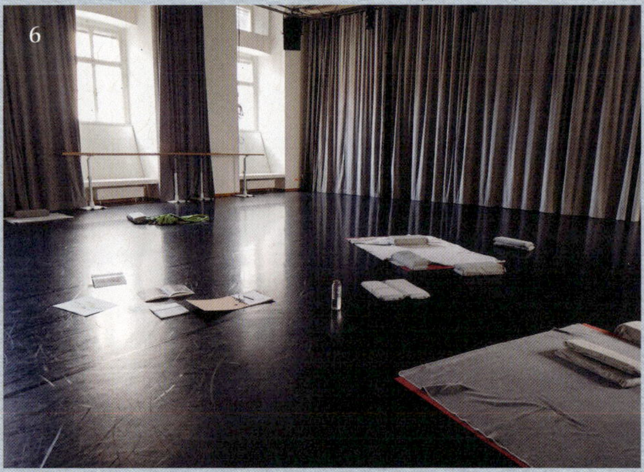

the autonomous subject of the modern philosophical tradition. Rather, *selves* are nodes within networks of relational intensities, always constituted in and through their connections from the beginning.

Such selves are not autonomous monads, nor do they wholly dissolve into the collective flux. In my experience, they exist as thresholds – sites of exchange where forces converge and diverge, shaping singular yet porous performative articulations. In embodied research, these performative selves become palpable through relational exposure rather than self-enclosure: as the body – bare in its existential dimension – that gestures towards another, as the writer's phrasing that responds to rhythm, as the sound that both emanates from and vibrates within multiple bodies.[12] Selves are felt not as self-contained units but as relational capacities, as nodal condensations of embodied, environmental, and affective vectors. To conceive of selves in this way requires us to rethink the notion of agency. Agency is not possessed but distributed, enacted across verbal and non-verbal registers. In the 'Diffractive Dialogue Score',[13] movement, sound, photography, and writing are not separate activities but interpenetrating modalities of articulation. Each becomes an extension of embodied inquiry, a mode of thought in motion. These practices radiate cosmopoietically: they expand outward into their *Umwelt* (this German word literally means *surrounding world*), sourcing vital force from the textures, rhythms, and resonances that surround them, while simultaneously projecting forms of attention, care, and intensity into these environments. This conception of the node resonates with posthuman and ecological philosophies that destabilise anthropocentric boundaries. Yet within choreo-ethical assemblages, a critical attitude manifests that breeds the theoretical along with the experiential: the performer who feels her movement taken up by the texture of the floor, the listener who hears sound as both emanating from and reshaping the atmosphere, the writer whose words trace the rhythms of a diffractive dialogue across agencies. Each encounter demonstrates that the self is not an origin but a passage, not an interiority but a relay of forces. These forces circulate and proliferate into practices of thinking-reading-annotating. These practices purposefully risk appearing incoherent or inconsistent, because they are already plural; however experience has shown that the practice of scoring, the choreographic environment, and its networks of relations offer artistic as well as spatial *containment*.[14] This term is mostly used in psychotherapeutic contexts, signalling a safe space for opening up towards the other who has the ability to take in undigested content or projections, which are reflected back in a structured way. Ethically, this nodal articulation of plural selves across agencies foregrounds responsibility as something shared and distributed. The Levinasian impossibility of

12. As part of the choreographic environment, there were two specifically tuned handpans (F-Bequinox – D♭ A♭ C D♭ E♭ F G♭ A♭ D♭ – and D♭ Lydian – D♭ A♭ C D♭ E♭ F G♭ A♭ D♭) available as instruments. They were made by Birgit Pestal as part of the choreographic environment. A handpan is a convex steel percussion instrument, played with the hands, that produces resonant, melodic tones through tuned notes hammered into its surface.

13. I explain the 'Diffractive Dialogue Score' as well as the 'The Dark Bag Score' in more detail in → Scores, 387.

14. Psychoanalyst Wilfried R. Bion developed the concept of *containment* in his 1962 book *Learning from Experience* (Maresfield Library, 1991), which is probably one of his most significant contributions to psychoanalytic theory.

escaping oneself implies that one is always already implicated in the relational field. To move, to speak, to write is to act from within a web of interdependencies. Responsibility is not an additional layer but these nodal selves' very mode of existence.

In this way, the choreo-ethical self becomes an aperture into cosmopoietic œkology, simultaneously situated and expansive, accountable and generative. To inhabit oneself as a plural node is to recognise that one is always more than oneself, that selves are a site where world-making forces converge and diverge.

The collaborative environment co-created with artist, architect, and performer Walter Lauterer exemplifies how space itself can become a co-constitutive participant in choreo-ethical assemblaging. Suspended from the ceiling, this lightweight, transparent structure resists enclosure. Suspended in the air, it creates an open, layered environment where light, shadow, and spatial permeability shape the unfolding of practice. Transparency here is not mere visibility but a relational condition. Participants suspended within a porous architecture, where each gesture reverberates in relation to others. This spatial condition amplifies the co-generative ground: it makes palpable the openness and stratification of embodied research. The suspended structure is both supportive and precarious. It draws attention to weight, balance, and interdependence. One cannot inhabit this environment without acknowledging the relationality it foregrounds: how lightness depends on suspension, how transparency depends on layering, how openness depends on subtle structuring. The environment allows multiple perspectives to intersect without solidifying into singular frames. Layers of fabric or mesh filter light, generating atmospheres that shift with movement, and when light and perspective come together in a specific way, they give rise to moiré patterns.

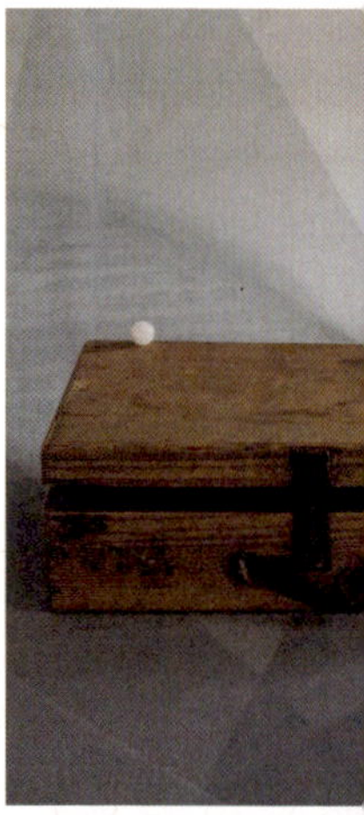

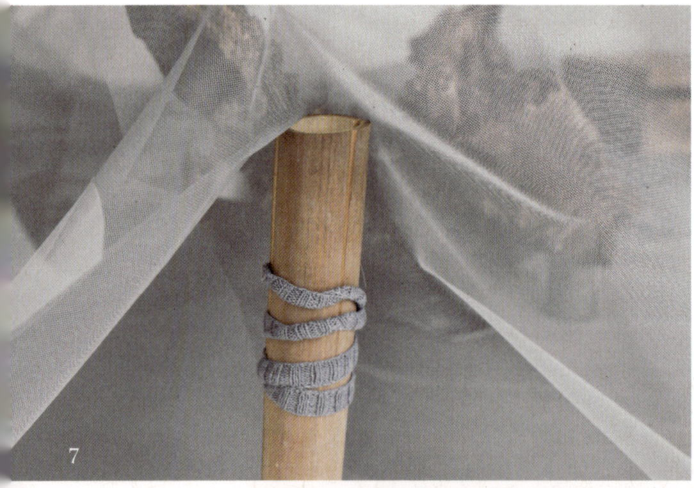

7

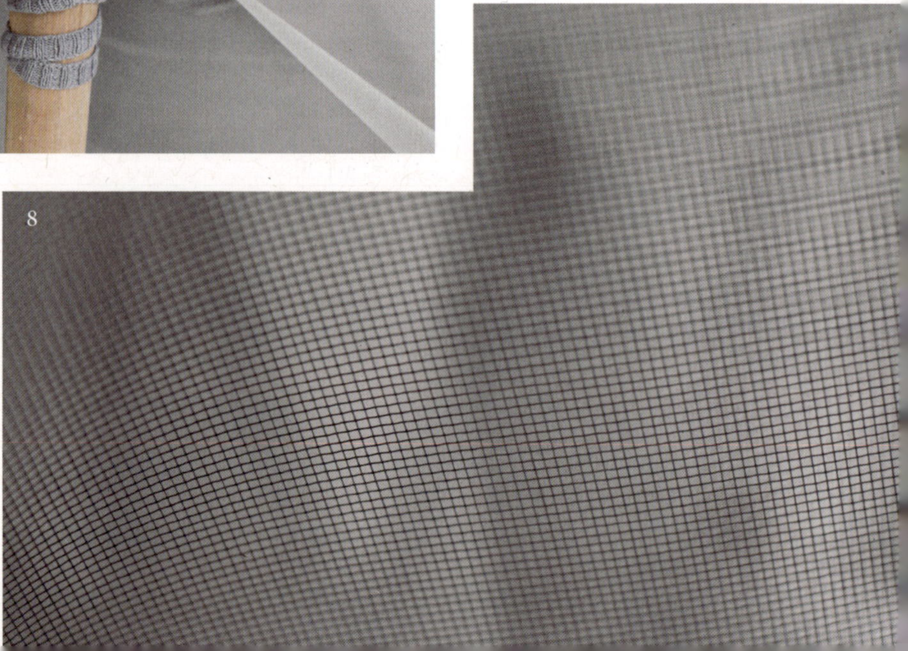

8

They are large-scale interference patterns that can be produced when a partially opaque ruled pattern with transparent gaps is overlaid on another similar pattern. For the moiré interference effect to appear, the two patterns must not be completely identical, but rather displaced, rotated, or have slightly different pitch. The term originates from *moiré* in its French adjectival form meaning a type of textile with a rippled or 'watered' appearance. Moire, or 'watered textile', is made by pressing two layers of the textile when wet. The similar but imperfect spacing of the threads creates a characteristic pattern which remains after the fabric dries.[15]

In our *choreographic environment*, we used synthetic fibre[16] and found an inspiring reference to physics, where the manifestation of wave interference can also be seen in the double-slit experiment.[17] Feminist theorist and physicist Karen Barad refers to this experiment when she discusses diffraction as 'cutting together-apart',[18] fundamentally altering conventional understandings. The wave-particle duality illustrated by the double-slit experiment reveals the intra-action between electrons and measuring apparatuses. I found the resonance between these concepts very apt within the choreographic environment. Through association and artistic reverie, I created connections between the moiré interferences and the

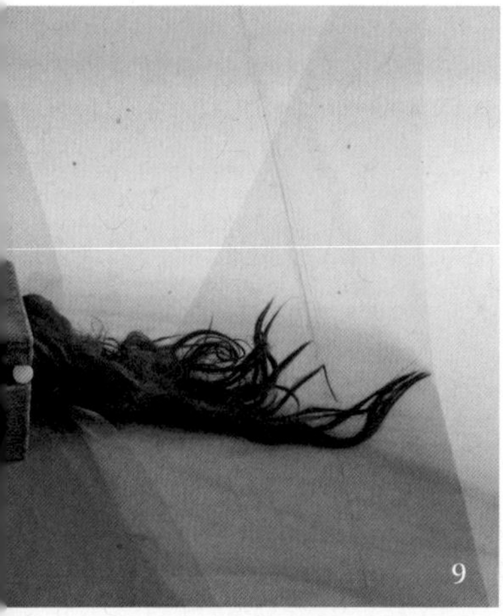
9

15. 'Moiré Pattern', *Britannica*, accessed 15 September 2025, https://www.britannica.com/science/moire-pattern.

16. The fabric will be reused after the project as a screen, as the project aims to be (environmentally) sustainable.

17. The double-slit experiment shows that particles like electrons or photons can behave as both particles and waves: when not observed, they create an interference pattern on a screen, as if each particle passes through both slits simultaneously. However, when a measurement determines which slit a particle goes through, this wave-like interference disappears, revealing the particle-like behaviour and highlighting the fundamental role of observation in quantum mechanics. 'Young's double-slit experiment', *Britannica*, accessed 15 September 2025, https://www.britannica.com/science/light/Youngs-double-slit-experiment. The beat phenomenon in acoustics is based on similar interference patterns: two close frequencies interfere, producing a pulsating sound that alternates between loud and soft at a rate equal to the frequency difference. 'Beat', *Britannica*, accessed 15 September 2025, https://www.britannica.com/science/beat-waves.

18. Karen Barad, 'Diffracting Diffraction: Cutting Together-Apart', *Parallax* 20, no. 3 (2014), 168–87.

Figs. 7–9: *Choreographic Environment*, 2020, © Mariella Greil and Walter Lauterer.

emergence of hypnotic watery patterns together with my deep dives into hydrofeminist[19] and post-humanist texts.

Choreo-ethical assemblaging in such an environment calls for a responsibility towards its fragility. The environment itself demands care, attunement, and reciprocity. It stages the fact that choreo-ethics is never self-sufficient but always embedded within conditions that exceed and sustain it. Thus, the structure that I co-created with Walter Lauterer did not merely house choreo-ethical assemblaging, it became a co-agent, shaping how relational intensities are distributed and perceived.

Consequently, inviting engagement with post-humanist hydrofeminism to permeate my artistic practice drove me to fully immerse myself in the medium of water. The diving tower[20] situated the embodied research within the medium of water.

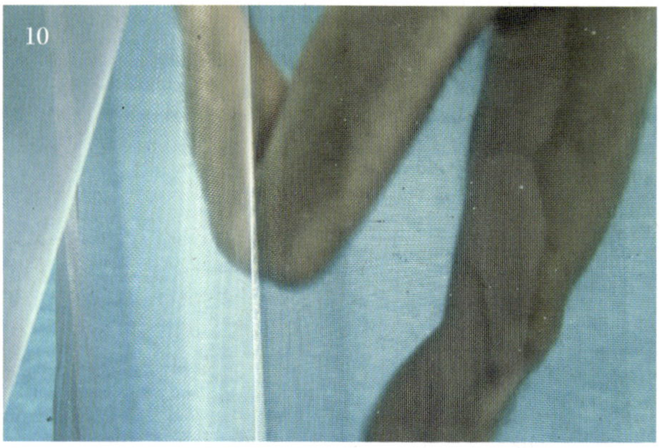

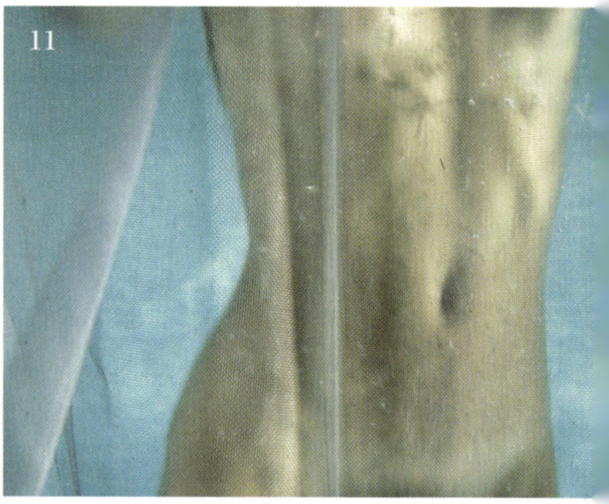

Here, immersion replaced suspension. Entering the aquatic environment, the performer confronted density, pressure, and the altered temporality of breath. Whereas the suspended architectural structure emphasised transparency and layering, the diving tower emphasised immersion and depth.

Water transforms movement. Gestures slow down, resistance increases, and gravity's pull is modulated by buoyancy. Sound transmits differently; vision refracts. The body must adapt to new laws of proprioception and survival: breath-holding, the equalisation of pressure, surrendering to currents. The medium is not neutral but constitutive, demanding new modes of attention and relation.

In this environment, the self-as-node is acutely aware of its vulnerability. Breath becomes the measure of time, and the possibility of submersion introduces both danger and release. The ethical dimension is heightened: immersion entails surrender, trust, and responsiveness. The medium itself becomes choreographic, shaping rhythm, intensity, and relationality.

19. Astrida Neimanis, *Bodies of Water: Posthuman Feminist Phenomenology* (Bloomsbury Academic, 2019).

20. We were performing and filming underwater and used the diving tower, a platform structure, to provide varying heights for diving to ensure controlled entry into the water for performers and the camera person.

Figs. 10 and 11: *Choreo-ethical Assemblages – Drowning in Depths*, 2025, © video still: Victor Jaschke, performance: Luisa Pisetta Ravanelli, concept: Mariella Greil.

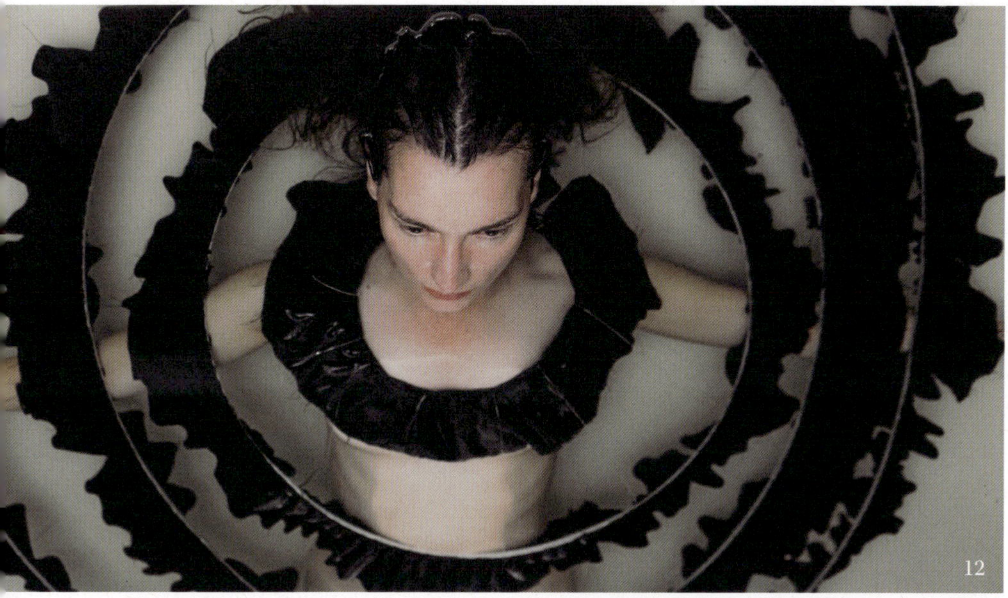

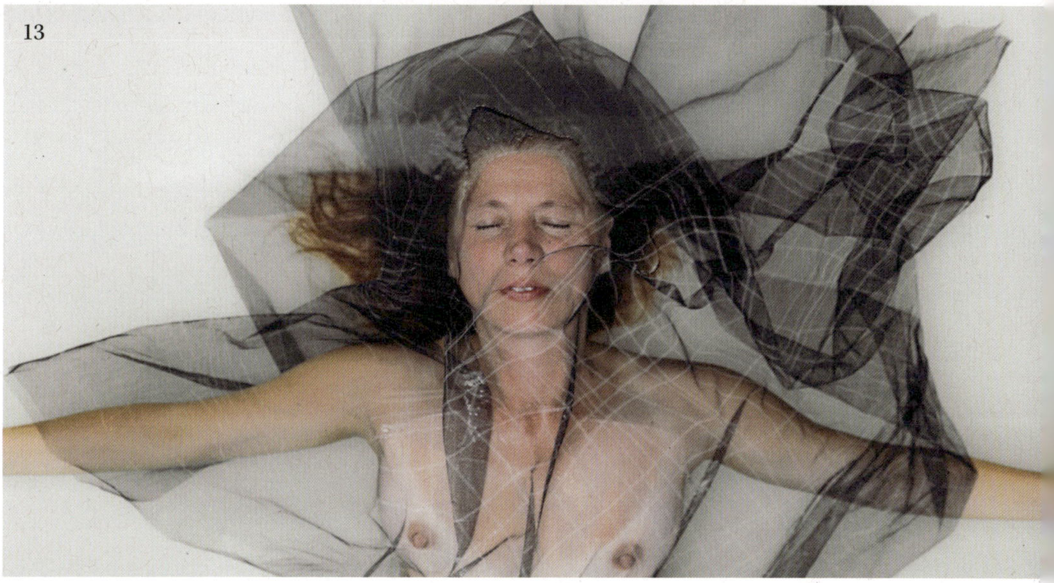

The diving tower exemplified how the environment-as-medium (→ Choreo-ethics as a Poetics of Being-in-the-Medium, 252) transforms the very conditions of embodied research. It situated practice not in transparency but in opacity, not in suspension but in immersion, foregrounding density, duration, and the precarious negotiation of limits.

The differentiations between these environments gave rise to the distinct choreo-ethical conditions to which the performative responses attuned themselves. The suspended architectural structure offered layering, transparency, and openness; the diving tower offered immersion, density, and temporal depth. One environment highlighted the airy and the visible, the other the aquatic and the opaque.

Yet both environments were defined by the contingencies of their own specific conditions.

Choreo-ethics is never free-floating but always shaped by the medium in which it unfolds. Each of the prepared choreographic environments demonstrated that space and medium are not backdrops but active significant participants,

Fig. 12: *Shaken Grounds – Sensory Deprivation Tank*, 2025, © video still: Victor Jaschke, performance: Lucie Strecker.

Fig. 13: *Shaken Grounds – Sensory Deprivation Tank*, 2025, © video still: Victor Jaschke, performance: Mariella Greil.

even co-constituents. This distinction clarified for me how different environmental affordances invite different ethical and aesthetic orientations: a care for fragility in the suspended structure, the surrender to density in the aquatic medium. Together, these orientations articulate the impact of the respective choreographic environments as conditions that were generative, ethically charged, and aesthetically effective. From plurality to co-generative ground, from œkological processes to nodal selves, from suspended architectures to an immersive medium, the following argument emerges as a thoroughly investigated consequence: the practice of choreo-ethical assemblage unfolds within environments that condition its very possibility. In other words, it is about a movement from the coexistence of elements (plurality) to a foundation that jointly produces a co-generative milieu. Choreo-ethical practice is embedded in this complex, interconnected environment – similar to ecological processes – and shapes entangled notions of subjectivity (nodal self-images) or, as in the jargon of post-human discourse, *trans-subjectivities.* Spatial dimensions are not just a background, they are the being-in-the-medium that emerges and actively inscribes itself into the practice, suspending an open, immersive, motile architecture. The performative practice of *choreo-ethical assemblaging* arises from dynamic, choreographed environments that enable its unfolding. These environments are not secondary but primary; they are not neutral stages but co-constitutive agents.

To speak of *choreographic environments as conditions* is thus to recognise that practice is inseparable from the milieus that sustain it. Responsibility emerges in the act of dwelling-with: with others, with materials, with atmospheres, with media. The choreo-ethical assemblage is this very articulation of practice and condition, of action and environment, of self and world.

Having established choreographic environments as conditions, my next task is linguistic: to name, describe, and verify the vocabulary through which my embodied practices become communicable. Vocabulary here is more than simply terminological precision; it is a choreo-ethical practice in itself, shaping how concepts move, resonate, and take hold. For me this is important, for to verify vocabulary is to acknowledge its performativity: words do not merely represent but participate in the constitution of the field. Just as environments condition movement, so, too, does language condition thought. In my view, precision[21] should be maintained together with openness, definition with resonance.[22] Rather than determining a lexicon, the task is to verify the relevance, weight, and viscosity of the terms – to allow them to remain mobile, relational, and accountable to practice.

We will now turn to the mini-lexicon, probing articulations of the vocabulary I developed in connection with this research and ensuring that language itself remains a co-generative participant in the cosmopoietic œkology of choreo-ethical assemblages.

21. In her text 'What if', Krassimira Kruschkova discusses *precise uncertainty.* Since I read about this, it has been one of the most influential paradoxa that I have been processing. See Krassimira Kruschkova, 'What If', in *Choreo-graphic Figures*, ed. Gansterer, Cocker, and Greil, 53.

22. I will pick up on this notion in more depth in → Aesthetics and Ethics are Twins, 271. See Hartmut Rosa, *Resonance: A Sociology of Our Relationship to the World*, trans. James Wagner (Polity, 2019), 358.

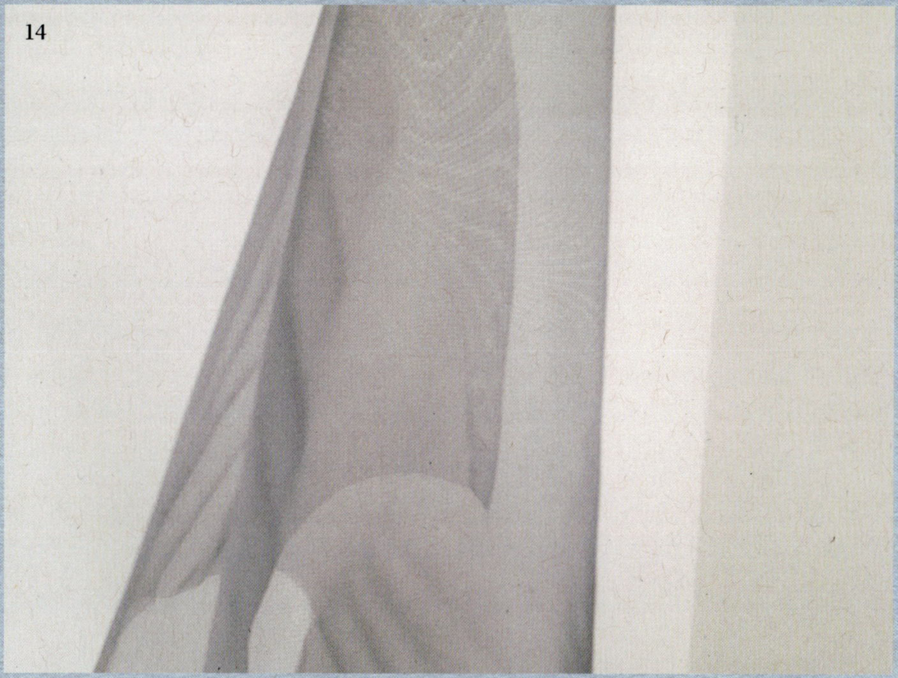
14

The Miroloi of Moire

To have no forms to rely on,
no shape to rest the hand upon,
finding no folds to hold or remember
the body by.
Moire interferes with oral modes of poetry;
songs of the space are not carried by breath alone,
heralding in a labile way of seeing.
Tilted fibres in motion,
patterns refusing to settle,
tiny gestures of haziness,
uncertain relation of grids,
switching lines.

She dreams of rerouted routines
eliciting a shift from textile sensation
to choreographic spell.
What once touched the skin
now choreographs the gaze.
Visual vibration unsettles the subliminal scope.

Neither veils of trauma
nor the losses of loved ones
appear as narratives or speeches of destiny.
These interferences of lament,
tears of curled effect,
bifurcate the grey in a dynamic, concentric manner.

Resisting closure, even temporary pause,
when space metabolizes slowly,
scaling up to silence, refracting the holding
of the moment.
The moire counters the marvel of an anechoic chamber,
where echoes are absorbed,
return differently.
Instead, within its choreographic environment,
visual waves interfere with each other,
a shimmering dance colliding through overlap,
layering intent.

The lightweight suspended architecture
structures the space for being,
rather than pausing.
This creates a fleeting centre.
However, she declines it,
instead moving towards the periphery,
wide awake with earthy elegance,
she feels the gravitational pull.

Never alone, towards the sweetest exhalation:
lungs emptied into wind,
intestines suspended from the sky.
The miroloi is sung where structure frays –
moireing song chanted at the gates of
the deepest sanctuary
in the world.

Verifying the Vocabulary

I understand writing not as the transcription of thought but as the rhythmic unfolding of embodied sense-making, the opening up of a choreographic dimension. Its cadence, interruptions, accelerations, and suspensions resemble the structuring of movement in time. Over the years, writing has become an integral part of my artistic practice. The rhythm of writing, the intense search for articulation, has become constitutive of my artistic practice and process of knowledge production in equal parts. To write in and through rhythm is to admit that thought itself moves – pulsating, staggering, pausing, drifting. For me, writing has become an event of embodiment, a corporeal inscription that gathers and disperses ideas, assembles and disassembles thoughts, much like choreography[23] unfolds through gestures and movements in relation to space, time, and other bodies. Writing is never innocent; it is always implicated in the very processes it seeks to articulate. When writing is approached as a form of choreographic practice, the text is not a neutral container but a vibrating field in which words enact the contingencies of embodiment. Thus, textual assemblages – patchworks of fragments, citations, voices, and rhythms – emerge as complex configurations: of words forming a specified vocabulary or transforming into a sounding board. Amid the plurality of language-based research, I seek to modestly form and probe modes of articulation – and in the end it will be up to you, the reader, to *verify the vocabulary* that I propose here.

Scholarship and assemblage have come together as a textual method for this book. Both forms of writing recognise that language itself is porous, that it carries its own histories, affects, and orientations. Gilles Deleuze and Félix Guattari's notion of the assemblage emphasises heterogeneity and connection; it is a constellation of heterogeneous elements provisionally brought into relation without subsuming difference under unity. A textual assemblage is a processual configuration – a writing-in-motion that choreographs language into constellations of proximity and distance, resonance and dissonance. In practice, I poetically condense my studio notes, artistic sketches, and mind maps into a text that runs in parallel and enters into a dialogue with scholarly writing.

This aligns with embodied research practices that engage with knowledge as something that emergences performatively – and, quite similarly, creative writing practices perform across the page. To choreograph language is to heighten awareness of its materiality: the weight of a comma, the silence of a pause, the sudden rupture of a dash. Writing moves in waves, beats, and counterpoints. It hesitates and leaps, much like a dancing body negotiating gravity and suspension. The rhythm of writing choreographs thought into a temporal unfolding, allowing meaning to arise slowly and through arcs of tension. Writing in this sense is less about representation than about evocation: it generates atmospheres of thought and sensibility, staging the ephemeral presence of embodiment.

23. The edited volume *Writing Choreography: Textualities of and Beyond Dance* articulates how the act of writing in dance scholarship and practice generates a textual body that does more than merely describe movement and actually enacts its own choreographic strategies. Together with Emma Cocker and Nikolaus Gansterer, I contributed a chapter entitled 'Choreo-graphic Writing – Towards More-than-One Means of Inscription' to the book. Leena Rouhiainen et al., eds., *Writing Choreography: Textualities of and beyond Dance* (Routledge, 2024).

From my perspective, embodied research requires writing that can sustain the proximity of sensation and concept, writing that does not merely abstract but re-sensitizes, where the writing itself delves back into sensation or uncovers other, additional layers of experience. Here, language[24] becomes a verb: writing is not about language as an object but about the continuous act of *languaging*, a process of shaping and reshaping perception into communicable textures. Languaging acknowledges that language emerges from the body's intra-actions with the world that it is a part of. It is a corporeal practice, shaped by breath, gesture, and attention, slides and slips of the tongue.[25] In this mode, the text is not supplementary to the embodied inquiry; it is one of its choreographic layers.

Textual assemblages together with scholarly reflections thus act as epistemic choreographies: they arrange words but also stage encounters – between disciplines, between theory and practice, between sensation and articulation. Each fragment of writing participates in a larger score, not unlike choreographic scores that hold open spaces for interpretation and improvisation. Writing as an assemblage has you, the readers, in mind and invites you to enter into a performative relationship with the text, moving with its rhythms, responding to its pauses, and being unsettled by its ruptures.

Besides clarity in the sense of argumentation, what matters for me is clarity as luminous resonance: writing's ability to create conditions in which the body of the reader senses the body of the writer, the movement of thought, the vibration of presence. Having spent years thinking about and critically questioning my own practice, I have come to understand (and have maybe learned the hard way) that to write choreographically is to affirm vulnerability and excess, to risk fragmentation and contradiction, to invite the reader into an ethical encounter with the incompleteness of embodied research. Rhythm and assemblage, in this sense, are not stylistic embellishments but methodological commitments: they affirm that knowledge arises through movement, through relation, through the choreographies of language itself.

Embodied Research It is not with abstraction that embodied research begins but with the elemental: the bare body. Stripped of any ornamentation, prior to representation, the body is encountered as a site of immediacy, vulnerability, and inexhaustible generativity. Setting aside the nostalgic search for authenticity, moving from within the bare body means acknowledging a radical beginning, an originary condition where perception is unmediated by conceptual overlays. Here, embodiment is not something one 'has' but something one continuously becomes.

24. Antrianna Moutoula, 'Unclogging the Ears: Nonstop Languaging as Autotheory in Art and Academia', *Arts* 11, no. 6 (2022): 114, https://doi.org/10.3390/arts11060114.

25. Mariella Greil, Victor Jaschke, Werner Moebius, and SCOBYs (symbiotic cultures of bacteria and yeast) within the scope of *Shaken Grounds* with Nikolaus Gansterer, Peter Kozek, and Lucie Strecker, 'Onomatopoetic Sound(e)scape: Slides and Slips Between Sonances and Symbiosis', 7 May 2025, meeting of the language-based artistic research special interest group, Society of Artistic Research (SAR) Conference, Porto, online video: https://www.researchcatalogue.net/view/2759372/3604371; and Mariella Greil and Werner Moebius, 'Onomatopoetic Sound(e)scape – Slides and Slips between Sound and Speech', 11 April 2024, SAR Forum, Tilburg, online video: https://www.researchcatalogue.net/view/835089/2686626.

Movement arises from the density of presence itself; dwelling in the bare body is to drop into direct experience. This dropping-in is less about intention than about surrender and suspension: a relinquishing of mastery, of the will to control, in order to allow sensation to guide action. This kind of practice resists the Cartesian separation of body and mind, affirming instead that knowledge arises immanently through corporeal encounter. As architect, author, and yogi Peter Sterios observes, 'Sensation is the body's native language.'[26] This phrase is instructive: rather than supplementing cognition, sensation is its ground, its originary articulation. To perform with and through the body is to pay attention to sensation as the elemental idiom of existence. Therefore, in embodied research, sensation is more than just registered – it is cultivated as an epistemic practice. The body becomes both subject and method, producing knowledge not through discursive analysis alone but through attunement to the micro-movements of breath, weight, balance, and vibration. Such a research approach places emphasis on 'moving from within', a practice that designates both a methodological orientation and an ethical stance. It calls for the relinquishing of external authority in favour of listening to the body's internal cues, to rhythms that unfold in subterranean strata of awareness. As I have elaborated elsewhere[27] in great detail, the bareness of the body is not just the absence of clothing or theatrical artifice; in my understanding, it is the exposure of corporeal vulnerability, the willingness to be seen, felt, and affected. It is in this exposure that embodied research acquires its generative force. Bare bodies are not neutral; we know with certainty that they are marked by histories, inscribed by social, political, and cultural forces. Yet when approached from within, bodies can also exceed these inscriptions. If we engage, they open up towards the not-yet-articulated, towards emergent possibilities that destabilise normative, rigid value systems. In this sense, bare bodies become a site of radical imagination, a place where new forms of trans*subjectivity and relationality can unfold.

Embodied research therefore demands a simultaneous double movement: an inward turn towards sensation and an outward articulation of what emerges in and through relational contexts, an opening-up towards the world (→ Cosmopoiesis, 129). This double movement parallels breathing: the inhalation of experience, the exhalation of expression. It also mirrors the rhythm of choreographic practice, oscillating between improvisation and composition, between the immediacy of the present moment and the reflective process of documentation, analysis, and synthesis. In my practice, writing and moving are interwoven modalities of embodied research, each feeding into the other, each carrying the trace of sensation. *She is movement, fully embodied.* I want to resist treating the body as an object of study or a vessel for symbolic representation. Instead, the body is acknowledged as a process, as kinetic unfolding. The body does not 'do' movement; the body *is* movement, always. To inhabit such an understanding destabilises hierarchical separations between subject and object, mind and body, theory and practice. I will keep repeating

26. Peter Sterios, personal communication with the author within the scope of the Inner Teacher Academy, 5 September 2025.

27. Mariella Greil, *Being in Contact – Encountering a Bare Body* (Edition Angewandte, De Gruyter, 2021); Mariella Greil, ed., *Bare Bodies – Thresholding Life* (Edition Angewandte, De Gruyter, 2024).

this mantra. Embodied research affirms a continuum of becoming, where corporeality and thought are entangled in a dynamic dance. This approach resonates – I would say loudly – with phenomenological insights, where embodiment is not a container for subjectivities (or trans*subjectivities) but their very precondition. Phenomenologist Maurice Merleau-Ponty's famous emphasis on the body as 'our general medium for having a world'[28] finds renewed force in embodied research methodologies that foreground movement as epistemic. Yet embodied research pushes on by describing as well as enacting the epistemic potency of the body in practice. It insists on the inseparability of research and performance, method and material.

Dropping into direct experience is a mode of resisting abstraction's premature closure and slows down the process of drawing conclusions. It allows research to remain porous, to be unsettled by what arrives unexpectedly. Embodied research therefore aligns with practices of receptivity, of sensibility, both qualities that resonate with psychotherapeutic approaches – in short, with the capacity to be affected by the unforeseeable. Working from within the bare body means to accept that research cannot be fully planned, that it must remain open to emergence, to the 'unexpected event' that interrupts categories. Sterios' proposition that sensation is the body's native language underscores the necessity of a methodological – maybe also linguistic – shift: one that recognises the equivalency of somatic articulation. Language in this sense is not confined to words; it encompasses gestures, tones, silences, movements, and their affective resonances. Sensation is articulation, and research must learn to listen. As a consequence, this requires a mode of thinking-feeling-writing that does not overwrite the body's voice but amplifies it, that allows textuality to resonate with corporeality.

In my practice, embodied research strives to cultivate a sensitivity to thresholds:[29] between stillness and motion, interiority and exteriority, vulnerability and power. It is at these thresholds that knowledge is generated – not as an abstract proposition but as a 'felt sense',[30] an embodied articulation that turns into sensed meaning when language or a symbol aligns with the sensation felt. The researcher becomes a choreographer, performer, witness – these roles alternative, with writing and moving across registers of practice seamlessly interweaving.

More than an escape into subjective indulgence, embodied research is an invitation to practice trans*subjectivity (→ Trans*formative and Performative Aesthetics – Performance Matter/ing as a Choreography of Ethics, 295). The bare body, exposed and vulnerable, radically invites relational[31] encounters. Its knowledge

28. Maurice Merleau-Ponty, *Phenomenology of Perception*, trans. Colin Smith (Routledge & Kegan Paul, 1962), 169.

29. Greil, *Bare Bodies*.

30. The term *felt sense* comes from Eugene T. Gendlin, a philosopher and psychotherapist who developed the practice of focusing in the 1960s and 1970s. Gendlin developed and worked with ideas like 'bodily felt sense', 'experiencing', and 'felt meaning' in his philosophical and psychological book *Experiencing and the Creation of Meaning* (1962), while the term 'felt sense' evolved in *Focusing* (1978). See specifically Eugene T. Gendlin, *Focusing* (Random House, 2003 [1978]), 14.

31. Petra Sabisch, *Choreographing Relations: Practical Philosophy and Contemporary Choreography in the Works of Antonia Baehr, Gilles Deleuze, Juan Dominguez, Félix Guattari, Xavier Le Roy and Eszter Salamon* (Epodium, 2011).

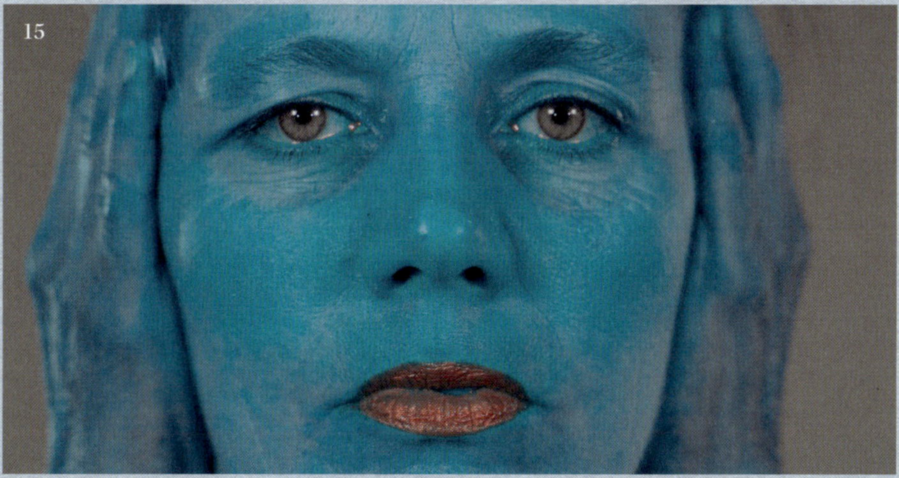

Direct Hit

A selfie is never grieving,
language never fully lost,
not at the principal turning point
near the oracle.
The chorus of the pomegranate
splits its seed-red mouth.
Glitching reverse language stutters,
a grammar of onomatopoiesis
where sense arrives
as a direct hit, no explanation.

Dirty spaces of consistently
pressing questions
blur the days passing.
The immediacy of tears in her eyes
refuses delay, refuses rehearsal.
A parapsychic playground opens,
where the axes of Martian dramaturgies
tilt the scene,
and gravity gently pulls on the fissures
of the self.

Avatar assurance, containment by death –
the sequencing of dreams takes place anyway,
drifts between frames of forgetful laughter,
the uncanny stability of being in the medium
holding us still while everything moves.
A counter-movement grows, quietly,
towards symbiotic cultures that breathe together.

Kinetic sequencing becomes prayer:
an ongoing improvised movement
between your eyes and my body,
mutual fondness looping into immersive embrace,
unwinding open perception.

I search for the reverberation of light in your iris,
the sensitive, unsettled recognition of
what cannot be known
before the encounter arrives.

Pivoting sensations teach vulnerable directness.
Embodied wording is nourished from within
– the visceral relational wisdom
entangled with the others' glance.

Lips open gently, hesitating,
forming a mark on another's soul
and proliferate excessive imagining,
an abundance of values, possibilities,
– realities that multiply from a single,
irreversible contact.

The Hydrofeminist

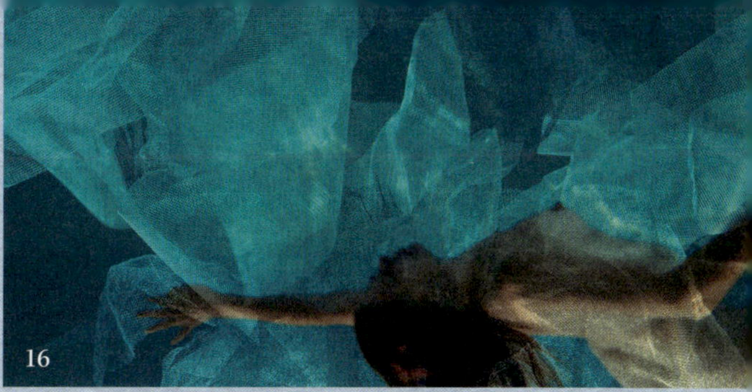

16

Diving into becoming
wet relations amidst
tides of endocrine release,
moist muscles that extend and bend.
She succumbed to the fabric,
its fluid movement
carried by subtle buoyancy.

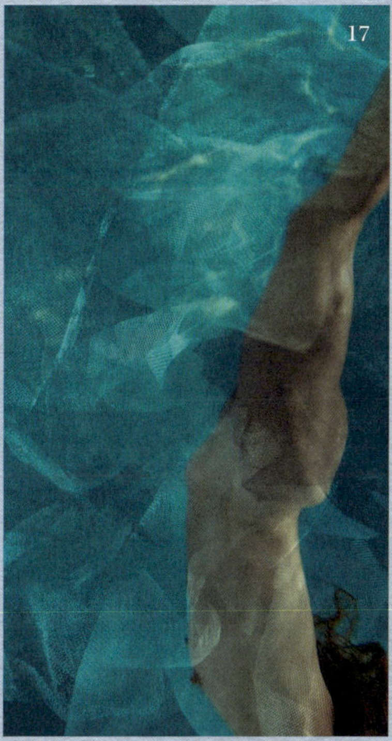

17

Shadowy probes of
intercellular fluids,
tissues of humble human water.
Substances that flow and stir,
breathe and dance.
Flushes of liquid drifts
suck her into eddies of elation,
slipping back into euphoria,
unguardedly.

She listens from a distance
to the fragility of chuckles,
otherworldly noises that come
from the deep.
Her lungs fill, she allows fluency
in her thought.
The bodies' fluids settle
like ocean dust.
Near the abyss, the seabed rises,
while the ripples arrive as surface
flows at the shore.

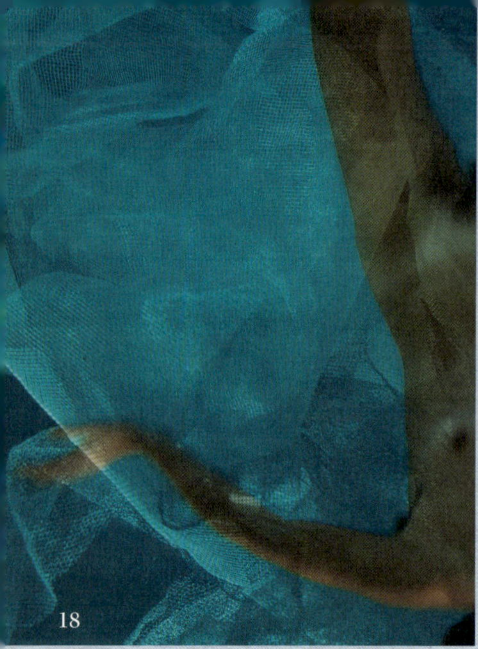

18

Drowning in her dissolution,
the hydrofeminist percolates
the waves,
cuts across the openings
of the fabric
in a gentle, surrendering dance.

Hydromorphic lust arises
as she falls into the darkness
of hazy notion.

In the depths of her viscera,
she encounters seismic, bittersweet Eros.
A vibrating body senses quivering excitement,
revealing blooms of intimacy
between the fleshy tissues.
No more abundant souls,
explicit aqueous jouissance.

Oxygen creatures carry the seeds in their mouths.
Tender and strong, a flower on tongue,
her beauty is porosity,
translucent skins touching
in luminous profundity.

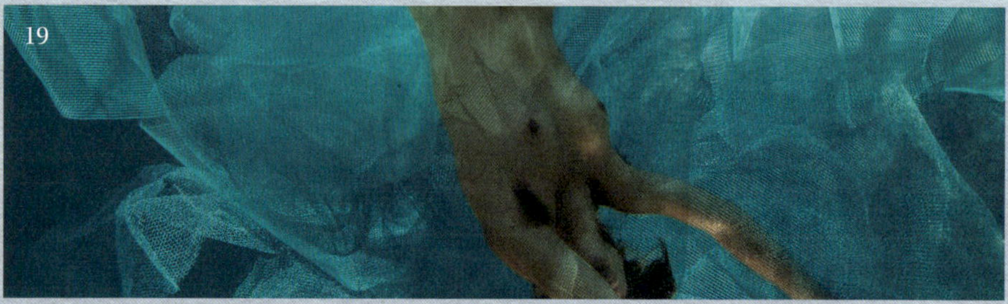

19

is not solitary but shared, not private but co-constituted. To move from within is also to move with and toward, to acknowledge that, from the outset, embodiment is always entangled with others – human and other-than-human. Research here becomes a series of choreo-ethical assemblages, staging encounters that transform both selves and others, always in the plural.

Ultimately, embodied research affirms that knowledge is not only thought but also felt, not only argued but also enacted. It situates the bare body as both a site and a method, sensation as both a language and a guide. In dropping into direct experience, research does not abandon its rigor but in fact becomes more rigorous, grounding epistemology in the immediacy of being. In doing so, it allows imagination to flourish – as an embodied response to its contingencies rather than as an escape from reality.

Practices of Polyvalence Polyvalence signifies diversity, a quality of simultaneous potentialities that resists reduction to a single meaning or a definitive form. As a practice, it invokes the generativity of excess: an embodied method for keeping contradictions, ambivalences, and layered registers of signification in play. Practicing polyvalence means affirming that knowledge, like movement, never exists in just one dimension; rather, it oscillates, resonates, and fractures.

The etymology of the term helps us to fathom its epistemic depth. From the Latin *poly* (many) and *valence* (strength, capacity), polyvalence designates a condition of 'many strengths' or 'multiple capacities'. The root *valere* means 'to be strong', 'to be well', 'to be able', evoking both power and vitality.[32] Polyvalence thus carries a sense of abundance and resilience: the ability to inhabit multiple positions, to generate meanings that are coexistent rather than mutually exclusive. In chemistry, 'valence' is an atom's capacity to form bonds with other atoms; polyvalence accordingly marks an enhanced capacity for relation, for multiple bonds. Applied to embodied research, this etymology suggests that polyvalence is not simply about variety but about relational potency, about the capacity to connect in diverse and unpredictable ways.

Polyvalent practices have emerged as a methodological anchor in my embodied research as they resist unilinear trajectories of meaning-making. In the practice of movement, they might appear as performative gestures or figures that are simultaneously intimate and public, vulnerable and forceful, opaque and transparent. In textual assemblages, they can take the form of writing that performs multiple registers – poetic, analytic, autobiographic, theoretical – without reconciling them into a single authorial voice. Polyvalent practices as an aesthetic and ethical stance align with hydrofeminist and post-human theoretical commitments to multiplicity and solidarity. As a concept, and practiced within the context of my work, polyvalence holds spaces open where differences can coexist without merging into each other. Polyvalent practices are committed to operating through negotiation,

32. 'Origin and history of *valence*', etymonline, accessed 12 July 2025, https://www.etymonline.com/word/valence.

by keeping as many options in play for as long as possible. They have been crafted as situated, as open-ended, and as capable of combining partly with one element, partly with another.

In my embodied practice, polyvalence is cultivated through attentional shifts. As a performer, I attune myself to multiple sensations simultaneously: the pull of gravity, the texture of skin against fabric, the awareness of another's gaze, the sound of breath. Each of these registers contributes to the polyphonic texture of the moment, a layered presence. Polyvalence demands an acute sensitivity to simultaneity, to the interweaving of heterogeneous forces. The body becomes a site where multiplicity does not fragment but intensifies experience. In the 'Diffractive Dialogue Score' as well as the 'Dark Bag Score' (→ Scores, 387), polyvalent practices are the key to dismantling hierarchies of experiences and meanings, and instead cultivating an openness towards choreo-ethical assemblages. In traditional epistemologies, knowledge is often stratified: some forms have been deemed more legitimate, others relegated to the margins. Polyvalence disrupts this order by granting equal valence to multiple registers of knowing. Sensation, affect, intuition, and imagination are not subordinated to rational cognition but stand as equally potent modes of articulation. Such a stance challenges academic conventions that privilege linear argumentation and singular authorship. Instead, polyvalence affirms the legitimacy of plural voices, of collaborative research practices that choreograph complexity rather than simplify it.

Textually, polyvalence manifests in hybrid forms of writing that weave theory together with diary entries, citation with imagination, critique with poetry. These assemblages are methodological rather than ornamental: they enact in language the very multiplicity that they advocate. Polyvalence thus becomes both theme and practice, subject and method. The text itself becomes a polyvalent assemblage, asking readers to inhabit the tensions and resonances between its layers.

Ethically, polyvalent practices articulate a commitment to relationality. Thus, whereas valence names the capacity to bond, polyvalence gestures towards the necessity of cultivating multiple relations across difference. In the setup of my research project *Choreo-ethical Assemblages – Narrations of Bare Bodies*, this often meant acknowledging the entanglement of human and other-than-human agencies, of cultural histories and personal experiences, of affective resonances and material conditions. Polyvalence dwells within that complexity and can become a strategy for resilience in contexts of precarity.

By cultivating multiple capacities, embodied research avoids the brittleness of singular definitions. Polyvalent practices distribute intensity across registers; they are a way of affirming that no single mode of articulation can capture the fullness of embodied knowledge. Instead, meaning arises in the shifting interplay of many strengths. In this sense, polyvalent practices are deeply generative. Practices of polyvalence do not merely represent complexity; they enact it, they choreograph it, they make it felt. The multiplicity itself produces new forms of knowledge and relation; polyvalent practices therefore affirm that strength lies in the capacity to sustain plurality, to allow contradictions and resonances to coexist as fertile grounds for research.

Epistemic Singularities The knowing heart is at the core of my understanding of epistemic singularities.[33] Let me begin with a memory. In 2007 when Sweet and Tender Collaboration was the first major group gathering at the Performing Arts Forum in St. Erme,[34] my colleague and friend Hajime Fujita said something that still resonates with me today: 'Mariella, you know, everything, really *everything*, has to pass through the heart.' Since then, I have been practicing passing things through my heart, which I honestly find to be a rather complex task – it has become the mantra of my ongoing embodied praxis. Phenomenologist Henri Maldiney introduced *transpassibilité* (transpassibility), a profound receptivity, a form of *pathic sensibility* to existence and to the *événement* (event), to what arrives unforeseeably and cannot be assimilated into pre-existing categories. It names the existential 'exposure' to that which disrupts or that which is *rien* (nothing),[35] or – in my own words – that which emerges as *bare bodies*.[36] From a pathic sensibility that registers the affective tremors of existence and exposes bare bodies as sites of both vulnerability and potentiality, imagination emerges as the generative force that transforms corporeal precarity into openings for ethical and aesthetic refiguration. As Maldiney writes, the 'primary principle' is

> that the thought of the heart is the thought of images, that the heart is the seat of imagination, that imagination is the authentic voice of the heart, so that if we speak from the heart we must speak imaginatively.[37]

Imagining for me lays the ground for epistemic singularity; the singular artistic voices that have demonstrated their radical receptivity to hearts articulate unique aesthetic positionings. In the Hibbard Lectures he gave at Manchester College on the present situation in philosophy (1909), psychologist William James emphasises

33. Here, I would like to make reference to the work of my esteemed colleagues Arno Böhler and Susanne Valerie Granzer, who are the Principle Investigators in the FWF research project *Arts in Philosophy: Philosophy in the Arts; On The Significance of the *Heart* in Artistic-Research and Performance Philosophy* at the Artistic Research Center located at the University of Music and Performing Arts, Vienna. I would also like to mention an early, but still inspiring work, namely Arno Böhler's *Singularitäten: Vom Zu-Reichenden Grund der Zeit; Vorspiel einer Philosophie der Freundschaft* (Passagen, 2005).

34. The Performing Arts Forum (PAF) is a place for practitioners and activists from the performing arts, visual art, literature, music, new media and the internet, theory, and cultural production, as well as scholars who seek to research and determine their own conditions of work. PAF is a place for people who are able to mobilise their own artistic production and knowledge production, and do not just respond to the opportunities given by the institutional market. Initiated and run by artists, theoreticians, and practitioners themselves, PAF is an informal, user-created institution; it is a platform for anyone who wants to expand their possibilities and interests in their own working practice. See Performing Arts Forum, accessed 29 August 2025, https://www.pa-f.net.

35. Henri Maldiney, *Penser l'homme et la folie*, 361–425, quoted in Mika Elo and Miika Luoto, eds., *Figures of Touch: Sense, Technics, Body* (The Academy of Fine Arts at the University of the Arts Helsinki, 2018).

36. Greil, *Being in Contact.*

37. James Hillman, *Thought of the Heart and the Soul of the World* (Spring Publications, 2021), 7.

'a pluralistic universe', the idea that the world is full of openness and unfinishedness. James argues against a single, unified, absolute whole. Instead, he advocates for the radical pluralism of 'each-form',[38] or, as we might refer to it today, 'idiosyncrasy', a quality that is often discussed in artistic research contexts. In the arts, a plurality of aesthetic voices makes itself heard. At the core of James' argument is the experience of intimacy, which he claims is only possible within a pluralistic universe. In this collection of lectures, he also argues that our beliefs form part of reality, which resonates with what I will introduce as *cosmopoietic practice* in → *Cosmopoiesis,* 129. James also unfurls why he thinks that pluralistic empiricism is a better ally than religion or rationalism,[39] as for him, *knowledge* arises *contextually* through *pluralistic, novel experiences* – no *single method* or *belief system* can fully capture reality's *epistemic uniqueness.* In resonance with James' radical empiricist and pluralist stance, I emphasise that reality is never totally unified and always unfolds through (hopefully) diverse, context-dependent experiences. For me, nothing is *fully* encompassed by a singular scientific method or monistic truth; instead, I am convinced that knowledge emerges in fragments, in the spaces between knowledges, radically contingent upon unique experiential encounters as *epistemic singularities.*

In conclusion, for me, epistemic singularities are not isolated phenomena; they are nodal intensities within a wider meshwork of relations. Rather than precluding connection, their uniqueness insists upon situatedness – each singularity shines in the specificity of its own conditions while resonating across practices and contexts. They are not universals but idiosyncratic constellations of embodied knowledge, emerging each time anew when the research is communicated. To engage epistemic singularities is to commit to a form of attentiveness that honours the irreducibility of the moment while also acknowledging the relational field that makes such singularities perceivable and transmissible. I am aware that my perspective is shaped by a predominantly Eurocentric framework, assuming familiarity with European contexts, practices, and references, which inevitably limits its scope of address. I acknowledge this limitation and recognize the necessity of further situating my references in relation to diverse epistemologies, particularly those emerging from the Global South. I wish I had the expertise to engage more substantially with these perspectives, to more fully attend to the entanglements of colonial histories, Eurocentric framings, and their enduring effects on artistic and theoretical practices. However, I hope to offer methodical bridges as I practice the 'Diffractive Dialogue Score' and the 'Dark Bag Score', which are clearly embedded

38. James introduced the concept of 'each-form' in distinction to 'all-form' at the end of 'Lecture I: The Types of Philosophy' and picks it up again at the beginning of 'Lecture II: Monistic Idealism'. Later in 'Lecture VII: The Continuity of Experience', he discusses experience which in a passage relevant to our context: 'It is the general conceptualist difficulty of any one thing being the same with many things, either at once or in succession, for the abstract concepts of oneness and manyness must needs exclude each other. In the particular instance that we have dwelt on so long, the one thing is the *all-form* of experience, the many things are the *each-forms* of experience in you and me. To call them the same we must treat them as if each were simultaneously its own other, a feat on conceptualist principles impossible of performance.' William James, *A Pluralistic Universe: Hibbert Lectures at Manchester College on the Present Situation in Philosophy* (1909; Project Gutenberg, 2024), Lectures II and VII, accessed 13 October 2025, https://www.gutenberg.org/cache/epub/11984/pg11984-images.html.

39. See ibid., especially Lectures I and VIII.

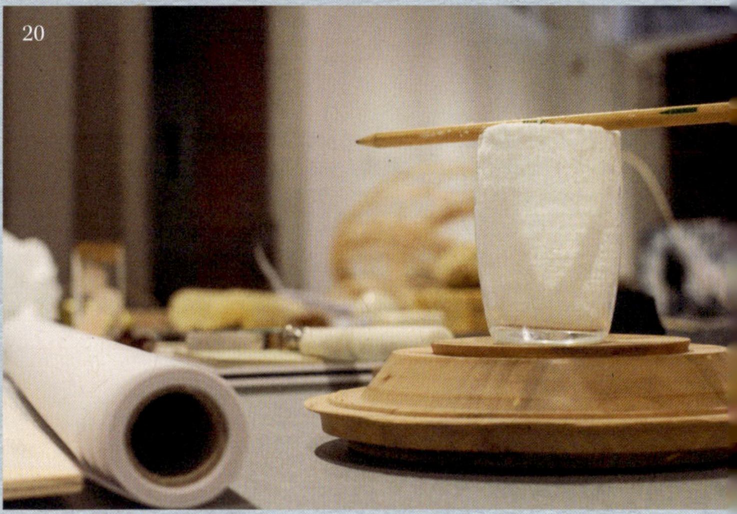

Crystals

Salt of the earth
– sibling of snowflake and diamond –
you land in quiet.
We hark back to spellwork
to break symmetry temporally,
daring the boundaries of time crystals.
You know oceans by compression,
you know pressure without a scene.
Through the dismantling of any impurities,
metamorphic processes of molecular
bonding occur.

The mineral structures figure out the
dew point,
murmurs of molten magma,
ice crystals suspended in the air.
Duration is folded.
Temporality hesitates, loops itself.
Teeth and bones are the crystalline forms
of the body.

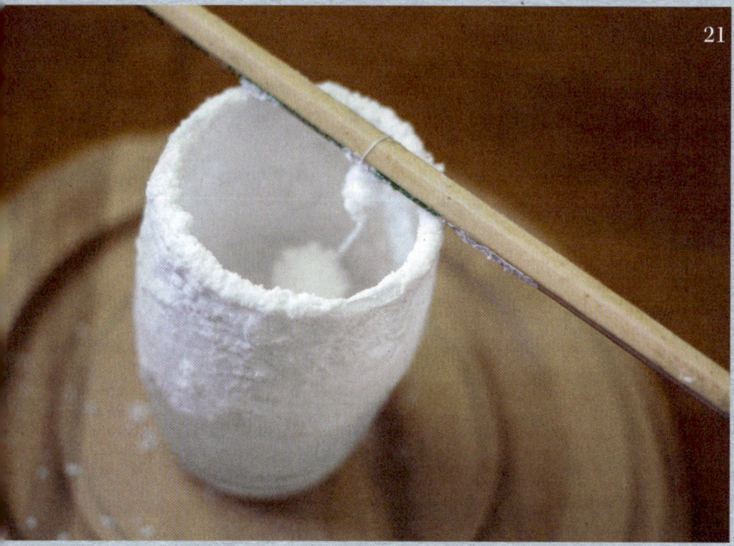
21

Glass half-full or half-empty,
quartz half-transparent or half-opaque,
body half-flesh and half-vessel,
bone half-sensation and half-architecture.

Double tongues, double pack,
double bind, double logic,
double exposure, double movement,
double risk, double address.

A crystal is matter that has decided to
remember itself.
It grows molecule by molecule –
until chance becomes pattern.
Solids form because they have learned
to hold still.
Light enters, is broken, doubled,
returned altered.
Duration exceeds witness,
chaos persuaded into rhythm,
metaphoric intimacy – clasp, release,
clasp again.

within their culturally and kinesthetically specific milieu, and I believe that these artistic research methods are accessible across diverse contexts.

Collective Contingencies Collectivity is never simply a given; it is always contingent. Choreography and dance as artistic practices lend themselves to collaboration. To gather, to act together, to think or move together requires the constant negotiation of differences, vulnerabilities, and emergent conditions. Collective practices are actual choreographies of contingency, unfolding through unpredictable dynamics that resist mastery. They demand an ongoing attentiveness to what exceeds planning – the unforeseen alignments, frictions, and dissonances that will always emerge when bodies, voices, and materials collaborate, often in the heat of group dynamics and conflicts. However, in the artistic research project *Contingent Agencies* (2019–25), artist and researcher Nikolaus Gansterer and artist-researcher Alex Arteaga creatively directed these volatile structures and atmospheres into their lively, generative dimensions, thereby emphasizing co-emergence. Gansterer writes, 'What apparatus do we conjure to diagram and analyze the rhythms of life as they pulse through our collective becoming?'[40] In my understanding, contingency is not an obstacle to collectivity but its very precondition, for it is only in the openness of indeterminate situations that collective action becomes meaningful. This observation crystallises into a crucial methodological insight: collectivity is not about overcoming contingency but about inhabiting it, choreographing with its instabilities. To work collectively across agencies is to surrender the fantasy of control and embrace the generative potential of uncertainty. Embodied research offers fertile ground for practicing such collective contingencies. My improvisational scores – the 'Diffractive Dialogue Score' and the 'Dark Bag Score' – attuned themselves to the shifting dynamics of the choreo-ethical assemblages as they emerged within the choreographic environments. Movement arose not from individual intention alone but from the relational field: gestures emerged in resonance or dissonance with others, decisions unfolded in the shared present, and the choreography was co-constituted moment by moment. This was a fragile process, for it could never be guaranteed; yet it was precisely this fragility that enabled the emergence of the not-yet-known.

Collective contingencies include other-than-human agencies (→ Human Index, 410, and → Other-than-Human-Index, 414) and foreground the ethical dimension of assemblages across various forms of existence. To work together contingently across trans*materialities means to (at least in part) relinquish sovereignty, to acknowledge interdependence, to remain open to being affected. It requires the cultivation of practices of listening, waiting, and responding without foreclosing. In this sense, collectivity becomes a practice of vulnerability[41] – where the

40. Alex Arteaga and Nikolaus Gansterer, eds., *Contingent Agencies: Inquiring into the Emergence of Atmospheres* (Hatje Cantz, 2025).

41. Erinn C. Gilson, *The Ethics of Vulnerability: A Feminist Analysis of Social Life and Practice* (Routledge, 2014).

strength of the collective fabric lies in its capacity to sustain difference, to linger[42] in the discomfort of alienation, and to embrace the challenges posed by the multiplicity of forces at play. The tree trunk, the broken shoe, the wooden suitcase, and the plant; a soft, filthy, deep-purple woollen bundle; stone flour and sponges – the aesthetics of collective assemblages are inseparable from their ethics. Each encounter is singular, and yet the practice itself is durable precisely because it embraces ephemerality as constitutive. The aesthetics of contingency resist commodification; they refuse to be stabilised into a product, insisting instead on the value of process, of the lived intensity of collective presence that extends beyond human actors, inviting other-than-human agencies to be present. Moreover, the temporality of collective contingencies is distinct; it unfolds through *kairos*, the opportune moment that arises unpredictably.

In the setup of the prepared choreographic environment, we affirmed a distributed creativity that arose in the interstices between bodies, thoughts, and materials. Knowledge co-emerged through collective processes. I contend that contingency is constitutive rather than accidental: it is the condition under which collectivity can come into being.

Talk with Walter Lauterer – Choreographic Environment
Edited transcript
13 July 2020

Mariella Greil: The choreographic environment creates a basis, a sort of framing.

Walter Lauterer: Yes, of course, because the dialogue partners will be practically entering into dialogue with you and the space. Exactly, so they will actually be communicating indirectly with me.

Mariella: Yes, yes, exactly.

Walter: That's the interesting thing.

Mariella: Yes, I mean, that's an exciting question that will be a topic between us, this form of response to, and performativity of, the crafted environment. So, if I can go into more detail about what I have in mind or what my requirements are for the space: it's not a vacuum, but a situated or prepared environment. And speculative ideas are there, rudimentary, as potentials to be taken up and shaped, or as a sort of calling for artistic practice, for embodied research. That's what I think will be exciting, how this space for choreo-ethical negotiation will open up, what it will then enable, and how it will be possible to be inside or outside of this dialogue zone created by the interplay of diverse materials, or where and in what way places and actions will be defined. I believe that there will probably also be a certain fluidity, because you will suggest something, and then I will respond to it, and it will be a dialogue with phases where everyone works autonomously, and then we meet again.

Walter: Yes, and then it will be reviewed or researched again.

Mariella: Ideally, this will lead to a point of calm where everything will align. When the choreographic environment has settled, I will begin to invite dialogue partners. This space will then become the environment for those dialogues.

Walter: ... which will really remain in place as a basic manifesto, so to speak. It should be a kind of neutral space, so to speak... but neutral can't be right. Not neutral. That's not possible.

42. I discussed the generativity of lingering in my lecture '... denn das Denken der Hand/ lungert herum' (14 November 2014) within the scope of the *TONGUES OF ARTISTIC RESEARCH* double lecture series with artists and theorists (concept and curation: Krassimira Kruschkova) held at TanzQuartierWien, accessed 13 October 2025, https://mediathek.tqw.at/tanzquartier-wien-online-archiv?tx_tqwmediathek_pi1%5Baction%5D=detail&tx_tqwmediathek_pi1%5Bcontroller%5D=Video&tx_tqwmediathek_pi1%5Bvideo%5D=236&cHash=9158f2488bfa7694928f76f50f4aeceb.

Mariella: No, neutral is not right at all because we are entering a designed space that is prepared for dialogue.

Walter: Ultimately, through the meeting between you and the invited dialogue partners alone, the space will automatically become different and will have a different effect on each person. Exactly, and that's why it makes sense not to change the space. That's clear to me now. Actually, the choreographic environment will have to remain unchanged because otherwise you will no longer be able to see the different reactions of the different people, you will no longer be able to assign them. Exactly, the space will remain a kind of matrix that will make the person visible.

Mariella: Yes, the person will come to the foreground. Through interaction with the environment, with our choreographic environment, and then also in contact with me. So, the 'Diffractive Dialogue Score' proposes that, first, there is an encounter with the space. The person is alone inside, then they come out, and I go in without the dialogue partner, and only in the third step do we come together. That is the rough concept that methodologically underlies the 'Diffractive Dialogue Score'.

Walter: So, there is simply this very strong interaction between body, person, mind, and space.

Mariella: I mean, it's more than a trace that resonates within the space. It's also the imagination, it's this entire space for thinking, the space for creation, play, analysis.

Walter: The energy field that is created there.

Mariella: Yes, exactly.

Walter: That works on very different levels.

Mariella: So, a term that I would very much like to explore in more depth is the concept of *emergence*, i.e., what can arise, but also the ground, the foundations, the depths from which something emerges. And I believe that there are some materials that have more of these emergent qualities than others. There are certainly things that invite more interaction, for example, the handpan, which for me is as much an instrument as it is a sound sculpture or an extension of the body. The choreographic environment is really a kind of experimental setup.

Walter: I find it totally exciting, as a kind of snapshot of movement, of things, bodies, and spaces.

Ultimately, within the framework of my research project *Choreo-ethical Assemblages*, collective contingencies (one of which was certainly the pandemic) taught me to reconceive of agency itself. Agency is an emergent property of relational fields rather than an attribute of autonomous subjects. It arises not despite contingency but because of it. To embrace collective contingencies is to affirm that knowledge, movement, and meaning emerge through exposure to unpredictability, through the vulnerability of co-presence, through the choreographic labour of being together in difference.

Œkological Cultures

It must arise in the heart in order to mediate the world truly, […] it is that subtle organ, which perceives the correspondences between the subtleties of consciousness and the levels of being. This intelligence takes place by means of images that are a third possibility between mind and world. […] '[I]ntelligence of the heart'

connotes a simultaneous knowing, and loving by means of imagining.[43]

The term *ecology* has long been mobilised across disciplines to denote the interconnectedness of organisms and environments. Yet in its etymological origins – from the Greek *oikos* (house, dwelling) and *logos* (discourse, study) – ecology is not only a descriptive science but a discourse of dwelling, a reflection on how we inhabit.[44] This etymological return opens up towards an expanded understanding that I call *œkology* – where the ligature *œ* signals a merging (literally of letters) and a shift away from systemic order toward relational openness, from models of homeostasis to practices of coexistence that emphasise vulnerability, fragility, and the porousness of boundaries.

The linguistic shift from *eco-* to *œko-* foregrounds the question of how cultures articulate, rehearse, and reconfigure forms of dwelling together. *Œkological cultures* bring together communities to reinvent and reflect on practices of co-habitation that attend to multiplicity and difference across different modes of existence. They resist the homogenising tendencies of ecological discourses that often aim at balance or sustainability, understood in managerial terms. Instead, our research engaged with the instability and contingency of living systems (→ Assemblages #4, 189), recognising that dwelling is never static but always a process (→ Assemblages #7, 345) of negotiation, improvisation, and reconfiguration.

Tracing the etymology further, *oikos* in ancient Greek did not simply mean 'house' but encompassed the household as a sphere of relations: family, property, resources organised under a certain order, or perhaps disorder. To speak of *œkological cultures* is thus to rethink the order and discourse of dwelling beyond the economy (*oikonomia*) and its calculative rationality. It is to cultivate a poetics of dwelling that is attentive to excess, to the unruly forces that disrupt household order, and that teases out the wild within the domestic.

This reorientation resonates with Félix Guattari's call for an 'ecosophy' that insists on the inseparability of environmental, social, and mental ecologies.[45] Yet *œkology* emphasises not the triadic balance of these registers but their transversal entanglement, their capacity to transform one another in unpredictable ways. Rather than *managing* difference, an œkological culture seeks to sustain its generativity, to hold open the space where new forms of relation can emerge.

In the practice of choreo-ethical assemblage, œkological cultures manifest in the cultivation of prepared environments. Rather than a controlled container, the studio is a porous milieu where breath, sweat, sound, and light mingle with gestures and words. It shapes its milieu. In the context of our research, the choreographic

43. James Hillman, *Thought of the Heart and the Soul of the World* (Spring Publications, 2021), 9.

44. Again, the Covid-19 pandemic in that sense bound us to our homes in a way I had not experienced before. It truly changed my connection to the *oikos*.

45. Félix Guattari, *The Three Ecologies*, trans. Ian Pindar and Paul Sutton (Continuum, 2000 [1989]).

score was less a script than a membrane – an interface (→ Scores, 387) that allowed for exchange between human and other-than-human agencies.

A persuasive articulation of this relational openness can be found in Haraway's *Staying with the Trouble*: 'We become-with each other or not at all.'[46] This simple yet profound statement encapsulates the ethos of œkological cultures: dwelling is never solitary; it is always co-practiced, always dependent on the fragile threads of relation that bind us to human and nonhuman others. Though *never* and *always* might sound polemic, dwelling is an imaginary that was tested in practice in the Polylogic Labs (→ Polylogic Labs, 178). The commitment to œkological cultures affirms interdependence and recognises that existence is co-existence, that to be is to be-with.

As a consequence, the aesthetics of œkological cultures foreground processes of attunement rather than representation. Performance becomes a site of sensing-with, of allowing the trans*materialities of the world to resonate through the body. Rather than being an isolated agent, the performer is part of an assemblage that includes air, sound, light, and the presence of others. In this regard, choreography is œkological, not in the sense of ordering space but of facilitating co-dwelling, of enabling encounters that transform both participants and environments.

Ethically, œkological cultures demand the reconfiguration of responsibility. To dwell œkologically is to be accountable to one's immediate companions as well as the extended webs of relation that sustain life. This responsibility cannot be fulfilled through managerial control; instead, it requires a practice of care, of listening to the subtle signals of imbalance or asymmetry, of responding to the needs of others. Care here is not the application of external norms but the ongoing responsiveness that emerges from being-with.

Finally, œkological cultures open out onto questions of futurity. Whereas ecology often aims at sustainability, understood as preserving systems for the future, œkology insists on the unpredictability of what is to come. It calls for practices that do not secure futures in advance but remain open to their emergence. This orientation is reflected in choreo-ethical assemblages: each encounter is an experiment in dwelling-with, a rehearsal for futures that cannot be known, that can only be enacted through the contingencies of the present.

46. Donna J. Haraway, *Staying with the Trouble: Making Kin in the Chthulucene* (Duke University Press, 2016), 4.

There is an experience of the visible thing as pre-existing my vision, but this experience is not a fusion, a coincidence: because my eyes which see, my hands which touch, can also be seen and touched, because, therefore, in this sense they see and touch the visible, the tangible, from within, because our flesh lines and even envelops all the visible and tangible things with which nevertheless it is surrounded, the world and I are within one another, and there is no anteriority of the percipere to the percipi, there is simultaneity or even retardation. For the weight of the natural world is already a weight of the past. Each landscape of my life, because it is not a wandering troop of sensations or a system of ephemeral judgments but a segment of the durable flesh of the world, is qua visible, pregnant with many other visions besides my own; and the visible that I see, of which I speak, even if it is not Mount Hymettus or the plane trees of Delphi, is numerically the same that Plato and Aristotle saw and spoke of. When I find again the actual world such as it is, under my hands, under my eyes, up against my body, I find much more than an object: a Being of which my vision is a part, a visibility older than my operations or my acts.

Maurice Merleau-Ponty, *The Visible and the Invisible*, ed. Claude Lefort, trans. Alphonso Lingis (Northwestern University Press, 1968 [1964]), 123.

Assemblages #2

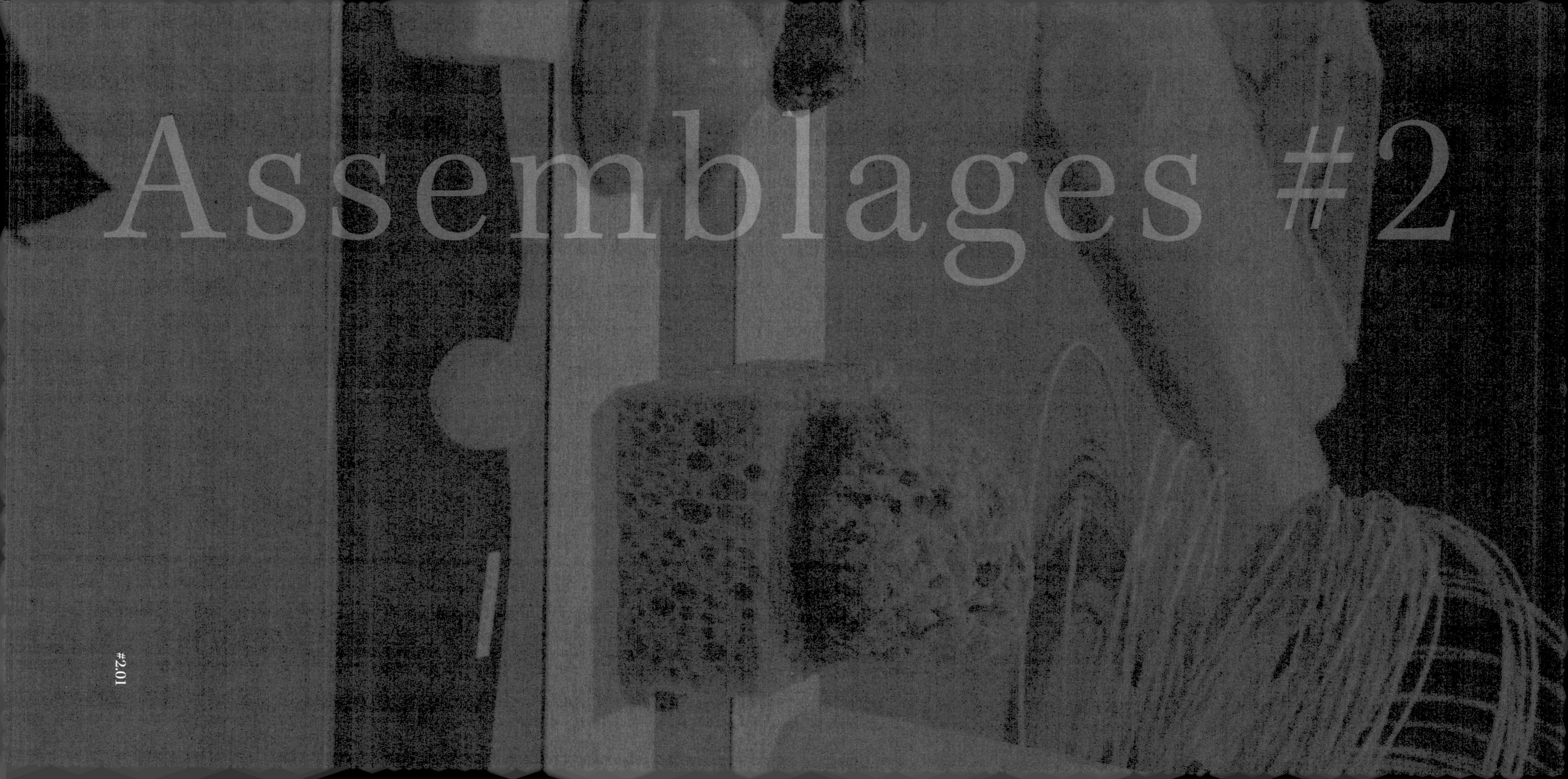

#2.01

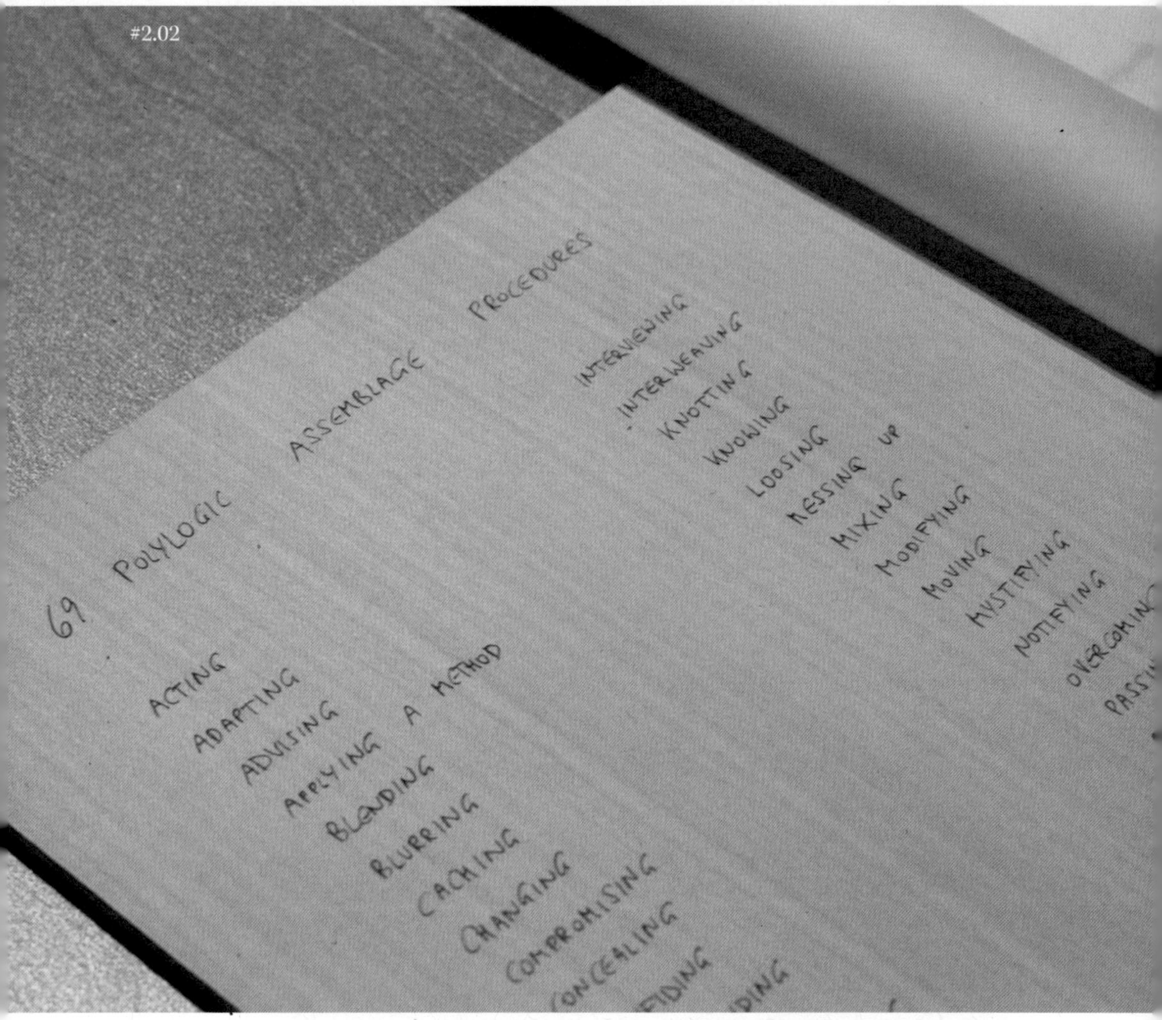
69 POLYLOGIC
ASSEMBLAGE
PROCEDURES
ACTING
ADAPTING
ADVISING
APPLYING A METHOD
BLENDING
BLURRING
CACHING
CHANGING
COMPROMISING
CONCEALING
INTERVIEWING
INTERWEAVING
KNOTTING
KNOWING
LOOSING
MESSING UP
MIXING
MODIFYING
MOVING
MYSTIFYING
NOTIFYING
#2.02

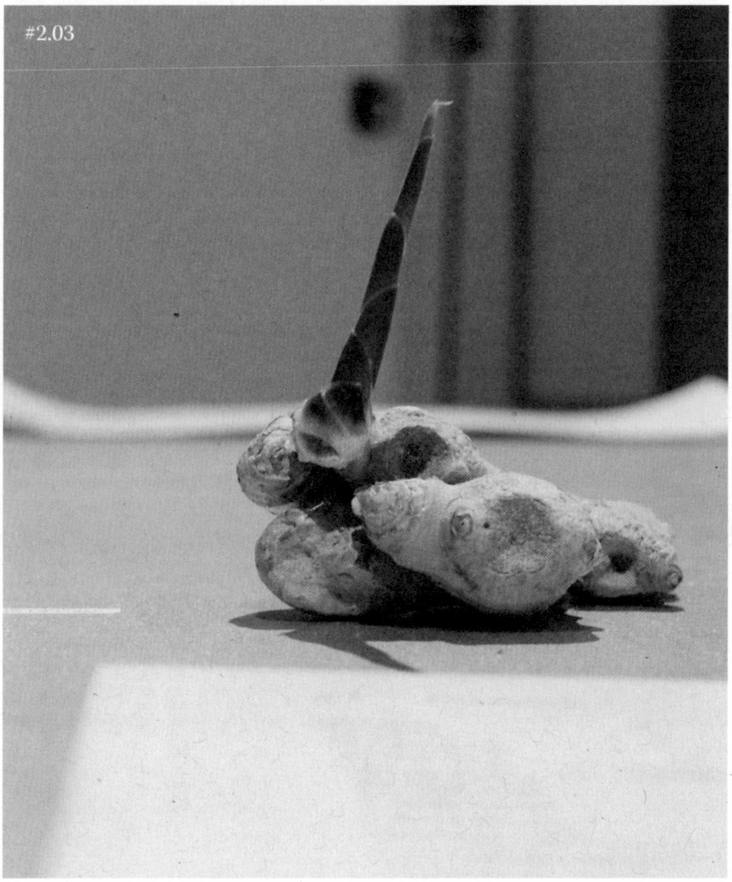
#2.03

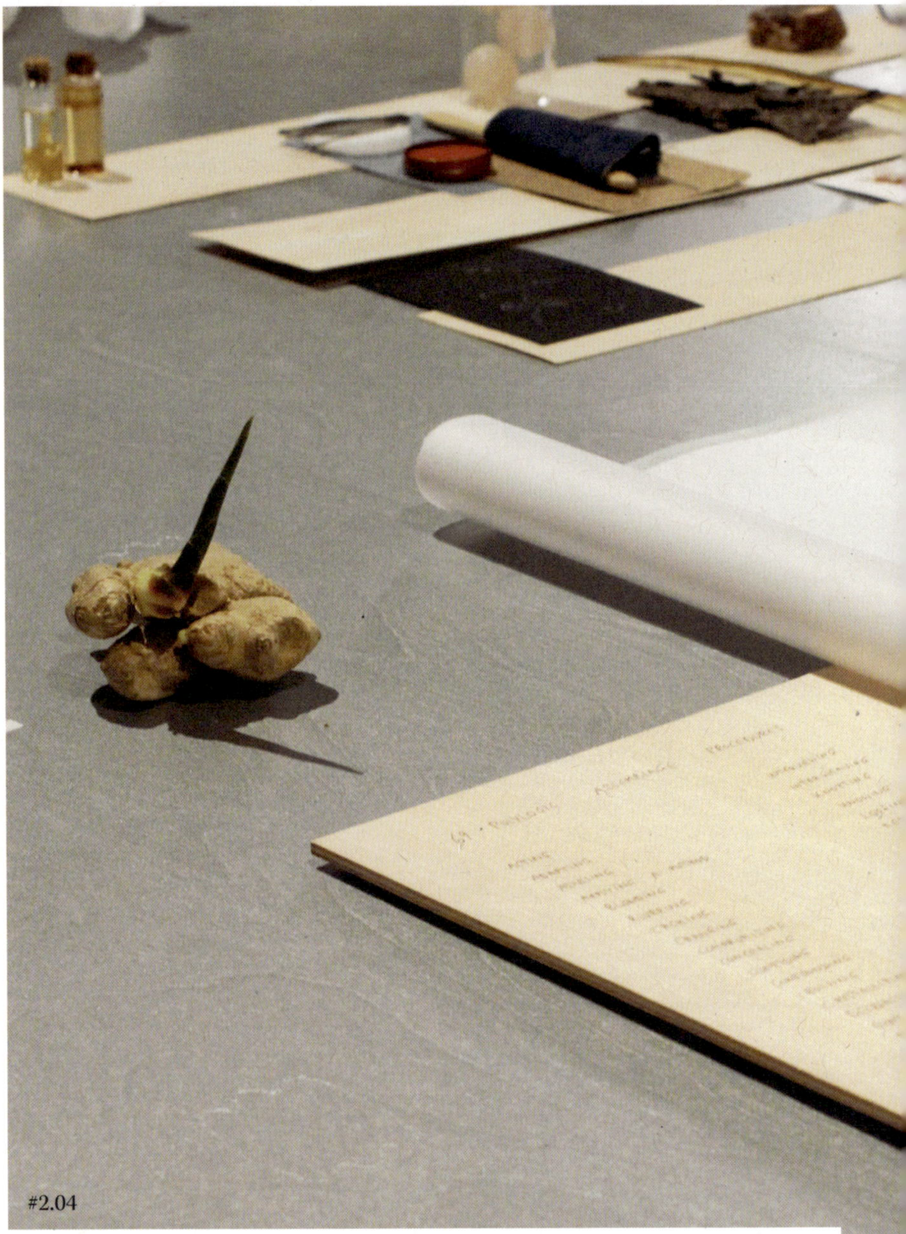

#2.04

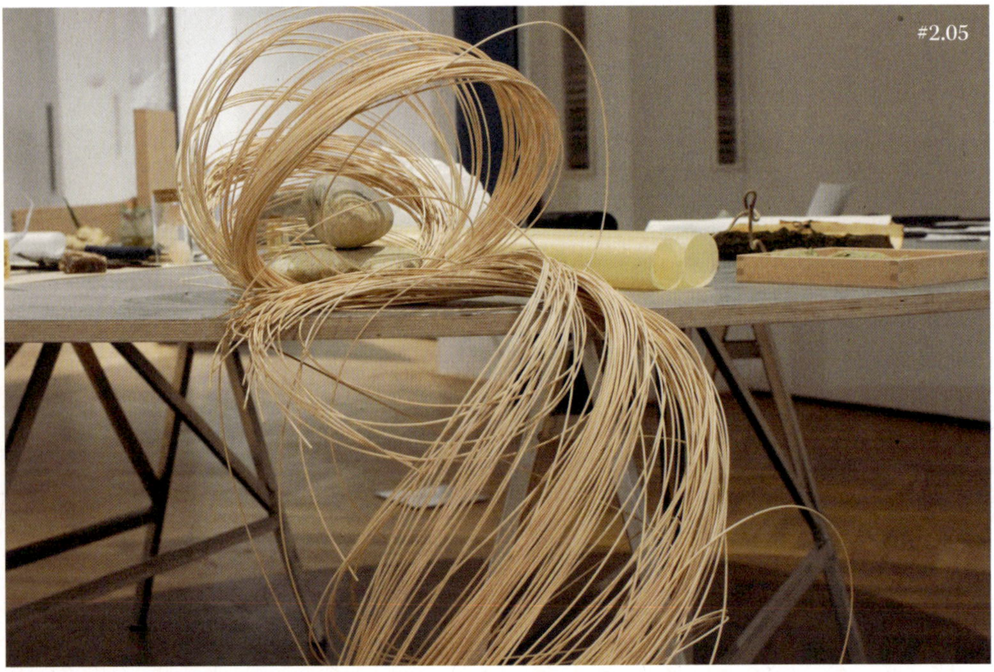

#2.05

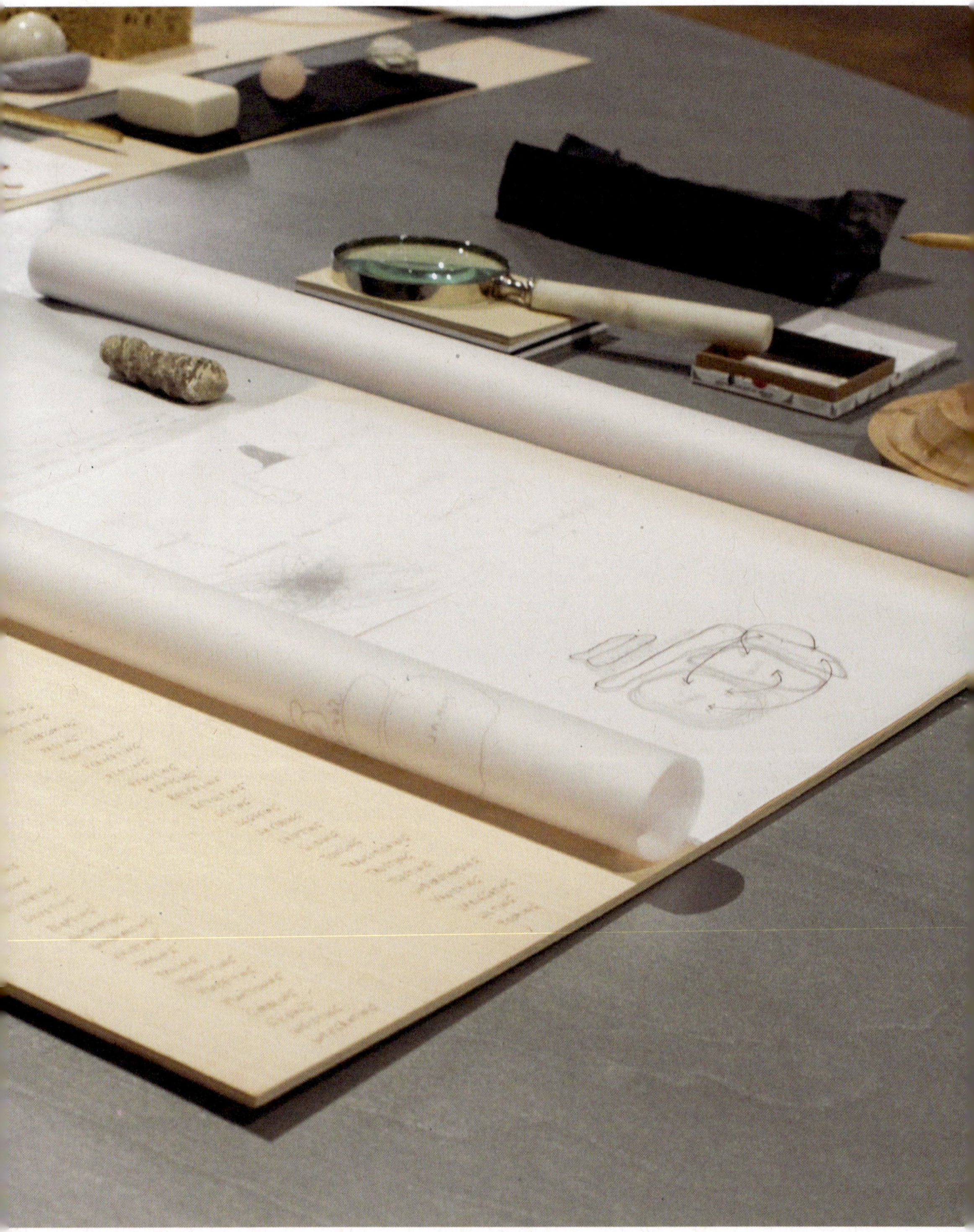

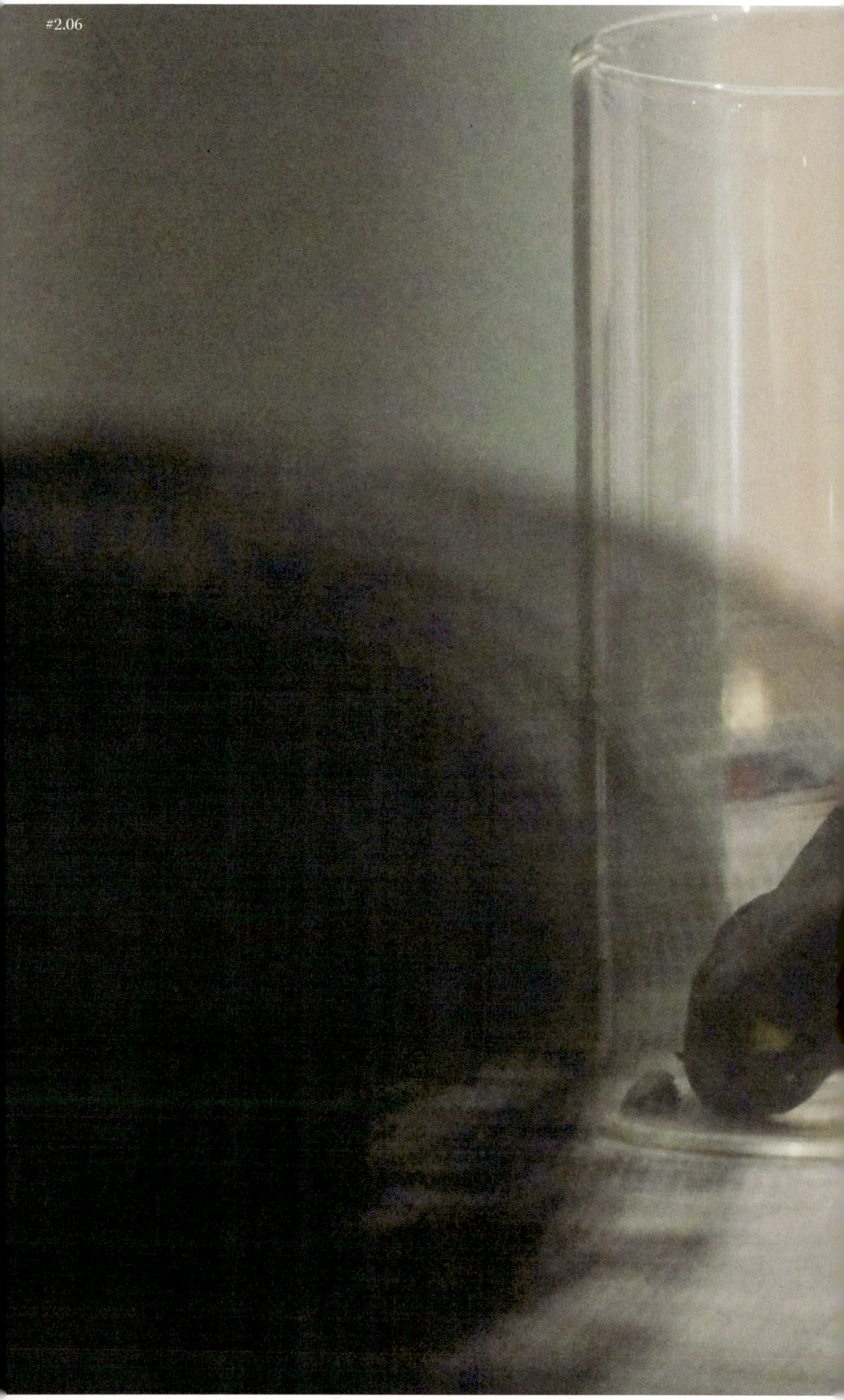
#2.06

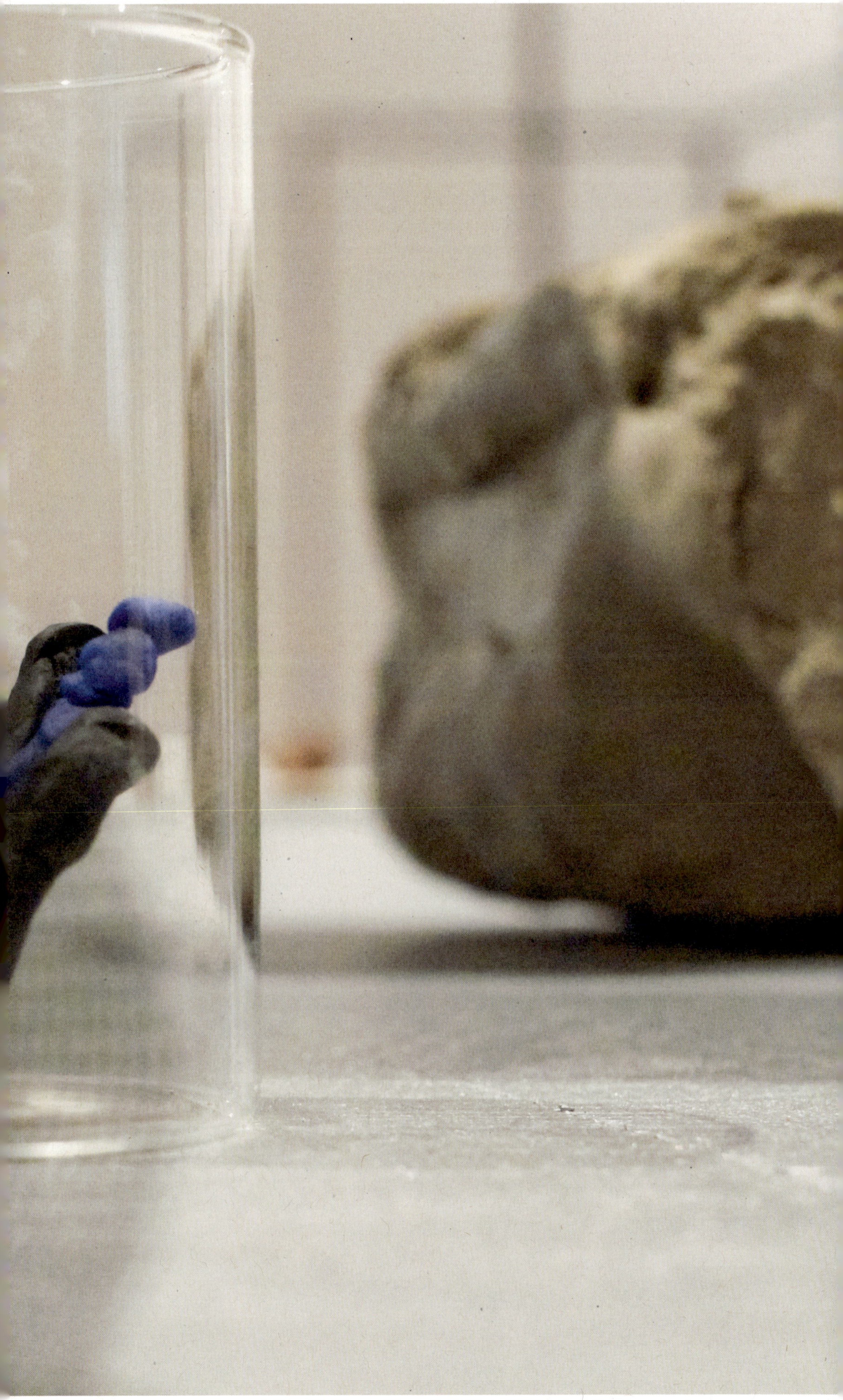

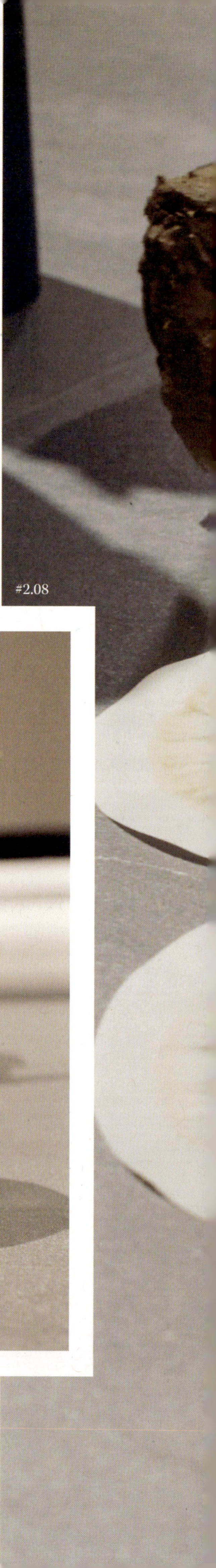

#2.08

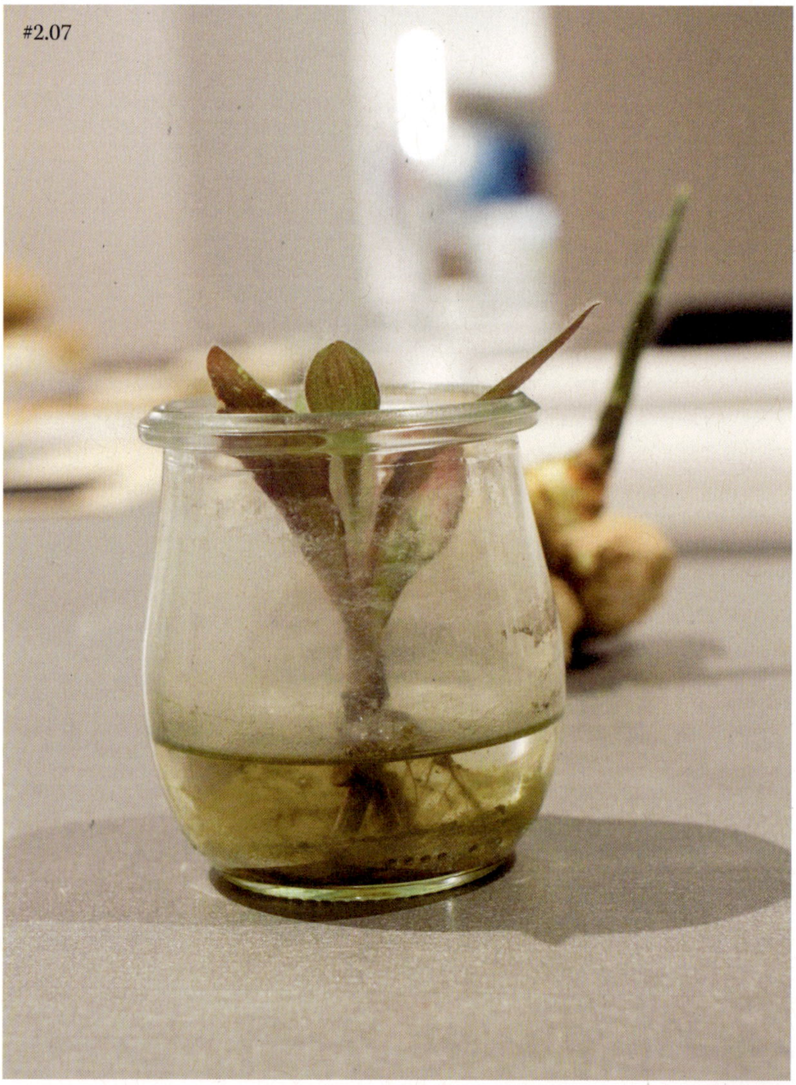

#2.07

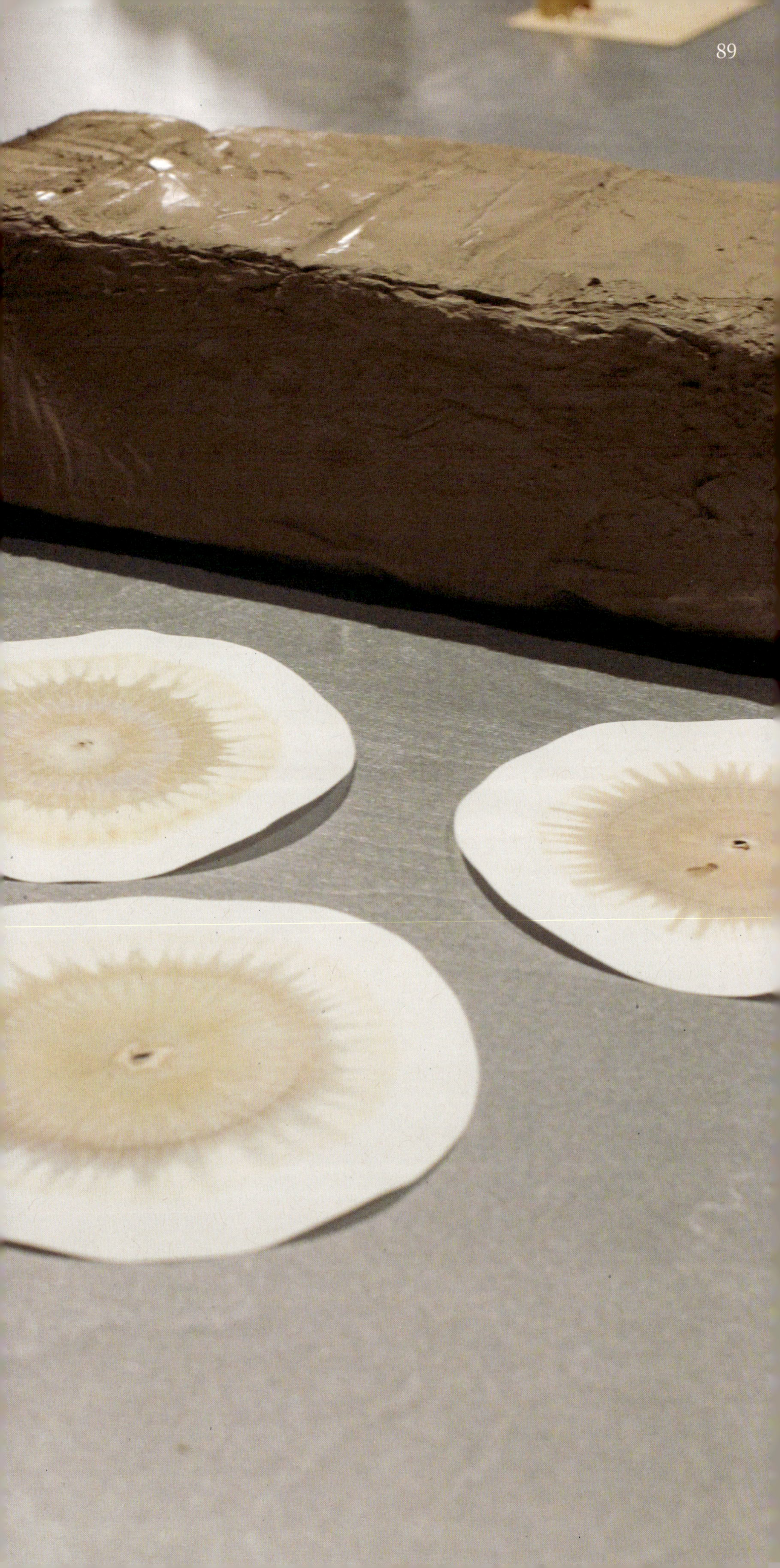

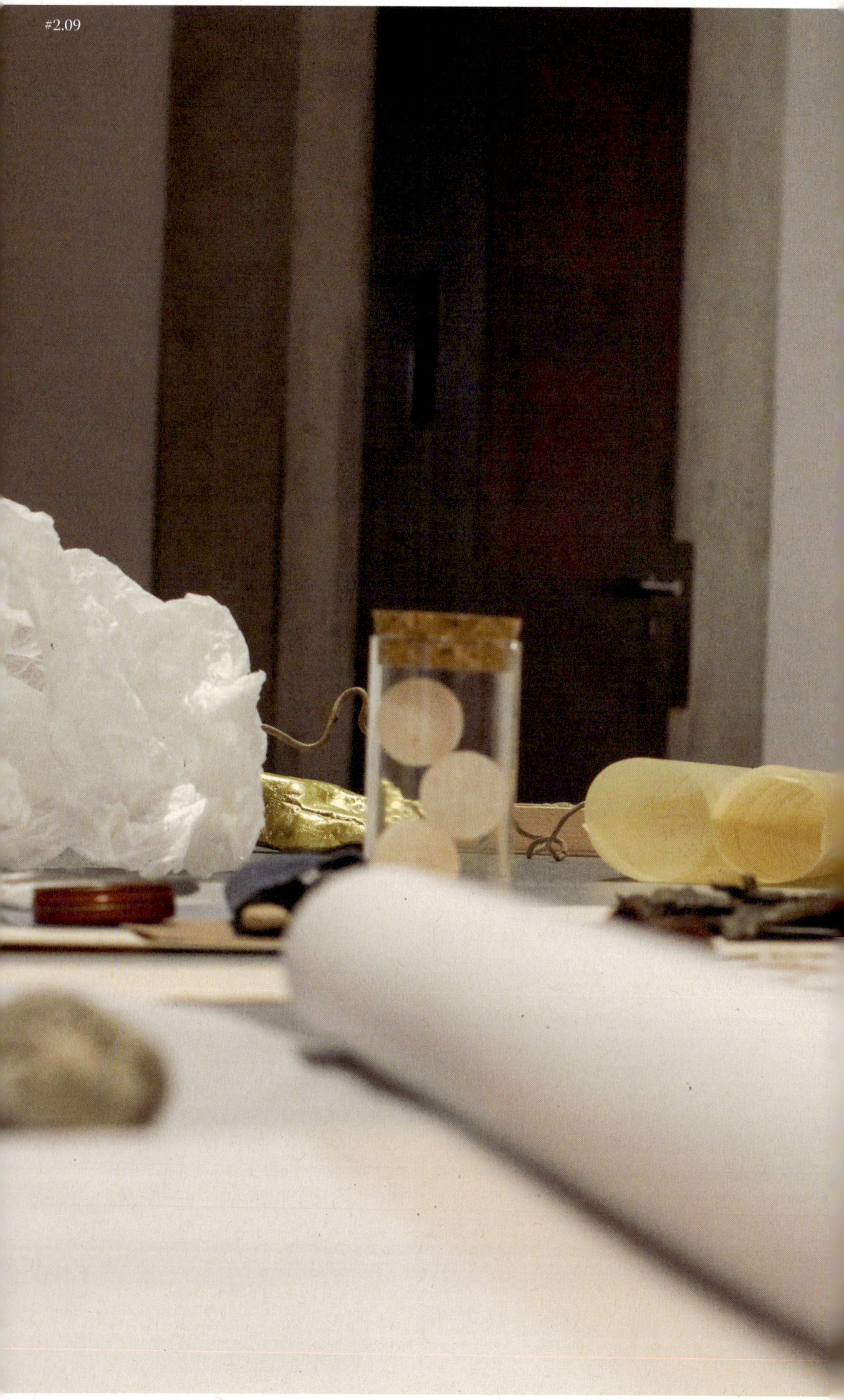

#2.09

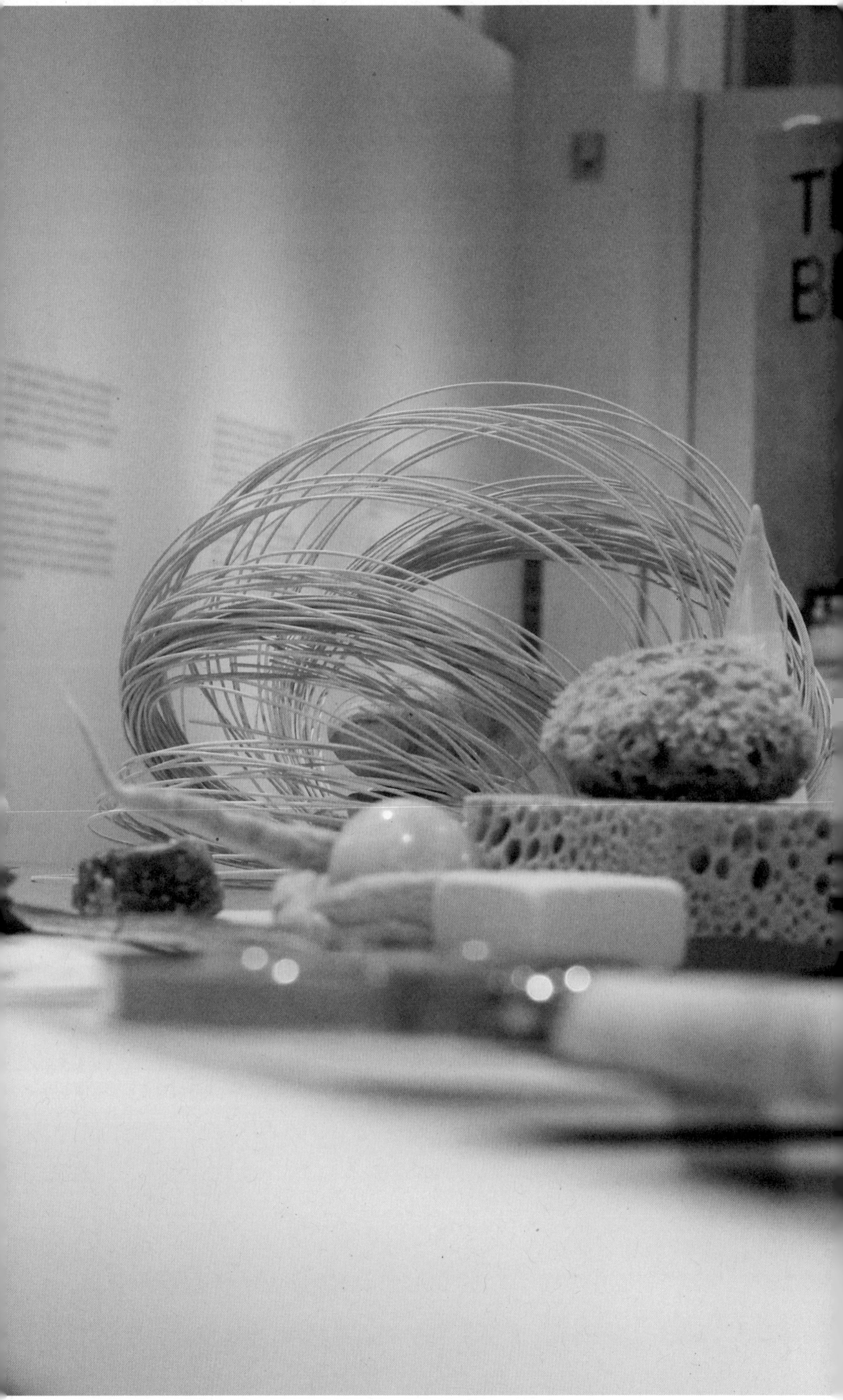

#2.10

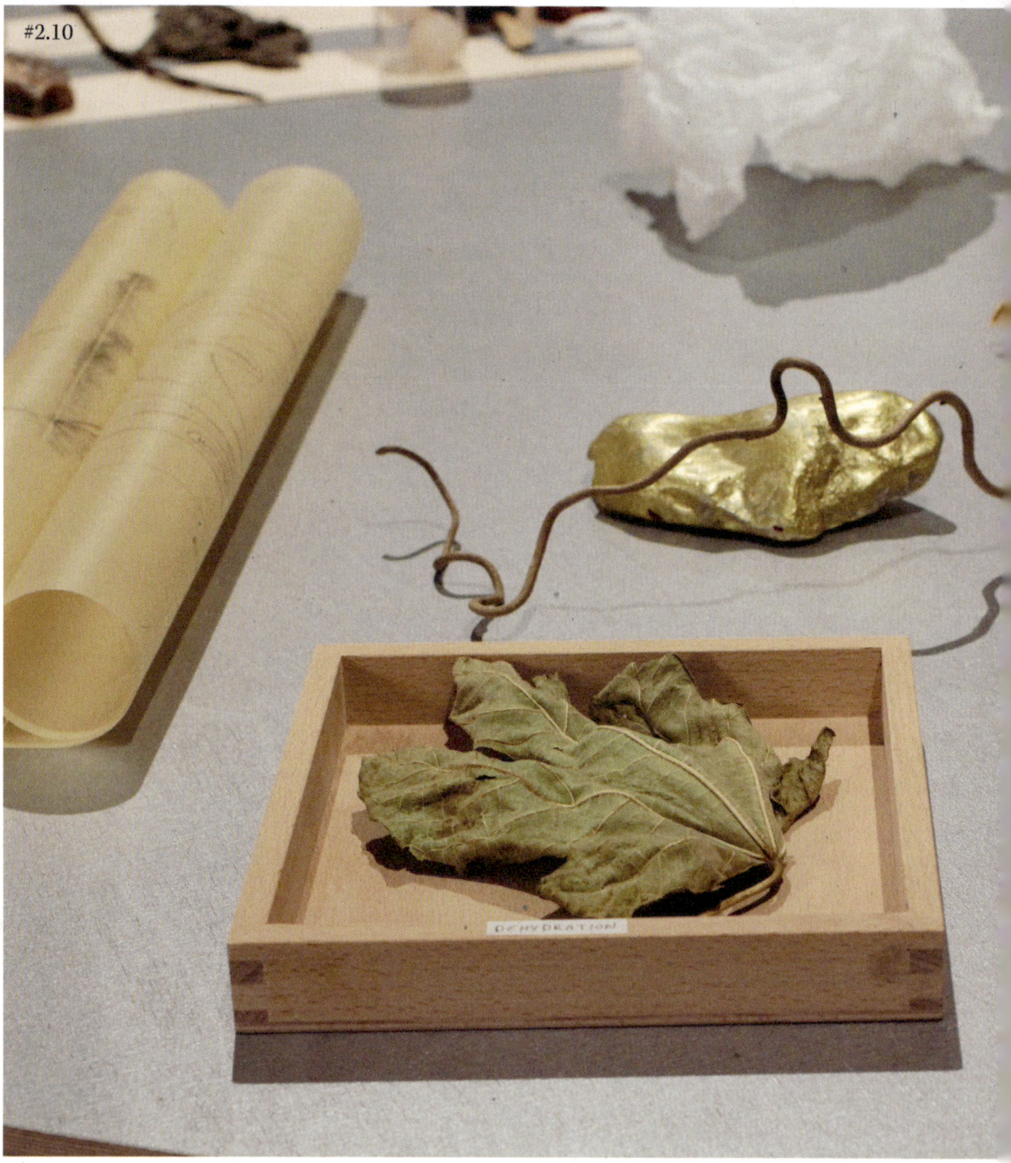

#2.11

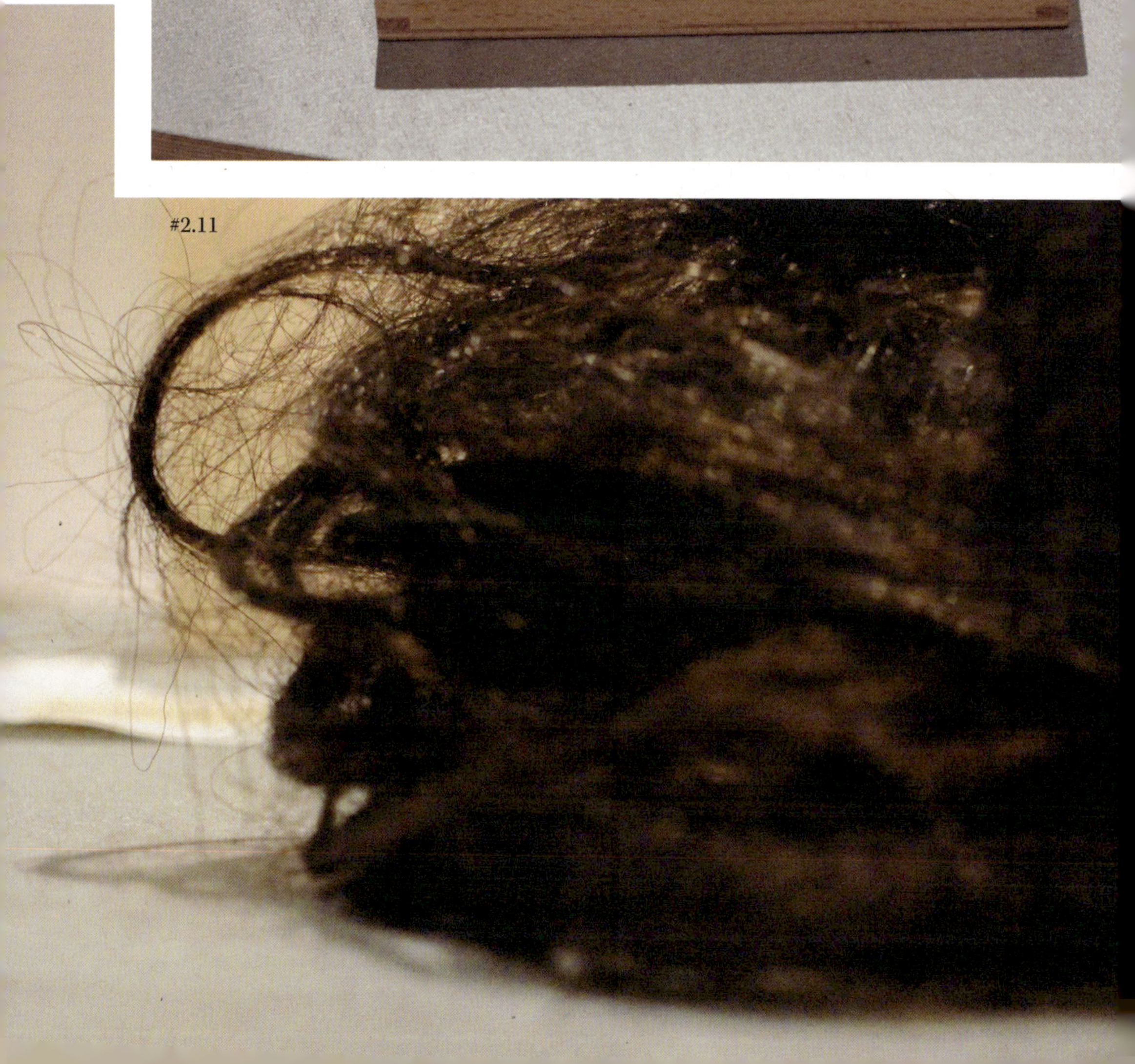

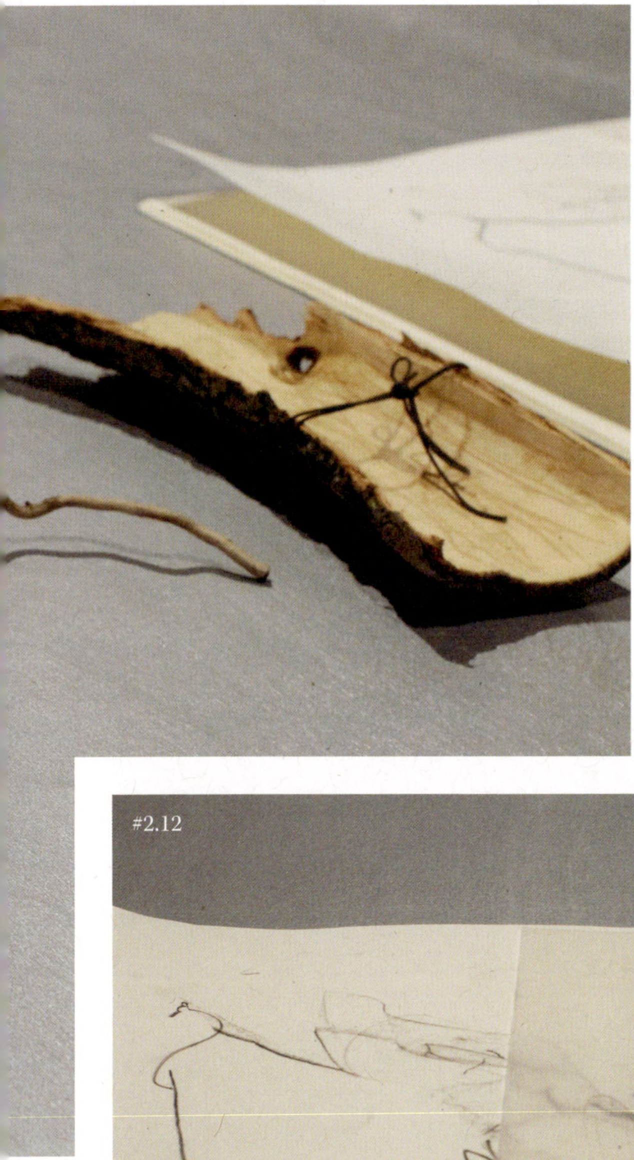

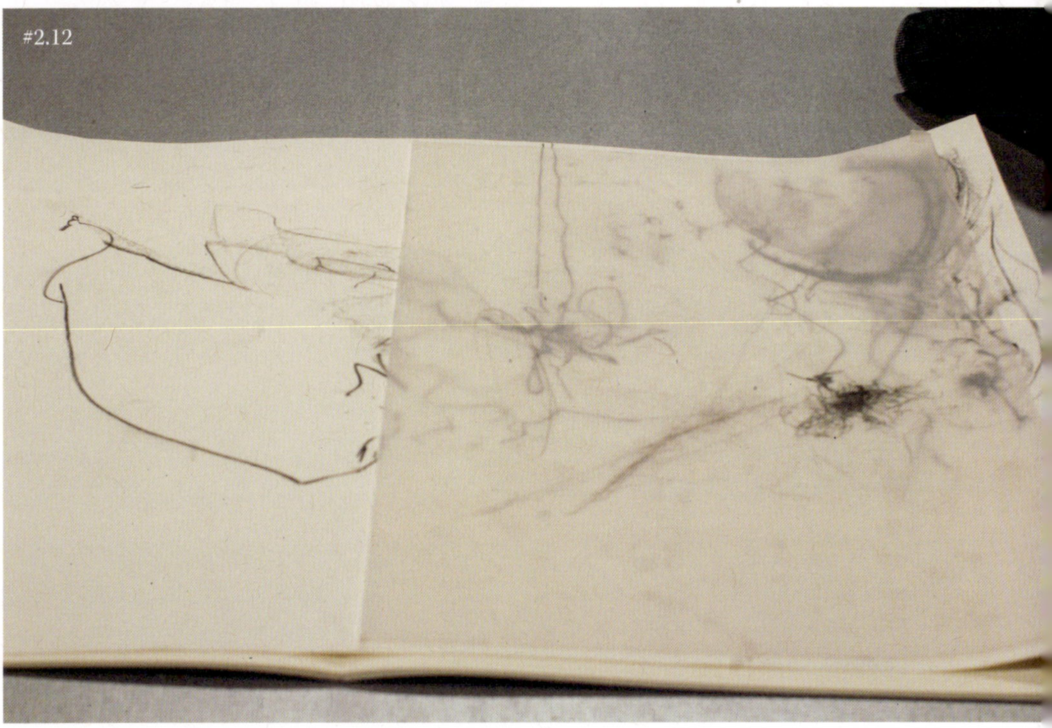
#2.12

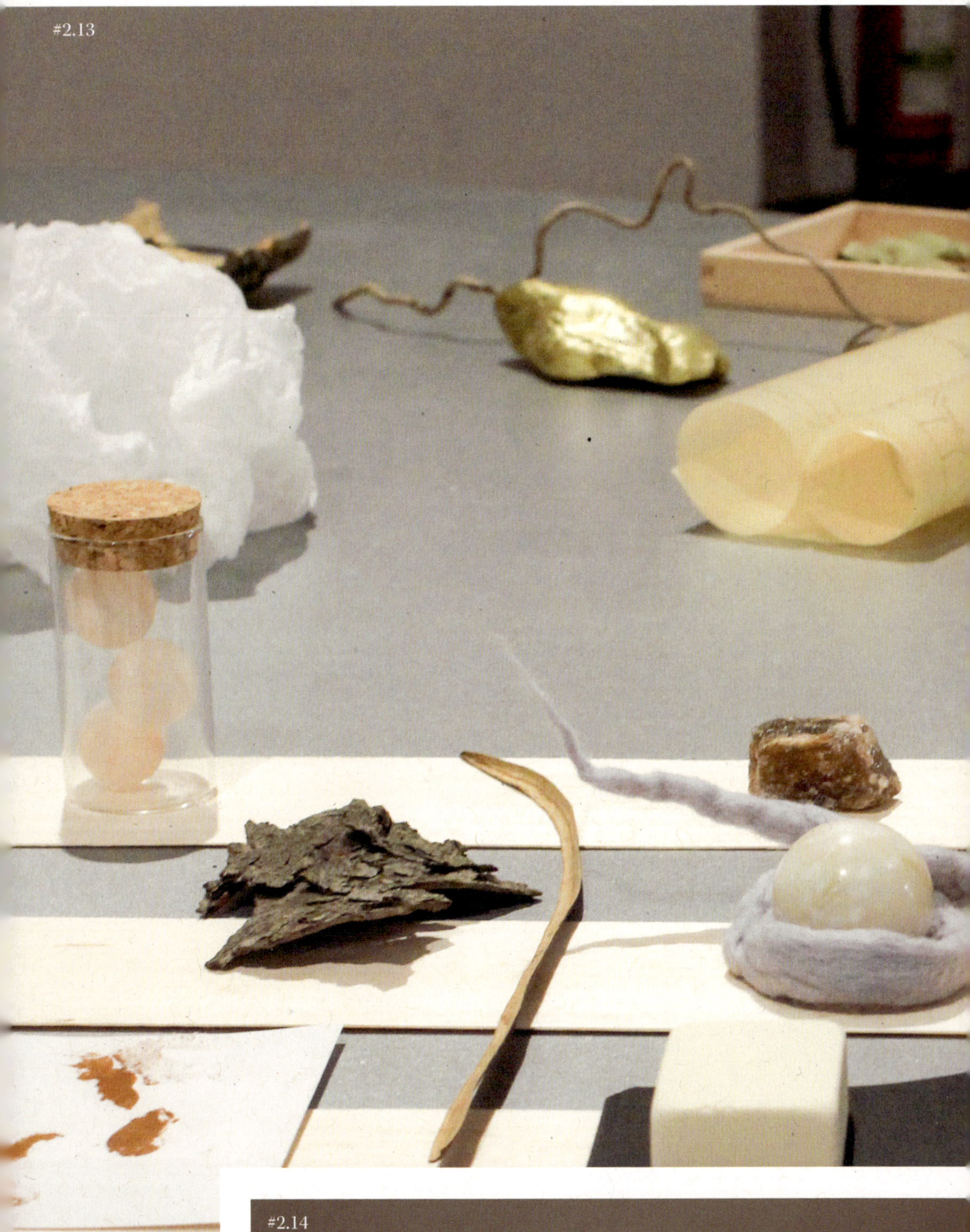
#2.13

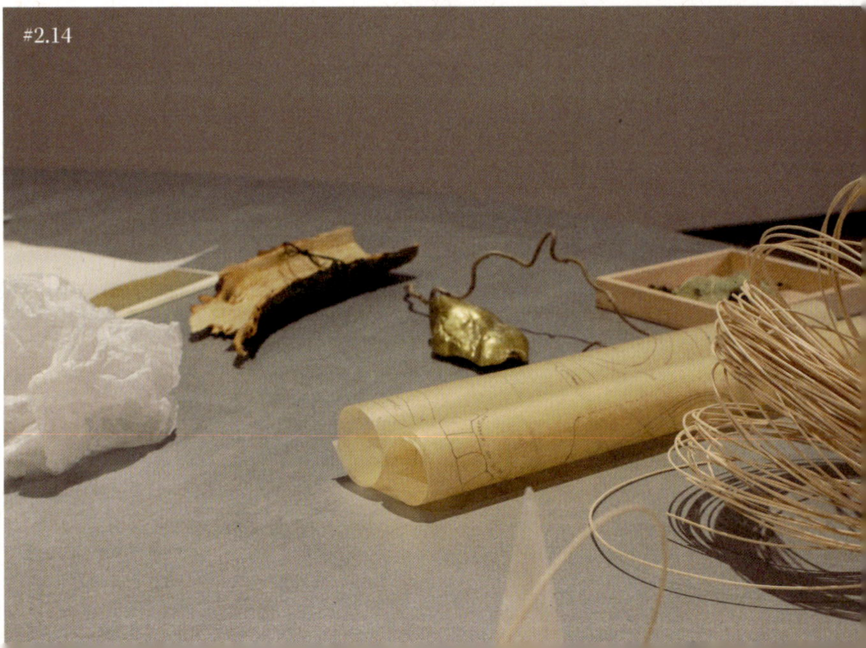
#2.14

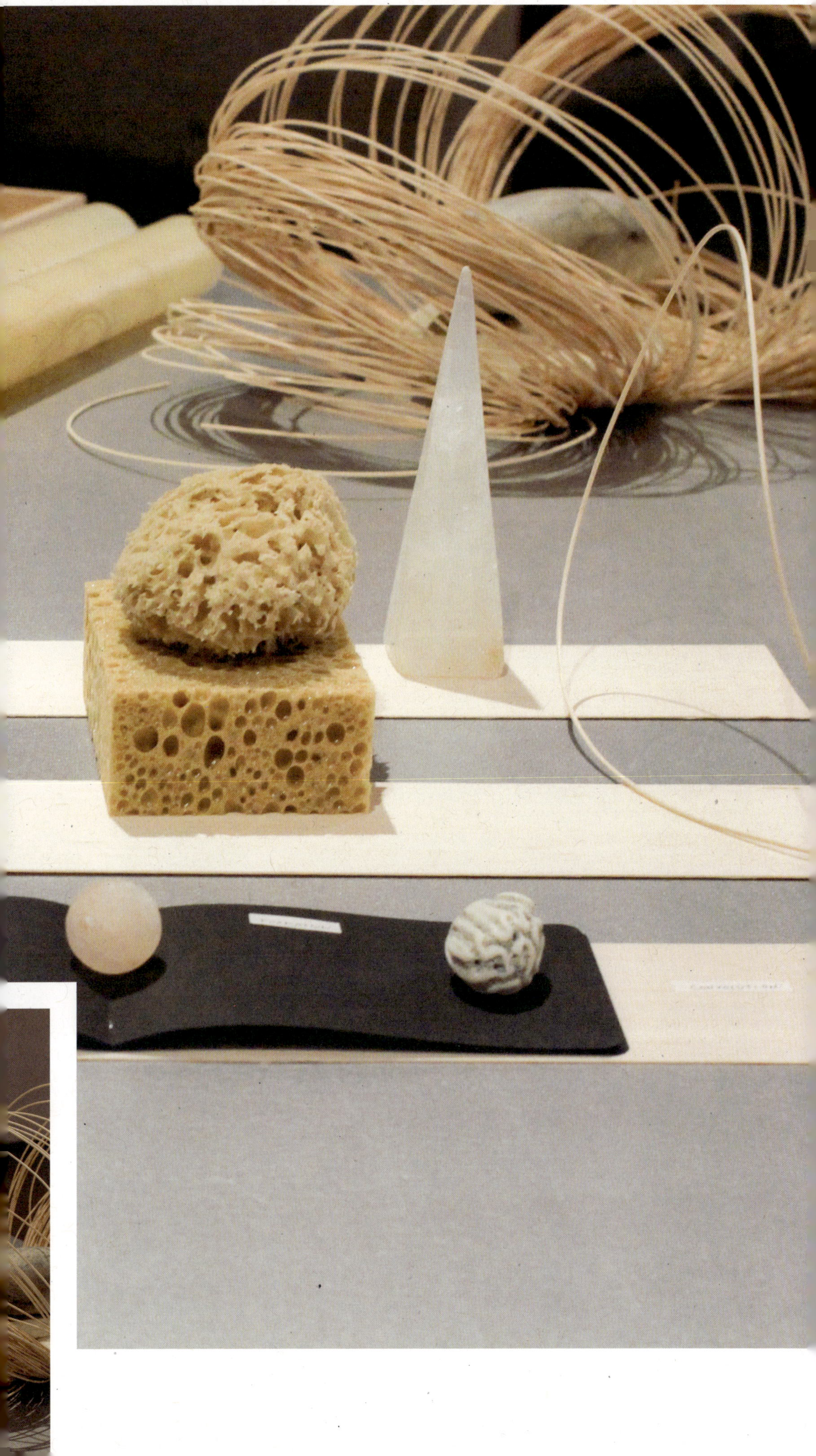

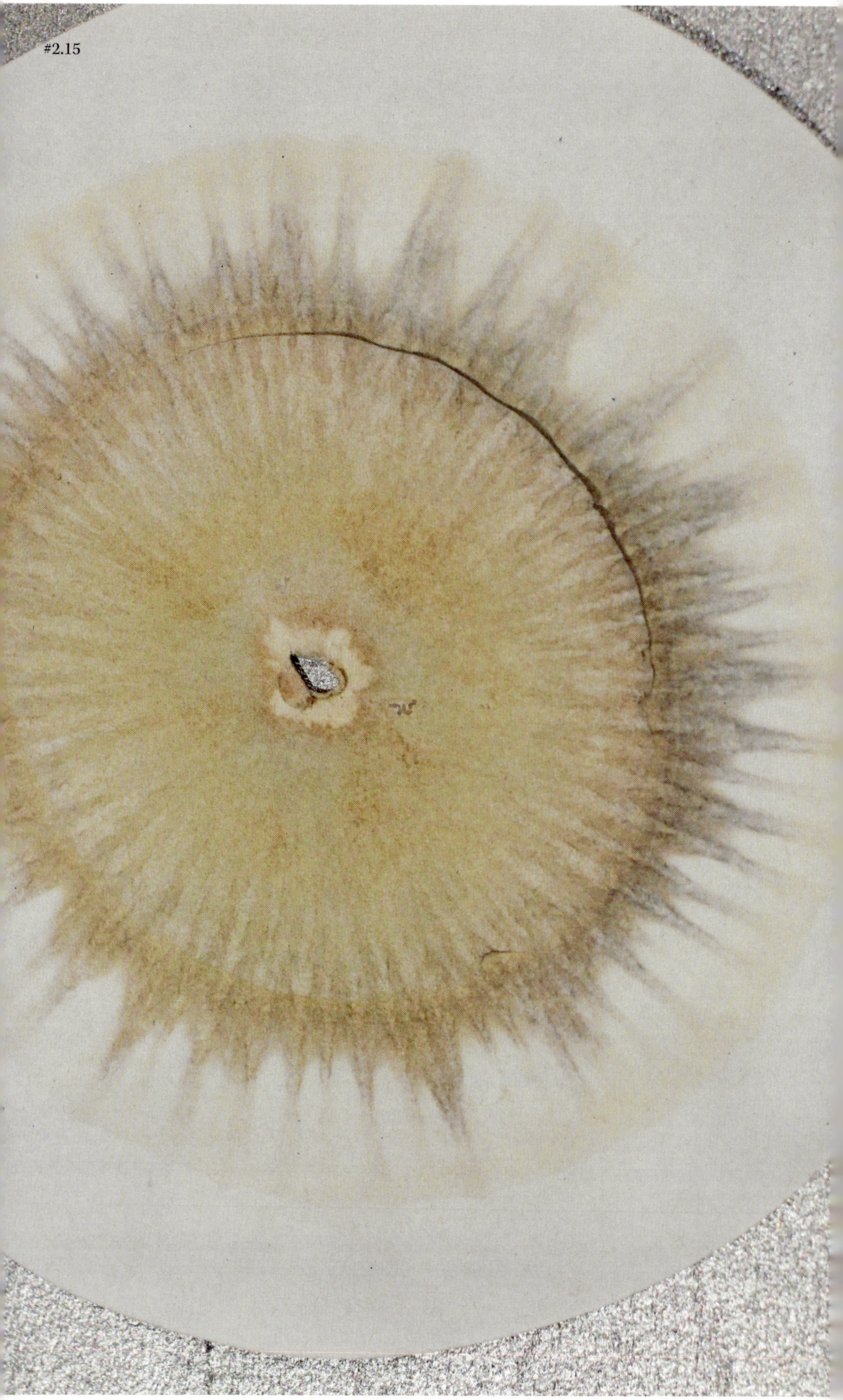
#2.15

#2.01: *Choreo-ethical Assemblages* in the exhibition *UNDERSTANDING – ART & RESEARCH*, MAK – Museum of Applied Arts, Vienna, 2019, © photo: Mariella Greil and Simona Koch.

#2.02–#2.14: *Choreo-ethical Assemblages* in the exhibition *UNDERSTANDING – ART & RESEARCH*, MAK, 2019, © photo: Mariella Greil.

#2.15: *Chromatography* as part of *Choreo-ethical Assemblages* in the exhibition *UNDERSTANDING – ART & RESEARCH*, MAK, 2019, © photo: Mariella Greil.

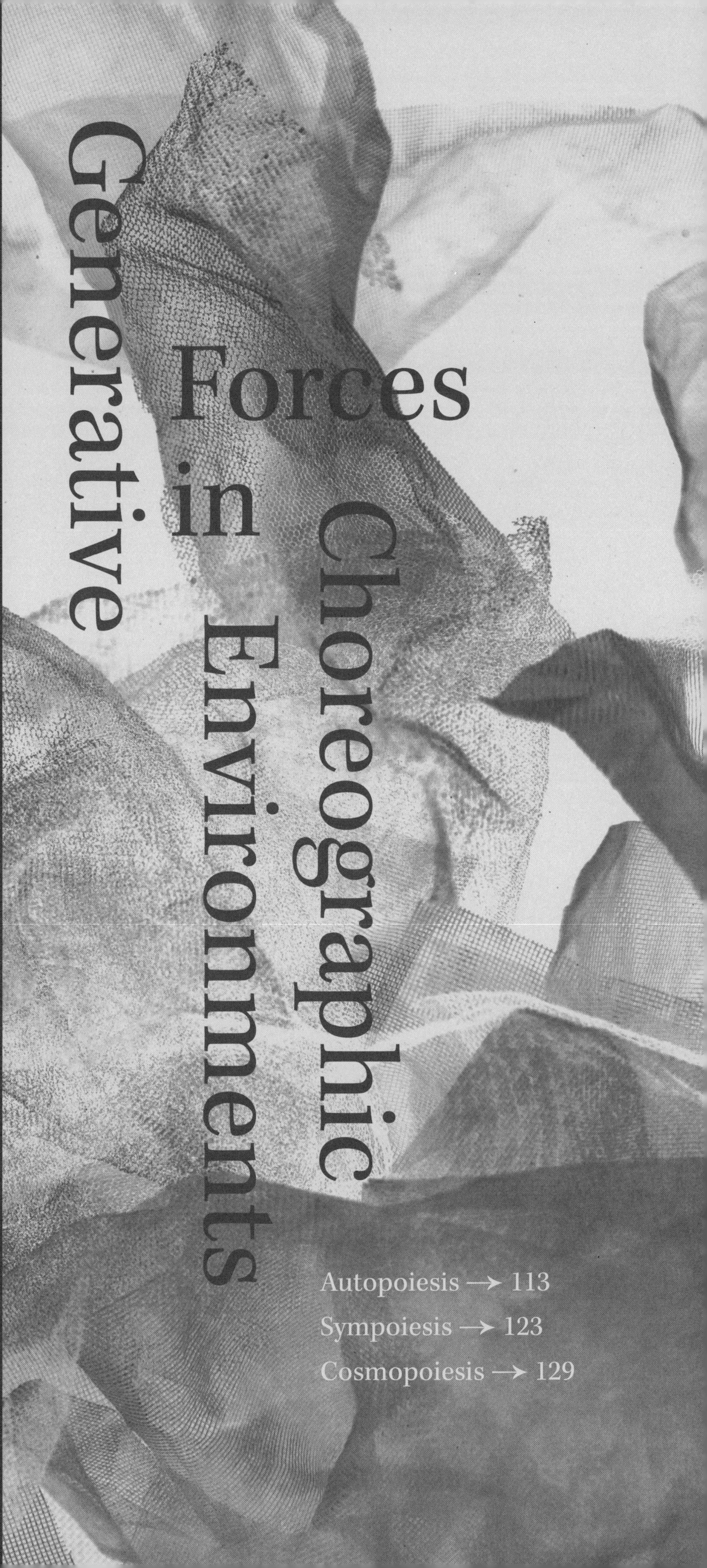

Generative Forces in Choreographic Environments

The notion of the *generative* invites us to think about processes of emergence, relation, and transformation that move beyond the static or representational and instead linger in the terrain of becoming. The term itself derives from the Proto-Indo-European root *genə-*, meaning 'to give birth' or 'to beget'.[47] This etymological ground already sets a dynamic tone, emphasising the act of creation as well as the vitality of arising, of something not-yet, of unfolding potential. Not merely productive in a linear sense, the generative reverberates across time and form, hosting multiplicities of emergence.

Micro-phenomenological Interview with Evfa Lilja
Excerpt, edited transcript
14 April 2023

Evfa Lilja: How did you come to this specific topic of choreo-ethics?

Mariella Greil: Everything started when I was collecting materials that held an ambiguity that made them open. I mostly chose them due to their tactile quality, which is a strong informative channel for me, as well as the visual one. Some of them came from the woods; this extreme habitat where millions of micro and macro organisms co-exist. I was fascinated by the atmosphere in the woods, this *very slow time.*

Evfa: Like the stone…

Mariella: Exactly. I was really attracted to the deep, slow time of the stone. And I had so many questions about whether I could actually take objects from the woods into the studio, whether I can ethically account for such a displacement. I went through different stages. First of all, I was spending time in the garden, and I got caught up in my curiosity to see some of its elements in the artificial setting of the studio. Each object brings along its own story. For example, I was interested here to see the SCOBYs (symbiotic cultures of bacteria and yeast). Over time, I brought several SCOBYs along, they have a valuable, cyclical nature. Some of them have been here with me since the pandemic started. This living, fermenting organism can nourish my body as kombucha and also morph into sculptural, paper-like forms when dried. I usually massage the SCOBYs into paper to let them dry into organic structures, which are too beautiful to simply discard. I consider this transformation into art as an act of palliative care. Another water-retentive object that caught my attention is the sponge. However, when the sponge dries out, it doesn't feel nice to the touch. But then, as soon as it's full of water, it becomes soft and pleasant again. It's this ongoing cycle of drying and rehydrating, hardening and softening, nourishing and being nourished by the environment that I find appealing – its hygroscopic nature.

This same root gives rise to a constellation of words: *genes*, from the Greek *génesis* – meaning 'formation', 'origin', or 'creation', introduces a biological and structural resonance; *gender* – referring to 'kinds', 'categories', or 'kinships' – underscores relational fields; and significantly, the Latin *genius*, which denotes not only 'wit' or 'talent' but also 'guardian spirit' – a daimonic[48] force that watches over one's *becoming*. This genius is not to be domesticated into a supernatural agent or intelligence, but is instead understood in its ancient form – as a mediator between immanence and possibility, between the singular and the universal. It is this genius, in all its

47. 'Gene', etymonline, accessed 16 May 2025, https://www.etymonline.com/word/*gene-.

48. This is a transliteration of the Greek *daimōn* – 'deity', 'divine power', 'lesser god', 'guiding spirit', or 'tutelary deity' – and is used here in its ancient Greek sense as 'supernatural agent' or 'intelligence lower than a god', 'ministering spirit', not in its later malignant Christian or Jewish translations as a 'god of the heathen' or 'unclean spirit'. I am especially interested in the dimension of the *daimonion*, a 'divine principle' or 'inward oracle' that anticipates the potential of a situation. In our project this is the encounter in the choreographic environment that manifests as the Polylogic Lab, where diffractive dialogues take place.

Sponging

Bound to the seabed, sponges teach
the grammar of pressure,
while hydrofeminism gently yields an ethics
of absorbent softness.
The marine invertebrates follow the weight
of vegetation,
keep breathing through their channels and pores,
round, unwilling to resolve.

The sponge in its industrial shape,
the cavities are edged in abstract form.
Synthetic organisms are silent,
there is no turning back.

Amidst the constant flow of water,
the assembly of living filter feeders
seem hesitant to enter a plantoid zone.
Through their squishy bodies
unspecialized cells circulate oxygen.
They become their own proliferation,
ancient and wild.

For the gathering, they provide an abundance
of micro-stories.
Chatter travels in space as prerogative sound.
It smells like slight disobedience,
stored in pores, seams, sediments.

Radical softness is gravitational.
Time is different underwater,
thicker, slower,
its phylogenetic adaptation in movement,
a form of listening for motile orientation.

Joining in or dropping out becomes
a tidal decision,
accelerating the process of embracing
the given freshwater.
Ritualistic jokers spin in the vortex of
the depths
and maintain trust in the matrix of minerals.

Laughing softly, encrusting the surface
of rocks,
the conference of the ocean sponges
goes dormant until conditions improve,
then they will last longer and
multiply through slow cell accumulation.
Squeezing and squishing what we thought
was solid,
remoulding their bodies,
then the porous tissues learn
to flow again.

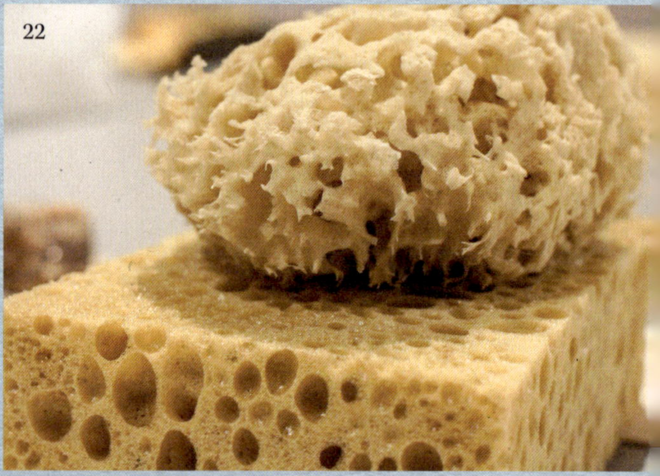

ambiguity and full of creative fervour, that permeates performative encounters and choreographic assemblages.

Within performative practices, particularly those attuned to *choreo-ethical assemblages* (→ Choreo-ethical Assemblages, 205), the generative is dispersed across the field of interaction, movement, gesture, and resonance, rather than being confined to a singular moment of inception. These assemblages, inherently entangled and ethically charged, are governed less by prescriptive logics than by their sensitivity to the micro-dynamics of attention, relation, and transformation. The generative thus operates as a force that exceeds individual intention and invokes collective thresholds of emergence – across agencies.

In the *choreographic environment* (→ Choreographic Environments, 41), phenomena of transmission unfold – not transmission as a unidirectional act of delivery but as a porous, multi-directional web of sensation and sense-making. In this context, rather than denoting the abstract or bland, *generic* signals that which is open, shared, and receptive: a ground *of* – or better, *for* – potentiality. What is being *generated*, then, is not confined to action, but includes preparation, attunement, and the cultivation of conditions from which something may emerge. It is in this sense that choreographic environments become generative – as spaces in which relations form, dissolve, reconfigure; where time stretches and compresses, where states of attention shift and intensify.

Generosity, too, becomes the conceptual kin of the generative – as a mode of abundance, of giving beyond measure, of holding a space open for the other to emerge, rather than as a moral gesture. This generosity is spatial, temporal, and affective. It marks the choreographic not as a product to be consumed, but as a field of practice and response, an œkology of touch, time, and transformation. The choreographic is both what is choreographed and that which choreographs – how bodies, forces, gestures, and frames organise and re-organise themselves and form an aesthetic.

In tracing the genealogy of the aesthetic, we encounter the formative gesture of Alexander Gottlieb Baumgarten, who introduced the term *aesthetics*, which at the time was a neologism emerging from the Greek αἰσθητική (*aisthētikē*), relating to sensory perception. The *Habilitation* thesis that he submitted to the University of Halle in 1735 was 'a booklet of not more than 40 pages'.[49] Significantly, however, he writes at the end of § CXVI of the *Meditationes philosophicae de nonnullis ad poema pertinentibus*,

With the existing definition, a more definitive term can be easily devised, and it is quite obvious that the Greek Philosophers and fathers do not equate the αισϑητα (aisthēta) with sense-perceptions alone, since that which

49. Hans Meyer, *Leibniz und Baumgarten als Begründer der deutschen Aesthetik* (Plötz'sche Buchdruckerei, 1874), X, Münchner Digitalisierungszentrum Digitale Bibliothek, accessed 16 May 2025, https://www.digitale-sammlungen.de/de/view/bsb11185869?q=Baumgarten&page=2,3.

is sensually cognised in its absence, namely the imagination, is also honoured with this name. Thus, the νοητα (noēta) – that which can be recognised through the higher faculty – is the subject of logic, whereas the αισθητικη (aisthētikē) is the subject of επιστημη αισθητικη (epistēmē aisthētikē) the aesthetic science or AESTHETICS.[50]

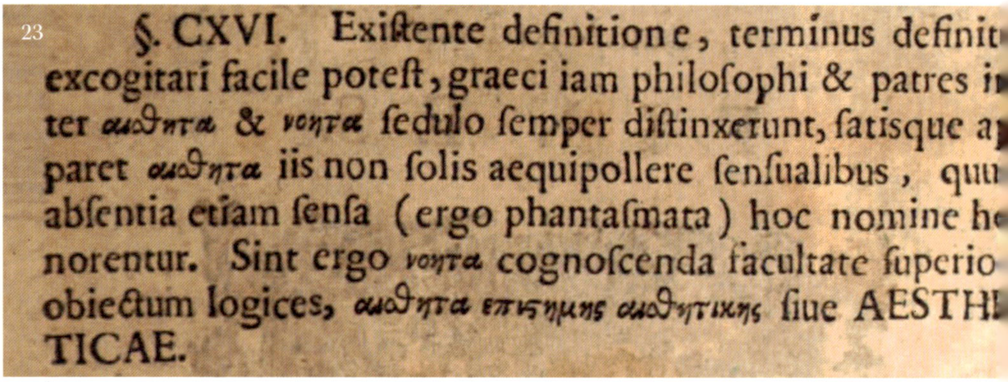
23

§. CXVI. Exiſtente definitione, terminus definit
excogitari facile poteſt, graeci iam philoſophi & patres in
ter αισθητα & νοητα ſedulo ſemper diſtinxerunt, ſatisque ap
paret αισθητα iis non ſolis aequipollere ſenſualibus, quu
abſentia etiam ſenſa (ergo phantaſmata) hoc nomine ho
norentur. Sint ergo νοητα cognoſcenda facultate ſuperio
obiectum logices, αισθητα επιστημης αισθητικης ſiue AESTHE
TICAE.

In this brief yet decisive statement, Baumgarten proposes a bifurcation: the νοητά (*noēta*) – the intelligible, that which is grasped by the mind – is the domain of logic, while the αισθητικά (*aisthētika*) – that which is apprehended through the senses, including the imagination – constitutes the subject of επιστημη αισθητικη (*epistēmē aisthētikē*), the science of sensory cognition. This move enacts a fundamental shift – treating sense, sensation, and imagination as legitimate, autonomous sites of knowledge.

This epistemic legitimacy of *the aesthetic* lays the foundations for understanding generative forces as more than solely rational or purely emotive, that is, as embodied, affective, and experiential – operating in the intervals between perception and articulation, between form and formlessness. Within the framework of my embodied research, the aesthetic is a method of knowing that moves with the instability of emergence, rather than stabilising into identity or structure. It is a process of dwelling and daringly acknowledges precariousness as a generative force.

50. Alexander Gottlieb Baumgarten, *Meditationes philosophicae de nonnullis ad poema pertinentibus* (Ioannis Henrici Grvnerti, 1735), 39, Münchner Digitalisierungezentrum Digitale Bibliothek, accessed 17 May 2025, https://mdz-nbn-resolving.de/details:bsb10820766 (my translation). Original Latin: '§ CXVI Existente definitione, terminus definitius excogitari-facile potest, graeci iam philosophi &patres inter αισθητα (aisthēta) & νοητα (noēta) sedulo semper distinxerunt, satisque apparet αισθητα iis non solis aequipollere sensualibus, quum absentia etiam sense (ergo phantasmata) hoc nominee honorentur. Sint ergo νοητα cognoscenda facultate superior objectum logices, αισθητα επιστημη αισθητικη (epistēmē aisthētikē) fiue AESTHETICAE.'

Fig. 23: Screenshot, © Mariella Greil / text by Alexander Gottlieb Baumgarten (Alexander Gottlieb Baumgarten, *Meditationes philosophicae de nonnullis ad poema pertinentibus* [Ioannis Henrici Grvnerti, 1735], 39, Münchner Digitalisierungezentrum Digitale Bibliothek, accessed 17 May 2025, https://mdz-nbn-resolving.de/details:bsb10820766).

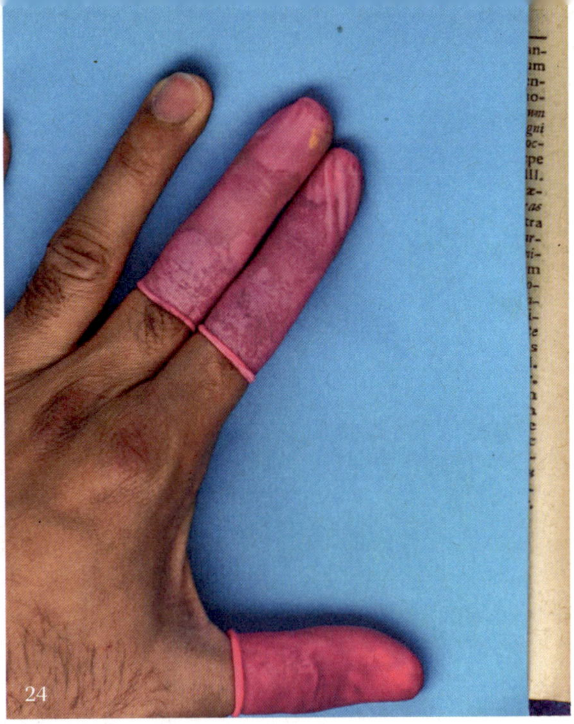

Taking the generative force further into the terrain of subjectivity and artistic creation, philosopher Immanuel Kant, in §46 of *The Critique of Judgment*, 'Fine Art is the Art of Genius',[51] elaborates on the figure of the *genius*. In his writings, the genius does not follow rules but is instead the origin of them – not by intention but by inspiration. The genius creates works of art whose rules cannot be fully explained or taught, which points to a dimension of the subject that goes beyond conscious, rule-governed action. In contrast, contemporary *generative* forms in this sense are a perpetual, ongoing regeneration, a revival and transformation of ideas. Kant's genius is an anomaly of subjectivity: it produces without fully knowing how, as he claims its works are exemplary, not imitable in method, and thus point towards the limits of pedagogy and artistic instruction. It might seem outdated, but it is worthwhile taking a closer look at this line of thought. In contemporary art, the artistic subject is decentred and no longer occupies a sovereign or central position; instead, it emerges as a distributed, post-human assemblage, entangled with the material, technological, ecological, and more-than-human. This shift marks a radical departure from the humanist paradigm in which the artist was construed as the autonomous subject – *genius, author, origin*.

As philosopher and researcher Jan Völker[52] argues in his analysis of Kantian aesthetics, the genius is not simply an *Ausnahmesubjekt* – 'exceptional subject' – but rather marks an *Ausnahme des Subjekts von sich selbst*, 'the subject's exception to itself'. This displacement is crucial: the generative emerges precisely at the edges of the subject, in the folds where intention gives way to affect, where mastery is suspended in favour of exposure. Rather than affirming the ego, the generative suspends and exceeds it.

In today's epistemic constellation, influenced by feminist materialisms, post-anthropocentric philosophies, and performative ontologies, the notion of subjectivity is refracted into relational, processual, and decentred *modes of becoming*. The subject no longer 'expresses' or 'represents' the world and instead co-emerges with it in a field of dynamic intra-actions. In this sense, the contemporary artistic subject is not a discrete entity but a distributed intelligence – a term which

51. Immanuel Kant, *The Critique of Judgment*, trans. Werner S. Pluhar (Hackett Publishing, 1987 [1790]), 307.

52. Jan Völker, *Ästhetik der Lebendigkeit* (Wilhelm Fink, 2011).

Fig. 24: Screenshot, © Mariella Greil / hand of anonymous archivist (Alexander Gottlieb Baumgarten, *Meditationes philosophicae de nonnullis ad poema pertinentibus* [Ioannis Henrici Grvnerti, 1735], 1, Münchner Digitalisierungszentrum Digitale Bibliothek, accessed 17 May 2025, https://mdz-nbn-resolving.de/details:bsb10820766).

references technological networks and algorithmic environments as well as dispersed cognition across bodies, tools, ecologies, and affects.

In her critical aesthetic considerations, Juliane Rebentisch extends this notion of generativity by positioning art as that which resists its own convention, which revolts against the framing devices through which it is captured. She writes,

> The idea is [...] that it is appropriate for all art worthy of the name to turn against its own conventionalisation, in other words to rebel against the contexts of aesthetic expectations and to upset the categories or framing with which we try to grasp it.[53]

This insurgency of form is itself generative: it does not destroy the aesthetic but reanimates it, forces it to become otherwise. It is through this continual renewal, this refusal to settle, that art maintains its force.

In the choreographic,[54] this rebellion against settling, but also critique of neoliberal working conditions and the superlatives of economisation, can be sensed in the micro-political movements of the body, in the reconfiguration of gesture, in the resistance to representation.

Micro-phenomenological Interview with Rosa Wernecke
Dark Bag Score excerpt, edited transcript
7 February 2025

Mariella Greil: These surfaces you have just described have very different qualities. You have said they are cold, but also warm, angular and smooth, rough. Can you zoom in on all these impressions and choose one of these qualities?

Rosa Wernecke: Just one?

Mariella: Just one, yes. It's their complexity that has appealed to you, right?

Rosa: Yes.

Mariella: So, the complexity is that one quality?

Rosa: Or 'angular', but that's not quite right either. It's like – I don't know. What's a word that combines angular, sharp, and pointed? What I find interesting is that you don't expect

53. Juliane Rebentisch, 'Singularität, Gattung, Form', in *Generische Formen – Dynamische Konstellationen zwischen den Künsten*, ed. Kirsten Maar, Frank Ruda, and Jan Völker (August, 2017), 14. German original: 'Der Gedanke [...], dass es aller Kunst, die den Namen verdient, eignet, sich gegen ihre eigene Konventionalisierung zu kehren, also gegen die Kontexte ästhetischer Erwartungen zu rebellieren und die Kategorien, mit denen wir sie zu fassen versuchen, außer Fassung zu bringen.'

54. I refer here to Jenn Joy's expanded notion of *the choreographic*. Joy treats *choreography* in its more conventional sense: as the art/practice of arranging movement, working with bodies, and producing what is referred to as dance performance. But *the choreographic*, for her, is broader: it encompasses theory, critical practice, affect, perception, and a field of address comprising bodies, viewers, the artwork, space, and time. The choreographic does not stop at what is visibly performed; it includes what is felt, what is awkward, what ruptures or trembles. Jenn Joy, *The Choreographic* (MIT Press, 2014).

it, and then suddenly it's there. Do you know what I mean?

Mariella: Yes. So that means there's also something that's kind of…

Rosa: … that sticks out or something…

Mariella: … that comes to you… comes towards you?

Rosa: Yes. Or like when you're walking on a smooth floor, and then there's a splinter that gets stuck in your foot. It's a bit like that.

Mariella: So, it's a quality that kind of stops you and holds you back a little.

Rosa: Yes. Yes, yes, totally.

Mariella: And this coming towards you or somehow drawing your attention to itself – can you give it a colour or describe it in more detail?

Rosa: You mean how it feels?

Mariella: Exactly, how does it feel? How did you know it suits you? How did it catch your attention?

Rosa: Well, I think it's because the object itself is completely different, or feels completely different. And then there's a spot that suddenly stands out.

Mariella: So, you have actually discovered something there…

Rosa: Like a counterpoint.

Mariella: Yes. So, something that goes against what you think it is reveals itself.

Rosa: Yes. Yes, and then there's a brief moment of resistance, and it stops or something.

Mariella: And what does this feeling of resistance do to you? Can you describe it a little?

Rosa: Well, I found it surprising, at least for a moment. And then it kind of stung a little. And it was like you had to go back and double-check. And then it's maybe a bit of a mix of: it's kind of interesting, you want to find out what it is, and at the same time it's a bit annoying.

Mariella: It's a bit annoying. But you wanted to find out exactly what it was. You went back, so to speak, and felt that sharp, angular edge again. And at that moment, you decided, 'This is the object I want to stick with.'

Rosa: Yes, but also in combination with the rest of the object's surface. The combination was decisive. I think if it had only been that one element, I wouldn't have chosen it.

Mariella: And that other element, can you describe it a little?

Rosa: Yes, well, it's kind of hilly, dented, and there are also some depressions or valleys and mountains, so to speak. And it's also a bit smooth and a bit rough. Quite firm. Or rather firm. And then I have also found it – now I think I've adjusted it a bit to the temperature of my hand – but I have also found it to be different in terms of cold and warmth. Yes.

Mariella: Do you have any idea what it could be?

Rosa: I think it's some kind of fruit, like an apple that has shrunk. But I don't know exactly what. But I think it's something natural that has a stem and that's shrivelled. I think. I have no idea, yes. That's it.

Mariella: Is there anything else you haven't talked about yet, any other qualities you have been able to discern?

Rosa: The body of the object itself feels very much like a stone or volcanic rock, a bit like dried lava, not as heavy as a stone, but a little lighter, and yet it has this mixture of smooth and rugged.

Mariella: And does it also have a porous quality like lava rock?

Rosa: Exactly.

Mariella: So, something fragile, porous?

Rosa: Yes, because I don't think the object is heavy. It's actually quite light. But the structure also has something stony about it. Except for the stem. If it didn't have the stem, for instance, I would think it was a stone.

Mariella: Maybe that was also the deciding moment when you said, 'I'll stick with it,' or did it have nothing to do with that but with its complexity instead? Before, you said complexity was an important deciding factor.

Rosa: I think it's also in contrast to the other things, of course, that I then felt the other things. And with all the other things, there was an element or a thing that was so central. And then with this one, for the first time, there was something else, so there is complexity, but that is also in relation to the other objects. And also the stem, that's already full – yes, maybe that's true, like a puzzle: 'Wait a minute, maybe that's not what I thought.' Although I haven't felt like I'm always desperately trying to figure out what it is. I have tried to let myself get involved in what I find exciting. But maybe the 'wanting to know' is still there underneath. I don't know.

Mariella: Are there any other impressions, sensations there that you haven't mentioned yet but that are important?

Rosa: Well, I find it interesting what it's done to my hands, this lace. That it is a little bit – well, it's not hurting me at all, but it's a little bit uncomfortable, maybe in a good way. I think that is perhaps one of those moments that you hold on to. And I also really like that it's so compact. I can say that in contrast to some of the other things. Yes, maybe I actually think it's quite cool that it fits in one hand and isn't so big.

Mariella: Yes, it's easy to hold.

Rosa: Yes.

Mariella: Right, I'll try to summarise again. So, that moment when you felt a slight irritation, thinking, 'Maybe it's not what I thought it was after all,' was something that reinforced your decision to stick with the object. And the fact that it's compact and fits in your hand feels pleasant. Although you've emphasised again that it wasn't really about finding the most comfortable object, but rather one that's surprised you for a moment, which is precisely what is interesting about it, that it's a little uncomfortable or a little irritating, that there's a resistance there and a quality of complexity. Does this tactile level perhaps reveal something that is also present on another level?

Rosa: Yes, yes, yes. Yes, absolutely.

Choreographic environments are not static compositions but living topologies – terrains that shift as bodies pass through them. Rather than novelty for its own sake, the generative force here is about a fidelity to transformation, to the event of *becoming*.

Moreover, an expanded understanding of choreography and contemporary performance manifests in translational processes – from one modality to another, from sensation to movement, from gesture to sound – operating as cross-modal invitations to further unfold aesthetic potentials. Thus, translation is transfiguration rather than duplication: a movement that alters, reshapes, and reinterprets. Within generative choreographic environments, such translational practices reveal the porousness of media and the instability of form. This is where the aesthetic becomes ethical – in the sense of responsiveness and attentiveness to what might emerge, what might come into being if the conditions are gently held open.

In sum, generative forces in choreographic environments are neither programmatic nor free; instead, they are attuned to the rhythms of emergence, relation, and transformation. They operate across the conceptual, the embodied, and the affective. They insist on process instead of identity. These forces work through generosity rather than possession. And perhaps most importantly, they invite us to reimagine the subject – not as the originator of action but as a participant in a field of becoming that is always more-than-individual, more-than-intentional, and always already in motion.

To understand the generative capacities of *choreographic environments*, it is instructive to return to *aesthetics* as *aesthesis* – the sensory mode of knowing, still aware of the resonances of its ancient Greek roots in *aisthesis* (αἴσθησις), meaning sensory perception as a fundamental mode of being-in-the-world. For Baumgarten, aesthetic experience was a way of thinking through the senses, a form of knowledge that does not culminate in logical clarity but in perceptual richness. In the *choreographic environment*, this notion becomes vividly operative: the environment 'thinks' by generating movement, sensation, space, and temporal relationships. Rather than producing potentiality and knowledge through spatio-temporal propositions alone, it generates them through the conscious activation of agencies and by attuning itself to contingencies and embodied events. The body is key in this active process of attuning. I personally first encountered practices of attunement as a core concept in music therapy[55] as well as various other forms of psychotherapy, especially in relation to early bonding processes between parent and child, and in understanding the foundational role of mutual human attunement.

In my artistic work, I draw on my longstanding attunement practice as a therapist and expand beyond the human towards all kinds of life forms and existences. In 2024, contemporary Romanian choreographer Alexandra Pirici performed her work *Attune* at Hamburger Bahnhof in Berlin, stating in the accompanying catalogue, 'The reality is that no fundamental distinction exists between matter that is alive and matter that is not, and that means that we are part of a continuum.'[56] On this continuum, and reflecting on its aesthetic regime, the environment is not a backdrop but a sentient field, a force of emergence – and so is the movement of the body: each shift in weight, each modulation of breath, each sonic vibration becomes a unit of thought. Rather than illustrating an idea, then, the choreographic environment produces it. It composes thinking. In this sense, this environment is a site of aesthetic cognition, a dynamic space where embodied wisdom exceeds representational logic and takes shape as a constellation of gestures, sensations, and relations.

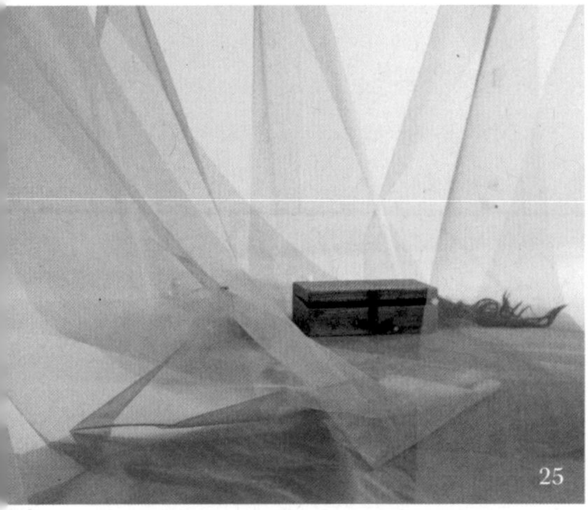

Once more, my point is that the choreographic environment has generative qualities. To extrapolate this in detail, let me return to Kant's notion of *genius* as 'the innate mental predisposition (*ingenium*) through which nature gives the rule to art'[57], for it becomes relevant here – though it must be radically reworked. For Kant, genius was the origin of the artwork, the site from which beauty emerges in an unteachable manner. Yet in the expanded field of

55. I graduated from the University of Music and Performing Arts Vienna in 2004 with a degree in music therapy and have since worked as an artist and therapist in the field, mostly in multidisciplinary teams. I currently teach within the scope of the 600-hour course that works towards the Further Education for Embodied Myoreflex Practitioner Certificate at ImPulsTanzFestival Viennna (https://www.impulstanz.com/en/emp) and in the Psychotherapy Sciences department at Sigmund Freud University (https://ptw.sfu.ac.at/en).

56. Alexandra Pirici et al., *Alexandra Pirici – Attune* (Silvana Editoriale, 2024), 47.

57. Kant, *The Critique of Judgment*, 307. This corresponds again to § 46, where the definition of genius appears. The original German: 'Genie ist das angeborene Gemütsvermögen (ingenium), durch welches die Natur der Kunst die Regel gibt.'

Fig. 25: *Choreographic Environment*, 2020, © Mariella Greil and Walter Lauterer.

choreography, genius is displaced from the singular subject to the relational fabric of the environment itself – the *ingenium* of the choreographic environment, meaning its disposition, nature, or soul. The choreographer does not singularly possess genius; instead, the environment *acts* with genius, gives rise to unforeseeable articulations through its very composition.

This notion of *distributed generativity* aligns with Rebentisch's rethinking of aesthetics[58] as a theory of *art's autonomy* – not as detachment but as a mode of *self-reflective engagement.* Here, I would like to emphasise reflection, which etymologically means 'the action of throwing back light or heat', based on the Late Latin *reflection,* literally, 'bending back'. For Rebentisch, aesthetic autonomy lies in art's ability to expose and interrogate its own conditions, a form of bending back into its aesthetic generativity and autonomy.[59] In choreographic environments, such autonomy is enacted through processes that render visible the production itself – exposing rehearsal as form, revealing collaboration as substance, and embedding failure or repetition into the repertoire of compositional, aesthetic strategies. The choreographic environment folds in on itself, revealing its scaffolding, its seams, its labour. It reflects itself while moving forward.

Here, the generative force is more than productivity; it is about *potentiality* – a force that sustains ambiguity, invites contradiction, and holds open the possibility of transformation. Autonomy, in this context, does not signal withdrawal from the world but indeed cultivates a heightened responsiveness to it. The choreographic environment becomes an ethical space of encounter, where difference can be maintained without assimilation, where form is always provisionally inhabited. Thus, the generative force of a choreographic environment is both ontological and political: it generates movement and meaning, as well as modes of co-being, co-sensing, and co-knowing.

It is *fortis* in the sense of inner resilience, ethical courage, and the capacity to maintain the force of emergence or structural coherence and the bravery of staying in motion, of moving without knowing where you are going. It equates to a steadfastness in flux, where strength is not rigidity or resoluteness, the establishment or cohesion of ideas, but rather the ability to endure, adapt, and create within indeterminacy, in a bold commitment to openness. In her keynote presentation at the 2021 SAR Conference in Vienna, Emma Cocker developed the notion of an attitude of openness with great care, advocating what is not predetermined. She did so both in terms of the aesthetic of her presentation and its content. Her keynote was entitled: 'Towards an Attitude of Openness'.[60]

Rather than through linear progress, the deliberate devotion to an attitude of openness proceeds through recursive improvisation, affective feedback, and

58. Juliane Rebentisch, 'Autonomie? Autonomie! Ästhetische Erfahrung heute', in *Ästhetische Erfahrung: Gegenstände, Konzepte, Geschichtlichkeit,* ed. Sonderforschungsbereich 626 (2006), accessed 19 July 2025, https://www.geschkult.fu-berlin.de/e/sfb626/veroeffentlichungen/online/aesth_erfahrung/aufsaetze/rebentisch.pdf.

59. Ibid.

60. Emma Cocker, 'Towards an Attitude of Openness', keynote presentation, 12th International Conference on Artistic Research, Society for Artistic Research, Vienna, 7–9 April 2021, online video, https://www.researchcatalogue.net/profile/show-exposition?exposition=1220981.

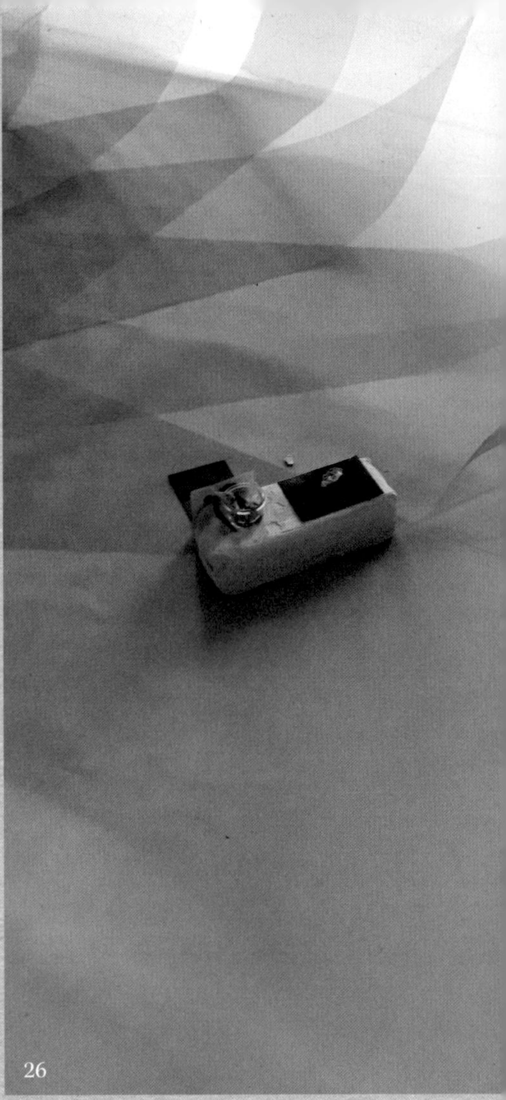
26

Astringent Reflection

Sandpapery sensation
lingers as an aftertaste,
dirty drugs scraping the
palate of thought,
their residue clouding
the mirror.

Clay binds fast the
reflections
before they can escape,
hardening into terracotta logic,
kiln-warm cognition.

Wild mirror images thrown back on pink,
feral and fresh, on the inside of seeing.

The unripe, delicate seedling leans,
not towards light but sideways,
towards the shadow of the mineral.
Besides it, a salt rock –
small enough to disappear in the mouth –
reflects the rays of light emerging from the surface,
hoarding brightness, at the layer of the skin.
Lucency rebounds, meets the stubborn
limit of matter.

At every threshold, waves encounter the
boundary of the material:
reflections, absorptions, and refractions –
the trinity of contact.
They break into frequencies and diffuse into
the aether.
Its sources are reinforced and multiply
through dialogic oscillation,
glossy spectra diffract,
reverse themselves –
up becomes down, back and front shift.

Visibility thins,
the diaphanous spectaculum is almost gone
interfaces dissolve into rosé-like shimmer.
Yet, drying processes continue,
time works slowly, astringently,
intensifying, especially on the surfaces.

Generations of figures –
kneaded from clay and water –
pause in their forming,
take their time to solidify.

They resist collapse,
wait for evaporation,
welcome the hardness
as it arrives.
Its inevitability is
patient,
granular memories
of touch and
sandy sedimentations
of sensation.

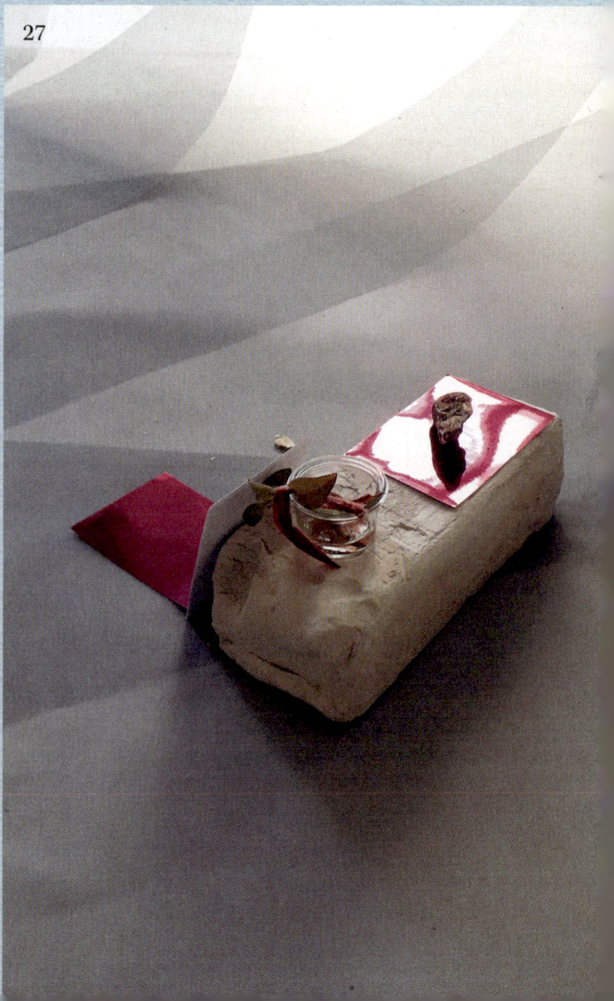

27

durational attunement. In the field of performative, artistic research, thinking and moving become inseparable – a mutual choreography of ideas and bodies, time and material, self and world, spirit and matter that folds, senses, and performs the *differences* of materials while simultaneously emerging as a *continuum* of performative and choreographed figures[61] moulded by generative forces.

Autopoiesis

Across the humanities, the prefix *auto-* has served as a marker of self-referentiality, interiority, and experiential authority. However, its proliferation across diverse conceptual domains such as autobiography, autofiction, autotheory, and autopoiesis demands a re-examination of its ontological and epistemological significance. I suggest interrogating the aesthetic and structural properties of these *auto-* formulations and situating them within a broader framework that considers the interrelation of narrative, embodiment, and œkology.

Autobiography has conventionally been understood as the narrative of a life, a genre anchored in coherence, memory, and authorial continuity. In her recent text *Passed Out – An Autobiographical Emergency*, Kath T. Zakravsky challenges this paradigm by presenting autobiography not as a cohesive story but as an archival remainder, a fragmented archive.[62] Her works embrace fragmentation, opacity, and the impossibility of full self-representation. This insistence on interstitiality subverts the autobiographical tradition, challenges the conventions of truth-telling and identity-assertion, and aligns the interstice with a poststructuralist critique of the subject.

Zakravsky's method can be likened to what feminist critic and writer Leigh Gilmore terms 'limit-case autobiographies'.[63] The authority of personal experience is complicated by the ruptures and contradictions of narrative form. While acknowledging the crisis of legitimacy, she deftly foregrounds the fragmented, multiple, and performative self.

In a series of publications spanning the last three decades, Leigh Gilmore has compellingly analysed the centrality of autobiographical storytelling in

61. I differentiate here between *choreographed* and *choreo-graphic* figures insofar as in the latter there is an emphasis on the figuration of notation, indicated by the hyphen that sets the *graphic* apart from the *choreo*. For further discussion, see Nikolaus Gansterer, Emma Cocker, and Mariella Greil, eds., *Choreo-graphic Figures: Deviations from the Line* (Edition Angewandte, De Gruyter, 2017), which can be downloaded at https://www.choreo-graphic-figures.net/publications/book.

62. K. T. Zakravsky, 'Passed Out – An Autobiographical Emergency', in *Bare Bodies – Thresholding Life*, ed. Mariella Greil (Edition Angewandte, De Gruyter, 2024).

63. Leigh Gilmore, *The Limits of Autobiography: Trauma and Testimony* (Cornell University Press, 2001), 18–19. Leigh Gilmore is Professor Emeritus at Ohio State University and is an expert in autobiography. She writes, 'Innovation in contemporary memoir derives in no small part from a history of literary and autobiographical experimentation' (18) and addresses 'the centrality of fictional and autobiographical intermingling to the development of autobiography' (22). As she emphasises, 'When self-representation entails the representation of trauma, the autobiographical paradox of representativeness is intensified' (19). Moreover, Gilmore is the author of *The #MeToo Effect: What Happens When We Believe Women* (Columbia, 2023); *Tainted Witness: Why We Doubt What Women Say About Their Lives* (Columbia, 2017); and *Autobiographics: A Feminist Theory of Women's Self-Representation* (Cornell, 1994). She is also an anti-rape activist.

intersectional activism.[64] Such autobiographical accounts challenge the ethical and epistemological premises of testimonial writing, emphasising instead the performative and constructed dimensions of self-narration, the discursive signature of the subject, and agency in self-representation.[65]

French writer and filmmaker Alain Robbe-Grillet developed autofiction through narrative estrangement as a fictional apparatus. His notion of autofiction presents a deliberate contamination of autobiographical truth by fictional devices. In works such as *Le Miroir qui revient* (1985),[66] Robbe-Grillet displaces the subject by rendering it a product of narrative operations. Autofiction, in his hands, functions less as a personal revelation than as a procedural apparatus. As Serge Doubrovsky, who coined the term *autofiction* in the 1970s, suggests, it is a 'fiction, of events and facts strictly real'[67] yet subjected to the logics of fiction.

In contrast, autotheory emerges at the intersection of embodied experience and critical reflection as a form of situated knowledge and epistemic intervention. Writer, curator, and artist Lauren Fournier defines it as a mode of writing that 'entails self-reflexive engagement with theoretical discourse, articulated through lived experience'.[68] Rather than subordinating the autobiographical to the theoretical, autotheory stages a dialogical relationship in which both are mutually constitutive.

Lauren Fournier draws upon feminist epistemologies, particularly those of Audre Lorde and bell hooks, to advocate for a mode of theorising that is situated, affectively charged, and politically responsive. The form it takes challenges the normative distinctions between academic and creative writing, privileging an aesthetics of vulnerability and openness, and a form of contextualisation that generates a broader meaning beyond the personal. In this sense, autotheory exemplifies feminist scholar Donna Haraway's notion of 'situated knowledges',[69] where knowledge is understood as partial, embodied, and contingent. The *auto-* here is not a sovereign self but a node in a network of relational intensities, articulated through both textual and extra-textual modes, writing and embodiment extending and entangling research into its *Umwelt.*

64. In the late 1980s, the term *intersectionality* was coined by American civil rights advocate and critical race theory scholar Kimberlé Crenshaw. Intersectional activism engages diverse identities across race, class, and gender, and stands up for political and social equity. See Brittney Cooper 'Intersectionality', in *The Oxford Handbook of Feminist Theory*, ed. Lisa Disch and Mary Hawkesworth (Oxford University Press, 2016).

65. Leigh Gilmore, 'The Mark of Autobiography: Postmodernism, Autobiography, and Genre', in *Autobiography and Postmodernism*, ed. Kathleen Ashley, Leigh Gilmore, and Gerald Peters (University of Massachusetts Press, 1994), 8.

66. *Le Miroir qui revient* (1985) by Alain Robbe-Grillet is a self-reflexive autobiographical 'fiction-autobiography' in which the author weaves together fragments of memory, familial myth, and invented episodes around the character Henri de Corinthe to explore the instability of identity, the unreliability of memory, and the tension between life and literary invention. Alain Robbe-Grillet, *Le Miroir Qui Revient* (Les Éditions de Minuit, 2010).

67. Serge Doubrovsky, *Fils* (Galilée, 1977), back cover.

68, Lauren Fournier, *Autotheory as Feminist Practice in Art, Writing, and Criticism* (MIT Press, 2021), 7.

69. Haraway reclaims the sensory system of vision for a particular, unmarked form of feminist embodiment while rejecting the male gaze. She instead argues for situated knowledge as 'a doctrine of embodied objectivity that accommodates paradoxical and critical feminist science projects'. Donna Haraway, 'Situated Knowledges: The Science Question in Feminism and the Privilege of Partial Perspective', *Feminist Studies* 14, no. 3 (1988): 581.

Finally, the concept of autopoiesis that gives this chapter its title was introduced by Chilean biologists Humberto Maturana and Francisco Varela,[70] and refers to the self-producing capabilities of living systems. These self-referential systems are operationally closed yet structurally open, maintaining their identity through recursive operations. In a next conceptual step, philosopher Niklas Luhmann extends this logic to social systems, in particular communication, proposing that society is not composed of individuals but of communicative acts that reproduce the system itself.[71]

When applied to cultural production, each creation is autopoietic in that it generates the rules and distinctions that constitute its identity. In this sense, autopoiesis suggests that embodied research practice is idiosyncratic and does not represent culture; rather it produces the conditions for the vital creative self to emerge through autopoiesis. Of course, art, then, becomes a privileged domain for autopoietic emergence because it stages this recursive process visibly and sensuously. Structurally coupled (to use Varela's term) with its environment, culture becomes a co-generative ground for autopoietic emergence, including its historical sedimentations and discursive formations. I understand autopoietic practices in the context of embodied research to be part of an œkology, the interlacing of mental, bodily, social, and environmental practice as emergent self-organisational processes. In this sense, a deepening into self-actualization takes place through cultural sedimentation, historical reflection, and œkological responsiveness.

Taken together, auto-configurations and autopoiesis reveal the limitations of viewing the self as a pre-discursive, complete, or indisputable essence. Instead, they foreground the self as a relational and procedural phenomenon, emerging from psychodynamic and systemic processes of inscription, performance, and discourse. This perspective aligns with recent turns in new materialism and performance philosophy, which have emphasised entanglement, emergence, and affective relationality – both as intrapsychic processes and relational patterns, which are equally sensitive to the temporal depth of lived experience.[72]

I am convinced that an œkological perspective allows for a non-hierarchical understanding of auto-configurations and autopoietic practices. Each mode (emerging as a *figure* or *practice*[73]) operates within an interdependent system that is structurally linked to the socio-material environments in which it is embedded. The aesthetics of autopoiesis are thus inseparable from their epistemic and ontological implications.

70. Humberto R. Maturana and Francisco J. Varela, *Autopoiesis and Cognition: The Realization of the Living* (Springer Science+Business Media, 1991). The Spanish original was published in 1972.

71. Niklas Luhmann, *Ecological Communication*, trans. John Bednarz, Jr. (University of Chicago Press, 1989), The German original was published in 1986.

72. In particular, the stretching of the temporal through a focus on micro-moments of lived experience and the thin-slicing of time is an activity that the research method of micro-phenomenological interviews embraces.

73. See Nikolaus Gansterer, Emma Cocker, and Mariella Greil, 'Epilogue – How to Play the Score', in *Choreo-graphic Figures*, 383. We elaborated three main categories of *figure* (elemental, empathetic, and transformative) in relation to the arc of creation and differentiated *practices* of attention, conversation, notation, and wit(h)nessing that were performatively activated within the score.

I would like to advance the daring proposition that the proliferation of *auto-* concepts in contemporary theory signals a paradigmatic shift away from representational to performative understandings of the self. It also resonates with post-humanist thought, which challenges the exceptionalism and coherence of the human subject. The performative selves co-emerge with their environments, temporally unstable, and materially distributed. Here, the *auto-* signals not a return to the sovereign self but an insistence on reflexivity, entanglement, and incompleteness.

Autobiography, autofiction, autotheory (even autodomestication[74]), and autopoiesis each interrogate the boundaries of subjectivity, authorship, and living systems. So, again, what also unites these diverse *auto-* formations is their departure from representational fidelity and their embrace of performativity as an ontological and methodological condition. Rather than delineating and spelling out clear distinctions among these genres, I argue in favour of a relational approach that situates these modes within a shared œkological matrix of meaning-production. While the performative turn as a broad cultural, philosophical, and methodological shift gained momentum in the late twentieth century (though its roots stretch back further[75]), it appears to mark a significant movement away from representational and structuralist models of understanding the self towards relational action, enactment, and becoming-with – that is, understanding phenomena as being *performed into being* rather than statically described. The *auto-* is not a claim to sovereignty but a site of recursive negotiation, a dynamic interplay between form, discourse, and embodiment. This also has an impact on the conception of the self. In my research, the self is no longer a pre-existing entity to be represented but a contingent and situated emergence, enacted through movement, verbal and non-verbal exchanges, writing, theory, and relational entanglements. Rather than a mark of individual selfhood, the *auto-* becomes a performative strategy – a way of staging the instability, fragmentariness, and constructedness of artistic subjectivity.

The performative field has long since abandoned the stable ontology of the 'artwork' as an object of contemplation. Instead, it has become a site of processual intensities and relational events – vibrant, flickering between *being* and *becoming*.[76] In this terrain, aestheticity is not merely attributed to form or content, nor is it located solely in the symbolic. Rather, it is an emergent field – a responsive, affective, and reciprocal space of transformation at the limen of the event. This field is shaped through presence, co-constitution (*being*), and the unfolding dynamics of interaction, entangling human and non-human agents, sensorial registers, and temporal modalities (*becoming*). The work of art is playing an increasingly peripheral role in aesthetic practices, and Erika Fischer-Lichte has clearly identified a shift away from the idea of the work of art (*Werkbegriff*) towards the concept of the event

74. Performance artist Krõõt Juurak concludes her research into *Autodomestication* as a blend of humour, provocation, and a persistently sticky metaphor. For further details, visit her blog: https://autodomestication.wordpress.com.

75. John Langshaw Austin introduced the concept of *performative utterances* in *How to Do Things with Words* (Harvard University Press, 1962).

76. Mariella Greil, 'Being and Becoming', in *Being in Contact – Encountering a Bare Body* (Edition Angewandte, De Gruyter, 2021).

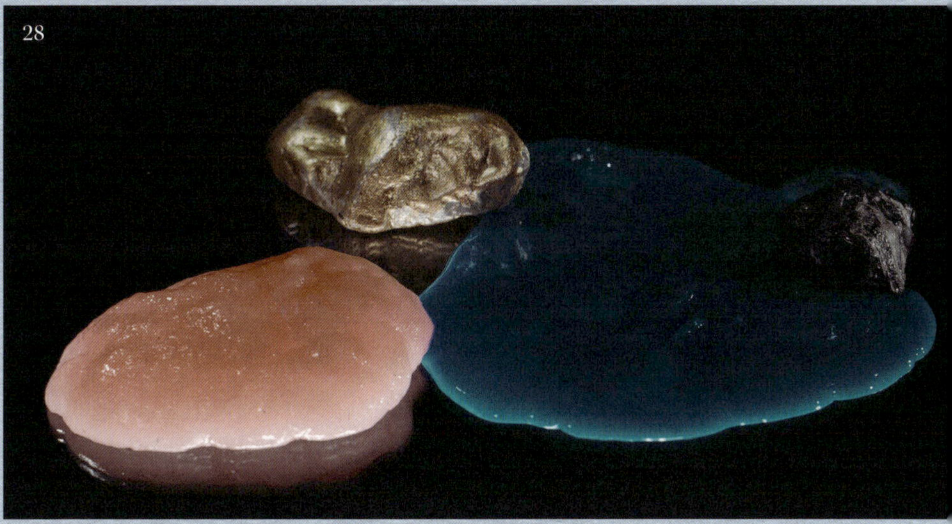

Slime

Slime is matter that slows movement until
touch is forgotten.

Mucus oozes across shared metabolic zones,
wrapping the relentless and unforgiving.

Snail slime's glamour and glibber
drags softly, thickening time along.
Some molluscs taste the world with their feet.

SCOBYs are cellulose slime sheets,
grown by bacteria and yeast symbiosis.
Gelatinous resistance made flesh
secretes mellowness into the system.

Slugs prolong contact by pressing their
tongues into the world,
an immersion from within extended feelers.
Their bodies know by touching,
trailing between figure and ground,
leaving wet vulnerability as a track.
Their sensory organs smear across the surface,
signalling outsourced sensation.

29

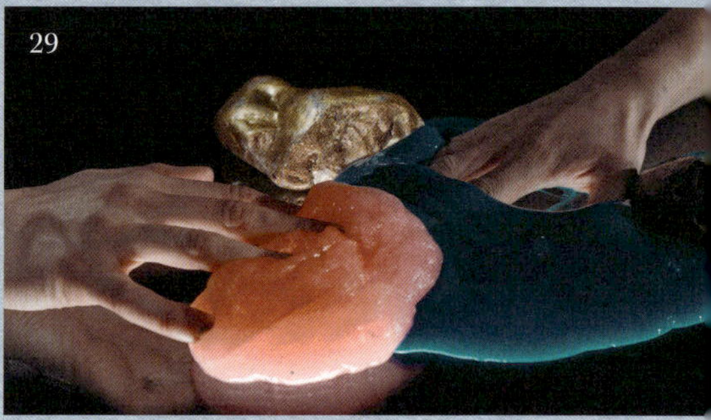

The grunge of slime is not
on its surface;
it rests voluptuously within the
tangible traces it leaves.
Residues cling onto the planes
when it pours itself across areas
of disgust,
biased against living fermentation,
cyanobacterial mats,
rotting compost or pond scum.

30

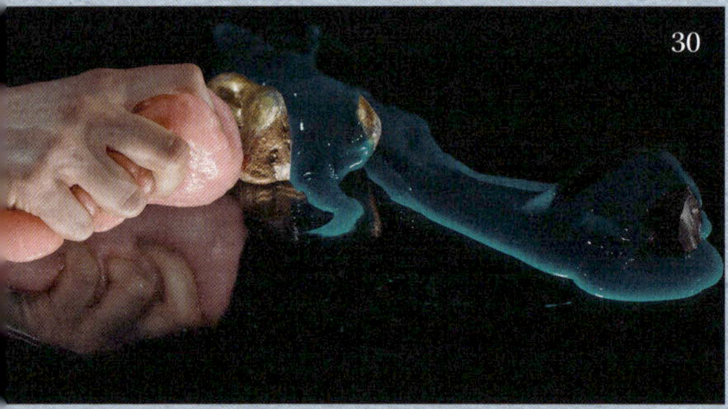

Slime is abject lubrication and excess
in softness.
It leaks, sticks, drips into regimes of
viscous transition.
Movements overspill the intention
of sidestepping ontological
ingratiation.
They sustain porosity,
perform consistent permeability,
erode good taste.

31

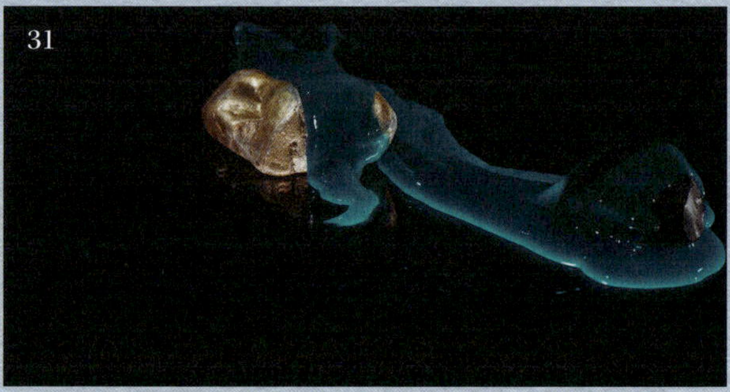

(*Ereignisbegriff*).[77] Contemporary performance artists are creating and experimenting with the crafting of specific situations and initiating experiential processes that demand response-ability from participants. Fischer-Lichte states that, upon entering the feedback loop of autopoiesis, the presence of actors, the *extasis* of things, the atmospheres, and the circulation of energy generate perceptions, affects, imaginations, and thoughts in both the performers and participants.[78]

This notion of *response-ability* – which we might understand in the twofold sense of the capacity to respond and the ethical imperative to do so – suggests that aesthetic practices no longer function as one-directional transmissions. Instead, they constitute a multiplicity of potential relations. (Un-)Fortunately, these relations are not given in advance; they arise, mutate, and dissolve within the processual fabric of the performance event. What is activated is a topology of becoming-with, where aestheticity is embedded within the reciprocal enfolding of movements, atmospheres, and intensities, and manifests as what I refer to as diffractive dialogues (→ Scores, 387).

In my research, anchored within the field of expanded choreography and contemporary performance, the aesthetic is not defined by the formal qualities of an autonomous object but by the way that it configures and transfigures relational œkologies. These œkologies are composed through sensing, through perception, but also through disturbance, rupture, and the ungraspable. Transformations occur due to autopoiesis and emergence, the destabilisation and dissolving of contrasts and liminalities. It is precisely in these liminal spaces – in the interstices between dialogue partners, material and immaterial, intention and accident – that the aestheticity of the Polylogic Lab (→ Polylogic Labs, 178) takes shape. Liminality here is not a threshold to be crossed but a dynamic state of indeterminacy, a resonant in-betweenness that sustains difference without fixation and keeps diversity fluid.

In this sense, performance as embodied research is not the presentation of preformed content but a site of potentialisation. It activates modes of attention and presencing that defy the closure of representation. As such, it becomes an ethical and aesthetic proposition – one that calls upon the participants (both as performers and dialogue partners) to enter into a relationship of co-creation. This relationship is not necessarily harmonious. It may be riddled with friction, failure, opacity. But it is precisely this instability that makes transformation possible.

Autopoiesis, as reconceived by Fischer-Lichte, draws on the cybernetic and biological origins of the term[79] as developed by Maturana and Varela, but relocates it within the aesthetic realm. The performance event is thus understood as a self-organising system in which all participants are implicated. The feedback loop she describes is not only energetic but ontological: presence affects presence. The circulation of attention, breath, gesture, gaze, sound, and silence produces shifts in the field. These shifts cannot be rehearsed in advance – they are evental in nature. They *emerge*. They unfold in time, in space, in the precarious co-habitation of difference.

77. Erika Fischer-Lichte, *Ästhetik des Performativen* (Suhrkamp, 2004), 282.

78. Ibid., 283.

79. Maturana and Varela, *Autopoiesis and Cognition.*

To speak of the *extasis of things* – as Fischer-Lichte does – is to evoke a condition in which objects, bodies, and environments exceed their boundaries, opening themselves up to transformative encounters. The extatic is more than ecstatic in the usual sense of joy or abandon; it is ex-stasis: standing outside oneself, a decentring. Thus, the aesthetic becomes a movement towards alterity, towards that which unsettles and unmoors. This is not a loss of self but a reconfiguration of the relational self – one that is situated, permeable, and co-constituted.

The aestheticity of performance, then, might be conceived of as a field of emergence in which form and content – as I have stated many times in diverse contexts[80] – are continuously being renegotiated through the interplay of forces. These forces include affective intensities, atmospheric pressures, cultural inscriptions, corporeal rhythms, and the temporality of lived experience, as well as all the infinitely numerous situations that are unpredictable and indeterminable because they can only occur and actualise themselves in performance. The work of contemporary performance artists – such as Mette Ingvartsen, Antonia Baehr, Philip Gehmacher, Meg Stuart, and Angela Schubot and Jared Gradinger – often dwells precisely in these thresholds, staging conditions of emergence rather than fixed narratives or visual spectacles. Their choreographies are movements in space as well as invitations into altered modes of perceiving, becoming, and being.

In my chosen context, the *Werkbegriff* becomes an anachronism, while the *Ereignisbegriff* foregrounds the evental nature of aesthetic experience. Yet even the term *event* risks reification if it is not considered through its *becoming*. It is not the event as a rigid temporal unit that matters but the eventfulness – the capacity of a moment, a gesture, a breath to open up a field of potential transformation. Though in my practice the choreographic environment is crucial as a spatial setting for embodied research, I would like to draw a line between my practice and the aesthetic theories of Rebentisch,[81] who argues in favour of understanding aesthetic experience as something essentially temporal and relational. In this view, the event is not what happens but what *could* happen. Aestheticity is thus linked to potentiality – in the embodied, situated here-and-now, rather than in the abstract. For me, this is the active staging and purposeful sustaining of potential encounters until they occur within their *prepared choreographic environments*. It is not by chance that this term, 'prepared environment', has been borrowed from a field that is dedicated to creative play, the autonomy of actions, and the development of selfhood, namely Pikler pedagogy.[82] Emmi Pikler, a Hungarian paediatrician and reform educator, developed a

80. On various occasions in public lectures or panels – most controversially in the double lecture series curated by Krassimira Kruschkova at TanzQuartierWien and most celebrated at the finissage of the exhibition *Körpereinsatz*, to which I was invited by Stella Geppert for a performative dialogue activation of her installation *Hieroglyphendecke* at Kunsthalle in Leipzig. See Gesa Ziemer and Mariella Greil, 'Vorträge: Künstlerische Forschung: Wozu? ... denn das Denken der Hand / lungert herum', 14 November 2014, Tanzquartier Wien, https://mediathek.tqw.at/tanzquartier-wien-online-archiv?tx_tqwmediathek_pi1%5Baction%5D=detail&tx_tqwmediathek_pi1%5Bcontroller%5D=Video&tx_tqwmediathek_pi1%5Bvideo%5D=236&cHash=9158f2488bfa7694928f76f50f4aeceb; Mostly however, the students at ArtEz, Codarts, and the Angewandte have heard me talk about keeping the ongoing circulation between content and form alive.

81. Juliane Rebentisch, *Ästhetik der Installation* (Suhrkamp, 2003).

82. For further information, see Pikler International, accessed 16 September 2025, https://www.piklerinternational.com/en.

radically respectful approach to infant care, emphasising autonomous motor development in prepared environments that foster agency and trust. At the Lóczy orphanage in Budapest, in the period after World War II, she created environments that were structured for self-initiated movement, relational continuity, and secure attachment, thereby challenging institutional norms. Her work foregrounded bodily competence as foundational for subjectivity, influencing contemporary infant pedagogy and somatic developmental approaches globally – it has also inspired my thought and practice surrounding what I call *choreographed environments.*

If I asked artist Nikolaus Gansterer how to define autopoiesis in performance, he would most probably say that performance as an aesthetic practice is the probing of contingency[83] – a material and discursive exploration of what might emerge when bodies, temporalities, and sensoria are unsettled from their habitual alignment.

In this sense, performance as I understand it is neither illustrative nor representational; it is – and this is the point of this whole chapter – *generative*, an open-ended poiesis that rehearses modes of *cohabitation*, *perception*, and *embodied reconfiguration*, rather than a world that is already given. Crucially, performance is *rehearsing how we might live together*: not by prescribing ethical norms but by exposing the fragility and mutability of relational structures. In the shared space of the event, it invites *experimental togetherness* – a practice of being-with that foregrounds proximity, risk, and response-ability. Through its temporal and corporeal specificity, performance is staging *how we might sense differently*, disrupting the habits of perception that accumulate like sediment and shape the distribution of the sensible (a nod to Jacques Rancière).[84] Instead of through abstraction, it does so through the *micro-politics of attention, rhythm, breath, and gesture*, making palpable the forces that shape our bodily orientations.

As artist and philosopher Erin Manning writes, 'The force of the micropolitical, its power, is its capacity to infrathinly infiltrate the hardenings into form.'[85] Manning's notion of the micropolitical as *infrathin infiltration* reveals how form is subtly unsettled from within – where sensation shifts before it settles. This is where aesthetic force operates: not as a fixed property but as an emergent potential. Performance operates in this register – it rehearses other modes of sensing and living. How might we sense differently, undo and redo our embodied habits of perception? It brings forth a *poiesis* not of objects but of relations, where *aestheticity* arises as a force: a dynamic constellation, a sensate resonance, intensity, expansion, ecstasy.

In the extasis of things, those things are not given as self-enclosed objects. Rather, they step forward, show themselves, appear in a particularly intense

83. Alex Arteaga and Nikolaus Gansterer, eds., *Contingent Agencies: Inquiring into the Emergence of Atmospheres* (Hatje Cantz, 2025).

84. Jacques Rancière, *The Politics of Aesthetics: The Distribution of the Sensible*, ed. Gabriel Rockhill (Bloomsbury, 2013); Mariella Greil, ed., 'Special Issue: Figure of the Sensible', *Activate* 2, no. 1 (2012).

85. Erin Manning, *For a Pragmatics of the Useless* (Duke University Press, 2020), 81.

> way as present [...]. Since it is both the presence of the performers and the ecstasies of things that constitute atmospheres, atmospheres appear to the perceiver with special intensity; they envelop him, he immerses himself in them; they penetrate his body as light, sounds, and odours.[86]

It is precisely this *showing*, as emergence and autopoiesis, that gravitates towards performativity and transforms situated, embodied research through the felt sense[87] into an aesthetics of potentiality. It hangs there as a vague movement between an emergent showing, an intimate encounter, and the presencing of embodied research.

In this light, performance becomes a poietic force – the making of relations rather than objects. Rather than being bound to production in the conventional sense, this kind of poiesis is tied to emergence, resonance, and transformation. It enacts a shift from ontological fixity to relational plasticity, where forms are continually negotiated through affective, kinetic, and perceptual interaction. All in all, it is in this very poiesis that *aestheticity* emerges: not as a static property or formal category but as a force field, a *dynamic constellation*, a felt resonance that exceeds representation. Aestheticity here is linked to the intensity of co-perception, the becoming-sensible of potentiality, the friction and shimmer between bodies in a process. It is not located *in* the work, nor can it be reduced to the artist's intention. Instead, it circulates as an immanent relational quality – a 'more-than', a 'not-yet', a *vibration* in the ecology of encounter.

Thus, performance as an aesthetic practice does more than reflect the world; it exercises and reconditions the very ways in which *worlding* occurs. It is, at its most potent, a *site of perceptual and relational experimentation*, a field where we practice how to see and move in a different way as well as how *to become* differently with others.

To dwell in the aestheticity of performance as embodied research is to suspend the binary of artwork and audience, product and process, subject and object. It is to linger in becoming, in the unstable, in the porous. It is to attune oneself to the event as a site of emergence, where presence is not given, but performed – time after time, each moment a bare and ephemeral touch of what comes into *be*ing, a *be*coming. This attunement requires practice, the practice of embodying, of listening empathically, of transforming relations into encounters across agencies. It takes vulnerability, openness, and a willingness to be affected. It is a mode of laying bare and knowing that

86. Fischer-Lichte, *Ästhetik des Performativen*, 289 (my translation). The German original: 'Bei der Extase der Dinge sind diese nicht als in sich abgeschlossene Objekte gegeben. Sie treten vielmehr aus sich heraus, zeigen sich, erscheinen in besonders intensiver Weise als gegenwärtig [...]. Da es sowohl die Präsenz der Schauspieler als auch die Extasen der Dinge sind, welche Atmosphären konstituieren, erscheinen Atmosphären dem Wahrnehmenden in besonderer Intensität; sie umhüllen ihn, er taucht in sie ein, sie dringen als Licht, Laute und Gerüche in seinen Körper ein.'

87. Eugene T. Gendlin, *Focusing* (Random House, 2003 [1978]).

exceeds cognition, a mode of being that exceeds the individual and instead practices the œkology of the dividual.[88]

In conclusion, the shift from *Werk* to *Ereignis*, from the object to the relational field, is more than just a terminological one. It signals a profound rethinking of the aesthetic as such and, in particular, the aesthetic dimension of performance as embodied research. The aestheticity of performance is no longer anchored in the static, the representational, or the sublime but in the minor movements, the in-between spaces, the precarious togetherness of bodies, things, and times. It is there – in the interstitial, the emergent, the affective – that *autopoietic performance* becomes a site of potential, a space of *becoming* something different.

Sympoiesis

In this section, I engage with entangled vitalities and symbiotic choreographies, and speculate about bare genes and microbial kinships in relation to *sympoiesis*. As cultural historian Nicoletta Isar[89] explains, sympoiesis was both a core term in ancient Greek natural philosophy – particularly in the field of atomism and for the pre-Socratics studying the physical universe in its complex interplay of relations – and a literary term used in the arts to describe co-creative processes such as *τραγωδίας συμποίησις* (*tragôdías sympoíesis*, the co-creation of the tragedy) and *μεταλλικοῦ ἀγάλματος συμποίησις* (*metallikou agalmatos sympoiesi*, the co-creation of a metal statue). *Choreo-ethical assemblages* are somewhat akin to all these fields.

It was Canadian environmental studies scholar Beth Dempster who introduced the term *sympoiesis* to the fields of ecological humanities in her 1998 master's thesis, where she wrote,

> I propose the conceptualization of boundaryless systems and have constructed the term *sympoiesis*, from the Greek words for *collective* and *production*, to describe such systems. In contrast to autopoietic systems, they are characterised by cooperative, amorphous qualities. [...] The concept emphasises linkages, feedback, cooperation, and synergistic behaviour rather than boundaries.[90]

88. The conception of the *dividuum* was reintroduced and theorised by Gerald Raunig. It has been extremely useful in helping me to think beyond the individual. See Gerald Raunig, *Dividuum: Machinic Capitalism and Molecular Revolution*, trans. Aileen Derieg (Semiotexte, 2016), 11–68.

89. We will encounter Nicoletta Isar again later, as she developed an understanding of chorography that has proved relevant for our discussions of *choreographic environments*. For more, see Nicoletta Isar, 'Sympoiesis', *Environmental Humanities Glossary*, Department of Arts and Cultural Studies, University of Copenhagen, accessed 10 July 2025, https://artsandculturalstudies.ku.dk/research/art-and-earth/environmental-humanities-glossary/sympoiesis.

90. M. Beth Dempster, 'A Self-Organizing Systems Perspective on Planning for Sustainability' (master's thesis, University of Waterloo, 1998), 4.

The term was then later popularised by Haraway, who expanded and elaborated the concept, stating, 'Sympoiesis enfolds autopoiesis and generatively unfurls and extends it'.[91] She further argues that "[...] autopoiesis and sympoiesis, foregrounding and back-grounding different aspects of systemic complexity, are in generative friction, or generative enfolding, rather than opposition'.[92]

In the context of my Polylogic Labs, I was certainly able to feel and affirm this mutual generative force. I perceived slips and slides between auto- and sympoietic processes together with the various agencies as highly creative, inspiring, and generative movements. The *sympoietic dynamics* in their 'cooperative, amorphous qualities' – as Dempster describes them – deepened both processual *experience* and emergent *aesthetics*. Slowly but surely, the more I became aware of this dynamic, vitalising phenomenon, the more it became a cornerstone of my unfolding research methodology.

'Partners in symbiosis, fellow symbionts abide in the same place at the same time, literally touching each other or even inside each other.'[93] In this statement, evolutionary biologist Lynn Margulis offers more than scientific insight – she gestures towards a poetics of cohabitation, a reimagining of life as a constellation of entanglements, both visceral and invisible. In my practices and reflections on sympoiesis, I attempt to move with such poetics, to think-with, feel-with, and move-with different forms of kinship, including tiny and cosmic ontologies (→ Cosmopoiesis, 129), and the aesthetic-philosophical implications of 'bare genes' – a conceptual speculation that I will introduce in the next section. I would like to emphasise that, while not the main focus, I made a deliberate attempt to expand my awareness of these agents and players – whether biological, chemical, material, or digital – that compose a rich landscape of more-than-human co-existence and mobilise non-scalar agency. The idea was to extend outwards to post-human performativity, unsettling human-scaled epistemologies and conventional aesthetic regimes. Accordingly, my research project *Choreo-ethical Assemblages* proposes a choreographic enquiry into how sympoiesis – as an artistic research practice and process – unfolds across different scales: cellular, social, conceptual.

We know that we are, in every sense, bathing in microbiomes (→ Assemblages #4, 189) – not one, but many – a plural worlding of bacterial cohabitations, generative precisely because they resist the logic of hygiene as separation. However, the idea that we have survived not *in spite of* microbes but *because of them* reorients how we perceive health, identity, and even intelligence. Rather than in isolation, evolutionary resilience emerges through intra-action[94] – becoming-with others,

91. Donna J. Haraway, *Staying with the Trouble: Making Kin in the Chthulucene* (Duke University Press, 2016), 58.

92. Ibid., 61.

93. Lynn Margulis, *Symbiotic Planet: A New Look at Evolution* (Basic Books, 1998), 2.

94. See Karen Barad, 'Posthumanist Performativity: Toward an Understanding of How Matter Comes to Matter', *Signs* 28, no. 3 (2003): 801–31. Barad writes, 'It is through specific agential *intra-actions* that the boundaries and properties of the "components" of phenomena become determinate and that particular embodied concepts become meaningful'. She continues by writing that 'the notion of intra-actions constitutes a reworking of the traditional notion of causality' (815). In the footnote she adds, 'There are no such independently existing objects with inherent characteristics' (816n21).

exchanging, responding, and engaging in sympoietic practices. This is more than coexistence – it is metabolic choreography, deeply responsive and wildly generative. As I have gradually come to understand, sympoiesis narrates the lives of thresholds: nucleation, growth, maturescence, death, and the metabolic processes of sprouting, blossoming, and decomposing that occur on thresholds and during transitions.[95] Each stage carries within it a process of *becoming-with* others – of decomposition as much as composition. The SCOBYs (symbiotic cultures of bacteria and yeast) that I became entangled with turned into a living diagram of this process. They were not just fermenting membranes but also choreographic agents, modelling distributed agency and shared metabolic time. They enacted sympoietic[96] systems, cultivating the collective for survival. Composed of over sixty microbial species,[97] these living mats offered complexity through their tactile skin of encounter, folding their metabolic rhythms viscerally into our own. Metabolism is emergent – relational, porous, and durational rather than self-contained.[98] What if we thought of ourselves as complex sympoietic cultures? What if choreography was fermentation?

This is not a rhetorical or metaphorical question; this is methodology. It proposes a post-human dramaturgy imbued with the messiness of slime, with liquid chaos and oozing wisdom. Fermenting cultures operate at the pace of rot and re-formation, inviting a different kind of attunement: one that metabolises impatience, composts linearity, and digests ambition into relational care. In sympoietic choreography, behaviour is no longer the province of autonomous bodies but an echo of *interactions* – timed, tuned, and tender – as well as *intra-actions* – embodied, experimental, and existential. Symbiotic fermentation cultures invite us to dwell in connection with a pulsating environment where growth and decay are inseparable: a microbially inspired, sympoietic aesthetics of survival. This is an existential aesthetics emerging from what I have introduced conceptually as *bare bodies*[99] – in intra-actions with each other and in tune with life cycles.

Sympoiesis is not neat; it refuses stable categories. In my research project *Choreo-ethical Assemblages*, it is an attempt to *feel into* the complexity of microsymbiotic kinship – we *know* that on a bacterial level we are exceeding species boundaries all the time. Still, the taxonomies of science – useful as they are – fail to contain the *unruly intimacies* of bacterial life. Microsymbiotic kinship defies linguistic

95. Mariella Greil, 'Amaryllisation: The Uncovering of the Life Cycle', in *Bare Bodies*, 9–26.

96. Donna J. Haraway, *Staying with the Trouble: Making Kin in the Chthulucene* (Duke University Press, 2016), Chapter 3, 58–98.

97. Andrew Adamatzky et al., 'Kombucha Electronics', preprint, Scientific Reports, 14 February 2023, https://doi.org/10.21203/rs.3.rs-2562074/v1.

98. Here is a small digression on the subject of temporality and duration: in *A World of Becoming* (Duke University Press, 2011), political scientist William E. Connolly ponders on time and duration, especially in Chapters 1 and 3. Remarkably, he quotes William James, who, in *A Pluralistic Universe*, wrote, 'The essence of life is its continually changing character; but our concepts are all discontinuous and fixed'. William James, *A Pluralistic Universe: Hibbert Lectures at Manchester College on the Present Situation in Philosophy* (1909; Project Gutenberg, 2024), accessed 13 October 2025, https://www.gutenberg.org/cache/epub/11984/pg11984-images.html. This prompted William Connolly to reflect on the fact that 'experience itself – during those moments when you suspend action and are acutely sensitive to its flow – discloses a flux in which elements from the past flow into the present and both of those fold into future anticipation' (Connolly, *A World of Becoming*, 33).

99. Greil, *Being in Contact*; Greil, *Bare Bodies*.

clarity but performs in the folds of artistic, diffractive, embodied encounters across agencies. Or – as I would argue – emerges as sympoietic practices. Terms like *species*, *individual*, and even *identity* begin to wobble. What unfolds is a continuum of dividual[100] beings, perpetually fusing, refusing, and transforming. Amoebic chaos becomes the site of future epistemologies, of what Mary Catherine Bateson might have called *peripheral visionaries*[101] – those operating at the edges, embodying the unknowable, proposing knowledge that ferments and leaks. Assemblages emerge

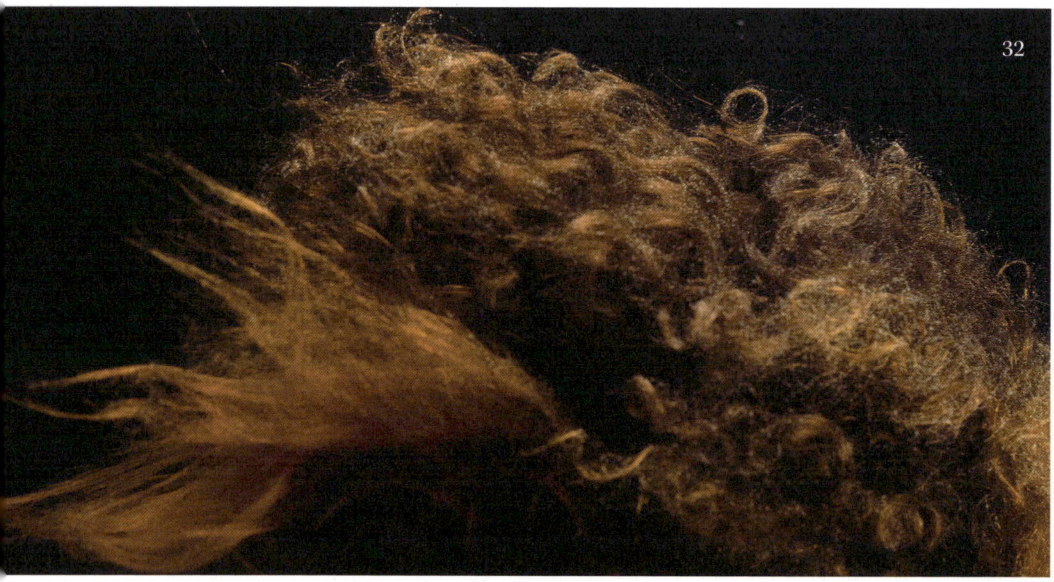

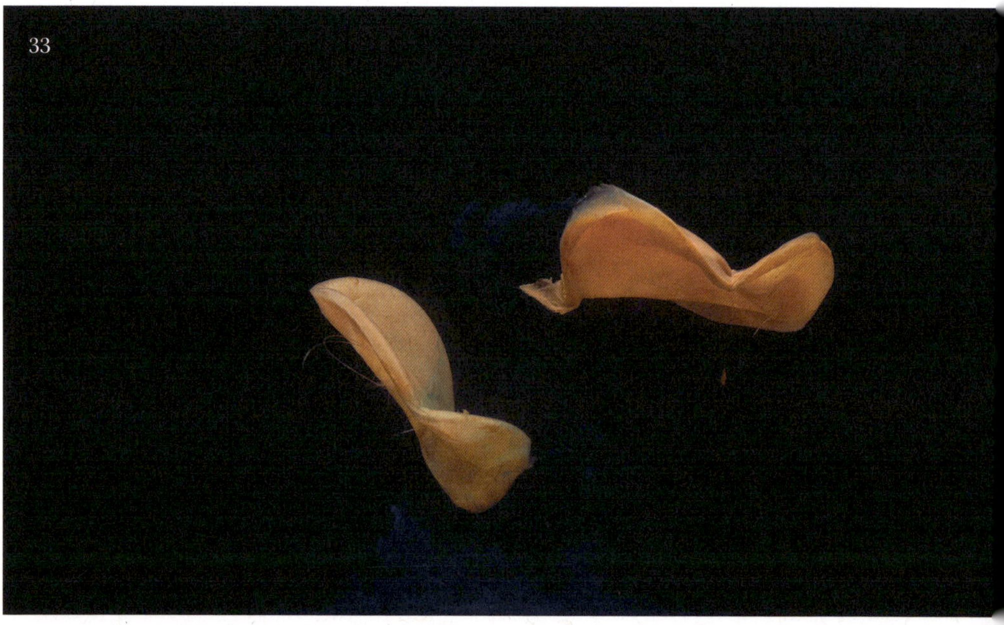

100. For more discussions about dividuality, see Raunig, *Dividuum*, 11–68.

101. Mary Catherine Bateson, *Peripheral Visions: Learning Along the Way* (HarperCollins, 1995).

Fig. 32: *Choreo-ethical Assemblages – Drowning in Depths*, 2025, © video still: Victor Jaschke, performance: Mariella Greil and Luisa Pisetta Ravanelli, concept: Mariella Greil.

Fig. 33: *Choreo-ethical Assemblages – Drowning in Depths*, 2025, © video still: Victor Jaschke, performance: SCOBY, concept: Mariella Greil.

as interdependent sympoietic entities, or – if you like – microbial acquaintances and their sexy fusions or confusions, which now unfold as peripheral visionaries[102] of future kinships.

It is against this backdrop, following this line of flight, that the notion of the *naked gene*, a term coined by H. J. Muller[103] and later critically recontextualised by Lynn Margulis emerges. Margulis criticised the naked gene as a figure of reductionism: a gene imagined in isolation, clean, stripped of its cellular, bacterial, and environmental context.[104] In her view, the gene was not a self-sufficient script but a relational node in an ancient and ongoing improvisation. Genes *do not act alone.*

To think with Lynn Margulis, then, is to resist the fantasy of purity. It is to embrace the biological and aesthetic necessity of entanglement. If we imagine the gene as a mover at the thresholds penetrating neighbouring zones, it is never solipsistic, nor can it be fully understood without the messy world to which it belongs. It is always embedded – dancing with other agencies, shaped by timing, affect, proximity.

Scientifically, Margulis states, 'Bacteria, not naked genes, did reside outside the nucleus but inside the cells[105] of many protists, yeasts,[106] and even plants[107] and animals.'[108]

Artistically, I would like to speculate and build on my differentiation between nude, naked, and bare bodies, expanding my conception into the world of genes.[109] So, let us entertain this experimental abstraction: could *bare genes* philosophically suggest a kind of *exposure in symbiosis*, one that is always already present at the heart of life – materially, symbolically, and aesthetically entangled?

102. Mary Catherine Bateson coined this term in relation to modern women, with their octopoid attentions, who pass on their traits to their descendants and thereby influence the futures. Margulis, *Symbiotic Planet*, 18.

103. H. J. Muller 'The Gene Material as the Initiator and the Organizing Basis of Life', *The American Naturalist* 100, no. 915 (1966): 493–517.

104. Margulis, *Symbiotic Planet*, 28.

105. Artist Mary Maggic biohacks and 'diysects' hormones, chemicals made by cells. Their work can be found at https://maggic.ooo.

106. My artistic collaborations with SCOBYs have been featured in the films *Shaken Grounds – Shifting Skies* (2024) and *Drowning in Depths* (2025), both of which were created in collaboration with Victor Jaschke. I would also like to draw attention to the work that my esteemed colleagues Barbara Graf and Monica LoCasio have carried out with SCOBYs as artistic material.

107. *Amaryllisation* (2020–23) is an artistic research project on the quest for knowledge about cultivating ddwelling places – an œkology (from the Greek *oikos*) – sensitive to the thresholds of metamorphosis. Through embodied attunement to the micro-phenomenological processes of growth, decay, and rebirth, *Amaryllisation* fosters an aesthetic and ethical practice of 'accompanying change' – witnessing and co-creating with the rhythms and temporalities of a more-than-human other. The project blends photographic documentation, poetic writing, and performative acts, such as dancing for the plant, as practices of co-sensing that challenge anthropocentric aesthetics and invite a vegetal modality of attention. For further details, see Mariella Greil, ed., *Bare Bodies – Thresholding Life* (Edition Angewandte, De Gruyter, 2024), especially 9–26.

108. Performance artist Krõõt Juurak concludes her research into *Autodomestication* as a blend of humour, provocation, and a persistently sticky metaphor. For further details, visit her blog: https://autodomestication.wordpress.com. Margulis' work is, of course, another relevant reference. Margulis, *Symbiotic Planet*, 28.

109. Greil, *Being in Contact.*

This probably biologically impossible, conceptual concatenation of *bare genes* – I traced the etymological root of *genə* earlier (→ Generative Forces in Choreographic Environments, 99) – carries within it the generative impulse of origin, evoking processes of *emergence* and *becoming* that resonate across biological, conceptual, and aesthetic registers with existential urgency. Is it through sympoiesis that *bare genes* (indifferentiated from naked genes) gain both their vulnerability *and* exposed openness? A bareness that invites merging rather than denying symbiosis? Here, I draw on a distinction between the stylised, aestheticised *nude* – a classical gesture often related to shame, the *naked* person as someone stripped, unshielded – and *bareness* as something open, connoting a kind of relational readiness – being ready for exposure to otherness and sympoiesis as co-creation in order to survive.

As I understand it, genes are located on chromosomes, which are found in the nucleus of most cells, and they are instructional units of DNA that guide how living organisms grow, function, and evolve.[110] In contrast to Muller's *naked genes, bare genes,* then, might signal a conceptual (though not a biological) shift – affirming the idea of a gene understood not as isolated information but as something vulnerable, entangled, generative, with an openness to touch, to the influence of other agencies, to co-creation.

Such a paradigmatic turn allows the genetics of ideas to open up a more speculative, more aesthetic lineage. Bare genes, as I imagine them here, are less about biological essence than about epistemic openings – scores for future relations, symbolic membranes of the ongoing becomings of the world.[111] In this sense, artistic, embodied research – like fermentation – is slow, processual, messy. It does not demand clear outcomes. Instead, it cultivates entanglement. In post-human performative practice, like in microbial symbiosis, the body is not a boundary but a site of passage, a host, and at the same time a guest in its environment. To perform with bare agency is to enter a space of co-poiesis, where exposure is generative and boundaries are permeable. Here, the choreographic environment is not a container but compost; it transforms and moves between auto- and sympoietic processes. It embodies a mode of knowing through doing, of metabolising relationality as a practice. And it is this practice – from the microbial to the choreographic – that offers us new tools for thinking about life not as an identity but as a series of *contact zones,*[112] not as control, but as care, performance, and metabolism.

If we are to survive – artistically, ecologically, philosophically – it may be because of these viscous, generative kinships.

110. 'Gene', *Genetics Glossary,* National Human Genome Research Institute, accessed July 12, 2025, https://www.genome.gov/genetics-glossary/Gene.

111. Connolly, *A World of Becoming.*

112. Donna J. Haraway, *When Species Meet* (University of Minnesota Press, 2008).

Cosmopoiesis

In the flickering tension between the ephemeral and the generative, between what disappears and what insists on becoming, the term *cosmopoiesis* finds fertile ground in performance as *choreographic world-making.* Far from metaphorical abstraction, the notion of world-making becomes a situated, embodied, and choreographic practice – a responsive interweaving of time, space, body, and matter. Within this œkology of emergence, performance is no longer conceived of as the representation of a world but rather as the proposition, activation, and negotiation of a world. Following such threads, guided by a choreographic mode of thought, I endeavour to unfurl the potential of *cosmopoiesis* in performative practice.

The term *cosmopoiesis* – literally, the making of a cosmos – appears across disparate disciplines and always carries with it the resonance of a political and aesthetic gesture. My Polylogic Lab practice (→ Polylogic Labs, 178) engages in and emphasises, even amplifies, the creation and emergence of multiple singular cosmologies, each unfolding in dialogue with a plurality of agencies. Anthropologist Eduardo Viveiros de Castro argues that Amerindian cosmologies are not just different cultural beliefs but different ontologies, each enacting their own cosmic consistency.[113] Plural genealogies reveal how different cosmologies enact different ontologies. Worlds in the plural. Cosmopoiesis denotes the capacity of a cosmology not only to describe but to generate a world and its beings, always relationally, always in motion.

In philosophical contexts, Isabelle Stengers gestures towards cosmopoiesis through her concept of *cosmopolitics*,[114] foregrounding the necessity of composing worlds *with* – never alone. Her cosmopolitical œkology resists universalism and attends instead to the situatedness of practices – as she argues, her 'ecology of practices'[115] affirms the collective and embraces the fragile liaisons that hold worlds together. Stengers calls for a slowing-down of thought, for us to engage with the interferences that alter what worlds may come. In my view, *cosmopoiesis* thus emerges as a form of care and ethical experimentation, emphasising practices of attention and enabling growing awareness and a practice of diffractive dialogues while staying radically attuned to frictions, doubts, and, of course, sincere criticism. *Choreo-ethics* – a neologism I found and began to develop[116] in my previous project – resonates with and affirms 'a "cosmopolitical" space where the hopes and doubts and fears and dreams they engender collide and cause them to exist'.[117] To me, this reads as a call for the cohabitation – and even co-creation – of heterogeneous worlds. As Stengers continues, she wants

113. Eduardo Viveiros de Castro, 'Exchanging Perspectives: The Transformation of Objects into Subjects in Amerindian Ontologies', *Common Knowledge* 25, nos. 1–3 (2019 [2004]): 21–42.

114. Isabelle Stengers, *Cosmopolitics I* and *II*, trans. Robert Bononno (University of Minnesota Press, 2010 and 2011); originally published in French as *Cosmopolitiques* (Éditions La Découverte, 1997).

115. Ibid., vii.

116. Greil, *Being in Contact*, 249–88.

117. Stengers, *Cosmopolitics I*, viii.

to 'slow down' the movement, make interesting the moment when the various ingredients of an ecology of practices come into *play*: requirement, value, and obligation. And I especially want to 'slow down' the transition from the problem of values [...] to the apparently 'purely physical' solution [...].[118]

In my practice of *choreo-ethical assemblaging* (→ Choreo-ethical Assemblages, 205), this stretching of time[119] and magnification of experiences and their value was intensified through micro-phenomenological[120] interviews and by creating a specific *choreographic environment*, which I will address later in greater detail (→ Polylogic Labs, 178), when I reflect on the Polylogic Labs. These Labs invited participants to engage in play in all its complexities, flows, decision-making-processes, imaginations, agencies and contingencies, resonances, and relations to time and space. Stenger's cosmopolitics as a *form of speculative pragmatism* – which does not seek consensus but instead ensures that the world is not prematurely unified under a single epistemological regime – acted as a backdrop for challenging neoliberal paradigms such as quick fixes, instant gratification, and final judgments based on (enforced) conformity.

Another appreciated scholar who informed my cosmopoietic practice is William E. Connolly, who does not use the term *cosmopoiesis* explicitly, but his work – particularly *A World of Becoming*[121] – in my view deeply resonates with the concept of cosmopoiesis. Connolly explores how multiple interacting systems (biological, geological, political, economic) create a plural polity of becoming, a world that is always in formation. He emphasises the plural, asynchronous dimension of temporality and how interactions and intra-actions can generate unpredictable, emergent – and maybe profound – changes within the world. In my artistic research project, the Polylogic Labs served as models and manifested as spaces where attunement to emergent assemblages and co-creation through temporal resonance were practiced. Connolly describes speculative potentials, including the imperfections of self-regulating systems, as possible alternatives to economic and social conventions of neoliberalism:

118. Ibid., 180.

119. In *A World of Becoming*, Connolly argues that our cosmos consists of 'multiple zones of temporality, with each temporal force-field periodically encountering others as outside forces'. William E. Connolly, *A World of Becoming* (Duke University Press, 2011), 7.

120. Claire Petitmengin, 'Describing One's Subjective Experience in the Second Person: An Interview Method for the Science of Consciousness', *Phenomenology and the Cognitive Sciences* 5, nos. 3–4 (2006): 229–69; Claire Petitmengin, Anne Remillieux, and Camila Valenzuela-Moguillansky, 'Discovering the Structures of Lived Experience: Towards a Micro-Phenomenological Analysis Method', *Phenomenology and the Cognitive Sciences* 18, no. 4 (2019): 691–730.

121. Connolly, *A World of Becoming*.

> in a cosmos composed of innumerable, interacting open systems with differential capacities of self-organisation, set on different scales of time, agency, creativity, viscosity, and speed.[122]

While he does not describe these assemblages as 'cosmopoietic', his language – 'open systems', 'ethos of pluralisation'[123] and 'resonance', 'multiple temporality', 'creative evolutions' as well as 'entangled humanism' – maps onto the idea of worlds co-emerging through relational, affective processes.

These genealogies orbit a central concern: *worlding* as a dynamic, co-emergent practice. A decade ago, Manning introduced the term *worlding* to contemporary choreography and performance discourse in a significant and thorough way – framing movement and dance, scene-making, and spatial practice as acts of world creation and transformation. Manning discussed the interdependency of *worlding* and the emergence of the subject:

> Worlding occurs in the process of a world becoming subject, or a subject becoming world. Or, to extend the analysis, subjects are transitory individuations in a processual worlding whereby certain actualities take form in a nexus of 'contemporarily independent' events.[124]

For me, *worlding* unfurls as an affective choreography – an emergent practice of attuning, sensing, and composing-with. Whereas autopoiesis focuses on the emerging self (or selves in the plural) – not egocentric, but rather always already in relation – in sympoiesis there is a clear dedication to merging with the other. Now, the third notion that I would like to introduce in this chapter – cosmopoiesis – resists enclosure, cultivating porous thresholds where bodies, materials, and temporalities co-articulate a world and bring it into being. Not a noun but a verb, worlding gestures towards an ethics of co-becoming, where the world is not given but continually danced into resonance. In my view, there is great relevance today in revisiting the Renaissance concept (if not myth) of *cosmopoiesis*, which describes the active agencies in the cosmos, not only because we are approaching the doom of climate catastrophe but, even more so, because of humanity's capacity to evoke actual and possible worlds

122. William E. Connolly, *The Fragility of Things: Self-Organizing Processes, Neoliberal Fantasies, and Democratic Activism* (Duke University Press, 2013), 25.

123. William E. Connolly, *The Ethos of Pluralization* (University of Minnesota Press, 1995).

124. Erin Manning, 'Choreography as Reading Practice', in *Thought in the Act: Passages in the Ecology of Experience*, ed. Erin Manning and Brian Massumi (University of Minnesota Press, 2014), 66.

through imagination and processes of making. I find *cosmopoiesis* – as acts of artistically constructing worlds – specifically present in artistic research practices, maybe even forming the core of creative embodied methods and thereby significantly contributing to shaping our contemporaneity. Experimental artistic research, with its wild – in the sense of untamed – ideas and idiosyncratic methodologies, will continue to dream up and shape future contemporaneities.[125] It will keep doing so despite the prolonged – and, from my perspective, quite scandalous – and persistent presence of Machiavellian power structures and strategies in global politics, but of course while also operating within those very institutional frameworks and standing up against violence and discrimination in favour of change and sustainable future contemporaneities. On the website of the 2016 Dance Congress, we read,

> Since the early 20th century, it has been understood as the artistic and theoretical demand to deal with the conditions and radical changes of the present and to position oneself in one's own times aesthetically, politically, socially and in dance, not least in a physical way.

Monica Gilette and Gwen Hsin-Yi Chang will share the leadership for the 2026 Tanztriennale in Hamburg and have stated that they are interested in cultivating 'a space of solidarity'. They foreground the potential of dance

> to excite, to soothe, to provoke, to inspire, to bring together, to reflect, to heal – and [wish] to engage with dance not only as a performative art form for the stage, but also for its unique ability to create more cohesive societies and to stimulate new approaches for reinvention and transformative thinking.[126]

The fact that such acts of reaching out into the world through the performing arts and weaving artistic practices into the very fabric of society are a central mission of such a cultural lighthouse project is extremely positive and gives rise to the hope

125. In 2016, the thematic focus of the Tanzkongress in Hanover, curated by Sandra Noeth, Sabine Gehm, and Katharina von Wilcke, was 'Contemporaneity – Zeitgenossenschaft' and served as a space for sharing politicised somatic, discursive, and curatorial experiments relating to how dancers, performers, and choreographers engage with the phenomenon of contemporaneity.

126. 'Tanztriennale', Kulturstiftung des Bundes, accessed July 13, 2025, https://www.kulturstiftung-des-bundes.de/en/programmes_projects/theatre_and_movement/detail/tanztriennale.html.

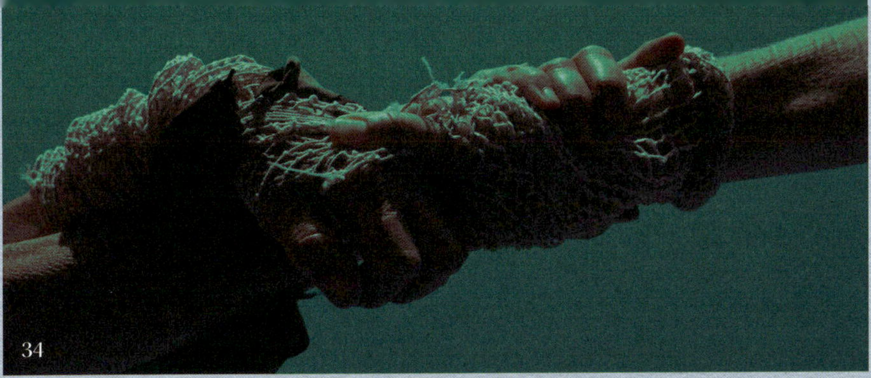

34

Hope Beyond Daylight

Extractivist tongues still scrape the ground.
The Earth is wounded, its guts wail.
At the shore of the insides between wine
and lithium,
alternative togetherness comes into being
on an ocean of grief.

In their unsorcery,
they form below practices
not ready for the eyes.

Alliances in darkness long to
meet the stranger within us
– unfinished kin.

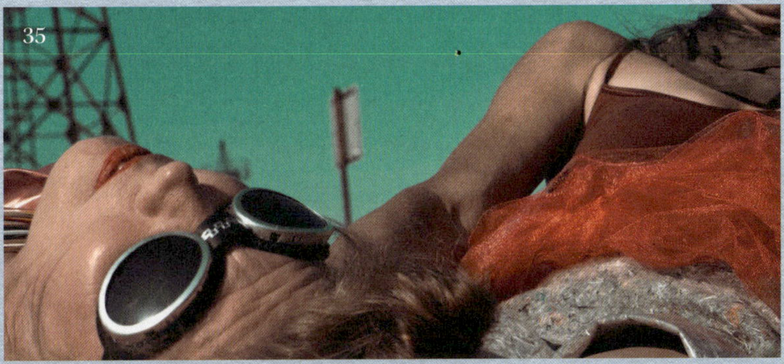

35

The breaking movement,
the swarming act of becoming,
landscapes of resistance,
riot and read, my radical friend!
We chose to nourish our beloved practices
of resourcing,
carrying the perpetual tremor within our being
– as hope – beyond the daylight pulsing
underground.

A flotilla of trembling bodies and hands gather.
Their friendships grow slow and feral,
mycelial, unannounced.

36

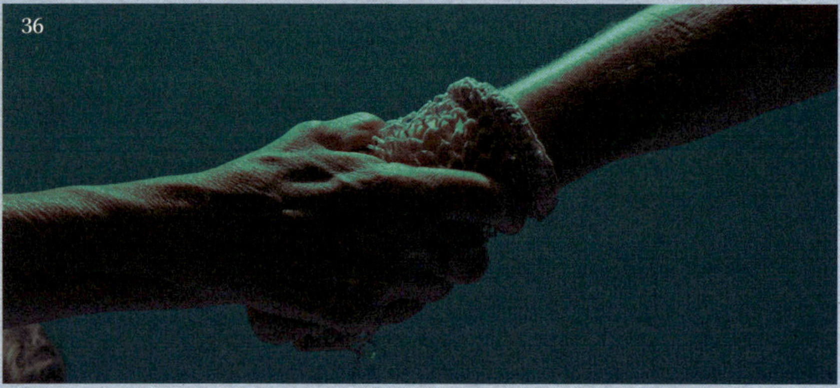

Without warning –
a crack in habit,
a loosening of the clenched future.
From this fracture,
many voices, one vibration,
no centre holding command.

They breathe, erode, reassemble,
between the lines of what was never meant
to survive.
They compost, durable enough to pass
from body to body.

37

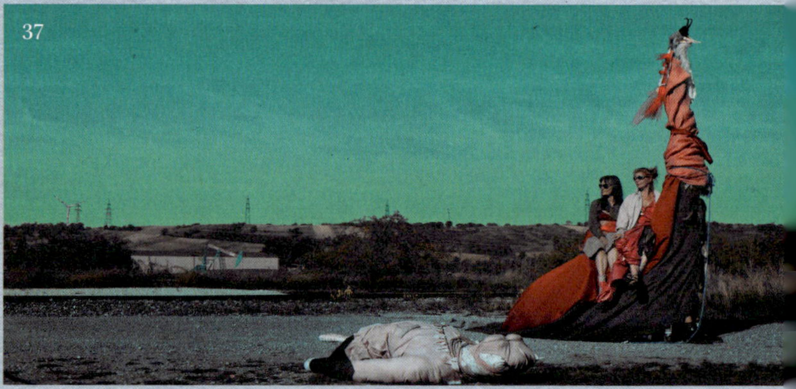

that it will thereby be possible to promote further dissemination of the results of embodied research projects.

I deliberately position myself in proximity to the Renaissance term *cosmopoiesis* and a Spinozian perspective. Yet, in light of the assertion of a contemporary choreographic position that sees the world as all-encompassing, scopic, and entwined with the cosmos, I strongly feel that my re-working of these concepts is radically interconnected with artistic practice as 'sustained life practices of experimentation'[127] and thus represents a clearly contemporary position. Economist, futurist, and education activist Lene Rachel Andersen has introduced the term polymodernity[128] as a framework for understanding ourselves and our societies in a much more complex way, encompassing Indigenous, premodern, modern, and postmodern cultural elements, and thus providing social norms and a diverse moral fabric for intimacy, spirituality, religion, science, and self-exploration, all at the same time.

Today's philosophical and artistic cosmologies, nourished by both scientific knowledges and spiritual wisdom, are responding to the paradigm shift indicated by current accelerated developments both in technology (geoengineering, aerospace, AI) and the sciences (neurosciences, microbiology, quantum physics). Moreover, restitutive and integrative efforts to validate Indigenous cultures and post-human philosophies are vital to contemporary performance practices. All together, these blended understandings of worlds offer potential alternatives for organising *future communities*,[129] which are speculative formations of collective life that resist normative temporality and hegemonic sociality. Emerging through artistic or activist œkological praxis, they enact forms of *anticipatory worlding*[130] and *commoning*[131] that reimagine relationality, care, and survival beyond capitalist extraction and colonial continuity. These alternative future communities evoke creative models

127. Adrian Heathfield in dialogue with Mariella Greil and Emma Cocker, 'Sedimentations of Sensitivities', in Bodies', in *Choreo-graphic Figures*, ed. Gansterer, Cocker, and Greil, 216.

128. Lene Rachel Andersen is specifically critical of postmodernism and remarks, 'Postmodernism is laying open our societies for hypermodernism and algorithm take-over. Postmodernism is not the perpetrator but it provides no spiritual or governance alternative to market forces.' I think that she hits the nail on the head. Lene Rachel Andersen, *Polymodernity: Meaning and Hope in a Complex World* (Nordic Bildung, 2023), 76.

129. Towards the end phase of my research project *Choreo-ethical Assemblages*, I was invited to join the *Futures of Communities* initiative (https://www.futuresofcommunities.earth), which emerged in 2023, inspired by the work of Fritz Hinterberger and Barbara Bulc. They met at the Wellbeing Summit in Bilbao and, in collaboration with artist Simona Koch and Daniel Gratzer, the founder of the flourishing society in Vienna, developed this initiative. I connected deeply with their declared value of social equity and economic prosperity coexisting harmoniously with nature, and was encouraged (without their knowing) to keep elaborating on the notion of œkology (→ Verifying the Vocabulary, 61).

130. José Esteban Muñoz introduced the idea of queer futurity, the then and there of what I call an *anticipatory worlding*. In my reading, his claim is to not only *desire* but *practice* such ecstatic future imaginings of collective political becoming (189). This he bases on a practice or – as he writes – 'a mode of contemplation or consciousness that is not self-enclosed, particularly in regard to being conscious of the other. [...] Knowing ecstasy is having a sense of timeliness's motion, comprehending a temporal unity, which includes the past (having-been), the future (the not-yet), and the present (the making present).' For me this means that each performativity proposes an aesthetics that in turn maps future social relations. José Esteban Muñoz, *Cruising Utopia: The Then and There of Queer Futurity* (NYU Press, 2009), 185–89.

131. The mode of being-in-common affirms a transversal relationality and, according to Rosi Braidotti, is 'a process of redefining one's sense of attachment and connection to a shared world'. Rosi Braidotti, *The Posthuman* (Polity, 2013), 193. For further discussions about communing, see also Michael Hardt and Antonio Negri, *Commonwealth* (Belknap, 2009), 139–40.

for the construction of other possible worlds. In my research practice, speculative scenarios that manifest in embodied, performative ways crystallise into artistic forms. The work of art could be the emblem of an anthropocentric understanding of world-making; however, in my understanding, I outline and propose *cosmopoiesis* as co-creation between human and other-than human agencies, such as vibrant matter,[132] atmospheres,[133] and their relations.[134] In the Renaissance, Giordano Bruno, an Italian philosopher, poet, and alchemist, as well as a dedicated astrologer, cosmological theorist, and esotericist, conjured up a vision of innumerable and infinite worlds as he rediscovered the Pythagorean myths of the cosmos, proposing the idea of *cosmic pluralism*.[135] In his conception, there are multiple imaginary worlds alongside and in parallel to pre-existing worlds. This resonates with my approach to choreo-ethical assemblages: I envision the unearthing of pluriversal future potentials – as a terrain where speculative, œkological, and commons-oriented cosmologies might yet emerge as post-digital futures – fully invested in artistic, critical, and meaningful world-making that resists dystopia and technocracy.

In contemporary discourse, there is a renewed urgency to reconcile the medieval *vita contemplative* – a mode of introspective, often monastic life oriented towards spiritual or philosophical insight – with the *vita activa*, which emerged during the Renaissance and privileges worldly engagement and pragmatic agency. This convergence signals a paradigmatic shift towards modes of living that resist binary separations, advocating instead for integrated practices that sustain both reflective depth and participatory presence within increasingly complex socio-ecological systems.

In particular, post-human philosophy's differentiations between agencies are well suited to blurring the boundaries between contemplation and activation. The post-human notion of agencies dissolves rigid subject-object divides, allowing for fluid interplay between contemplation and activation, where thinking becomes doing and perception itself enacts transformation across human and other-than-human fields.

Above all, post-human philosophy's nuanced articulations of agency have unsettled entrenched subject-object binaries, fostering permeability between contemplation and activation. In this framework, within which I reflect on my own embodied research, sensate cognition and discerning action co-emerge, rendering perception an operative force that participates in world-making.

Thinking is no longer preparatory or posterior to doing but is itself a form of enactment – folded into and distributed across human and other-than-human assemblages – thereby reconfiguring agency as relational, entangled, and performative.

132. Jane Bennett, *Vibrant Matter: A Political Ecology of Things* (Duke University Press, 2010).

133. Alex Arteaga and Nikolaus Gansterer, eds., *Contingent Agencies: Inquiring into the Emergence of Atmospheres* (Hatje Cantz, 2025)

134. Erin Manning, *Relationscapes: Movement, Art, Philosophy* (MIT Press, 2012).

135. Giuseppe Mazzotta, *COSMOPOIESIS: The Renaissance Experiment* (University of Toronto Press, 2001), xiii.

Alchemical Gold and White Cloud

Temperatures leaning into each other.

First: calcination.
A silent mineral enough to scrape.

Then dissolution.
Words loosened into vapour,
memory softened,
liquid bodies forgetting their edges.

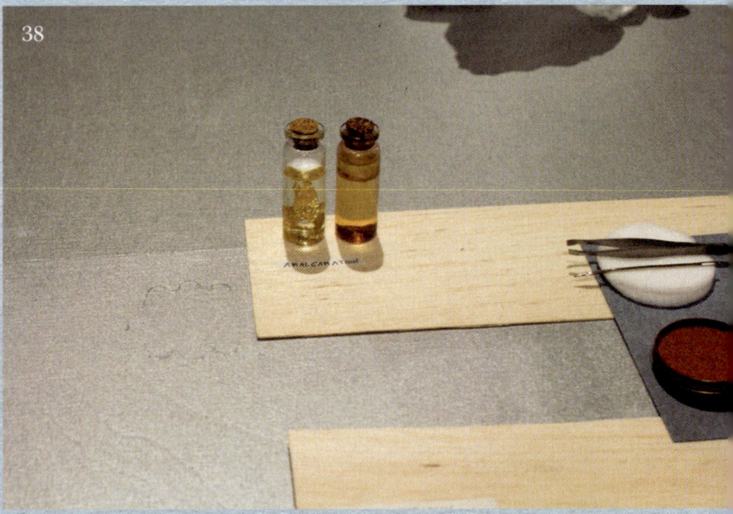
38

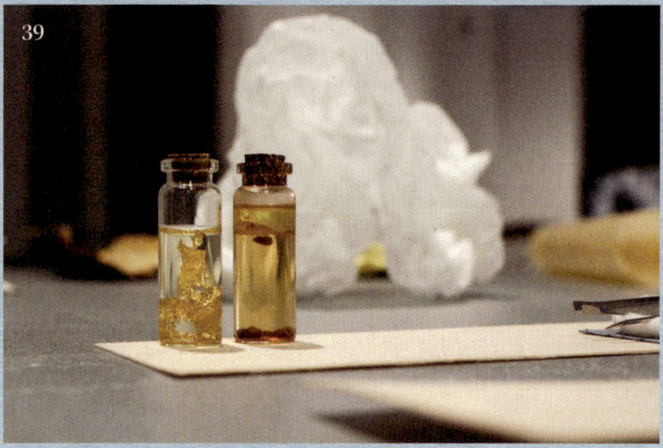

The cloud absorbed us without judgement.

In separation,
I noticed these tools were not mine:
reflex to gather, shadows of fear, all set down
carefully.

Conjunction came quietly.
A glance aligned with breath,
a pause thickened,
time briefly agreed to stay.
Nothing spectacular –
yet the air changed colour.

Through fermentation,
something old died sweetly:
the need to keep the warmth tenderly steady.

At last, coagulation:
gold not as metal
but as conduct –
the way the encounter learned to shine
and then let go,
amalgamation.

The cloud closed.
The gold remained,
circulating.

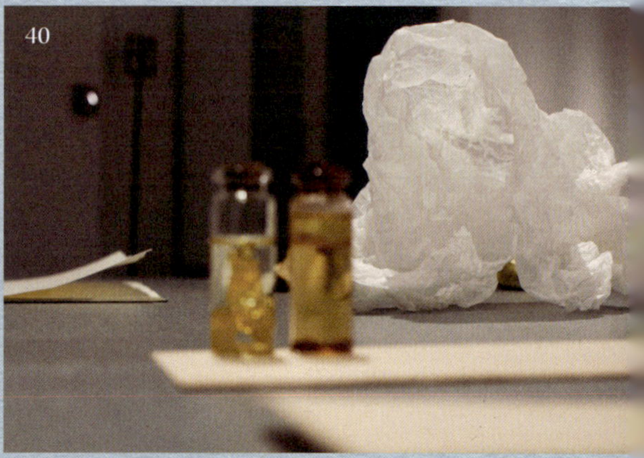

After all, rather than being an individuating act of creation, cosmopoiesis is an ongoing, situated, performative process in a twofold sense: first, as the gerund of creating meaning and, second, in the literal sense of materialisation. As Haraway writes,

> It matters what matters we use to think other matters with; it matters what stories we tell to tell other stories with; it matters what knots knot knots, what thoughts think thoughts, what descriptions describe descriptions, what ties tie ties.[136]

And, as I would add, it matters what worlds world worlds. In a daring line of flight, I outline cosmopoiesis as a practice of cosmic artisans. The *cosmic artisan* is a figure drawn from philosophers Gilles Deleuze and Félix Guattari's minor science[137] and revived in Kay Sidebottom's post-human educational theory.[138] If we imagine the cosmic artisan (aka the artist) as the one who enacts *cosmopoiesis* – world-making – then they do so as an immanent operator of material flows, as a subject-less agent embedded within the dynamics of matter itself, an immanent field of forces that coagulate, deterritorialise, and recompose. The cosmic artisan attunes themselves to emergent materialities, crafting with and through the rhythms of becoming. This is co-composition within the pluriverse, where ontologies are multiple and entangled. As a practitioner of transversal thought, the cosmic artisan engages with cosmopoietic practices, forging otherwise relational sensibilities and activating speculative, ethical futures immanent to the more-than-human cosmos. The cosmic artisan views the world not as a resource but *as a potentiality*, as a field of interpenetrating forces and relations. The artisan's ethics is experimental, attuned to the 'in-between', to thresholds and becomings. Thus, this ethics is about practicing a form of creativity aligned with life's immanent powers.

136. Haraway, *Staying with the Trouble*, 12.

137. Gilles Deleuze and Félix Guattari, *What Is Philosophy?*, trans. Graham Burchell and Hugh Tomlinson (Columbia University Press, 1994), 196.

138. Kay Sidebottom, 'Cosmic Artsan', in *More Posthuman Glossary*, ed. Rosi Braidotti, Emily Jones, and Goda Klumbytė (Bloomsbury Academy, 2023), 23–25.

P34: *The greater the affect with which we imagine a thing we love to be affected toward us, the more we shall exult at being esteemed.*
Dem.: We strive (by P33), as far as we can, that a thing we love should love us in return, that is (by P13S), that a thing we love should be affected with joy, accompanied by the idea of ourselves [as cause]. So the greater the joy with which we imagine a thing we love to be affected on our account, the more this striving is aided, that is (by P11 and P11S), the greater the joy with which we are affected. But since we rejoice because we have affected another like us with joy, then we regard ourselves with joy (by P30). Therefore, the greater the affect, with which we imagine anything we love to be affected toward us, the greater the joy with which we shall regard ourselves or (by P30S) the more we shall exult at being esteemed, q.e.d.

Benedict de Spinoza, *Ethics*, ed. and trans. Edwin Curley (Penguin Classics, 2005), Part III, Proposition 34, Dem., 88.

Assemblages #3

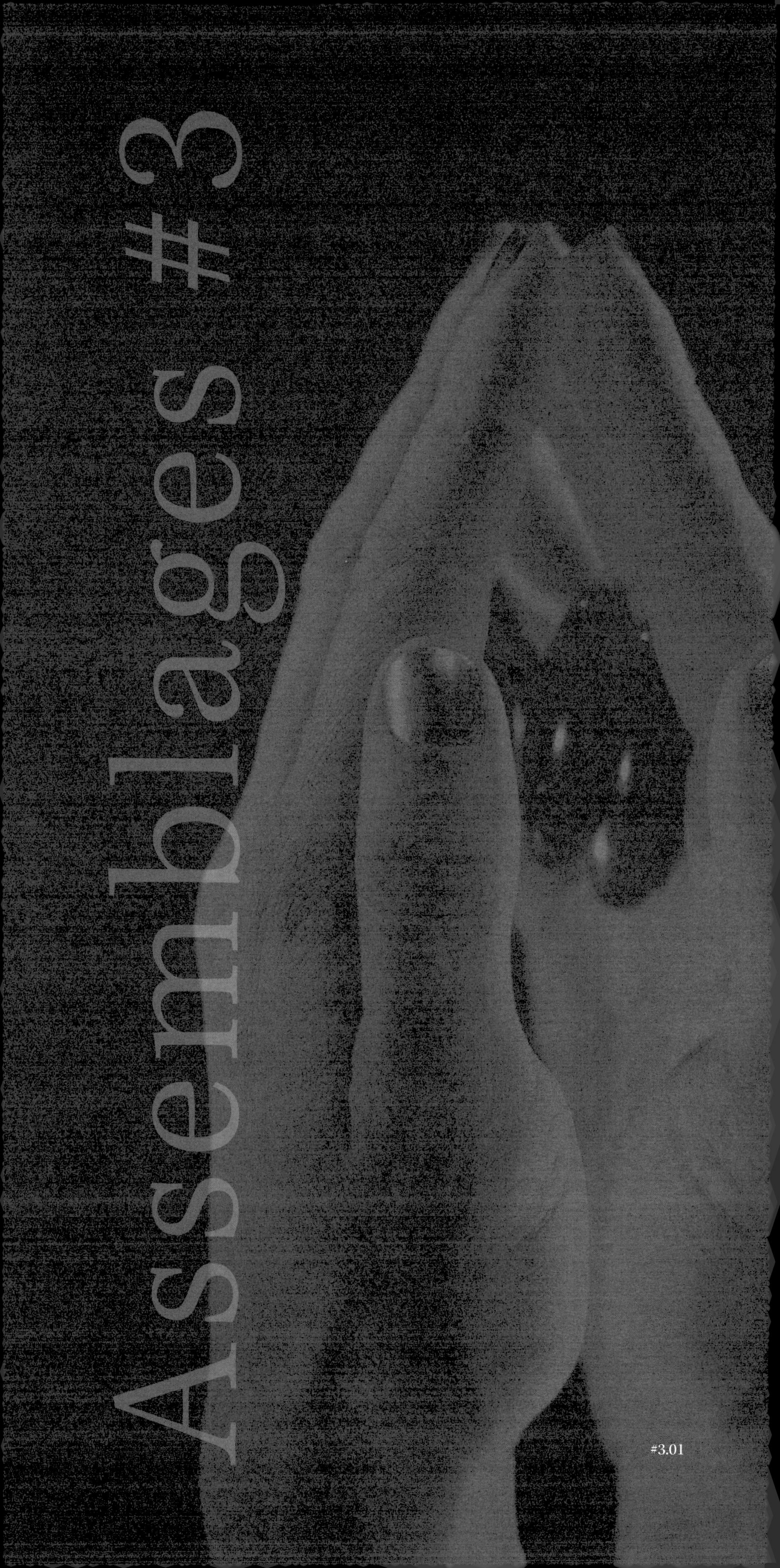

#3.01

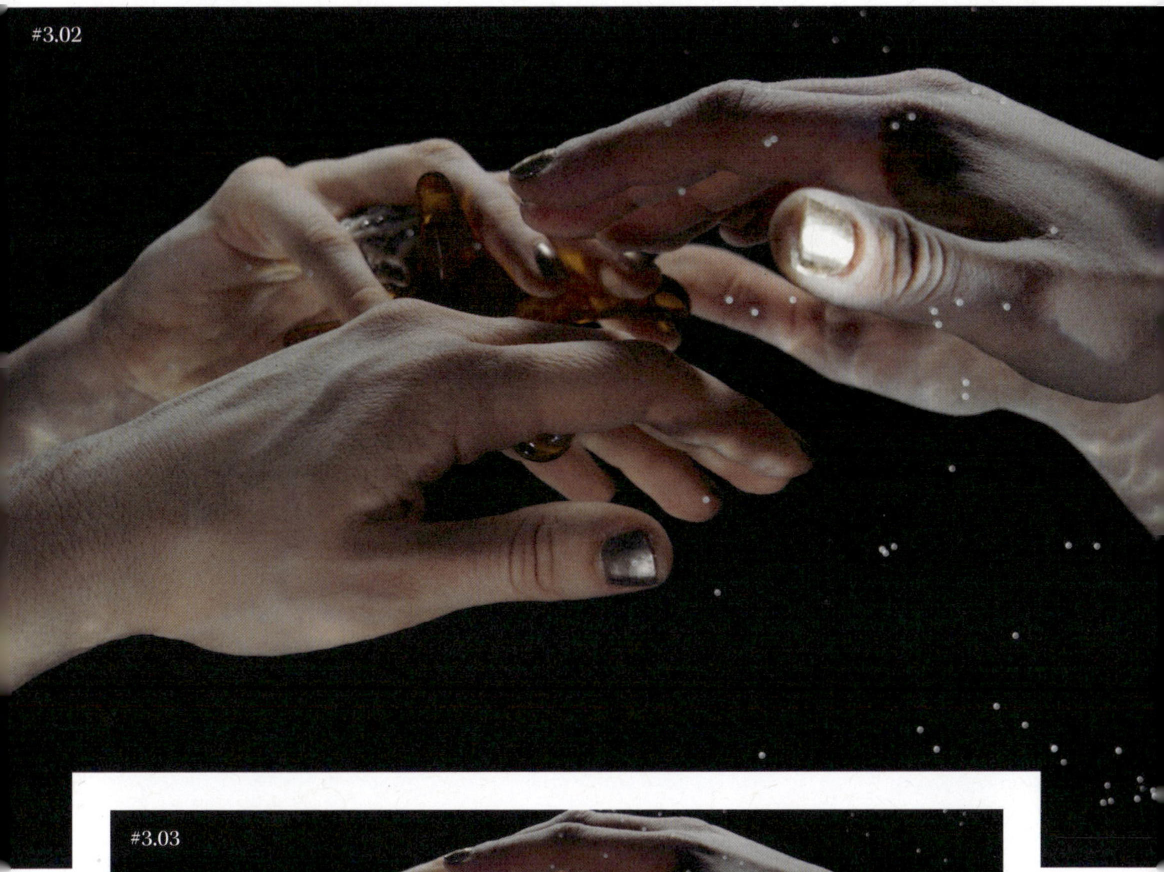
#3.02

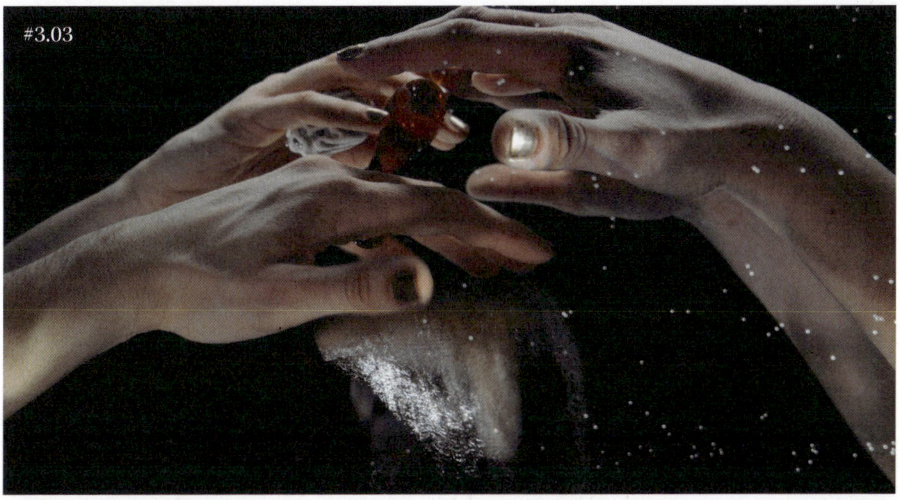
#3.03

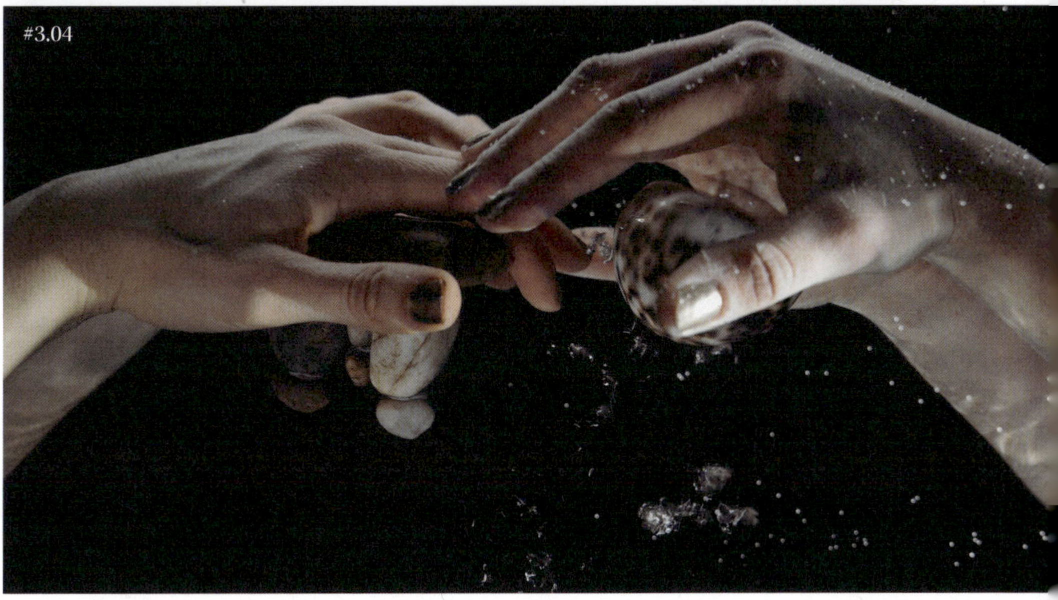
#3.04

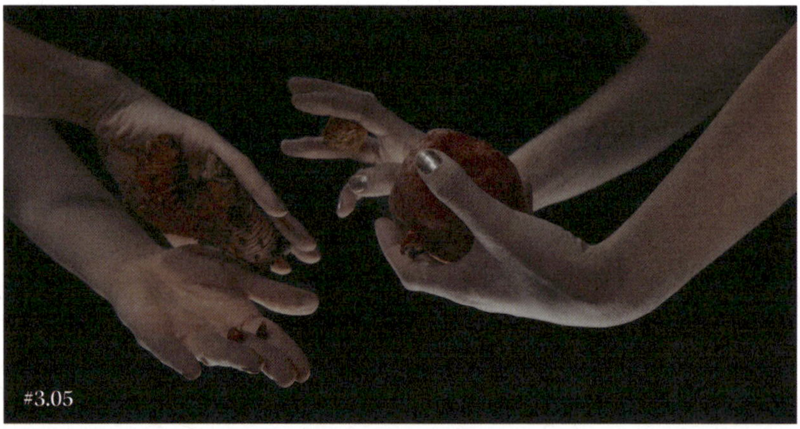
#3.05

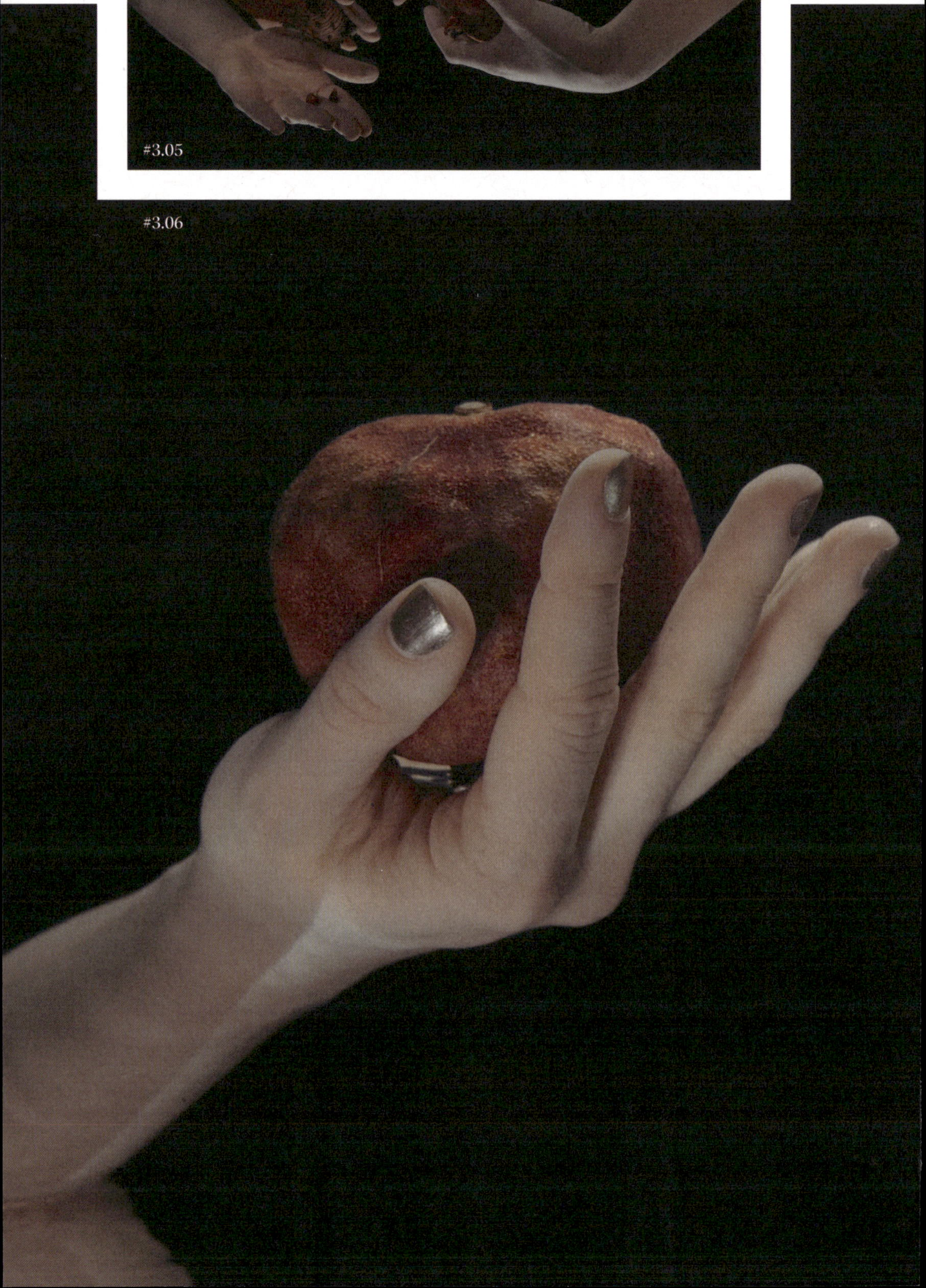
#3.06

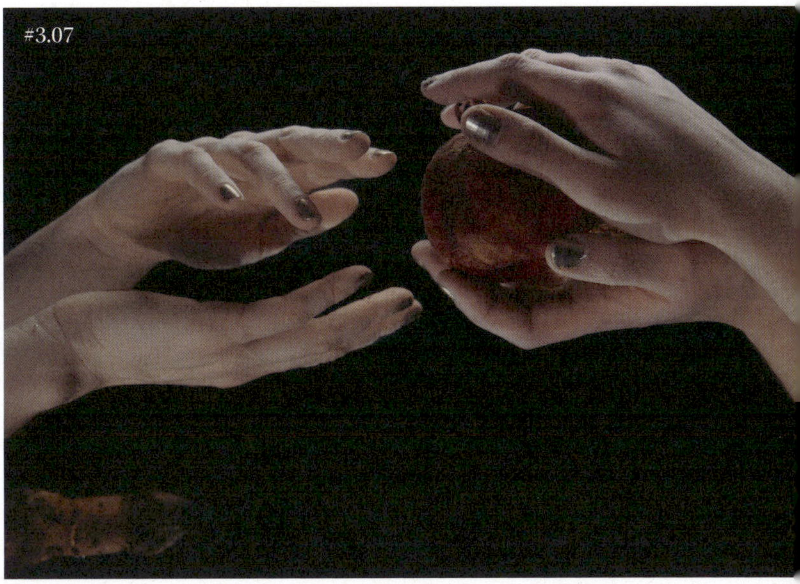
#3.07

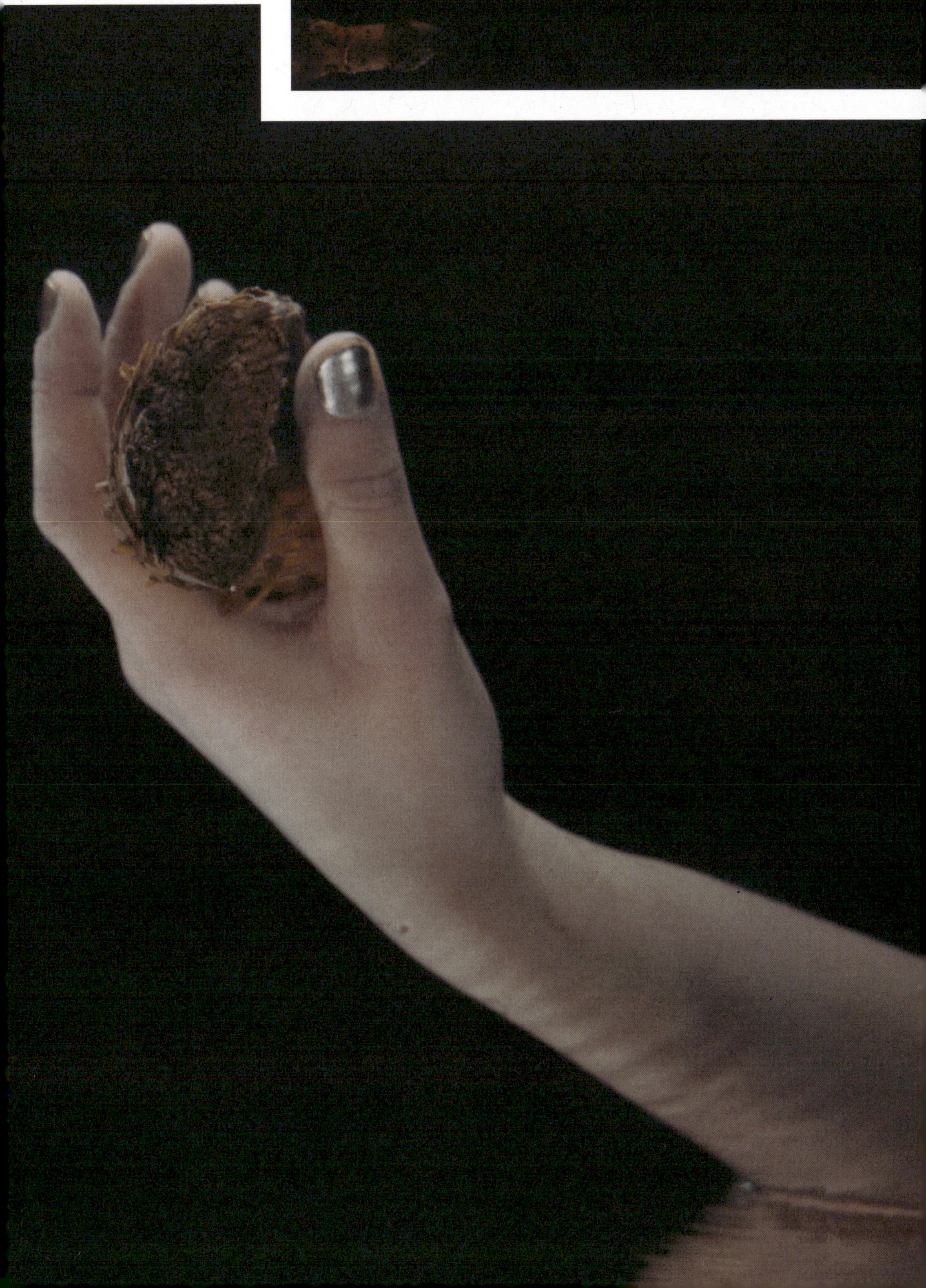

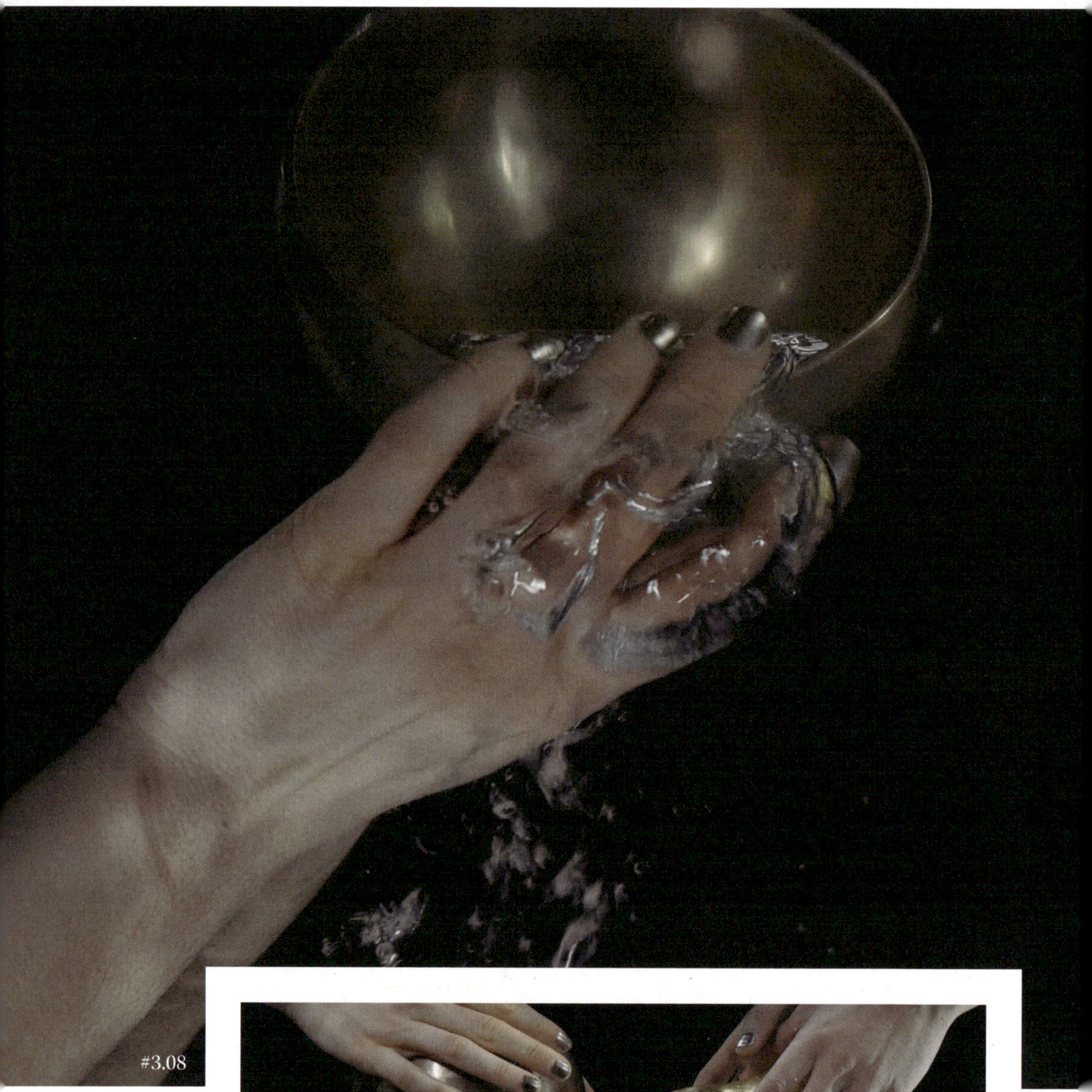

#3.08

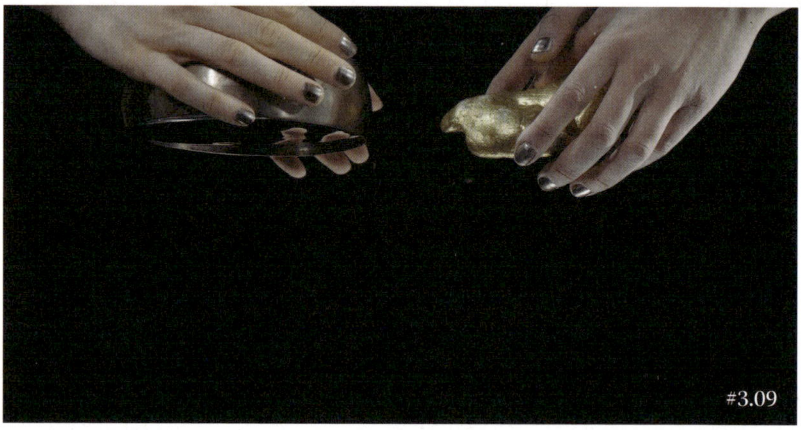

#3.09

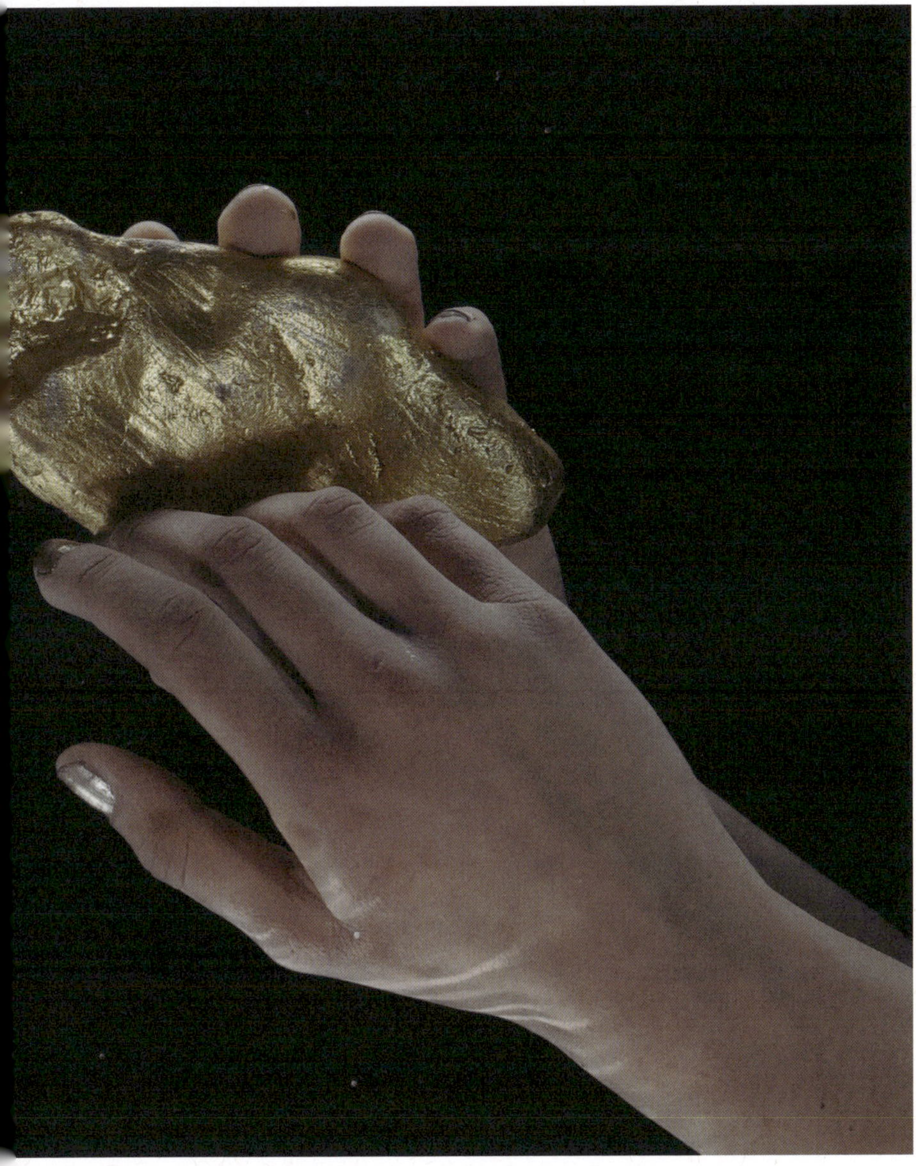

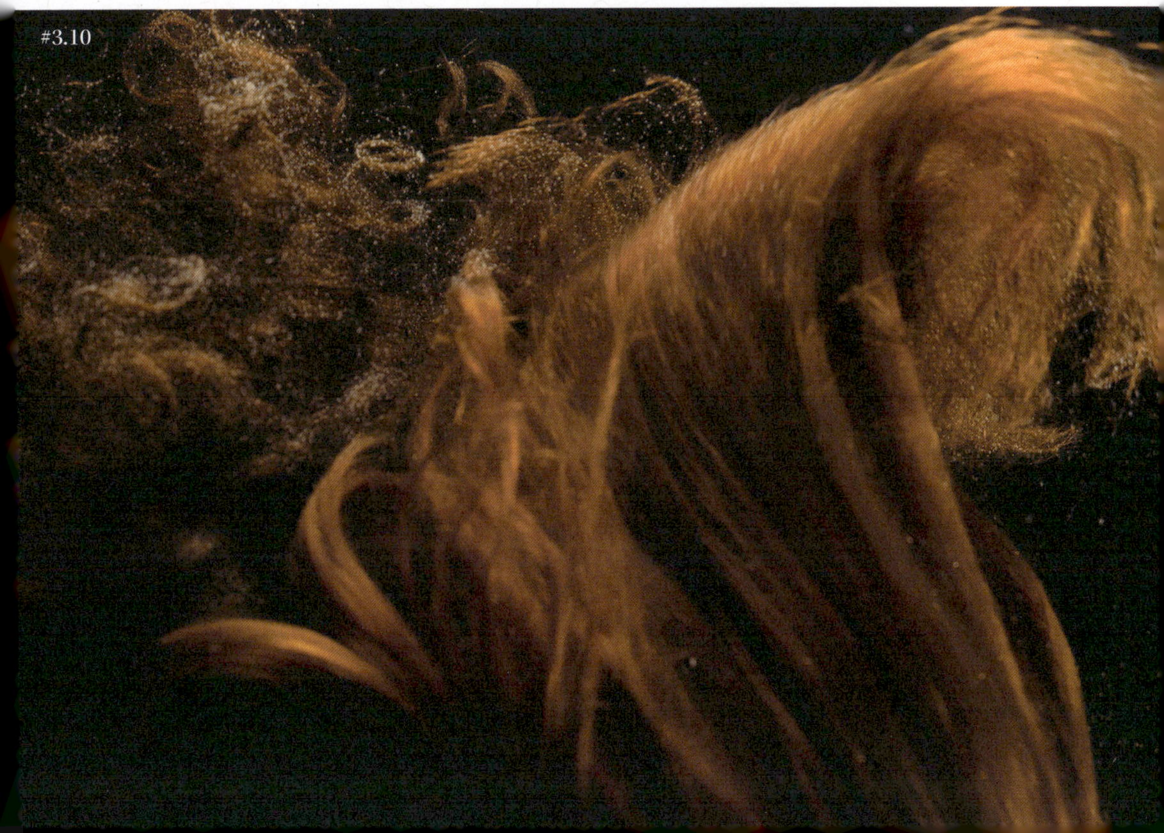
#3.10

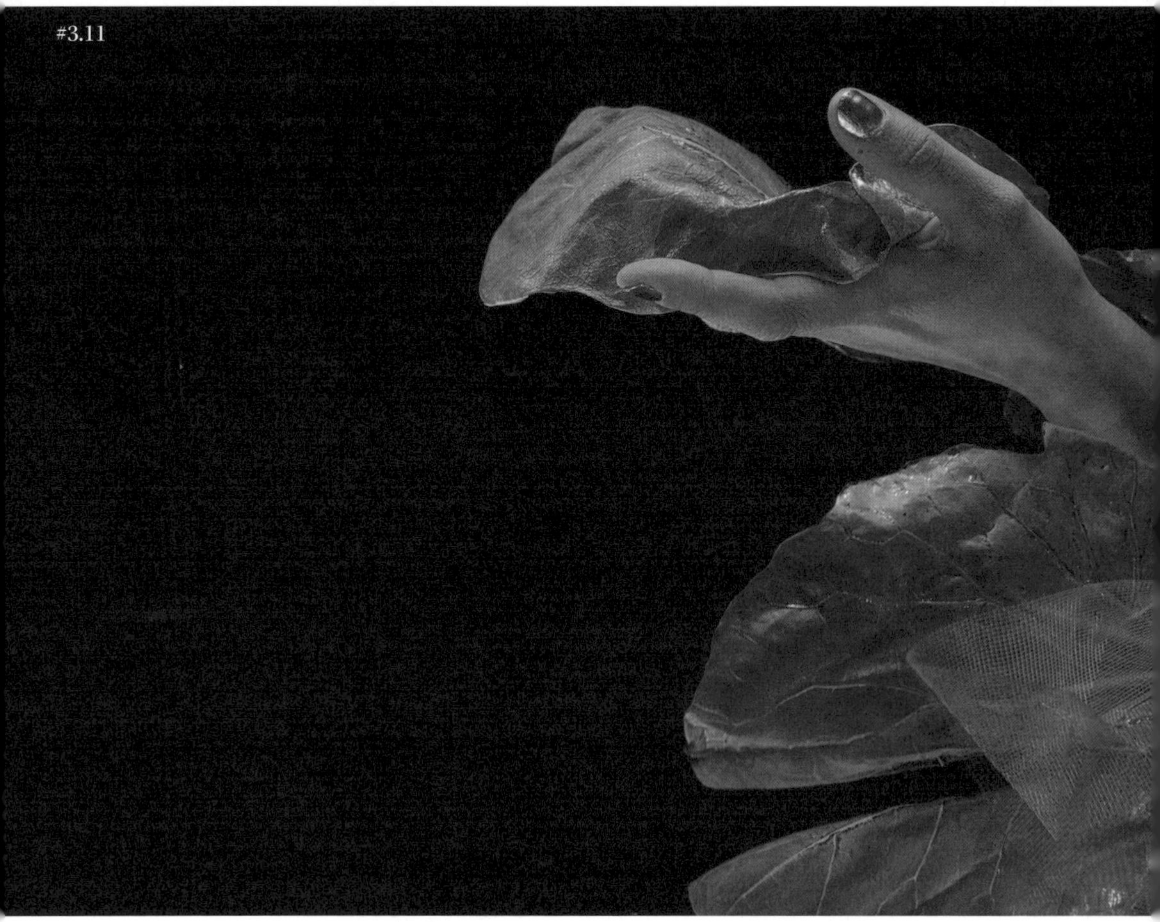
#3.11

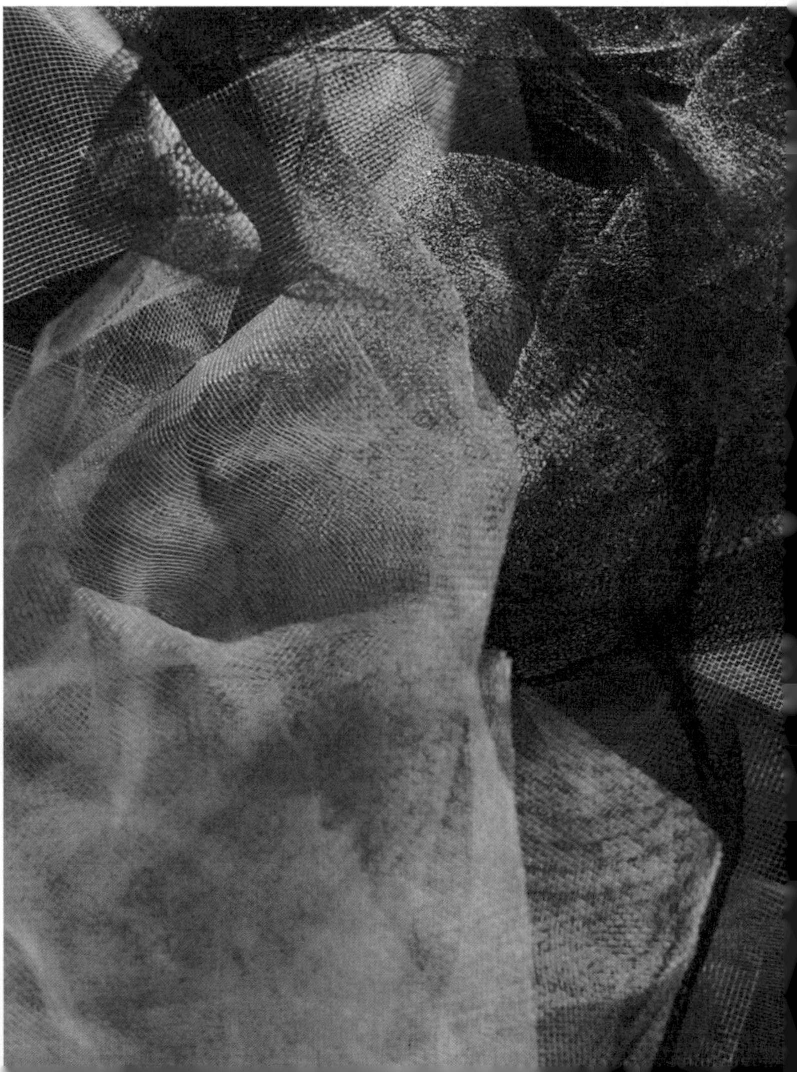

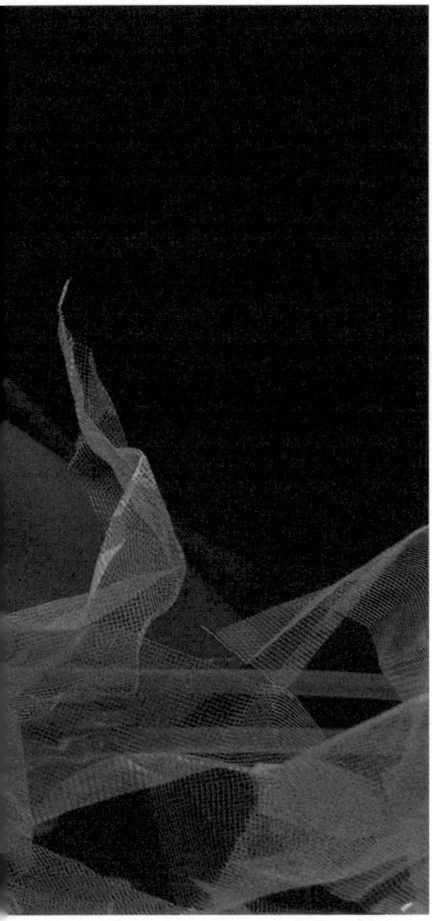

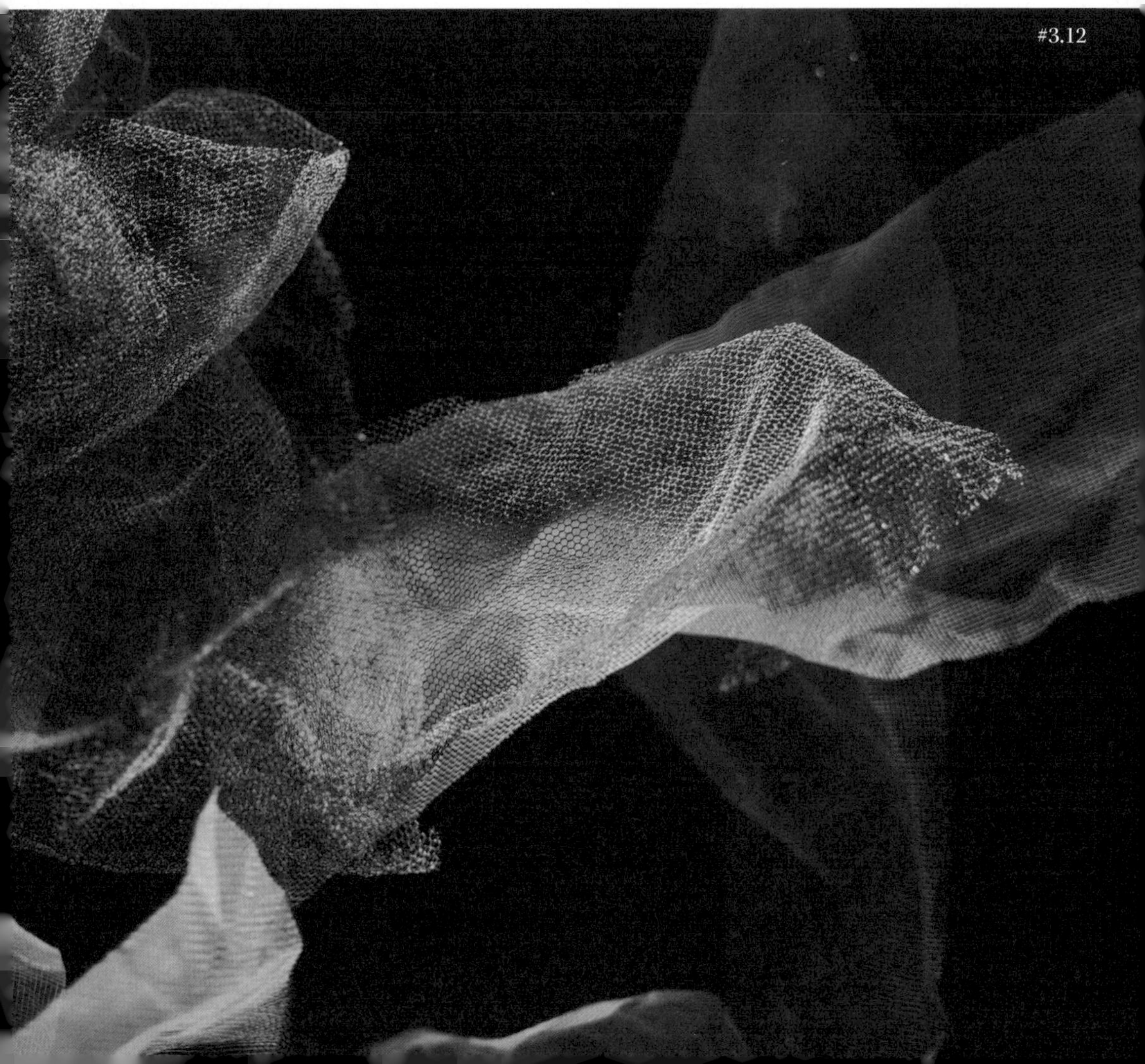
#3.12

#3.13

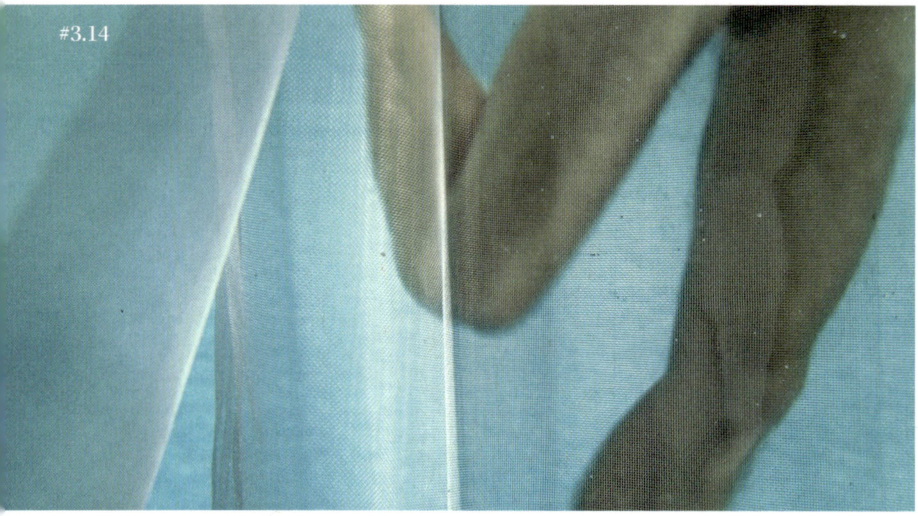

#3.14

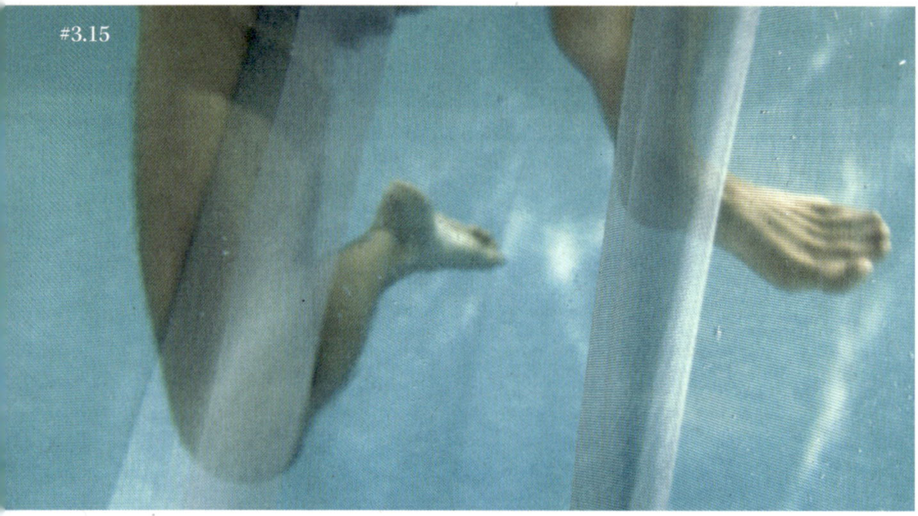

#3.15

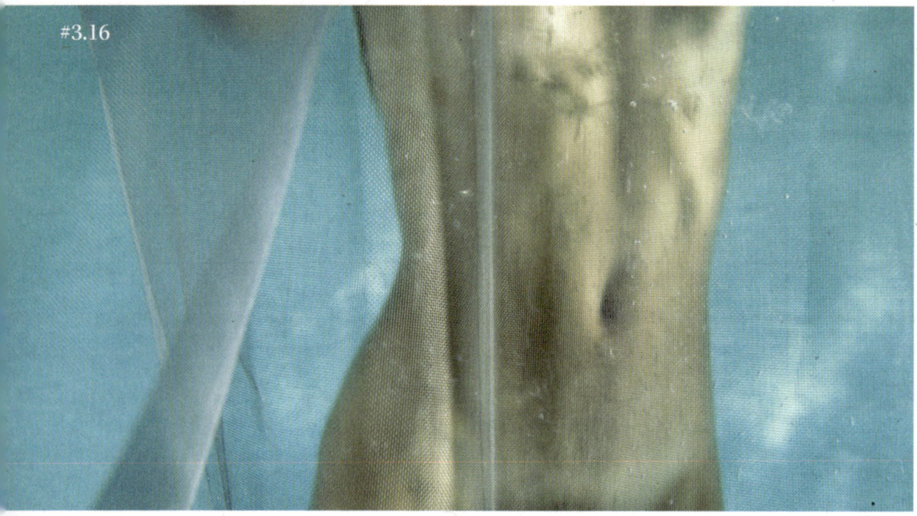

#3.16

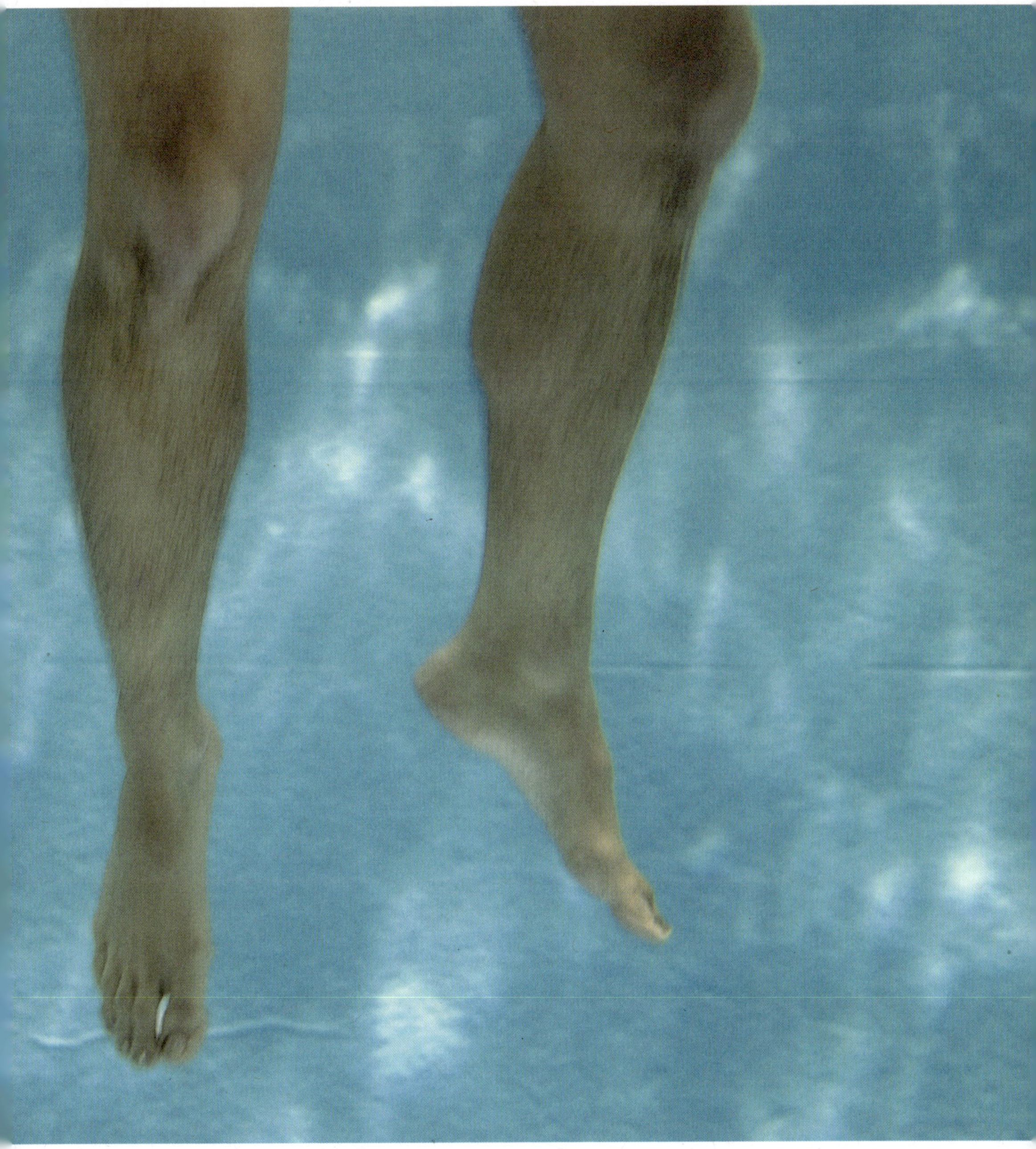

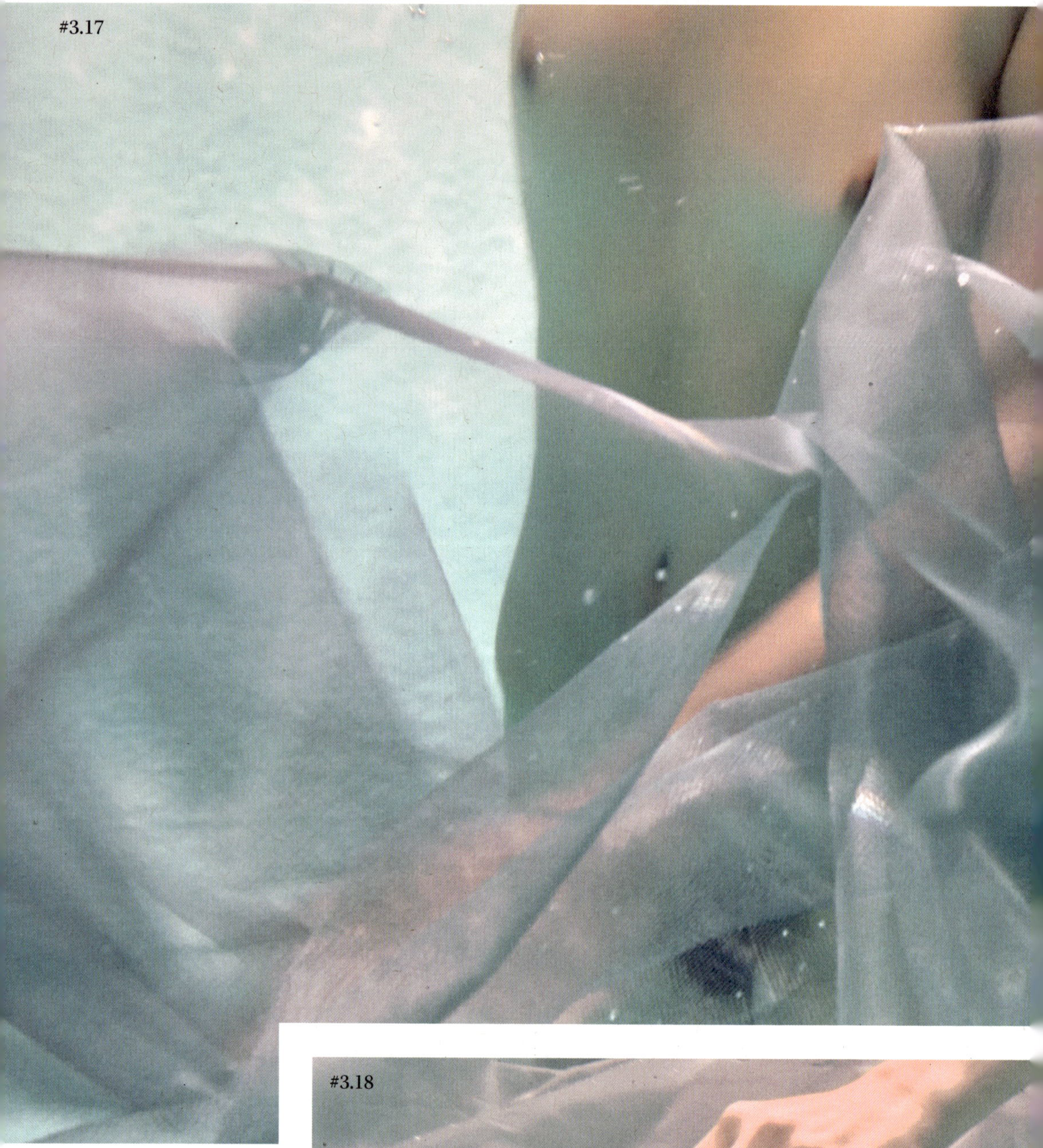
#3.17

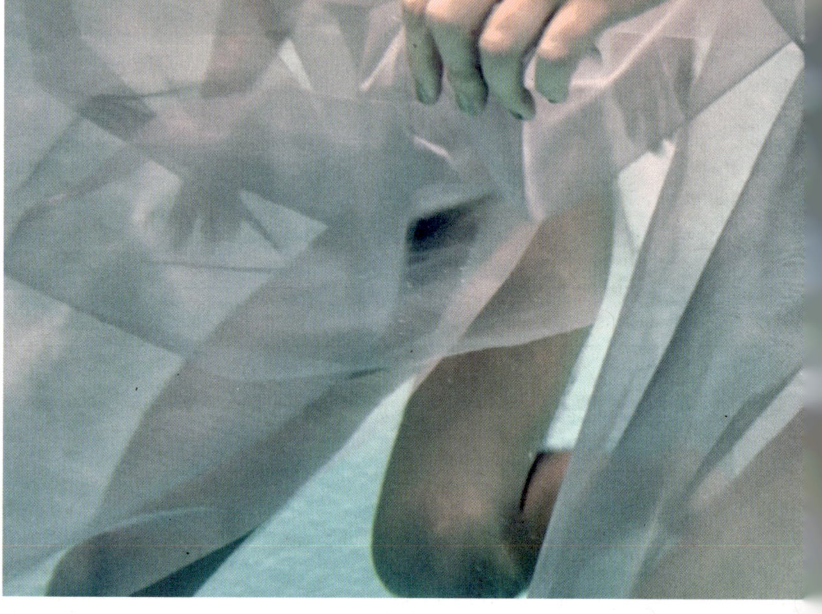
#3.18

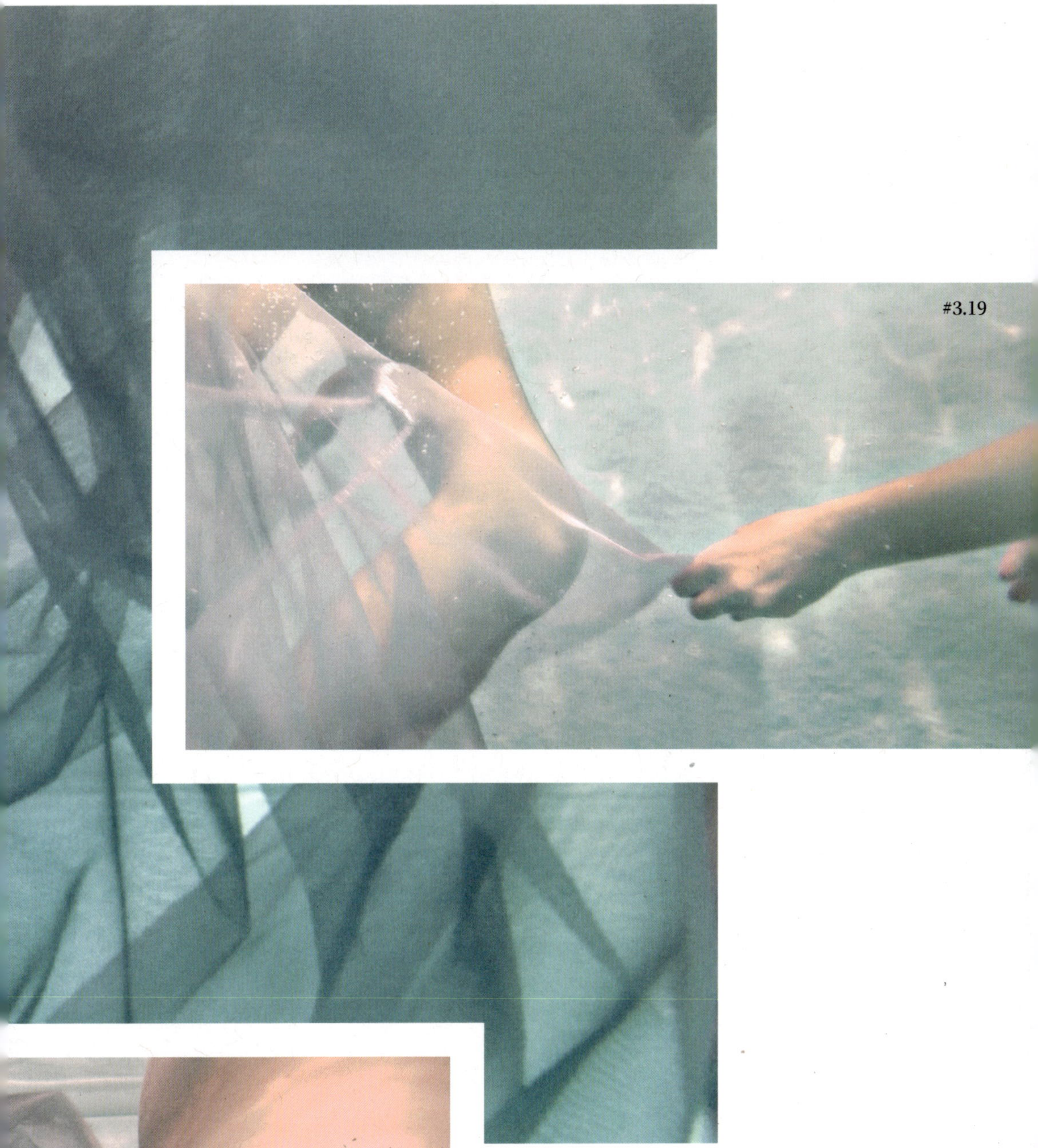

#3.19

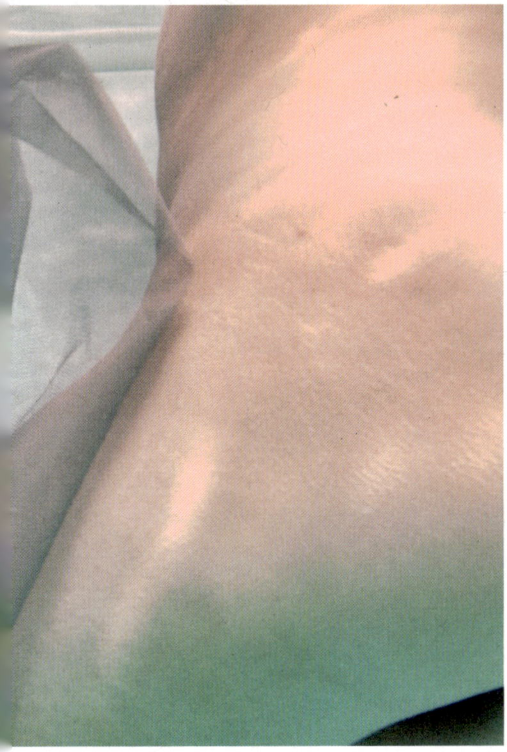

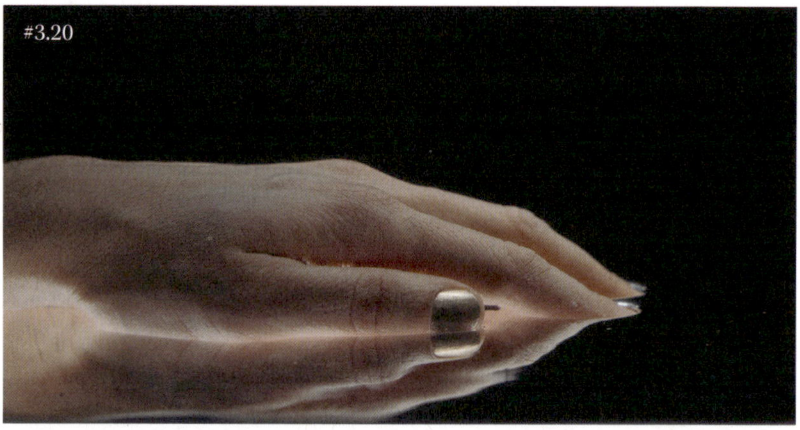
#3.20

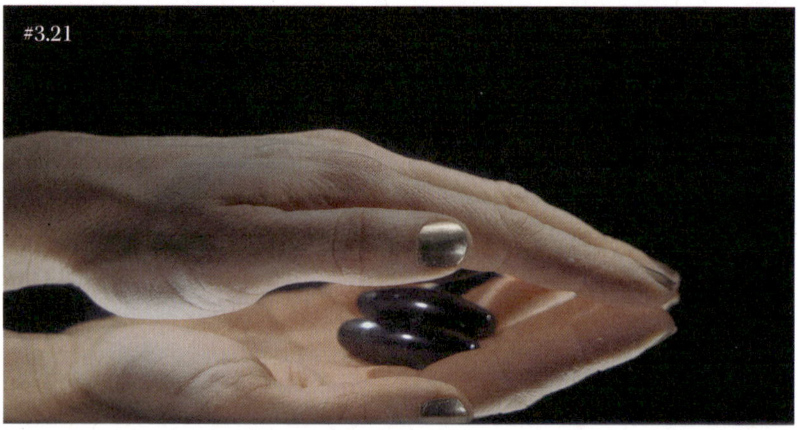
#3.21

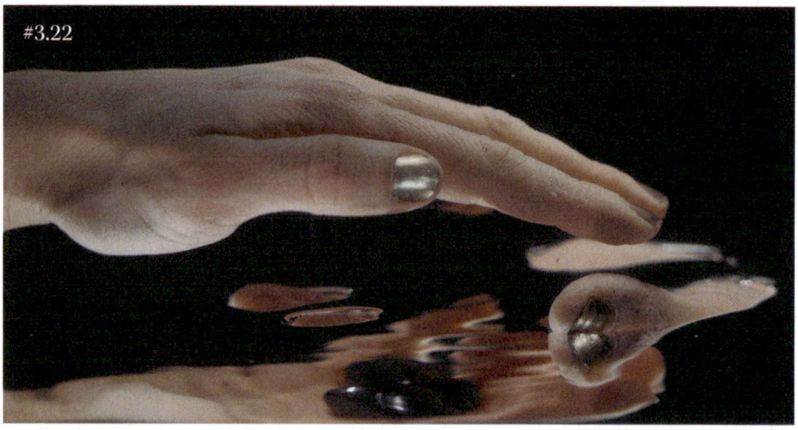
#3.22

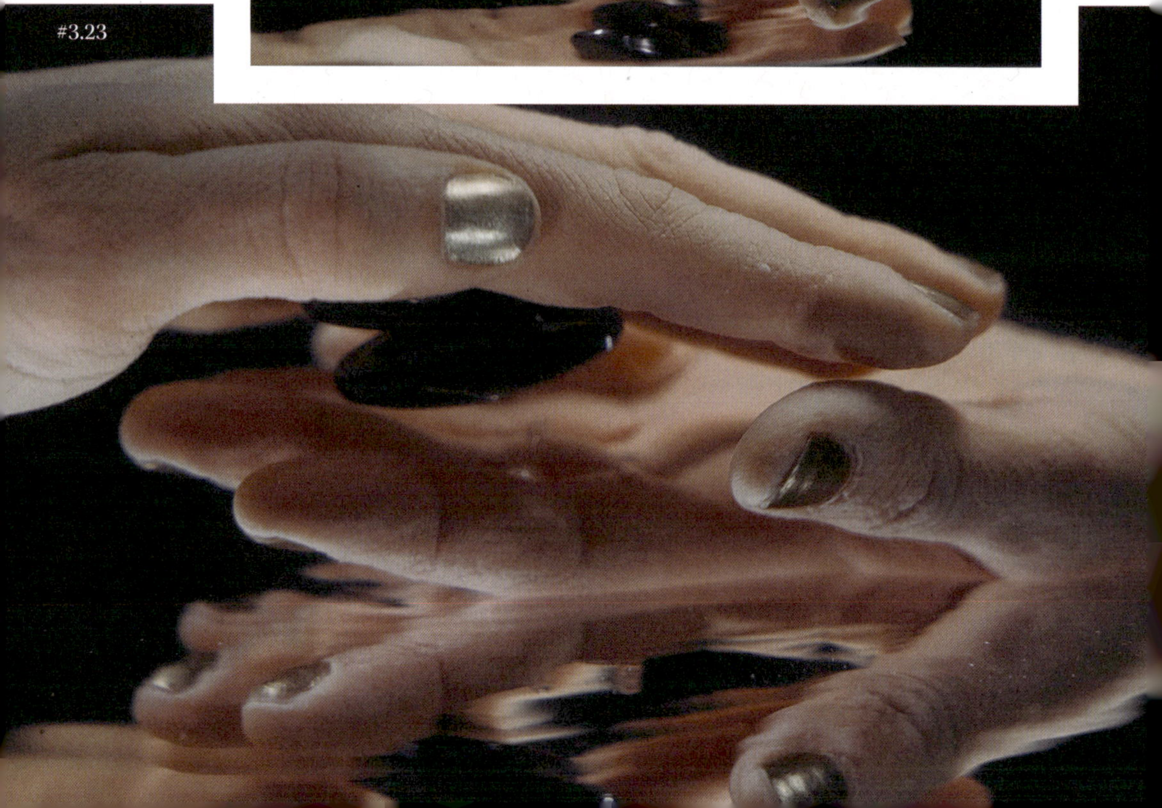
#3.23

#3.01: *Choreo-ethical Assemblages – Drowning in Depths,* 2025, © video still: Victor Jaschke, performance: Mar Esteban Martin and magnets, concept: Mariella Greil.

#3.02–#3.04: *Choreo-ethical Assemblages – Drowning in Depths,* 2025, © video still: Victor Jaschke, performance: Mar Esteban Martin, Luisa Pisetta Ravanelli, stones, scleractinia, cypraea tigris, concept: Mariella Greil.

#3.05– #3.07: *Choreo-ethical Assemblages – Drowning in Depths,* 2025, © video still: Victor Jaschke, performance: Mar Esteban Martin, Luisa Pisetta Ravanelli, pomegranate, root, concept: Mariella Greil.

#3.08– #3.09: *Choreo-ethical Assemblages – Drowning in Depths,* 2025, © video still: Victor Jaschke, performance: Mar Esteban Martin, Luisa Pisetta Ravanelli, singing bowl, golden stone, concept: Mariella Greil.

#3.10: *Choreo-ethical Assemblages – Drowning in Depths,* 2025, © video still: Victor Jaschke, performance: Mariella Greil, Luisa Pisetta Ravanelli, concept: Mariella Greil.

#3.11: *Choreo-ethical Assemblages – Drowning in Depths,* 2025, © video still: Victor Jaschke, performance: Mariella Greil, kohlrabi, concept: Mariella Greil.

#3.12: *Choreo-ethical Assemblages – Drowning in Depths,* 2025, © video still: Victor Jaschke, performance: fabric, concept: Mariella Greil.

#3.13–#3.16: *Choreo-ethical Assemblages – Drowning in Depths,* 2025, © video still: Victor Jaschke, performance: Luisa Pisetta Ravanelli and fabric, concept: Mariella Greil.

#3.17–#3.19: *Choreo-ethical Assemblages – Drowning in Depths,* 2025, © video still: Victor Jaschke, performance: Mariella Greil, Luisa Pisetta Ravanelli and fabric, concept: Mariella Greil.

#3.20–#3.23: *Choreo-ethical Assemblages – Drowning in Depths,* 2025, © video still: Victor Jaschke, performance: Mar Esteban Martin, Luisa Pisetta Ravanelli, and fabric, concept: Mariella Greil.

Purposeful Polysemy

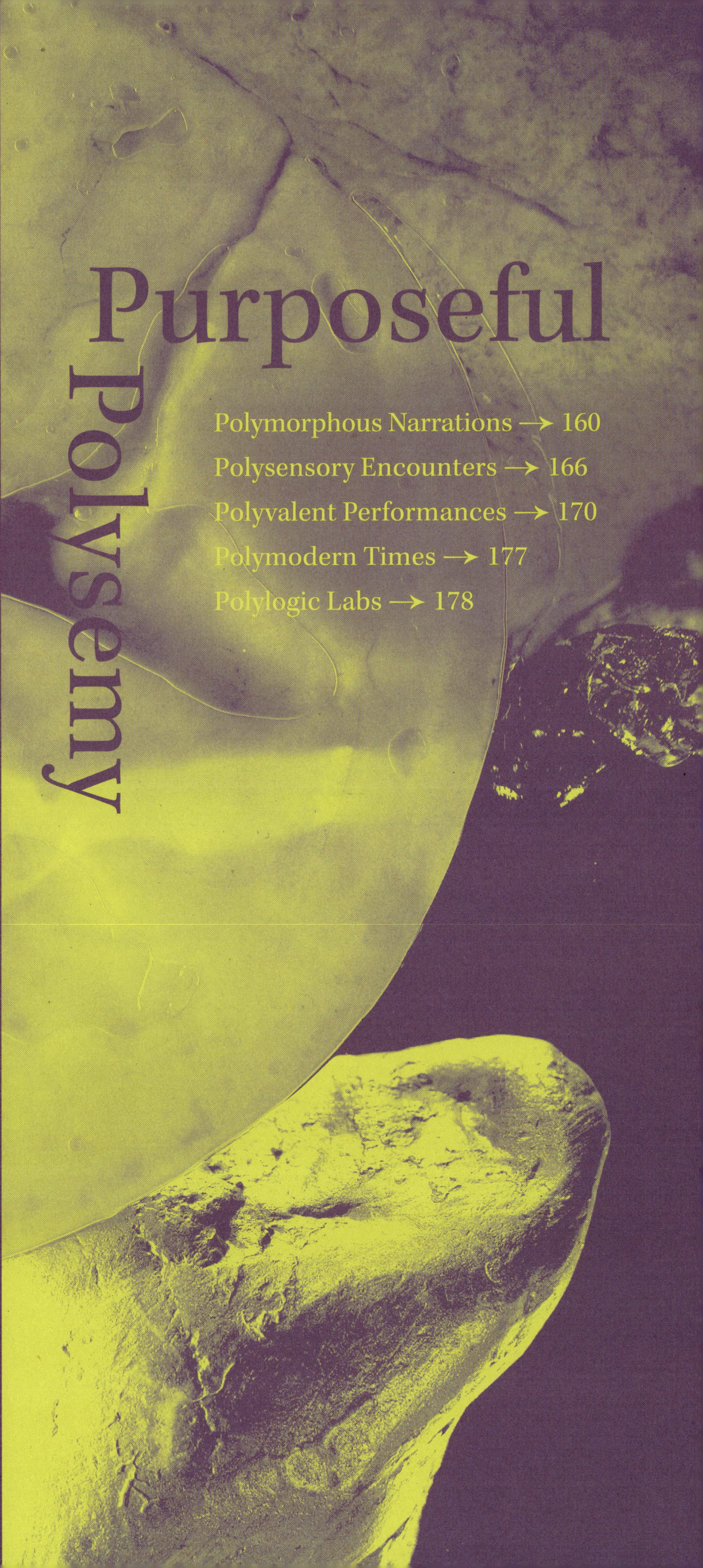

My research project *Choreo-Ethical Assemblages – Narrations of Bare Bodies* outlined the craft and mechanics of contemporary performance-making and artistic research, but also expanded into a shared space and encounter, blurring the lines between artist/creator and spectator/receiver. The contours of the project were formed by shared storytelling and performative vignettes, and were sourced from both individual and collective memory. Even more broadly, the project's purpose was to interrogate the subjectivities produced by language, matter, and performativity. Through this research project, it was my intention to advocate for embodied, ethical encounters with other agencies as well as with the audience – or as cultural theorist Irit Rogoff proposes, with those implicated[139] – across effects and flows. The wit(h)nesses in diverse forms become 'us' through – as Rogoff puts it – 'narrative implication'.[140]

In relation to what I term 'bare bodies',[141] narrative implication operates less as a linear storytelling device than as a performative field in which bodies are inscribed with, and inscribe, layers of meaning. Bare performing bodies, stripped of theatricality, codified roles, and (at times, but not always) costumes, do not present themselves as neutral surfaces; rather, they are already charged with histories, sociopolitical inscriptions, and sensory presences that implicate both the performers and wit(h)ness in an ongoing act of narration. I remember Xavier Le Roy's *Product of Circumstances* (1999), a lecture performance that combined artistic and scientific methods with embodied research. The staged autobiography critically traced mechanisms and hierarchies that are widespread in science and art – as products of circumstances – while roguishly implicating the audience as witnesses to the shift in professional context, from molecular biology to choreography. Le Roy sharply and astutely exposed the way the body thinks ('Thinking became a corporeal experience,' Le Roy said), its failings (earnest attempts to perform formal dance technique sequences with a poker face), and the innocence he once brought to both professional worlds, molecular biology and choreography, through the humour that resides within his body. This humour lived in the proportions of his limbs and their combination with scientific facts, creating absurdity. The mutual implication culminated in moments of laughter, and when there was no laughter or giggling, it would render the presence of the other mutually insignificant.

This implication is reciprocal – even more so in the one-on-one performance situation. Interpretive projections meet the body's resistant opacity, producing a relational narrative œkology. Here, narrative is neither imposed from without nor solely authored from within, but emerges through the choreography of attention, touch, and spatial co-presence. In this sense, bare bodies function as narrative thresholds – sites where the implied narration is felt before it is told, and where the body itself becomes a contingent, co-authored text in motion while cultivating polysemy. Polysemy invites multiple related meanings and allows for layered interpretations,

139. The implication of the other into the artistic work or act is discussed in this conversation between Irit Rogoff, and Marina Vives and Sonia Fernández Pan, 'A Conversation with Irit Rogoff: Where Do We Sit Within All of This?', *A*Desk: Critical Thinking*, 15 November 2015, https://a-desk.org/en/magazine/a-conversation-with-irit-rogoff.

140. Ibid.

141. Greil, *Being in Contact.*

the intentional, multifaceted encoding of certain aspects of artworks. An act or movement, a material or term can evoke several associations at once, enriching the encounter's polysemic resonance, which has the power to unearth surprising links as well as the unforeseen depths of embodied, artistic research.

Purposeful polysemy became a guiding principle for my artistic, embodied research, and I will therefore weave this chapter together by mapping the plural ontologies and the coexistence of heterogeneous 'spaces of being' that emerged through the practice of choreo-ethical assemblage. The topology traverses *polymorphous narrations, polysensory encounters*, and *polyvalent performances*, before reflecting on *polymodern times*, and concludes by discussing the Polylogic Labs that I established within the framework of my research.

The Greek roots of the prefix *poly-* (πολύς) mean 'many', 'a lot', while the Proto-Indo-European *pelə-* means 'to fill', with its derivatives referring to abundance and multitude. For this reason, I will strive not to overload this chapter and to keep abundance at bay. However, it seems worthwhile including a brief digression on polyvagal theory, which has significantly influenced various psychotherapeutic approaches to trauma and also resonated materially in the co-design of the setting of the choreographic environment as well as in the scores that I developed and probed throughout my research. The choreo-graphic environment that I developed in collaboration with artist and architect Walter Lauterer was mindfully designed to host the Polylogic Labs. The notion of the Polylogic Labs formed the core of my research project's methodological framework. I will outline how purposeful polysemy evokes what I call *polyvalent practices* in the field of embodied research.

Embodied research articulates itself through the body as both its epistemic locus and methodological apparatus, privileging enactment over abstraction. In performance, it mobilises lived corporeality, kinaesthetic intelligence, and the relational dynamics that emerge in co-presence, thereby producing modes of knowing that are situated, intersubjective, and contingent. Such a framework resists the instrumentalisation of the body as a mere object of analysis, instead positioning it as an active agent in the co-constitution of meaning. The knowledge generated is not singular but distributed, arising in the shifting interrelations among performers, wit(h)nesses, and the wider socio-cultural field, and remaining open to transformation beyond the moment of encounter.

As Irit Rogoff has stated,

> The conversation that I am interested in is one that extends whatever project, and takes it elsewhere, through us. The most important thing in the world to me is 'us'.[142]

142. Irit Rogoff, 'A Conversation with Irit Rogoff'.

In this register, 'us' names a performative collectivity in which narration is co-authored – its trajectory shaped by the generative force of *we*-ness in the collective's material and ethical stance across agencies and matters. Beyond its grammatical usefulness, the *we* refers to situational co-authorship and operates as performatively enacted we-ness and communal agency (including the other-than-human), undermining the individual and instead emphasising the dividual.[143]

Polymorphous Narrations

The heart *we* carry is not singular. It pulses through multiplicities, through the layered folds of psyche, soma, and relationality. In the evolving landscape of my project, *Choreo-ethical Assemblages – Narrations of Bare Bodies*, embodied research traversed contemporary performance, psychotherapy, and philosophy; a call was made to think beyond methods that are individualising towards a polyvalent ethics of attunement – an ethics not grounded in rigid protocol but in a responsiveness to the singular textures of each encounter. My project explored how performative, philosophical, and psychotherapeutic approaches take shape (establish their own contours) around the deep recesses of the psyche, particularly through the prism of daydreaming, memory work (including trauma), and embodied resonance, as these resonances emerge through the body *in* or *as* experimental performance.

To explore the psyche is to enter terrain shaped by paradox and polarity. In my view, the maturing of artistic work necessitates an ethical anchoring that holds space for such paradoxes without collapsing them into binary thought. I emphasise here the notion of *framing*,[144] the capacity to sustain ambivalence – or better, polyvalence – ambiguity – or better, polyguity – and fragmentation without rushing to coherence in the event that there is no coherence. Here, ethical anchoring is not an act of moralising but a practice of sustaining a field where creation and integration, rupture and repair, memory and forgetting can coexist in a fertile tension.

From true consideration – understood as the reflective engagement with ethical responsibility in human action – emerges ethical narration, wherein narrative form and discursive strategies themselves enact, question, or redistribute responsibility. Here, narrativity becomes a site for performing ethics, not merely representing it, shaping how otherness, agency, and accountability[145] are articulated and received.

Micro-phenomenological Interview with Emma Cocker
Excerpt, edited transcript
26 September 2022

Emma Cocker: The shoes were definitely worn. Maybe the thing that I'm less interested in or that I feel less drawn to is if it feels like the narrative is being closed down. So, there was something to do with trying to evacuate narrative.

143. Gerald Raunig, *Dividuum* (Semiotext(e), 2016).

144. Stephan Trinkaus, *Ökologien des Prekären – Zu einer Theorie des Haltens* (transversal texts, 2022).

145. Irina Baldini, *Accountable Temporary Expedients* (Brave New Books, 2022).

Mariella Greil: What an interesting word. Because evacuation is when you when empty a site, when you rescue people.

Emma: Yeah, is that what it is? I don't know the etymology of evacuate. I would imagine it's emptying. Yeah. To empty a scene would be to evacuate it, to take something out. Yes. So, to evacuate narrative, I think, would be to try and almost exorcise, to empty a space of narrative, explicit human narrative. Maybe this is the actual thing, to empty something of a strong human narrative. Or the narrative of the performer, even, maybe? Yes. Maybe the narrative of the performer. Yes, the performer was very present in the collection of objects, a collection of photographs. Maybe the handpan contains the narrative or the histories of performance. And some of the photographic images that can very evidently be read as performance works are very interesting. But I think there's something about human agency that's very strong in them. As if they are trying to make the agencies between human and nonhuman more interrelated rather than using them as props or objects that are activated in some kind of way through human narrative. And then they become about unfoldings, I think something is unfolding, the gesture of holding...

Mariella: Yeah, I think we are back to the topic of fitting and not-fitting. I think there's something in there that I find very interesting, as well as in the evacuation of narrative. I wonder what the difference is between narrative and narration?

Emma: Narrative feels as if we'd be more in the key of 'There's a reader of this story that is already there.' Yeah, this I don't know. Actually, *narrative* feels as if there is already a story that creates the contexts and almost like the logic of relations between objects, when *narration*, I guess, has a sense of unfolding.

Mariella: Yes, narration is in a process of becoming. Yeah, that was what I had in mind when I decided on the subtitle of my project 'Choreo-ethical Assemblages – Narrations of Bare Bodies'.

Emma: That's interesting, then, yeah.

Mariella: I was relieved you didn't say narration there, but spoke about the evacuation of narrative.

Emma: It's not to say that it's a problem. It's just that if I think about it in terms of bodies, narrative, the narrative of a bare body actually feels as if it's much more concerned with what is already inscribed. So, I think I will place that almost in the field of histories and memories and autobiography. Whereas narration, I think, is the sense of... I don't know yet...

Mariella: Yes, it was also speculative and more oriented towards what is to come than going back to the histories, or the autobiographic.

Emma: In that sense, the bare body also feels as if it's been evacuated of narrative. I mean that, in order to narrate now, in order to engage with narration as a live process of unfolding, I wonder whether there is something to do with the evacuation of narrative, like letting go of histories in order to just really be the real bare body.

Mariella: To come to this existential level. Yeah.

Emma: A radical emptying of all autobiography: Identity. History. Memory.

Mariella: Yes. The interesting thing for me is that with this opening up, with this emptying, there's always an opening.

Emma: Yeah, exactly.

Mariella: Because when we think about 'emptying', we think about losing something. But for me, I always feel that it's actually enriching, that it's actually opening up possibilities, inviting more possibilities through the conscious making of space, evacuation.

Emma: And for relation, I mean the sense of pure relation. It is almost like the sense of having the facility of the body as if you've never seen it before. And then there are all of these objects; it felt almost like being a baby again – where babies don't really know: What's in their hand? And what is an object? There's that kind of like, 'Wow!', I mean, 'Amazing!' before habit develops, before certain histories and expectations and conventions are inscribed into us. There's just this radical openness of 'anything is possible' in a way. You don't even know yet, at that point, subject – objects. There's no dualism even, in that sense, it's just relation.

Mariella: That reminds me of course of the work of the developmental psychiatrist and psychoanalyst specializing in infant development Daniel Stern.
I was thinking about bonding, cultivating different forms of bonding...

Emma: ...and how different bonds forms, which I think lie in this touch of binding.

Mariella: Yes, exactly, the narration of being-in-contact.

Across both literary and performative, choreographic history, narrative form has persistently sought to destabilise linear temporality and redistribute and experiment with narrative agency. The *branching narrative* (*verzweigtes Narrativ*) designates a mode in which the diegesis proliferates into multiple potential continuations, articulated through nodal decision points that foreground contingency and polysemy. In this configuration, the reader or – in the case of choreo-ethical assemblages – the wit(h)ness is reconstituted as a co-producer of the narrative trajectory, performing a series of selective acts and movements that determine both the sequence and resolution of events. Within the context of scripts and writing, a historically specific instantiation of this form is the *gamebook*, which emerged as a distinctive publishing format in the late twentieth century. Here, the formal apparatus of the codex is mobilised to simulate ludic interactivity: numbered segments function as narrative lexis, and page-turning becomes an embodied enactment of diegetic choice. This ludic, embodied dimension of choice-making is at the heart of performance and the unfolding of the compositional, agential choreography of bodies, things, atmospheres, and the relational space-time between them.

More capaciously, *nonlinear narration* operates as an umbrella category encompassing all departures from a strictly chronological organisation of events. Such narrations may enact temporal disjunctions, anachronic sequencing, or parallel plotlines without necessitating reader intervention. While branching narratives constitute one subset of this paradigm, nonlinearity can also manifest in structurally closed works, for example, through analepsis (flashbacks), prolepsis (flashforwards), framed narratives, or montage-like fragmentation.

Furthermore, in my research, I found a genealogically earlier but formally distinct precedent: the *entrelacement,* a compositional technique prominent in medieval romances that interweaves multiple narrative threads. Unlike the contingent bifurcations of the branching form, *entrelacement* alternates between plotlines as different voices narrate from their respective perspectives, deferring resolution and rhythmically oscillating between narrative strands. I refer to this compositional technique as it was an inspiration for the weaving of the creative texts in my research project.

Taken together, these four modes – branching narrative, the gamebook, nonlinear narration, and *entrelacement* – constitute discrete yet interrelated strategies for reconfiguring narrative temporality, causal coherence, and the distribution of agencies.[146] Juxtaposing and comparing them reveals a *longue durée* of formal experimentation in which the *telos* of storytelling is neither fixed nor singular but an open field of structural and experiential possibilities.

As I focus on the unfolding *narrations* of bare bodies, and because my project unfolds exclusively through being in dialogue, I have decided to share my reflections on Wagner Schwartz's performance *Dialogue with La Bête* (2025).[147]

146. More specifically, I refer here to authorial/performative versus readerly/wit(h)nessing agencies.

147. Wagner Schwartz's original performance *La Bête* was created in 2005. The *Goldring↔Schwartz* project *Dialogue avec « La Bête »* is a 24-minute film and was first presented in 2020. The ImPulsTanz / mumok collaboration curated by Chris Standfest marked the bringing together of both the live performance and the screening of the art film, presented on a double bill.

This performance work was a bodily meditation on mobility and agency refracted through the prism of Lygia Clark's *Bichos* (1965), which offers a compelling space in which to consider the precariousness of the body within a participatory framework. The *Bicho* replica, devoid of inherent animation, became a poignant stand-in for the artist's own vulnerability, a material echo of the potential for manipulation. By extending the invitation to intervene *not* to the object but to himself, Schwartz destabilised the traditional power dynamics of performer/spectator, object/subject. He exposed a raw nerve, a palpable tension residing within the very act of offering one's malleable selves up for interaction.

The invitation was, of course, deceptive. The gesture of participation, while seemingly empowering, also implicated the audience in a choreography of potential exploitation. This is where the work's strength lay: in its refusal to offer easy resolutions or comforting illusions of shared agency. Instead, it lingered in discomfort, in the ethical quagmire of consent and control, focusing on the polymorphous body of Schwartz and the diverse narrations that the spectators created.

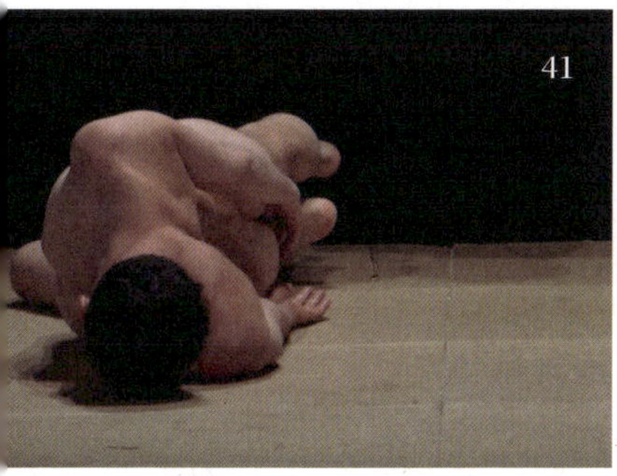

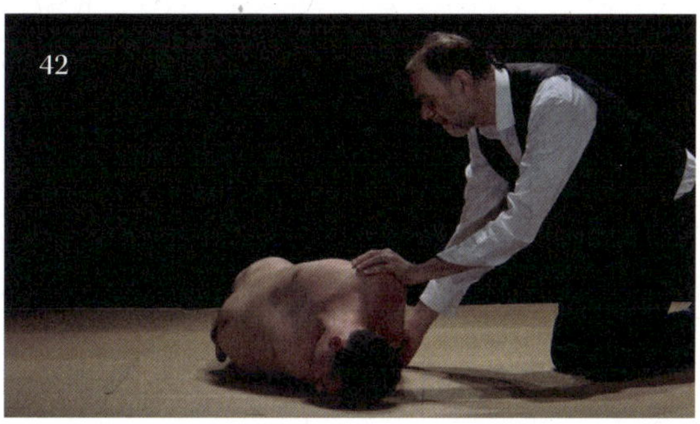

Laurent Goldring's *Dialogues* series, born from this very collaboration with Schwartz, provides a further layer of reflection. It allows us to see Schwartz's performance refracted through another artist's lens,[148] highlighting the generative depth and potential of artistic exchange and the interwovenness of the tactile and the visual, nonverbal, and verbal dialogue with the body, as well as its limitations and its capacity for transformation. In their layered complexity, performance and film together serve as a vital reminder that both participation and dialogue are more than simply feel-good exercises – they are complex processes of negotiating power, responsibility, and the enduring question of what it means to be embodied in a world that constantly seeks to objectify and manipulate.

Goldring's series becomes a contemplation on what the body can do, how it folds and unfolds, silent, expanding into the depths of time, as we witness the

148. At the 2025 ImPulsTanzFestival, I saw both the performance and the film. In the film, the painter Alex Amann manipulates Schwartz according to Goldring's instructions, as he had asked Amann to take on the role of the audience, giving him instructions on how to move and mould Schwartz's body. In this performance for the camera, Amann's hands serve as an intermediary for Goldring's voice, which makes visible and emphasises the tactile, mediating role of the hands while ultimately remaining in close dialogue with the visual and communicative dimension of the flesh, materiality, and sculpturality of the body and its movement. Goldring once again brilliantly works on his long-standing (since the 2000s) exploration of the image of the body as seen through the lens of the camera.

Figs. 41–42: *Goldring↔Schwartz* project *Dialogue avec 'La Bête'*, 2025, © video still: Laurent Goldring, performance: Wagner Miranda Schwartz and Alex Amann.

polymorphous narration. It can be read as a form of relational experimentation, addressing issues of power dynamics and consent, but also as an approachable performance work that needs the audience's hands to come into being. From this tactile co-creation, a state emerges that gestures beyond the pragmatic coordinates of waking life, with its norms and conventions relating to proximity and distance, towards a perceptual field in which boundaries relax and the imagination operates with fewer constraints. It feels as though we are engaged in a form of *co-dreaming* – an intersubjective drift into a shared oneiric field[149] in which perceptual, affective, and mnemonic[150] traces entangle. In this mode, the boundary between individual and collective psychic life becomes porous, enabling a generative oscillation between self and other – or, in the plural, between selves and others. Such a state can be understood as the mutual inhabitation of a transitional space, akin to psychoanalyst and paediatrician Donald Winnicott's 'potential space',[151] yet extending into the simultaneity of multiple embodied subjectivities, where dreaming operates not as solitary psychic production but as a relational, co-constituted event. It is a form of moving together in the choreographic environment as we co-dream encounters across agencies in the here and now, there and then, and potential futures – all at once.

The capacity to remain 'innerly spacious' and to fully inhabit inner space during periods of acute upheaval[152] – maintaining perceptual openness, cognitive elasticity, and polyvalent tolerance – is not merely a coping mechanism but, it seems to me, a pivotal existential and epistemic competence of the twenty-first century. In my view, this inner expanse counters the contraction of reactive reflexes, fostering a relational mode of thought and action that is sensitive to complexity and essential for creative and ethical agency in uncertain times.

Such creative and ethical agency, however, presupposes not only deliberate ethical reflection but also what I call a practice of 'inner spaciousness' – a cultivated openness that resists defensive contraction when certainty dissolves. This receptivity extends beyond the waking mind into psychic states where the coordinates of linear logic and reality-testing are suspended, and intuitive-creative action emerges. In such states, permeability is more than a symptom of vulnerability[153] – it is

149. *Oneiric* comes from the Greek *oneiros* (ὄνειρος), meaning *dream*. In literary, artistic, and philosophical contexts, it describes dream-like states, atmospheres, or processes. 'Oneiros', etymonline, accessed 16 May 2025, https://www.etymonline.com/search?q=oneiros.

150. It is the Latinised form of the Greek *μνημονικός* (*mnēmonikos*, 'of or pertaining to memory', from *mnēmōn* (genitive, *mnēmonos*) 'remembering', 'mindful', stemming from the Proto-Indo-European root **men-*, 'to think', which quite subtly undoes time by bringing mindful thinking and remembering (as preserving the unforgotten) together in Schwartz's performative act. 'Origin and history of mnemonic', etymonline, accessed 14 August 2025, https://www.etymonline.com/word/mnemonic.

151. Winnicott's *potential space* is the imaginative, relational area between self/selves and other/others, where creativity and play emerge. Donald Woods Winnicott, *Playing and Reality* (Tavistock, 1971), 51–70.

152. The inhumane conditions in Palestine, as well as the wars in Ukraine, Myanmar, Sudan, Ethiopia, etc., and climate catastrophe are just a selection of the turmoil that instantly and deeply unsettlingly comes to mind.

153. Erinn C. Gilson, *The Ethics of Vulnerability: A Feminist Analysis of Social Life and Practice* (Routledge, 2014).

mode of potential generative cognising through the senses and an ethical resource, enabling encounters with aspects of plural selves and worlds that are otherwise inaccessible. The nocturnal theatre of dreaming offers a paradigmatic example: as psychoanalyst and neuropsychologist Mark Solms' neuropsychoanalytical reframing suggests, dreaming cannot be reduced to the neurophysiological mechanics of the REM cycle, instead constituting a liminal mode of being – a space where the self becomes porous to regression, fragmentation, and the return of what has been repressed.[154] J. Allan Hobson and Robert W. McCarley's 1977 'activation-synthesis hypothesis' laid the groundwork for a critical view of psychoanalytical dream work, positing that dreams are random neural firings interpreted by the brain and thereby challenging the hermeneutics of classical dream analysis.[155] This provoked an ongoing debate: is the interpretation of dreams an artistic pseudoscience, as philosopher Adolf Grünbaum critiqued it in his book *The Foundations of Psychoanalysis: A Philosophical Critique* (1984), or a legitimate psychodynamic practice? But this question is itself perhaps limited by disciplinary purism. As Solms explains, 'dreams safeguard a good night's sleep',[156] while the dream state is, paradoxically, a generative state. In artistic practice, the cultivation of reverie and daydreaming functions as a form of knowledge production – which could be termed a *poetics of psyche*. Fantasising and daydreaming intensify affective experience; they loosen the ego's grasp on narrative coherence, inviting in the unpredictable.[157] In this sense, the practice of associating is an encounter with the unconscious in its raw, generative form. As Solms explains, dopamine agonists enhance the vividness of dreams and psychotic symptoms alike, while antipsychotic medications blunt both. This biochemical modulation underscores the materiality of the psyche – it cannot be reduced to the mind alone. Dreaming, then, is neither wholly neural nor wholly symbolic – it is a liminal practice straddling the neurochemical, the imaginal, and the interpersonal. The practices of association and assemblage in my project invited neuroplasticity in the sense that both activities practice and cultivate polymorphous narrations that amalgamate performance practice, imagination, and action. In my research project, the convergence of creative performative craft with dreaming and imagining constitutes a dynamic interplay wherein embodied practice and imaginative cognition co-constitute modes of material engagement. Dreaming and imagining, traditionally situated within the realm of the intangible, are reconfigured here as vital vectors of material sensitivity – enabling practitioners to apprehend latent potentials within matter itself. This fusion destabilises the

154. Karen Kaplan-Solms and Mark Solms, *Clinical Studies in Neuro-Psychoanalysis: Introduction to a Depth Neuropsychology* (Karnac, 2000); and Mark Solms, *The Hidden Spring: A Journey to the Source of Consciousness* (W. W. Norton & Company, 2021).

155. J. Allan Hobson and Robert W. McCarley, 'The Brain as a Dream State Generator: An Activation-Synthesis Hypothesis of the Dream Process', *American Journal of Psychiatry* 134, no. 12 (1977): 1335–48.

156. Mark Solms, 'The Dreaming Mind vs. The Dreaming Brain', keynote, World Congress of Psychotherapy, July 17, 2025, Sigmund Freud University, Vienna.

157. Danielle Knafo and Kenneth Feiner, *Unconscious Fantasies and the Relational World* (Analytic Press, 2006).

dichotomy between abstraction[158] and concretion, as performative craft activates the body's tacit knowledge to translate ephemeral visions into tangible form through concrete action. Such praxis embodies a somatic epistemology where materiality is not a passive substrate but an active interlocutor in the creative process. Within this framework, dreaming is reimagined not as mere fantasy but as a generative state that informs, and is informed by, hands-on making, allowing unforeseen trajectories to unfold. Thus – and this can be extended to embodied research in general – creative performance emerges as a site of reciprocal entanglement between mind, matter, and movement, inviting a profound reconsideration of agency within artistic materiality.

Polysensory Encounters

Through embodied research, the artistic research community is expanding the classical scholarly paradigm. In the following paragraphs, I will introduce the notion of *polysensory encounters*, which refers to experiences and interactions that engage multiple sensory modalities simultaneously or in a complex interplay of experimental performance and living life. These encounters challenge the traditional privileging of vision and auditory perception as the dominant sensory channels in Western epistemology and aesthetics. Instead, they prepare fertile ground for embodied, transdisciplinary research, spanning philosophy, the psychotherapeutic sciences, art theory and practice, cultural studies, dance-making, choreography, and performance, as well as anthropology and ethics. The study of polysensory encounters emphasises how meaning, affect, and experimental knowledge generation emerge through the integration and negotiation of diverse sensory inputs – such as touch, smell, proprioception, and interoception[159] – beyond the narrowly defined scope of isolated sensory modalities.

This chapter seeks to critically explore the concept of the polysensory encounter by addressing its theoretical underpinnings, methodological implications, and cultural significance. It will also situate polysensory encounters within the broader discourse of multisensory integration and sensory ethnography, underscoring their relevance to contemporary artistic and particularly performative practices.

In the following, I will propose a shift from sensory hierarchies to sensorial œkology. Western epistemology, shaped by Cartesian dualism and Enlightenment

158. In decolonial studies, the notion of *abstraction* is frequently identified as a 'white term', operating as a conceptual marker that defines what is not figurative and therefore not legible within the analytical framework of the Western gaze. Such a deployment of abstraction functions less as a neutral aesthetic category than as a *dispositif* of exclusion, demarcating epistemic boundaries that naturalise Eurocentric modes of perception. In contrast, decolonial aesthetics seek to unbind abstraction from its hegemonically codified meanings, foregrounding plural modes of signification and sensorial registers that resist capture by (Western) analytical rationality. The very etymology of the term – from the Latin *abstrahere*, 'to draw away', 'to pull from' – already signals a movement of separation, of taking something from its context, that resonates with the colonial gesture of extraction: to abstract is not merely to generalise but also to dispossess. Decolonial critique re-reads this genealogy, insisting on the possibility of abstractions that are not severed from their situated, embodied, and relational grounds, but rather emerge from within pluriversal worlds.

159. Proprioception articulates kinaesthetic self-localisation within space, while interoception designates affective and perceptual attunement to visceral, metabolic, and homeostatic corporeal states. In interplay, they weave together spatial orientation and internal regulation, generating a dynamic continuum of embodied self-awareness that undergirds both perceptual consistency and aesthetic experience, which is crucial for performing choreo-ethical assemblages.

rationalism, has historically marginalised the body's sensory complexity by privileging sight and hearing as the primary modes of perception and cognition. In his introduction to philosopher Michel Serres' 1985 book *The Five Senses – A Philosophy of Mingled Bodies (I)*, Steven Connor argues that this sensory hierarchy reflects a conceptual 'tyranny of panoptical vision',[160] where the eye is considered the sovereign organ of truth and knowledge. The resurgence of interest in the multisensory body in the late twentieth and early twenty-first centuries has challenged this ocularcentrism by reclaiming the sensory plurality inherent to human experience. Polysensory encounters extend this critique by emphasising the simultaneous activation and entanglement of multiple sensory channels in the making of meaning. This perspective aligns with the emerging field of sensorial œkology, which foregrounds the relational and œkological nature of sensory experience. Sensorial œkology posits that senses do not function in isolation but as dynamic, context-dependent systems[161] influenced by environmental, cultural, and bodily factors.[162]

Phenomenologists like Maurice Merleau-Ponty have provided foundational insights into the embodied nature of perception, emphasising the pre-reflective, lived experience of the body as a sensory locus. Merleau-Ponty's concept of the 'flesh of the world'[163] articulates how perception is a process of corporeally intertwining with the environment, a notion that resonates with the understanding of polysensory encounters as events that are inherently relational and situated.

Advances in neuroscience have revealed that sensory modalities are not discrete or isolated within the brain but interact extensively through processes of *multisensory integration*. The brain synthesises inputs from different senses to construct coherent perceptual experiences, as shown in research on the superior colliculus and the temporoparietal junction.[164]

160. Steven Connor, introduction to *The Five Senses: A Philosophy of Mingled Bodies* (I), by Michel Serres (Continuum, 1985), 6.

161. Within the framework of the Researchers' Exchange, a format hosted by Angewandte Performance Laboratory (APL) for dialogue between artist-researchers, we were invited to a dialogue practice with the FWF PEEK-AR 776 research project *SENSING LIVING SYSTEMS: Exploring the Potential of Multisensory Scenography for Systems Awareness* by artists Paul Divjak and Jeanette Müller (Angewandte Performance Laboratory (APL), University of Applied Arts Vienna, 28 May 2024). I sensed the urgency of gaining a deeper understanding of how direct sensory experiences form living systems both within the artistic context but also beyond. Advocating for the Sustainable Development Goals (SDGs) and systems literacy will prove to be vital to future sustainability, 'for the shaping of a life-affirming social, ecological and economic transformation of our world' (as stated in the abstract of the project).

162. Tim Ingold, *Being Alive: Essays on Movement, Knowledge and Description* (Routledge, 2022 [2011]).

163. Maurice Merleau-Ponty, *The Visible and the Invisible*, ed. Claude Lefort, trans. Alphonso Lingis (Northwestern University Press, 1968 [1964]), 248–51.

164. Besides the visual inputs in superior layers, the deeper layers of the colliculus also receive auditory and somatosensory inputs that are connected to many sensorimotor areas of the brain. Alexander A. Kustov and David Lee Robinson argue that there is shared neural control of attentional shifts and eye movements ('Shared Neural Control of Attentional Eye Shifts and Eye Movements, *Nature* 384 [1996]: 74–77), which is especially interesting in relation to the attention practices that I introduced as part of the project, mostly in preparation for the 'Diffractive Dialogue Score' within the frame of a Polylogic Lab, such as stilling eye movements, focusing on the inner motion, expanded listening, or various movement tasks based on sensorimotor awareness. Mark T. Wallace and Barry E. Stein develop a line of argument stating that multisensory integration and complex combinations of cross-modality cues develop as and alongside maturing processes. See Mark T. Wallace and Barry E. Stein, 'Development of Multisensory Neurons and Multisensory Integration in Cat Superior Colliculus', *Journal of Neuroscience* 17, no. 7 (1997): 2429–44.

Such neuroscientific findings provide an empirical basis for polysensory theory, showing that perception is inherently multimodal and adaptive. However, polysensory encounters, as discussed here, extend beyond neurological integration to encompass the phenomenological and sociocultural dimensions of sensory experience. They interrogate how social and cultural contexts mediate sensory perception and how sensory modalities are variously valued and interpreted across different communities. I would therefore like to briefly digress to consider polysensory encounters in anthropology and sensory ethnography.

In the last few decades, anthropologists have increasingly adopted a polysensory approach to ethnographic research, focusing on how sensory practices shape cultural knowledge and social relations. Scholars like Steven Feld, Keith H. Basso,[165] and David Howes have demonstrated that sensory hierarchies vary significantly across cultures, where smell, taste, or touch can carry profound social and symbolic meanings that are absent or devalued within Western frameworks.

Sensory ethnography seeks to document and analyse such embodied experiences, emphasising sensory labour, affective atmospheres, the social life of senses, and their tuning to and through culture. In the context of my research on choreo-ethical assemblages, polysensory encounters are understood as events where multiple sensory modalities are interwoven with cultural meaning-making, challenging Western assumptions of thought processes limited to cognition, which lack sensory depth and complexity.

Contemporary art and performance practices have been at the forefront of exploring polysensory encounters to expand aesthetic experience and critique dominant sensory hierarchies. Of course, the non-Western and diasporic practices of artists and scholars have recently informed this broadening and questioning of Western research methods within the West, especially in relation to disciplines such as the environmental sciences, ecology (Robin Wall Kimmerer[166]), systems thinking, sustainability, and education (Tyson Yunkaporta[167]).

Artistic interventions often deploy smell, touch, temperature, and proprioception, alongside sound and vision, to create immersive environments that provoke new modes of perception and affect. They engage the audience's whole body through tactile and visceral encounters, destabilising the spectator's role and foregrounding embodied co-presence. Similarly, installation art often employs olfactory and tactile elements to evoke memory, intimacy, or alienation, drawing attention to the non-visual registers of meaning.

The polysensory encounters in art unfold not as a chronology but as a force field where senses intermingle and reconfigure each other. From antiquity's synaesthetic imaginaries – the 'harmony of the spheres' – to the Gothic and Baroque staging of light, music, and architecture, perception has been cultivated as excess,

165. Steven Feld and Keith H. Basso, *Senses of Place* (University of New Mexico Press, 1996); see also Steven Feld and Katell Morand, 'Representing the Poetics of Place: A Conversation with Steven Feld', *Éc(h)opoétiques* 87 (2020): 89–98; David Howes, ed., *Empire of the Senses: The Sensual Culture Reader* (Berg, 2005).

166. Robin Wall Kimmerer, *Braiding Sweetgrass* (Milkweed Editions, 2014).

167. Tyson Yunkaporta, *Sand Talk: How Indigenous Thinking Can Save the World* (The Text Publishing Company, 2023).

as immersion, and has prepared the ground for the vision of the *Gesamtkunstwerk*, inscribed with this longing for convergence.

This term made its earliest appearance in German philosophical writer Eusebius Trahndorff's *Ästhetik oder Lehre von der Weltanschauung und Kunst* (Aesthetics or the Doctrine of Worldview and Art; 1827), where it entered discourse as both a concept and a neologism. It was later popularised by the composer Richard Wagner. Yet it was in the ruptures of the avant-gardes – Futurism, Dada, Surrealism – that ocularcentrism was most provocatively unsettled through noise, touch,[168] and even smell. Fluxus and Happenings carried this further, dissolving the separation between the senses and spectators, choreographing participation as a political gesture. Today, installation and performance art are extending these gestures towards ecological and relational sensibilities, distributing perception across humans and other-than-humans, across bodies, environments, and technologies. To trace transversal polysensory encounters across epochs is to sense art as a vibrant, generative ecology where touch, sound, smell, vision, and movement interlace – a choreography of perception itself, perpetually becoming.

Polysensory encounters in art challenge conventional spectatorship by making sensory engagement explicit, relational, and participatory. They encourage us to reconsider the boundaries between subject and environment, human and other-than-human agencies.

However, working through polysensory encounters demands multimodal methodologies capable of capturing the complexity of sensory interplay. Though its complexity is beyond our current understanding, we still need to commit to dealing with and attempting to expand on what we know so far in accordance with the methods we have developed. Traditional research methods that prioritise verbal articulation or visual documentation risk occluding the embodied and affective dimensions of polysensory experience. Thus, embodied methods such as sensory mapping, participatory observation, and affective ethnography, alongside micro-phenomenological interviews, offer promising avenues for engaging with polysensory phenomena. However, I am critically aware of the potential for sensory reductionism and self-indulgence. Especially in the face of harsh realities like the current contexts of socio-political crisis, war, and climate catastrophe, I believe it is urgently necessary to engage in a deep practice of embodied research to explore what choreo-ethical assemblages could mean. Polysensory encounters call for reflexivity regarding the researcher's own sensory positioning and the power dynamics inherent in sensory regimes.[169] This includes interrogating how senses are validated or marginalised within specific cultural and institutional contexts.

Recent theoretical frameworks such as post-humanism and new materialism have further expanded the significance of polysensory encounters by decentring the human subject and recognising the agency of other-than-human actors

168. My two favourites, which have been acknowledged as relevant reflections on touch, are Constance Classen, *The Deepest Sense: A Cultural History of Touch* (University of Illinois Press, 2012); and Erin Manning, *Politics of Touch: Sense, Movement, Sovereignty* (University of Minnesota Press, 2007).

169. I find Pauline Oliveros' reflections on values, power, and the senses deeply thought-provoking. Pauline Oliveros, *Quantum Listening* (Spiral House Editions, 2024), 8–15.

and environments. Within the context of choreo-ethical assemblages, polysensory encounters become sites where boundaries between human and non-human, subject and object, animate and inanimate blur.

This ontological reconfiguration resonates with the concept of *sympoiesis* (making-with) that I introduced earlier (→ Sympoiesis, 123), which emphasises collaborative and entangled processes of becoming. In this light, polysensory encounters are not simply human experiences but co-constituted events involving multispecies, technological, and œkological agencies.

My embodied research into choreo-ethical assemblages invited a radical rethinking of perception, knowledge, and embodiment. By acknowledging the multiplicity and interdependence of sensory modalities, polysensory encounters open up new horizons for ethical and aesthetic engagement with the world. Ethically, they call for greater attention to be paid to sensory diversity and the inclusion of marginalised sensory experiences. Aesthetically, they encourage innovative practices that expand the sensory palette and foster more inclusive and immersive modes of encounter.

In sum, polysensory encounters constitute a crucial paradigm for contemporary research in performance practice as I seek to move beyond sensory reductionism, embrace complexity, and honour the full spectrum of embodied experience across agencies with the practice of choreo-ethical assemblage. Paying attention to practices and breath work, I tune into my body and dance with all my senses alert, *open to experiencing* the *complexity of the encounter* between myself as a body and as space. I practice to feel both at the same time – the mesmerising *inner spaciousness* and the instigating *outer set-up*. In collaboration with Walter Lauter, I created what I call a *choreographic environment*, specifically designed for these encounters, which formed a crucial part of the diffractive dialogues and the emergence of choreo-ethical assemblages. The practice is demanding, at times hypnotic, as I deeply tune into being with all agencies and presences – my *own* and the *others* and the *other others*. Precariousness,[170] the vulnerability of living beings and a condition of play, precedes the framing, while a prepared environment[171] maintains the framework and somewhat tames contingencies. Taming contingencies for me means the slow and consistent process of building trust into the situation of the encounter. I remember the story of the Little Prince meeting the fox in Antoine de Saint-Exupéry's narrative,[172] a courageous and heartfelt commitment to the process of befriending the stranger.

Polyvalent Performances

Polyvalence in performance unfolds as a multiplicity of semantic, sensorial, and relational potentials cohabiting within a singular aesthetic event, which consequently has ethical and political significance. Rather than aligning with univocality, which

170. Judith Butler, *Precarious Life: The Powers of Mourning and Violence* (Verso, 2006).

171. Emmi Pikler, *Friedliche Babys – zufriedene Mütter* (Kösel, 1982).

172. Antoine de Saint-Exupéry, *The Little Prince*, trans. Katherine Woods (Farshore, 2023).

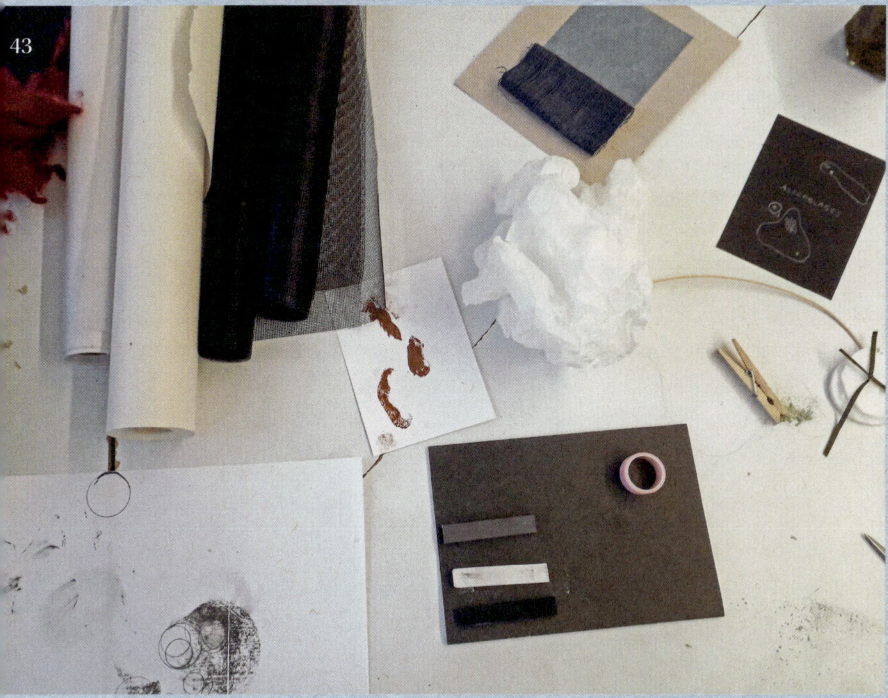

Arrangements

Arrangements are the birth of the space
between things and shadows,
between stance and rule.
They begin as touch,
fingers nudging a circle,
choreographing a reading of material and space.

Patience negotiates sweat.
Marriages are arranged and forgotten,
the right of freedom of movement.
The pulling and pushing about of bodies,
objects and abjects,
coils views of life across biographies.

Negotiating the gravity of affect
and ties to one's habitat
by following the call of where you want to die.
A place for each thing, a honey for each spoon,
lining things up for no reason it seems,
still, a polylogic persists.

Their positions loosen again, reshuffling the pack.
In the lean of a wall,
in the way power sits closer,
they promise reframing.
Their orientation pauses for a moment,
before they turn again.
Rules forgetting their edge.
To rearrange is to risk relation:
hands crossing, plans crossed.
On the map something slips, something holds.
The environment exhales,
the order becomes generous.
We stand inside its offer, move towards it,
survive repetition and feel
undecided once again.

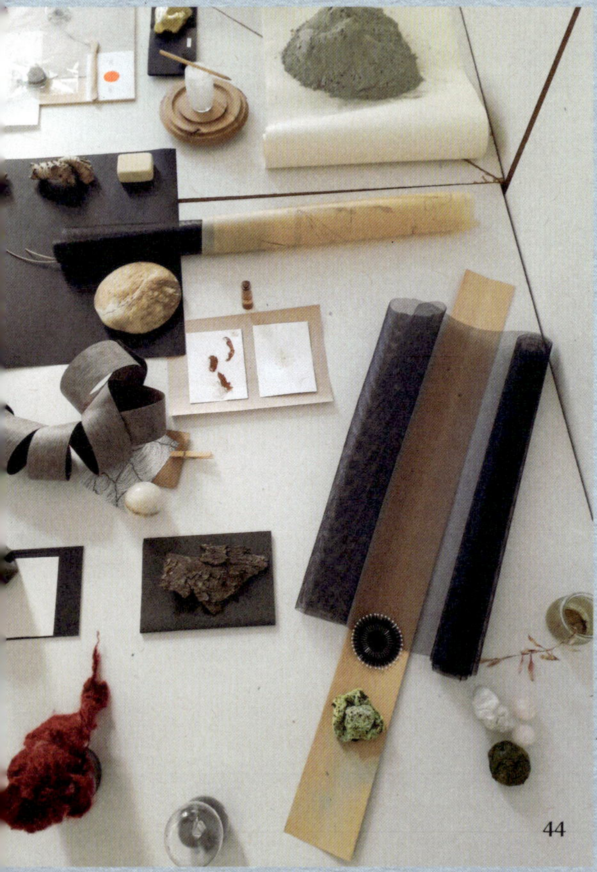

After all, fresh
arrangements will age,
they will crease,
will be misread.
Silence made them,
broke them,
revealed the stories of the
bodies that made them.
How will we arrange our
shared tomorrow?
Which asymmetries will
we decide to mend?

secures meaning through closure, polyvalence operates through openness, maintaining divergent readings, affective registers, and embodied experiences without resolving them into a singular interpretive frame. In the performative field and in the scores developed and tested in the framework of *Choreo-ethical Assemblages*, this manifested as a simultaneity of meaningful and incidental gestures and movements, in which choreographic structures and improvisatory impulses co-existed, enabling shifts in attention, rhythm, and meaning-making in the plural.

Polyvalence resists the binary logic of either/or, instead inhabiting an *and/and* condition in which movements, utterances, and spatial arrangements retain their layered potentialities. Instead of diluting coherence, this multiplicity deepens the work's relational fabric, enabling it to meet each wit(h)ness from a distinct trajectory of engagement. In this way, the performer's body functions as a polysemic agent – an embodied score that oscillates between precision and indeterminacy, inviting wit(h)nesses into a participatory act of reading the performative situation.

From a dramaturgical perspective, polyvalence activates what might be termed a 'relational elasticity', in which the work can stretch to accommodate contrasting, even contradictory, readings while maintaining its integrity. This elasticity is not arbitrary; it is choreographed through attentiveness to thresholds – between movement and stillness,[173] intention and accident, presence and withdrawal.[174] The polyvalent performance thus becomes a site of co-production, where meaning is neither fixed by the maker nor passively received by the spectator, but continually renegotiated in the porous space between them. In this sense, polyvalence is less a strategy than a mode of being-with, attuned to the generative tensions of multiplicity.

This mode of being-with is dependent on attunement to the moment with full presence – which is elaborated in psychotherapy as '[c]ultivating presence and engaging in present-centered relationships'.[175] Psychologist, musicologist, and health science researcher Shari Geller and psychiatrist Stephen Porges, who proposed polyvagal theory[176] in 1994, discuss the impact of the vagus nerve in relation

173. Stillness can refer to both physical and mental states. And even if we know that there is an ongoing multitude of processes happening within the body, the German *Stille* refers to a state of peace, tranquillity, or calm, maybe clarity of mind, and spiritual growth.

174. In 2020, during the pandemic lockdowns, I was invited to contribute to the INTRA project *Withdrawing the Performer*, led by performers Charlotta Ruth and Jasmin Schaitl in collaboration with dancer and neuroscientist Imani Rameses. See https://www.dieangewandte.at/jart/prj3/angewandte-2016/main.jart?rel=en&reserve-mode=active&content-id=1609322325777&projekt_id=1609322330666. In the labs, I had an opportunity to discuss and experiment with the framing of performance situations and the withdrawal of the performer, together with collaborating dialogue partners Philipp J. Ehmann, Nikolaus Gansterer, Margarete Jahrmann, Dennis Johnson, Anne Juren, Krõõt Juurak, Christian Schröder, and Lucie Strecker.

175. Shari M. Geller and Stephen W. Porges, 'Therapeutic Presence: Neurophysiological Mechanisms Mediating Feeling Safe in Therapeutic Relationships', *Journal of Psychotherapy Integration* 24 (2014): 178.

176. Stephen Porges proposed that the vagus is not a single, uniform system but has multiple evolutionary layers of organisation with distinct physiological and behavioural implications. In his model, the 'dorsal vagal complex' (phylogenetically older, unmyelinated fibres) is linked to immobilisation and shutdown responses. The 'ventral vagal complex' (newer, myelinated fibres from the *nucleus ambiguus*) supports social engagement, affects regulation, and calms parasympathetic states. Together with sympathetic activation, the dorsal and ventral vagus nerves form a *hierarchy* of autonomic responses and compose a dynamic modulation.

to attuned presence and resonance in encounters. When we collaborated on the project 'Passenger Diaires', philosopher and colleague Kath T. Zakravsky once argued that anatomical knowledge is completely overrated. I disagree and find, on the contrary, that understanding the very materiality of the inner body in its entangling of emotions, movements, drives and inputs is highly relevant and inspiring.[177] In his – admittedly still widely criticised and disputed – polyvagal theory, Porges argues that the cranial *nervus vagus*, predominantly known for its parasympathetic influence on viscera such as the heart and gut, constitutes a central pathway of interoceptive signalling and homeostatic regulation between brain and viscera. Porges and Geller investigate *neuroception* as a process influencing our autonomic nervous system and acting as an adaptive mechanism, and introduce the term 'social engagement system', which I find relevant for my reflections on choreo-ethical performance:

> Through brainstem mechanisms, the phylogenetically newer vagal circuit is also neuroanatomically and neurophysiologically linked to the cranial nerves that regulate the striated muscles of the face and head, which are the primary structures involved in social engagement behaviors. This neuroanatomically based 'face-heart' connection provides mammals with an integrated 'social engagement system' through which vocal prosody and facial expression functionally convey an individual's present physiological state to others.[178]

The multidirectional communication required to recognise and read the psychophysiological presence of others (including *other others* with diverse agencies[179]) influences positionalities and movements, expressions and prosody, creating a significant, facilitative choreo-ethical environment for embodied polysensory assemblages and polyvalent performances.

177. And indeed fantastic. I recommend engaging with Anne Juren's PhD project, 'Fantasmical Anatomies', the written component of which is accessible here https://www.diva-portal.org/smash/get/diva2:1607139/SPIKBLAD03.pdf.

178. Shari M. Geller and Stephen W. Porges, 'Therapeutic Presence: Neurophysiological Mechanisms Mediating Feeling Safe in Therapeutic Relationships', *Journal of Psychotherapy Integration* 24, no. 3 (2014): 178–92.

179. The notion of *other others* comes from the performance lecture *Thinking Matters Other Others – A Translecture*, a collaboration with Nikolaus Gansterer at Tanzquartier Wien (28 November 2014, SCORES N°9). The term designates agencies that elude human-centred frames of perception and call for a choreographic practice attentive to their autonomy. In this sense, matter articulates itself and demands listening organs attuned beyond the human sensorium. In my experience, perception continually reorganises itself in response to such encounters, while responsibility extends to the environments that we co-shape together. At the same time, things themselves emerge as choreographers of human experience and movement, generating reciprocal fields of agency that complicate distinctions between subject and object.

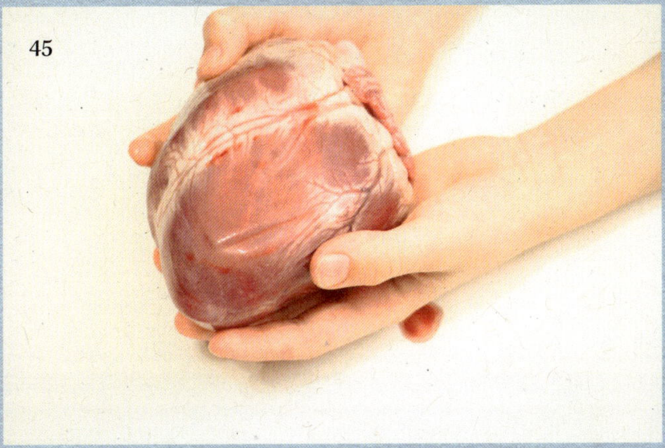

Holding a Heart Tenderly

Walking backwards into the future,
we saw history unfold in front of us.

Retrospectively we see the rotting,
the fruit turned wrinkled,
the time will have floated away like
dandelion parachutes.

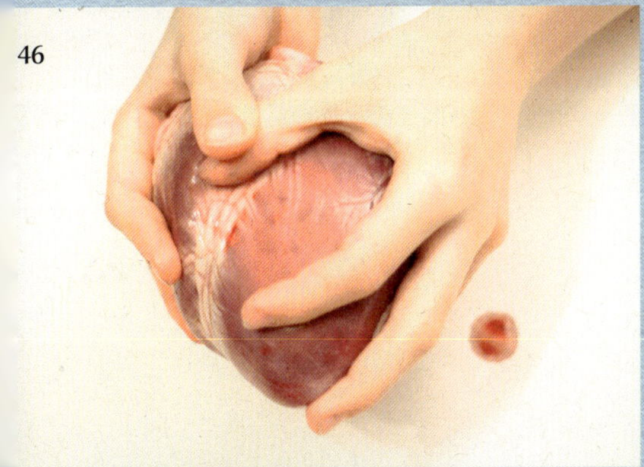

From above, I will
blow the scattered
clouds of sensations
back into your hands,
the hands of a child
holding a heart
tenderly.

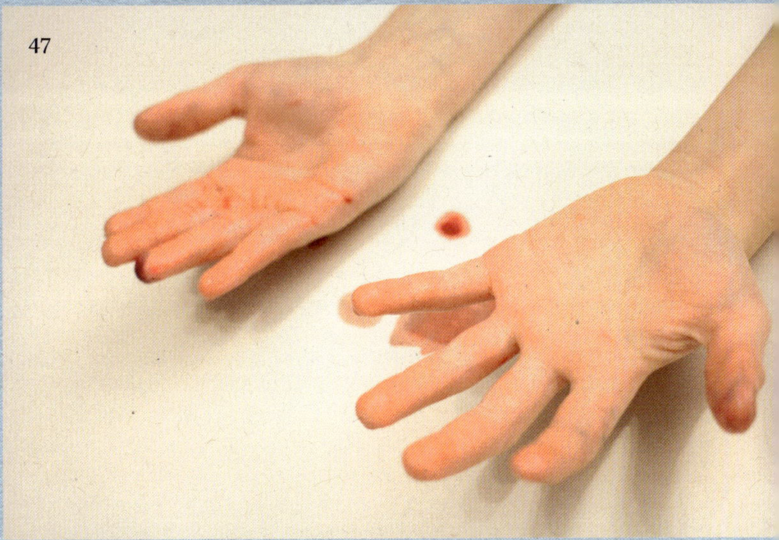

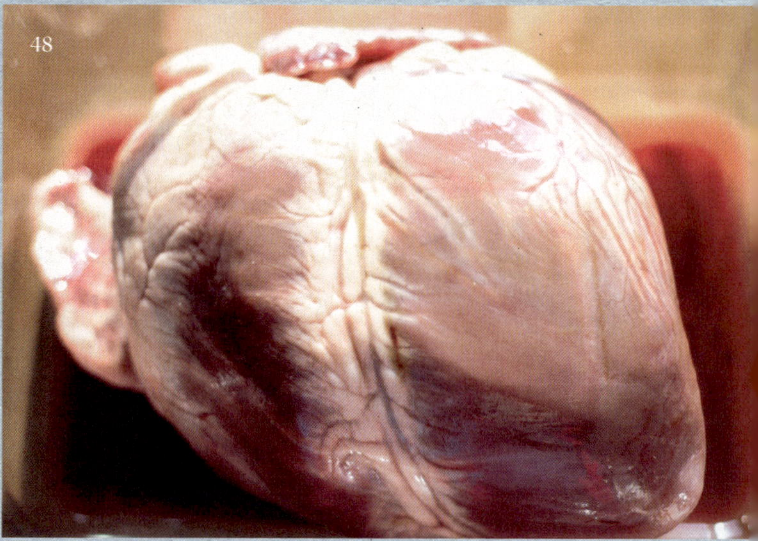

There are different veins and arteries,
the layers of connective tissue.
Within each skin another shiny glaze emerges,
with its fleshy parts
embedded in fluid architecture.
Fascia is always flowing, never arriving,
in constant motion,
an elastic structure of dripping fibres,
textures, temperatures.

Words become breathable membranes.

Polymodern Times

Polymodernity, as theorised by Lene Rachel Andersen, denotes a structural condition of culture: the coexistence, entanglement, and mutual influence of multiple modernities – temporal, cultural, and epistemic – within a shared yet non-unified historical field. It is an analytical and descriptive term, identifying the heterochronic and polycentric nature of contemporary modernity. Polymodernity thus belongs to the register of *conceptual frameworks*, offering a lens through which artistic, political, and social phenomena can be understood in their simultaneity while remaining in a generative tension with each other.

Rejecting the idea of a singular, teleological modernity unfolding along a universal axis, Andersen foregrounds heterochronicity: divergent rhythms of development, persistence, and transformation operating simultaneously within and across sociocultural spheres. This perspective recognises the polyphony of modernist inheritances, where avant-garde experimentation, Enlightenment rationalism, and diverse non-Western trajectories intersect without collapsing into a single narrative of progress.

Within this framework, modernity is not superseded (as in postmodernity) but multiplied – its ideals refracted through plural histories, materialities, and positionalities. Rather than linear evolution or nostalgic revivalism, polymodernity proposes a layered palimpsest on which temporal strata remain visible and legible in their overlapping. As such, it belongs to the register of conceptual frameworks, offering diagnostic and descriptive means with which to grasp artistic, political, and social phenomena in their simultaneity, contradictions, and productive tensions.

By contrast, *polymodern times* function less as a condition and more as a *temporal designation* – a way of naming the lived present as shaped by polymodern dynamics. It emphasises experiential and phenomenological dimensions: how we – as dividual agents, collaborative souls, or collectives – embody artistic practices and inhabit the overlapping, asynchronous temporalities that the term *polymodernity* describes. In this sense, polymodern times are not only the historical moment *produced by* polymodernity but also the perceptual and affective register through which that multiplicity is navigated.

Whereas polymodernity is diagnostic, delineating a meta-structural reality, polymodern times situate us *within* that reality, foregrounding the phenomenology of life and work across multiple modernist inheritances. The former is a theoretical condition; the latter is its temporal experience – an embodied 'now' characterised by simultaneity, relational negotiation, and the constant reweaving of diverse temporal strands.

All in all, the scope, conceptual function, and ontological status of polymodern times differ from their conceptual and terminological predecessor. Polymodernity is the diagnostic condition of multiplied modernities; polymodern times are its embodied temporality – an expanded agora in which diverse inheritances engage in an ongoing, often dissonant, but profoundly generative dialogue.

Polylogic Labs

My research is rooted in post-Judson dance, performance studies with a focus on European contemporary experimental dance, and somatic practices as they were developed mostly in the last century. In the light of this, in my longstanding artistic practice, I investigate an aesthetic and responsive rhetoric of the body in movement – as non-verbal and verbal relational practices (thinking – moving – speaking). Within the framework of the research project, these psychophysical practices met, at times collided, and were negotiated in Polylogic Labs, as I called the events where I met with a dialogue partner in a performative one-on-one-setting within the prepared installation of the choreographic environment, to perform the 'Diffractive Dialogue Score' and/or the 'Dark Bag Score'.

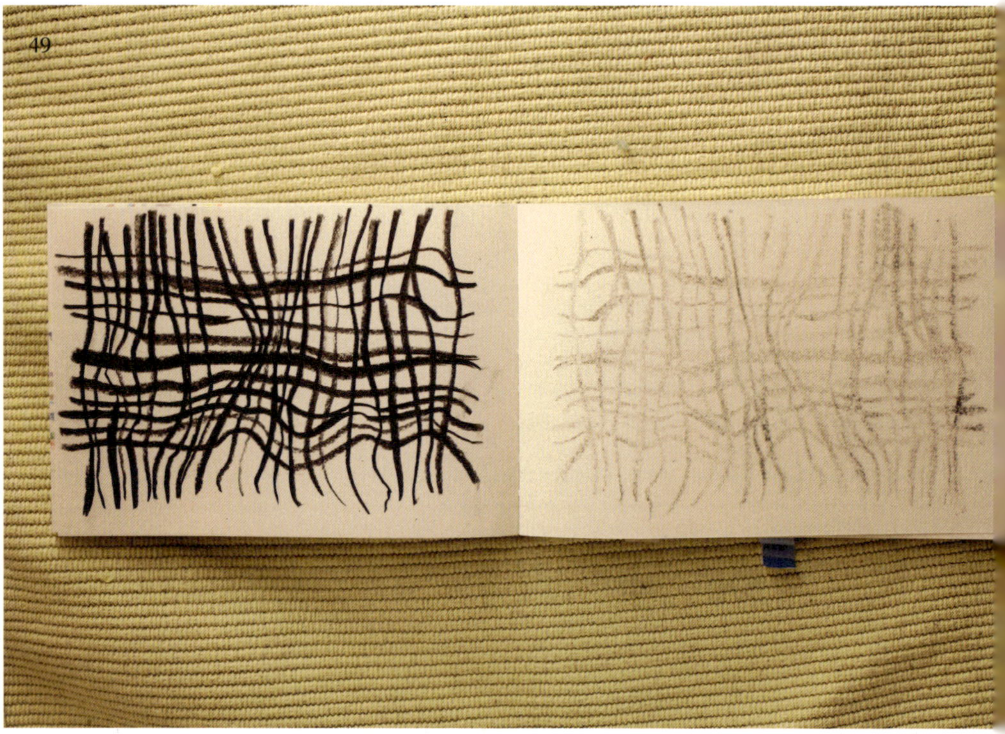

Allow me to translate and develop the metaphor of *weaving* into a performative score structure. In my reworking of this metaphor, the three foundational techniques of logotherapy – Socratic dialogue, paradoxical intention (involving humour), and dereflection – constitute the warp. The weft is formed by the emergent performative and conversational material created with various dialogue partners (human and other-than-human) as transversal movement. These discrete threads achieve cohesion through interdependence, generating a fabric that is simultaneously structural, aesthetic, and functional. Beyond its technical mechanics, weaving exemplifies a relational ontology of matrix (warp) and transversal movements and gestures (weft) – composing a cyclical temporality that combines repetition with incremental difference. Each pass is the same yet not identical, while patterns emerge through sustained variation as temporal, spatial, and material layering that regulates attention through rhythms and processes of attunement. If I may stretch the metaphor a little further, the subtitle of a book on Chinese medicine *The Web*

Fig. 49: *we aver*, 2025, © photo: Mariella Greil.

Knitting Infinity

Knitting stitch by knitting stitch,
the endless strip presents unobtrusively.

The texture of the impossible
performs unexcitedly a loop without edges.
In the softness of the woollen thread,
a murmuring topology: Oikos. Kosmos.

In the heat of the moment,
it is about taking up the thread of the conversation
that is leaning into itself in
unforgetful twists and openings,
through breathing together.

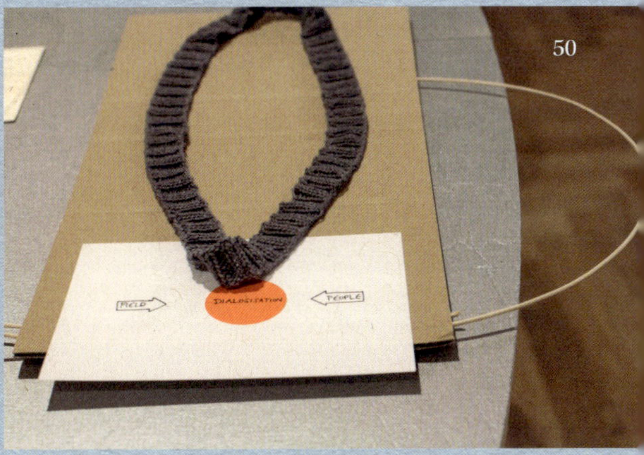

With every stitch, a gentle turn occurs,
dialogisation takes place
between the arrows of people and field.
At this point, a continuous becoming-thread
across I and you,
crafted directions bend time and space,
without breaking.
Instead, the needles have tuned into the humming
of the field,
touching people by their relations
and how they hang together by a thread.

Entangling the here with the now,
these lost threads of an argument
are spinning a gone thought.
The sutures open out into
a web without a weaver
between beings and matters.
Still the wool unwinds.

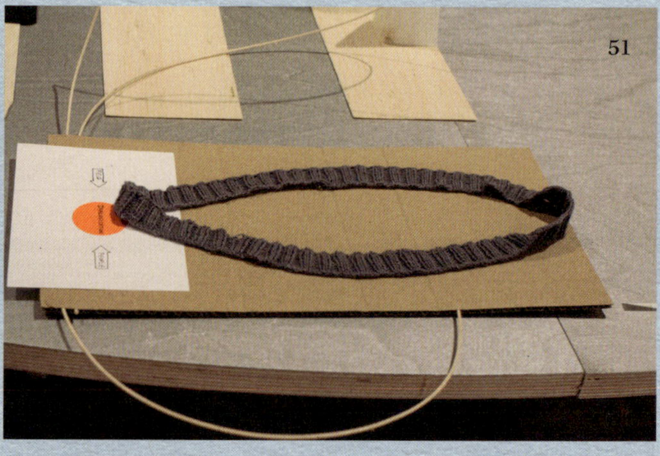

That Has No Weaver comes to mind. Medical researcher Ted Kaptchuk, who is the author of this classic in somatic practice education, chose the metaphor of the *web* due to the interconnectedness of phenomena it represents, pointing out that there is no autonomous weaver behind it. He writes, 'The desire for knowledge is the desire to understand the interrelationships or patterns within that web, and to become attuned to the unfolding dynamic.'[180] This resonates with my research interests, seeking to understand deeper relational and communicative dynamics – which take shape in movement – of what I call choreo-ethical assemblages as well as the cosmopoietic œkology that emerges from them.

I had started out in the early stages of my project with the concept of choreo-logics, which I used as distinct from Joan and Rudolf Benesh's *Choreology* (unhyphenated), which they coined in 1955. Choreology is the aesthetic and scholarly study of all forms of human movement using movement notation. My use of *choreo-logics* (hyphenated and in the plural), however, was etymologically committed to the notion of 'more-than-one' (as in *choreo* or *chorus*), indebted to philosopher, textile artist, and dancer Erin Manning's elaborations,[181] and *logos*, understood in resonance with Viktor Frankl's concept of logotherapy.[182] As the project unfolded, I realised that it was important to acknowledge the abundance (*poly-*) of logics that emerged in the lab. Accordingly, after the first year, I adapted my terminology to refer to Polylogic Labs (instead of Choreo-Logic Labs), which also reflects an openness to emerging embodied and expanded polyvalent practices, and which recognises and commits to *the undisciplinary* as a deliberate methodological node while maintaining an awareness of the gravity and plural rootedness of choreographic research.

Despite various shifts and necessary tunings throughout the project – due to its methodological evolution but also the pandemic working conditions during lockdowns – my research was concerned with giving tangible articulation to (previously untold) narrations from a diverse range of bare bodies[183] and worked with the articulations, actualisations, and contaminations of *embodied knowledges* and *expanded choreographies* through undisciplinary methodological formats that emerged in Polylogic Labs, publications, and presentations.

Another quite significant shift took place in the wake of my explorations of the nature of 'singularities'[184] generated through choreographic practices and

180. Ted Kaptchuk, *Chinese Medicine: The Web That Has No Weaver* (NTC Contemporary Publishing Group, 2000), 15.

181. Erin Manning, *Always More Than One: Individuation's Dance* (Duke University Press, 2013).

182. Viktor Frankl, *Man's Search for Meaning: An Introduction to Logotherapy*, trans. Ilse Lasch (Beacon, 2006); originally published in German as *... trotzdem Ja zum Leben sagen: Ein Psychologe erlebt das Konzentrationslager* (Verlag für Jugend und Volk, 1946).

183. Based on the rich field of practice as research undertaken within the scope of my doctoral dissertation with the title 'Being in Contact: Encountering A Bare Body' (University of Roehampton, 2019), this enquiry is thematically a practice – as – research project that further develops the notion of the *bare body* proposed in my dissertation. See Mariella Greil, *Being in Contact: Encountering A Bare Body* (Edition Angewandte, De Gruyter, 2021).

184. André Lepecki, *Singularities: Dance in the Age of Performance* (Routledge, 2016).

choreo-somatics, which share 'spectral forces of eventness'[185] with immanent political and ethical forces, emerging specifically where meetings, collisions, and generative resistances occur between people, but also between fields of practice. Performance, philosophy, and therapy have a long-standing, uneasy relationship with each other, which is why it seemed temptingly promising to bring them together and closely investigate their interrelatedness.

Through shared personal practices and the development of the collaborative Polylogic Labs, my research project attempted to find ways to better understand and make tangible processes of baring and concealing within the various choreographies of embodied or expanded practices. A particular focus was directed at areas of overlap within the three research areas (performance, philosophy, and therapy), forming around the nodes of hands-on approaches, transmissions, documentation, and their immanent ethical and epistemological concerns. While performing movement and sound, or drawing and writing, the main interest was to assert the epistemological significance of these foremost (for different reasons) undisclosed aspects of a performer's / philosopher's / therapist's epistemic work – a call for the exchange of views and a prompt for articulation in diffractive dialogues.

I conceptualised the Polylogic Lab as a space for diffractive dialogue and courageous experimentation. It was the core methodological framework of my project – a dedicated allotment of space, time, and *energeia.* Following Aristotle, *energeia* is 'the principal to realise potentiality' or, as translator Joe Sachs renders it, 'being-at-work'. Sachs says that 'we might construct the word *is-at-work-ness*[186] from Anglo-Saxon roots to translate *energeia* into English'.[187] I came together physically with each invited guest in the studio space to engage in dialogue, practicing thinking-moving-understanding relationally and uncovering *poly* (many) *logics* (meanings). Each dialogue followed a proposed score to discuss and develop sharable forms of practice-as-research conversations – both non-verbally and verbally.

Four intensives with choreographer Evfa Lilja, writer-artist Emma Cocker, myoreflex therapist and somatic movement educator Kerstin Kussmaul, and sound artist Werner Moebius were organised to create inventive working conditions for the project's polylogic research – the Polylogic Labs – where ideas, tools, and methods were conceived, developed, tested, and documented through bespoke *dialogical practice.* Socratic dialogue is a technique applied by logotherapists as a method of listening intently, identifying patterns, and finding (new) meanings for what has been said. The 'Diffractive Dialogue Score' and the 'Dark Bag Score' can

185. Athena Athanasiou states, 'Our earlier conversation speaks to the subversive potentialities of dispossessed subjectivities, the possibility of becoming embodied differently. As we have already discussed, performativity is about a differential and differentiating process of materializing and mattering, which remains uninsured and unanticipated, persistently and interminably susceptible to the spectral forces of eventness. The political challenge is thus to engage with points of contestation that have the potential to hold intelligibility open to what you have called "the political promise of the performative."' Judith Butler and Athena Athanasiou, *Dispossession: The Performative in the Political* (Polity, 2013), 140.

186. Joe Sachs, introduction to *Metaphysics,* by Aristotle, trans. Joe Sachs (Green Lion, 1999), Book 9, 1048a, 30 (emphasis added); see also Joe Sachs, 'Aristotle: Motion', *Internet Encyclopedia of Philosophy,* accessed 13 October 2025, https://iep.utm.edu/aristotle-motion.

187. Ibid.

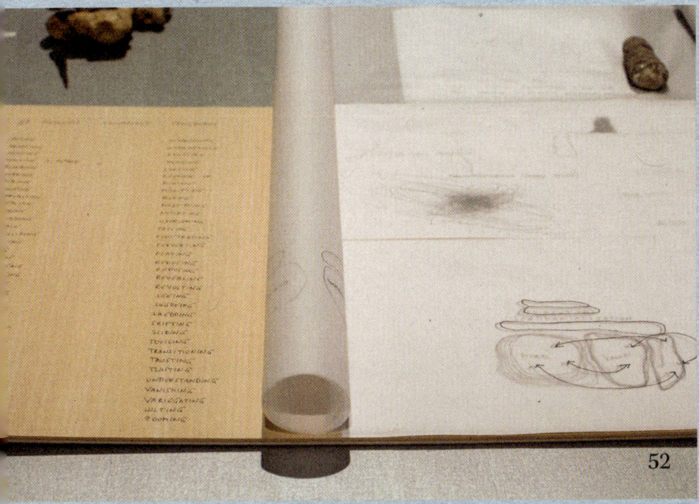

52

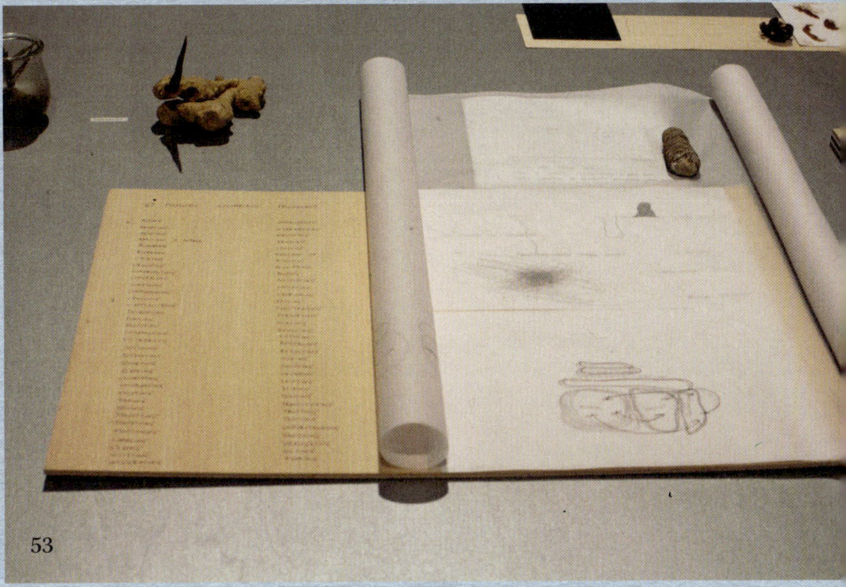

53

69 Polylogic Assem

acting adapting advisi
blending blurring caching
concealing confiding
crystallizing decreasi
disarranging discharging
doubting elapsing enc
existing fading forfeitin
gambling gliding insisting
interweaving knotting kno
mixing modifying movi
overcoming passing penet
reducing refusing reve
segueing shedding sh
transitioning trusting t
vanishing variegati

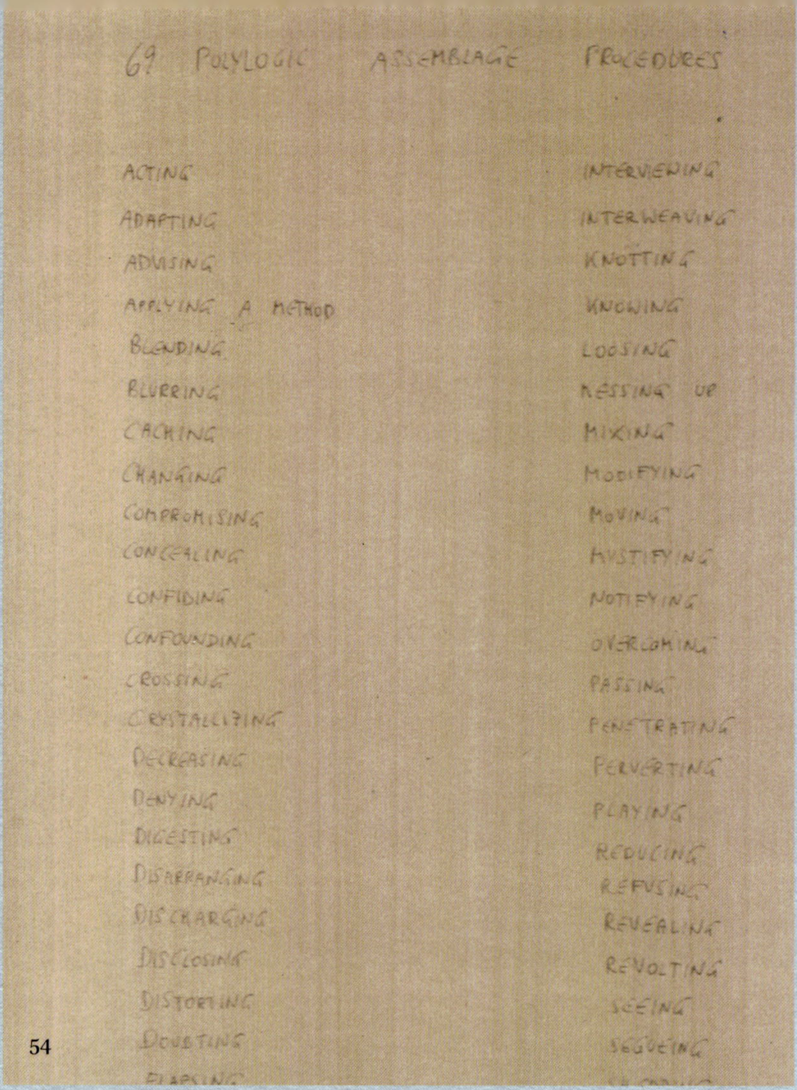

69 POLYLOGIC ASSEMBLAGE PROCEDURES

ACTING
ADAPTING
ADVISING
APPLYING A METHOD
BLENDING
BLURRING
CACHING
CHANGING
COMPROMISING
CONCEALING
CONFIDING
CONFOUNDING
CROSSING
CRYSTALLIZING
DECREASING
DENYING
DIGESTING
DISARRANGING
DISCHARGING
DISCLOSING
DISTORTING
DOUBTING

INTERVIEWING
INTERWEAVING
KNOTTING
KNOWING
LOOSING
MESSING UP
MIXING
MODIFYING
MOVING
MYSTIFYING
NOTIFYING
OVERCOMING
PASSING
PENETRATING
PERVERTING
PLAYING
REDUCING
REFUSING
REVEALING
REVOLTING
SEEING
SEGUEING

nblage Procedures

ing applying a method
g changing compromising
confounding crossing
ing denying digesting
ng disclosing distorting
crypting enigmatizing
ıg forgetting functioning
g integrating interviewing
wing loosening messing up
ing mystifying notifying
trating perverting playing
ealing revolting seeing
ıifting sliding tousling
twisting understanding
ing wilting zooming

enable a focus on *forms of contact*, the development of *narrations* and *polysensory and affective labour of encountering* at the intersections between the performative, philosophical, and therapeutic fields.

The Polylogic Labs functioned as experimental laboratories or relational environments, an intimate zone or simultaneous platform for exchange *and* generative pressure, immersion *and* transfer, deceleration *and* intensity, creating the initial conditions crucial for developing sustained cross-disciplinary, dialogical enquiry. The Polylogic Labs were conceived as the making of a *milieu* for thinking in-and-with practice, a 'making space', or the composing *of* space (and time, potential, and actual *energeia*), dedicated to focusing on the processes of encounter, exploration, and experimentation. These processes unfolded as performances, manifested as narrations of sensorial (bare) bodies, and formed choreo-ethical assemblages.[188] The term *Polylogic Lab* invokes both the facilitating milieu and the actions and movements that take place in that milieu; it describes a 'space of thinking-feeling-understanding', which, as Henk Borgdorff notes, 'creates room for fundamental reflection – a free space to think – in and through artistic practice of creating and performing. [...] there is a real need for this free space for material thinking.'[189] The score was composed of both (nonverbal) material studio-practice dialogues – a tracing of processual movements and a choreography of residues – and (verbal) diffractive, dialogical encounters, infused with micro-phenomenological interviews as well as the collaborative building and interweaving of narrations. Dialogical exchange is a fundamental part of the Polylogic Lab for exploring points of affinity and connectedness (a shared vocabulary and philosophy) in relation to the research questions, for instigating open processes, and for reflecting on related methods and techniques of query, rather than being oriented towards production, resolution, or outcomes.

In the amalgamation of studio, retreat, and research residency, the laboratory follows a polylogic, building on the strength of scores as generative frameworks for explorations within contemporary art and performance. In this context, I engaged in the production of a body of work based on dialogues made of movements, words, and materials together with guest researchers. The collaboratively developed narrations were documented and traced, exposing the working processes of the performative, philosophical, and therapeutic practices in their diffractions.

In *Metaphysics,* Aristotle writes,

When the agent and the patient meet in accordance with the potency in question, the one must act and the other be acted upon;

188. Arno Böhler, 'Sensorial Bodies', in *Choreo-graphic Figures: Deviations from the Line*, ed. Nikolaus Gansterer, Emma Cocker, and Mariella Greil (Edition Angewandte, De Gruyter, 2017).

189. Henk Borgdorff, 'Where Are We Today? The State of the Art in Artistic Research', in *Art and Research*, ed. Janet Rittermann, Gerald Bast, and Jürgen Mittelstraß (Springer, 2011), 67.

but in the former kind of potency this is not necessary, for whereas each single potency of the latter kind is productive of a single effect, those of the former kind are productive of contrary effects, so that one potency will produce at the same time contrary effects (if every potency must act automatically whenever agent and patient meet). But this is impossible. Therefore, there must be some other deciding factor, by which I mean *desire* or *conscious choice*.[190]

In my reading, Aristotle conceives of change (*kinesis*) as involving two poles: *the agent*, who is the one doing and the active source of change bringing a potency into actuality, and *the patient*,[191] the one undergoing, the being (in its double meaning as a noun and a verb) that is changed or affected. This is what supplies the potency, the material possibility for that change. So, the patient is not just passive; they are the seat of potentiality that makes change possible. Without the patient's potential, the agent's act would not have anything to actualise. It is crucial that active and receptive capacity come together in vital relation in order for an action to occur.

In the Polylogic Labs, we were attending to and uncovering decision-making processes and their evolution. Together with my dialogue partners, I explored the dynamics of affective labour, and we formed gyrational points of contact. These encounters closely addressed the intimate process of 'laying bare' within 'thinking-making'.

Resonating with Aristotle's articulation of kinesis as a dynamic between agent and patient, the Polylogic Labs were sites where potency and actuality were continuously negotiated through the medium of collaborative scores. What emerged was neither a simple causal chain nor a linear act of transmission, but rather a recursive choreography in which agency and receptivity were interwoven in polyphonic constellations. The 'deciding factor' that Aristotle attributes to desire or conscious choice found its contemporary articulation here as a collective attunement to relational processes: a polylogic disposition that resisted the closure of univocal outcomes and instead foregrounded the simultaneity of divergent potentials. By cultivating this field of encounter, the laboratory revealed how thinking and making, acting and undergoing transformed into each other and generated an epistemic as well as aesthetic surplus. The work of the Polylogic Labs thus extended

190. Aristotle, *Metaphysics* (Green Lion, 1999), Book 9, 1048a.

191. From Latin *patientem*, 'bearing', 'supporting', 'suffering', 'enduring', 'permitting'. See 'Patient', etymonline, accessed September 23, 2025, https://www.etymonline.com/word/patient.

Aristotelian thought beyond its binary poles by installing multiplicity as an operative condition – where decisions were no longer singular but dispersed, where desire was pluralised, and where potency unfolded through the mutual entanglement of bodies, materials, and discourses. In this way, the laboratory became not only a place of research but a performative and ethical practice of co-actualisation, in which the very structure of potentiality was rendered visible, audible, and tangible.

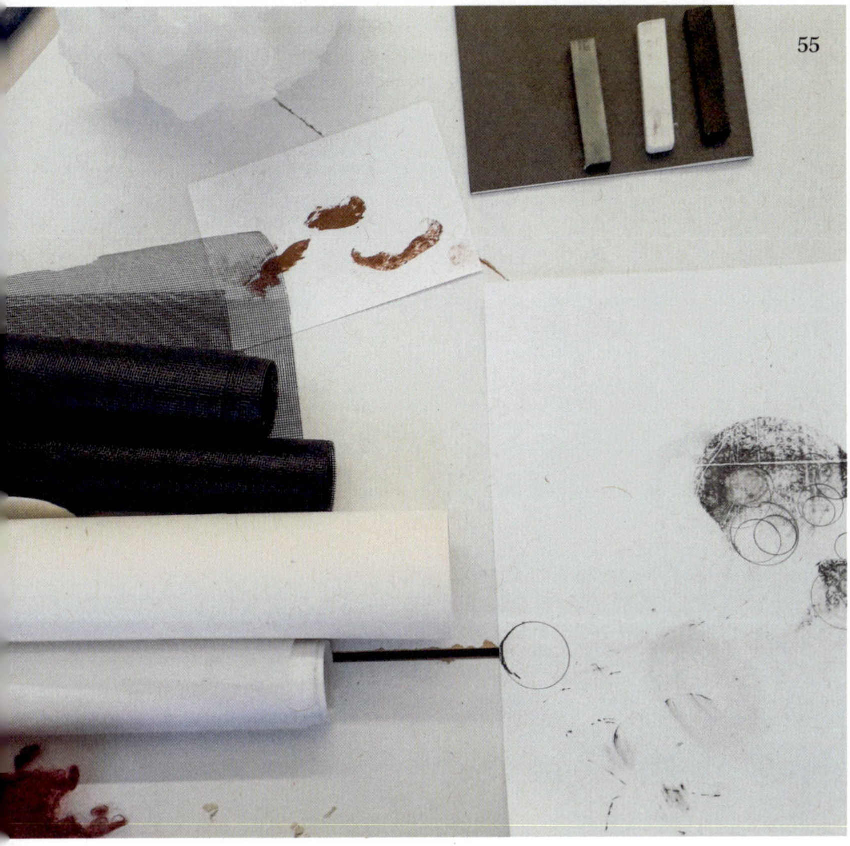

Fig. 55: *Choreo-ethical Assemblage*, 2024, © photo: Mariella Greil.

'...the beautiful carries new possibilities for affective apprehending and produces new artistic effects where aesthetics converges with ethics even beyond the artist's intentions or conscious control. The aesthetic is trauma's transformed affectability in wit(h)nessing in/by art, beyond time and in different sites and spaces, yet it has ethical and even therapeutic consequences. The new healing potential offered by the idea of wit(h)nessing is ethical, yet profoundly aesthetic, or transferred by aesthetic means. Today, the beautiful is that which brings out whatever is able – as object, subject or event – to offer reaffectation-as-redistribution and can absorb traumatic traces of Thing-event, Thing-encounter, and wit(h)ness-Thing, diffracted.'

Bracha L. Ettinger, 'Wit(h)nessing Trauma and the Matrixial Gaze', in *The Matrixial Borderspace*, ed. Brian Massumi (University of Minnesota Press, 2006), 148.

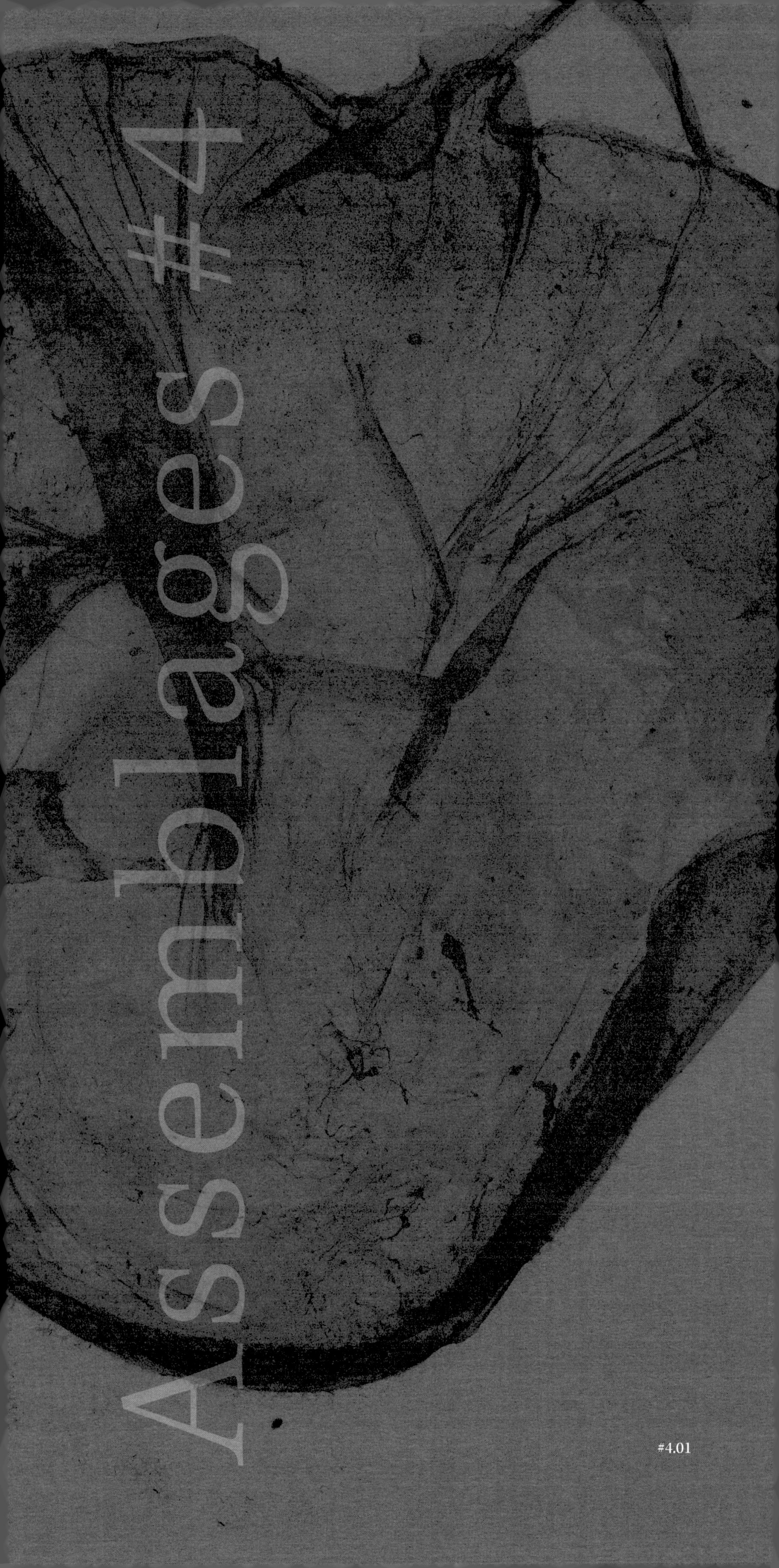

Assemblages #4

#4.01

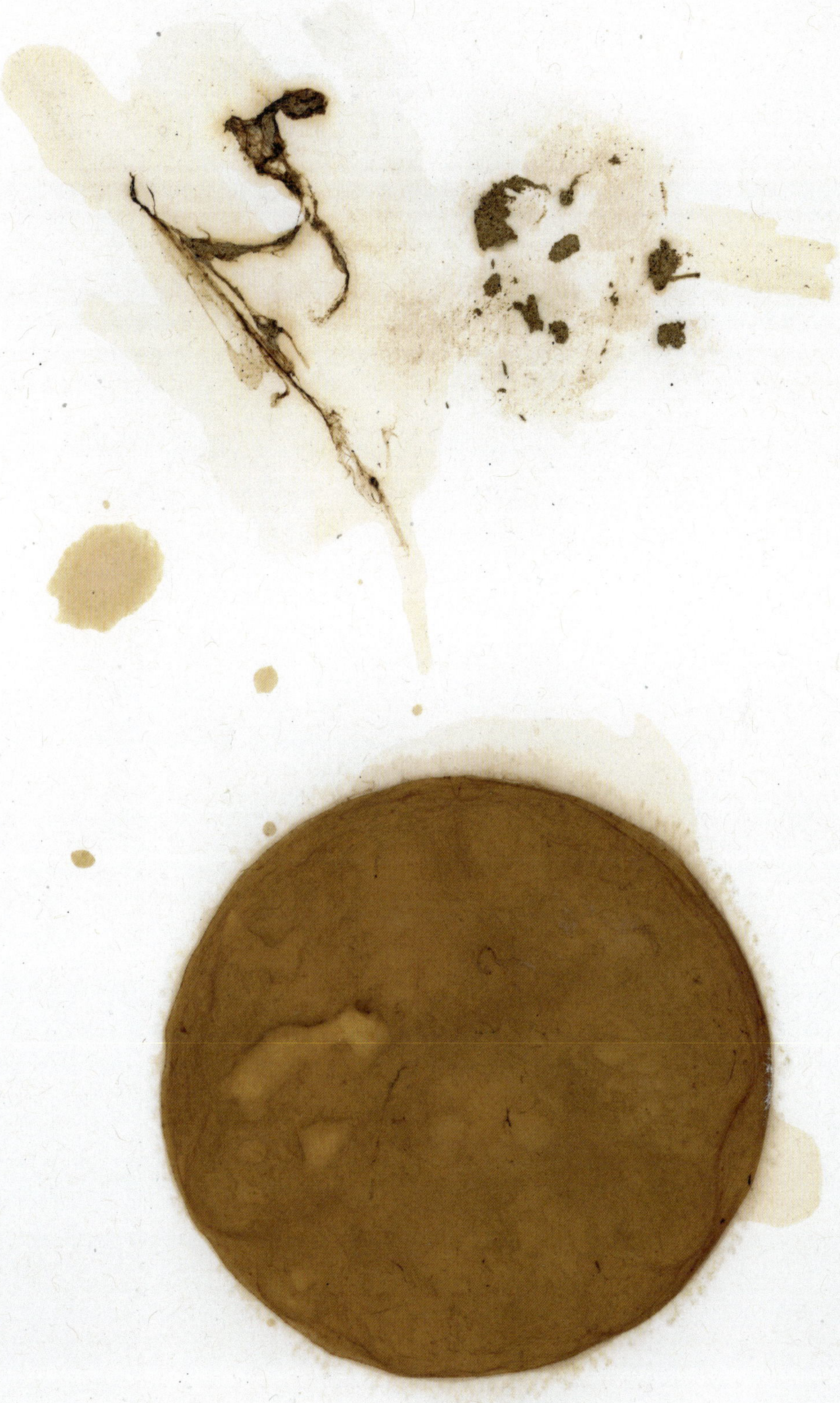

#4.02

#4.03

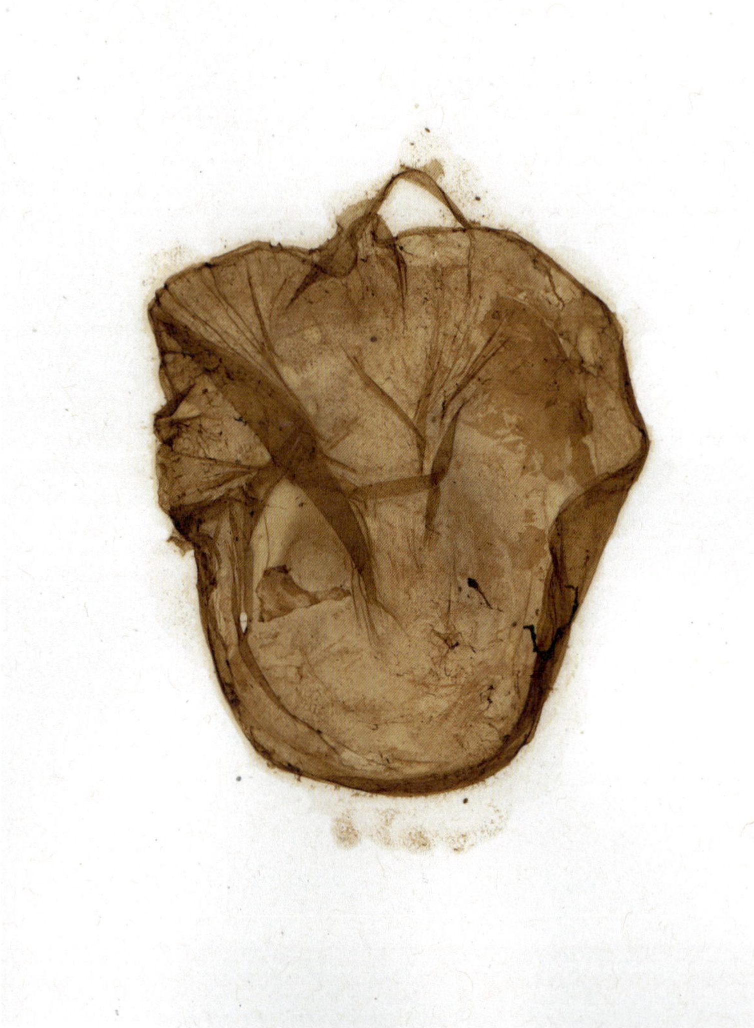

#4.04

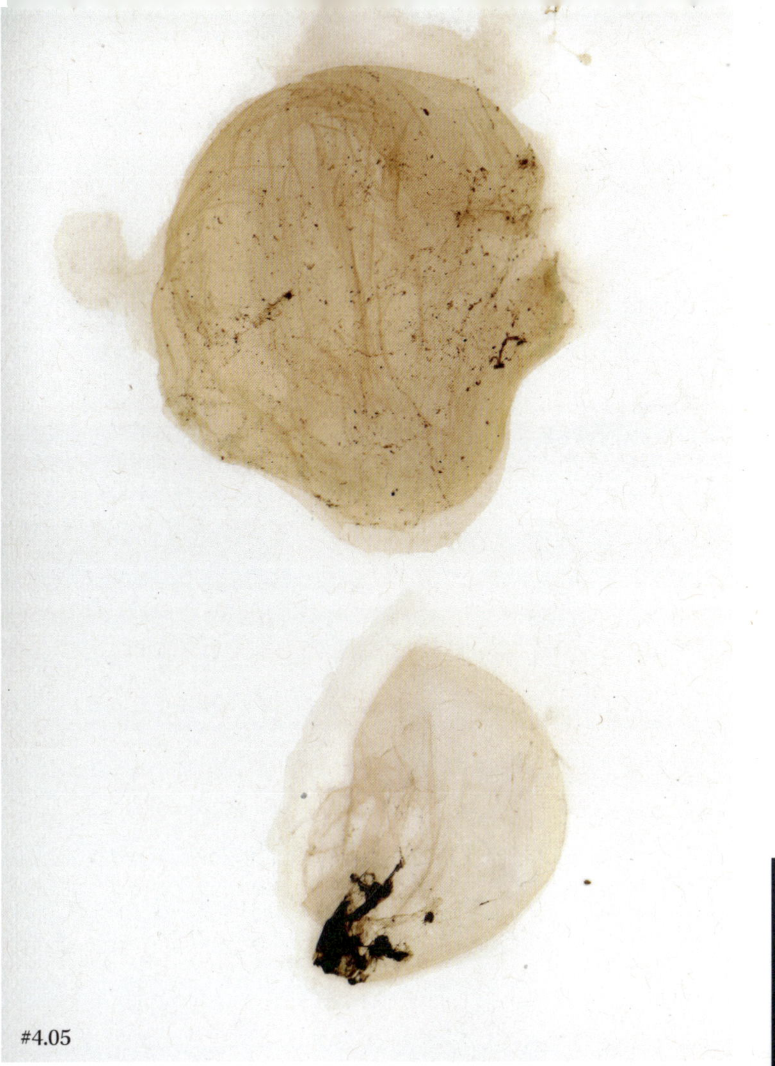

#4.05

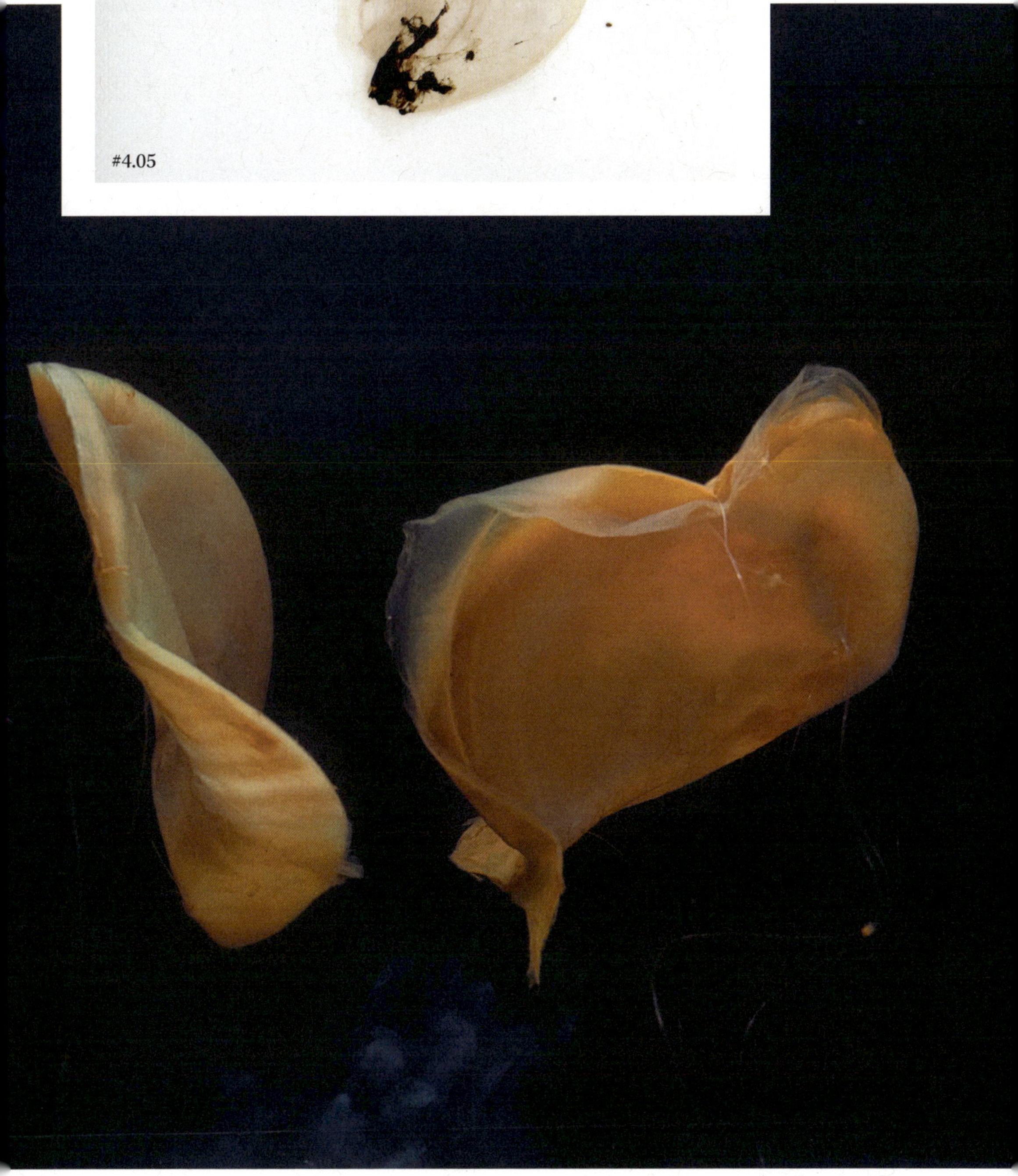

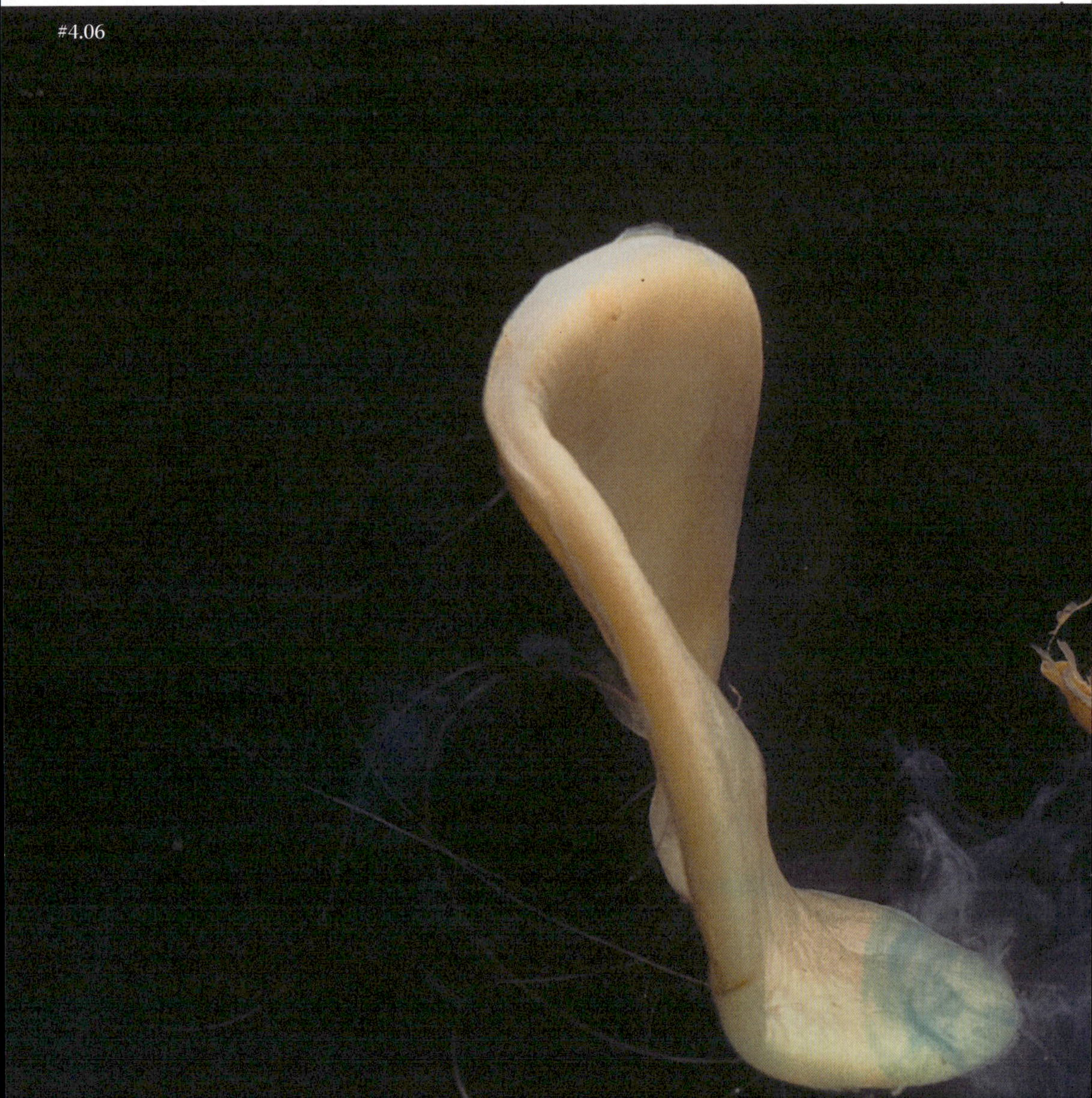
#4.06

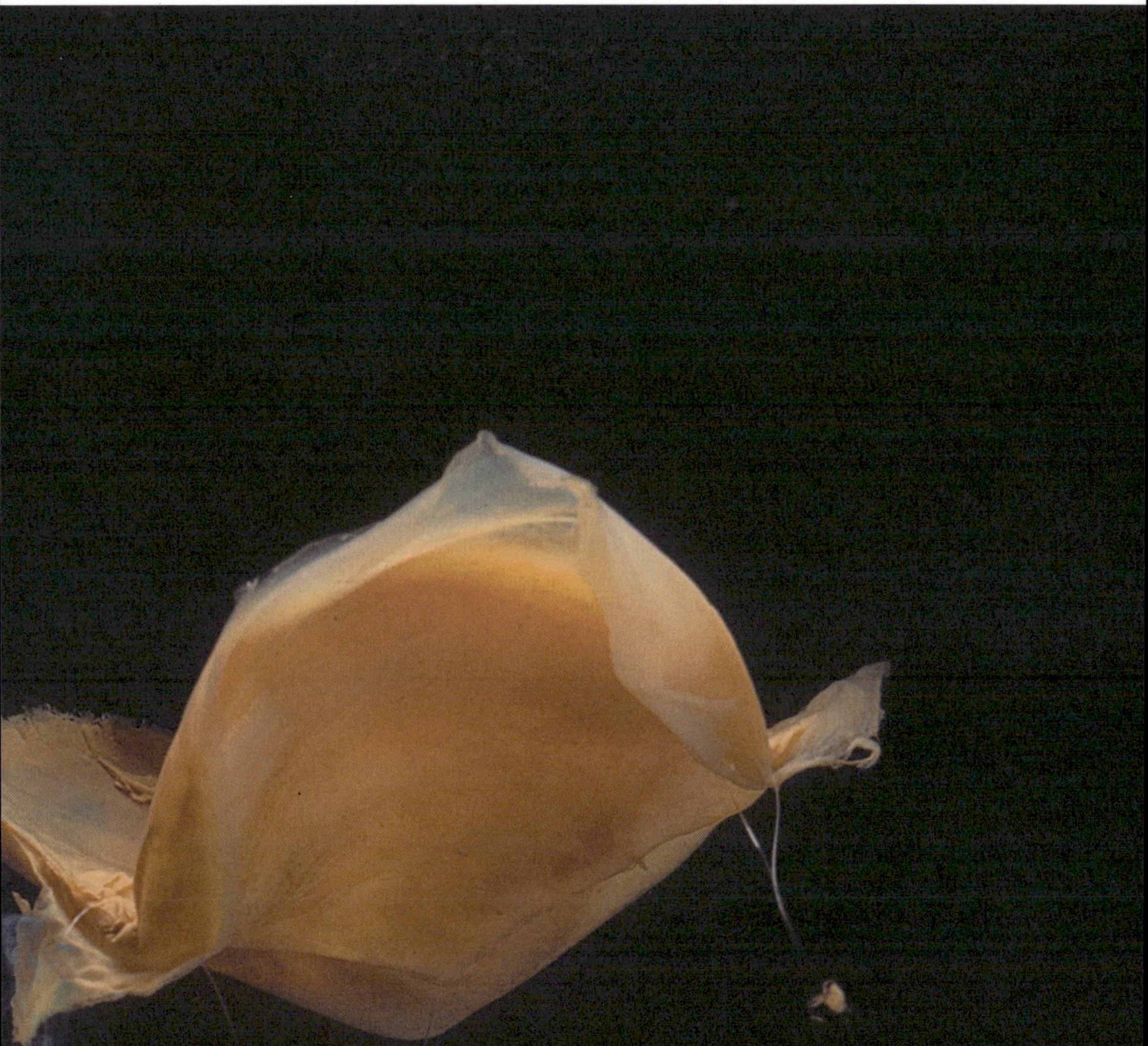

#4.07

#4.08

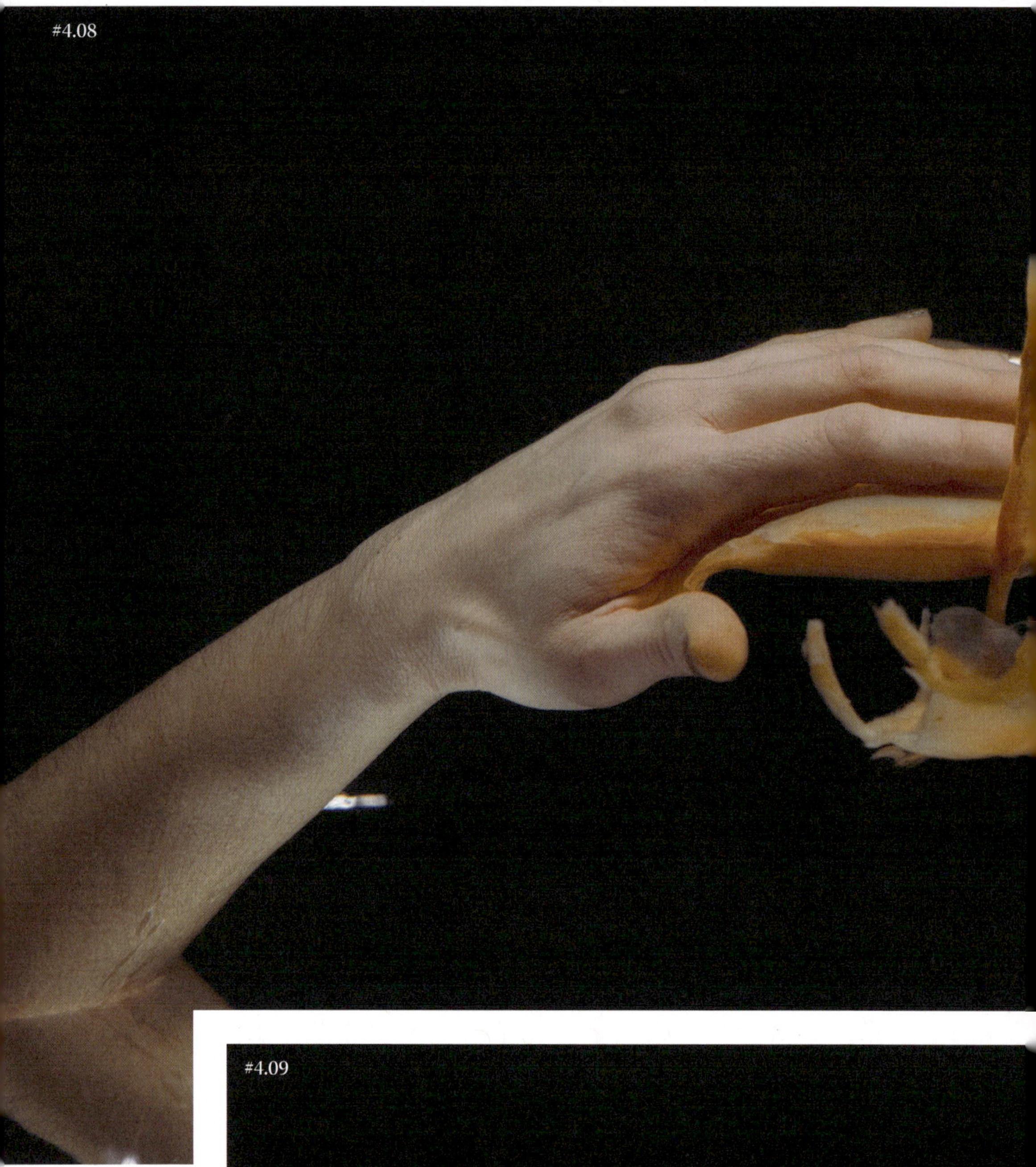

#4.09

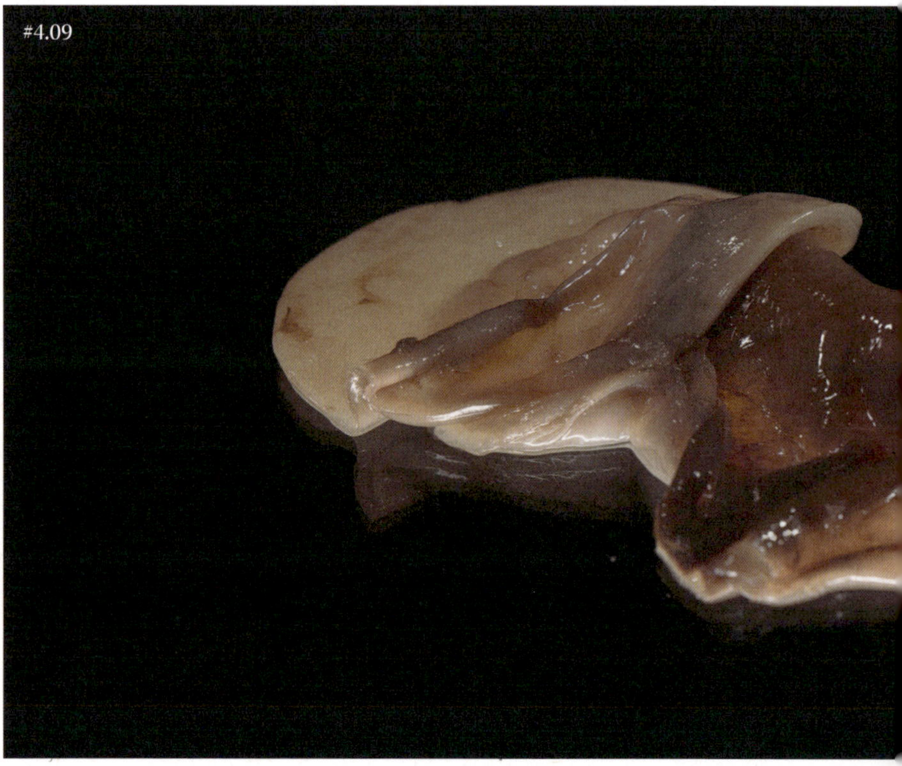

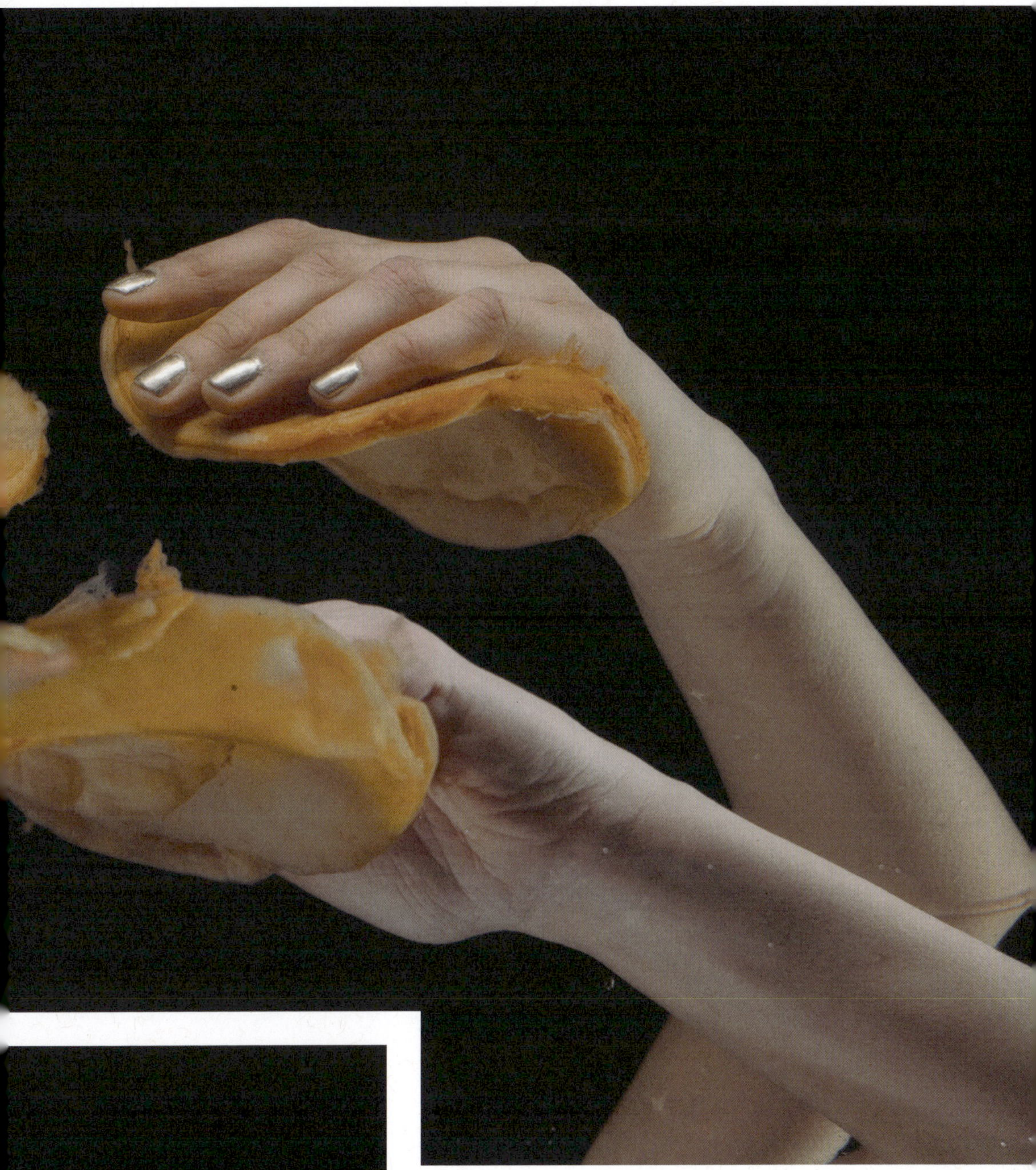

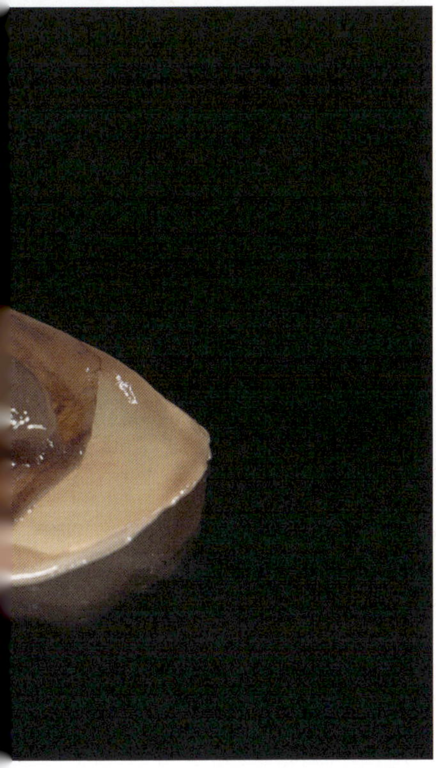

#4.10

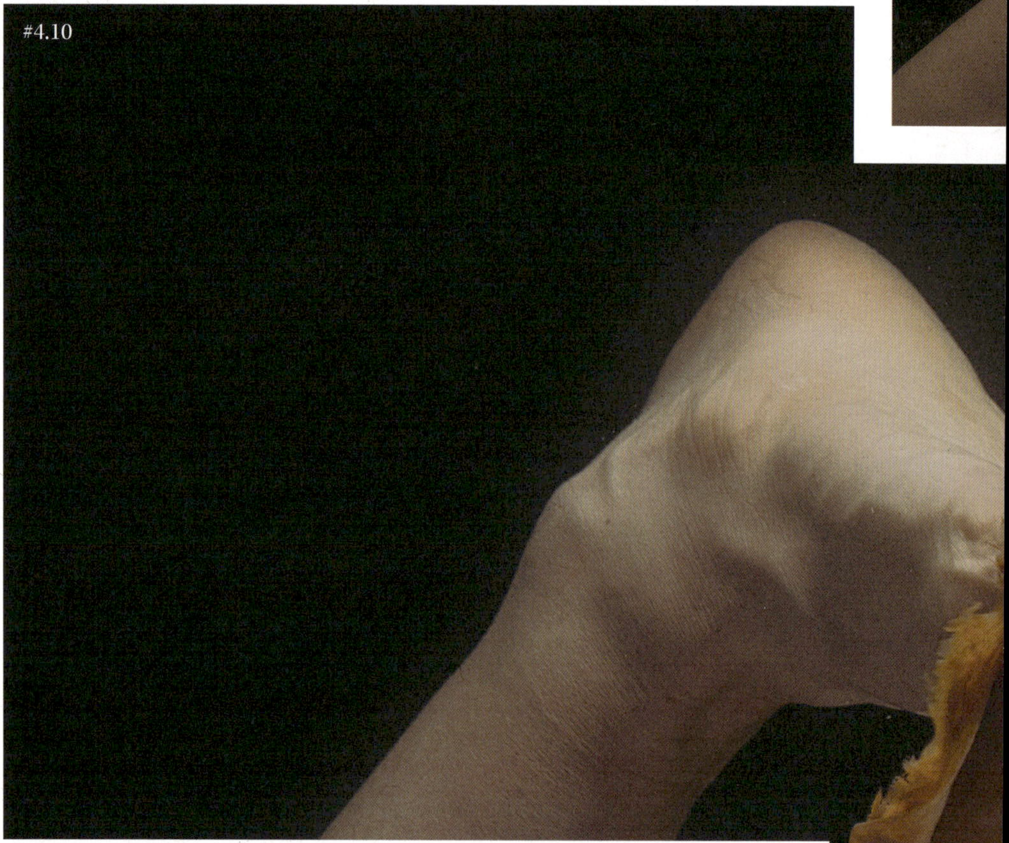

#4.11

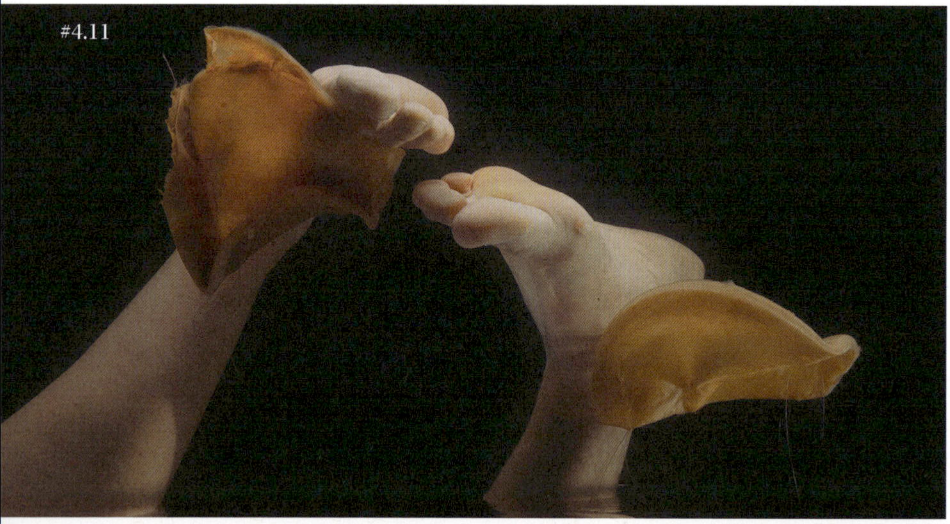

#4.12

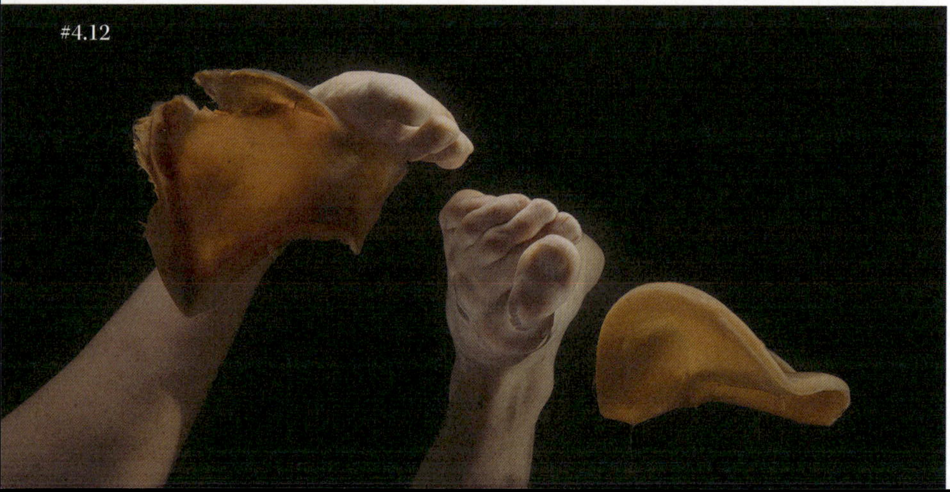

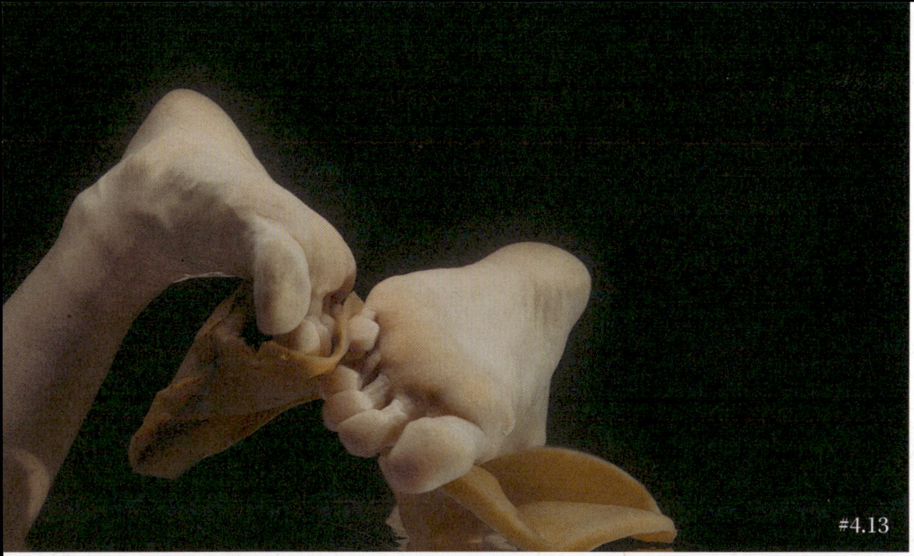

#4.13

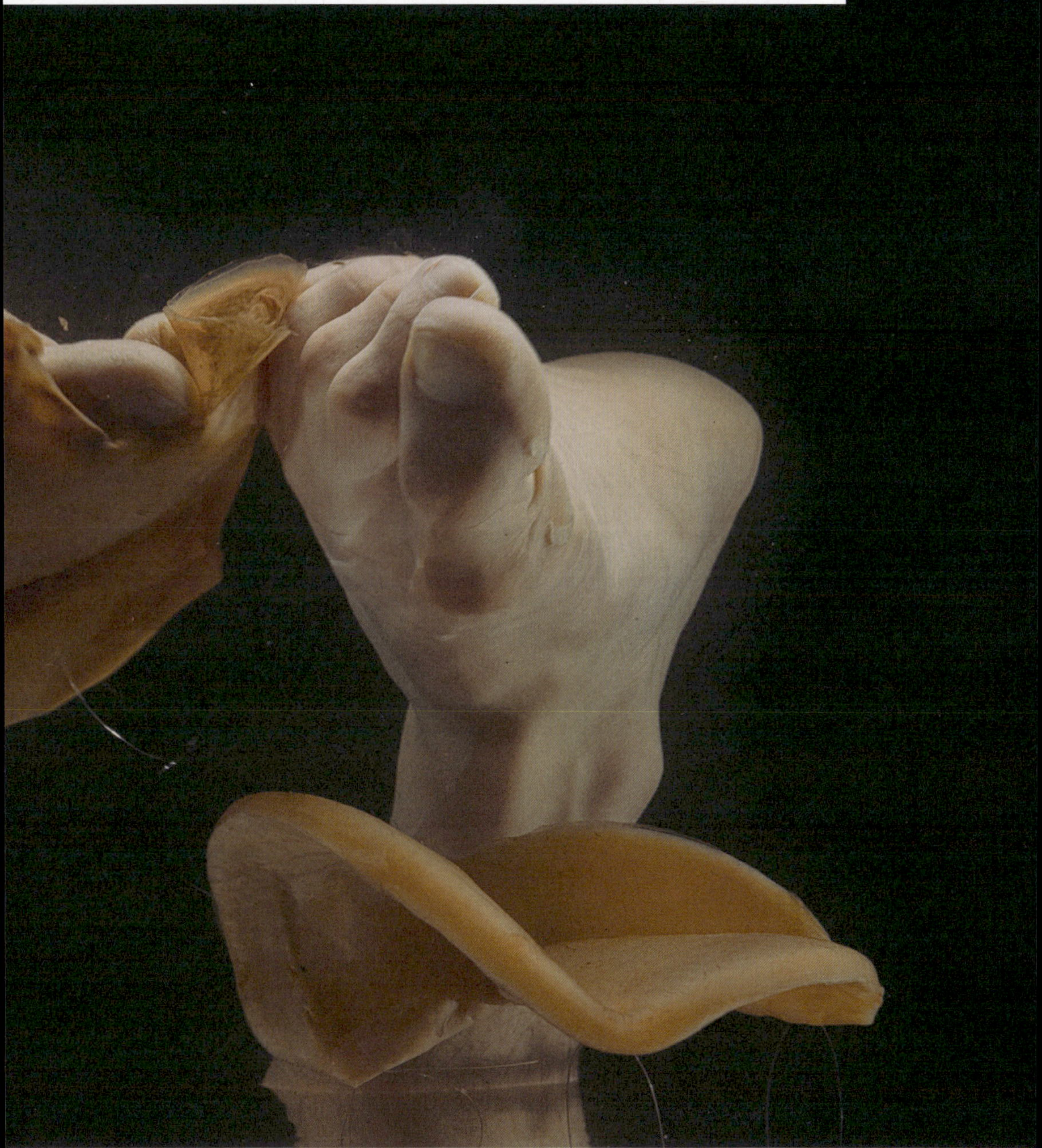

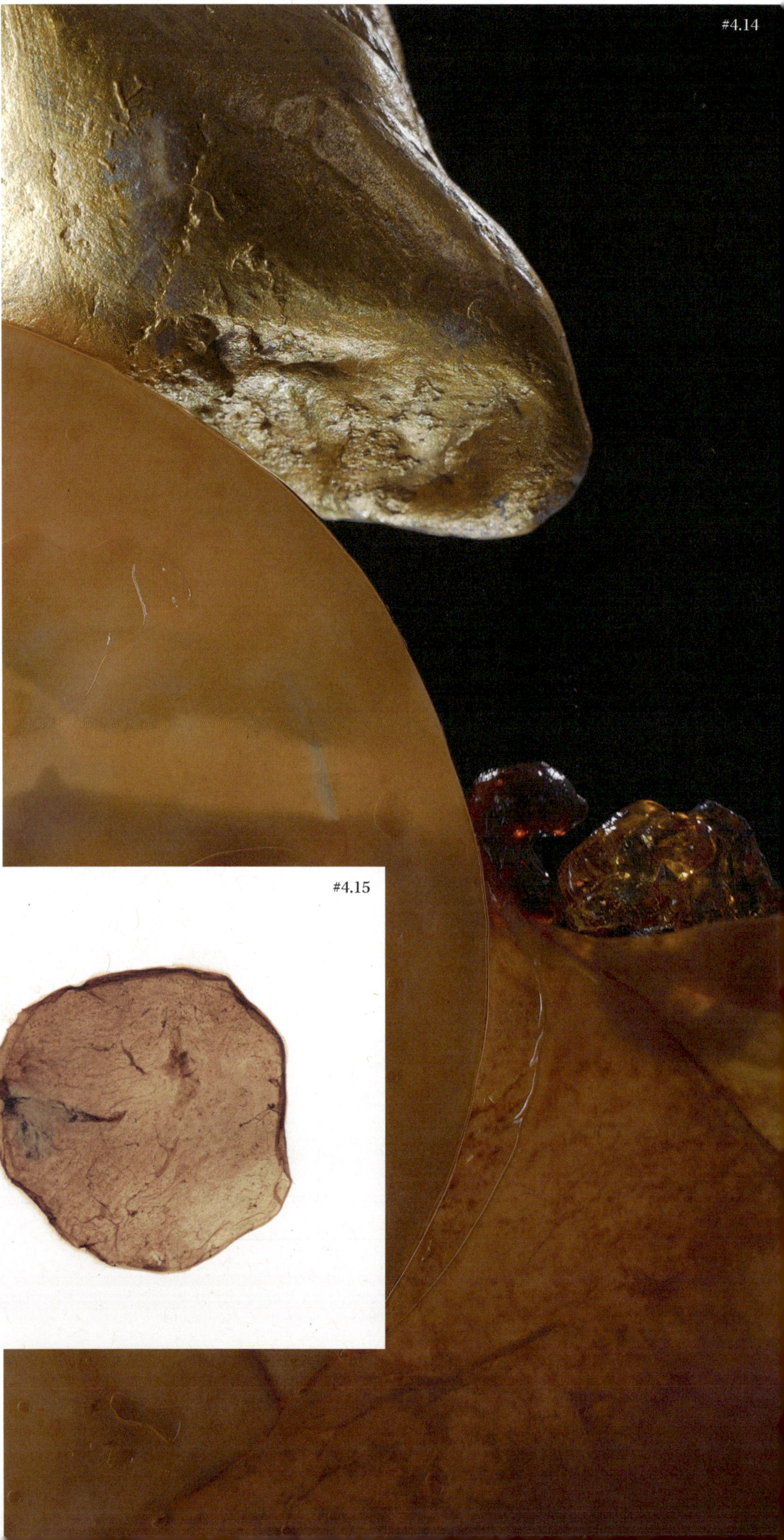

#4.14

#4.15

#4.01–#4.03: *SCOBY (symbiotic culture of bacteria and yeast)*, 2021, © scan: Mariella Greil.

#4.04: *Choreo-ethical Assemblages – Drowning in Depths*, 2025, © video still: Victor Jaschke, performance: SCOBYs, concept: Mariella Greil.

#4.05: *SCOBYs*, 2021, © scan: Mariella Greil.

#4.06: *Choreo-ethical Assemblages – Drowning in Depths*, 2025, © video still: Victor Jaschke, performance: SCOBYs, concept: Mariella Greil.

#4.07: *SCOBYs*, 2021, © scan: Mariella Greil.

#4.08: *Choreo-ethical Assemblages – Drowning in Depth*s, 2025, © video still: Victor Jaschke, performance: Mar Esteban Martin, Mariella Greil, Luisa Pisetta Ravanelli, and SCOBYs, concept: Mariella Greil.

#4.09: *Choreo-ethical Assemblages – Drowning in Depths*, 2025, © video still: Victor Jaschke, performance: SCOBYs, concept: Mariella Greil.

#4.10–#4.13: *Choreo-ethical Assemblages – Drowning in Depths*, 2025, © video still: Victor Jaschke, performance: Mar Esteban Martin, Luisa Pisetta Ravanelli and SCOBYs, concept: Mariella Greil.

#4.14: *Choreo-ethical Assemblages – Drowning in Depths*, 2025, © video still: Victor Jaschke, performance: Mar Esteban Martin, Mariella Greil, Luisa Pisetta Ravanelli, and SCOBYs, concept: Mariella Greil.

#4.15: *SCOBY*, 2021, © scan: Mariella Greil.

Choreo-ethical Assemblages

Choreo-ethical assemblage is the core concept that this chapter will unravel in relation to my research project, bringing two terms[192] together: the neologism *choreo-ethics* and *assemblages*, the latter a now established concept that philosopher Gilles Deleuze and psychoanalyst Félix Guattari developed in the 1980s.[193] The three components of this compound construction are *choreo* (more than one), *ethics* (disposition and characteristic spirit, principles and practices of a time and place), and assemblage (an act of coming together). By way of brief explanation: *choreo* refers to the chorus, to the many, or, as Walt Whitman puts it in *Leaves of Grass*, to the idea that 'I contain multitudes'.[194] *Choreo* – as a *dispositif* – configures bodies, affects, and spaces into relational assemblages. The other half of the compound *choreo-ethics* affirms *ethics* as an orientation towards life-sustaining practices. For me, choreo-ethical assemblages are constellations in which various vectors – assembling and dissembling (each other?) – interlace. They are always provisional, open to rearrangement, and conditioned by the relational intensities that circulate among bodies, gestures, and environments. Ethics here is not a code of conduct but a matter of attentiveness: the responsibility of moving-with and moving-apart.

A/Effective Assembling and Dissembling

The entangled processes of assembling and dissembling constitute a dynamic tension that is particularly generative when considered through the lens of choreographic practice and ethical reflection. Choreo-ethical assemblages – emergent constellations of movement, relation, and responsibility – foreground this tension in ways that problematise fixity and invite the reconfiguration of subjectivities, spaces, and temporalities. If assembling is understood not as the construction of closed wholes but as an open-ended practice of connection, juxtaposition, and provisional cohabitation, then dissembling manifests as more than dismantling; it becomes a necessary and productive unravelling. The oscillation between these poles delineates the preconditions for what I call choreo-ethical assemblages.

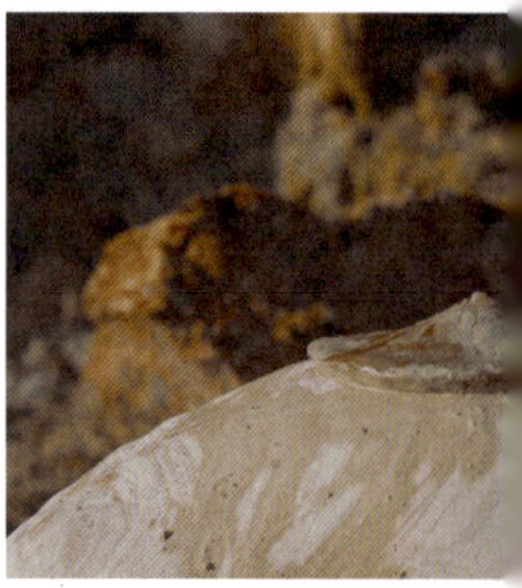

Philosopher and art theoretician Gerald Raunig's articulation of 'concatenation' (*Verkettung*) – a transversal mode of linking heterogeneous practices – provides a crucial entry point for thinking about acts of assembling beyond totalising logics. In *Art and Revolution* (2007)[195] and later in *Factories of Knowledge, Industries of Creativity* (2013),[196] Raunig insists that concatenations resist the

192. I developed and elaborated on these terms separately in my doctoral dissertation (University of Roehampton, London, 2018), which was published as *Being in Contact: Encountering a Bare Body* (Edition Angewandte, De Gruyter, 2021).

193. Gilles Deleuze and Félix Guattari, *A Thousand Plateaus: Capitalism and Schizophrenia*, trans. Brian Massumi (Continuum, 2004).

194. Walt Whitman, 'Book III: Song of Myself', in *Leaves of Grass* (Project Gutenberg, 2008), https://www.gutenberg.org/ebooks/1322.

195. Gerald Raunig, *Art and Revolution: Transversal Activism in the Long Twentieth Century*, trans. Aileen Derieg (Semiotext(e), 2007).

196. Gerald Raunig and Antonio Negri, *Factories of Knowledge, Industries of Creativity*, trans. Aileen Derieg (Semiotext(e), 2013).

closure of representation and instead privilege the open series, the non-hierarchical connection. Assemblages are less about unified structures than about transitory nodes or temporary closures[197] in a field of potentiality. In choreographic terms, this translates into the ways in which bodies, gestures, affects, and spatial conditions align contingently, creating relational intensities without permanence, at times leaving traces or creating resonances. Some of the diffractive dialogues that I carried out with my dialogue partners articulated how these intensities can leave affective *imprints* on the space – either in the form of memories in the acting bodies or as material traces in the room – and they can be factors that influence subsequent movements. The ethical dimension emerges precisely in this impermanence: in an attentiveness to how the *coming-together* of bodies and forces is always

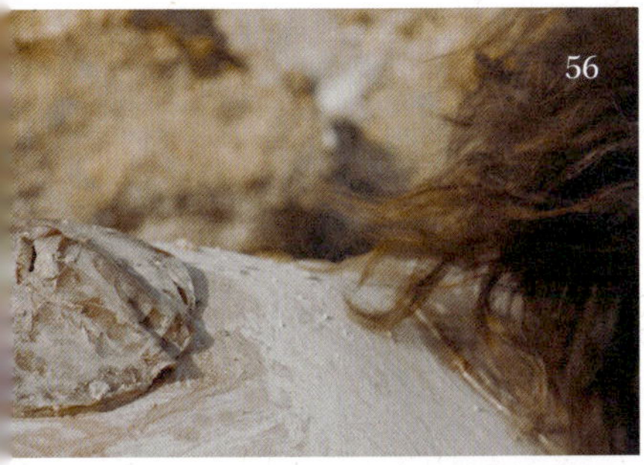

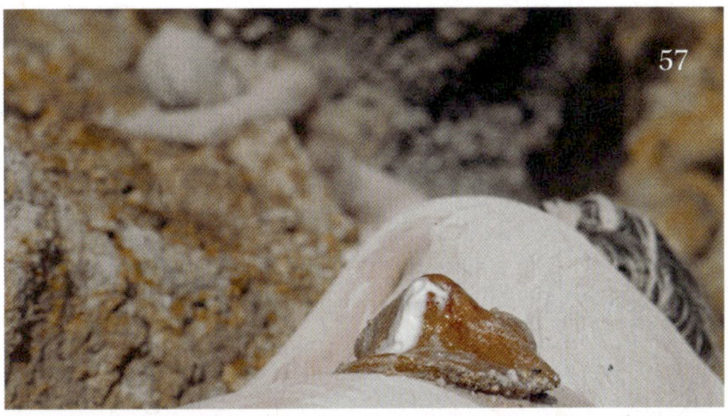

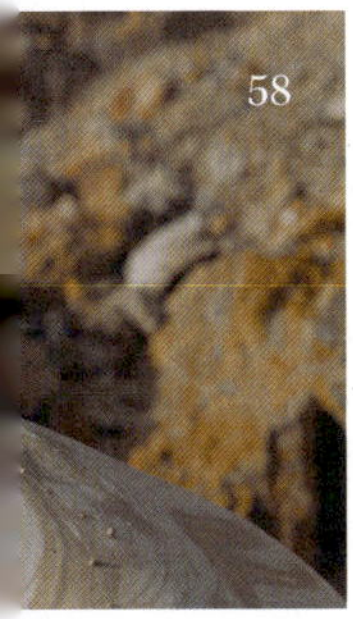

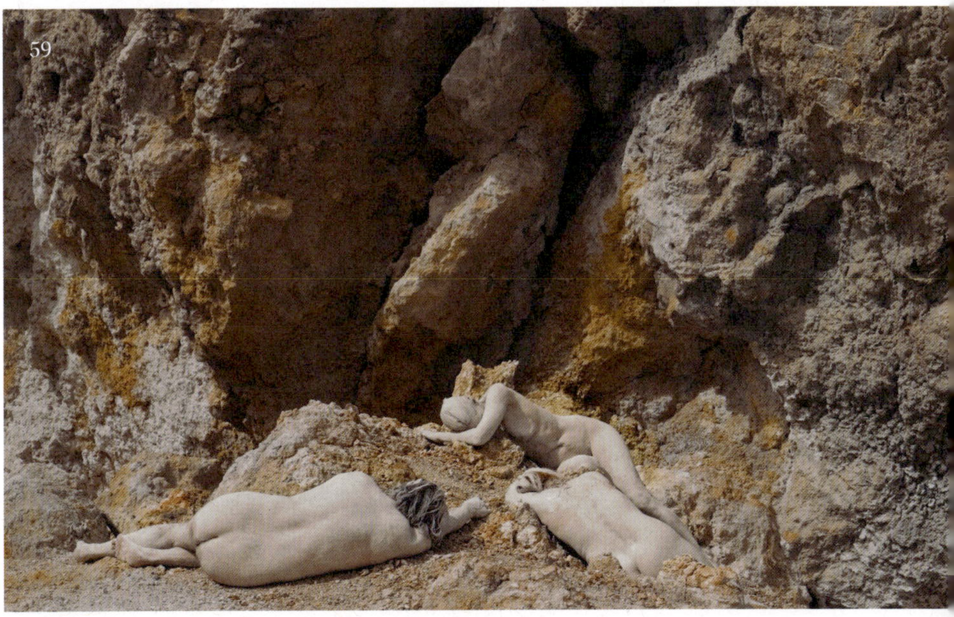

197. Nikolaus Gansterer, Emma Cocker, and Mariella Greil, 'Figure of Temporary Closing', in *Choreo-graphic Figures: Deviations from the Line*, ed. Nikolaus Gansterer, Emma Cocker, and Mariella Greil (Edition Angewandte, De Gruyter, 2017), 100–10.

Fig. 56: *Shaken Grounds – Onomatopoetic Sound(e)scape: Slides and Slips Between Sonances and Symbiosis*, 2025, © video still: Victor Jaschke, performance: Mariella Greil, Lucie Strecker, and SCOBY.

Fig. 57: *Shaken Grounds – Onomatopoetic Sound(e)scape: Slides and Slips Between Sonances and Symbiosis*, 2025, © video still: Victor Jaschke, performance: Peter Kozek, Lucie Strecker and SCOBY.

Fig. 58: *Shaken Grounds – Onomatopoetic Sound(e)scape: Slides and Slips Between Sonances and Symbiosis*, 2025, © video still: Victor Jaschke, performance: Mariella Greil and SCOBY.

Fig. 59: *Shaken Grounds – Onomatopoetic Sound(e)scape: Slides and Slips Between Sonances and Symbiosis*, 2025, © video still: Victor Jaschke, performance: Mariella Greil, Peter Kozek, Lucie Strecker and SCOBY.

shadowed by dispersal, disassembly, and reconfiguration, a continuous process of assembling and dissembling, forming and reforming, sonances and resonances.[198]

I would also like to point out here that Deleuze and Guattari's conceptualisation of *agencement* is implicit in how I use *assemblage*. In *Mille Plateaux*, they note that an assemblage is composed not of discrete units but of relations of exteriority, of 'lines of flight' that deterritorialise as much as they conjoin. In their writings, *agencement* refers to the contingent co-functioning of heterogeneous elements – bodies, statements, affects, codes, materials. The relation itself transforms the elements; they do not pre-exist their arrangement. An *agencement* is therefore ontologically generative. *Agencement* insists on dynamism: it describes *how* heterogeneous elements are arranged, aligned, and made to function, and how these alignments can shift.[199]

Rather than aggregates, assemblages are processes that constantly alter the very elements that they link. The choreography of assemblages, then, is not the imposition of a form upon inert matter but a continual process of co-composition, where movement, sensation, and thought are mutually implicated. Ethics is immanent to this operation: it inheres in the decisions, intensities, and responsivities that govern how bodies touch, separate, resist, and flow together. Dissembling here acquires a doubled meaning: it is the capacity to undo and to mask, to reveal the fragile contingency of structures, and to allow alternative distributions of the sensible in the sense intended by French philosopher Jacques Rancière.[200] Consequently, what emerges is assembling and dissembling as a/effective practices.

The prefix *a/* in *a/effective* names a productive ambiguity between the *effective* – which produces tangible outcomes – and the *affective* – which modulates sensation, intensity, and relational attunement. A/effective assembling thus refers to a practice of bringing-together that is simultaneously material and affective, structural and atmospheric. Likewise, a/effective dissembling denotes not only the dismantling of structures but also the recalibration of affective textures: the atmospheres of trust, suspicion, openness, or withdrawal that contour the very possibility of collective formation.

The affective turn in the humanities and social sciences has underscored this dimension of collectivity and perception – that bodies feel, vibrate, and move before they signify, that they are contagious with effervescences. Sociologist Patricia T. Clough has argued that affect indexes 'the bodily capacity to affect and be affected [...], the felt aliveness given in the preindividual bodily capacity to act, to engage,

198. I was invited to present *Onomatopoetic Sound(e)scape – Slides and Slips Between Sonances and Symbiosis* at the Special Interest Group Session for language-based artistic research at the 2025 Society for Artistic Research (SAR) Conference, which was the 16th International Conference on Artistic Research hosted by i2ADS, at the University of Porto.

199. Here, I am following the route that Brian Massumi took in his 1987 translation of Deleuze and Guattari's *Mille Plateaux*, where he rendered *agencement* consistently as *assemblage*. Still, I would like to acknowledge that scholars such as artist and philosopher Manuel DeLanda have worked hard to clarify that *assemblage* must be understood in Deleuze and Guattari's sense of *relations of exteriority* rather than as a mere aggregate. See Manuela DeLanda, *Assemblage Theory* (Edinburgh University Press, 2016).

200. Jacques Rancière, *The Politics of Aesthetics*, trans. Gabriel Rockhill (Continuum, 2004).

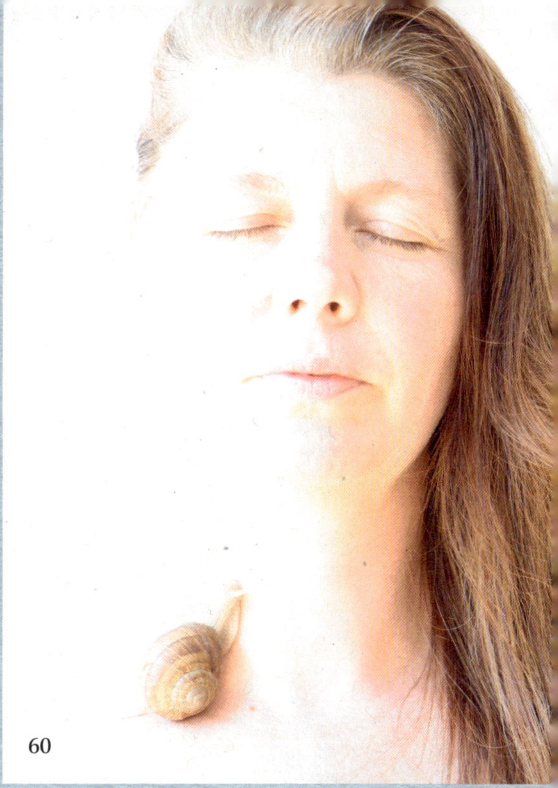

60

Mollusc Myths

Light touch,
crossing the interface
to the other,
fully retreating into you,
then we suddenly remove the touch.

No, we are not going into dark places,
molluscs are survivalists.
Some munch on algae and incorporate the
algae's chloroplasts,
allowing them to photosynthesize sunlight
like plants.

My favourite snail can sleep for up to three years.

When conditions get too dry, certain land snails
enter a state called *estivation*
– a kind of super-powered nap –
sealing themselves into their shells until the
environment becomes hospitable again.

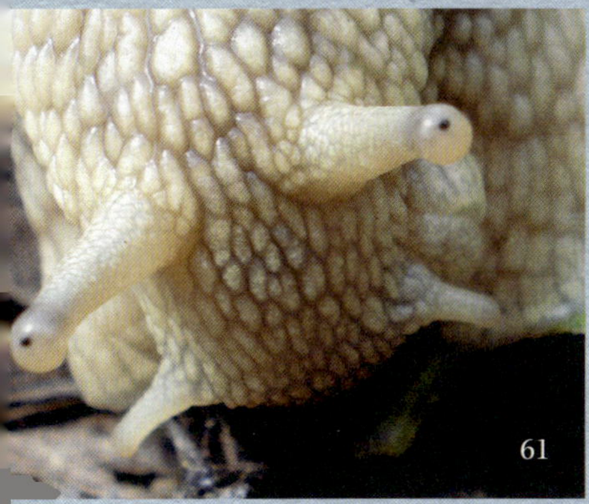

61

Octopuses have three hearts and their blood is blue.
Their blue blood comes from a copper-based molecule
that is superefficient in cold, low-oxygen environments.

The snail crawls on me,
it is a gradual approach to tactile intensity,
I think about the fragile selection of one part
of the experience,
its diachronic unfolding,
the feeling of expectation before the touch.

Tingling at the surface,
a sweet rush on my skin,
my hair stands on end like antennae,
stretching towards the touch,
a longing, a desire, an excitement.
When the touch occurs,
calm returns, and we are on the next plateau.
Perception moves on.

The unfolding is connected,
I experience it from within,
softening from the heart,
red, but not in its
loud version.

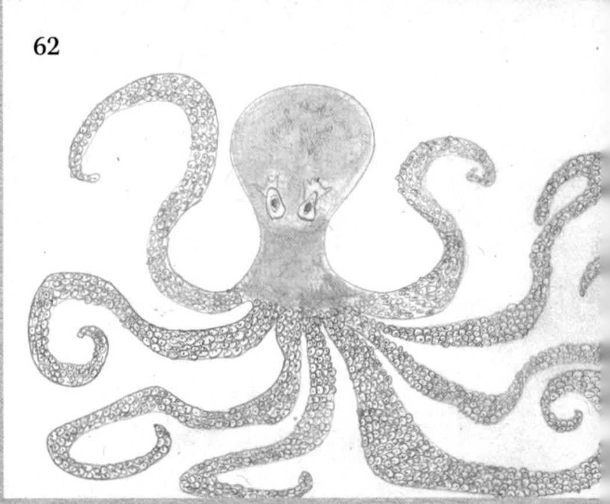

Breathing becomes deeper.
My weight sinks into the
floor through the soles
of my feet.
I go for a bath in this sensation,
bridging the abyss between our hearts.

Our bodies are ecstasiated.
The things stretch towards us,
trusting the mystics,
dismantling the layers of the bare,

and to connect'.[201] These bodily intensities exceed the subject – they are intensities that circulate across and through assemblages. Sociocultural theorist and ethnographer Melissa Gregg and philosopher of science Gregory Seigworth's influential *Affect Theory Reader* (2010) similarly foregrounds affect as a relational force, as 'an impingement or extrusion of a momentary or sometimes more sustained state of relation *as well as* the passage (and the duration of passage) of forces or intensities'.[202] They describe affect as being 'born in *in-between-ness* and resid[ing] as accumulative *besides-ness*', and also as the 'supple incrementalism of ever modulating force-relations – that rises and falls not only along various rhythms and modalities of encounter but also through the toughs and sieves of sensation and sensibility'.[203]

Micro-phenomenological Interview with Kerstin Kussmaul
Excerpt, edited transcript
10 November 2022

Mariella Greil: What kind of responses to your actions did you read in the environment? Can you identify a moment?

Kerstin Kussmaul: I found a clear response when you walked up on the tables. I think it happened in the second half.

Mariella: Was it the fact that you were there too before that caught your attention?

Kerstin: I was up there before, but it's not about the location. When I was sitting, I was seized by the desire to change the configuration of the tables, but every step felt so significant that I didn't get around to it. In the end, I did climb up. I sat down and decided to become my own object in my object world. I started to paint with my feet. Later, you stepped up, painted with your hand, took a few steps, and eventually came down again. When you went up, I could read a curiosity about prints that I felt was a material resonance from this kind of greyish powder. I would say, it was sort of an entanglement, rather than a response.

Mariella: Yes, that ground stone powder.

Kerstin: I was really drawn to that too. The fact that you used it to make prints stayed with me. Also, the act of getting up: I think, by getting up, you totally destroyed the idea of display. And in that sense, I found that to be a response.

Mariella: What changed when you started watching me sitting on it? Can you recall a physical memory?

Kerstin: Breaking the idea of the display created a feeling of satisfaction in me. It also set off a reverberation that made me hear what I had done. This was because your action was not exactly the same as mine. If you had done exactly the same, I would have felt that you were just copying me. Because you did something else I could relate to, I sensed you had an understanding of what I was doing before.

Mariella: Can you situate that satisfaction in your body?

Kerstin: Maybe in my face and in my belly. It wasn't very strong, I must say. In the face it took the shape of a little smile, and in the belly it took the form of relaxation, like a little exhale.

Mariella: So, you saw me stepping up there, you heard your printed feet, and you reacted with a little smile, and your belly relaxed.

Kerstin: Yes, it was a smile and the relaxation of being recognised. I saw this recognition as a response to what I had done. As I said before, the response was not perfect, but it was a variation.

201. Patricia Ticineto Clough and Jean O'Malley Halley, *The Affective Turn: Theorizing the Social* (Duke University Press, 2007), 2.

202. Melissa Gregg and Gregory J. Seigworth, *The Affect Theory Reader* (Duke University Press, 2010), 1.

203. Ibid., 2.

Mariella: Variation. And that variation was recognised by seeing the physicality of the action, so tactility was involved.

Kerstin: Yes, there was definitely a haptic resonance. Also, I do remember that when I went up there, I did see the sense of risk I felt.

Mariella: Yes, it was strong. Okay, so basically, I was activating the response that you were able to read in the space. How did you know that the moment had started when you saw me stepping up there? Can you situate it again in the body?

Kerstin: In my belly. But I'm wondering now, how did I recognise that as a response? I think that's an essential question. Because this is really the problem with phenomenological research. How do I know what I know? Where does my experience come from? Once, during a party in New Zealand, I almost got into a fight about somatics with a Māori woman. Since then, I've been questioning my knowledge a lot. She told me that she is in touch with her ancestors, that she has one in Chile with whom she communicates. At first, I didn't find it very credible, so I kind of doubled down on trying to understand her story. I was so busy trying to figure out how she did that, whether it was a cultural imaginary or a conceptual idea. But it became clear that we come from two different cultures. It seemed like she couldn't really explain how she perceived it. Then we got into a discussion: where does our physical perception actually start? Can I call it a somatic experience or not? We couldn't resolve it that evening. We were so entangled in the conversation that other people actually left the space. In that moment, I became so deeply invested in Māori knowledge about experiencing. Ever since, I've realised that she actually challenged my own perception. How do I really know what I know? If I see a moment of recognition in her words, is that just my own interpretation? Can I know if she has recognised me? Can she know? There's something inside me sometimes that just knows, I feel it physically. But it's something you can't argue or prove.

Affective assembling, then, involves the cultivation of atmospheres of resonance and receptivity, while affective dissembling interrupts habitual circuits, creating ruptures that open up new forms of ethical relation. For example, in dance improvisation, the refusal to sync with another's gesture may dissemble emergent mimetic cohesion, thereby redirecting collective attention towards difference rather than sameness. The ethics here is not normatively codified but situational and negotiated: it is probed through the micro-adjustments of weight, gaze, timing, and intensity that determine how bodies co-compose in difference.

The term *choreo-ethical* designates a practice of negotiating proximity, touch, potentiality, and temporality – *how* one moves with and against others (including other others), *how* one reflects on vulnerability[204] and opacity, *how* one modulates intensities of presence. Assembling is the act of weaving together relations of trust and experimentation, while dissembling ensures that such relations do not harden into exclusionary or coercive structures.

Here, ethics, or, more precisely, the choreo-ethical dimension, is understood in closer proximity to the Levinasian attentiveness to alterity than to the Kantian sense of universalizable imperatives – namely, as irreducible exposure to the *other* (including other others). Yet choreography complicates even Levinas, for it demonstrates that exposure is never one-directional; it is distributed, kinetic, multiple. The choreo-ethical assemblage is therefore both methodological and political. Methodologically, it describes how research and practice can operate through the assembling of fragments, gestures, and discourses without demanding their synthesis into a singular narrative. It negotiates the dynamics of control – not as a set regime but as a shifting distribution of constraints and affordances that shape how bodies, affects, and relations come to matter.

204. I am specifically inspired by Hélène Cixous' notion of 'feminine economy', as paraphrased by Erinn Gilson in her description of vulnerability as 'a virtue of sorts, one enabled by "feminine economy"', in *The Ethics of Vulnerability: A Feminist Analysis of Social Life and Practice* (Routledge, 2014), 129.

Micro-phenomenological Interview with Evfa Lilja
Excerpt, edited transcript
14 April 2023

Mariella Greil: As a researcher you are usually not so much in control…

Evfa Lilja: No, I mean, life is chaos. So, you have to organise it somehow to gain control over it. I mean, that's what we've been doing all morning, trying to control the space, right? Organise it in favour of revealing something. As a choreographer, I know I could never reach the point of total control. But I try and try and try – at least – to create new situations, new settings, new stagings, new relationships. It's all a continuum. And maybe that's why I am drawn to these kinds of objects that are so hard, that pretend to be stable, because nothing else is. Choreography has something to do with this idea that someone has to be brave to organise space and bodies to make life happen.

Politically, it insists on disassembling the dominant regimes of movement – such as the disciplining of bodies in neoliberal labour markets or the spectacle logics of cultural industries – in order to create spaces for alternative modes of being-together.

Let us take a closer look at resonances and divergences, and reflect on the embodied research methods that evolved out of the Polylogic Labs. While Deleuze and Guattari theorise assemblages ontologically, as the very fabric of reality's relationality, Raunig emphasises their political dimension as transversal concatenations. Both perspectives converge in their insistence that assembling is not unification but multiplicity, and that dissembling is necessary to keep multiplicity alive. In my view, the strength of assemblages derives from their inclusive ontologies and the potential for generating democratic relations.[205]

In my diffractive choreographic and dialogical practice, this translates into criticality towards fixed structures of authorship or hierarchy. Assemblages emerge through temporary distributions of agency, where dialogue partners[206] and wit(h)-nesses, spaces and affects co-compose the *encounter*.[207] They relate to each other in a phenomenological, sensuous spell[208] and ethical agility.[209] Dissembling ensures that these distributions remain fluid. The site-specific choreographic environments purposefully disassemble conventional spatial divisions of stage and audience, reconfiguring how bodies encounter one another in dialogue in one-on-one settings and exploring how attention circulates.

Sara Ahmed's work on affect and emotion deepens this trajectory by insisting on the 'stickiness'[210] of affect: how histories of encounter cling to bodies and spaces, shaping possibilities of movement. In choreo-ethical assemblages, affect is not supplementary but constitutive. Assembling entails the orchestration of rhythms,

205. Hans Asenbaum, 'Democratic Assemblage', in *What Makes an Assembly?*, ed. Anne Davidian and Laurent Jeanpierre (Sternberg, 2022), 249–60.

206. These can be human agents such as dancers, philosophers, therapists, sound artists, etc., or other-than-human agents such as tree trunks, broken shoes, a handpan, a suitcase, a glass vase, needles, felt, rotten apples, etc. (see human and other-than-human INDEX).

207. Greil, 'Encounter, Affect and Response', in *Being in Contact*, 79–126.

208. David Abram, *The Spell of the Sensuous: Perception and Language in a More-than-Human World*, 20th anniversary ed. (Vintage Books, 2017).

209. Noyale Colin, Catherine Seago, and Kathryn Stamp, *Ethical Agility in Dance: Rethinking Technique in British Contemporary Dance* (Routledge, 2024).

210. Sara Ahmed, *The Cultural Politics of Emotion* (Edinburgh University Press, 2014), 91.

tones, speeds, and hesitations that exceed semantic meaning; instead, intensities, atmospheres, and vulnerabilities are foregrounded as we navigate the dialogue. Dissembling, conversely, disrupts habitual affective alignments, introducing dissonance or hesitation that can resensitise participants to dynamics of power or exclusion.

In my project, this kind of negotiation had more to do with unfolding in the spirit of collective improvisation, following the 'Diffractive Dialogue Score', where interlocutors were instructed to continually enter and exit the choreographic environment. Assembling is evidence of the various configurations of fleeting cohesion, while dissembling prevents closure and emphasises an ongoing process of negotiation. The affective atmosphere oscillates between intimacy and estrangement, resonance and dissonance. The result is an ethical sensitivity to the fragility of togetherness.

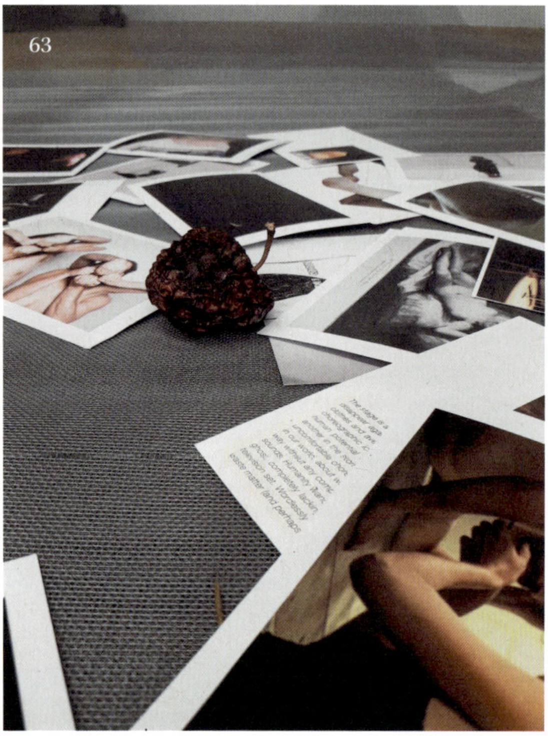

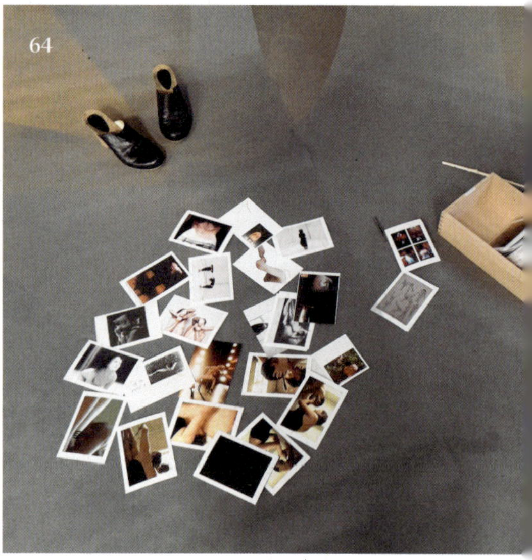

Micro-phenomenological Interview with Emma Cocker
Excerpt, edited transcript
26 September 2022

Mariella Greil: How was it for you to enter the space?

Emma Cocker: At first, I was overwhelmed by the presence of so many objects. In the space, there was a sense of waiting, where objects stood ready to be activated in an awesome, reactive environment. It almost resembled a clearing, or a glade, or even a wood in which those objects were organised. Yet *in their arrangement, they were already acting.*

Mariella: How would you describe your interaction with the objects?

Emma: Since the beginning, I felt I was facing their histories. I was wondering, 'Who else has been here? How did previous bodies intervene in them and their arrangement?' These questions were moving me between *here* and *there*. It seemed that certain objects were carrying very *strong histories*, while others *called for relation.* The call for relation, for example, made me reflect on the *objects' obviousness*, their clear goal and conventional use. So, in deciding where to place them, I followed their call for a connection with other objects in the room.

Figs. 63 and 64: *Choreo-ethical Assemblages – As/Dissembling*, 2022, © photo: Mariella Greil.

Mariella: How did you sense that call? Can you go back to that moment and describe it a bit?

Emma: I think it happened somewhere in the movement between objects that were waiting to be activated and those that already seemed to carry a kind of presence, as if they were already on stage. I guess the call had something to do with the idea of *fit*. I noticed it in some of the photographs: a desire to make things fit, to fold or enclose one another; there was a longing for things to come into contact. That piece of wood, for example, felt very much like it was calling. It had a presence that seemed to invite other objects to meet it, to come close. And some of them just felt like they belonged there where they were. There was no need to force it. They just fit. They belonged.

Mariella: Did you place the objects directly in one spot or would you try different spots?

Emma: There were a few objects that went *magnetically* straight to the spot. The call was in both ways, and all I had to do was carry it. And it just fit.

Mariella: So, for some objects you adopted the role of the carrier.

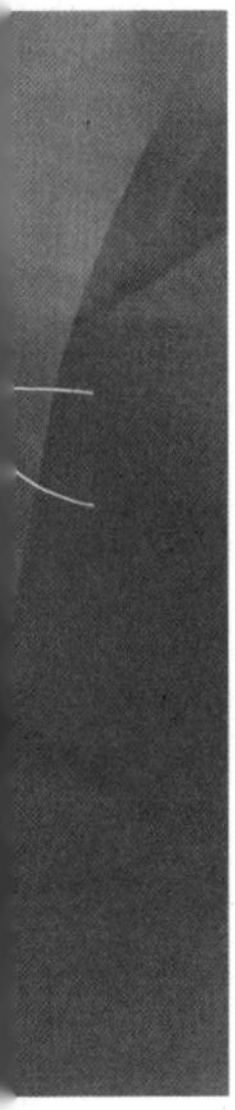

To think about this movement of assembling and dissembling is to refuse the binary of construction and destruction, stability and chaos. Instead, the acts of assembling and dissembling form the core of my œkology of practices – with a nod to Isabelle Stengers.[211] In this sense, assemblages (Deleuze and Guattari) and dissemblages (Raunig)[212] constitute temporary, transitional acts and processes of shaping that in turn condition potential future practices. They are comparable to aggregates, where one miniscule electron makes the difference and can change the phenotype of a substance from liquid to solid or gas. Choreo-ethical assemblages thrive on the oscillation between gathering and scattering, attunement and interruption. This oscillation is not a flaw but a generative condition: it ensures that assemblages remain open, porous, and capable of transformation, available for choreo-ethical negotiation – the crucial point of the project.

Micro-phenomenological Interview with Emma Cocker
Excerpt, edited transcript
26 September 2022

Mariella: It is a very open setting for focusing on making a decision; I'm really curious about where you anchored yourself in order to be able to do it. While you were moving, orienting yourself within the space and moving the objects, did you think first and then act? Or did you move something and recognise it afterwards?

Emma: The first two actions were intuitive. I don't think there was any thought at first. Something just called. The openings were already there. They belonged. I saw the sponge first. It felt like it needed placing. There, without full awareness, I imagined it together with the trunk.

Mariella: So, you noticed both of them before you acted?

Emma: Yes, and I wasn't specifically focused on one or the other. I was just drawn to that space. Then I had the intention for the sponge to become part of the trunk; I was looking for one new body to emerge. *It wasn't about blending them, because they were still separate. But I was folding, or enveloping them. Like hands folding into themselves.* With the second object, the golden rock, it went differently: I was actively searching for something. I had a thought about which shape might fit. This process was quite embodied; *I believe there is a correlation to the body, how one part fits into another with comfort or stuckness. It's definitely neither about force nor balance. Maybe it is more akin to how joints work, a kind of natural articulation between two parts that just know how to meet. The bones work in separation. But they cooperate.*

211. Isabelle Stengers, 'Introductory Notes on an Ecology of Practices', *Cultural Studies Review* 11, no. 1 (2005): 183–96.

212. Gerald Raunig, *Dissemblage: Machinic Capitalism and Molecular Revolution* (Minor Compositions, 2022).

Mariella: And there's something about the bones that means that they need to be in the right spot. Yeah. Because if they get a little displaced, the whole muscular, fascial, and, consequently, endocrine and nervous systems will have an issue. It's interesting that what each of you did was articulate the space. Articulating something can mean making it more precise in one way or another. Although, I'm not sure that's always true. When you're lifting your leg, for example, that gives it a certain direction. So, there's something about positioning something through an articulation, *but at the same time, that articulation is also yet to be interpreted or to be received by somebody in order to be read as an articulation.* You were saying, *this is where it needed to go.* And the uncanny thing did need to be there. And I can clearly read your articulation. So, my big question is: how do aesthetics form, and how can we communicate through them? What does it mean to communicate *through* aesthetic decision-making? And of course, aesthetics can vary widely, be very...

Emma: ...completely different. I mean, in this aesthetic decision there is something about fit, fit-ness, like a hip and hip socket. But in some moments, it didn't feel like that at all; I rather felt like I was trying to ram something. And then, there were also decisions driven by my wish to prevent casual interaction, meaning almost unconscious gestures that weren't really embodied. For example, the way the drum calls to be touched. But in that context, it felt a bit off. Similarly, the box of images invited an interaction that felt very familiar; I could have flicked through it casually, without much attention, like flipping through a magazine. I did flick through them. But it became stressful, especially because of the time constraints. Like with the drum, I was trying to find ways to disable that kind of skimming through the material. And that's why I wanted to find a way to prevent that kind of superficial interaction. I wanted to create a situation where, if I was going to interact with something, it would have to be intentional.

Practicing a/effective assembling and dissembling is not simply a matter of indulging in artistic practices; rather, the urgency of the research is based on the need to articulate how these practices reconfigure ethics, politics, and collectivity. Choreography here becomes a conceptual laboratory, a site where the logics of assembling and dissembling can be experimented with, where ethical attunement can be rehearsed, and where alternative futures of relationality can be imagined. My endeavour is actually trying to get the text itself to perform this gesture: assembling artistic-choreographic, ethico-philosophical, psychotherapeutic, and socio-aesthetic strands while dissembling inherited disciplinary boundaries.

A/effective assembling and dissembling, understood through choreo-ethical assemblages, foreground the necessity of both connection and rupture, composition and decomposition. Drawing on Raunig's transversal politics, Deleuze and Guattari's ontological emphasis on assemblages, and the affective turn's attention to intensity and atmosphere, we can understand choreographic *assemblaging* as a practice that continually negotiates thresholds between togetherness and separation.[213] Ethics, in this sense, is choreographic: it is about how we move with and against one another, how we assemble and dissemble relations in ways that keep multiplicity alive and foster conditions for unforeseen modes of co-existence.

The figures of thought, movement, and speech, together with various related material manifestations, form a choreography of residues. These traces of processes are the beginnings of documentations; they are a collection of loose ends that bear witness to 'what happened before' and anticipate the emerging potentialities

213. These topics of coming together and falling apart are embedded broadly in the ethos and creative identity of dancer and choreographer Raja Feather Kelly. As related in an interview, 'Feather is the middle name he gave himself at age 13. "It has nothing to do with movement," he says. "I just like how feathers come together and fall apart."' Jonathan Mandell, 'How Raja Feather Kelly Gives Shows All the Right Moves', *tdf*, accessed 9 September 2025, https://www.tdf.org/on-stage/tdf-stages/how-raja-feather-kelly-gives-shows-all-the-right-moves/?utm. The levity of this statement is emphasized in the image of the floating feathers, which resonates with a quality that I strive for in *assemblaging*.

of future practices. When we follow πολύ (*poly*, more than one),[214] λογική (*logiki* or in English, 'logics', from Greek λόγος (*logos*, meaning 'statement', 'understanding', 'speech'),[215] it can reveal[216] latent unfoldings of trajectories to come. Due to their very plural quality and their synchronicities, these future potentials unfold in discourses, conversations, and performances that are diverse and layered. They often employ queer, punk, or camp aesthetics and can at times be existential, wild, or unruly. However, during the diffractive dialogue practices, it became clear to me that the practice of dissembling was at least equally important and deserved just as much attention as the practice of assembling. Raunig writes, 'The dissemblage lets itself fall and falls apart, into dispersed bracing, into joinings out of joint [...].'[217] Falling apart and falling into place, falling down and falling in love, falling out and falling up, falling asleep and free falling.

In the *Choreo-ethical Assemblages* project, there was a strong commitment to the *analogue* in the Polylogic Lab while remaining firmly embedded within a post-digital context. The act of following a score of encounters built on residues of actual, material presence. A choreography emerged that was radically based on the traces lingering in the studio space: the purposeful message, letters, or instructions for the next guest, or the unintentional leftovers, forgotten things or half-baked thoughts, scribbles, vacancies. Researchers as private investigators searched out the agency of remnants of presence in the space, the reverberations of bodily movements, recorded sound traces archived in various formats, as well as memories, touch, smells, etc., stored and reactivated in the studio space. The body performed as an archive of encounters with others (human bodies in space) and other others (other-than-human bodies, materials, things in space), a sort of actualising, maybe a form of *thing*-ing,[218] in its original sense of assembly, affirming the common as its *telos*.[219]

214. *Poly-* is the Greek word-forming element, the equivalent of the Latin word *multi-*, meaning many, much. See 'poly', etymonline, accessed 23 September 2025, https://www.etymonline.com/word/poly-.

215. Interestingly, the root word *logos* is translated differently in connection with *logic* than when it is etymologically explained on its own terms. In connection with *logic, logos* is translated as 'reason', 'idea', 'word'. 'Logic', etymonline, accessed 24 August 2025, https://www.etymonline.com/search?q=logic.

216. Besides his continued attempts to rehabilitate aesthesis (αἴσθησις) (→ Aesthetics and Ethics are Twins, 271), Dieter Mersch also clearly gets to the point, when he explains the *performance problem* in one long sentence: 'Husserl, like Wittgenstein after him, [...] tried to distinguish between different modes of use and thus developed the problem of the mode in the direction of a performance problem, as it was ultimately taken up again by pragmatic linguistics, in particular in the speech act theory of John Langshaw Austin and John R. Searle: one and the same utterance can, depending on the situation or context, be understood as an assertion, a request, a question, or a threat, without any other sign expressing its practical status: rather, it reveals itself by virtue of its execution' (my translation). Dieter Mersch, *Was sich zeigt – Materialität, Präsenz, Ereignis* (Fink, 2002), 238.

217. Raunig, *Dissemblage*, 255.

218. The Editors of Encyclopaedia Britannica, 'thing', Brittanica, accessed 24 August 2025, https://www.britannica.com/topic/thing-Scandinavian-political-assembly. In the project *Contingent Agencies* led by Nikolaus Gansterer and Alex Arteaga, a 'þing' (thing) is the term used to designate the situation when practices of notation are simultaneously performed. In the context of *Choreo-ethical Assemblages*, thing-ing is used in a wider sense and with an emphasis on mutual performative encountering of things and the related, perceptual shifts.

219. Michael Hardt and Antonio Negri, *Assembly* (Oxford University Press, 2017), 239.

Animisms and Assemblages

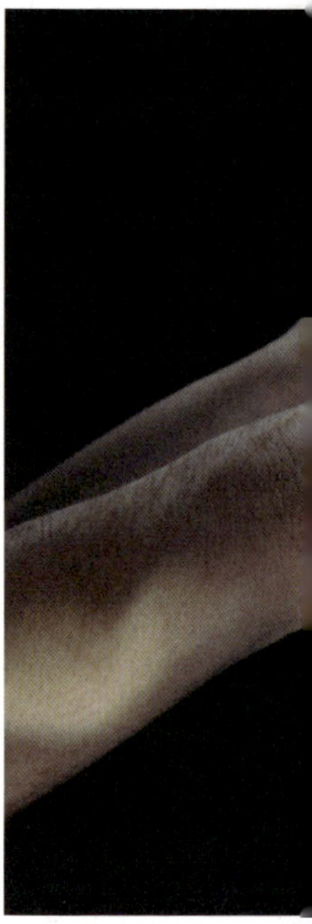

From assemblies, where the common is the telos, emerges a porous horizon where assemblages, reconfiguring relational worlds, intertwine with animisms. In my continued references to choreo-ethical assemblages, I must point out that they are inevitably as much made up of practices of dissembling as they are of assembling, as well as both immanent and related affects and effects (or as Fischer-Lichte would have it, *effective affects*[220]). However, I do not feel the urgency to shift the terminology towards *dissemblages* as I purposefully apply a thorough (in terms of conceptual depth) but lenient (in terms of artistic practice) understanding of the noun *assemblages*, taking advantage of its soft boundaries and terminologically deliberately open outlines. In my artistic work, practicing and engaging with the dynamics of choreo-ethical assemblages, as well as reflecting on and finding out about them, I have realised that the contingent constellation of aesthetic structures has become inhabited by sentient (in the widest possible sense) bodies. I have found these bodies to be prone to negotiation and ready to explore 'the distributive agency of the many things at play, open(ing) the preceptive conditions for serendipitous becoming'.[221]

Animism, from the Latin *anima* – 'life', 'breath', 'soul', 'coming alive', or, as Hans Asenbaum, a research fellow at the Center for Deliberative Democracy and Global Governance puts it, 'serendipitous becoming'[222] – both depend on actualisation and animation, but also on care and attentiveness. Animism, as the 'attribution of living souls to inanimate objects',[223] struck me as surprisingly relevant notion, really only through the practicing of diffractive dialogues and, through them, the befriending of others. Over time, I found myself, through my artistic practice, establishing friendships with subjects and objects[224] (at times even kinships in Haraway's terms[225]) across agencies. Materials and their movements, sounds, smells, and atmospheres captivated my attention, as I was struck by the relational depths I sensed – at times sudden, at others with these seemingly mutual affections being built over time. These depths – or maybe I can describe the phenomenon a bit more precisely (in the plural) as *absorptions*, immersions, obsessions – guide my reflections on the research process (see the textual accounts). It was from this sensation that the film *Drowning in Depths* (2025) evolved, a collaboration with filmmaker Victor Jaschke and performers Mar Esteban Martin and Luisa Pisetta Ravanelli.

220. Erika Fischer-Lichte, *The Transformative Power of Performance: A New Aesthetics*, trans. Saskya Iris Jain (Routledge, 2008 [2004]), 151.

221. Hans Asenbaum, 'Democratic Assemblage', in *What Makes an Assembly?*, ed. Anne Davidian and Laurent Jeanpierre (Sternberg, 2022), 255.

222. Ibid.

223. 'Animism', etymonline, accessed 24 September 2025, https://www.etymonline.com/word/animism.

224. See → Assemblages #2, 81.

225. Donna J. Haraway elaborates: 'Kin is a wild category that all sorts of people do their best to domesticate. Making kin as oddkin rather than, or at least in addition to, godkin and genealogical and biogenetic family troubles important matters, like to whom one is actually responsible.' Donna Haraway, introduction to *Staying with the Trouble: Making Kin in the Chthulucene* (Duke University Press, 2016), 2.

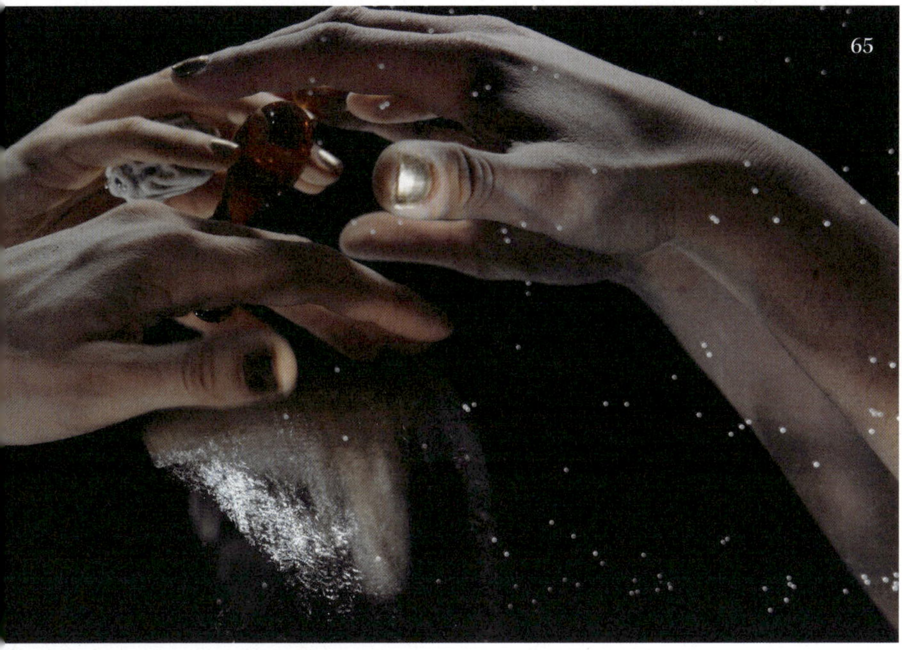

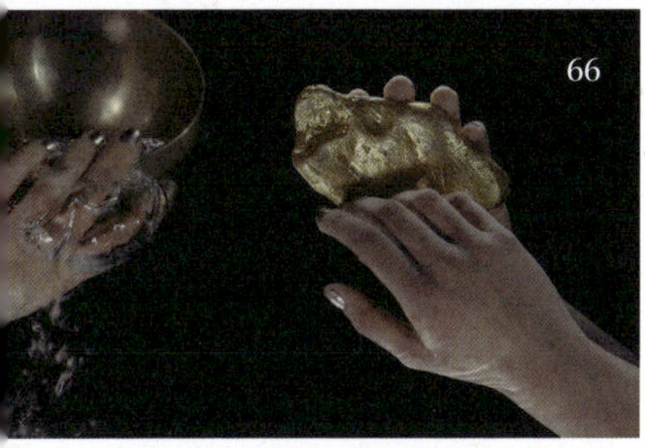

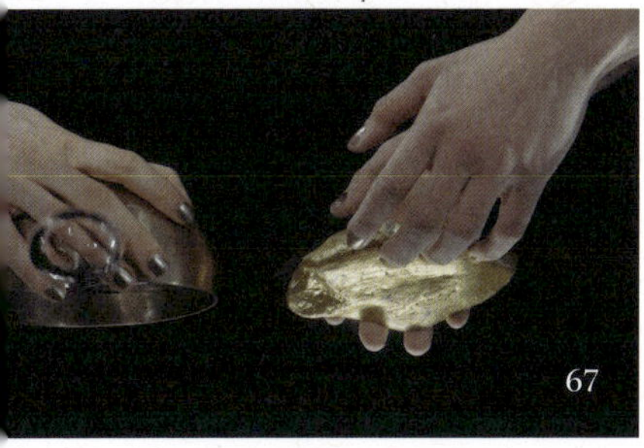

However, when I started to investigate and write about animisms, I found that contemporary theory and artistic practice has been paying renewed attention to animism. This fact calls – I think – for a careful rethinking of categories that have long been banished to the domain of the 'primitive', the 'irrational', or the 'non-modern'. The figure of animism, once relegated to the anthropological imaginary as a prescientific worldview, has returned under conditions that question the ontological stability of the human, the object, and the social. It is within this discursive resurgence that the entanglement of animisms and assemblages gains its relevance. Both concepts attempt to destabilise a model of ontology organised by separability, hierarchy, and instrumental rationality; both open up towards a recognition of relational ontologies in which agency circulates across heterogeneous actors and materials.

Jane Bennett's *Vibrant Matter* provides one influential articulation of distributed agency. In her account of 'thing-power' and 'vital materiality', Bennett pursues a materialist ontology attentive to the lively capacities of matter – capacities that cannot be reduced to human intention or mastery.[226] The term 'assemblage',

226. Jane Bennett, *Vibrant Matter: A Political Ecology of Things* (Duke University Press, 2010), 3–4.

Fig. 65: *Choreo-ethical Assemblages – Drowning in Depths*, 2025, © video still: Victor Jaschke, performance: Mar Esteban Martin, Luisa Pisetta Ravanelli, scleractinia, scleractinia, and somatic interface, concept: Mariella Greil.

Figs. 66 and 67: *Choreo-ethical Assemblages – Drowning in Depths*, 2025, © video still: Victor Jaschke, performance: Mar Esteban Martin, Luisa Pisetta Ravanelli, singing bowl, and golden stone, concept: Mariella Greil.

drawn from Deleuze and Guattari, indicates a provisional gathering of actants – human and other-than-human – whose efficacy arises from their conjunction. What matters in an assemblage is not the discrete essence of each element but the emergent force produced by their relations. Bennett discusses this approach against the backdrop of ecological crisis, where the belief that matter is inert underwrites extractivist regimes. To encounter matter as vibrant is thus a political and ethical provocation: it calls for new forms of responsibility attuned to other-than-human agencies.

Anselm Franke's curatorial project *Animism* (2010–12) staged a parallel but differently inflected intervention. Rather than simply rehabilitating animism as a worldview, Franke probed the epistemic violence embedded within the modern construction of *animism* as the Other of rationality.[227] In Franke's framework, animism denotes both a colonial projection and a counter-concept through which the exclusions of modernity can be made legible. Post-human animism, in this sense, does not imply a naïve return to pre-modern beliefs but a strategic reanimation of the political unconscious of modern thought. By exhibiting works of art alongside ethnographic materials and theoretical documents, Franke dramatised the oscillation between the animistic and the rational, exposing their co-implication rather than their opposition. Animism, for him, became a mode of critique – destabilising the categorical distinction between subject and object, nature and culture, human and other-than-human.

Placed in connection to choreo-ethical assemblages and imagining a dialogue between them, the discursive assemblage of Bennett's vibrant matter and Franke's post-human animism reveal complementary trajectories. While Bennett foregrounds the immanent vitality of matter and the distributed character of agency, Franke foregrounds the epistemological and political stakes of naming and framing animism. Both approaches converge in their resistance to anthropocentrism and integrate themselves into my practice, yet they differ in emphasis: Bennett tends towards redescribing materiality ontologically, whereas Franke insists on the historical entanglement of knowledge, power, and representation. To consider them together is to insist that any renewed animism must be simultaneously ontological and political; an attentiveness to material vitality cannot be abstracted from the histories through which animism has been constructed as alterity.

What emerges under the rubric that I would like to introduce in this chapter – 'animisms and assemblages' – is conceptual terrain on which agency is always pluralised and contested. Assemblages articulate the way in which forces gather without central command, producing emergent orders that exceed intentionality. Animism, reframed through a post-human lens, acknowledges that agency is never exhausted by human reason but reverberates across the registers which modernity has attempted to silence. However, contemporary embodied practices (as I proposed them in my research) could bring them back and give them a voice. In their convergence, the amalgam of animism and contemporary embodied practices, we

227. Anselm Franke, 'Much Trouble in the Transportation of Souls, or: The Sudden Disorganization of Boundaries', in *Animism*, ed. Anselm Franke (Sternberg, 2010), 12–14.

Complementary

Assimilating trans*materialities:
surfaces incline towards one another,
the trunk carrying what the vacancy releases,
dovetailing with the log.
Tangible things fall into line by quiet agreement,
a soft yes whispered to matter,
consent offered to material presence,
as it tunes itself to micro-frequencies
below the threshold of form
of hesitant articulations,
not yet formed.
They hover.

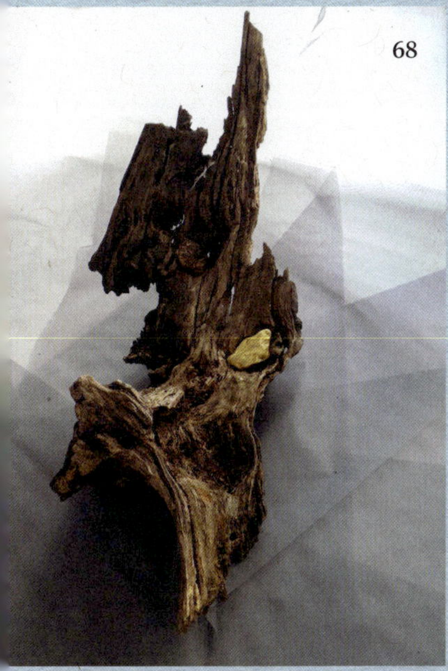

Testing the fit of liminal
spaces,
where apprehension means
sensitivity to edges,
– sharpening contact.
Words touch bare bodies
without claiming them.
They brush, withdraw,
return in a rhythm.

A coming event gathers
density,
coalesces through relational circuits,
breeds a taxonomy of invisible processes,
yet actively composes
the dark side of matter.

Sudden rage flares,
heat as generative pressure,
fuel for transformation.

Crafting openform compositions
a culture of choice that embraces exposure,
bows to the discrepancies between trust and risk.
The urgency to take a stance enters.
The forming of an aesthetics follows behind it,
slightly out of breath, puzzling
– a consequence.

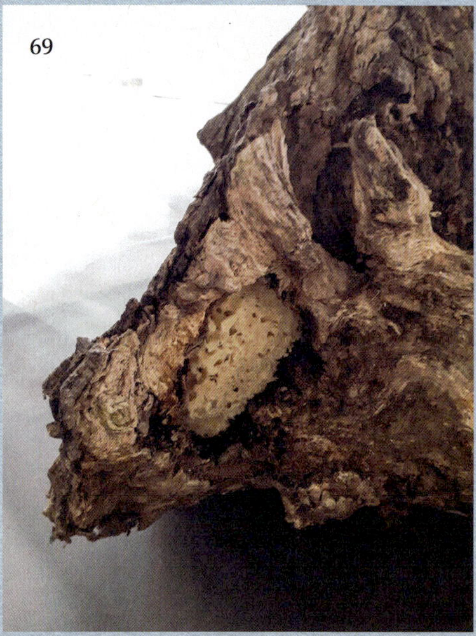

Bodymentation: begins
inside out
– the readiness to *sense*,
self-spawning activity,
lucid horizontality.
Resting in the depths,
undoing through slow-burn
processes
to radically meet what
stands before you.

Leaving space for contradictions,
for the courage to keep up the practice.
Unbound future,
hitting it right in the heart (yes, Rebecca Horn)
so that it begins to vibrate.
Tomorrow completes the interval
that yesterday has left open.
Complementary times mind asymmetries
by holding on to the differences.
Each component sustains
what the other cannot contain.

perceive the outlines of a post-human ethics that resists both the instrumentalisation of the other-than-human and the romanticisation of its alterity.

This convergence carries methodological implications. For philosophy, it requires thinking *with* rather than *about* the other-than-human. For artistic practice, as Franke's curatorial work demonstrates, it suggests formats that allow heterogeneous ontologies to coexist without immediate assimilation. For socio-aesthetic politics,[228] it proposes a shift – or maybe, better, an expansion – from sovereignty to co-agency, from governance over inert matter to participation in assemblages of vibrant matter. To address climate change, extinction, and technological saturation, the conceptual pair of animism and assemblage enables us to perceive the world not as a resource but as an interlocutor – and an entangled one at that. If I zoom in onto the Polylogic Labs for a moment, in these encounters, I notice these specific dynamics in the activation of the 'Diffractive Dialogue Score' and in being in contact with the various dialogue partners – both non-verbally and verbally: in the material conversations across various agencies and modalities of sense-making, there was an emphasis on *responding* to the space, while in the micro-phenomenological interviews, there was an emphasis on *questioning*. Obviously, the medium brings about and influences how we process and articulate experiences. However, it felt meaningful to shift between these modalities as it clearly unearthed a different understanding, created the mutual implication, the being folded into each other's existences, that emerged as constitutive and felt deeply integrative.

In my view, the implications of encountering the world as an interlocutor that is already entangled extend into aesthetics. Bennett's sensitivity to the affective dimensions of thing-power resonates with a tradition of aesthetic theory that seeks to register that which resists being captured conceptually. Similarly, Franke's animism foregrounds how aesthetic forms themselves mediate the oscillation between visibility and invisibility, between the human and its others. Thus, the coupling I suggest here between animisms and assemblages might be understood as an aesthetic and political project: to create forms, narrations, and encounters that reveal the vibrancy of matter and the multiplicity of agencies without re-colonising them under a new universalism.

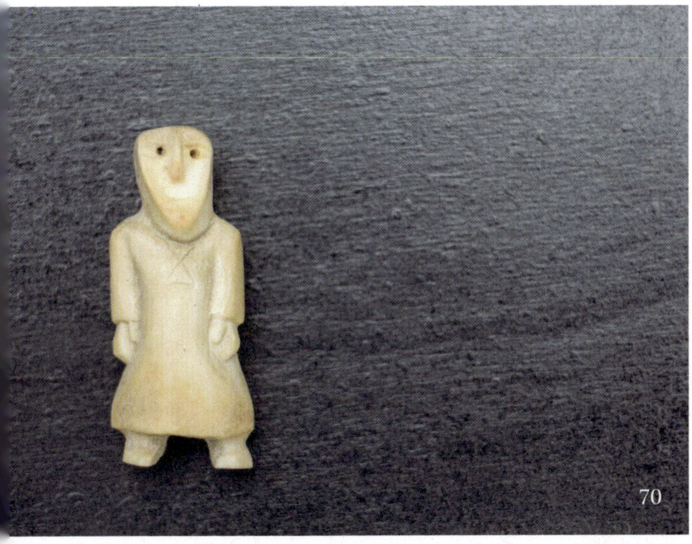

228. I will take up this notion in more depth in → Socio-aesthetic Emergence, 312.

Fig. 70: *Russian Talisman*, guest object of Efva Lilja, 2023, © photo: Mariella Greil.

In conclusion, the encounter between Bennett's vibrant matter and Franke's post-human animism invites us to imagine a world in which the commons – I mean those spaces where practices of commoning actually take shape – is no longer the exclusive domain of human subjects but an assemblage of animated agencies. To think-feel-activate these notions together is to orient thought towards the porous, the plural, and the performative: a world where stones, spirits, infrastructures, and imaginaries co-constitute each other, and where the task of embodied research is less to master than to be attentive towards.

Micro-phenomenological Interview with Efva Lilja
Excerpt, edited transcript
14 April 2023

Mariella Greil: And this other object... is a bone?!

Efva Lilja: It's a Russian hand craft. I had this collaboration with Russian director Anatoly Vasiliev. I worked with him for quite some years. He invited me to start a company in Moscow. He was very challenging to work with. When he entered a space, people just rose. That Russian way – he was worshipped. He could spend hours sitting with the actors, eyes closed, and then suddenly he would open his eyes and start working [laughs]. As if it was too painful to watch the world. He was very difficult. But he made very beautiful performances. And when I said goodbye after our first collaboration, he gave me that. I think it's a very traditional figure [see Fig. 26], and it was given as a symbol of respect. It means a lot to me. He was a very radical theatre man – still is. He started in Taganka and later got his own theatre in central Moscow, near Arbat. It had everything – a stage, TV studio, mask and costume studio, plus a guesthouse, where I stayed. Then the city built him a new, fully customised theatre near the Kremlin – huge, white, very Grotowski. It even had a Globe replica, many rehearsal studios, a rooftop chapel (I didn't know he was religious), and a restaurant. It was a big, big building. But then the political situation changed. He was forced to sell tickets. He held the political view that theatre belongs to the people – it should be free, paid for by the state. But policy changed, and he was required to generate income. He refused. There was a big conflict. The staff tried to save the theatre. While he was on tour, they rented out the space to Mercedes-Benz – for world exhibitions without him knowing. But eventually, he had to leave the country. He went to France for a number of years. Now he's back in Moscow, but I don't know how things are. I have to go back.
I lived there from 1998 to 2005, back and forth between Stockholm and Moscow. It just showed how complicated the Russian situation is. Such beautiful people. But the political situation created by Putin is absolutely disgusting. People are suffering so badly from it.

Mariella: And do you carry this object as a reminder of that respect?

Efva: As a reminder of something that really moved me. Also, because my heart is somehow Russian. There's something in that energy, among the people... It's like what I felt in New York: you have to give it your all or you fail. And I loved that intensity. It's a long paragraph; I don't know if you are interested in this story.

Mariella: You mean it's a kind of all-in commitment?

Efva: Exactly. For example, in the first production I did with him, there were about fifty people on stage: actors, a choir, musicians, everyone exhausted after months of work. We were close to premiere, and one day he just came in, sat down, and said, 'We are not doing our best. I've cancelled the opening.' No drama. Just conviction. He believed we hadn't reached our potential. And so we kept working and delayed the premiere to January. Everyone was shocked – imagine the cost! But he didn't care. 'We haven't reached our capacity.' But during the process, there was so much exchange. I would suggest something, ask, 'What if I do this or that?' and it was welcome. And even after rehearsals, we'd all go home and keep working – thinking, preparing, digesting. It wasn't about clocking out at five. It was about honouring the work.

Mariella: Yeah. Our job doesn't really separate life and work like that...

Efva: No. It was a shared ethic. It was about dignity. You know? A painter who's proud of their work can finish the day with dignity. But if you just throw paint on a canvas and walk away without caring... well, that's something else. And it's the same with us, whether it's theatre or dance or anything else.

Mariella: And still, in our field, everything is organised around deadlines, premieres, short production cycles...

Efva: Exactly. And that's why I had to restructure my company. We knew we needed a year-long process to finish something meaningful. So, we created a system: a repertoire we can perform immediately while continuing to develop new work over longer periods. That way, we can take time – pause, reflect, return. Let things breathe. Not everything should be adrenaline and fast turnovers.

Mariella: It's like slow cooking. A kind of commitment to time.

Efva: Yes, but hard to explain in a culture that values immediacy. The arts have become so dominated by trends, by conceptual shortcuts. You're expected to present something based on an impulse, and that's it.

Mariella: Adrenaline-based.

Efva: And sure, there's value in that. But if it becomes the only mode, we lose depth. There's a lack of trust in the process. People ask, 'Why do you do what you do?' – especially when public money is involved. And I think, fine – just don't ask me to *justify* it. Ask me to *articulate* it. That's a different thing.

Mariella: Right. Why is it relevant?

Efva: Exactly. We have to train ourselves to speak about what we do – not to reduce it but to give it context. In Russia, when I showed my work, people rarely said, 'I don't get it.' They had opinions. They'd say, 'Why didn't you do it this way?' They engaged. Even if they didn't like it, they had a reason.

Mariella: So not just, 'I didn't understand,' and then walk away…

Efva: Right. I still get that response sometimes. But if I ask them, 'Well, what did you experience? What were you feeling?' they often come out with something extraordinary. And I say, 'That's it. That's your understanding of the piece.' And then we can have a conversation – your experience and mine. But we're so trained to associate understanding with right and wrong. And that kills trust in subjective experience.

Mariella: And alongside that, there's a kind of diminishing of the role of aesthetics.

Efva: Yes. Because aesthetics can't always be explained in words. And we've come to rely too much on verbal rationality. In Western culture, it's all timelines – beginnings, endings, logic. But in other cultures, time is circular. There's trust in the moment. You can feel something deeply without needing to define it.

Mariella: Or maybe just be more nuanced and precise about the feeling itself. More phenomenological.

Efva: Exactly.

Animae and *Objecti*

Here, I would like to introduce another promising juxtaposition – between *animae* and *objecti*. It generates a productive tension, I find, as both terms are grounded in classical languages – Latin and Greek – yet they reverberate differently in the present. *Animae*, the plural of *anima*, denotes, as introduced in the last chapter, breath, soul, life force, and the intangible capacity of vital movement; *objecti*, as the plural of *objectum*, signifies what is 'thrown against' or 'placed before', that which confronts perception and is thought of as externality. To explore their divergences and convergences is not to return to a solely philological exercise but to situate their etymological traces within contemporary concerns about trans*materialities and trans*subjectivities – fields in which boundaries between bodies, materials, and agencies are less stable than classical metaphysics has presumed. In diffractive dialogues, we practice trans-bodied conversation and explore *other forms* of relating to singular, shared, infradimensional *worldings*. In her book *Relationscapes – Movement, Art,*

Philosophy, philosopher and artist Erin Manning discusses the interval as a 'quality through which the relation is felt'.[229] She writes,

> This singularity is what expresses the virtual fullness of the interval, its plentitude. This plentitude is the worlding of the movement. That interval is worlding does not mean that it contains the world, but that it potentially expresses the infradimensional, which is the worlding of pure plastic rhythm.[230]

In my micro-phenomenological practice, I found a tool to expand the interval, and the choreographic environment similarly performed this act of attuning to the plentitude that is present in the space-between, that which Manning terms 'the interval'.

The breath of our body performs this fullness and rhythm of the interval. Etymologically, *anima* derives from the Indo-European roots *ane-*, meaning 'to breathe'.[231] From breath to spirit, *anima* becomes that which animates the corporeal. It resonates with the Greek Ψυχή (*psyche*), again tied to breath and life, but also to affectivity, imagination, and the invisible dimensions of existence. *Objectum*, by contrast, stems from *obiciere*; its roots are, as I said, 'to present', 'to throw against', or 'to cast before'. It presupposes an intentional subject to which the object is opposed, positioning the object as an obstacle or a fact in the field of perception. The metaphysical drama of Western thought is rehearsed in this polarity between *animae* and *objecti*: life force and soul on one side, inert externality on the other.

Yet in contemporary aesthetics, particularly within performance and installation practices, this polarity is destabilised. *Animae* find resonance in performances where breath, voice, and affect emerge as carriers of presence beyond representation. Performative bodies do not merely signify; they materialise the *anima* through gestures, intensities, and rhythms that are just as energetic as they are symbolic, just as factual as poetic. The *animae* of performance cannot be reduced to psychological interiorities; they are trans*material: they circulate between performers and spectators, across atmospheres and environments, producing collective embodiments that exceed individual subjects.[232] Performance thus foregrounds the vitality and transmissibility of *animae*, aligning with contemporary theories of affect and with post-human accounts of distributed agency.

229. Erin Manning, *Relationscapes: Movement, Art, Philosophy* (MIT Press, 2009), 17.

230. Ibid., 35.

231. 'Animus', etymonline, accessed 24 August 2025, https://www.etymonline.com/word/animus. In 'BREATHE – An Introductory Dialogue', Sandra Noeth and Janez Janša speak about the vital, physical act they want to connect to fundamental questions about life and its inequalities. Sandra Noeth and Janez Janša, 'BREATHE — An Introductory Dialogue', in *Breathe: Critical Research into the Inequalities of Life*, ed. Sandra Noeth and Janez Janša (transcript, 2023), 6.

232. André Lepecki, *Singularities: Dance in the Age of Performance* (Routledge, 2016), 45–47.

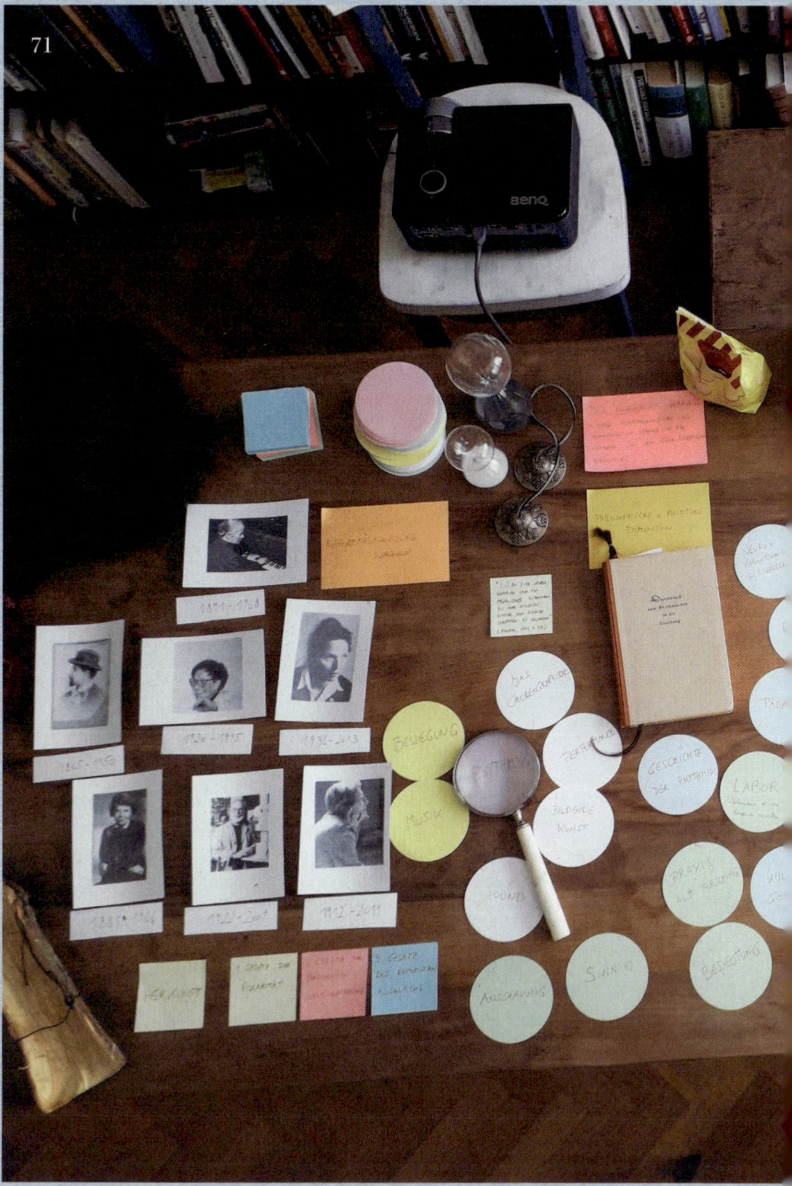

If you...

If you respect history,
history will respect you back!
– said Peter Pleyer in a 1997 dance class.

Climate catastrophe, wars, pandemics,
vulnerabilities proliferate, angst and
anxiety spread.
Desperation crops up,
a scar rehearsed until it dances back.
These days, history answers only
when activated:
through repetition, deviation,
through breath interrupting form,
refusing to stay past.

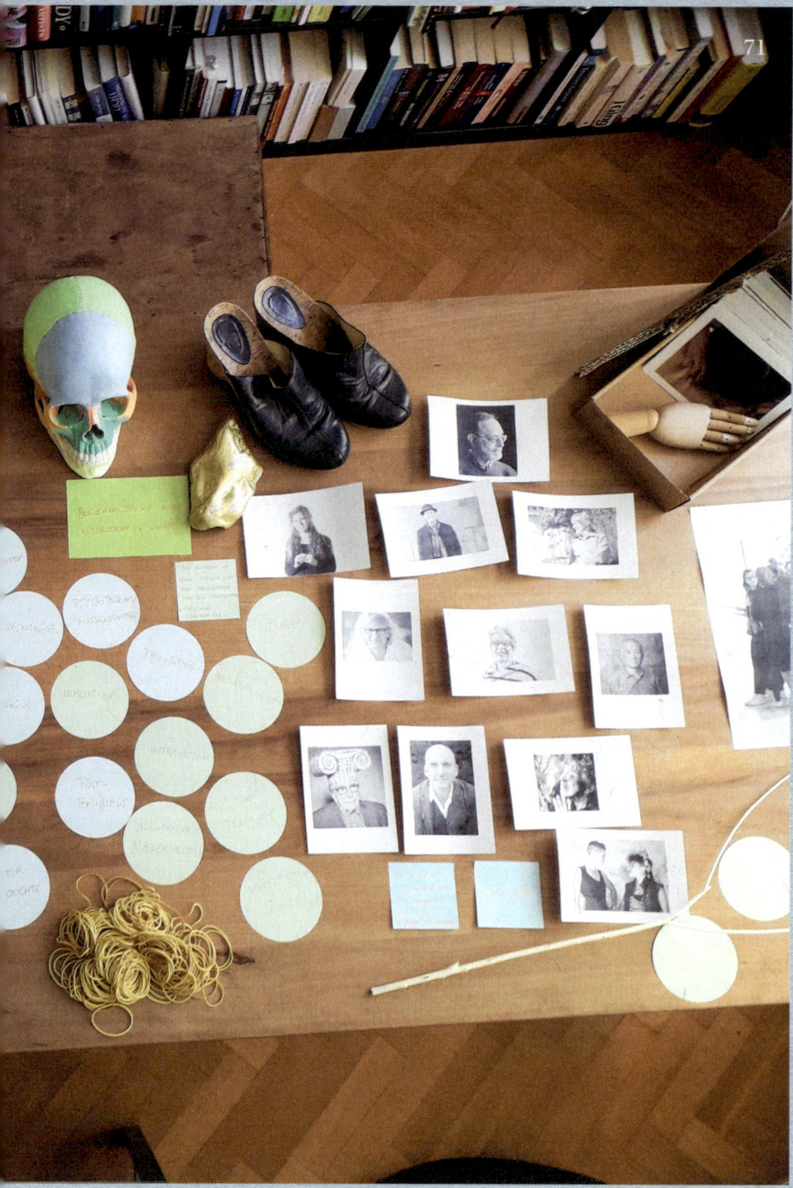

Are we willing to become the material of histories?

A fundraiser for 300 warm-help boxes for elderly people in Kyiv
arrives in my winter mailbox
with the unchanged belief that dance and art matter
– writes Peter Pleyer in his 2026 newsletter.

There is another question lingering:
If you respect the future,
will the future respect you back?

Conversely, *objecti* occupy a privileged place in fine art installations. Installations confront visitors with spatialised arrangements of objects that are neither inert nor self-sufficient. They are staged to interrupt habitual perception, to reconfigure relations of scale, materiality, and perspectival orientation.[233] The *objectum* here is not a passive datum but a participant in assemblages that demand bodily negotiation and sensory recalibration. The object in the installation is always already relational: it organises pathways, choreographs movements, and invites tactile or haptic engagement As artist and art critic O'Doherty writes, 'Things make space happen.'[234] Whereas the object in classical metaphysics was conceived of as mute externality, in contemporary installations, it becomes an interlocutor that speaks through spatial dramaturgies and performs trans*materialities.

Micro-phenomenological Interview with Emma Cocker
Excerpt, edited transcript
26 September 2022

Mariella: So, for you, touching with your hands here didn't feel right?

Emma: I think it's because it is a way of interacting with materials that already have a history, belonging to the lineage of the 'correct' way to do it. I think some of my enquiry was about trying to thwart that established way of becoming present by inviting another kind of presence. So, flicking through the images or playing the drum felt like that tactility is already *prescribed* by the objects. It's something to do with the way history invites or doesn't invite certain ways of interacting, setting in motion some interactions and disabling others.

Mariella: Are those histories imagined?

Emma: Yes. Imagined and cultural.

Mariella: Yes, and imagination is influenced by cultural belonging and vice versa.

What links *animae* and *objecti* is the reconfiguration of their boundaries under conditions of trans*materiality and trans*subjectivity. Trans*materiality designates the porosity of materials, their capacity to exchange forces, affects, and energies across categories once conceived of as discrete. I remember two performances that made their trans*materiality intensely tangible. In the first, *Agnus Dei* (2012) by performer and architect Viktor Fuček, the warm breath of the performer's body melted an ice lamb, a traditional symbol of sacrifice and purity, over a duration of 173 min., 53 sec. The performer amplified the transition between aggregate states. He attuned himself to the measure of existence in search of the 'right' rhythm for a breath between body and world, between the material and the spiritual. The other work, which I witnessed live in Liverpool, is *BLEU REMIX* (2007) by Yann Marussich, where the heat within an installation cube made of glass altered the circulation of the performer's bodily fluids. Blue-tinted biological liquid oozed through the layers of his skin like strange blue perspiration.

233. Claire Bishop, *Installation Art: A Critical History* (Tate Publishing, 2005), 6–13.

234. Brian O'Doherty, *Inside the White Cube: The Ideology of the Gallery Space* (The Lapis Press, 1986 [1976]), 39.

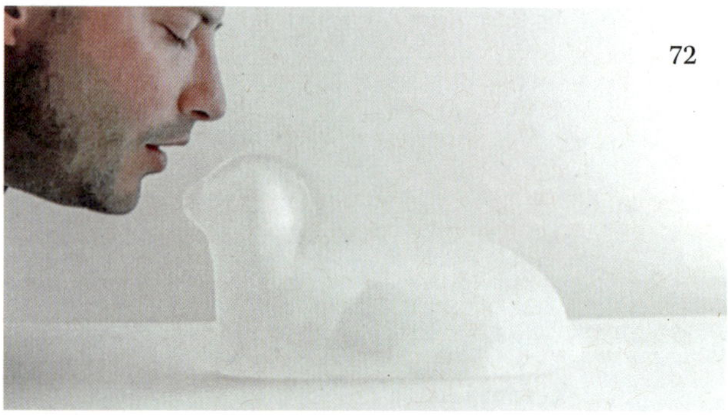

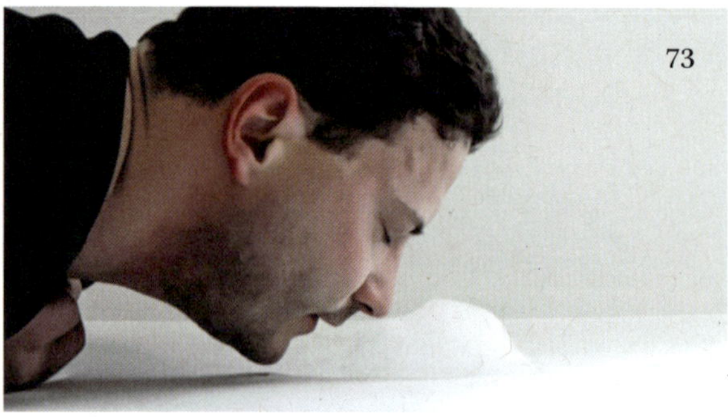

These two performances were two quite memorable instances of trans*materialisation, where *animae* and *objecti* co-constituted each other. Trans*subjectivities, correspondingly, mark the dispersal of subjectivity across assemblages. Neither the performer's psyche nor the spectator's consciousness can claim ownership of the experience; rather, subjectivity emerges in the in-between, shaped by material mediations or, as contemporary philosopher and feminist theoretician Rosi Braidotti states, by 'a new way of combining ethical values with the well-being of an enlarged sense of community, which includes one's territorial or environmental inter-connections'.[235]

In this terrain, phantasms and realisms are not strict oppositions but at times strangely entangled. *Animae* commonly conjures up phantasmatic associations: soul, spirit, ghostly presences that elude empirical capture. Yet in performance, phantasms are real forces; they have an impact on perception, reconfigure temporality, and inscribe themselves into collective memory.[236] Similarly, *objecti*, conventionally the guarantors of realism, become spectral when staged in installations: stripped of their utilitarian contexts, they hover between presence and absence, solidity and the imagined or sensed. The phantasm thus belongs equally to the realm of *objecti*, while realism can be claimed by *animae* as the reality of affective transmission. Together, they manifest a transmaterial aesthetics.

235. Rosi Braidotti, 'Posthuman Ethics', in *The Posthuman* (Polity, 2013), 190.

236. Fischer-Lichte carefully differentiates between episodic and semantic memory, and emphasises physical articulations such as emotions and sensations as meanings. Erika Fischer-Lichte, *The Transformative Power of Performance: A New Aesthetics*, trans. Saskya Iris Jain (Routledge, 2008 [2004]), 150–60.

Figs. 72 and 73: *Agnus Dei*, 2012, © video still and performance: Victor Fuček. Slovakian artist, architect, and performer Victor Fuček writes, 'Our culture has developed through labour on fields. Our culture has evolved in the rhythm of peasant life, but we don't live in this rhythm now and instead we run. When we learn how to breathe correctly we learn how to live.' This short description accompanies the video documentation of the performance *Agnus Dei* (Rome, 2012), accessed 13 October 2025, https://www.youtube.com/watch?v=NF4z9UfBwJ8. Further information on his work can be found on his website: https://www.viktorfucek.net.

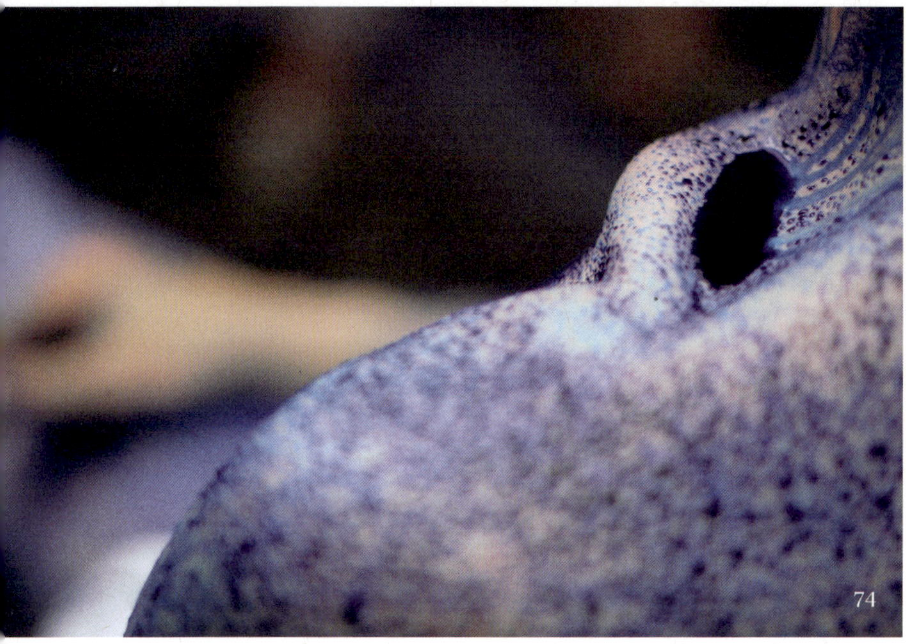

Micro-phenomenological Interview with Kerstin Kussmaul

Excerpt, edited transcript

10 November 2022

Mariella: That's the whole question about awareness and consciousness. And if we bring in sensitivity, I perceive the experience as a hypersensitive space. My starting point is to develop preconditions and dive in. And it was really beautiful to see how you were there. In this practice, my big fear is that someone will enter and then collect information, rather than experiencing the materials.

Kerstin Kussmaul: It really felt like a huge invitation, that's for sure, which was made possible by the kinds of materials and how they're presented.

Mariella: That moment of recognition: does it have maybe a colour or temperature besides the feeling of release in the belly?

Kerstin: It's warm, fuzzy, and light – because it gives me a feeling of being understood, which is always something that makes relationships smoother. The way you responded acknowledged a journey I had made in the space and shaped what it became in that moment. It was also a recognition of the linearity of time and its constant change. So, there was also this act of recognising together that time is evolving.

Mariella: Yes, even though I have to say, when I was in it, it felt timeless.

Kerstin: Yes!

Mariella: There's something about the various ways of relating to time, since at several points I was the timekeeper. In holding the timeline, there was a gravitational pull of presence drawing me into the moment.

Kerstin: I know, I had the same experience when I was in the space, I could have gone on for another hour. There is an element of timelessness, and yet I strongly sensed a metaphor of time's harvest, where awareness of the changes taking place made me observe everything as if it were unfolding right now, before rearranging elements of confusion.

Ultimately, the differences between *animae* and *objecti* remain significant. *Animae* emphasises interior motion, vitality, the invisible force of animation; *objecti* emphasises exteriority, confrontation, and resistance. Yet in contemporary artistic practices, both are continually being resituated within aesthetic practices and processes,

Fig. 74: *BLEU REMIX*, 2008, © photo: Jakub Wittchen, performance: Yann Marussich.

rather than essences. In my experience, performance shows that *animae* are not metaphysical souls but an intercorporeal force field, while installations reveal *objecti* to be not inert givens but activated nodes within experiential choreographies.

Thus, as my embodied research into choreo-ethical assemblages affirms, *animae* and *objecti* today necessitate a double gesture: to recover their etymological depth and to reimagine them through transmaterial and transsubjective practices. This gesture aligns with the broader shift occurring in philosophy and aesthetics towards post-dualistic paradigms. The once stable division of phantasm and realism, subject and object, life and matter, nature and culture is dissolving into a continuum where the breathing body of performance *and* installation object both articulate modes of presence, affect, and relation.

Finally, *animae* and *objecti* no longer stand in opposition to one another as spirits and matter but are entangled figures in the aesthetic negotiation of our contemporary moment, as artists, researchers, and also as human agencies. Their convergence in the domains of performance and installation – concretely in my research as diffractive dialogues in choreographic environments – underscores a broader rethinking of artistic ontology: one in which trans*materialities and trans*subjectivities[237] shape a field where phantasms are real, and realism is haunted.

Birthing Cosmogonies

Despite the mutual contamination and fluid boundaries between the imaginary and the factual, I am reminded of what Deleuze and Guattari call 'the smooth space' in their tome *A Thousand Plateaus.*

Micro-phenomenological Interview with Evfa Lilja
Excerpt, edited transcript
14 April 2023

Mariella Greil: We organise it in different taxonomies. The practices and techniques we engage with come with their own epistemologies. For example, inviting you to do the 'Dark Bag Score' opens up certain epistemological movements. And now I'm wondering, how do you know that you have this curiosity? How do you recognise your desire to know when touching the object?

Evfa Lilja: My curiosity feeds my will. It just drives me forward in life, and I simply trust my curiosity to guide me. Whether it has to do with manoeuvring through everyday life or with art-making. And it is not that I'm after all the answers. I don't need to know the answers. I just need this drive. Curiosity gives me the strength to approach life. If I lose my curiosity – which happens sometimes – I lose my motivation. Because what I already know is not enough, right?

Mariella: Which brings us back to the researcher, right?

Evfa: Yes.

Mariella: Okay, so now it is me who has to make a decision about which object we are going to discuss. I got the peeler. I have it in my hands now. This decision was made pretty sensorially because I like the way I hold it in my hands. It feels useful. I also think of peeling the skin. I was thinking of when you take off the skin off a person – quite a heavy image, but that is what comes to mind. Basically, this is what we do to the cucumber: we take off

237. Leticia Glocer Fiorini, 'Trans-Subjectivities: The Analyst's Attempts to Classify and Their Effects on Countertransference', *The Psychoanalytic Review* 109, no. 3 (2022): 257–75, https://guilfordjournals.com/doi/10.1521/prev.2022.109.3.257.

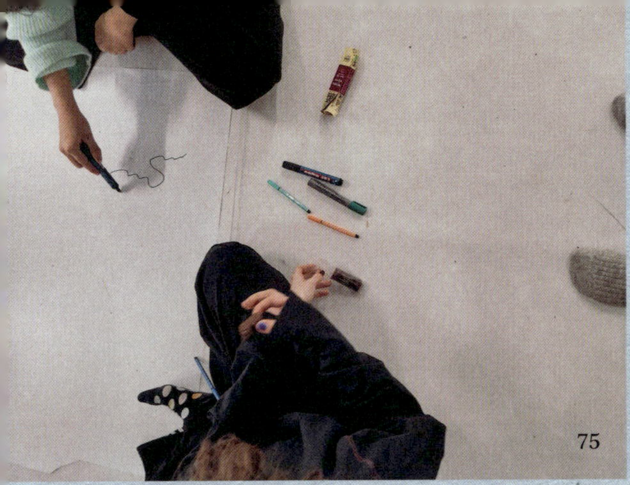

Noise of Human Consciousness

Hi, my name is Welcome!

I share this generously empty space with you
and have decided to emphasize listening.
At the peak of toomuchness,
it is my attempt to exit the endless pink noise.
It is my ongoing practice,
maybe located, half-forgotten,
jamming in the hollowness of human
consciousness,
where we find snippets of pop culture.
Wrong direction, wrong direction, stupidity
let go!

Exploded whales, flags of fog,
the ironing of mamaninipupulalatitionon,
after which expanded strategies of imagination
came to the fore,
replacing choreographic hints or the art
of facilitation.
As a matter of fact,
all goals have been removed;
Instead, today, ethics inspires
politics,
making time to explore
an entry point
for performing in public spaces.

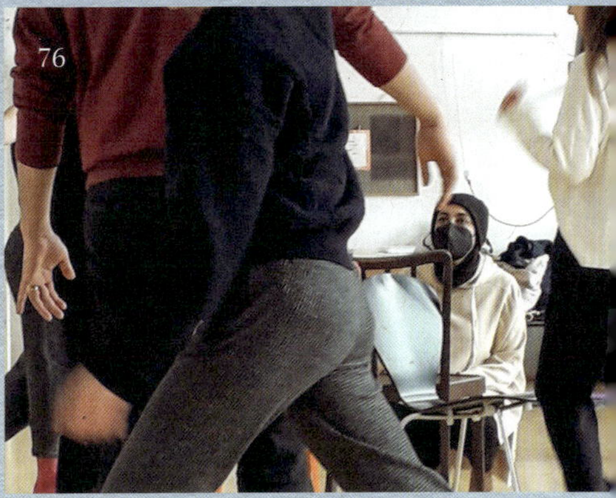

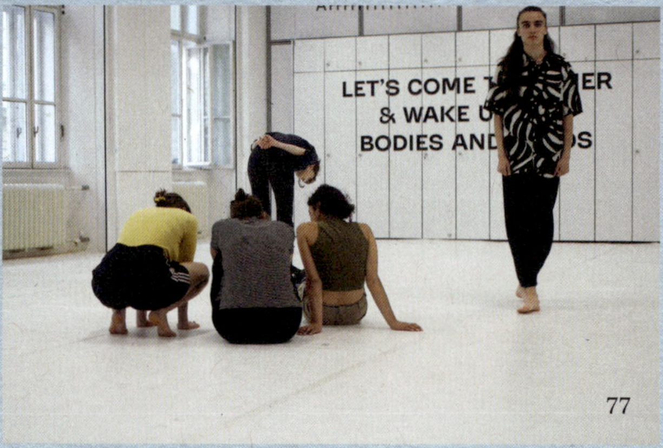

77

Who are you?
I am
a vibrating tectonic plate,
a fissure, a gap of knowledge,
a strange ministry of inner affairs.
I deal with tremors and traumas
and dance towards the centre of gravity
I try to move my body in alignment with the Earth.

I am a choreo-ethical assemblage
that will never have happened.

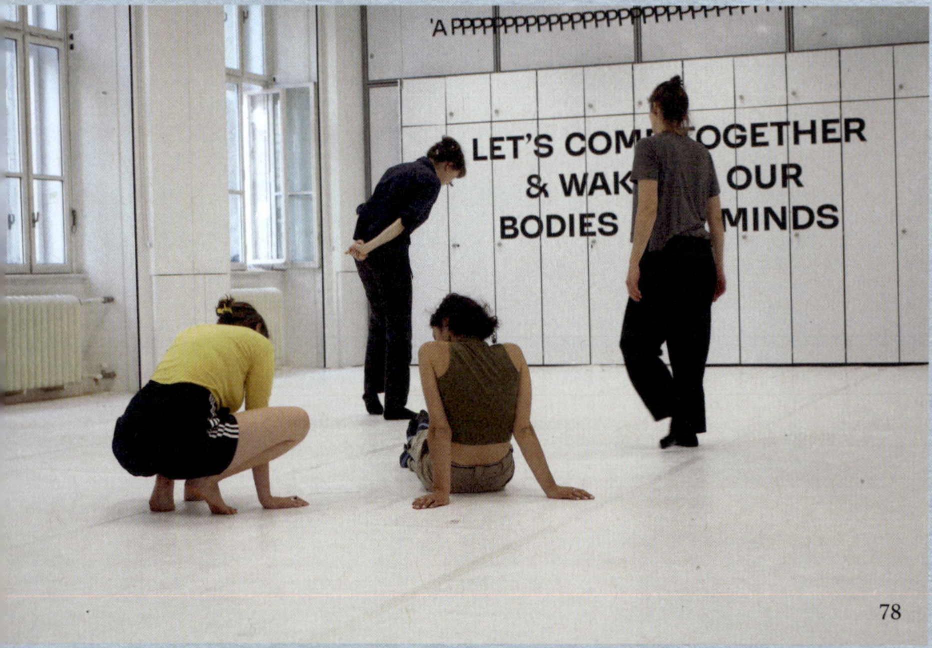

78

the skin in order to eat it. So, preparing it for our own nourishment and pleasure. Sometimes I peel carrots until I only have the strings of them. I feel some pleasure in that. There's something about taking off the outer layer to go deeper inside. That what interests me. And the peeler is a tool for this. I think creating tools was part of our evolution when we differentiated ourselves from animals. We are surrounded by so many tools in this moment. But this is a peeler so it's helping us to take off the skin. The skin is actually the biggest organ that we have. We would probably not be able to breathe if our skin was gone.

Evfa: Yeah. So, I think it's beautiful when you talk about utilisation. Peeling off. You can peel off so many different layers of consciousness to get closer to you, to your being.

Mariella: Yes, and of course I have always associated it with bare bodies, as this has been an obsession.

Evfa: I have such an intense feeling towards that object, my stomach is crampy. I thought I'd never use it. I got it as a gift from a person with whom I had a very intense love affair, two years ago. We were absolutely passionate. We were talking about getting married, moving in together; everything was so intense. Then suddenly, he became psychotic and disappeared into nowhere. He was admitted into an institution where he didn't want to be. I was not allowed to follow. He didn't want to reveal or expose his vulnerability. He wanted to be the strong one, and suddenly he was not. This was his first experience of absolute depression in his life. He had a lot of problems as an effect of medications and had cancer for many years. He had never talked to anyone about it. He wanted to stand on his own two feet and show up strong, until it was just too much and his system collapsed. And the last time he was in my house he brought me that kind of peeler. I never used it. It's useless. It peeled off all of my defence. It left me completely naked in that situation. So, that failed relationship is still a bare sore in my soul. This peeler was staring at me in my drawer when you asked me to pick some sort of object.

Mariella: A really intense relationship, a whole world and a love story condensed in this peeler.

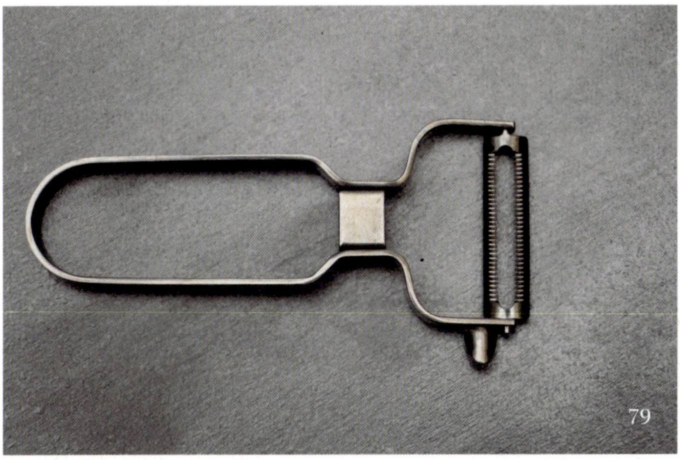

The following passage about *birthing cosmogonies* focuses on choreo-ethical assemblages of care, in which artistic practice, philosophical speculation, and socio-political imagination intersect. The cosmogony, as I propose it, fuses cosmogenesis with co-agency: it is not the origin of a cosmos from a singular source but the ongoing birthing[238] of worlds through collective, entangled acts of becoming. This articulation opens up a horizon for thinking about creation beyond the logics of singular authorship or hierarchical genealogy. Instead, birthing is understood as distributed, multiple, and processual – a cosmogony of plurality rather than of origin.

238. In the July-August 2025 issue of *tanzraumberlin*, choreographer, performer, and writer Claire Lefèvre 'reflects on creative processes as birthing metaphors. She introduces the figure of the "performance doula", a protagonist who would support people emotionally and physically before, during and after the gestational work of art making'. Claire Lefèvre, 'The Performance Doula', *tanzraumberlin*, July-August 2025, https://www.tanzraumberlin.de/en/tanzbuero/trb-magazine/article/the-performance-doula.

Fig. 79: *Peeler*, guest object of Efva Lilja, 2023, © photo: Mariella Greil.

Proliferating viewpoints, refracting perception through multiplicity, and cultivating what can be called the fantastic perspective is generative: it births altered spatialities (or as I call them, choreographic environments) that, in turn, permit alternative ways of relating. Cosmogonies emerge precisely in such perspectival bifurcations, where the frame of the worlding – as I introduced it earlier in relation to the Renaissance idea of cosmopoiesis – is not given but continuously assembled, destabilised, and reconstituted. Rather than coming out of the blue, the emphasis on birthing brings into focus questions of artistic care, reproduction, and intergenerational responsibility in connection with artistic creations and the passing on of cosmopoietic practices.

Cosmogonies are not only cosmological gestures but also lived practices of interdependence, where the birthing of worlds is inseparable from the birthing of relations of care. Amid shifting cultural imaginaries, cosmogonies articulate themselves as choreo-ethical processes; they choreograph relations, distribute agencies, and reconfigure the ethical space of coexistence. To perform is to orient oneself towards a shared, improvisational process of becoming. Animist resonances are not incidental, and, especially in contemporary accounts of animism, distributed personhood is foregrounded, as well as reciprocal agency and the recognition of nonhuman forces as co-constitutive of worlds. To birth[239] a cosmogony is to affirm, question, and challenge how life unfolds in mutual accompaniment rather than being unilateral production.

The aesthetic implications of birthing cosmogonies are profound. Performance art stages cosmogonies by foregrounding processes over products, presence over representation. The performer births worlds of affective resonance that exceed individual subjectivity, drawing spectators into co-agential assemblages. Installation art participates in a similar way, as material arrangements shape conditions for emergence rather than merely representing a given order. In both cases, the artwork becomes less a stable object than an ongoing birthing of relations – a fantastic perspective enacted in time and space.

The fantastic lies in the generative, in creativity, revealing the contingent plurality of world-making. Thus, cosmogonies are not fantasies in the pejorative sense but fantastic operations: perspectival inventions that open up towards co-created future cosmologies.

Ethically, the act of birthing cosmogonies challenges the sovereign figure of the solitary subject. It insists on co-becoming as constitutive of existence. This resonates with feminist and decolonial accounts of relational ontology, where life is always shared from the outset and care is foundational rather than supplementary. The parental is not only a private role but a site where global inequalities, technologies, and politics intersect and impact the beginning of a life enormously. To conceive

239. Cordula Daus' research project *Outer Woman* (2020–26) and Dorottya Vékony's work address birthing, midwifery, and ectogenesis. See 'Outer Woman', FWF, accessed 28 September 2025, https://doi.org/10.55776/V797; Cordula Daus, accessed 28 September 2025, https://corduladaus.com; Dorottya Vékony, accessed 28 September 2025, https://dorottyavekony.com. In my own explorations, I focus on the connections and differences between cosmogonies and cosmopoiesis, and how material configurations can act as generative thresholds, birthing perceptual and affective shifts. Emphasising porous materials and precarious balances foregrounds cosmogony as a fragile, ongoing negotiation between forces – human, material, and environmental.

Material Births

Growth in plural –
a field of roots and glass
then humble stepping aside:
affects, winds, streams,
learning their ordainment
long after the collapse.

How does realness enter material births –
through a trembling refusal to be seamless?
When is it time to initiate a cosmogony?
Mid-breath, the heart of the plant
is moist and full of sap of life,
matter doesn't hesitate,
pressing sweetness into fibre.

Even if forgotten,
whirlwinds of encounter return like dreams,
folded into sleep.
Freedom to navigate the joy of missing out,
tender suffering and taking refuge in a future
that has not yet grown a body.

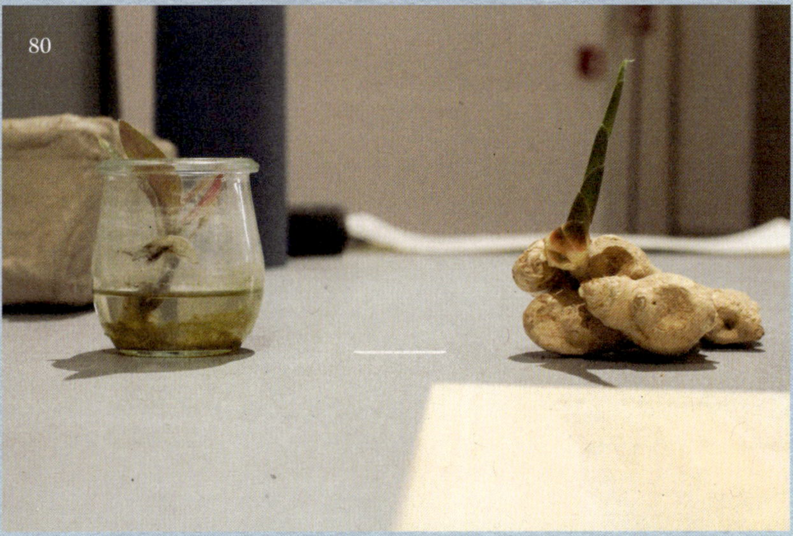

A house of lucent opacity stands,
striving to be understandable.
Its transparent walls become thin,
sensitive to touch,
tuning the ear to encounters across agencies,
vegetal, mineral, human,
vibrating in dense intimacy.

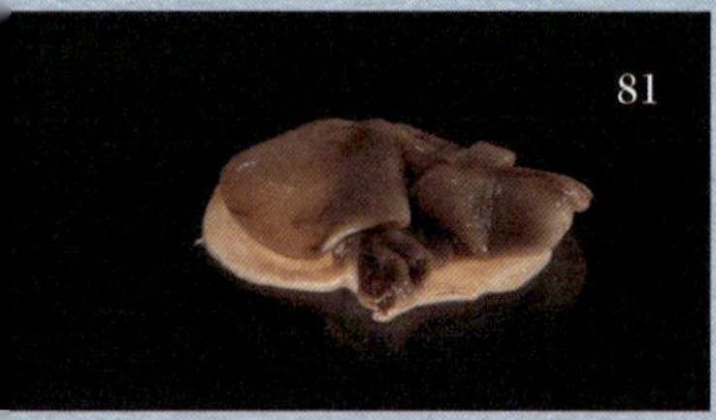
81

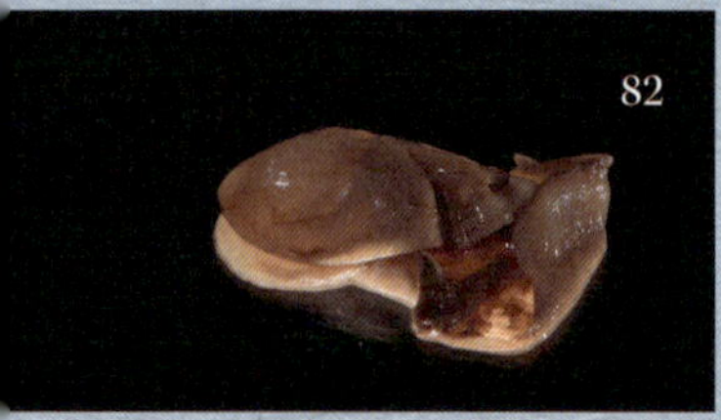
82

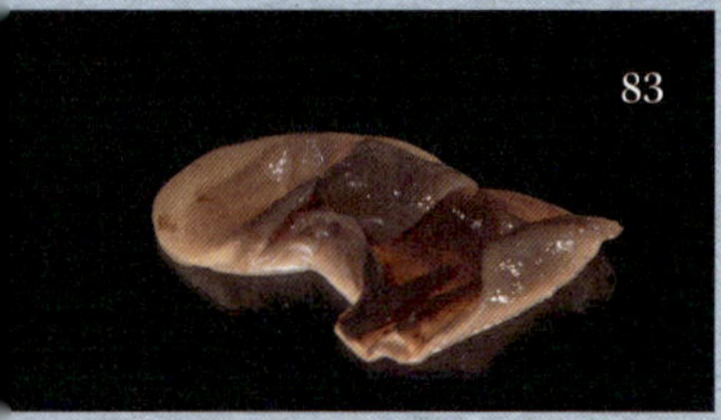
83

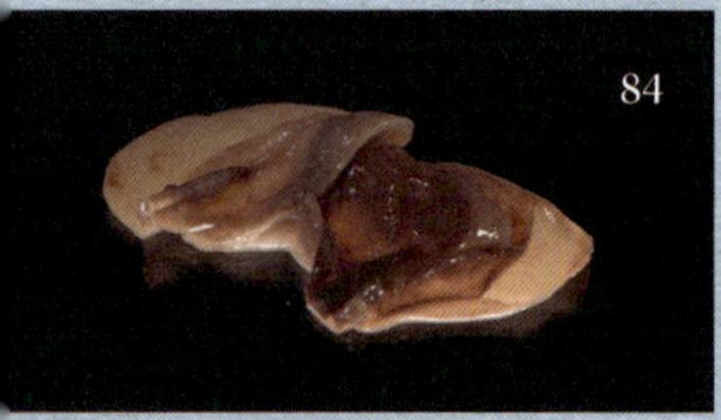
84

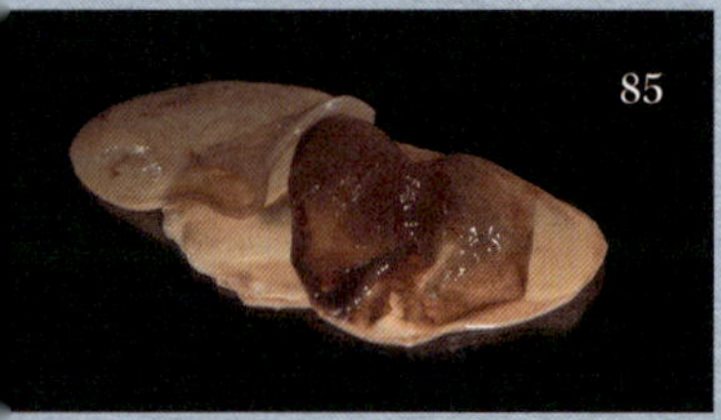
85

There are revolutions that invest
in new relations
with vibrating vital forces,
slow, risky.
The adventure of creation
in common cosmogonies
will flourish with many tremulous
voices.
Quivering, becoming –
an echo of Édouard Glissant's dreams –
an archipelago of
interdependent works,
held apart by water,
connected by drift.

cosmogonies is therefore not a romanticised artistic metaphor but actually a site of intersection, where global inequalities, technologies, and politics need to be taken seriously as the entangled realities of birthing worlds – artistic, social, and cosmic.

Whereas traditional cosmogonies are often narrated through myths of singular creators – gods, demiurges, or founding fathers – cosmogonies practiced in the context of choreo-ethical assemblaging[240] in this sense resist centripetal narratives. They are plural, improvisatory, and fragile, sustained by acts of mutual care and continuous negotiations of difference. The birthing of cosmogonies is not so much an origin story as it is an ethics of ongoingness: worlds are always in the making, and responsibility lies in *how* they are midwifed.

In essence, *birthing cosmogonies* denotes a conceptual and practical orientation that draws on aesthetic, philosophical, and social-theoretical resources. It mobilises the fantastic as a technique of multiplicity, situates itself within lineages of smooth spaces of thought, and resonates with feminist re-conceptualisations of artistic, cosmopoietic acts as contested practices. As such, cosmogonies propose thinking about world-making as a process of collective birthing: not genesis from nothing, but genesis as co-agency – trans-subjective, trans-material, and profoundly ethical.

The SCOBYs (symbiotic cultures of bacteria and yeast) came into the project during the pandemic, when I needed to radically shift my research to the confines of my home, turning my living room into an atelier and creating desktop performances. The SCOBYs entered my artistic practice during that time in 2020. First, they appeared as an uncanny presence, at second glance nothing more than a gelatinous membrane, a curious by-product of fermentation. Yet the longer I spent exploring their form of existence and learning about their qualities and processes, the more fascinated I became. Finally, I trusted them and allowed them into my microbiome, drinking homebrewed and even double-brewed Kombucha. The SCOBY can be read as a living metaphor for processes of emergence, cohabitation, and finitude. It is a figure of birth and death that does not conform to human-centric rhythms but articulates interspecies entanglement and temporality. Rather than through a singular act of origin, a SCOBY comes into being through gradual sedimentation: invisible bacteria and yeast, suspended in a nourishing substrate of tea and sugar, align their metabolic activities until a surface mat forms. This pellicle, at once skin and scaffold, is more than the product of one organism – it is the excretion of many, a corporeal trace of metabolic excess. In this sense, the SCOBY is born through secretion rather than conception, through accretion rather than individuation. Its 'birth' is a slow coalescing, a choreography of cells layering themselves into coherence. Such a birth, if we may still call it such, challenges anthropomorphic notions of natality. Instead of rupture and singularity, it offers a mode of emergence based on continuous accumulation and interdependence. The SCOBY embodies symbiosis not as a harmonious fusion but as a fragile negotiation, a living compromise between yeast-driven fermentation and bacterial cellulose production. Its vitality is contingent on the ongoing circulation of nutrients – which

240. *Assemblaging* is a neologism I created for the practice of 'doing assemblages' that – as far as I can see in the field – has not been used elsewhere so far. However, I find it useful to have a verb for this key practice in my embodied research.

I provided it regularly according to the highest hygienic standards – or, in other words, the attentiveness of its environment and, of course, the porous interchanges across microbial species. Birth here is less an event than an œkological condition – a threshold between potential growth and decay. Yet just as its genesis unsettles the singularity of beginnings, so too does its decline disturb conventional understandings of death. A SCOBY does not die in a discrete moment of cessation. Rather, it undergoes a slow desiccation. As moisture evaporates and nourishing fluids recede, the pellicle loses pliancy, turning brittle, translucent, papery. Its microbial inhabitants retreat into dormancy, and what once was soft and generative hardens into fragility. This 'death' is, in fact, an extended process of withering, a dehydration that unfolds over days and weeks. The SCOBY's dying is not abrupt but spectral: life lingers, suspended, even as vitality diminishes. I developed an artistic practice of palliative care for SCOBYs, transforming them into artworks. I had been busy with withering processes in the *Amaryllisation* project, and I found resonances as I accompanied the SCOBYs through their drying-out processes. As I write this sentence, I am acutely aware that aridification is a real threat facing the world given the planetary climate catastrophe. However, the temporality of drying complicates any strict demarcation between life and death for the SCOBY. For unlike an organism whose cessation is final, a SCOBY retains, in many cases, the possibility of renewal. Should the desiccated pellicle be reintroduced to nourishing fluids – sweetened tea, warmth, and care – it may revive, reabsorbing liquid, softening, and awakening dormant microorganisms. This capacity for reanimation inscribes a paradox into the conventional logic of life cycles: the SCOBY is both fragile and resilient, mortal yet capable of resurrection under proper conditions. Not every dried-out SCOBY will return to vigour – if dehydration is prolonged or if microbial balance is lost, the culture may indeed perish or go mouldy. But the possibility of revitalisation complicates our imaginaries of finitude: the dried SCOBY can be read as a chrysalis-like suspension, a waiting, rather than an absolute ending.

In this way, the SCOBY stages a metaphor of relational vitality: birth not as a singular origin but as accretive becoming, death not as terminal cessation but as gradual drying out, and renewal not as a miracle but as œkological responsiveness. Its life is exemplary of symbiotic interdependence, an ontological reminder that vitality is not inherent but sustained, nourished, and, at times, restorable.

Being-in-Contact: Animating Assemblages and Relational Ontology

To speak of *being-in-contact*[241] is to invoke a mode of existence that resists isolation. Contact is not merely a surface touch or fleeting encounter but an ontological condition: entities become through their relational exposure, through their participation in fields of affect, materiality, and temporality. Within the framework of embodied research, especially in the project *Choreo-ethical Assemblages – Narrations of Bare Bodies*, assemblages and relational ontologies converge, opening

241. Greil, *Being in Contact.*

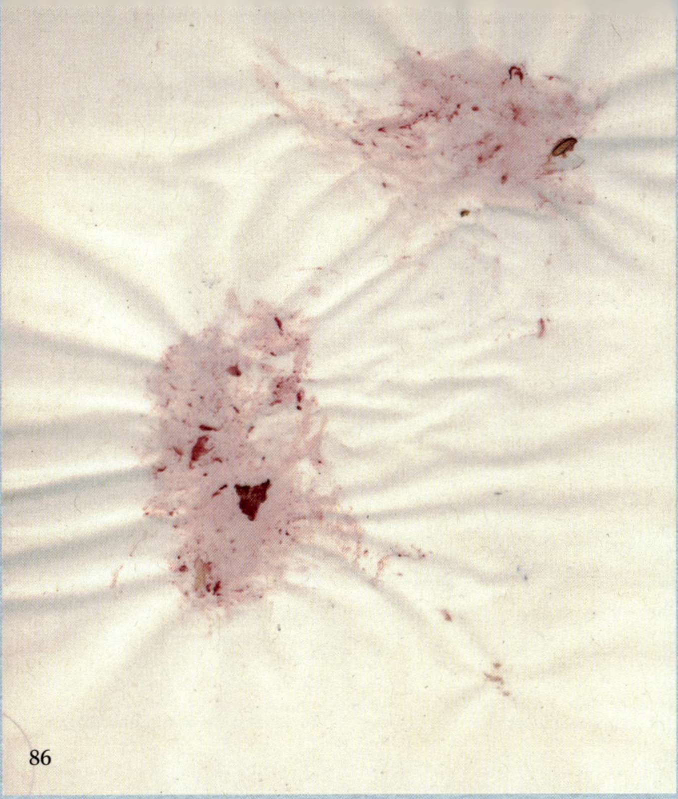

86

Amaryllian Squeeze – Visceral Embrace

**In the veins of the unexpected,
peripheral practices blossom.
Hidden in the cracks of the city,
we choose dance as our religion.
Squeezed for the tangible politics of care,
the 'we' principle survives in our shared souls.
Metaphysical exhaustion peters out
in short stories
while poetry rubs against incoherent realities.**

87

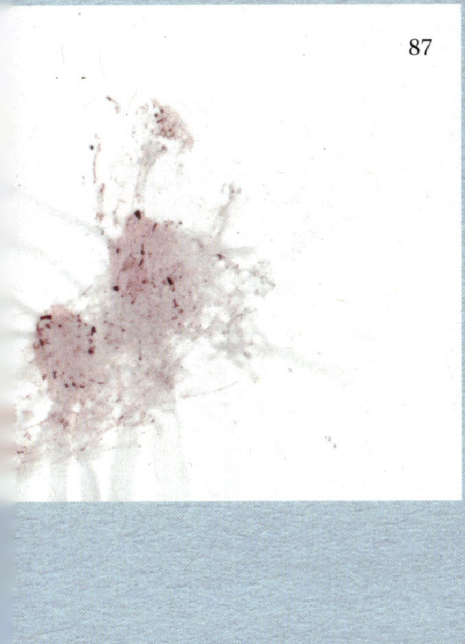

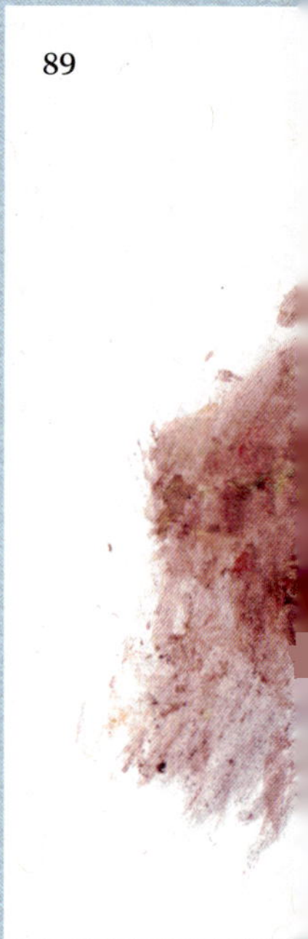

In the meadow of coexistence,
we sound out precious mystery
as we touch on imagination as the core of
(and not just addendum to) politics.
The cycle of life builds an ecology
that senses the needs of the landscapes
around us,
listens to the screams of endangered
environments,
and cares for the bodies trying to
recover from capitalism.
The glaciers, coral reefs, and polar ice caps,
as well as the plant world, the flora, the ferns,
present us with an enormous task,
call for our souls and hearts,
are direly in need of the bending of time –
time that we cannot afford to lose.

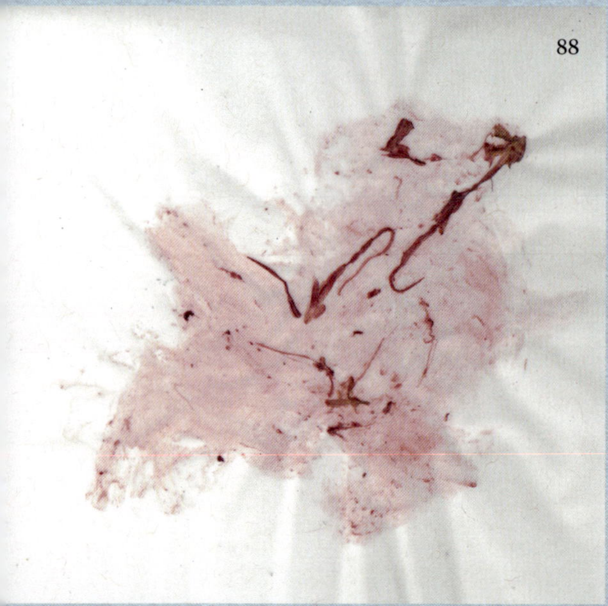

How to protect the generosity of the cycle?
What can we give, what do we need to snatch now,
and why is power in the hands of the reckless?
Pressing the blood of the plant onto the page,
before it even begins to rot away.
Damn it, where to take it from here?

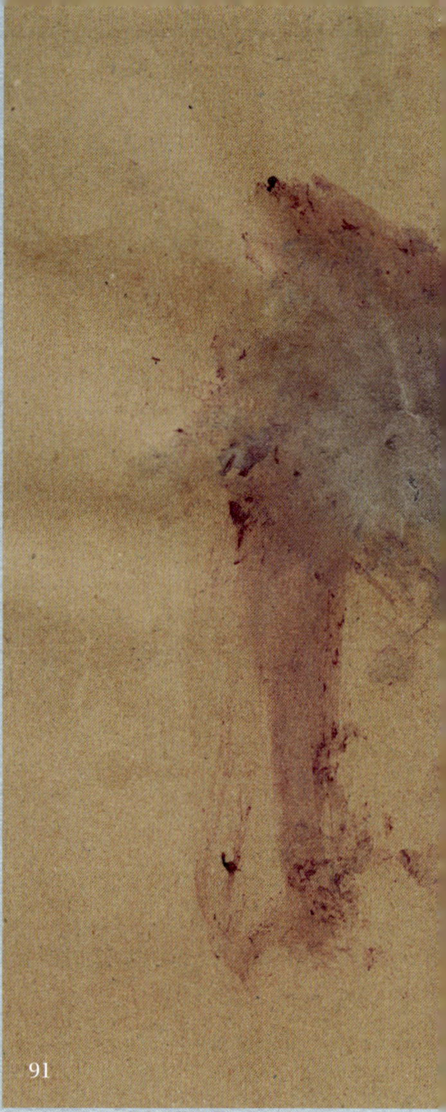

91

The images are formed
by milking the moment,
by trying and drying,
pollination and numbing,
creation and thumbing.

All the contents, the viscera of the blossoms,
pistils, pollen, petals, pedicels pressed upon paper.
Diaphanous presence and profane incarnation
at once.

92

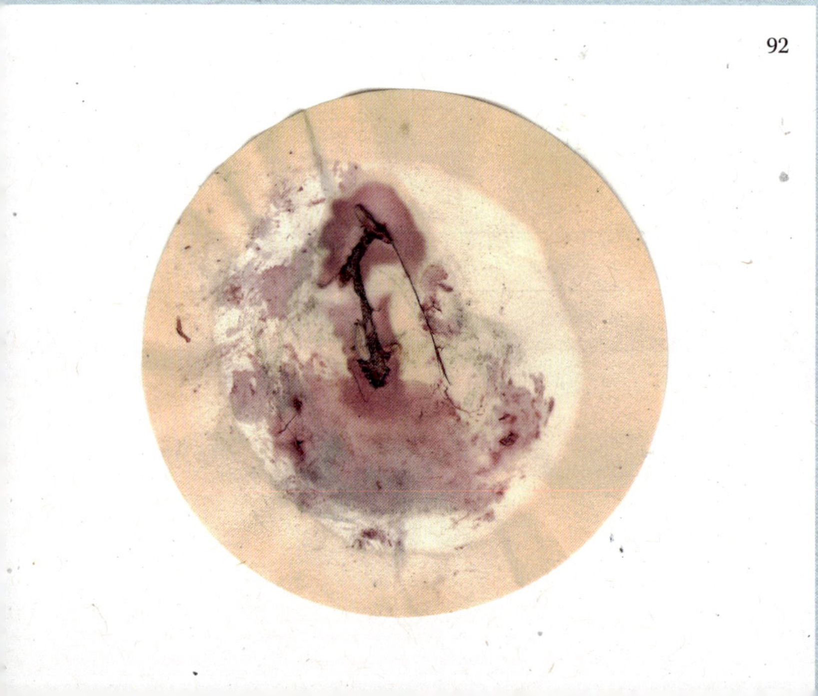

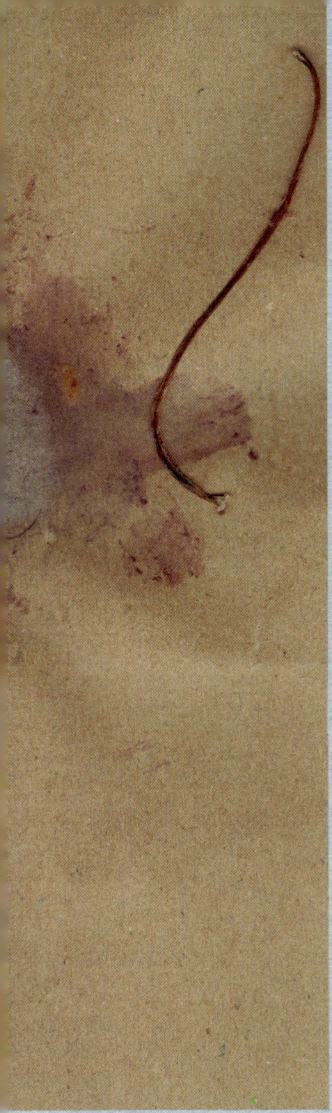

Withering Ovary

Change of life. Period.
Weight of the head.
Soft toes. Extended feelers.
The back senses the warmth,
the mouth is opening.
Dance.

One leg is here,
Another leg is there,
then they are folded, crossed,
hip and pelvis gently bend.
Meditate.

Blades (plants and shoulders), lifted,
are a vulnerable surface,
even if some think of weapons.
A leaf *cuts light* while constantly being cut
– by wind, insects, climate, human
maintenance.
Withering is to slacken, yield, decompose.
Weather.

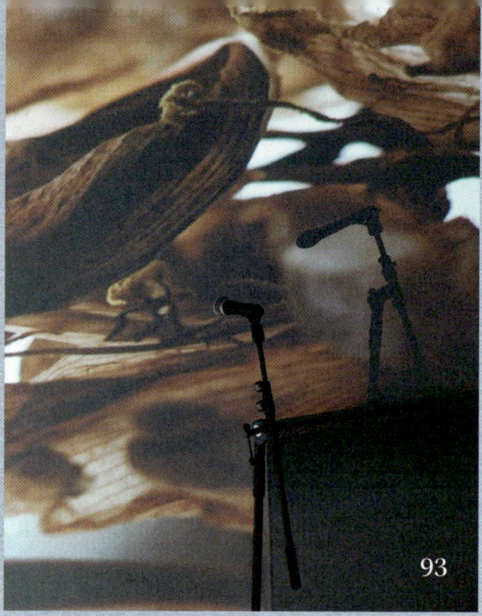

93

Folding inwards,
starch and scent retreat.
Petals fall without drama.
Time enters tissue,
relabels sweetness as seed,
fertility as memory.

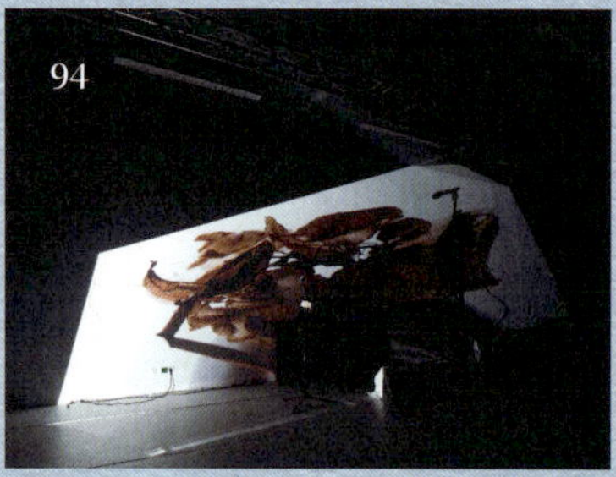

94

Still, sap circulates
in another rhythm,
another usefulness,
another season of staying.

After bloom ends,
silence bears patience,
decay bursts softly onward.

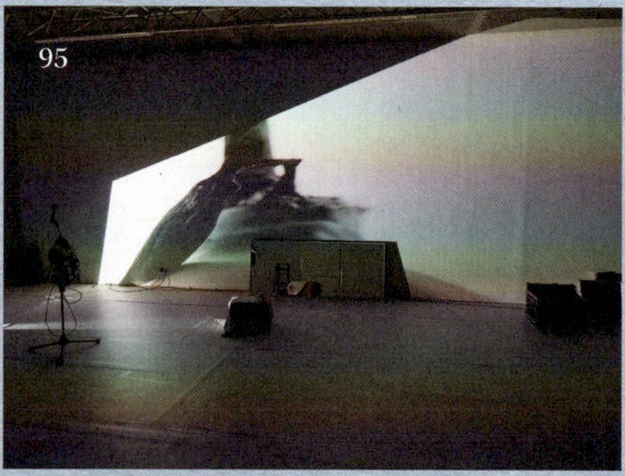

95

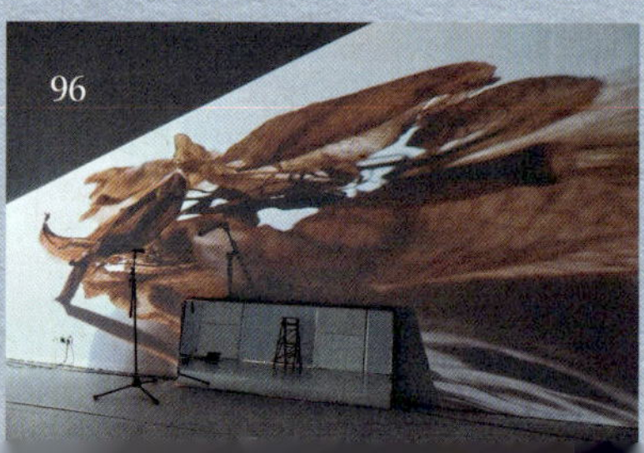

96

up a space for rethinking what it means to animate, to act, and to live in co-presence with human and other-than human forces.

Drawing on the work of Gilles Deleuze and Félix Guattari, assemblage theory provides a conceptual framework that moves beyond substance ontology. So, let us start with some basic terminology: an assemblage is a provisional constellation of heterogeneous elements – bodies, affects, objects, discourses, technologies – that acquire capacities and potentialities in and through their conjunction. Deleuze and Guattari write,

> There is no individual enunciation. [...] [E]nunciation has this social character [...]. [E]nunciation in itself implies *collective assemblages* [...]. [W]hat comes first [...] is a collective assemblage [...]. The notion of collective assemblage of enunciation takes on primary importance since it is what must account for the social character. [...]. If we wish to move to a real definition of the collective assemblage, we must ask of what [...] these acts immanent to language [consist] that are in redundancy with statements or constitute order-words.[242]

This approach has been radicalised in recent scholarship by thinkers such as Manuel DeLanda and Jane Bennett, who extend assemblage theory into social, political, and ecological domains – and in my project I intended to do so *in practice*. Bennett insists on the vibrancy of matter, proposing that other-than-human bodies or matter are not inert substrates but actants within assemblages of agency.[243] Such a move destabilises the privilege of human intentionality, repositioning humans as one node among many in distributed networks of vitality.

As Hans Asenbaum succinctly puts it, 'Assemblage thinking is in itself radically democratic. It aims to overcome the exclusion of non-humans by proposing a flat ontology.'[244] This line of thought captures the ethical and political stakes of assemblage practices. To think and act in flat hierarchies is to refuse to relegate stones, microbes, or infrastructures to the status of passive backdrops. It is to affirm

242. Gilles Deleuze and Félix Guattari, *A Thousand Plateaus: Capitalism and Schizophrenia*, trans. Brian Massumi (Continuum, 2004 [1980]), 88–89 (emphasis in original).

243. Bennett, *Vibrant Matter*, 20–21.

244. Hans Asenbaum, 'Democratic Assemblage', in *What Makes an Assembly?* (Sternberg, 2022), 252.

that the capacity to affect and to be affected[245] is not the exclusive domain of the human but circulates across scales and materials. Radical democracy here is not only a matter of political representation but of ontological inclusivity: a recognition of the plural agencies that constitute worlds.

Relational ontology, articulated in diverse strands of anthropology, philosophy, and aesthetics, resonates with this move towards cosmopoietic œkology. Whereas assemblage thinking emphasises the contingent gathering of heterogeneous elements, relational ontology emphasises the priority of relations over entities. For philosopher Alfred North Whitehead, reality is constituted by events and relations rather than enduring substances.[246] In anthropology, Eduardo Viveiros de Castro[247] and Philippe Descola[248] describe relational ontologies in which personhood and agency are distributed across human and other-than-human actors, challenging the modern divide between nature and culture. Both trajectories converge in the insight that beings do not pre-exist their relations but emerge through them.

To animate assemblages, then, is not to anthropomorphise matter but to recognise the already operative vitality of relational fields. In performance studies, for example, the body is understood less as a given substance than as a node in networks of gesture, atmosphere, and resonance. Fischer-Lichte has described performance as a transformative event that reorganises subjectivity by virtue of shared presence and affective contagion.[249] Here, being-in-contact becomes the constitutive condition of the aesthetic: performers and spectators co-animate an assemblage that exceeds both.

Similarly, if we look at installation art, objects are not static but relationally animated. Claire Bishop has shown how installation art produces immersive environments in which the viewer becomes a participant, entangled in spatial and material configurations.[250] The installation operates as an assemblage that animates not only objects but the perceptions, affects, and imaginaries of its guests as they move through the installation. Being-in-contact here designates the mutual activation of matter and perception, a choreography of objecthood and embodiment. The ethical implications of animating assemblages are profound. If assemblages are radically democratic, as the statement by Asenbaum above suggests, then ethical responsibility cannot be restricted to interpersonal obligations but must extend to other-than-human participants. Bennett's political ecology of things foregrounds precisely this demand: to acknowledge the *agency* of electricity grids, food networks, and waste

245. See my diagram in Greil, *Being in Contact*, 78.

246. Alfred North Whitehead writes, '"Actual entities" – also termed "actual occasions" – are the final real things of which the world is made up.' Alfred North Whitehead, *Process and Reality: An Essay in Cosmology*, ed. David Ray Griffin and Donald W. Sherburne, corrected ed. (Free, Press, 1978), 18. In the best-case scenario, the 'Diffractive Dialogue Score' created the conditions for '"actual occasions" to emerge'. Ibid., 18–19.

247. Eduardo Viveiros de Castro, *Cannibal Metaphysics*, ed. and trans. Peter Skafish (Univocal, 2014), 45–47.

248. Philippe Descola, *Beyond Nature and Culture*, trans. Janet Lloyd (University of Chicago Press, 2013), 82–84.

249. Fischer-Lichte, *The Transformative Power of Performance*, 155–58.

250. Bishop, *Installation Art*, 11–13.

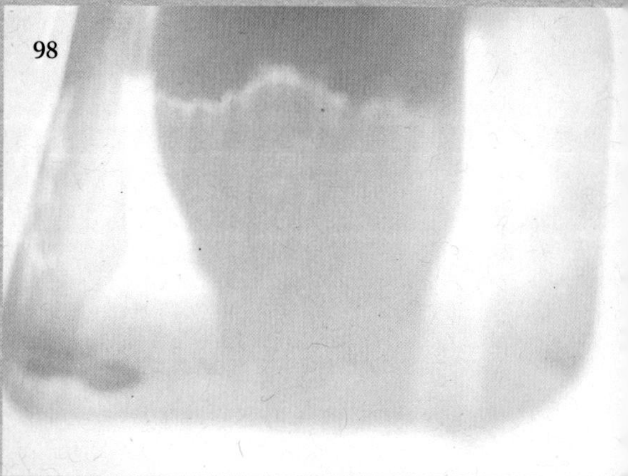

Falling or Fading

Bliblablurring
the lines between imagination and memory,
between felt sense and cognized feelings.
Is the message of the blackbird's song
in the singing or in its pausing?
This poem is a place for diffractive recollection,
for faded dances and choreo-ethical assemblages.
Poiesis cutting across the page,
differentiating space and time as affects fade,
falling into felt forms of knowing and forgetting
what will have been significant for the others?

Alive.
Implication by default.
Modelling the mind.
Minding the gap.
Slowly but steadily forming a topology of
forgotten moves and knowledges.
Habit of writing letters.
Untranslatable communication.

streams as co-determining human life.[251] In the research environment, this includes mobile configurations and atmospheric environments beyond that which functionally sustains everyday life. Being-in-contact means that no act is purely individual; each gesture resonates within a meshwork of dependencies and consequences.

Relational ontology deepens this ethical horizon. To affirm that beings emerge through relations is to insist that care and responsibility are not optional but constitutive. The feminist scholarship on the ethics of care has underscored how interdependence structures existence, countering the modern fantasy of autonomy.[252] Within a relational ontology, such insights acquire ontological force: care is not merely a moral choice but a mode of sustaining relational worlds. To animate assemblages responsibly is therefore to cultivate conditions in which humans and other-than-humans alike can flourish.

The political dimension of being-in-contact cannot be ignored. As we know, at least deep down, assemblages are differentially structured rather than neutral, and of course, we are aware that power circulates through infrastructures, institutions, and ecologies.

I envision a post-humanist, emancipatory 'politics of affirmation' and a sustainable (nomadic) ethic, as elaborated by Braidotti, which of course also has a significant impact on the concept of the subject (or trans*subjectivities). In her book *Tausend Subjekte* (A Thousand Subjects), Isabella Schlehaider speaks of the implicit presuppositions of a ramified nature. She concludes her introduction by stating that she sees her book project as an experiment, an attempt to explore the possibility of a post-humanist understanding of nature and thus of a truly *political ecology*. In the context of my *Choreo-ethical Assemblages* project, I felt an urgency to explore the potential of a *cosmopoietic œkology* through *embodied research* and, even more, to realise it where possible. The circulation of power within such a political cosmopoietic œkology sustains collective agency and resists fascist claims to power. Relational ontology, while emphasising interconnectedness, must therefore inevitably attend to asymmetries and exclusions. A flat ontology[253] does not mean the equal distribution of capacities but a refusal to ontologically subordinate certain entities. Politics, then, consists in negotiating the conditions under which assemblages are formed, maintained, or transformed.

Ultimately, I am convinced that being-in-contact designates an ontological, aesthetic, and ethical disposition attuned to the vibrancy of relational existence.

251. Jane Bennett discusses *adsorbsion*, a term that Deleuze and Guattari introduced in *What is Philosophy?* (trans. Hugh Tomlinson and Graham Burchell [Columbia University Press, 1996], 153) as agential impetus. Bennett, *Vibrant Matter*, 34–35.

252. Joan C. Tronto, *Moral Boundaries: A Political Argument for an Ethic of Care* (Routledge, 1993), 102–04.

253. The phrase 'flat ontology' has been popularised in part through the philosophical work of Manuel DeLanda, whose reinterpretation of Deleuze and Guattari articulates an ontology in which entities at different scales – molecules, organisms, institutions, cities – are treated with equal ontological dignity. In *A New Philosophy of Society*, DeLanda argues that assemblages cannot be reduced to their individual parts, nor can they be subsumed under overarching totalities; rather, they are emergent wholes whose properties depend on relations of exteriority. Manuel DeLanda, *A New Philosophy of Society: Assemblage Theory and Social Complexity* (Continuum, 2006), 10–12. This model contrasts sharply with hierarchical or tree-like ontologies that privilege certain levels – such as the human subject or the state – as the ultimate bearers of reality.

Assemblage thinking and relational ontology converge in an affirmation that worlds are composed – cosmospoietically – through contact, not in isolation. To animate assemblages is to participate in radical democracy at the ontological level: a democracy of forces, relations, and agencies. The challenge for thought and practice alike is to dwell in this condition with attentiveness and care, cultivating forms of contact that enable *shared flourishing*[254] across the porous boundaries of human and other-than-human, material and immaterial, actual and potential.

Choreo-ethics as a Poetics of Being-in-the-Medium

[M]edia structure how things are in the world and how things are known in the world.[255]
Jussi Parikka

To think and practice *choreo-ethics* is to move beyond the codification of choreography as a structural arrangement of steps and gestures. It is instead to inhabit choreo-ethical assemblages as a mode of relational practice, where ethics arises from the dynamics of being-in-contact, being-with, and being-through. Ethics here is less a system of prohibitions than a poetics of co-composition: an articulation of how relations are sustained, transformed, and animated in and through movement.

In his translator's foreword to *A Thousand Plateaus*, philosopher Massumi states that there have been various efforts to construct an open-ended, smooth space of thought. He outlines a lineage stretching from Spinoza's ethics[256] and Nietzsche's 'gay science',[257] through Artaud's 'crowned anarchy',[258] to Blanchot's 'space of literature'[259] and Foucault's 'outside thought'.[260] Each of the ideas and concepts mentioned resonates with me. Certainly, choreo-ethical assemblages grow from these roots – though certainly beyond the tree-model of knowledge – with branches extending towards animist and rhizomatic philosophies, including feminist theory (with a predilection for *écriture feminine*), new materialism, post-human philosophy, autotheory, enactivism, and micro-phenomenology.

This brief genealogy situates choreo-ethics as one articulation of evolving philosophical relations. Spinoza's ethics, grounded in the capacity of bodies to

254. See website of the flourishing society: https://flourishingsociety.org.

255. Jussi Parikka, *A Geology of Media* (University of Minnesota Press, 2015), 1.

256. Benedict de Spinoza, *Ethics*, ed. Stuart Hampshire, trans. Edwin Curley (Penguin Classics, 2005).

257. Friedrich Wilhelm Nietzsche, *The Gay Science: With a Prelude in Rhymes and an Appendix of Songs*, trans. Walter Kaufmann (New York: Vintage Books, 1974 [1887]).

258. Deleuze borrowed the notion of 'crowned anarchy' from Antonin Artaud, the founder of the Theatre of Cruelty. The term goes back to Artaud's *Heliogabalus, or The Crowned Anarchist* (Infinity Land Press, 2019 [1934]).

259. Maurice Blanchot, *The Space of Literature*, trans. Ann Smock (University of Nebraska Press, 1989 [1955]).

260. Michel Foucault, 'Maurice Blanchot: The Thought from Outside', in *Foucault/Blanchot*, trans. Brian Massumi (Zone Books, 1990).

affect and be affected,[261] aligns profoundly with embodied research, where movement is never isolated but always a vector of encounter. One might be tempted to say that Nietzsche's gay science destabilises the solemnity of philosophy, inviting art and experimentation as thoroughly ethical modes and valid research methods.[262] Artaud's *anarchic* visions of a theatre of cruelty expose the raw forces of affect and sensation, while Blanchot's literary space suspends subjectivity in the indeterminacy of language. From my perspective, Foucault's outside thought unsettles the interiority of subjectivity, opening onto relations of power and discourse. The rhizome spreads its rootlets towards Hélène Cixous' 'white ink' thinking and acknowledges the complexity of relations and matter in new materialist practices. From there, post-humanist terrains and enactivist ideas of the mutual constitution of the environment and organism proliferate as 'they enact a world'.[263] Autotheory and micro-phenomenological practice are handy tools for reflecting on choreo-ethics as a poetics of being-in-the-medium. Taken together, these trajectories converge in an ethos of relationality and openness, from which choreo-ethical assemblages emerge as a practice that is at once philosophical, artistic, and ethical.

To propose choreo-ethics as a *poetics* underscores its aesthetic dimension. *Poetics*, in the Aristotelian sense, is a theory of making and of bringing forth, which denotes the theoretical discourse on the structures, functions, and modalities of artistic (especially literary) production. *Poiesis* emerges from the same root, foregrounding the processual and generative dimensions of making; however, it often extends to encompass broader philosophical, aesthetic, and ontological registers, articulating enquiries into creation as an activity. In the context of choreo-ethical assemblages, *poiesis* is the crafting of relational situations. The ethical becomes aesthetic insofar as it is performed and sensed, in the same way that the aesthetic becomes ethical insofar as it concerns the conditions of living and being, but also for surviving together, for actualising and vitalising. This mutual inflection resonates with Juliane Rebentisch's claim that aesthetics cannot be reduced to the realm of beauty or taste but relates to the negotiation of autonomy and heteronomy, form and relation, as they are concretely negotiated through embodied research in the shared *live* space of performance:[264]

Liveness is the core of the performative poodle. It is therefore a paradoxical mediality that characterises performance: its specificity is that which is *no longer* specific – its materiality is immateriality. Consequently, the meaning

261. Spinoza, *Ethics*, Part III, Proposition 34, Dem., 88.

262. Nietzsche, *The Gay Science*.

263. Ezequiel A. Di Paolo, Marieke Rhohde, and Hanne De Jaegher, 'Horizons for the Enactive Mind: Values, Social Interaction, and Play', in *Enaction: Toward a New Paradigm for Cognitive Science*, ed. John Stewart, Olivier Gapenne, and Ezequiel A. Di Paolo (MIT Press, 2014), 38.

264. Juliane Rebentisch, *Aesthetics of Installation Art*, trans. Daniel Hendrickson with Gerrit Jackson (Sternberg, 2012), 125–26.

> of this art was no longer to be found in the thing itself, in its colours and forms, but in its occurrence and thus in the open.[265]

Within this field, choreo-ethical assemblages function as a generative matrix: movements, gestures, and rhythms become communicative events that both exceed and sustain sociality.

This perspective aligns with Erin Manning's concept of 'choreographic thinking' as an infra-sensory mode of relation, where movement is not subordinated to form but is understood as a field of pre-acceleration, always in the process of becoming.[266] Choreo-ethics, in this sense, is a poetics that attunes to the intervals, foldings, and elasticity of relation: it is about more than what is visible as assemblage – it is about how relations unfold in the very fabric of communicative beings.

Similarly, art and cultural theorist Bazon Brock has argued consistently that art is not a separate sphere of life but a medium of communication in its most emphatic sense:

> The nature of communication is always the same for all living things: it is about building relationships, a network of relationships between the living system and its environment [...]. Two abilities play a decisive role here: empathy and anticipation. Empathy means suffering in advance, anticipation means reacting in advance to events that have not yet occurred [...].[267]

For Brock, artworks are not mute objects but communicative devices that intervene in the structures of perception and thought. This perspective resonates deeply with choreo-ethics, understood as being-in-the-medium, being-in-communication: performance does not merely transmit messages but stages the very conditions of communicability. Brock also reactivates the notion of the artist as a *medium* – not

265. In German: 'Liveness ist der Kern des performativen Pudels. Es ist also eine paradoxe Medialität, welche die Performance auszeichnet: ihr Spezifisches ist das *nicht mehr* Spezifische – ihre Materialiät ist die Immaterialität. Nicht mehr im Ding, in seinen Farben und Formen war folglich der Sinn dieser Kunst zu suchen, sondern in ihrem ereignen und damit im Offenen (Rebentisch).' Ulf Otto, 'Going live: Performance Unter digitalem Vorzeichen', *Kunstforum International* 264 (2019): 166.

266. 'Proprioception provides us with clues that precede our cognitive understanding of where we are going. Preacceleration: we are going, always already.' Manning, *Relationscapes*, 14.

267. Bazon Brock, *Theoreme: Er lebte, liebte, lehrte und starb. Was hat er sich dabei gedacht?*, ed. Marina Sawall (Walther König, 2020), 322. Original: 'Auch ist das Wesen der Kommunikation für alles Lebendige stets das gleiche: Es gilt, Beziehungen aufzubauen, ein Netzwerk von Beziehungen des lebendigen Systems zur Umwelt [...]. Dabei spielen zwei Fähigkeiten eine entscheidende Rolle: die Empathie und die Antizipation. Empathie meint das Vorausleiden, Antizipation das Vorausreagieren auf noch nicht eingetretenes Geschehen [...].'

in the spiritualist sense of channelling otherworldly voices but as someone who makes palpable the invisible forces, tensions, and potentials that circulate within the social body. In this sense, the embodied researcher is a medium of relationality – or, as in the title to Petra Sabisch's book, the focus is on 'choreographing relations',[268] translating between the embodied and the atmospheric, the seen and the unseen, the singular and the collective.

Artist and co-founder of the German Green Party Joseph Beuys further radicalised the understanding of art as communication by proposing the concept of 'soziale Plastik' (social sculpture).[269] Quite famously, for Beuys, 'Everyone is an artist,'[270] not in the sense of producing objects but in shaping the social body through communicative action. In his famous dictum, art becomes coextensive with life, and art is understood as a medium through which society is sculpted. Beuys said, 'I did take the role of the shaman';[271] his role was 'mediumistic', channelling energies and intensities that exceed individual authorship. Moreover, Barbara Grondau writes that 'it becomes evident that the artist functions as a medium, a connection to the transcendent levels of reality'.[272] This is not unlike Brock's idea of the artist as a mediator of invisible forces, but Beuys gives it a more explicitly transformative, utopian dimension. In the context of choreo-ethics, these perspectives illuminate performance as a communicative medium that both registers and reconfigures the relational field. Choreo-ethical assemblages, like Beuys' social sculptor, function as a medium of collective transformation across agencies.

The ethical stakes of choreo-ethics are thus tied to its capacity to reconfigure relationality. Whereas communication is often reduced to linguistic or digital exchanges, choreo-ethics insists on the embodied, affective, and multisensory dimensions of communicative existence. For me, this strongly aligns with Jean-Luc Nancy's notion of 'being-with', where existence is always co-existence, exposed to the other and sharing the condition of finitude.[273] In choreo-ethical assemblaging, understood as the threshold where assembling becomes assemblage, the sphere of

268. Petra Sabisch, *Choreographing Relations: Practical Philosophy and Contemporary Choreography in the Works of Antonia Baehr, Gilles Deleuze, Juan Dominguez, Félix Guattari, Xavier Le Roy and Eszter Salamon* (Epodium, 2011).

269. 'With his "social sculpture", Beuys goes beyond Marcel Duchamp's readymade. He is no longer interested in the museum context, but rather in the anthropological context. For him, creativity is the science of freedom. All human knowledge comes from art; the concept of science has developed from creativity' (my translation). German original: 'Mit der "Sozialen Plastik" geht Beuys über das Readymade von Marcel Duchamp hinaus. Denn ihn interessiert nicht länger der museale, spndern der anthropologische Zusammenhang. Kreativität ist für ihn Freiheitswissenschaft. Alles menschliche Wissen stammt aus der Kunst, der Wissenschaftsbegriff hat sich aus dem Kreativen entwickelt.' Heiner Stachelhaus, *Joseph Beuys* (Heyne, 1989), 82.

270. Ann Temkin and Bernice Rose, *Thinking is Form: The Drawings of Joseph Beuys* (Thames and Hudson, 1993), 19.

271. Joseph Beuys, quoted in Uwe Schneede, *Joseph Beuys: Die Aktionen* (Hatje Cantz, 1994), 336.

272. Barbara Gronau, 'I Did Take the Role of the Shaman… The Artistic Rituals of Joseph Beuys', *Documenta* 28, no. 1 (2010): 51, https://doi.org/10.21825/doc.v28i1.10529.

273. Jean-Luc Nancy, *Being Singular Plural*, trans. Robert D. Richardson and Anne E. O'Byrne (Stanford University Press, 2000), 94. My colleague Iris Julian reflects on the concepts of *being-with* and *co-authoring* in the artistic, contemporary field. See Iris Julian, *Singular Plural Ways of Staging Together: Perspectives on Contemporary Dance, Art Performance and Visual Art* (transcript, 2024).

assemblage/dissemblage set in motion by the performer's body, the spatial configuration of agencies, and the resonances of sound, smell, and touch collectively constitute a *medium through which being-with is enacted.* Moreover, choreo-ethics opens out onto a post-human horizon. Jane Bennett's concept of 'vibrant matter' foregrounds the agency of other-than-human forces – objects, materials, movements, atmospheres – that participate in the choreography of relations. She explains that '[a]ssemblages are ad hoc groupings of diverse elements, of vibrant materials of all sorts. Assemblages are living, throbbing confederations that are able to function [...].'[274] A poetics of being-in-the-medium must therefore encompass not only human bodies but the assemblages of affects, infrastructures (choreographic environments such as the diving tower), and practices of diffractive dialogue (scores, desktop performances) as these œkologies shape current and future relational existences. In this sense, choreo-ethics is both intersubjective and transsubjective, spanning species and materialities, affirming what Guattari calls the *ecosophy* – the ecological articulation of subjectivity, environment, and sociality.[275]

At the artistic, aesthetic level, this orientation finds expression in contemporary performance practices that foreground relationality and co-presence. Works that blur the boundary between performer and spectator, or where the performance takes place at non-theatrical sites, enact choreo-ethics as a mode of co-habitation. Lisa Hinterreithner's *padded* (2024), which I experienced at the Tanzquartier in Vienna, invited participants to linger in a community comprising materials and bodies, feminist and luscious, yet also *containing* in the psychoanalytical sense of holding, processing, and transforming another's projected emotions. The hybrid performance-installation work comprised a series of delicate micro housings that emerged and transformed, turned into bolt-holes, or became sites for pleasure quests. The audience witnessed a practice of dwelling in softness, living and growing in gentle habitats. The ethical demand was not scripted but emerged immanently: how does one engage with both the set design and the performers, how does one move, how does one share space with others – human and other-than-human alike? Such practices elucidate what Fischer-Lichte describes as the 'autopoietic feedback loop'[276] of performance, where meaning is continuously generated through the interplay of performers and others (including other others) in set-ups that comprise flat hierarchies. As I argued earlier,[277] autopoiesis has become sympoiesis in the post-Anthropocene, and – out of acute urgency – I have extended it further toward cosmopoiesis. It is a Renaissance term that I propose to tenderly stretch, including and co-constituting other others through choreo-ethical assemblages.

274. Jane Bennett, *Vibrant Matter: A Political Ecology of Things* (Duke University Press, 2010), 23.

275. Félix Guattari, *The Three Ecologies*, trans. Ian Pindar and Paul Sutton (Continuum, 2000 [1989]), 43.

276. 'The feedback loop as self-referential, autopoietic system enabling a fundamentally open, unpredictable process emerged as the defining principle of theatrical work.' Erika Fischer-Lichte, *The Transformative Power of Performance: A New Aesthetics*, trans. Saskya Iris Jain (Routledge, 2008), 38.

277. I will take up this notion in more depth in → Generative Forces in Choreographic Environments, 99.

At this point, a short note on flat ontology and its genealogy seems expedient. I would like to dedicate some words to philosopher and artist DeLanda's later work, *Assemblage Theory* (2016), which sharpens this principle into a defence of 'flat ontology'.[278] Here, 'flatness' does not mean sameness or a lack of differentiation but denotes a refusal to posit ontological tiers of reality on which, for example, macro-level social structures dominate micro-level interactions. Instead, all assemblages exist on the same ontological plane, though they may differ in scale, stability, and capacity. As DeLanda notes, this orientation resists the 'sedimentation' of social ontology into rigid strata, emphasising instead the fluid interplay of emergent wholes and their component parts.[279] In this line of thinking, Asenbaum's claim that 'assemblage thinking is in itself radically democratic'[280] becomes clearer. A flat ontology disrupts hierarchies that would ontologically privilege the human, the macro-structure, or the transcendent idea. Instead, it foregrounds a democracy of existence: viruses, infrastructures, plants, and institutions are all recognised as participants in the world's becoming. Democracy here is not metaphorical but ontological: it redistributes agency across scales and entities, opening up the possibility of non-anthropocentric ethics and politics. I deliberately articulate it as an option, as something tentative, as it is a practice at which I regularly fail. I am not just paying lip service when I say that failure is a valid option; rather, failure is actually crucial for learning and contributes to the fine-tuning of my research and, ultimately, to the development of relevant future practices. This rough genealogy also highlights why assemblage thinking aligns and resonates with contemporary relational ontologies and post-humanist ethics. It links Deleuze and Guattari's anti-arboreal critique of knowledge, through DeLanda's materialist reformulation, to the more recent turn towards ecological and multispecies thinking. On this continuum, 'flatness' is not the flattening of differences but a recognition and retention of their singularity within a common ontological field.

All in all, where we land with all this is that choreo-ethics as a poetics of being-in-the-medium and in communication is not a theory of morality but a practice of relational, lived aesthetics and ethics. It emerges from a philosophical lineage that values openness, multiplicity, and relationality. It affirms poiesis as the crafting of shared situations and communication as the medium in which being-with is enacted. I find that Brock's conception of art as emphatic communication and Beuys' vision of social sculpture enrich this horizon by underscoring the artist's mediumistic role in translating invisible forces into shared, embodied experience and in shaping the collective body. Choreo-ethics thus figures not only as an ethics of relation but as a mediating practice of trans*subjective and trans*material communication, where art is inseparable from the poetics of co-existence.

278. DeLanda argues that 'the ontological status of all assemblages is the same'. DeLanda, *Assemblage Theory*, 19. Braidotti adds to the discussion by writing about how Deleuze 'thinks within the flat ontology on immanence, which encompasses both the embodiment of mind and the "embrainment of matter"'. Rosi Braidotti *Transpositions: On Nomadic Ethics* (Polity, 2006), 253.

279. DeLanda, *Assemblage Theory*, 21–23.

280. Asenbaum, 'Democratic Assemblage', 252.

A POETHICAL READING*

Valentina Desideri and Denise Ferreira da Silva

Valentina Desideri: A decision does not dissipate all the other possibilities.

Denise Ferreira da Silva : Yes, exactly. So, then, it suggests that a decision's not really a determination, since 'determination' implies that choosing one path or position eliminates the others.

Valentina: It's a way of making decisions that holds onto uncertainty, making room for the fact that the decision-maker might be wrong. It's a breed of decision-making that's more like betting than determining.

Denise: [Nodding] You live in that moment. You don't know whether it's good or not, and so you have to become comfortable with being unsure. I like that. Finally, the Seven of Cups is in the Unfolding position, i.e., what happens when there is 'connection and togetherness' in decision-making. Okay, so now what? [Laughter]

The Emperor intervenes

EMPEROR: What do you mean? If I'm removed from the center – if I'm to be comfortable with uncertainty and make decisions without certainty – what is my power, exactly? I'm all about power, remember: decisiveness and certitude. What is it that I'm supposed to do if I cannot decide with certainty?

Denise: In terms of ethical decisions, you'll have to live with the possibility that any decision you make carries everything along with it; and that you cannot delimit what is right or wrong, good or bad.

Valentina: Every decision you make is unsettled and unsettling.

[...]

The Devil speaks

DEVIL: I come calling after the guilt and shame provoked by activating an unclothed power.

Denise: I read you as an indication that the Seven of Cups wants to maintain The Emperor's fixed position on power because it fears its own irresolution.

Valentina: Or perhaps The Devil is a reminder that when you live with uncertainty, you must attend to the possible evil, or harm, implied by your moves. At the very least, you must become aware of it. When a subject like The Emperor operates on an over-simplified narrative of good and evil, he's trying to push the real evil out of sight, towards the periphery.

Denise: Yes, in attempting to constrain and eliminate evil, the subject may itself become evil.

DEVIL: Ladies, I am the problem with the Seven of Cups' fear of making decisions, which is to inhabit the position of power enabled by the decision to live with possibilities instead of resolving them.

Valentina: So we should image an ethics that is able to deal with that specific kind of power – 'the power to live with choices' – and not shy away from it...

Denise: In all its manifestations.

* With permission from the authors slightly edited excerpts from Valentina Desideri and Denise Ferreira da Silva, 'A Poethical Reading', *The Serving Library* 13, accessed 24 September 2025, https://www.servinglibrary.org/journal/13/a-poethical-reading.

[E]thical practice concerns more than a societal alignment with behavioural rules, and more than a revelation of philosophic debate. In relation to these thoughts, it is feasible to consider how the wealth of dance learning and experience resides in the micro-political practice of cooperative endeavours. Working in a polydisciplinary frame, we gather and generate experiences; embody and transmit ideas; and utilise creative practices of cooperation, transformation, identity making, and the sustaining of community. In these ways, the practice of making dances contributes to our ways of living. As we work and relate, we experiment, we think through visible ideas, we forge associations through making thoughts visible, and we examine ways to resolve complexities and to generate new ways of resolving our communicative intentions through choreographic problem solving. We can argue that dancing is about sense finding and sense making. It is a place where we each learn and are changed through the process.

Fiona Bannon, 'New Imaginaries: Dance Training, Ethics and Practice', in *Ethical Agility in Dance: Rethinking Technique in British Contemporary Dance*, ed. Noyale Colin, Catherine Seago, and Kathryn Stamp (Routledge, 2024), 27.

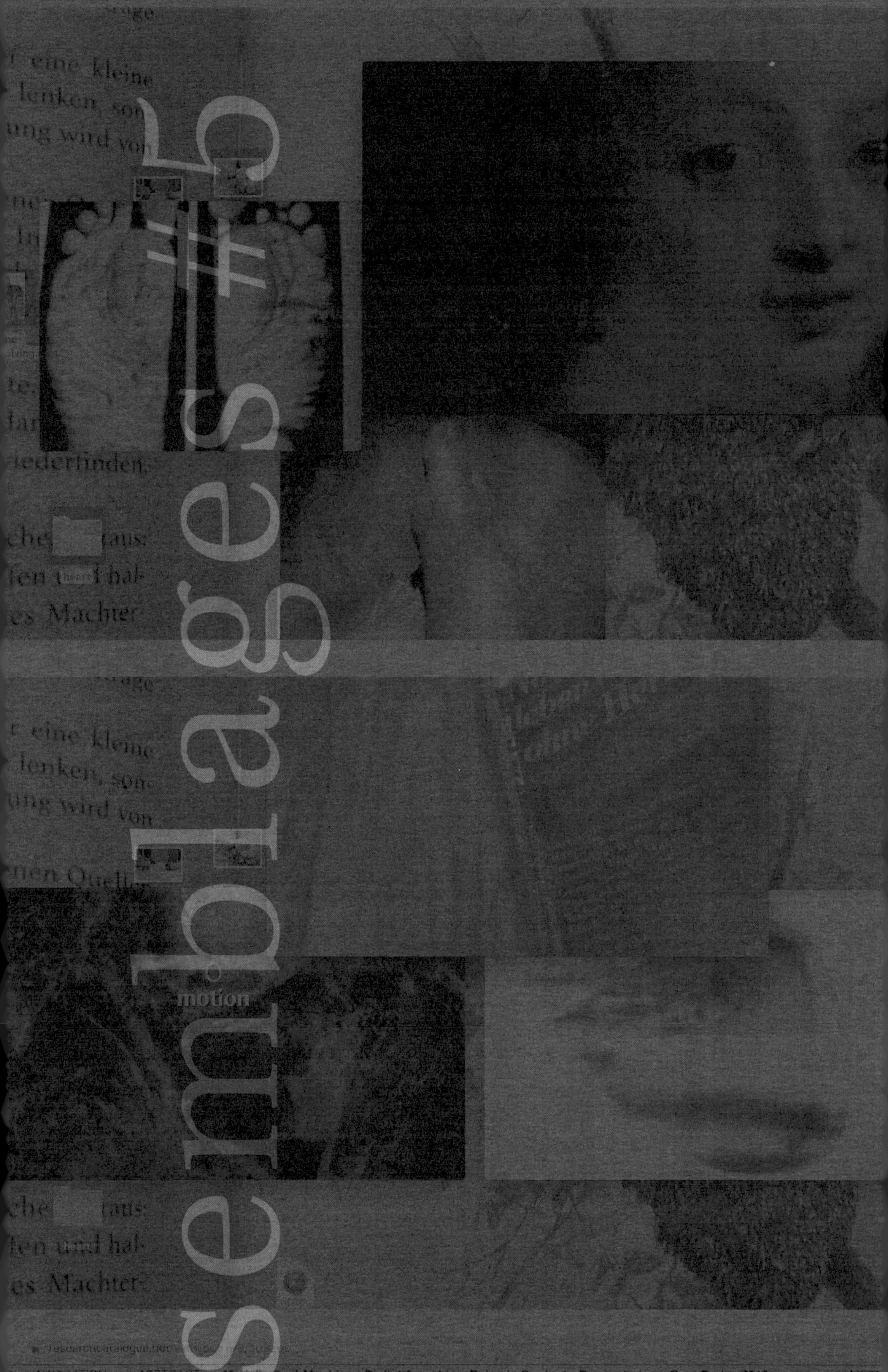

the emergence of a bare body

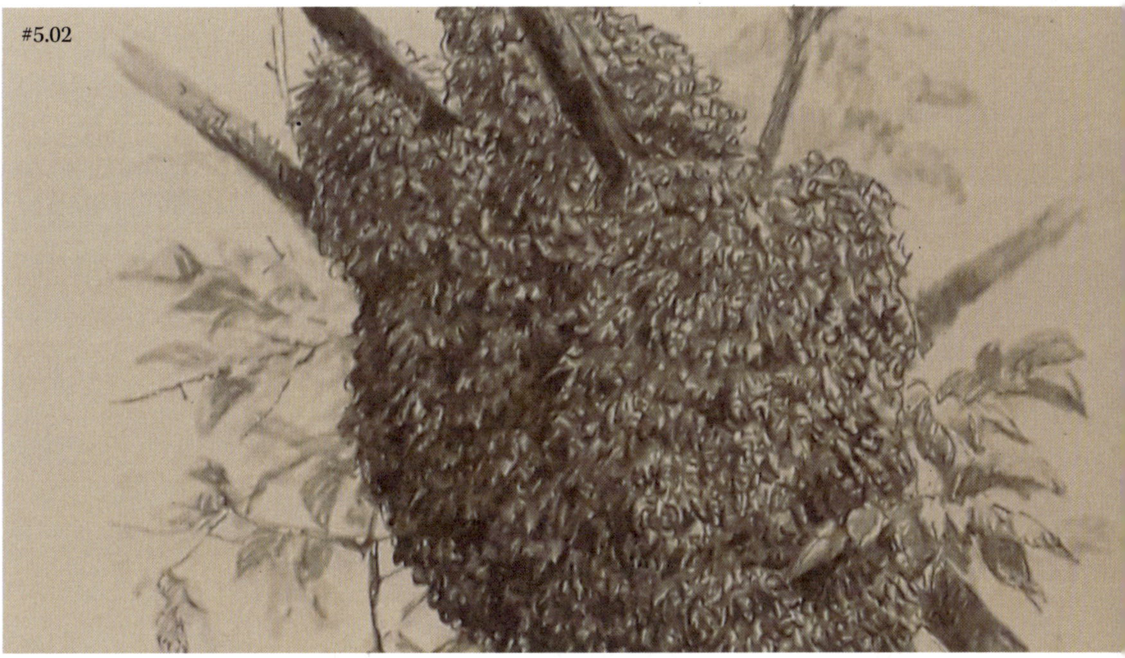
#5.02

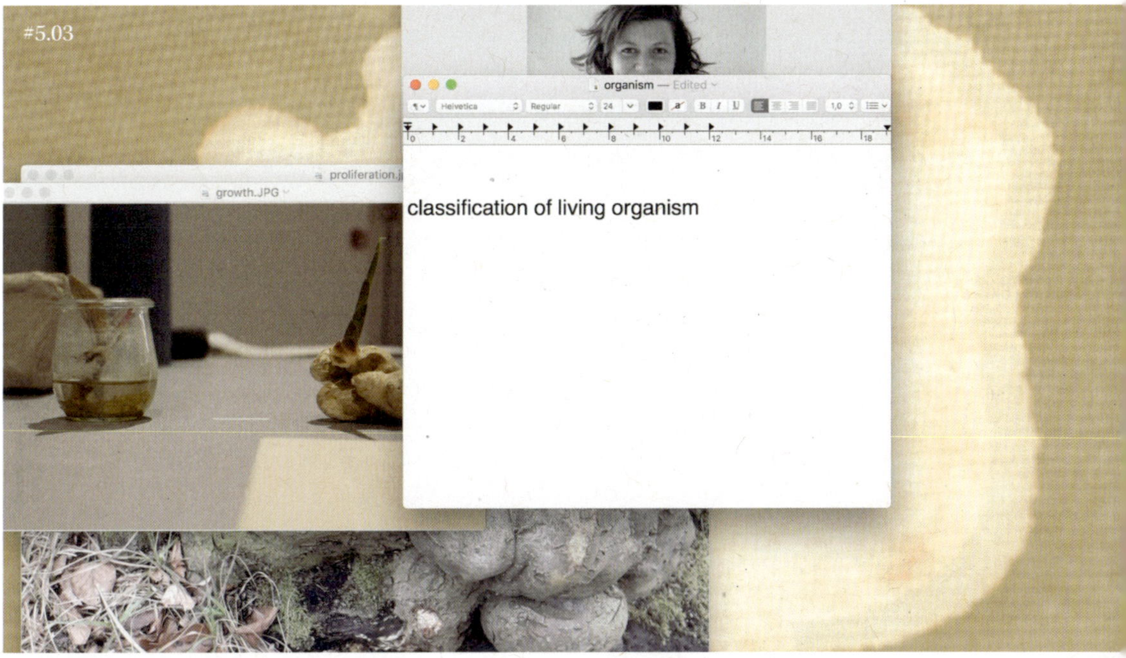
proliferation.j
growth.JPG
organism — Edited
classification of living organism
#5.03

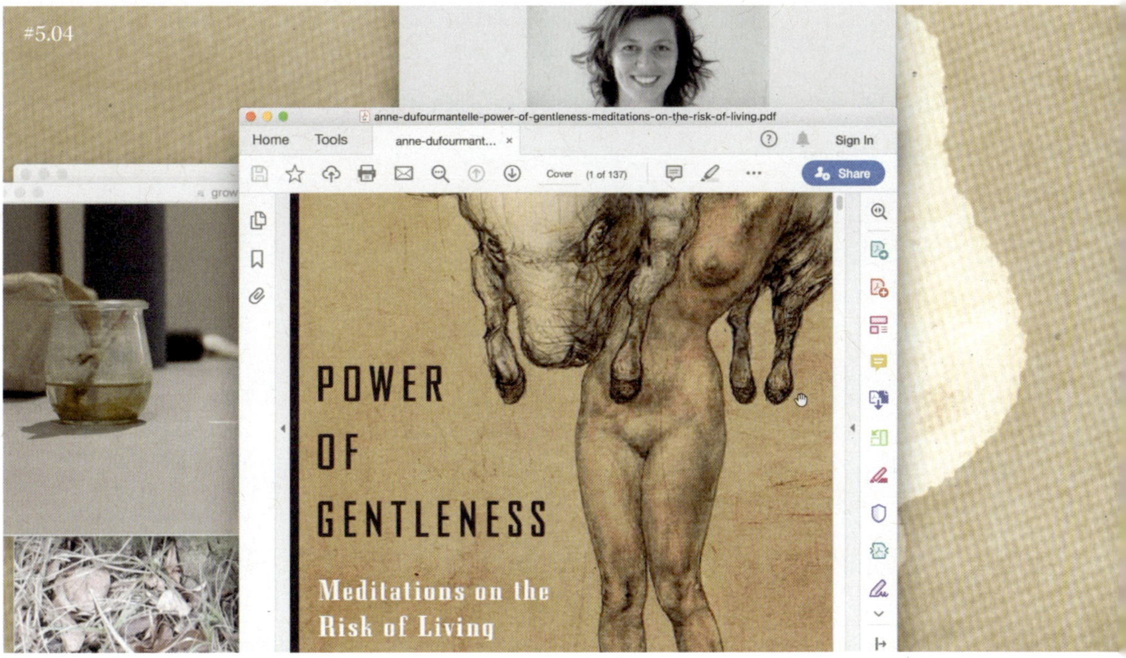
anne-dufourmantelle-power-of-gentleness-meditations-on-the-risk-of-living.pdf
Home
Tools
anne-dufourmant...
Sign In
Share
POWER
OF
GENTLENESS
Meditations on the
Risk of Living
#5.04

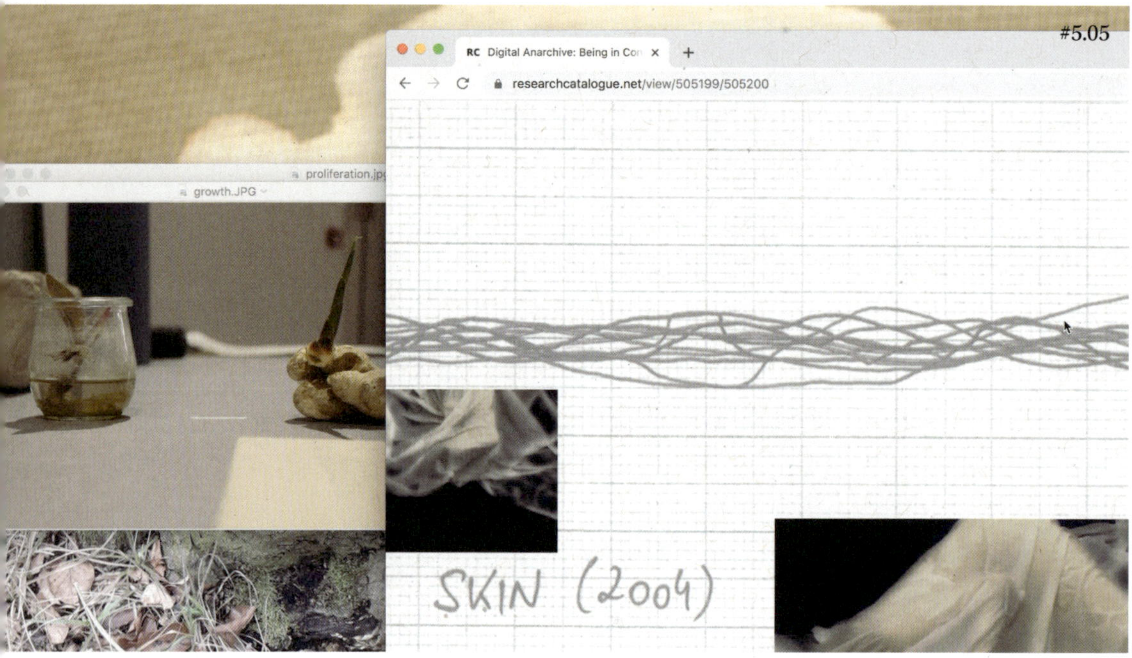
RC Digital Anarchive: Being in Con
researchcatalogue.net/view/505199/505200
proliferation.jp
growth.JPG
SKIN (2004)

#5.05

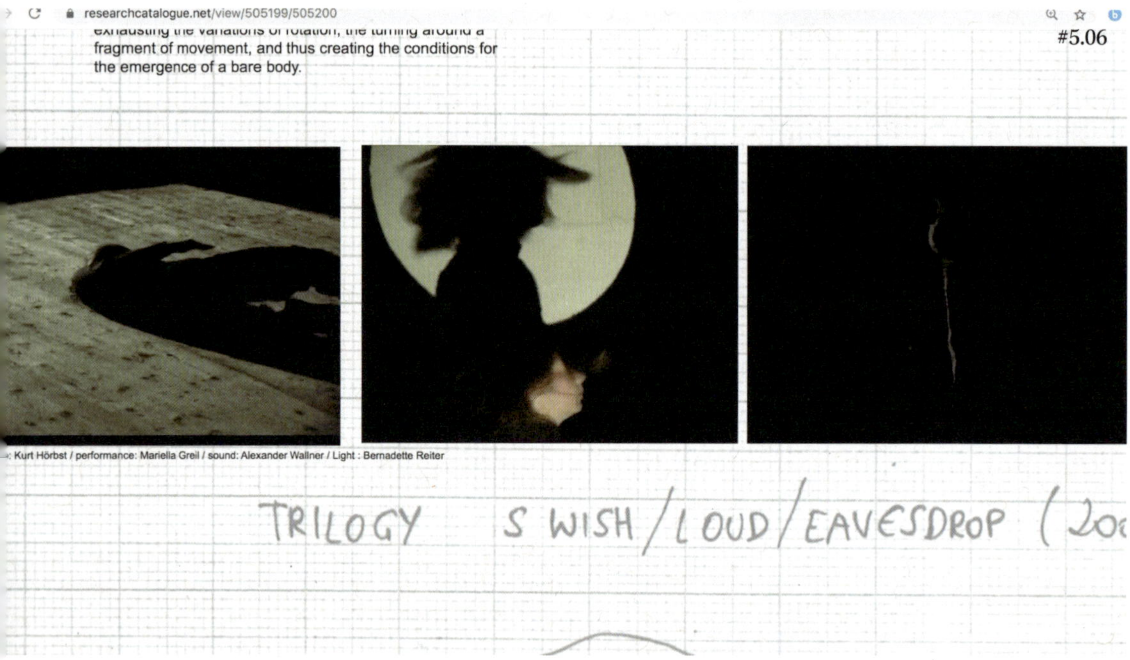
researchcatalogue.net/view/505199/505200
fragment of movement, and thus creating the conditions for
the emergence of a bare body.
Kurt Hörbst / performance: Mariella Greil / sound: Alexander Wallner / Light : Bernadette Reiter
TRILOGY S WISH / LOUD / EAVESDROP (20

#5.06

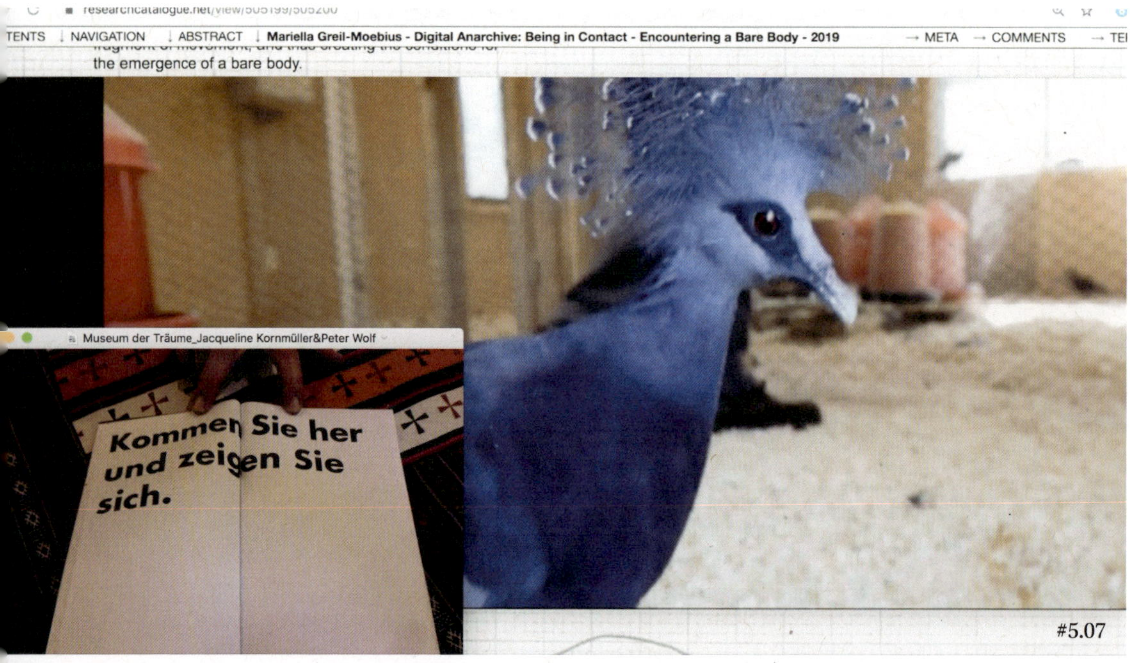
TENTS NAVIGATION ABSTRACT Mariella Greil-Moebius - Digital Anarchive: Being in Contact - Encountering a Bare Body - 2019 → META → COMMENTS → TE
the emergence of a bare body.
Museum der Träume_Jacqueline Kornmüller&Peter Wolf
Kommen Sie her und zeigen Sie sich.

#5.07

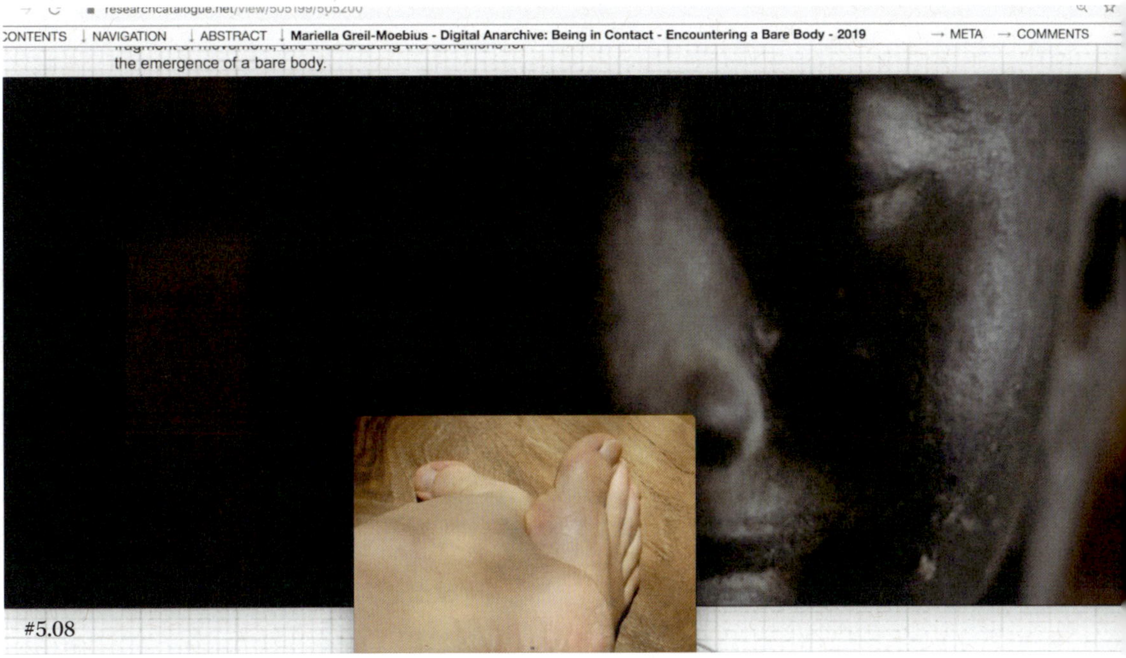
CONTENTS ↓ NAVIGATION ↓ ABSTRACT ↓ Mariella Greil-Moebius - Digital Anarchive: Being in Contact - Encountering a Bare Body - 2019 → META → COMMENTS
the emergence of a bare body.

#5.08

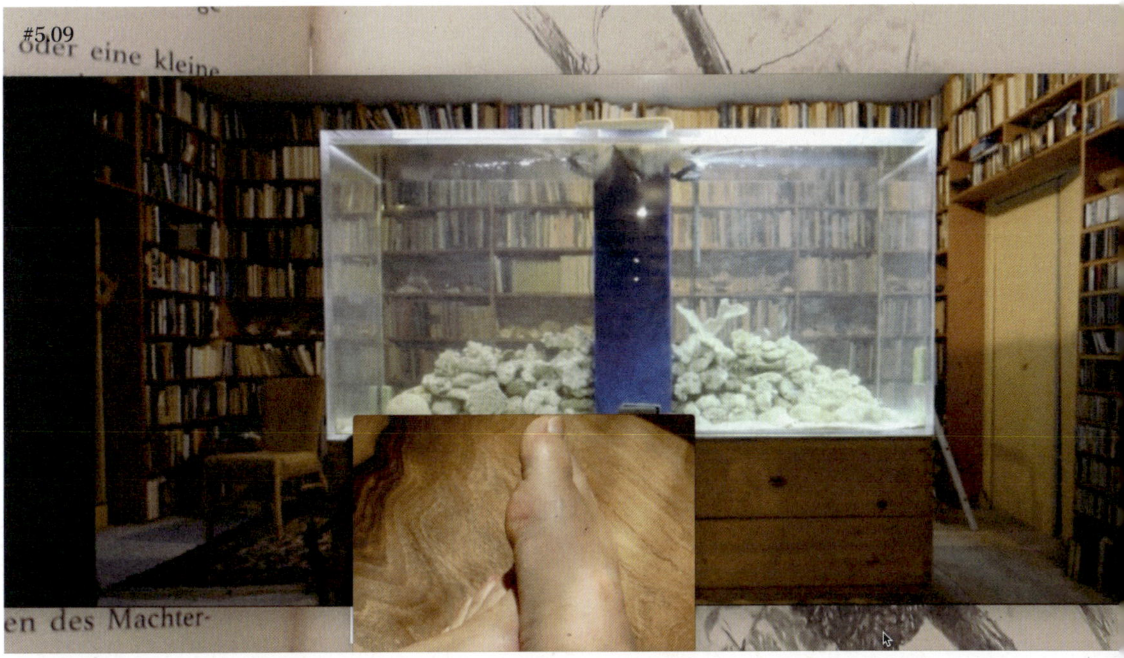
oder eine kleine
en des Machter-

#5.09

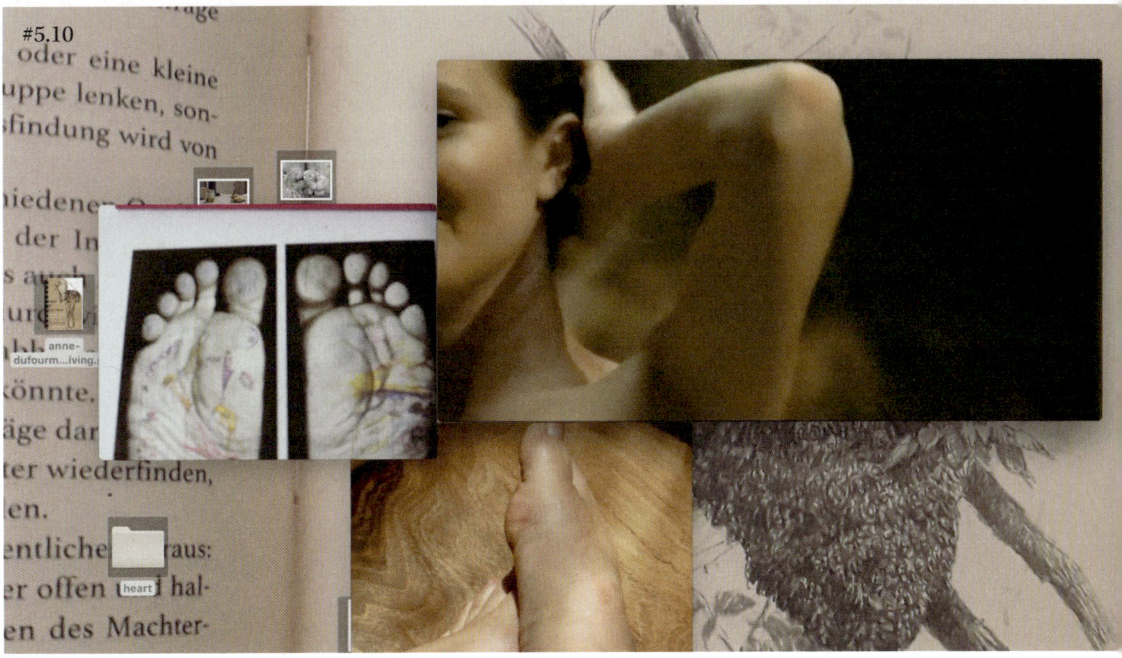
oder eine kleine
uppe lenken, son-
findung wird von
könnte.
ter wiederfinden,
en.
er offen
hal-
en des Machter-
anne-
dufourm...living.
heart

#5.10

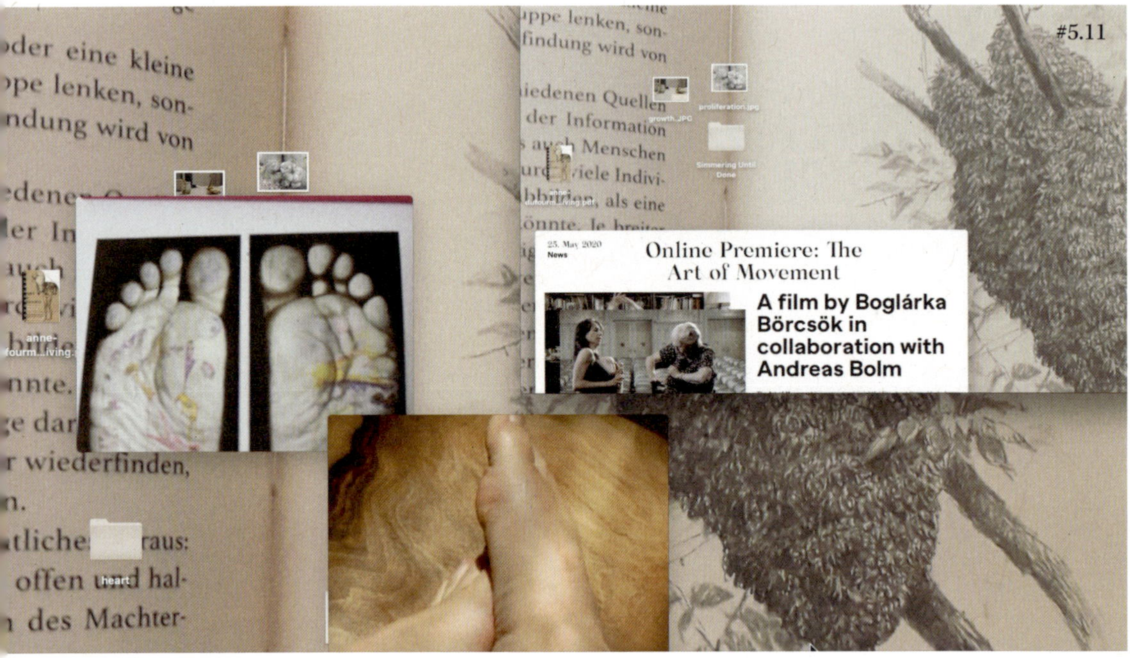
Online Premiere: The Art of Movement
A film by Boglárka Börcsök in collaboration with Andreas Bolm
heart

#5.11

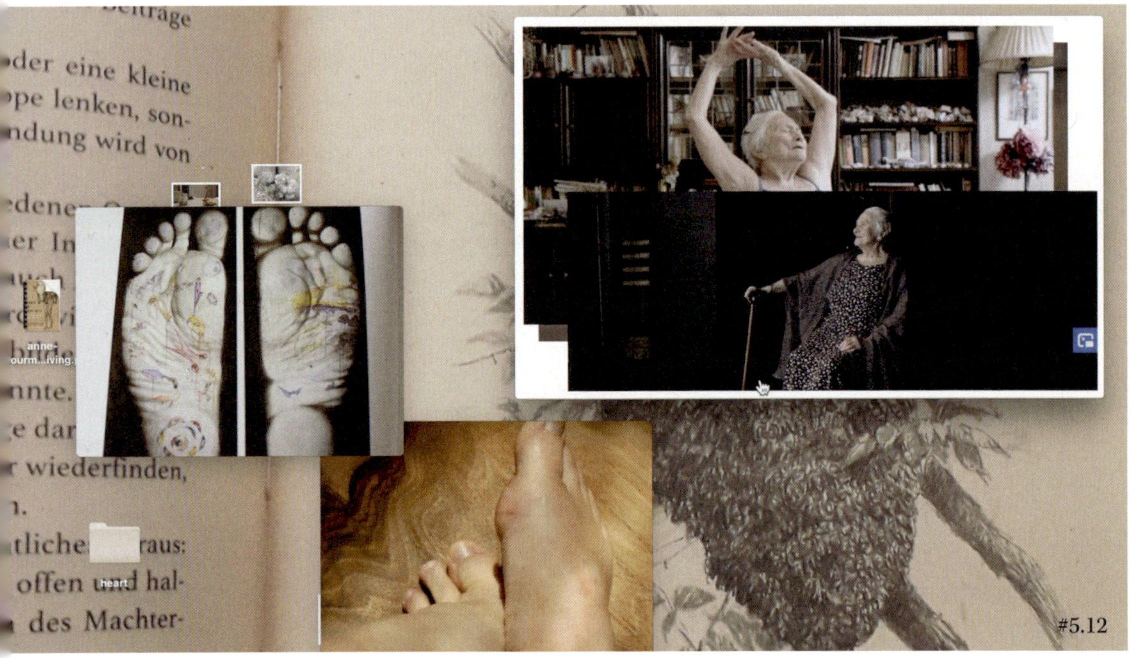
heart

#5.12

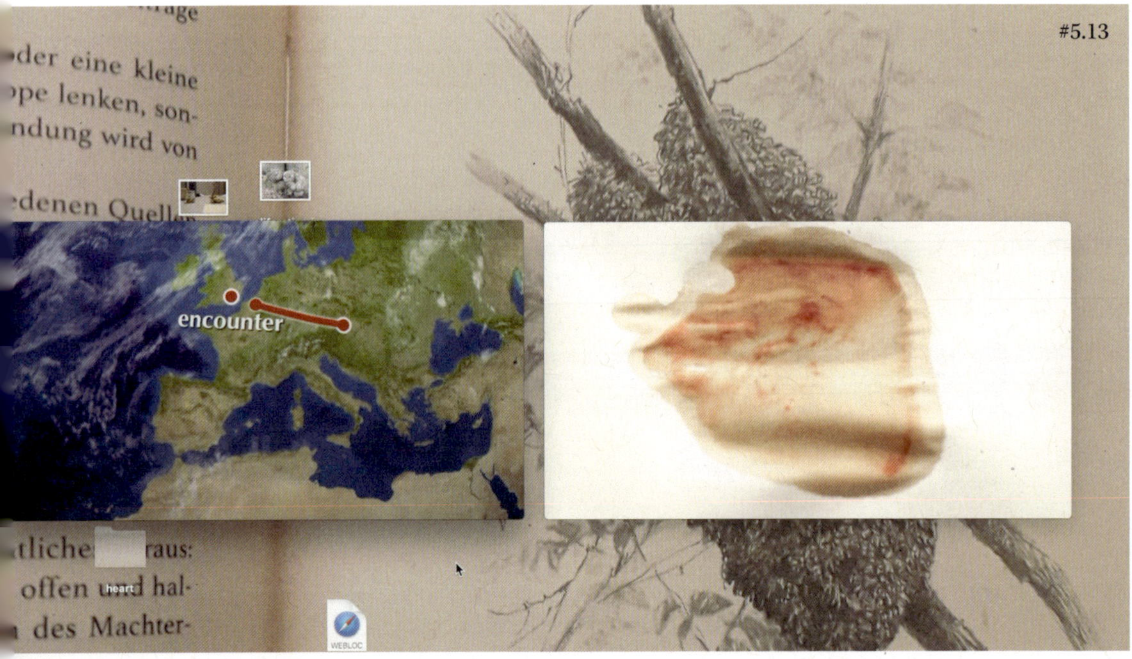
encounter
heart

#5.13

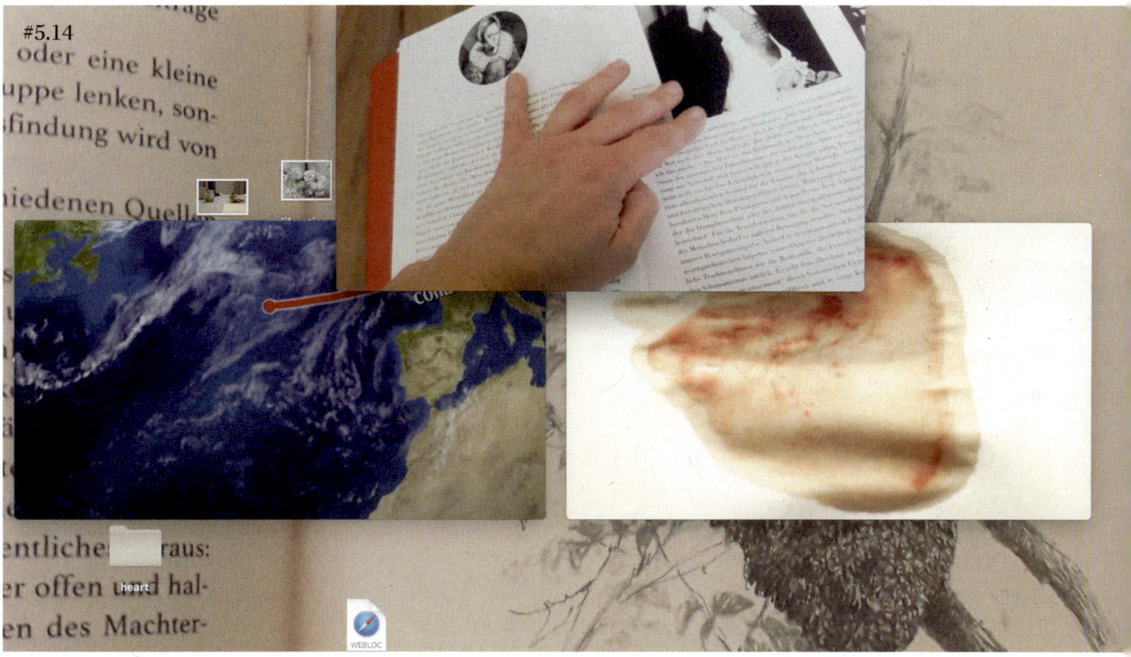
oder eine kleine
uppe lenken, son-
findung wird von
iedenen Quell
entliche raus:
er offen und hal-
en des Machter-
heart
WEBLOC

#5.14

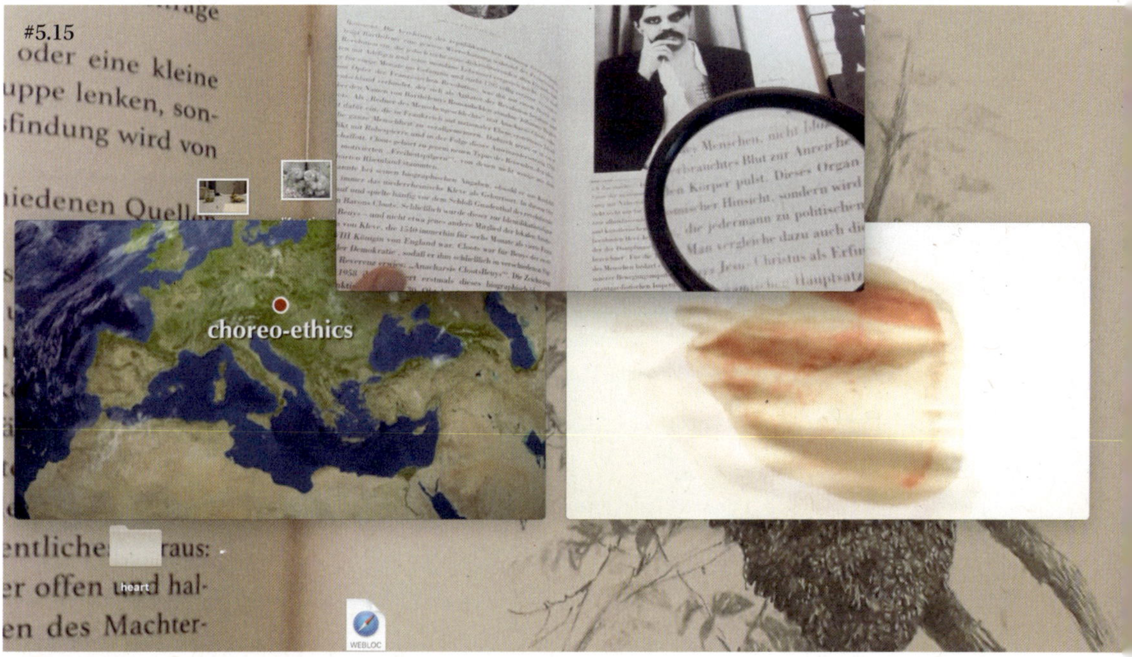
oder eine kleine
uppe lenken, son-
findung wird von
iedenen Quell
choreo-ethics
entliche raus:
er offen und hal-
en des Machter-
heart
WEBLOC

#5.15

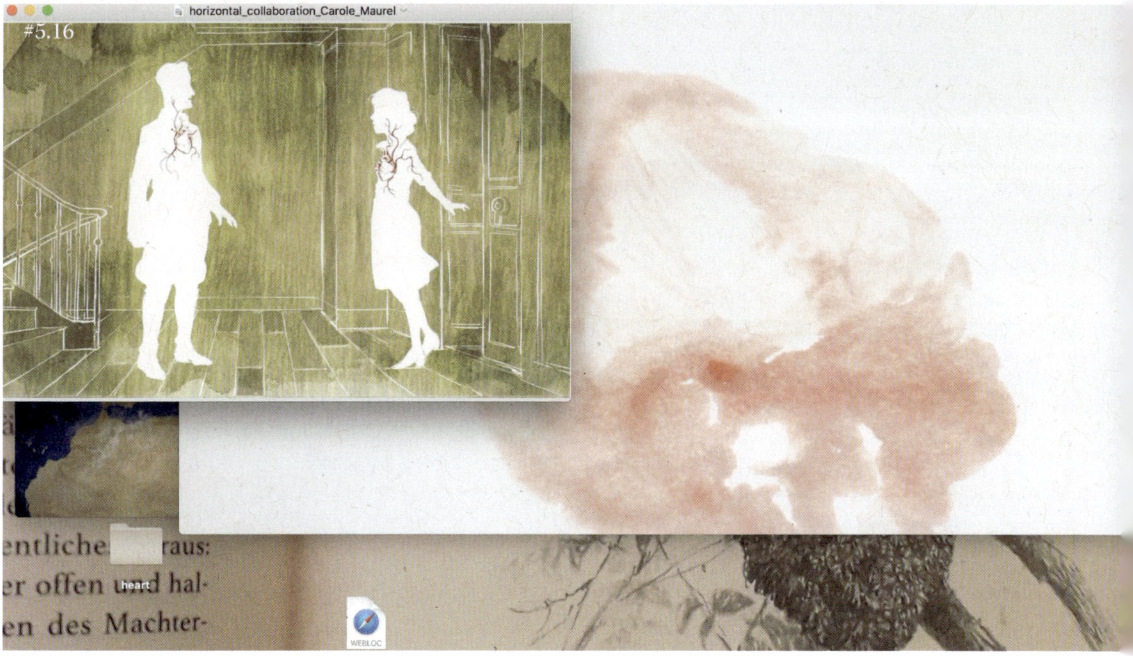
horizontal_collaboration_Carole_Maurel
entliche raus:
er offen und hal-
en des Machter-
heart
WEBLOC

#5.16

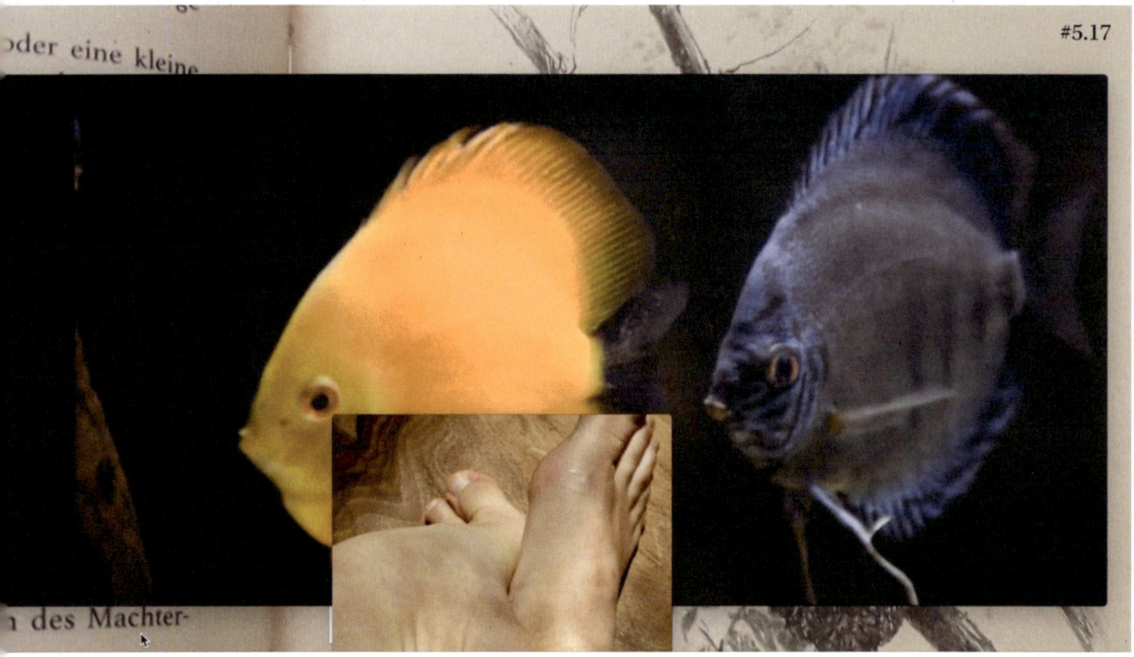

#5.17

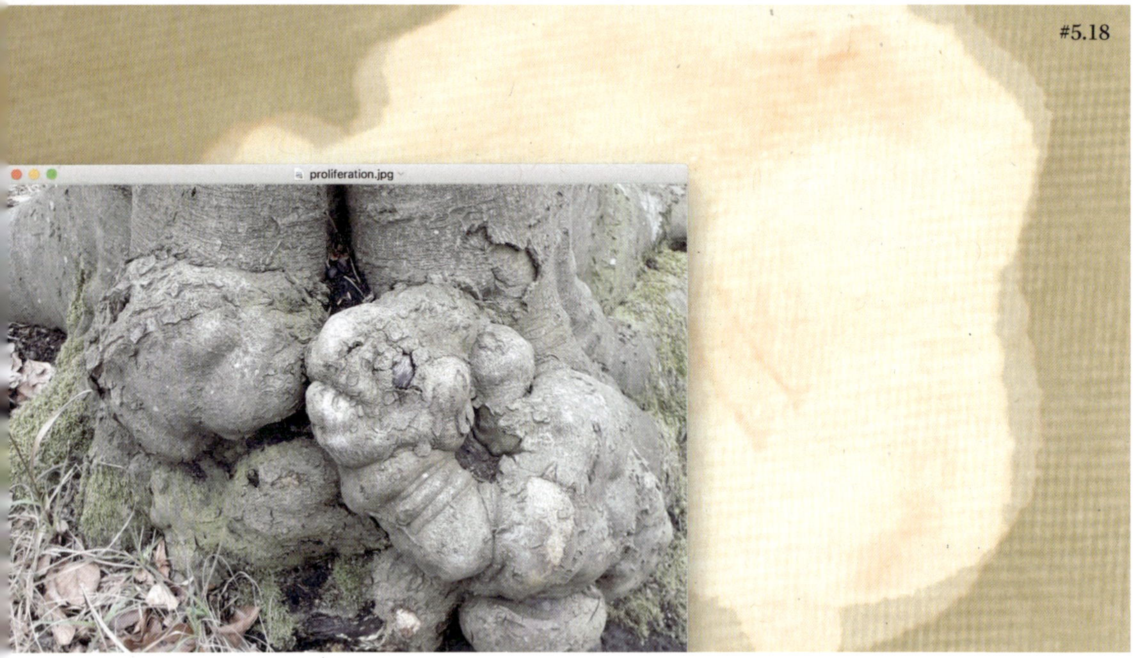

#5.18

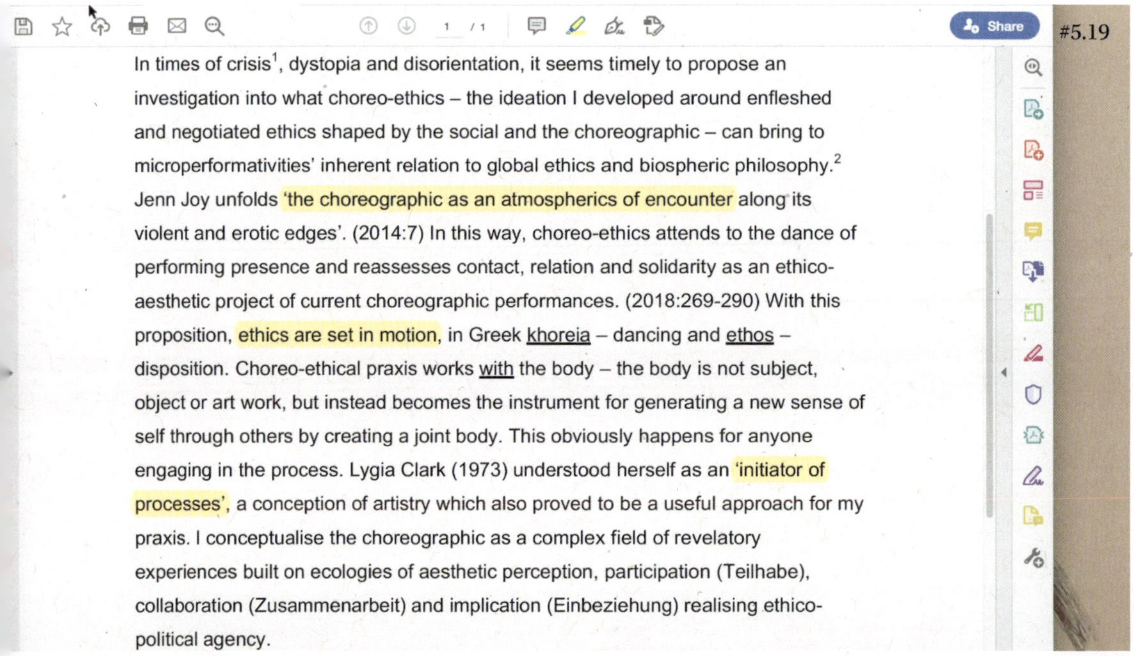

In times of crisis[1], dystopia and disorientation, it seems timely to propose an investigation into what choreo-ethics – the ideation I developed around enfleshed and negotiated ethics shaped by the social and the choreographic – can bring to microperformativities' inherent relation to global ethics and biospheric philosophy.[2] Jenn Joy unfolds 'the choreographic as an atmospherics of encounter along its violent and erotic edges'. (2014:7) In this way, choreo-ethics attends to the dance of performing presence and reassesses contact, relation and solidarity as an ethico-aesthetic project of current choreographic performances. (2018:269-290) With this proposition, ethics are set in motion, in Greek khoreia – dancing and ethos – disposition. Choreo-ethical praxis works with the body – the body is not subject, object or art work, but instead becomes the instrument for generating a new sense of self through others by creating a joint body. This obviously happens for anyone engaging in the process. Lygia Clark (1973) understood herself as an 'initiator of processes', a conception of artistry which also proved to be a useful approach for my praxis. I conceptualise the choreographic as a complex field of revelatory experiences built on ecologies of aesthetic perception, participation (Teilhabe), collaboration (Zusammenarbeit) and implication (Einbeziehung) realising ethico-political agency.

#5.19

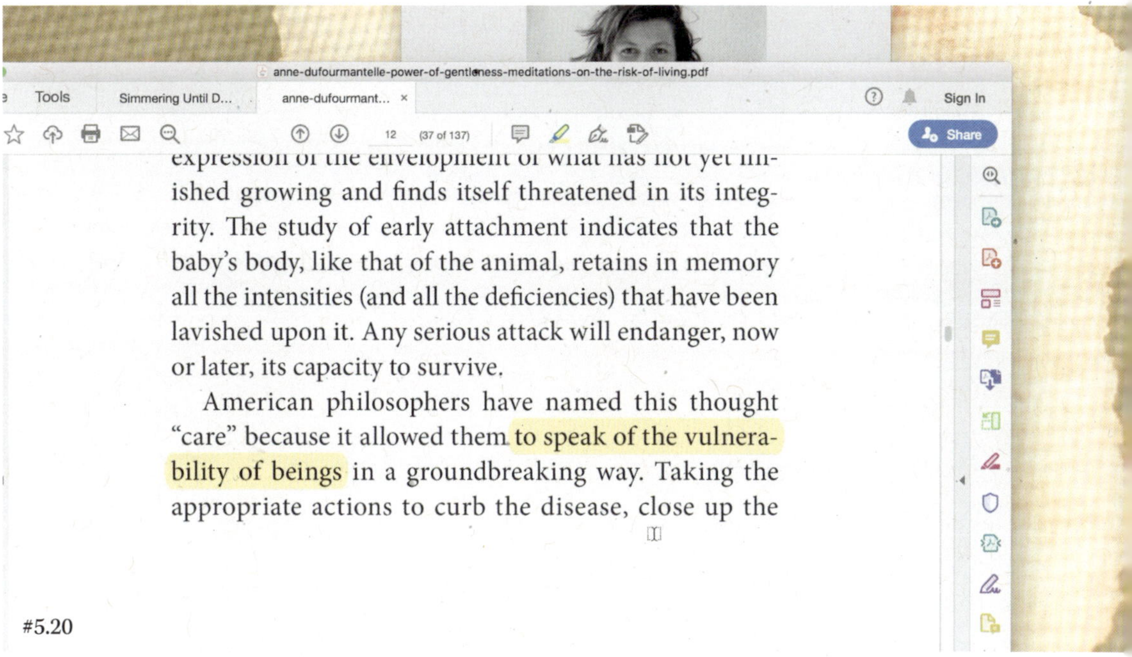
anne-dufourmantelle-power-of-gentleness-meditations-on-the-risk-of-living.pdf
Tools
Simmering Until D...
anne-dufourmant...
Sign In
12
(37 of 137)
Share
expression of the envelopment of what has not yet fin-
ished growing and finds itself threatened in its integ-
rity. The study of early attachment indicates that the
baby's body, like that of the animal, retains in memory
all the intensities (and all the deficiencies) that have been
lavished upon it. Any serious attack will endanger, now
or later, its capacity to survive.
American philosophers have named this thought
"care" because it allowed them to speak of the vulnera-
bility of beings in a groundbreaking way. Taking the
appropriate actions to curb the disease, close up the

#5.20

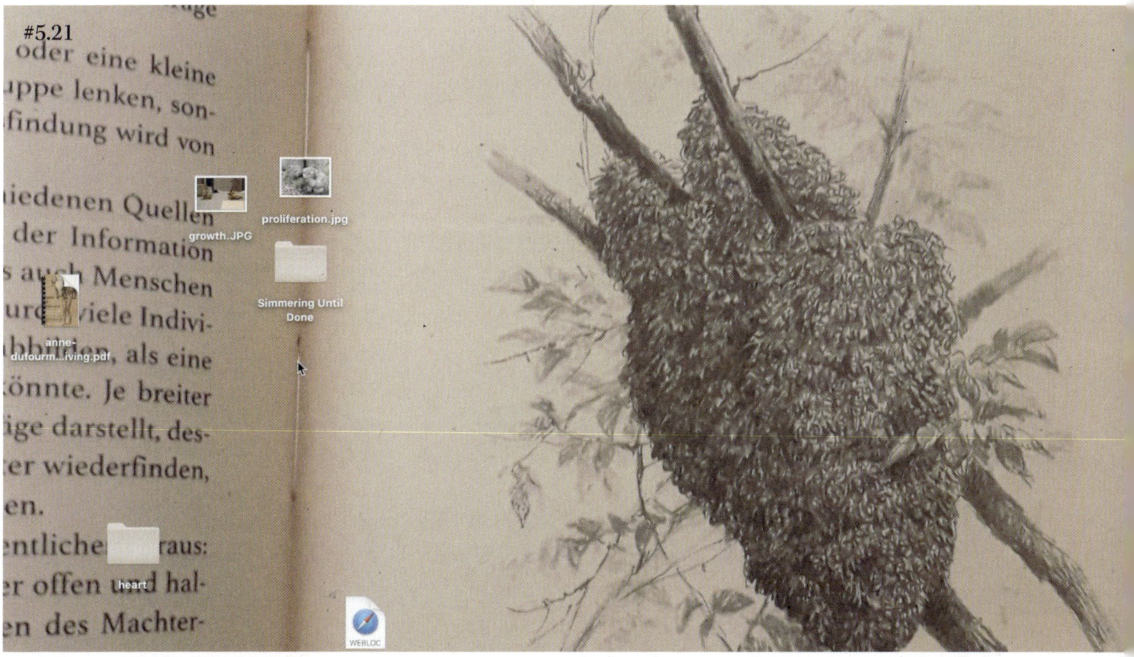
oder eine kleine
uppe lenken, son-
findung wird von
iedenen Quellen
der Information
Menschen
viele Indivi-
als eine
önnte. Je breiter
ige darstellt, des-
er wiederfinden,
en.
entliche
raus:
r offen
hal-
en des Machter-
growth.JPG
proliferation.jpg
Simmering Until Done
anne-dufourm...iving.pdf
heart
WEBLOC

#5.21

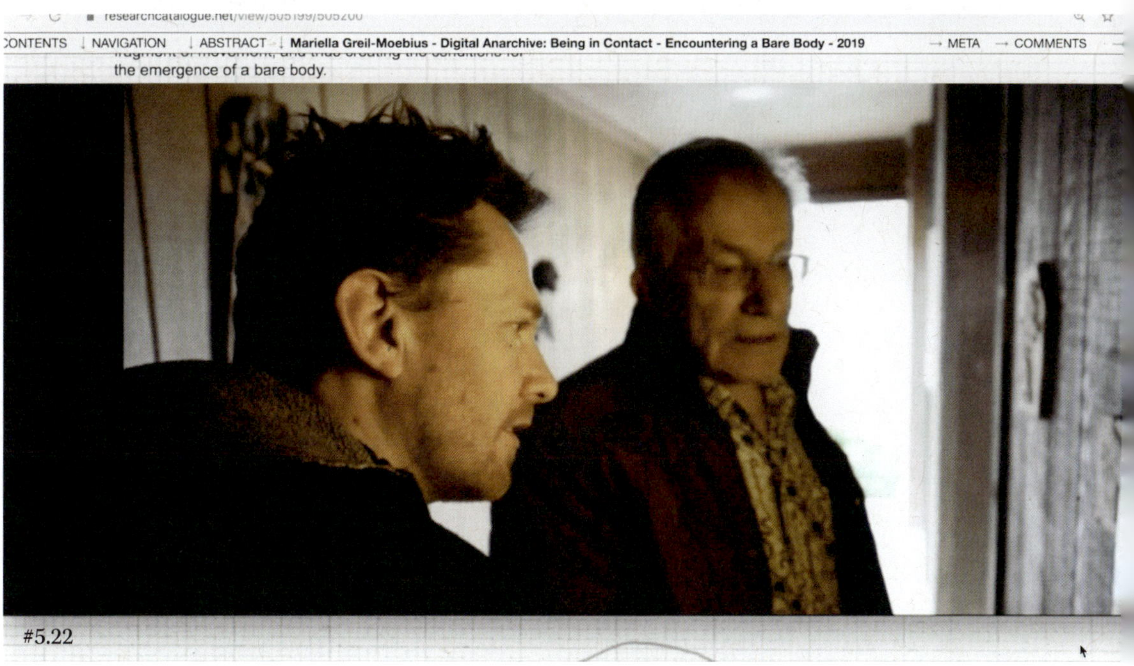
researchcatalogue.net/view/505199/505200
CONTENTS
NAVIGATION
ABSTRACT
Mariella Greil-Moebius - Digital Anarchive: Being in Contact - Encountering a Bare Body - 2019
META
COMMENTS
the emergence of a bare body.

#5.22

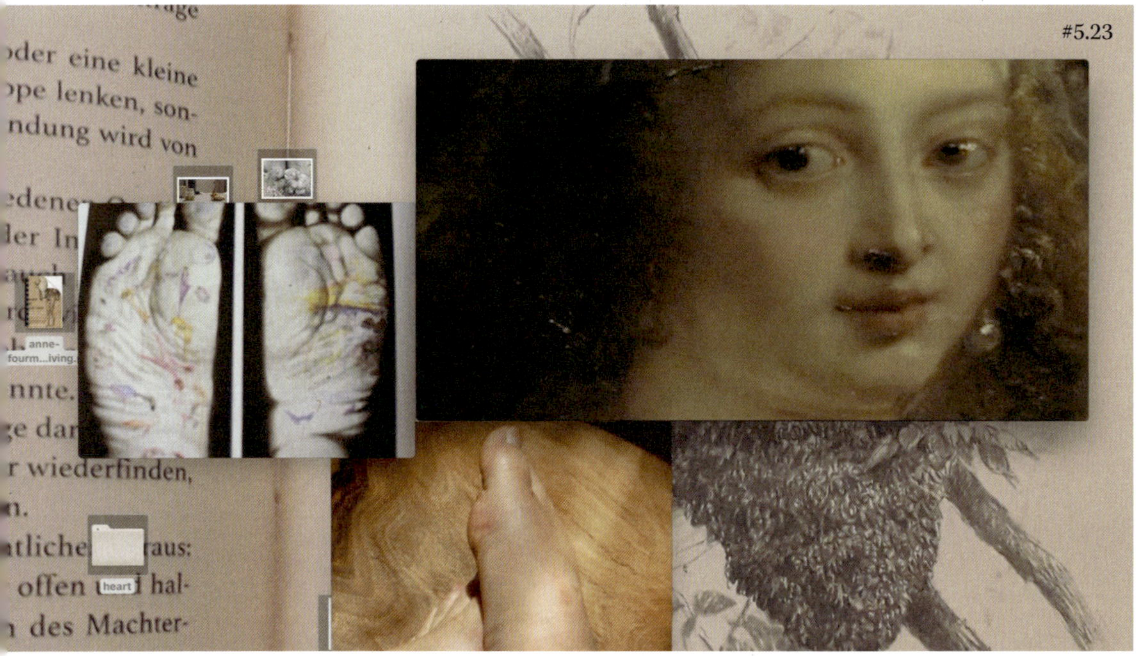
oder eine kleine
ope lenken, son-
ndung wird von
edene
ler In
anne-
fourm...living.
nnte.
ge dar
r wiederfinden,
n.
tliche raus:
offen hal-
heart
n des Machter-
#5.23

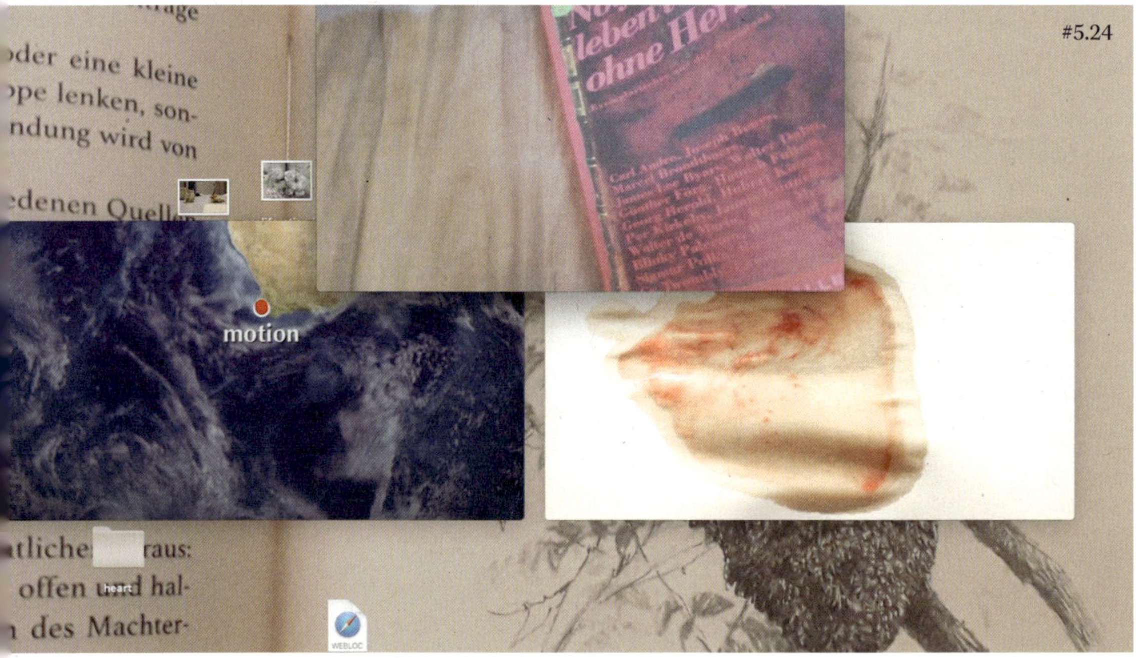
oder eine kleine
ope lenken, son-
ndung wird von
edenen Quell
motion
leben
ohne Her
tliche raus:
offen hal-
heart
n des Machter-
#5.24

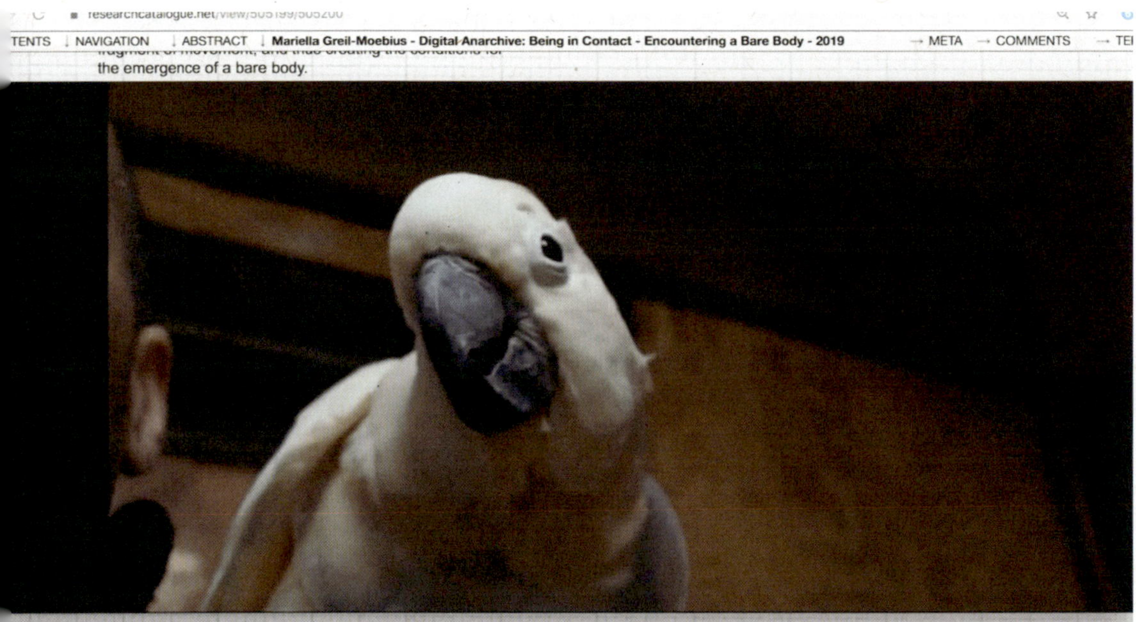
TENTS ↓ NAVIGATION ↓ ABSTRACT ↓ Mariella Greil-Moebius - Digital Anarchive: Being in Contact - Encountering a Bare Body - 2019 → META → COMMENTS
the emergence of a bare body.
#5.25

#5.01: *Simmering Until Done*, desktop performance, 2020, © video stills and performance: Mariella Greil and Simona Koch, with additional visual material by Boglárka Börcsök, Andreas Bolm, Paschalis Dougalis, Hugo Glenndinning, Anne Dufourmantelle, Mani Froh, Thomas Glavinic, Adrian Heathfield, Evá Kovács, Alphonso Lingis, Vivien Löschner, Carole Maurel, Annette Messager, and Peter Paul Rubens.

#5.02–#5.25: *Simmering Until Done*, desktop performance, 2020, © video stills and performance: Mariella Greil, with additional visual material by Boglárka Börcsök, Andreas Bolm, Paschalis Dougalis, Hugo Glenndinning, Anne Dufourmantelle, Mani Froh, Thomas Glavinic, Adrian Heathfield, Evá Kovács, Alphonso Lingis, Vivien Löschner, Carole Maurel, Annette Messager, and Peter Paul Rubens.

Desktop performances were a format explored in response to the Covid-19 pandemic, when live performances were cancelled. All desktop performances and video commentaries by Mariella Greil are available at https://choreoethicalassemblages.home.blog/publications.

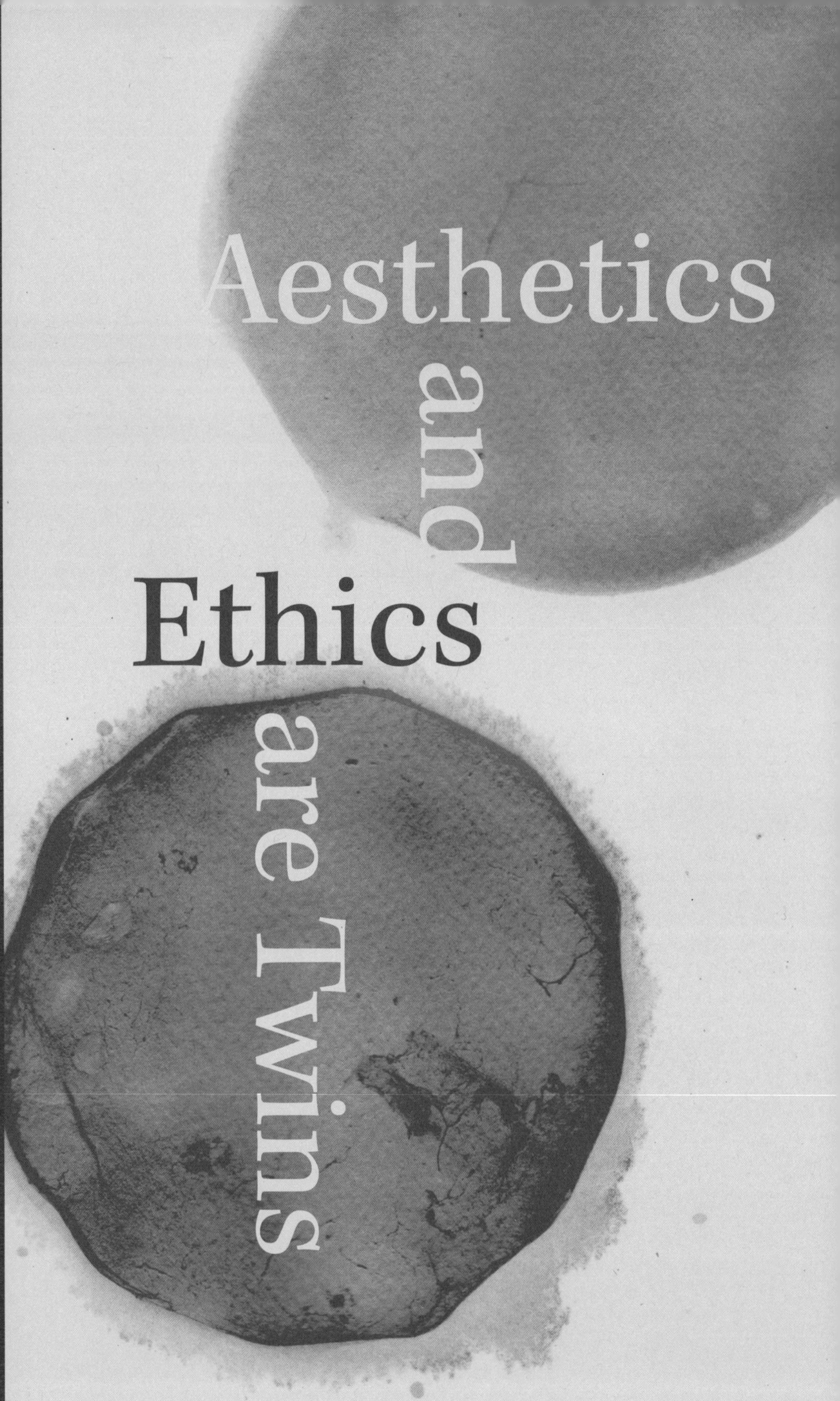

Aesthetics and Ethics are Twins

Art is the truth of feeling, the revelation of the hidden grounds.[281]
Henri Maldiney

To say that aesthetics and ethics are twins is to propose a relation that is more primordial than analogy and more intimate than metaphor. They are not merely parallel domains of philosophical reflection – one concerning the realm of perception and sensibility, the other concerning norms and conduct – but share an originary root in human responsiveness to the world. In approaching this idea, I follow phenomenologist Henri Maldiney's phenomenological investigations into art, existence, and the event, particularly where he introduces the horizon of *intellectus agens*[282] – the active intellect – understood here not in the Aristotelian, scholastic register of abstraction but as the power to open towards the unforeseeable. Through this lens, choreoethics can be regarded as a *poetics of being-in-the-medium*, a way of articulating the inseparability of aesthetic and ethical life. Being-in-the-medium and being-in-communication through *poiesis* builds on the 'radical openness towards the event' that Maldiney termed 'transpassibility' (*transpassibilité*).[283] Philosopher David-Augustin Mândruț discusses transpassibility in relation to the notion of *trust* and draws out how Maldiney addressed rhythm in regard to our attunement to the world. Given that the world is currently living through a triple planetary crisis (global warming, loss of biodiversity, pollution), the call made by dancer, choreographer, and artistic researcher Efva Lilja to 'trust in art'[284] (→ Choreo-ethical Relations and Diffractive Dialogues, 363) might sound not only vague but even slightly naïve. Still, it tickles my heart to read that call, and I firmly believe that art – like no other domain – has the tools to shift political and social values and to instigate change.

Micro-phenomenological Interview with Kerstin Kussmaul
Excerpt, edited transcript
10 November 2022

Mariella Greil: What has just happened in this session? I would like to invite you to recall one moment from this entire day together. Can you choose one specific response that you made to the environment?

Kerstin Kussmaul: When I lassoed you. In that moment I had been debating internally with

281. 'Die Kunst ist die Wahrheit des Empfindens, die Offenbarung des verborgenen Grundes.' Henri Maldiney, quoted in Till Grohmann, introduction to *Henri Maldiney: Drei Beiträge Zum Wahnsinn*, ed. Till Grohmann, trans. Grohmann and Samuel Thoma (Turia + Kant, 2018 [2007]), 15; quote originally published in French in Henri Maldiney, *Art et Existence* (Klincksieck, 1987), 27.

282. In reference to the Middle Ages, Maldiney differentiates between *intellectus agens* and *intellectus possibilis* – that is, *active* and *receptive* intellects – which he elaborates on in connection with his term *transpassibility.* Henri Maldiney, *Drei Beiträge zum Wahnsinn*, 126. David-Augustin Mândruț engages the couplet 'transpassibility-transpossibility' (*transpassibilité-transpossibilité*) and discusses with great nuance how Maldiney's account of trust, or original faith (which he borrows from Edmund Husserl's concept of *Urdoxa*), is related to our rhythmical relationship to the world. David-Augustin Mândruț, 'Martin Buber and Henri Maldiney on the Notion of Event', *META: Research in Hermeneutics, Phenomenology, and Practical Philosophy* 16, no. 2 (2024): 463–83.

283. Mândruț, 'Martin Buber and Henri Maldiney', 463.

284. Efva Lilja, *Art, Research, Empowerment: On the Artist as Researcher* (Regierungskansliet, 2015), accessed 24 September 2025, https://www.efvalilja.se/pdf/art-research-empowerment---the-artist-as-researcher.pdf.

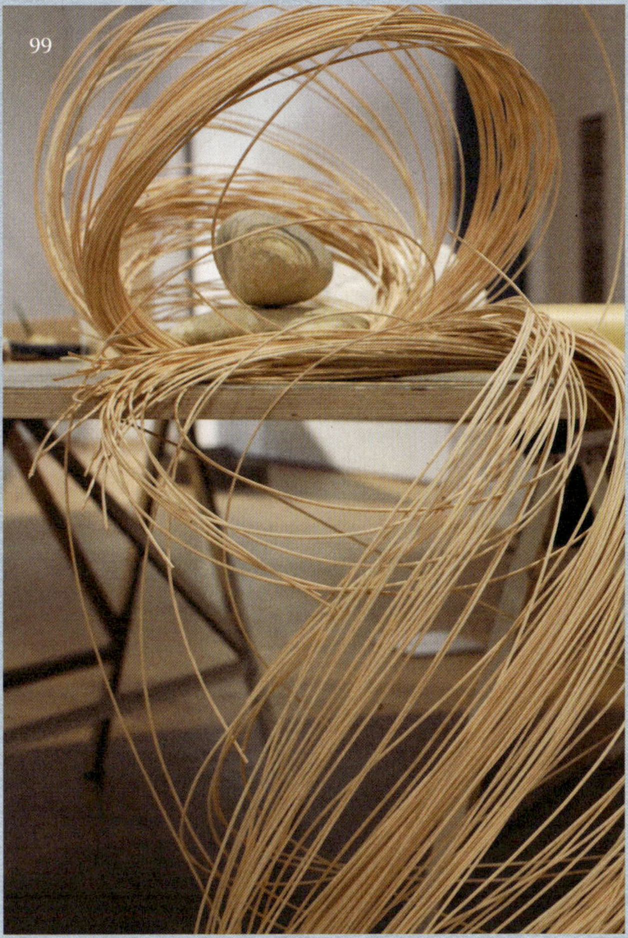

Dome of Swirls

Stony heart,
a vault of ribs,
architecture felt from inside.
Across the edge, a dynamic force
presses and pulls –
hidden people, gremlins,
sweet ideas smuggled into the system,
entering with a *ductus* of turning,
curved fluvial sequences of change.

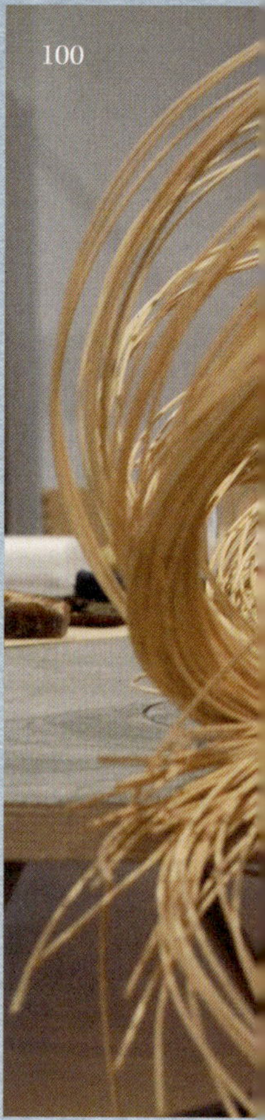

Wild cube, brave space, proliferation –
a cloud of somatic response
seeking sufficient ground.
Non-personal questions levitate,
advanced tinkering,
yet acceptable as deep work,
independent as sky,
dense as underwater forests.
Willowy structures bend without collapse,
overlapping and apportioning affect,
with atypical empathic timing.
Alternative relational rhythms,
circadian communication rustling
between body tissues and time,
matter and meaning.

Idiorhythmic forms – Roland Barthes whispers –
diaphanous dances,
and patterns of intuition flaring,
shifting out of and beyond circular frames.
Second-order reflections
on embodied synchrony
crystallize into metascience,
staging the swirls of research experiments,
debunking myths of knowledge theory,
the idealized sobriety of formal models.

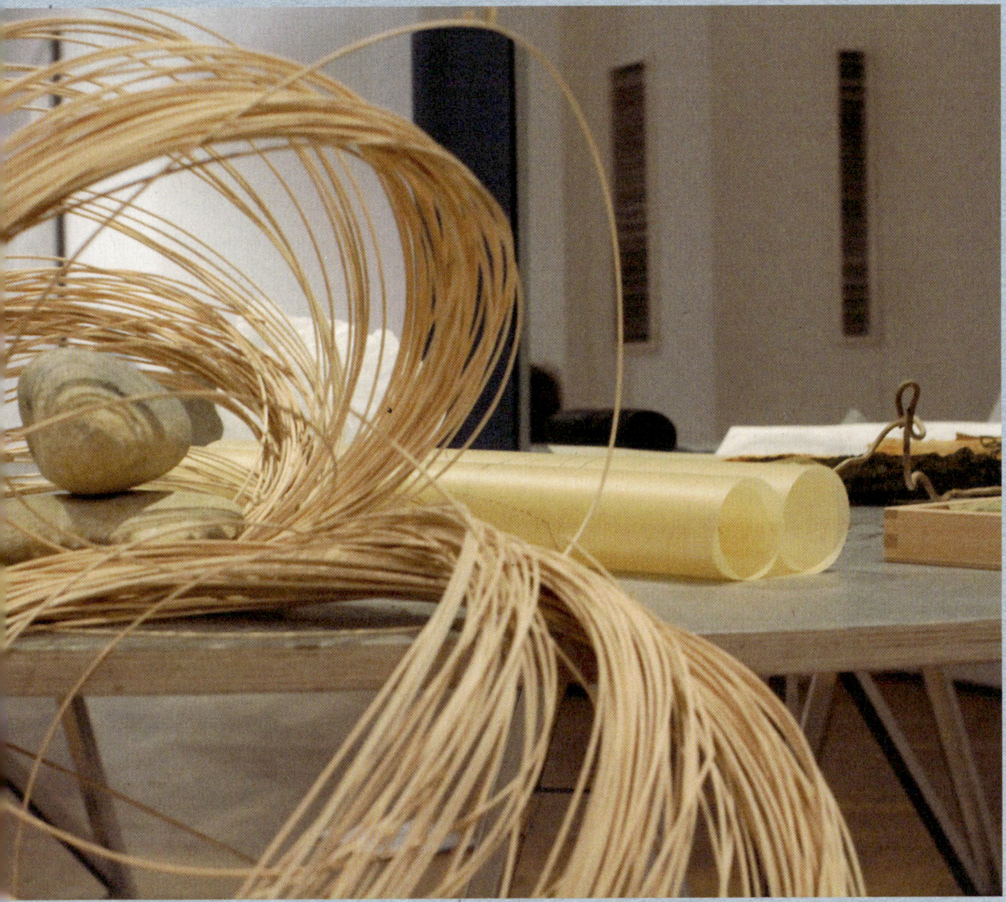

Embodied methodological activism persists:
diversity, epistemic humility,
the unmaking of the reproducibility crisis,
the loosening of logical inference and proof
in the field of artistic research.
In defence of epistemic and methodological pluralism,
standing up for situated knowledge
we carve out space for spirited experiments,
that do not yet know their names.

Witness this –
an act of trusting in art aloud.
Daring the cache of experience as matter,
a hypothesis of love,
trans-phrased as an ontological shift.
Found science, choreographed.
Ephemeral sequencing through body and soul.
Free-fall fascial transmission.
Protest, not against,
but *for* the joy of ethics.

Motionless, alive-with.
A vivarium released from enclosure
unfolding as being-amidst –
a site of mutual affect –
bodies, materials, microbes, climates
influencing one another.
Life uncoiling relationally
as an œkology of practices,
as process rather than specimen
and milieu rather than container.

The helical cathedral calls for co-presence
and ongoing transformation,
spiralling into ontologies of the living –
self-organizing, contingent, and irrevocably
relational.

myself about the different levels I was constantly engaging with. *What am I allowed to do?* And I was noticing my own judgments in the process. For example, I don't want to do it, because then, *poor Mariella, she would have to clean it up afterwards.* This was a moment where I noticed that you had been present in the space the whole time. And yet I knew it, because you were witnessing everything I was doing, but I did not take it into account. Suddenly in that moment, you became part of my environment, so strongly. You were within my world of relationships. And what I did, it was not pre-planned; it felt physically very spontaneous. I thought I would probably scare you a little.

Mariella: How did the lassoing action come into being?

Kerstin: Actually, I wouldn't have been able to verbalise the lassoing in the moment I did it. I can only do that now. I felt like I was trying to make connections with distance. As underscore,[285] I noticed that I wasn't just touching the centre, I engaged nearby, but I was also having indirect relationships to it. And in connecting actions, as well as with connecting objects, I found myself debating about my senses. Sometimes I had my eyes closed; sometimes I had them open. And I realised how touch is at the beginning of all that action. And the lasso was an image of touching: it extends, and rolls, opens up, and I could touch you.

Mariella: Was the visual sense guiding you in that action?

Kerstin: It was a combination of both visual and tactile senses, because we were two metres apart, and that action was a way of creating touch through distance.

Mariella: So, there was a desire to reach out, then there was the following action, right? Can we go a bit deeper into this gap between the motivation to do and the doing?

Kerstin: I remember noticing you photographing something that I had done just moments before. So, I felt like I was always a few steps ahead. And I saw you standing there in the middle, and I thought, Mariella is part of my world. How can I make that clear to her? Then I just looked around, not knowing how to do it. So, I saw the lasso, which I had already moved before. And then I was like, Yes, I will take that and throw it around her neck. Even though you were following my traces, I could sense you were not focused on me. In that moment, there was an inner debate about crossing boundaries, as I knew I was going to scare you. However, because of my personal history with you, I decided to cross that boundary. I do not do this enough; I need to be more *courageous*. I will not die; she will not die; she probably won't drop her camera. Everything else is negotiable. Individual care ethics. And I think I was also able to make that decision because I do know you, your physicality, your reflexes, and the state of your nervous system through our work together. I probably wouldn't have made that choice with someone I had just met.

Mariella: So, you felt that I – as part of the environment – was ready to encounter your crossing of a boundary, even if it was not often crossed from your side. It seems like you felt the trust and the support from the prepared environment to be negotiable, so that the thresholds were waiting for you.

Kerstin: You were ready for it, but you were unprepared. Nevertheless, you definitely have dealt with crossed boundaries before. So, because of my *trust* that you'd faced this topic already, I felt like you must be ready to do this.

Mariella: Yes. It's very interesting that such two very strong words came up: *courage and trust*. Can we go back to that very moment? Close your eyes. So, you're standing there, you have the lasso in your hand already, you see me with a camera, busy with tracing and documenting the movements. What happens in your body? Where do you sense that courage to throw it? Can you describe it?

Kerstin: I recognise that you're part of my world of relationships. Then I want to find a form to express this. I turn around and realise I have a lasso in my hand. I look at you again. I freeze. A bubbly feeling envelops my entire diaphragm area. It was a very short moment. But I think a leap of faith drove me to take action as well. My curiosity and eagerness to improvise overcame this little feeling of not being entirely sure if it was going to work or not. There was a potential for a true dramaturgical change of dynamics. And then I forgot.

Mariella: I would like to linger at this visceral, diaphragmatic, bubbly threshold moment. The diaphragm is there for breathing. Did you feel any change in your breathing? Can you recall that?

Kerstin: I'm not entirely sure. I wasn't very aware of my breathing. I might have held my breath, actually. So, there was definitely like an increase, from parasympathetic to sympathetic. With an inhale. Interesting, there was a mis-temporality.

285. This is dancer's jargon. The 'Underscore' was first introduced by dancer and founding participant in contact improvisation Nancy Stark Smith when she began developing it in the early 1990s. The 'Underscore' is the continuous, subtle awareness of internal impulses, bodily sensations, and environmental cues that inform and guide movement, fostering responsive, improvised, and relational dance experiences that follow several stages. You will find more information about the 'Underscore' here: https://www.contactimprov.com/underscore.html.

Mariella: How did the space sound in that *leap of faith* moment?

Kerstin: There was a clicking of a camera signifying where your attention was directed – that was quite dominant. The ongoing noise outside from the traffic, which was so depressing for me the whole time. There was a permeability between the inside and outside space. But the space in here had a listening quality for its objects.

Mariella: Can you describe the music and the materiality of the room?

Kerstin: Since, I'm a synesthetic thinker, I hear movements. The reverberation of the room exposed me to the constant reconfiguration of previous bodies during our thinking process. In my hand it was a mixture of senses, emotions, and memories, as if I was tapping into someone else's memory.

Mariella: When did this whole scene end?

Kerstin: Once I did it, it was done. The action itself was more important than what you did with it. I saw you photographing yourself and that was a feeling of *mission accomplished.* I think you stayed a little longer with it, but my attention dispersed somewhere else, such that I can't say the exact moment that it shifted because I was drawn to something else.

The claim that aesthetics and ethics are twins resists the disciplinary division that isolates aesthetic experience from practical life. While in the common understanding, aesthetics is reduced to questions of taste, beauty, or representation, and ethics is confined to moral prescriptions, their twinship affinity remains invisible. At a deeper register, both emerge from the same gesture of responsiveness: a capacity to be affected (→ A/Effective Assembling and Dissembling, 206), to let oneself be moved, to orient oneself within a world of meaning. Twins are not identical but rather have a kinship relation that, through the necessity of considering their differences, enables differentiation and mutual illumination.

Ethics without aesthetics would probably become somewhat rigid, potentially blind to the texture of lived situations, insensitive to the nuances of encounters. Aesthetics without ethics risks devolving into mere formalism, detached from the demands of responsibility. Their twinship signals that each calls forth the other and that both are born in the same natality of human and (perhaps a daring claim) other-than human existence – an originary attunement to the world as a polysensory encounter (→ Polysensory Encounters, 166) between multiple forms of existence.

Aesthetics of Openness – Ethics of Vulnerability and Exposure

Maldiney's philosophy is marked by a thinking of the event (*l'événement*), not as something predictable or manageable but as the unforeseeable irruption that exposes existence to its own openness or – as I suggest – its bareness.[286] For Maldiney, art exemplifies this openness, for it constitutes more than a reproduction of the world – it is the creation of a world through form, rhythm, and presence.

286. I introduce the conceptual ideation of *bare bodies* in Mariella Greil, *Being in Contact – Encountering a Bare Body* (Edition Angewandte, De Gruyter, 2021) and elaborate on and discuss it further with dialogue partners in Mariella Greil, ed., *Bare Bodies – Thresholding Life* (Edition Angewandte, De Gruyter, 2024).

Cosmopoietic practice in art invites us to experience the possibility of existence being re-founded.[287]

Ethics, then, cannot be reduced to codes or norms but arises in the moment when beings are confronted by the otherness of the event (*l'événement*) as what I call *choreo-ethics:* the call that demands a situated, live response beyond predictability that cannot be confined to given rules or foreseeable measures. Aesthetics cannot be diminished to taste but is the mode in which existence vibrates with form, rhythm, and sense. Both ethics and aesthetics are ways of being-in-exposure, of sustaining oneself in the face of contingencies. Maldiney shows that the aesthetic event is always an ethical event as well, for it implicates one's mode of being in relation to alterity, vulnerability, and possibility – the term he uses is *transpossibilité* (transpossibility). In my understanding, this means an openness to unforeseeable events exceeding known prior possibilities, as one attunes oneself to the phenomenology of the event and the art of co-existence. In embodied artistic research, we generally refer to this recognition of potentiality as improvisation.

In this light, the idea of the *intellectus agens* acquires renewed relevance. Traditionally, Aristotle's active intellect was understood as the immaterial principle that actualises the potentialities of thought, enabling abstraction and knowledge. In the scholastic tradition, *intellectus agens* was the faculty that illuminated phantasms and rendered intelligible the forms available to the human mind. Rebirthed in phenomenological and new existential terms,[288] the *intellectus agens* is less a faculty of abstraction than a power of opening: the capacity to let meaning emerge in and through encounter. It is not primarily a cognitive function but an ontological gesture – the act of receiving and transfiguring what comes to presence.

In Maldiney's sense, this rebirth of the *intellectus agens* corresponds to the necessity of a mode of thinking that is active in acceptance rather than mastery, in sustaining the rupture of the event rather than preventing it. Active and passive intertwine; ultimately, the base of sustained acceptance layered with continuous choreo-ethical navigation and experiment persists, while rupture profoundly interrupts. Yet both keep co-existing at the same time – generating tension where yielding and asserting co-constitute the event's unfolding and its transformative resonance as a process of ongoing negotiation. The intellect here is the active-passive power to remain open, to withstand exposure. As I have argued elsewhere,[289] performing bare bodies endure the fact that they are exposed, which is aesthetic insofar as it resonates with form and rhythm; it is also ethical insofar as it constitutes a responsibility for the otherness of the event.

287. In the project *Morphopoly*, led by artist-researcher and philosopher Kath T. Zakravsky, this constant re-founding of the world is concretely practiced as a game, where children (aged 7–11 years) are invited to reinvent worlds through building and rebuilding with a range of materials, 'models of the world', combining imagination, narration, and materialisation in dialogue with architects, photographers, artists, and media educators. Kath T. Zakravsky, *Morphopoly*, accessed 11 July 2025, https://www.morphopoly.org.

288. See the extensive work of Colin Wilson (1931–2013), the British philosopher and novelist who pioneered 'new existentialism', or what he also called 'phenomenological existentialism', exploring human potential and consciousness, and transcending ordinary perception. Wilson strove 'to create a new and optimistic existentialism', which I find quite sympathetic. Vaughan Rapatahana, 'Colin Wilson', *Philosophy Now* 101 (2014), https://philosophynow.org/issues/101/Colin_Wilson_1931-2013.

289. Greil, *Being in Contact*; and Greil, ed., *Bare Bodies.*

Let us now circle back and think again about what it means when we say that aesthetics and ethics are twins. In my view, their twinship becomes choreographically manifest in movement, in relation, and in the performative unfolding of being-in a situation. Choreo-ethics does not reduce ethics to rules for conduct during dance, nor aesthetics to criteria of beauty in movement. Rather, it names a poetics of *being-in-the-medium* – the medium being more than the materiality of the dance or performance, namely, the very milieu of relational existence.

To be in the medium is to inhabit the in-between: the resonance between bodies, the interval between gesture and perception, the spacing that makes relation possible. Maldiney reminds us that the aesthetic event is always temporal and rhythmic, a matter of form arising through the interval. Ethics, in turn, is not an exterior imposition but the way in which humans and other-than-humans comport themselves in relation to this interval – whether they allow space for the others and sustain the openness of the event. Choreo-ethics thus articulates an ethos of movement that is also an aesthetic of responsibility. To dance is to risk exposure, to entrust oneself to rhythm, to be vulnerable to interruption. This vulnerability is not a deficit but the very condition of the aesthetic, ethical twinship: it is where the poetics of being-in-the-medium emerges. There are three conceivable interrelated dimensions: resonance, responsibility, and relation. Aesthetics is first of all resonance[290] – the way forms vibrate, how gestures echo in perception, how bodies respond to rhythms. In the medium, resonance is not limited to artistic expression but extends to the very texture of existence, to the rhythms of encounter and the sonority of being-with-others. Rather than being a superimposed code, ethics arises as a responsibility to this resonance, the way one sustains or interrupts it. More than merely a moral responsibility, this is an ontological responsibility: it concerns how we allow the medium to speak, how we respond to its unforeseeable demands. And finally, the twinship of aesthetics and ethics culminates in relation. To be in the medium is to be in relation – not as fusion, but as intervals of coexistence, where distance and proximity co-constitute one another. Relation is choreographic insofar as it is structured through movement, rhythm, and spacing; it is ethical insofar as it calls for responsibility to the alterity of the other or other others.

In our contemporary situation, I propose the rebirth of the *intellectus agens* as embodied research, which in my project calls for choreo-ethical attunement. In a world marked by ecological crisis, technological acceleration, and socio-political fragmentation, the capacity to be open to the unforeseeable – to sustain resonance and relation – becomes crucial.

Choreo-ethics as a poetics of being-in-the-medium is a way of practicing this rebirth. It is not a doctrine but a lived praxis: the cultivation of attentiveness to rhythm, the endurance of exposure, the responsiveness to otherness. In this sense,

290. There might be 'dreams of a relationship to the world that is resonant through and through, in which body and psyche, spirit and nature, individual and collective history, the individual and society overcome their divisions, relate to each other as counterparts, and enter into vibrant responsive relationships to each other'. Hartmut Rosa, *Resonance: A Sociology of Our Relationship to the World*, trans. James Wagner (Polity 2019), 358. See also Renaud Hétier et al., 'From Resonance to Transformation of the World', *Réseaux: Communication, Technologie, Société* 235 (2023), 169–91.

aesthetics and ethics are reborn together as twins of existence, reoriented by the active intellect, embodied as openness.

Following Maldiney, one can see that art exemplifies the intertwining of the aesthetic and the ethical: each work of art is both a form and a call, both rhythm and responsibility. As an openness to the unforeseeable, the rebirth of the *intellectus agens* grounds – both in its transpassibilities and transpossiblities – this twinship of aesthetics and ethics that forms a renewed, contemporary phenomenology of existence.

Choreo-ethics, in this sense, offers a way to inhabit this twinship: by practicing resonance, responsibility, and relation in and through movement, the movement of thought is enacted as embodied, lived openness. In this poietic poetics, aesthetics and ethics are indeed twins – not as separate domains, but as interwoven aspects of the same event of being.

Let me zoom in onto the *ethics of vulnerability*, which – in my view – resists reduction to a discourse of weakness or deficit. Instead, vulnerability should be understood as a generative condition of relation, exposing the subject to modes of affectability that unsettle the fantasy of autonomy. To be vulnerable is not merely to risk harm but to be implicated in the constitutive openness of existence itself. In Levinasian terms, vulnerability arises in the face-to-face encounter, where the self is summoned beyond its own self-interest and called to respond by the irreducible alterity of the other. He writes,

> Hasn't the third dimension been forgotten? The direction toward the Other, who is not only collaborator and neighbor of our cultural work of expression, or a client of our artistic production, but interlocutor: the one to whom expression expresses for whom celebration celebrates, he who is both term of an orientation and first signification. In other words, before it is celebration of being, expression is a relation with the one to whom I express the expression and whose presence is already required so that my cultural gesture of expression can be produced.[291]

This presence and openness to cultural gestures is not accidental but ontological, grounding an aesthetic of exposure wherein the body – particularly the bare body – appears as the site of both receptivity and resistance. It requires the implicated other. In choreographic and performative contexts, the unveiled body refuses the coverings of convention and invites an encounter with alterity that cannot be reduced to spectacle. Here, nudity functions less as an object of vision than as an operation of relation:

291. Emmanuel Levinas, *Humanism of the Other*, trans. Nidra Poller (University of Illinois Press, 2006), 30.

an insistence on presence in its most precarious, and therefore most potent, form. Jean-Luc Nancy's reflections on *être-en-commun* (being-in-common)[292] illuminate this dimension of exposure: the body is always with others from the beginning, its surface a porous threshold where sense is shared and meaning emerges. To be exposed is not to be dissolved but to enter into the fragile negotiation of touch, distance, and resonance both within and between us. '[P]hilosophy needs to think in principle about how we are "us" among us, that is, how the consistency of our Being is in being-in-common, and how this consists precisely in the "in" or in the "between" of its spacing.'[293]

An 'aesthetics of openness'[294] describes this exposure as an active practice of permeability rather than as passive submission. The bare body – stripped of its protective layers (which does not just mean clothing) – foregrounds this very negotiation: it materialises the tension between withdrawal[295] and offering, between self-enclosure and intercorporeal attunement. In its vulnerability, the body becomes the threshold through which an ethical demand emerges, calling forth a situated response that cannot be pre-scribed by normative prediction. Thus, an ethics of vulnerability and an ethics of openness intersect as conditions for an ethic that, in my practice, is choreographic in nature: not mastery, but responsiveness to the unforeseeable. I call this the emergence of choreo-ethical assemblages.

Depth Aesthetics – Encountering Ethical Dilemmas

The contemporary discourse on aesthetics has increasingly moved beyond the narrowly construed realm of beauty or the sublime towards relational, œkological, and ethical terrains, I would like to locate within this shift the contours of what could be described as *depth aesthetics* – a concept that, while not yet formally canonised, resonates with existing philosophical and psychoanalytic traditions. Norwegian philosopher Arne Næss coined the term *deep ecology*.[296] More recent work by physicist and Jungian analyst Andrew Fellows has critically interrogated the ontological and ethical embeddedness of the human within wider œkological matrices.[297] *Depth*

292. Jean-Luc Nancy, 'Of Being-in-Common', trans. James Creech, in *Community at Loose Ends*, ed. The Miami Theory Collective (University of Minnesota Press, 1991); Jean-Luc Nancy and Christopher Fynsk, *The Inoperative Community*, ed. Peter Connor, trans. Peter Connor et al. (University of Minnesota Press, 2008 [1986]); Efe Basturk, 'Nancy and the Idea of "Being-in-common": An Alternative Existentiality for the Subjectivity'. *SATS* 21, no. 1 (2020): 61–80, https://doi.org/10.1515/sats-2019-0011.

293. Jean-Luc Nancy, *Being Singular Plural*, trans. Robert D. Richardson and Anne E. O'Byrne (Stanford University Press, 2000 [1996]), 26.

294. Emma Cocker, 'Towards an Attitude of Openness', keynote presentation, 12th International Conference on Artistic Research, Society for Artistic Research, Vienna, 7–9 April 2021, https://www.researchcatalogue.net/profile/show-exposition?exposition=1220981.

295. See the project *Withdrawing the Performer*, led by performers Charlotta Ruth and Jasmin Schaitl in collaboration with dancer and neuroscientist Imani Rameses, accessed 24 September 2025, https://www.dieangewandte.at/jart/prj3/angewandte-2016/main.jart?rel=en&reserve-mode=active&content-id=1609322325777&projekt_id=1609322330666.

296. The term was coined by Norwegian philosopher Arne Næss in 'The Shallow and the Deep, Long-Range Ecology Movement: A Summary', *Inquiry: An Interdisciplinary Journal of Philosophy* 16, no. 1–4 (1973): 95–100, https://doi.org/10.1080/00201747308601682. Næss expands on the concept of *deep ecology* in Arne Næss, *Ecology, Community and Lifestyle: Outline of an Ecosophy*, trans. David Rothenberg (Cambridge University Press, 1989).

297. Andrew Fellows, *Gaia, Psyche and Deep Ecology: Navigating Climate Change in the Anthropocene* (Routledge, 2019).

aesthetics can be conceived of as a parallel exploration of how aesthetic experience penetrates beneath the surface-level perception of the beautiful and subliminal. Given the interwovenness of aesthetics and ethics, the deeper layers of aesthetics potentially reveal strata of ethical dilemmas that challenge anthropocentric certainties. The notion of *depth* here becomes both metaphorical and literal: metaphorical in that it engages with psychic as well as existential profundity, and literal in its orientation towards œkological depth – soil, roots, and the non-human ground of existence.

In *Gaia, Psyche and Deep Ecology* (2019), Andrew Fellows develops a transdisciplinary approach in which Jungian depth psychology converges with œkological philosophy. For Fellows, the œkological crisis cannot be reduced to a technical problem but is symptomatic of psychic dissociation, of a collective repression of our interdependence with the other-than-human world. Rather than in a superficial appreciation of natural beauty or a romanticised perspective on nature, Fellows' articulation of 'deep ecology' thus situates the aesthetic within a psychically transformative encounter with the/an œkological being. The aesthetic, in this register, requires an opening into vulnerability – an exposure to the uncanny alterity of the other-than-human, which, genuinely and in its depths, resists instrumentalisation. Ultimately, and through an act of hermeneutic reverse engineering, I understand the claim of psychologist Don Kuiken, who says,

> An appropriate focus for the examination of the depth metaphor is aesthetic experience, especially if, as I submit, an experience is not aesthetic unless it invites depth. To suggest that aesthetic experience inherently invites depth is neither essentialistic nor stipulative. Rather, its epistemic force is comparable to saying that an animal is not a bird unless it has wings. Both claims require qualification (and perhaps apologies to graphic designers and penguins), but in a manner that generally reflects the complexity of empirical statements.[298]

Depth aesthetics, then, may be understood as cultivating this mode of fine attunement that Fellows discusses beyond the mirror concept of the *anima mundi*, where the organ of perception, the heart, responds directly to an experience. Fellows quotes psychologist and author of books on depth psychology James Hillman, who writes, 'Sensing the world and imagining the world are not divided in the aesthetic

298. Don Kuiken, 'Understanding the Depth Metaphor in Aesthetic Experience: Pressing the Limits of Psychological Inquiry', in *Toward a Psychology of Persons*, ed. W. Smythe (Erlbaum, 1998), 103.

response of the heart'[299] (→ Polymorphous Narrations, 160). Rather than being a disinterested Kantian contemplation[300] of form, depth aesthetics demands embodied resonance that risks destabilisation. Herein lies the first ethical dilemma: how to sustain aesthetic openness without collapsing into either romantic idealisation or despair in the face of œkological devastation. The aesthetic encounter carries ethical weight precisely because it destabilises the subject's secure boundaries and demands recognition of the responsibility towards that which exceeds human comprehension. The transfigured spaces of choreographic environments form the conditions for aesthetic grounding and thereby support the development of depth œkology. (→ Depth Aesthetics – Encountering Ethical Dilemmas, 282)

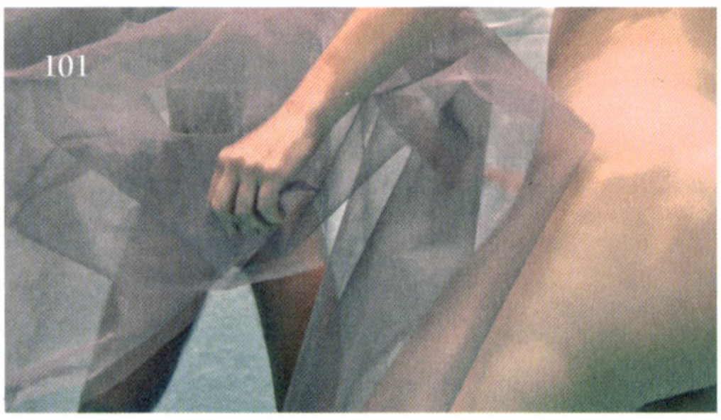

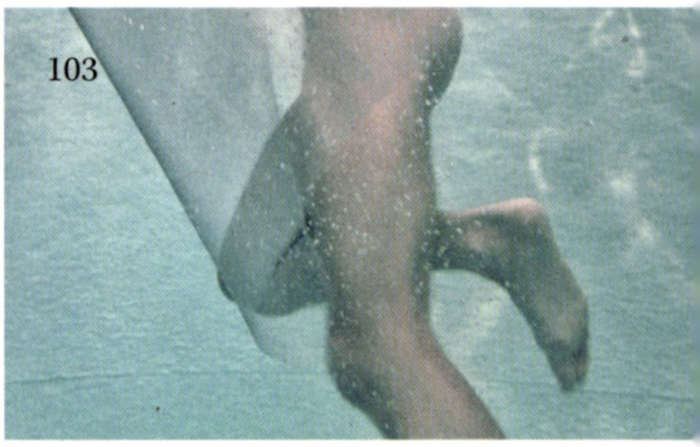

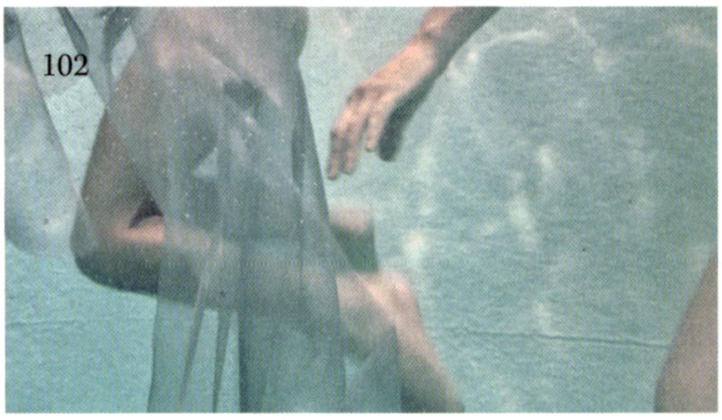

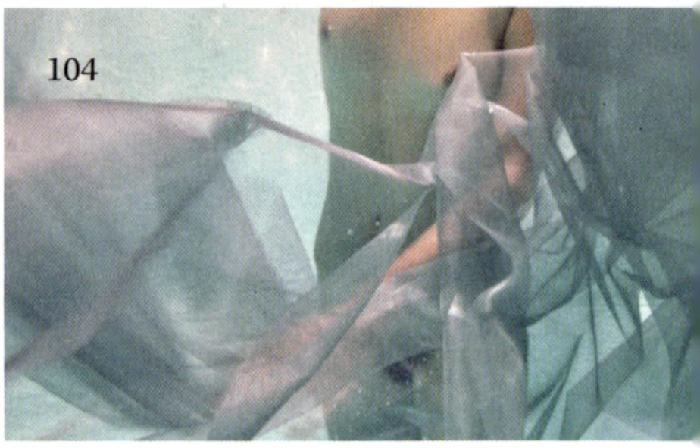

I met psychoanalyst Joseph Dodds within the scope of a Researchers' Exchange[301] at the Angewandte Performance Laboratory (APL). I then read his book *Psychoanalysis*

299. James Hillman, 'Anima Mundi: The Return of the Soul to the World', in *The Thought of the Heart and the Soul of the Worlds* (Spring Publications, 1992), 107.

300. Philosopher Bart Vandenabeele rectifies a common misconception of this notion of Kantian disinterestedness in his article 'Aesthetic Disinterestedness in Kant and Schopenhauer', *Estetika: The Central European Journal of Aesthetics* 49, no. 1 (2012): 45.

301. On 28 May 2024, a researcher's exchange took place, during which the two FWF PEEK research projects, *Sensing Living Systems*, exploring the potentials of multisensory scenography for systems awareness, and *Shaken Grounds: Seismography of Precarious Presences* engaged in dialogue with an audience of guest experts, including Joseph Dodds, to reflect on the current state of their artistic practice, methods, and approaches. A temporary landscape of ideas and a joint dinner provided space for exchange. See *Sensing Living Systems*, accessed 28 September 2025, https://ail.angewandte.at/explore/sensing-living-systems; and Shaken Grounds: Seismography of Precarious Presences, accessed 28 September 2025, https://shaken-grounds.org.

Fig. 101: *Choreo-ethical Assemblages – Drowning in Depths*, 2025, © video still: Victor Jaschke, performance: Mariella Greil and Luisa Pisetta Ravanelli, concept: Mariella Greil.

Fig. 102: *Choreo-ethical Assemblages – Drowning in Depths*, 2025, © video still: Victor Jaschke, performance: Mariella Greil and Luisa Pisetta Ravanelli, concept: Mariella Greil.

Fig. 103: *Choreo-ethical Assemblages – Drowning in Depths*, 2025, © video still: Victor Jaschke, performance: Luisa Pisetta Ravanelli, concept: Mariella Greil.

Fig. 104: *Choreo-ethical Assemblages – Drowning in Depths*, 2025, © video still: Victor Jaschke, performance: Luisa Pisetta Ravanelli, concept: Mariella Greil.

and Ecology at the Edge of Chaos,[302] where he extends the psycho-œkological inquiry by framing climate change and ecological destruction as crises that emerge at the intersection of psychic economies and systemic complexity. For Dodds, aesthetics are implicated in how we imagine, deny, or disavow œkological realities. He insists on the necessity of a nonlinear, psychoanalytic œkology – a critical practice that attends to unconscious strata, the meshworks of phantasies, and resistances that shape both individual and collective relations to the environment, deeply connecting them to the cosmos. An œkology of aesthetics forms like magma,[303] emerging from intense flows and nucleations, and from the crystallisation of affective nuggets that are then re-liquified. It is a merging of the ethical and aesthetic, the social and political stratification of values. In practice, this is the intuitive selection of the companions whom I bring into the choreographic environment.

In this sense, depth aesthetics must be attuned not only to overt aesthetic experiences of nature or art but also to the unconscious undercurrents that contour them. In the concrete case of my studio practice, this included, for instance, repeatedly and tenderly touching a pomegranate, moving it around, tracing its

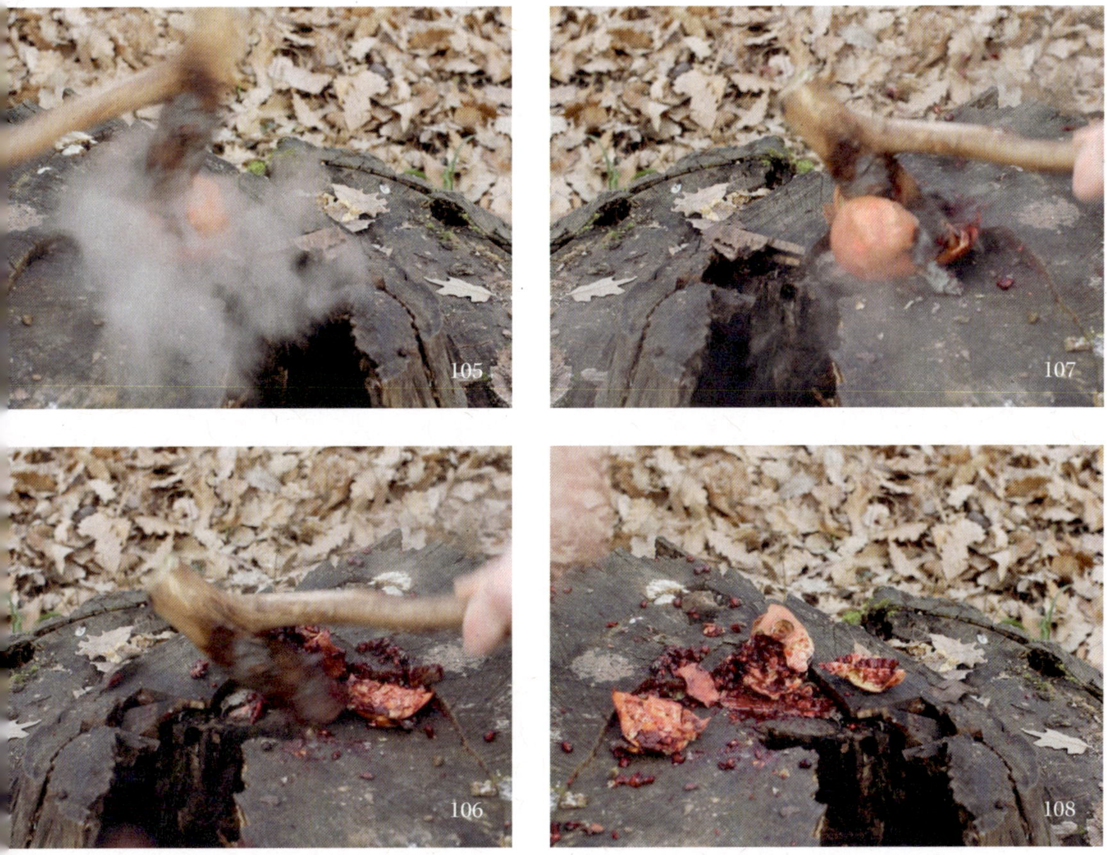

302. Joseph Dodds, *Psychoanalysis and Ecology at the Edge of Chaos* (Routledge, 2011).

303. Here I am picking up on the resonance of an older text by Manuel DeLanda that discusses stratified systems as products of structure-generating processes, which consolidated loose raw materials and sorted them into classes and, ultimately, into hierarchies of stratified, more permanent states. Manuel DeLanda, *A Thousand Years of Nonlinear History* (Swerve, 2005), 62–64.

Figs. 105–108: *Polylogic Organism – Performative Assemblages of Choreo-ethics* (*Gradually Slowing the BPM of the Pomegranate*), 2021, © video still: Werner Moebius, performance: Mariella Greil.

relations to various objects, and perceiving how the air progressively dried the skin until it hardened. One day, it became clear that I needed to get a hammer, take the pomegranate to the woods, and smash it.

My relations with the fruit shifted from tenderly caressing the pores of its fresh skin to witnessing the skin's aging, the changes in the shades of its colour. And finally, the pomegranate's rotten viscera violently opened up, setting free the spores of the decomposition process that had been invisible but became sensate through the smashing. In the sustained practice of choreo-ethical assemblaging, I became sensitive to

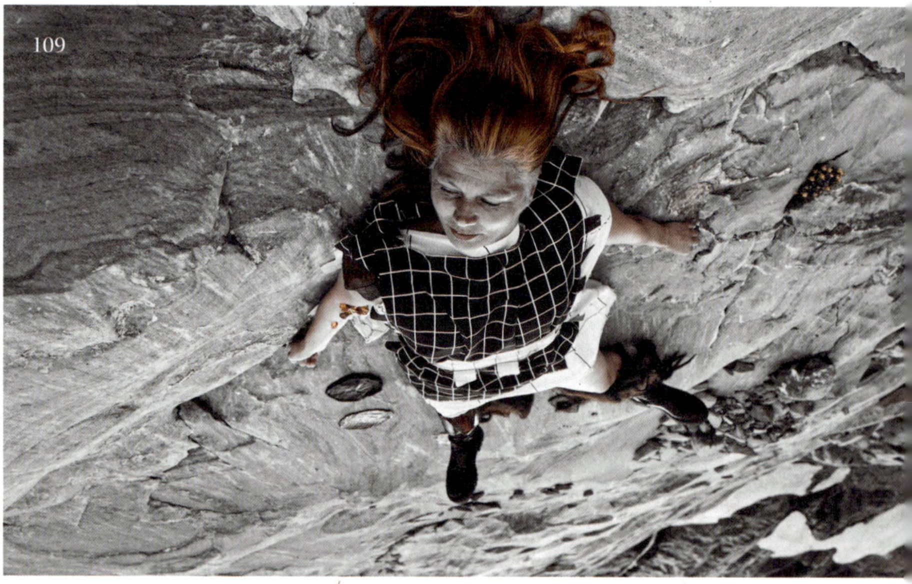

transformative processes and their ethical dilemmas. Another area in which I have encountered an ethical predicament is in the aestheticisation of catastrophes. Images of melting glaciers, raging fires, and polluted oceans are dominating current contemporary art production, potentially mobilising ethical concerns and risking commodification within a culture of the spectacle.

Dodds conceives of the *ecological self* not as an autonomous subject but as an ongoing process of entanglement with the environment, a condition that necessarily entails ethical implications and dilemmas.[304] The œkological self, as I suggest, builds on such a notion, but develops it further.

Certainly, these questions persist: How do we discern when aesthetic engagement deepens awareness and when it anesthetises? When does it opens up to an ethical response and when does it serve as a defence against unbearable realities? Psychologist Viktor Frankl referred to logotherapy as 'height psychology', as something different from and complementary to the Freudian expression 'depth psychology'. Contemporary depth psychology, complemented by height psychology, explores the affective interplay of body and mind (a spirited psychophysical

304. Dodds argues in favour of acknowledging the porous boundaries of the ecological self and its interdependency, and of growing an awareness for the whole spectrum of beings around us that constitute the environment. He dedicates a subchapter to the ecological self in his chapter 'Ecopsychology and the Greening of Psychotherapy', in *Psychoanalysis and Ecology at the Edge of Chaos* (Routledge, 2011), 77–101.

Fig. 109: *Shaken Grounds – Shifting Skies*, 2025, © video still: Victor Jaschke, performance: Mariella Greil.

The Decaying Shoe
and the Shavings of the Mason

The decaying shoe was walked across
countries and decades,
got lost, and in this very moment shines in
new morbid splendour.
It never asked, "Are we here yet"
(as Meg Stuart did);
instead, it left traces when it touched the ground,
passing through landscapes, contexts, thresholds,
and the porous edges of experience.

The decaying shoe prevented feet from
bleeding while carrying them forward
despite rocky paths and beyond
smoothed surfaces.
While the longing for the night to fall and
the day to yawn continued,
atmospheres steadily shifted.

In this gentle interstice, the shavings of
the mason performed their softest quality
as they piled up into a cone of stone dust.
Fingers sink into its silkiness,
still slightly disoriented as the eyes follow
the attraction
of the rough, rotten, remains of leather.

Materiaphiliac residue echoes in the silence of
the choreographic environment.
Did you hear the squishing sounds as you
touched the shoe?
Did you imagine how it imprinted itself on the
layer of stone dust that covered the ground?
Could you deepen your attention, or has your
gaze become prickly, restless, rambling like
tumble weeds?

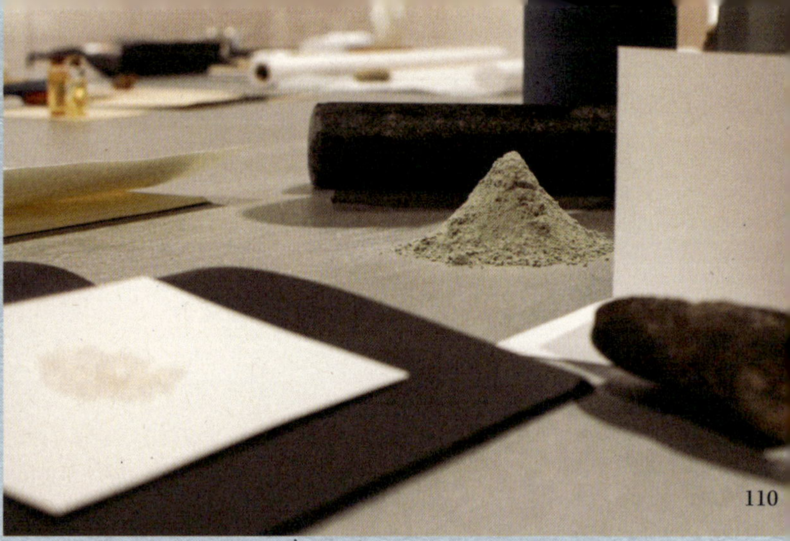

110

Stone dust drifts – the softest remnant of hardness –
grain settling into grain
like the slow exhale of the mountain,
a becoming and a yielding, from the
durable to the friable,
as if remembering
the pressure of a living foot.
For a moment, matter leans towards matter.

Long before the hominin fossils were
found in Jebel Irhoud,
the lithic layers conglomerated with
human ossifications, and
the mountain became evermore hypersensitized to
the countless feet in shoes.
Future pathfinders have understood that
even the geological layers will decay, and
the shoe will become ground leather.
Porous feelings fall in fine particles.

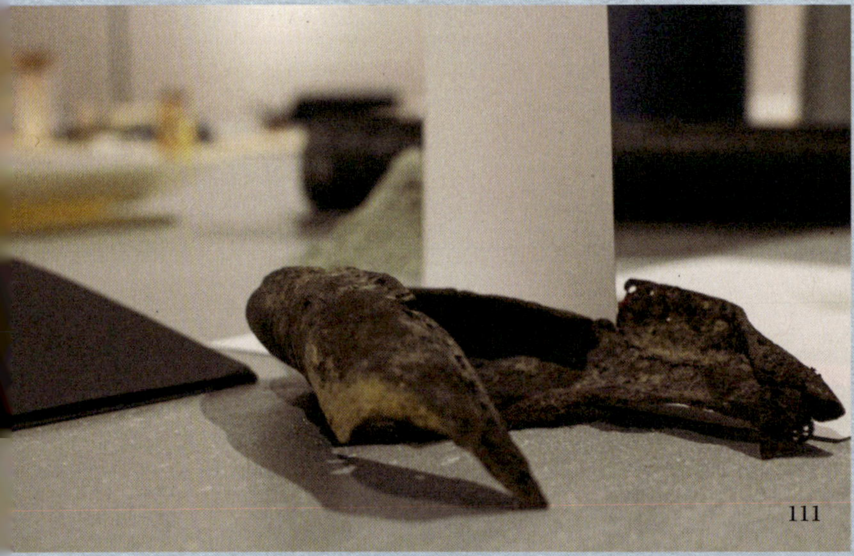

111

continuum) and – to use the language of my research – investigates the depths that animate *bare bodies. Height psychology* means turning towards the soul, the immaterial aspect of a living being, gesturing towards a transcendence. In my embodied research, these terms are not necessarily oppositional; instead, they make visible the existential fold within which this differentiation is embedded. The surfaces of ethico-aesthetics acknowledge a considerable degree of complexity and purposefully queer any polarising reading through embodied research informed by concepts of immanence and experience as a *deep surface.*[305]

Deep surface conveys a paradoxical but fruitful image: a *surface* suggests something exposed, flat, immediately there – that which appears – while *deep* suggests something hidden, interiority, layers beneath the visible. To boldly call immanence a *deep surface* means that what is given, what is right here, *the surface itself,* is not shallow or superficial but dense, rich, infinitely folded. Depth is not located 'behind' or 'underneath' but is manifest *in* the surface, as the surface's own intensity. In my reading, this resonates with Gilles Deleuze, who sees immanence as a plane rather than a hierarchy, as well as Maurice Merleau-Ponty, for whom perception always already embodies depth in the visible. It clearly breaks the old dualism of surface versus depth. Instead, the surface *is* depth – a shimmering field where, rather than pointing 'beyond', things draw us further *into* the immediacy of being, towards an emergent poetics of being-in-the-medium, mediating.

Beyond cognition we find *meaning* (in German *Sinn*) in this very form of existence: being bare bodies within the œkology of depth aesthetics.

When we zoom in on œkology, the relations and dynamics between self, other, and other others come to the fore. The œkological self is different from the *ecological self* insofar as it emphasizes forms of dwelling, it establishes communities of multiplicities and difference across diverse forms of existence. I find it pertinent how Dodds carefully contextualises the conceptual matrix of the ecological self:

> The concept of the ecological self builds on the work of Searle and is defined by the environmental philosopher Paul Shepard as a 'self with a permeable boundary. … Ecological thinking registers a kind of vision across boundaries'. Drawing on the new sciences of complexity and open systems, Joanna Macy argues that what 'had appeared to be separate self-existent entities are now seen to be so interdependent that their boundaries can be drawn only arbitrarily… *As open systems we weave our world,* though each individual

305. Mariella Greil, *Being in Contact,* 189, and 231–48.

consciousness illumines but a small section of it, a short arc in vaster loops.'[306]

So, the vision of the world – the cosmopoietic weaving – materialises in spiralling loops, diverse forms of being, circular communities,[307] and is deeply grounded in a foundation of values that is constantly being negotiated, positioning and carving out future perspectives. Moving and being moved, the constructive tension between polarities creates a vital oscillation between poles and generates energy. As artist Wassily Kandinsky wrote in 'On the Spiritual in Art',

> Each one of these artists, who can see beyond the limits of his present stage, in this segment of spiritual evolution is a prophet to those surrounding him and helps to move forward the ever obstinate carload of humanity.[308]

In my view, spirituality in contemporary performance art manifests as *embodied* enquiry, dismantling binaries of sacred and secular, forging experiential spaces where transcendence, immanence, and collective resonance become aesthetic, political, and somatic practices. In the field of psychotherapy, it was Frankl, the founder of logotherapy who said,

> The mind (*das Geistige*) is only known in connection with the body and psyche, which is why any separation of the spirit from the body and psyche is only heuristic. The mind (*das Geistige*) is what is free in human beings [...] and separates itself [...] as existence from facticity (actuality).[309]

306. Dodds, *Psychoanalysis and Ecology, 82–83* (my emphasis). The first quote is from Theodore Roszak, 'Where Psyche Meets Gaia', in *Ecopsychology: Restoring the Earth, Healing the Mind*, ed. Theodore Roszak, Mary E. Gomes, and Allen D. Kanner (Sierra Club Books, 1995), 1–17. The second quote is from Joanna Macy, 'Working Through Environmental Despair', in *Ecopsychology*, 279–87.

307. Mo Smit and Els Leclercq, *Circular Communities the Circular Value Flower as a Design Method for Collectively Closing Resource Flows* (TU Delft Open, 2023).

308. Wassily Kandinsky, *On the Spiritual in Art* (Solomon R. Guggenheim Foundation, for the Museum of Non-Objective Painting, 1946 [1911]), 17.

309. Original: 'Das Geistige ist nur in Verbindung mit Körper und Psyche bekannt, weshalb jede Trennung des Geistes von Körper und Psyche nur heuristisch ist. Das Geistige ist das Freie im Menschen [...] und sich abgrenzt [...] als Existenz von der Faktizität (Tatsächlichkeit)'. Karlheinz Biller and Maria de Lourdes Stiegeler, *Wörterbuch der Logotherapie und Existenzanalyse von Viktor Emil Frankl* (Süddeutsches Institut für Logotherapie und Existenzanalyse, 2020), 101. The quote refers to Viktor E. Frankl, *Der Leidende Mensch: Anthropologische Grundlagen der Psychotherapie* (Huber, 1998 [1984]), 143; and Viktor E. Frankl, *Logotherapie und Existenzanalyse: Texte aus sechs Jahrzehnten* (Psychologie Verlags Union, 1998 [1985]) 94n1.

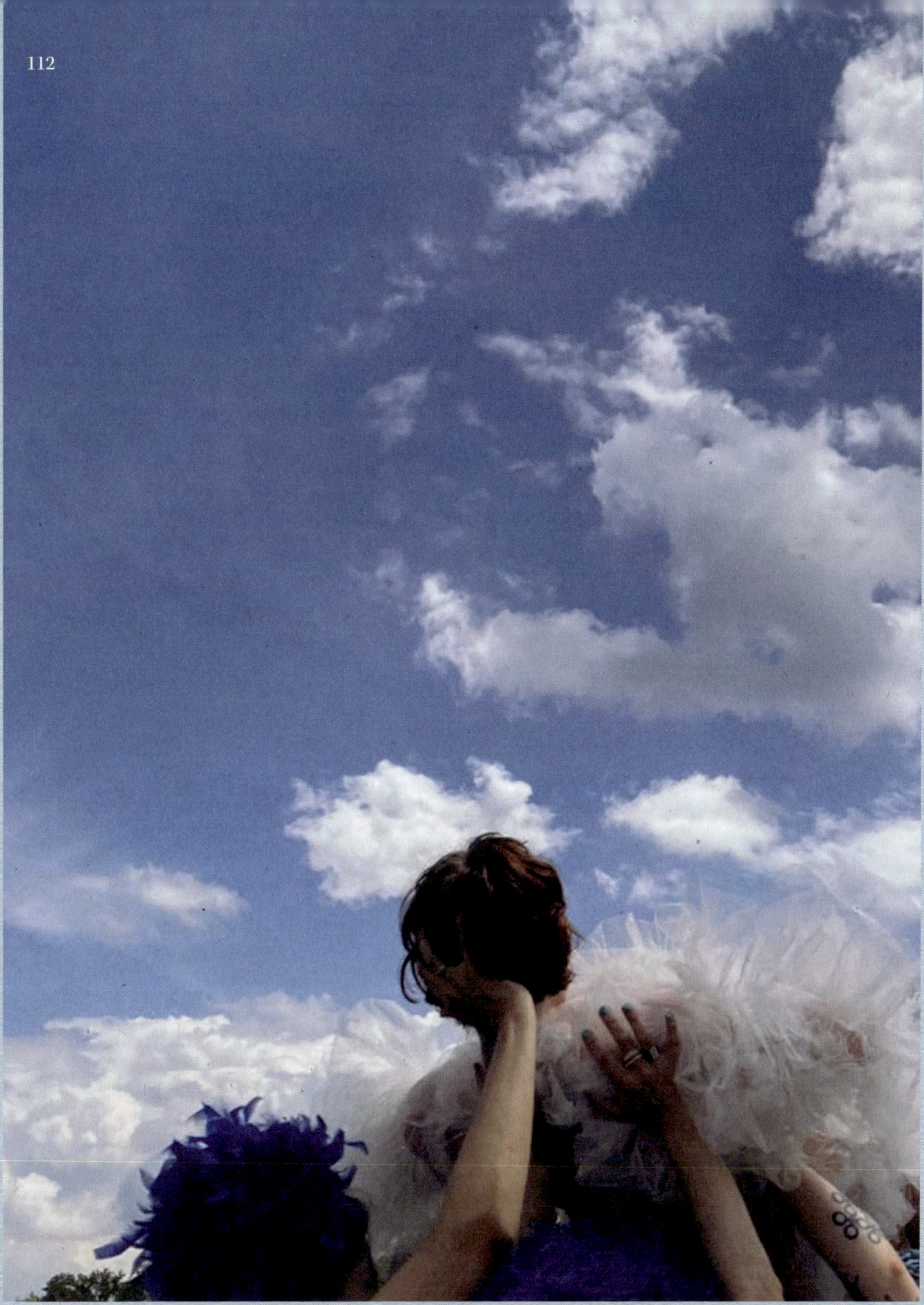

Aria on Air

The tender breeze of a memory of being immersed in air's materiality, and of expanded registers of perceptibility, blows through the marrow of our bones. A collective storm that has trespassed the many lungs, skins, bloodstreams – nourishing our cells, binding together absorbing bodies and their diaphanous environments.

Instasis. Extasis. Inhale. Exhale. Insistence. Existence.

A connection to the depths of our breaths that keep us earthlings alive *and* the unsettling toxicity of polluted air, floating invisible deadliness, that can touch us uncannily, unseen.
A porosity of clouds, whispers of love and fear surround the light touches of air.

Instasis. Extasis. Inhale. Exhale. Insistence. Existence.

Opening up to swallow air while surrendering to the peristalsis and anastalsis of dances by fire, water, and earth.
A queering of rhythms that cares for diverse liveable practices of intake and outpour, intimacy and assembly, love-making and fornication, lasciviousness and touch.

Instasis. Extasis. Inhale. Exhale. Insistence. Existence.

An ecology of phantoms that dissolve, winds that move the heat of the moment along. We keep shifting scenes, changing tonalities, mobilizing invisible frames, and ventilating meanings.
A black leaf floating away with lightness while our hands carry the cloud up into the sky.

Instasis. Extasis. Inhale. Exhale. Insistence. Existence.

Folding the mind into the body entwines facticity with vision; within this fold, the lived body becomes an event of transition – neither entirely material nor purely perceptual – where the senses think and thought touches matter, where suffering emerges as a generative crease, where corporeal vulnerability intensifies perception, exposing thresholds between immanence, transcendence, and the fragile architectures of becoming.

In *Climate Crisis, Psychoanalysis, and Radical Ethics* (2017), Donna M. Orange develops an ethics of radical responsiveness that foregrounds a form of ethical vulnerability and attunement. She thoughtfully considers that what 'keeps us avoidant [...] and too paralysed to respond appropriately [...]' is 'the loss of many kinds of hope and certainty for the future'.[310] Why do we feel so helpless when confronted by ethical dilemmas? In the face of planetary catastrophe, we are slowly understanding that the climate crisis cannot be reduced to statistics; it becomes an ethical summons that exposes our vulnerability and interdependence. When landscapes, species, or atmospheres reveal suffering, the question is whether art and theory anesthetise these disclosures into consumable forms or allow themselves to be unsettled and ethically obligated. Radical ethics, in this sense, is an aesthetic practice of staying-with – a cultivation of vulnerability that resists instrumentalisation and foregrounds the fragility and urgency of planetary life.

In his reformulation of Kant's maxim, philosopher Hans Jonas calls on us to '[a]ct so that the effects of your action are not destructive of the future possibility of such life'.[311]

Environmental philosopher J. Baird Callicott has been central in developing an environmental ethics grounded in ecological science yet attentive to cultural pluralism. In works such as *Beyond the Land Ethic*,[312] Callicott advances a relational ontology in which the value of beings is not intrinsic in the Cartesian sense but emerges from systemic interrelations. His approach complicates simplistic dichotomies of anthropocentrism versus ecocentrism by emphasising a communitarian pluralism (the circular communities as one model, but always culturally attuned) – acknowledging that ethical obligations span multiple scales, from intimate human relations to ecosystems. Integrating Callicott's perspective, depth aesthetics must confront the ethical dilemma of scale – how to navigate aesthetic experiences that resonate at the intimate, personal level – as depth aesthetics does in diffractive dialogues within choreo-ethical assemblages and simultaneously at the planetary level. Environmental ethical pluralism responds to global systemic crisis. Depth aesthetics here involves a capacity to sense across scales, recognising that ethical dilemmas can rarely be resolved within one framework. Aesthetic engagement thus becomes a practice of maintaining tension – between local attachment and global responsibility, between immediate affect and systemic analysis.

310. Donna M. Orange, *Climate Crisis, Psychoanalysis, and Radical Ethics* (Routledge, 2017), xiii.

311. Hans Jonas, *The Imperative of Responsibility in Search of an Ethics for the Technological Age* (University of Chicago Press, 1984), 11.

312. J. Baird Callicott, *Beyond the Land Ethic* (State University of New York Press, 2000).

To synthesise these perspectives, I propose depth aesthetics as an orientation that integrates ecological, artistic, psychotherapeutic, and ethical registers. It insists that aesthetic experiences are not merely matters of taste but are events of ethical provocation, where trans*subjectivities are confronted with their own limits, projections, and entanglements. The depth dimension is both psychological (unconscious processes, affective intensities) and œkological (the layered interdependence of life systems). Through my embodied research practice of choreo-ethical assemblaging, I experienced depth aesthetics as an ethical practice. The relational negotiation of proximities, inter- and intra- actions, but also transformation and destruction, decomposition and proliferation formed the core of my research processes.

The ethical dilemmas encountered in the space of the Polylogic Lab were manifold. The following are four such dilemmas that I found highly relevant for developing the 'Diffractive Dialogue Score':

- *The dilemma of representation:* how to represent ecological crisis aesthetically without commodifying suffering or dulling urgency?
- *The dilemma of attunement:* how to remain open to unsettling depth aesthetic experiences without collapsing into paralysis or denial?
- *The dilemma of scale:* how to mediate between individual affect and systemic complexity, between local and planetary dimensions?
- *The dilemma of action:* how to translate aesthetic insight into ethical and political practice without instrumentalising art?

Each of these dilemmas underscores that depth aesthetics cannot promise resolution. Rather, its contribution lies in cultivating the capacity to sustain ethical tension, resist pseudo-solutions, and fully inhabit uncertainty, transforming precarity into creativity. If depth aesthetics is to be more than an academic concept, it must be lived as a practice. This implies cultivating forms of aesthetic engagement – through performance, the development of contemporary rituals and myths, and ecological encounters with diverse agencies – that foster attunement to both depth and ethical ambiguity. In psychoanalytic terms, this practice leads to a capacity for *negative capability* – withstanding uncertainty and paradox, without defensive foreclosure. In ecological terms, it requires a willingness to experience the other-than-human as a partner in co-creation, not as an object of control. In ethical terms, it calls for responsiveness to suffering, without seeking quick redemption, as well as a sustained commitment to a praxis of depth aesthetics.

Depth aesthetics, as articulated through the resonances between my practice and my readings, foregrounds the profound intertwinement of aesthetic, œkological, and ethical registers. It proposes that aesthetic encounters are never innocent but always already ethically charged, demanding from us an attunement to the depths of the psyche and the depths of œkological interdependence. The ethical dilemmas that emerge in this domain – practiced in the Polylogic Lab and in its cosmopoietic transpossibilities[313] – are not obstacles to be overcome but essential features of a practice that resists simplification.

In encountering ethical dilemmas through aesthetic depth, we are invited to inhabit vulnerability, to acknowledge interdependence, and to bear witness to suffering in ways that may unsettle but also reconfigure the contours of ethical life. Depth aesthetics thus gestures towards a mode of existence that is neither detached contemplation nor sheer activism but a sustained practice of ethical responsiveness in the face of ecological and existential depth – the responsibility of depth.

Trans*formative and Performative Aesthetics – Performance Matter/ing as a Choreography of Ethics

As twins, ethics and aesthetics are more than a trope; they insist on a particular method of enquiry. As discussed earlier, both concern the cultivation of perception, the modalities of relation, and capacities for responsiveness. When approached through the lens of trans*formative and performative aesthetics, this kinship sharpens into a practice where art and performance do not simply illustrate but rather transform ethics and aesthetics into embodied encounters, as sensorially choreographed openings that demand a response. It was American academic and author Jack Halberstam who introduced the prefix *trans**, which I have taken up in the title of this subchapter to discuss trans*formative aesthetics. Halberstam writes,

> As we will see, the asterisk modifies the meaning of transitivity by refusing to situate transition in relation to a destination, a final form, a specific shape, or an established configuration of desire and identity. The asterisk holds off the certainty of diagnosis; it keeps at bay any sense of knowing in advance […]. [T]rans* can be a name for expansive forms of difference, haptic relations to knowing, uncertain modes of being, and the disaggregation of identity politics predicated upon the separating out of many kinds of experience that actually blend together, intersect, and mix.[314]

313. David-Augustin Mândruț writes that 'transpossibility would be the creative response given by Dasein to that event'. David-Augustin Mândruț, 'Martin Buber and Henri Maldiney on the Notion of Event', in *META: Research in Hermeneutics, Phenomenology, and Practical Philosophy* 16, no. 2 (2024): 465.

314. Jack Halberstam, *Trans*: A Quick and Quirky Account of Gender Variability* (University of California Press, 2018), 4–5.

In my reading of Halberstam, *trans** signals transition and translation as well as transgression: the traversing of disciplinary, ontological, and affective borders. The choreo-ethical does not lie in moral instruction or in the didactic deployment of modes of conduct, but in the way that performance insists on mattering through its trans*formative aesthetics, also in its singularity.[315] The activating of trans*formative and performative aesthetics to emphasise the mattering of *trans*subjectivities* and *trans*materialities* adds another layer, some nuance, and some buoyancy to the Butlerian sense of performativity as the reiterative practice through which meaning and bodies materialise.[316]

Trans*formative and performative aesthetics unfold as both a marker of vulnerability and a vector of power, suspending identity in states of becoming rather than arrival. It gestures towards thresholds, translations, and transgressions that resist closure, thereby embodying the precariousness of movement across categories while engendering a generative force. Halberstam reminds us that *trans** is not simply about crossing, but about unfixing, opening up aesthetic and ethical terrains where indeterminacy itself becomes a resource. In choreo-ethical assemblages, *trans** choreographs not only matter but also mattering – performative acts that render ethics palpable as a dynamic negotiation of permeability, porosity, and affective relationality. Performance as an art form operates as a threshold[317] practice, creating temporary constellations of trans*subjectivities that destabilise the conventional zones of how we encounter others and other others. It is this destabilisation of ontologies, agencies, and epistemologies that renders performance ethically charged. Performance matter/ing is therefore an aesthetic mode that choreographs ethical exposure, where diverse agencies, performers, and environments perform agential cuts. Karen Barad delineates the agential cut as a boundary within phenomena, enacting distinctions that simultaneously produce entities and relations through intra-active becoming. These performative and trans*formative practices simultaneously draw our attention to webs of co-affective obligation. These obligations can manifest as withdrawal from *or* confrontation with unethical propositions *or* also destructive impulses. They require a committed practice of keeping the situation open, maintaining the negotiations, and thus adopting an attitude of choreo-ethics as a cosmopoietic practice.

To describe performance as a choreography of ethics is to foreground its capacity to articulate responsibility as a lived and sensory event. Choreography, in this expanded sense, structures attention, intensity, and relation. It organises how we come to sense ourselves in relation to others, human and other-than-human, and how we might endure or transform the weight of this relationality. Choreo-ethical choreography is generative. It produces conditions in which the question of responsibility becomes unavoidable, even as answers are deferred; they bind us into situations where choices matter, where witnessing is never neutral, and where the

315. André Lepecki, *Singularities: Dance in the Age of Performance* (Routledge, 2016).

316. Judith Butler, *Gender Trouble: Feminism and the Subversion of Identity* (Routledge, 1990); Judith Butler, *Bodies That Matter: On the Discursive Limits of 'Sex'* (Routledge, 1993).

317. Greil, *Bare Bodies.*

refusal to respond is itself a response. This echoes psychoanalytic accounts of denial and resistance but re-situates them within the cultural field of performance amid an œkology of dilemmas.[318]

The Polylogic Lab rehearses *how*, in a climate crisis, *aesthetic practices* foreground vulnerability, fragility, or decay and are not simply artistic gestures but ethical interventions. These practices insist that we cannot bracket the œkological reality from the aesthetic realm because both converge in the field of experience.

The performative dimension of aesthetics complicates this further. Recognising that aesthetics is always performative is to radically claim that the effects of performances are not and should not be limited to representation. Rather, they operate through enactment, through embodied resonance, through the reconfiguration of sensoria. When spectators are unsettled, moved, or implicated, they are doing more than interpreting symbols; they are undergoing an ethical event – they become part of choreo-ethical assemblages. Performance matter/ing thus denotes this double register: performance matters because it materialises, and it matters because it obligates. Performance practitioner and researcher P. A. Skantze has discussed the practice of spectating eloquently. She writes from the perspective of the spectator and emphatically describes sensing and experiencing directly at the limen, right in that imaginary space where performance and imagination blend, as

> to insist upon the central nature of understanding what has been experienced, what has been sounded, what has been seen, what has been missed and must be lingered over, again and again, at the threshold.[319]

Radical ethics, as articulated by Donna M. Orange, insists on attunement and witnessing in the face of suffering and catastrophe. Trans*formative and performative aesthetics can be understood as the aesthetic corollary to this ethical position: they cultivate the capacity to stay-with, to linger at the threshold, to endure discomfort without collapsing into resolution. The performative becomes a training ground for ethical vulnerability, staging modes of being-together that are not predicated on mastery but on exposure.

At the same time, trans*formative and performative aesthetics gesture towards futurity. They ask how ethico-aesthetic practice might exceed its own conditions, how it might spill over into the domains of œkology, politics, and care. Here, performance as a choreography of ethics opens up a horizon where choreo-ethical practice is not the afterthought of aesthetic experience but its very engine. It suggests that in the interstices of movement, gesture, sound, and image, we encounter

318. Isabelle Stengers elaborates on an ecology of practices in the chapter 'Culturing the Pharmakon?' in *Cosmopolitics I*, trans. Robert Bononno (Univocal / MIT Press, 2010 [1997]).

319. P. A. Skantze, *Itinerant Spectator / Itinerant Spectacle* (Punctum, 2013), 202.

forms of responsibility that cannot be codified; rather, they are sensed, rehearsed, and remembered as choreo-ethical assemblages.

In this sense, trans*formative and performative aesthetics are more than ancillary to ethical discourse – they are indispensable to it. They show that choreo-ethics is not a matter of abstract principles but of tangible corporeal timing, affective tonality, and sensorial calibration. The twinship of ethics and aesthetics is lived in every encounter that unsettles and obligates, that exposes us to others and other-than-human agencies, and that demands a choreo-ethical response. Performance matter/ing, then, is its embodied enactment, its fragile and forceful rehearsal, its most incisive aesthetic form.

To bring into being other worlds beyond those of purely abstract information, [...] to dare to confront the vertiginous Cosmos so as to make it inhabitable; these are the tangled paths of the tri-ecological vision.
A new ecosophy, at once applied and theoretical, ethicopolitical and aesthetic, would have to move away from the old forms of political, religious and associative commitment... Rather than being a discipline of refolding on interiority, [...] it will be a multifaceted movement [...]. A collective and individual subjectivity that completely exceeds the limits of individualization, stagnation, identificatory closure, and will instead open itself up on all sides to the socius, but also to the machinic Phylum, to techno-scientific Universes of reference, to aesthetic worlds, as well as to a new 'pre-personal' understanding of time, of the body, of sexuality. [...].
We need new social and aesthetic practices, new practices of the Self in relation to the other, to the foreign, the strange [...].
By means of these transversal tools [*clefs*] subjectivity is able to install itself simultaneously in the realms of the environment, in the major social and institutional assemblages, and symmetrically in the landscapes and fantasies of the most intimate spheres of the individual, the re-conquest of a degree of creative autonomy in one particular domain encourages conquests in other domains – the catalyst for a gradual reforging and renewal of humanity's confidence in itself starting at the most minuscule level.

Félix Guattari, *The Three Ecologies*, trans. Ian Pindar and Paul Sutton (Continuum 2008), 44–45.

Assemblages #6

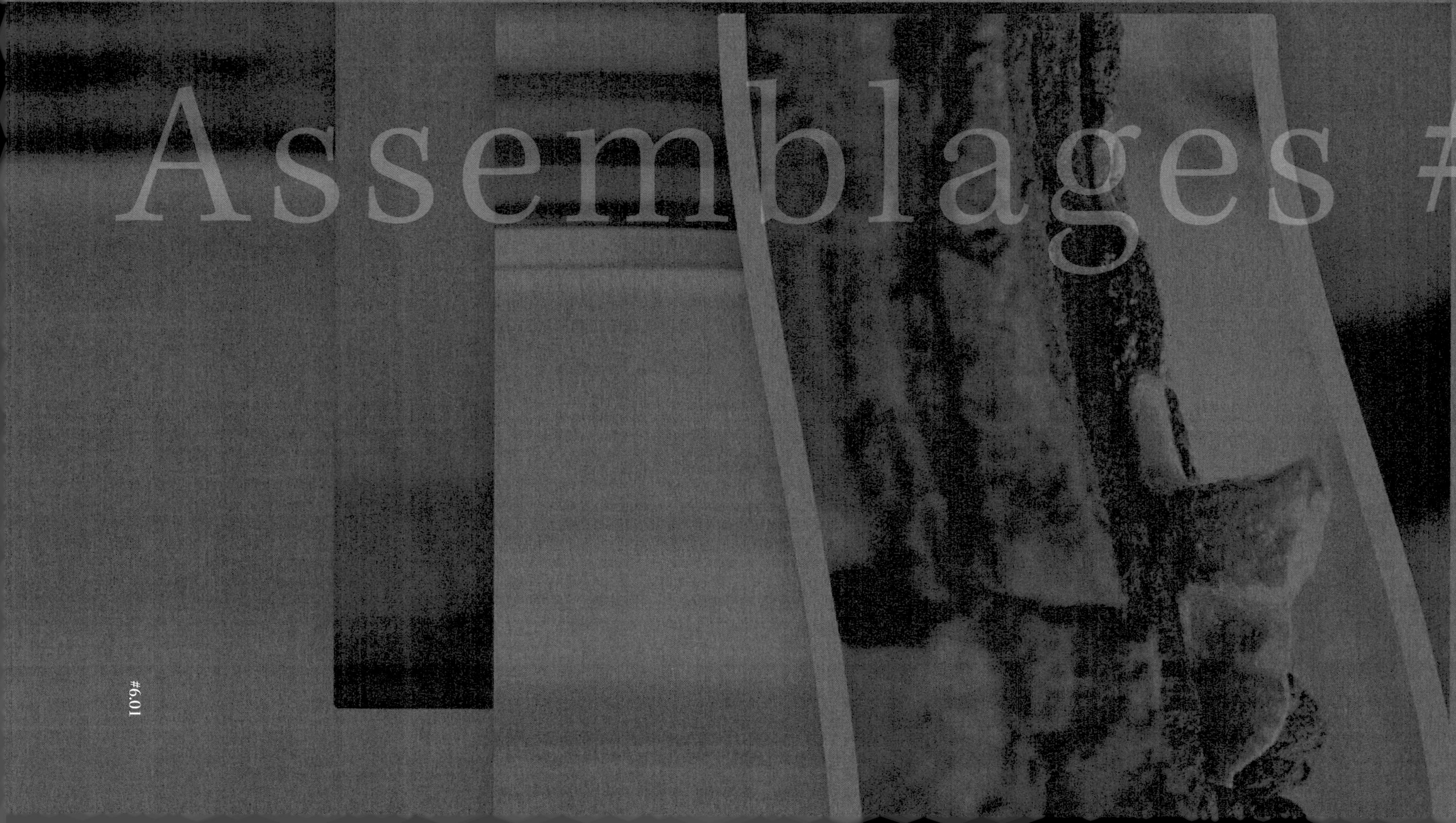

#6.01

#6.02

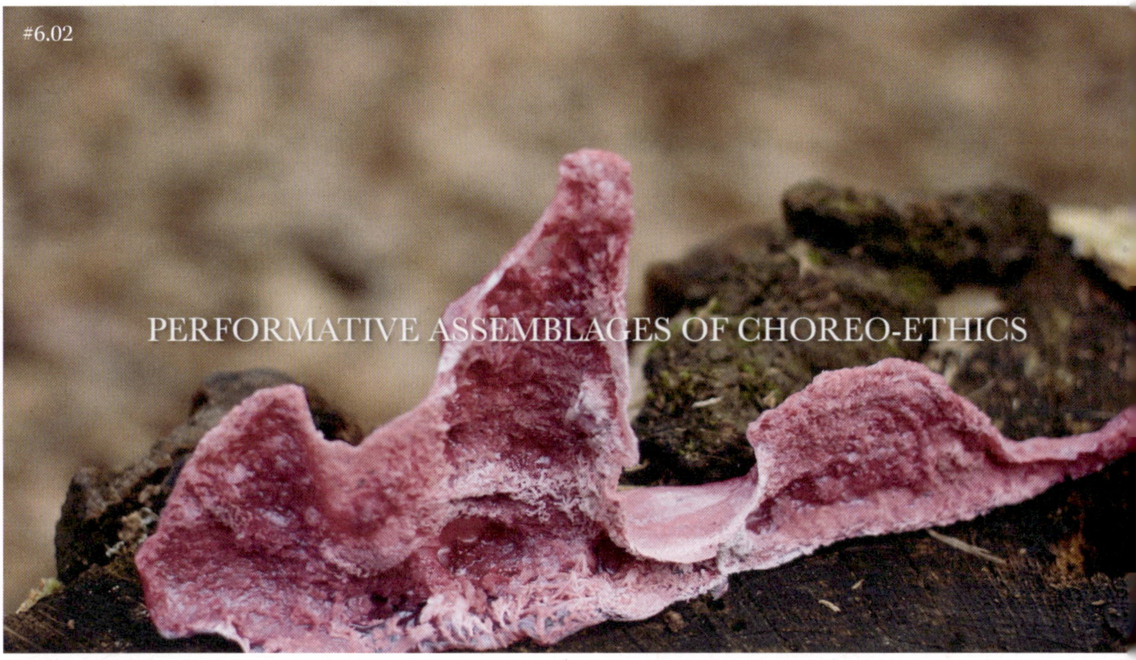
PERFORMATIVE ASSEMBLAGES OF CHOREO-ETHICS

#6.03

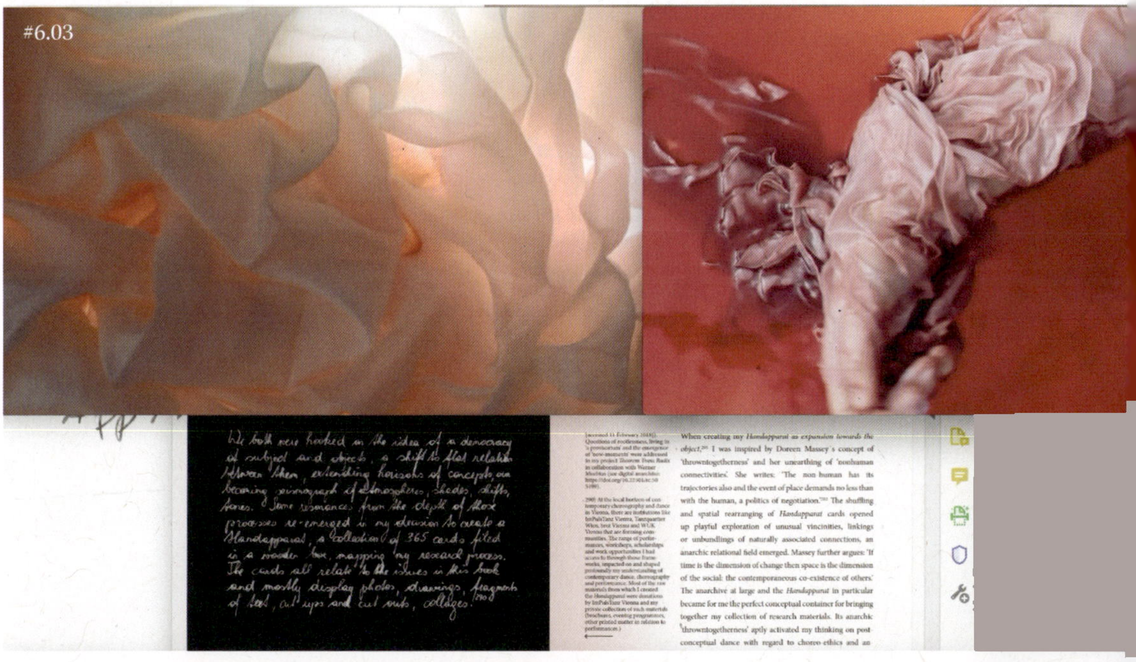
We both were hooked on the idea of a democracy of subject and objects, a shift to flat relation between them, extending horizons of concepts, our becoming seismograph of atmospheres, shades, shifts, tones. Some resonances from the depth of those processes re-emerged in my decision to create a Handapparat, a collection of 365 cards filed in a wooden box, mapping my research process. The cards all relate to the issues in this book and mostly display photos, drawings, fragments of text, cut ups and cut outs, collages.
When creating my Handapparat as expansion towards the object, I was inspired by Doreen Massey's concept of 'throwntogetherness' and her unearthing of 'nonhuman connectivities'. She writes: 'The non human has its trajectories also and the event of place demands no less than with the human, a politics of negotiation.' The shuffling and spatial rearranging of Handapparat cards opened up playful exploration of unusual vincinities, linkings or unbundlings of naturally associated connections, an anarchic relational field emerged. Massey further argues: 'If time is the dimension of change then space is the dimension of the social: the contemporaneous co-existence of others.' The anarchive at large and the Handapparat in particular became for me the perfect conceptual container for bringing together my collection of research materials. Its anarchic 'throwntogetherness' aptly activated my thinking on post-conceptual dance with regard to choreo-ethics and an

#6.04

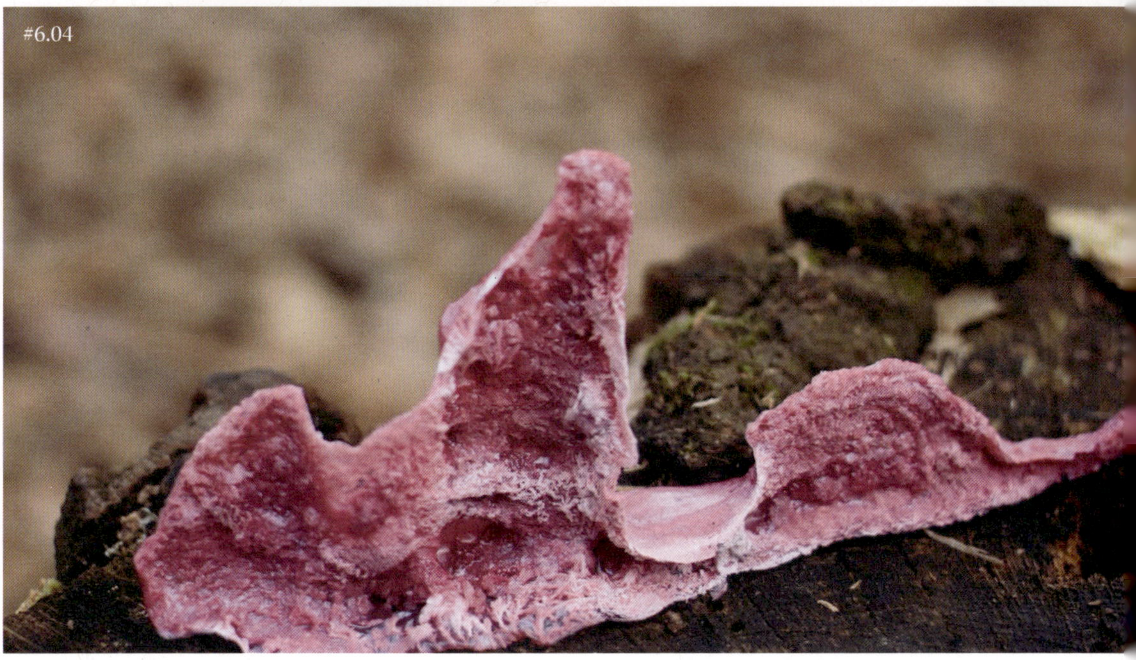

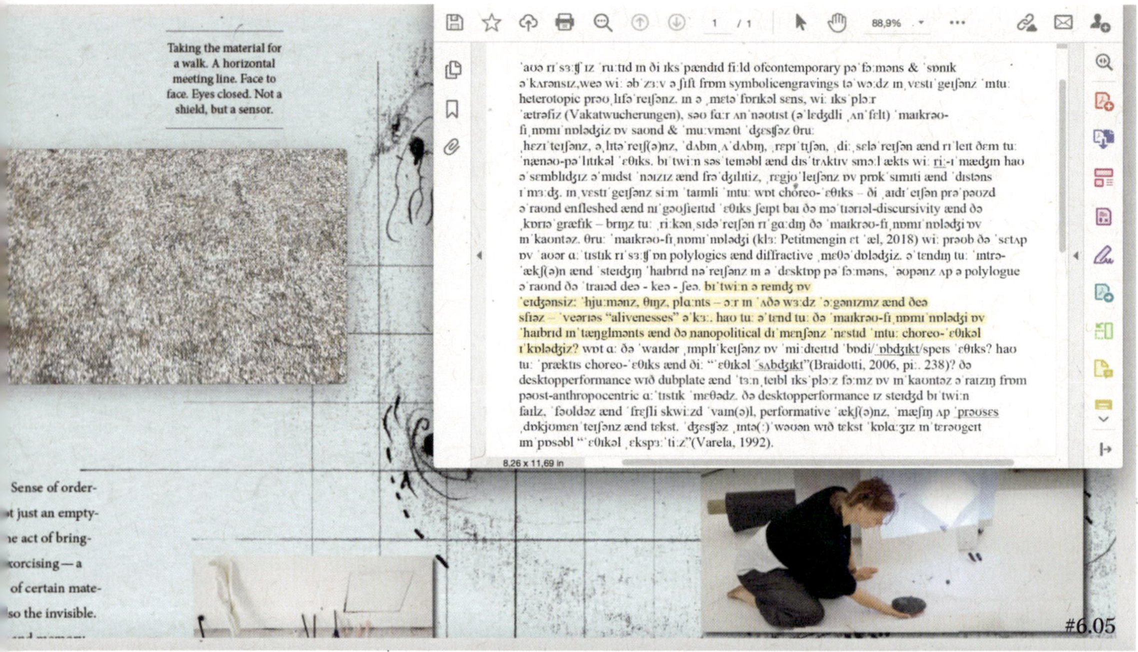
Taking the material for a walk. A horizontal meeting line. Face to face. Eyes closed. Not a shield, but a sensor.
Sense of order-
ot just an empty-
he act of bring-
xorcising — a
of certain mate-
so the invisible.

#6.05

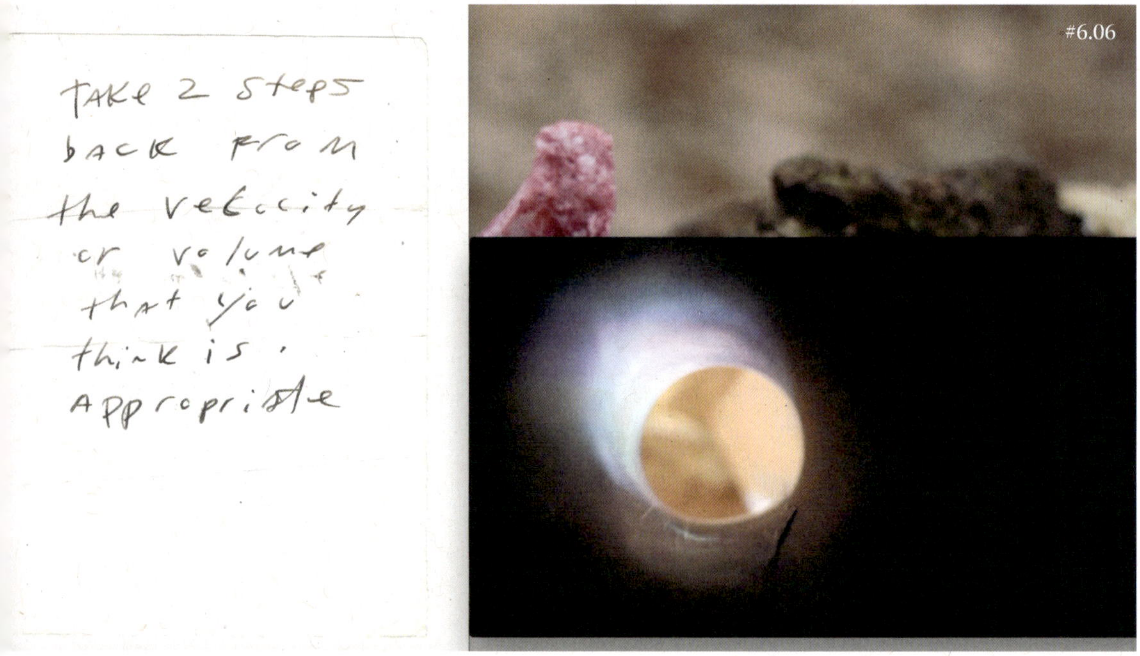
take 2 steps back from the velocity or volume that you think is appropriate

#6.06

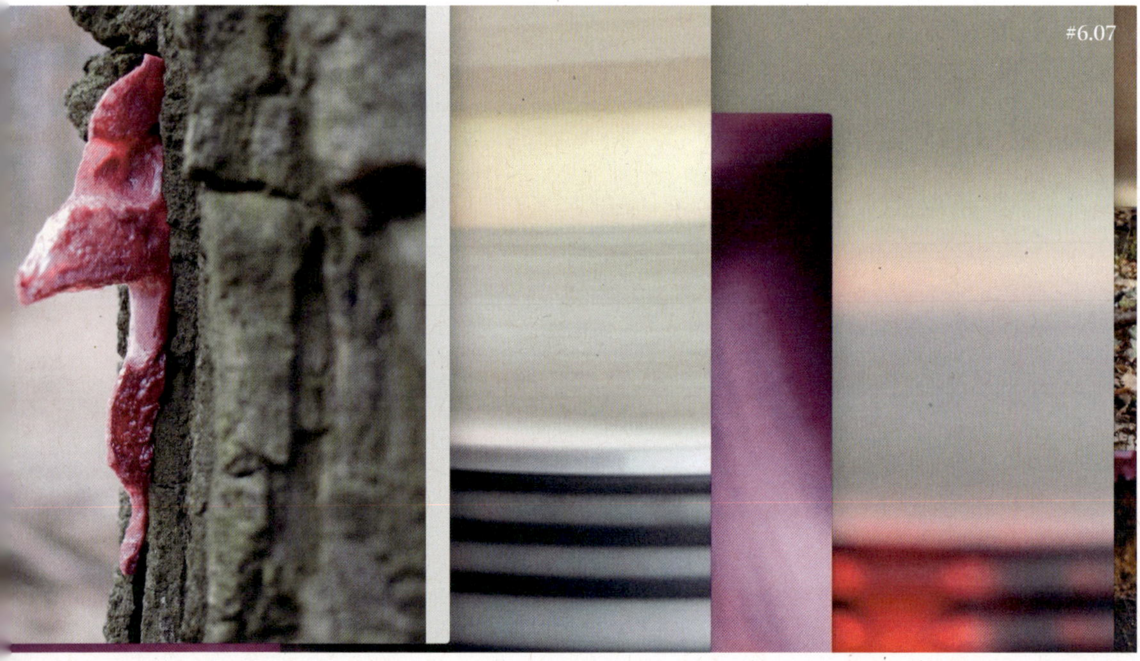

#6.07

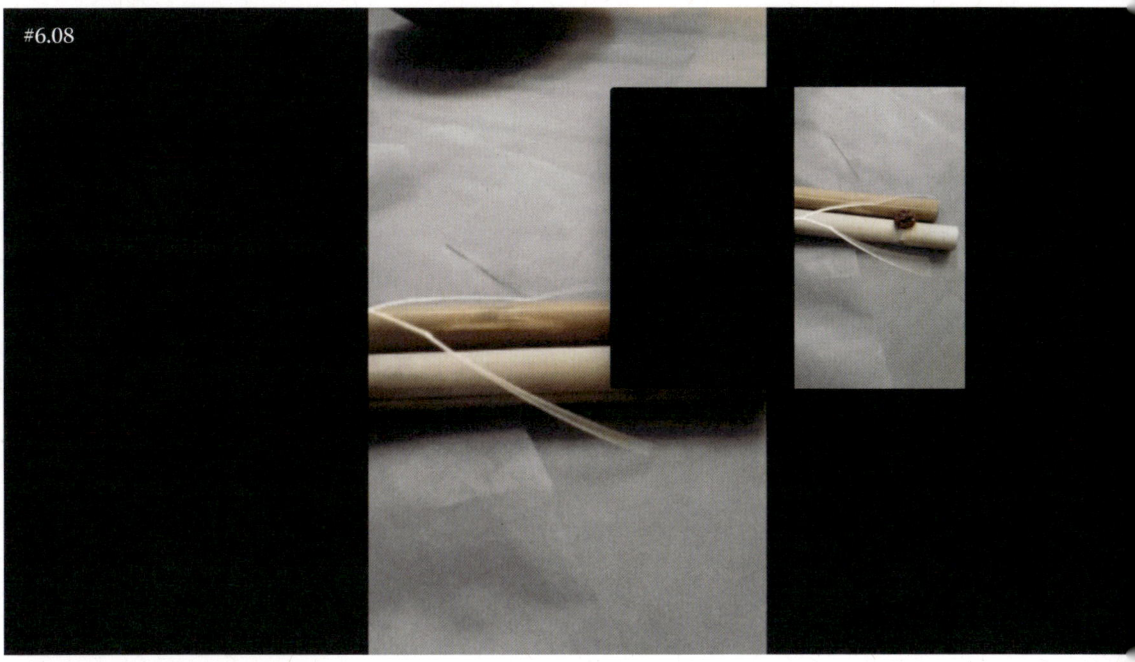

#6.08

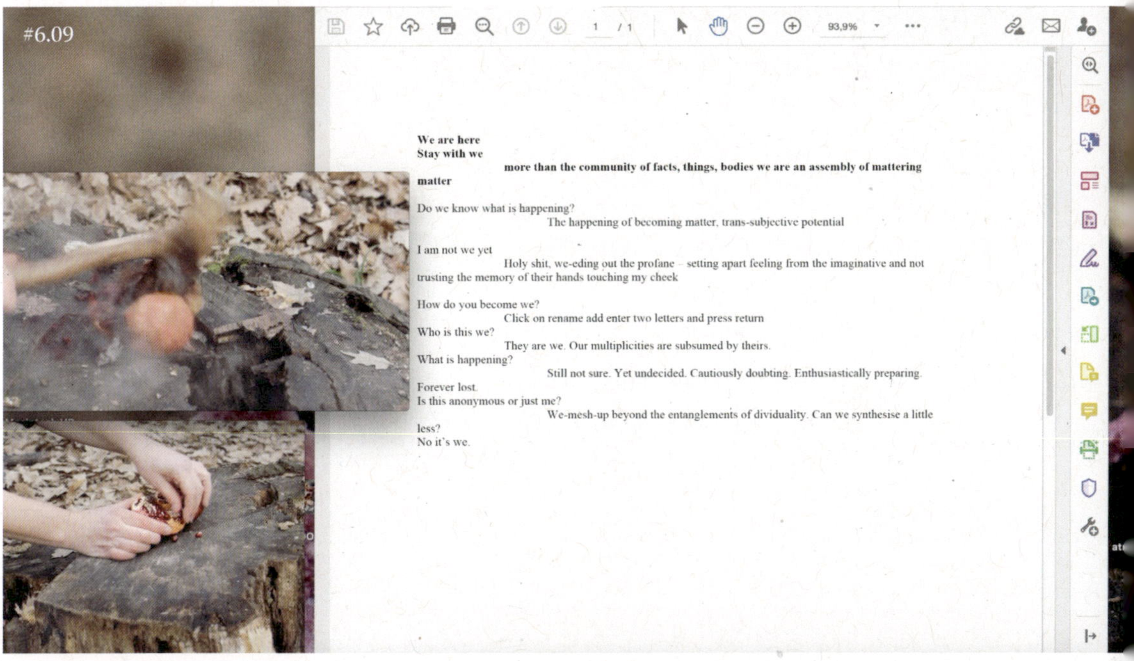

#6.09

Now that I have to save tomorrow, that I have to have a form because I don't sense that I have the strength to stay disorganized, now that, fatefully, I shall have to frame that monstrous, infinite flesh and cut it into pieces that something the size of the mouth can take in, and the size of my eyes' vision, now that I shall fatefully succumb to the necessity of form that comes from my fear of being unlimited – then let me at least have the courage to let that form form by itself, like a crust that hardens on its own, a fiery nebula that cools into earth. And let me have the great courage to resist the temptation to invent a form.

Clarice Lispector[2]

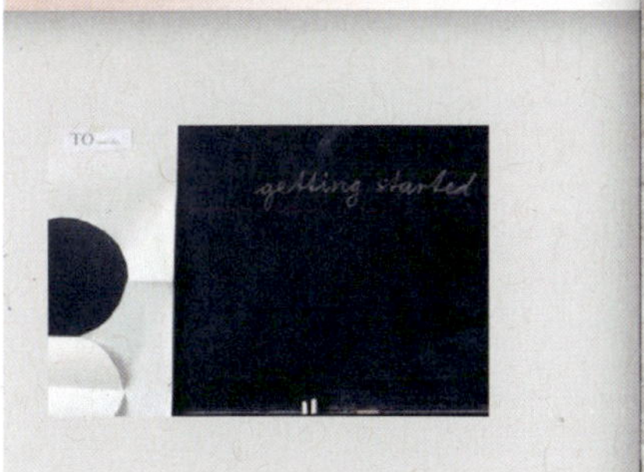

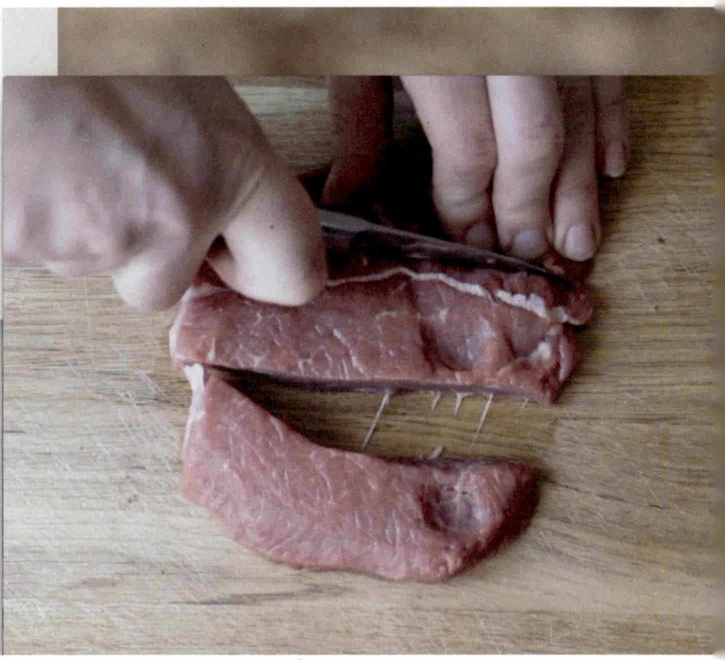

#6.10

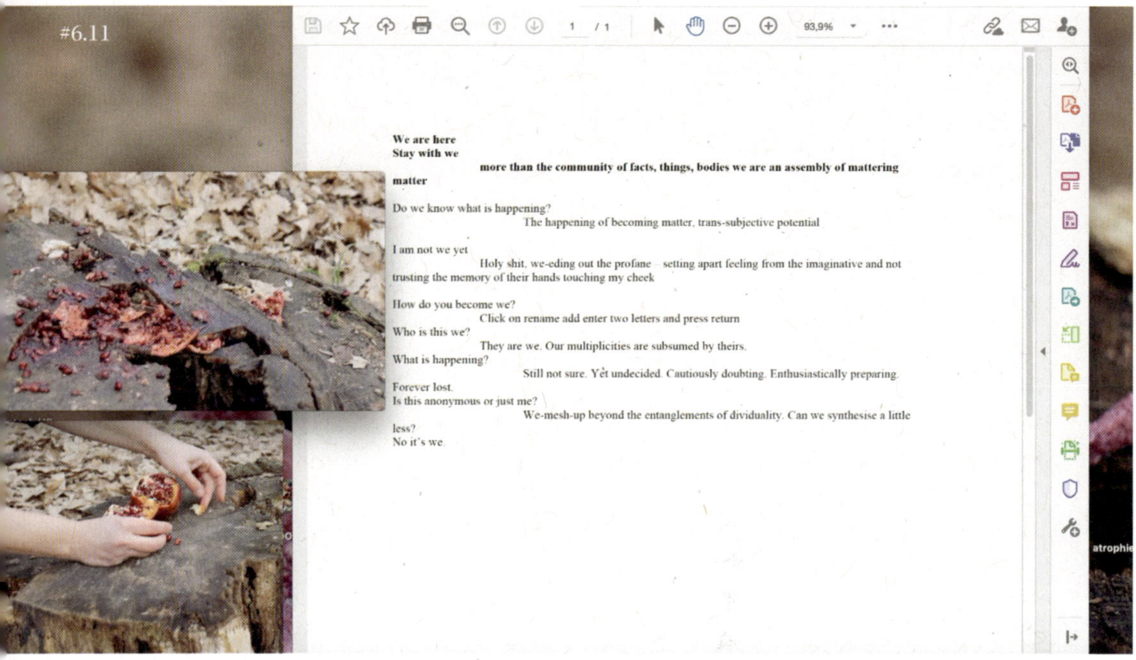
#6.11
1 / 1
93,9%
We are here
Stay with we
more than the community of facts, things, bodies we are an assembly of mattering matter
Do we know what is happening?
The happening of becoming matter, trans-subjective potential
I am not we yet
Holy shit, we-eding out the profane – setting apart feeling from the imaginative and not trusting the memory of their hands touching my cheek
How do you become we?
Click on rename add enter two letters and press return
Who is this we?
They are we. Our multiplicities are subsumed by theirs.
What is happening?
Still not sure. Yet undecided. Cautiously doubting. Enthusiastically preparing.
Forever lost.
Is this anonymous or just me?
We-mesh-up beyond the entanglements of dividuality. Can we synthesise a little less?
No it's we.
atrophie

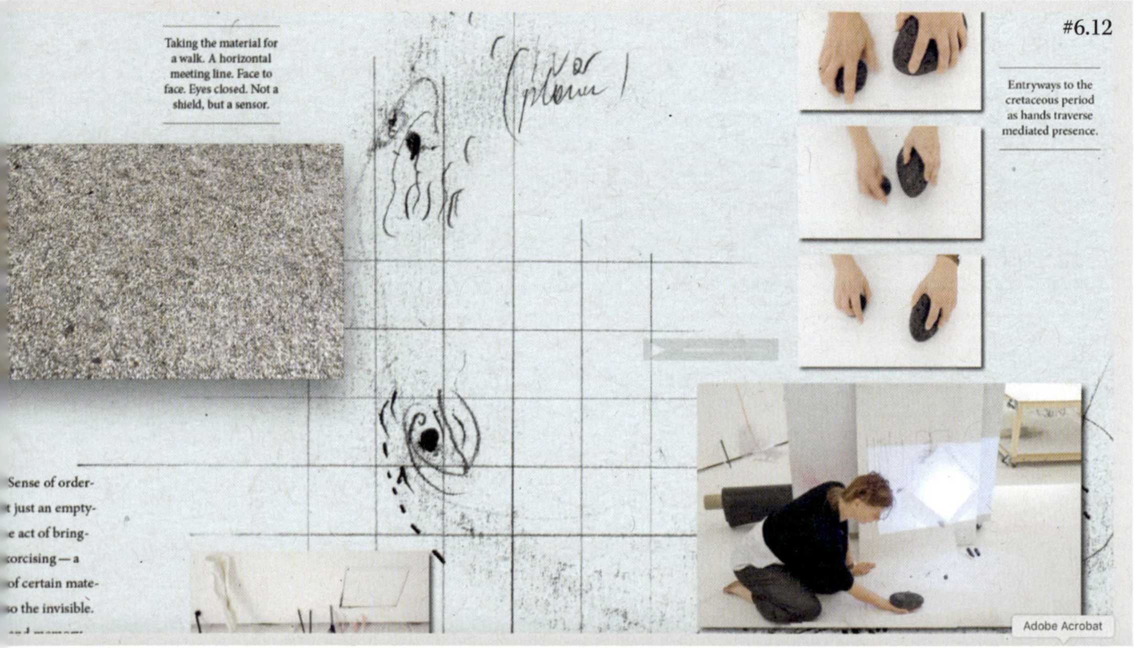
#6.12
Taking the material for a walk. A horizontal meeting line. Face to face. Eyes closed. Not a shield, but a sensor.
Entryways to the cretaceous period as hands traverse mediated presence.
Sense of order-
t just an empty-
e act of bring-
xorcising — a
of certain mate-
so the invisible.
Adobe Acrobat

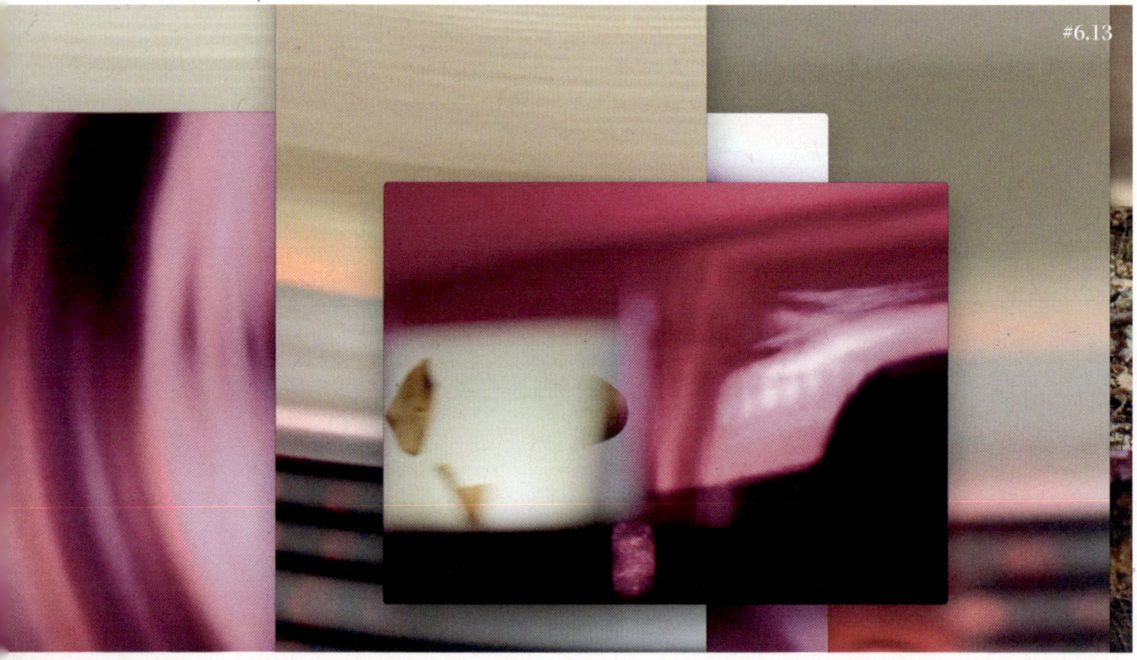
#6.13

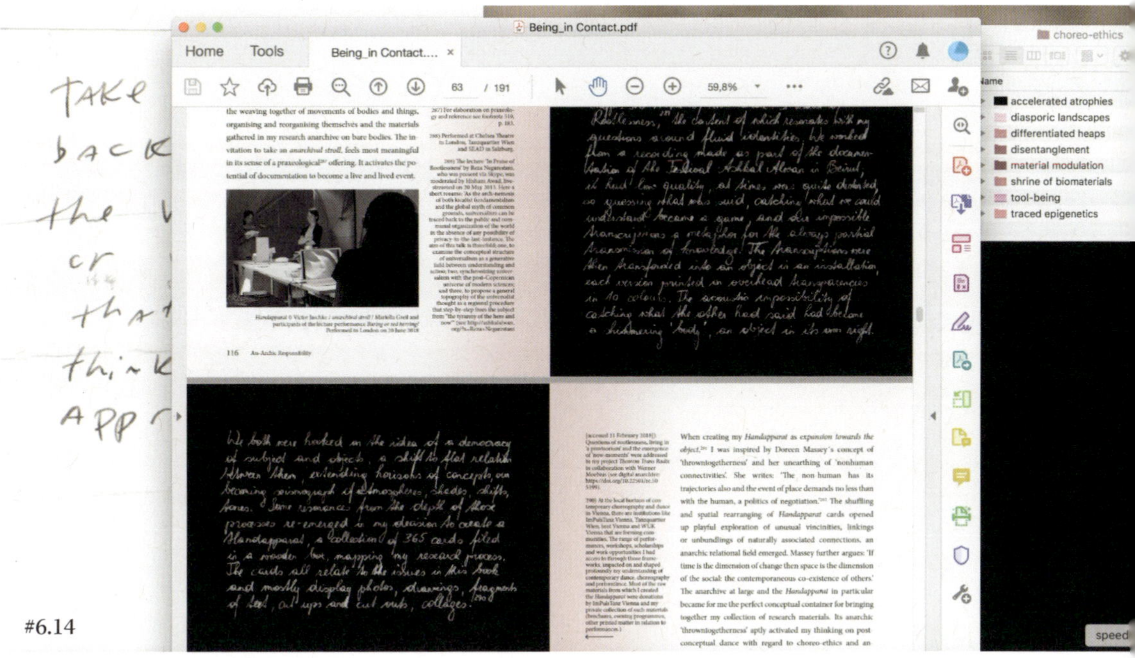
TAKE
back
the
cr
that
think
APP
Being_in Contact.pdf
Home
Tools
Being_in Contact....
63 / 191
59,8%
choreo-ethics
accelerated atrophies
diasporic landscapes
differentiated heaps
disentanglement
material modulation
shrine of biomaterials
tool-being
traced epigenetics
the weaving together of movements of bodies and things, organising and reorganising themselves and the materials gathered in my research anarchive on bare bodies. The invitation to take an anarchival stroll, feels most meaningful in its sense of a praxeological offering. It activates the potential of documentation to become a live and lived event.
116 An-Archic Responsibility
Rootlessness, the content of which resonates with my questions around fluid identities. We worked from a recording made as part of the documentation of the Festival Ashkal Alwan in Beirut, it had low quality, at times was quite distorted, so guessing what was said, catching what we could understand became a game, and the impossible transcriptions a metaphor for the always partial transmission of knowledge. The transcriptions were then transferred into an object in an installation, each version printed on overhead transparencies in 10 colours. The acoustic impossibility of catching what the other had said had become a shimmering 'body', an object in its own right.
We both were hooked on the idea of a democracy of subject and objects, a shift to flat relation between them, extending horizons of concepts, our becoming seismograph of atmospheres, shades, shifts, tones. Some resonance from the depth of those processes re-emerged in my decision to create a Handapparat, a collection of 365 cards filed in a wooden box, mapping my research process. The cards all relate to the issues in this book and mostly display photos, drawings, fragments of text, cut ups and cut outs, collages.
When creating my Handapparat as expansion towards the object, I was inspired by Doreen Massey's concept of 'throwntogetherness' and her unearthing of 'nonhuman connectivities'. She writes: 'The non human has its trajectories also and the event of place demands no less than with the human, a politics of negotiation.' The shuffling and spatial rearranging of Handapparat cards opened up playful exploration of unusual vincinities, linkings or unbundlings of naturally associated connections, an anarchic relational field emerged. Massey further argues: 'If time is the dimension of change then space is the dimension of the social: the contemporaneous co-existence of others.' The anarchive at large and the Handapparat in particular became for me the perfect conceptual container for bringing together my collection of research materials. Its anarchic 'throwntogetherness' aptly activated my thinking on post conceptual dance with regard to choreo-ethics and an
speed
#6.14

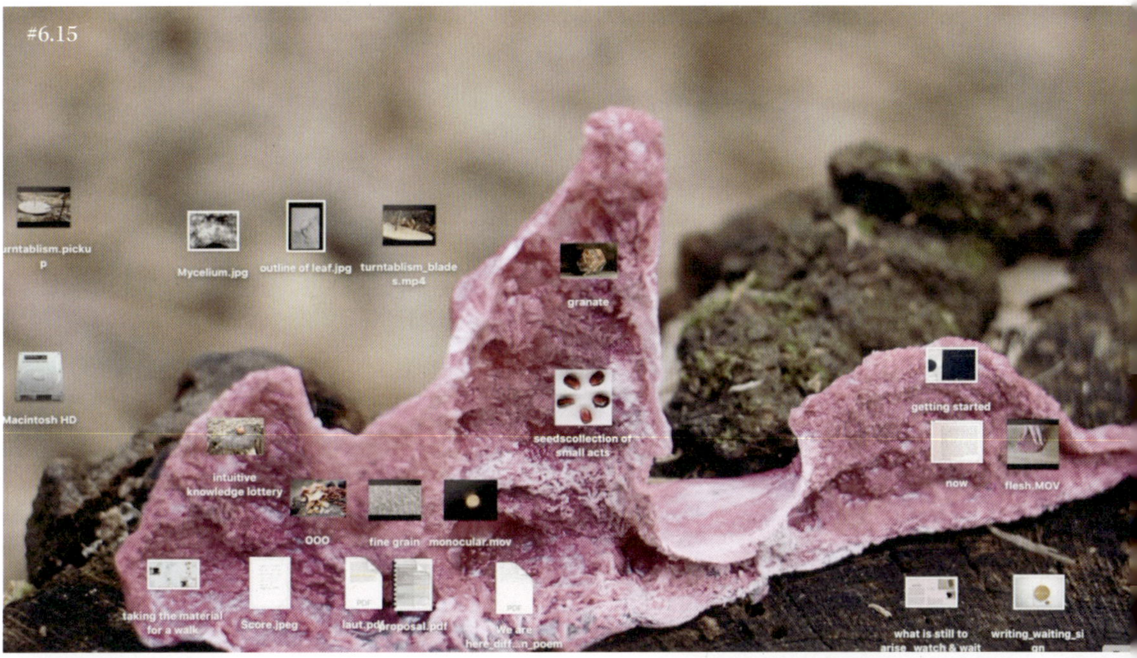
rntablism.picku p
Mycelium.jpg
outline of leaf.jpg
turntablism_blade s.mp4
granate
Macintosh HD
getting started
seedscollection of small acts
now
flesh.MOV
intuitive knowledge lottery
ooo
fine grain
monocular.mov
taking the material for a walk
Score.jpeg
laut.pdf
proposal.pdf
We are here diff...n_poem
what is still to arise_watch & wait
writing_waiting_sign
#6.15

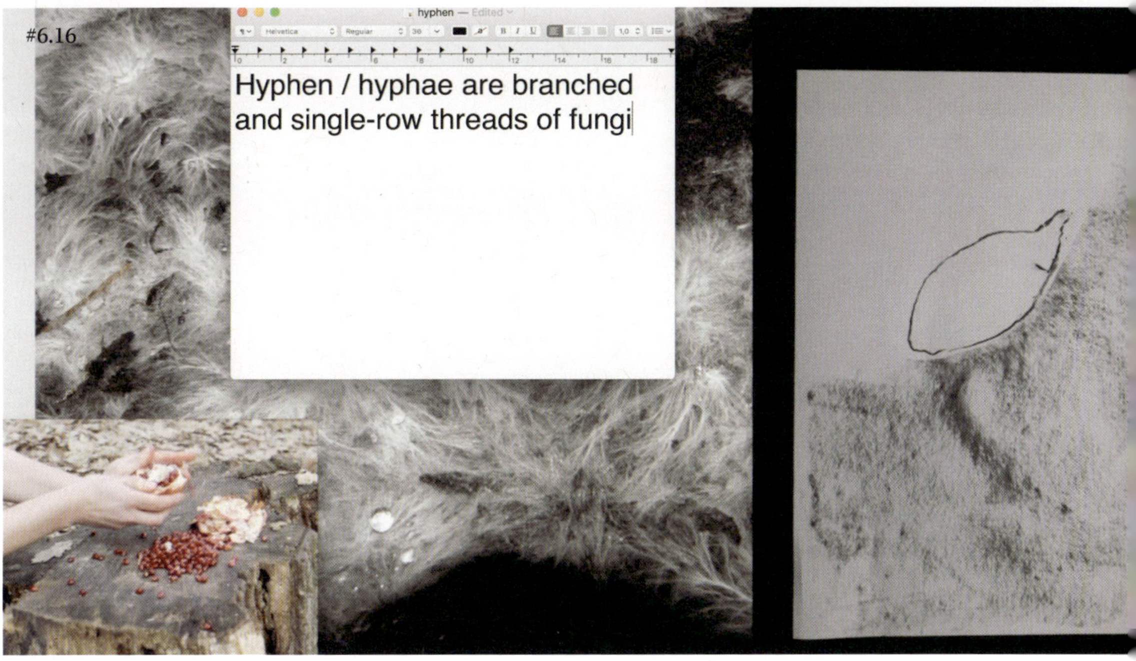
hyphen — Edited
Helvetica
Regular
Hyphen / hyphae are branched and single-row threads of fungi
#6.16

Now that I have to save tomorrow, that I have to have a form because I don't sense that I have the strength to stay disorganized, now that, fatefully, I shall have to frame that monstrous, infinite flesh and cut it into pieces that something the size of the mouth can take in, and the size of my eyes' vision, now that I shall fatefully succumb to the necessity of form that comes from my fear of being unlimited – then let me at least have the courage to let that form form by itself, like a crust that hardens on its own, a fiery nebula that cools into earth. And let me have the great courage to resist the temptation to invent a form.

Clarice Lispector[2]

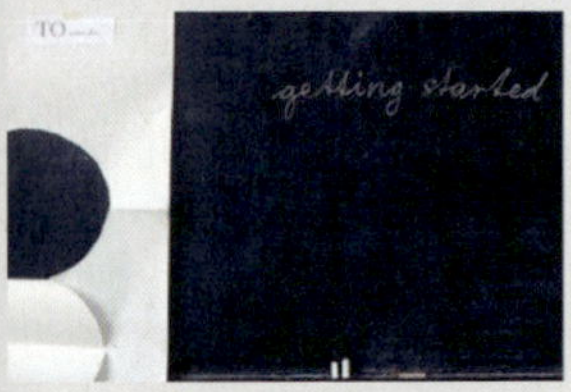

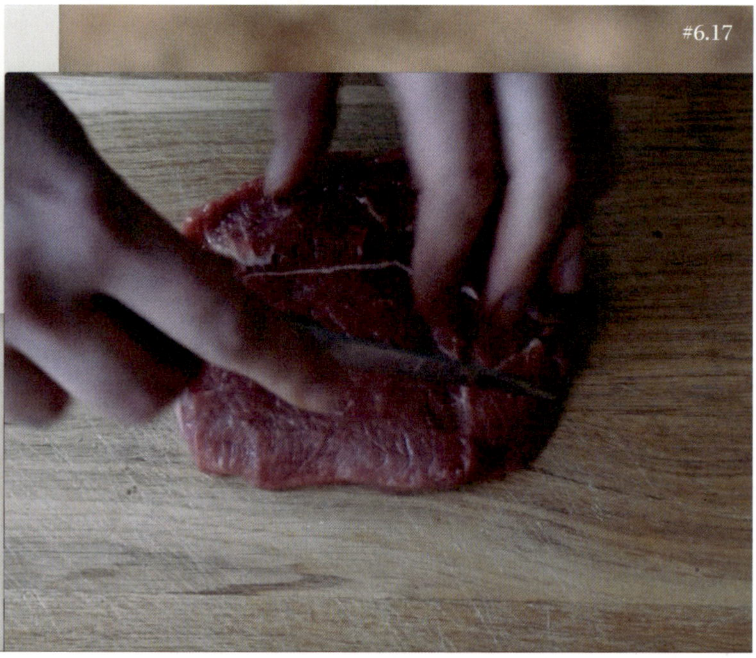

#6.17

Now that I have to save tomorrow, that I have to have a form because I don't sense that I have the strength to stay disorganized, now that, fatefully, I shall have to frame that monstrous, infinite flesh and cut it into pieces that something the size of the mouth can take in, and the size of my eyes' vision, now that I shall fatefully succumb to the necessity of form that comes from my fear of being unlimited – then let me at least have the courage to let that form form by itself, like a crust that hardens on its own, a fiery nebula that cools into earth. And let me have the great courage to resist the temptation to invent a form.

Clarice Lispector[2]

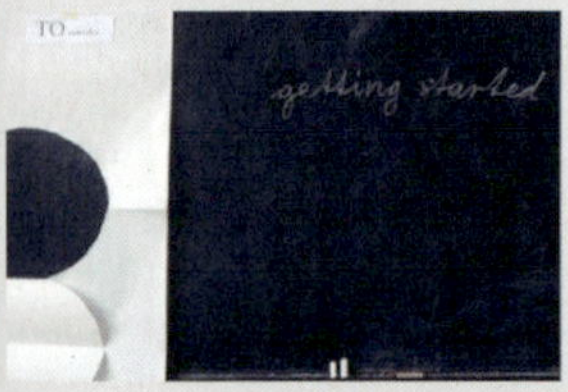

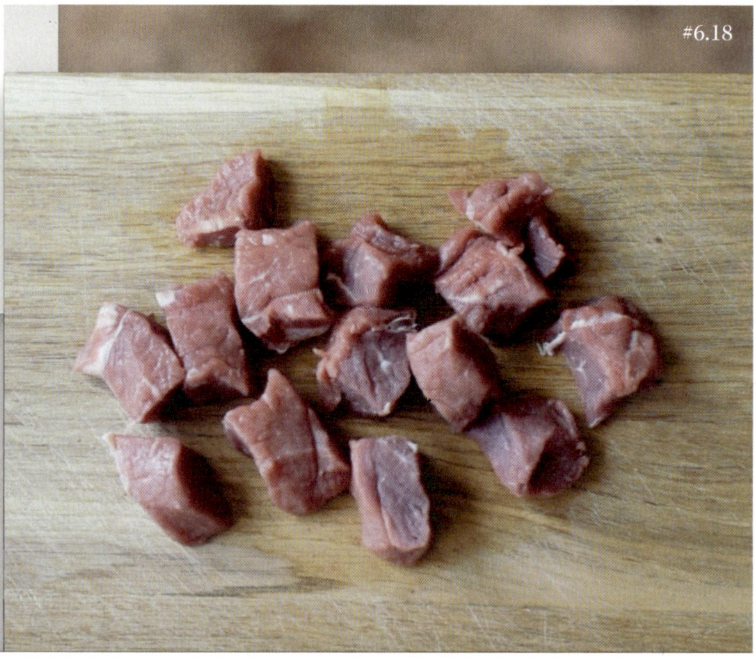

#6.18

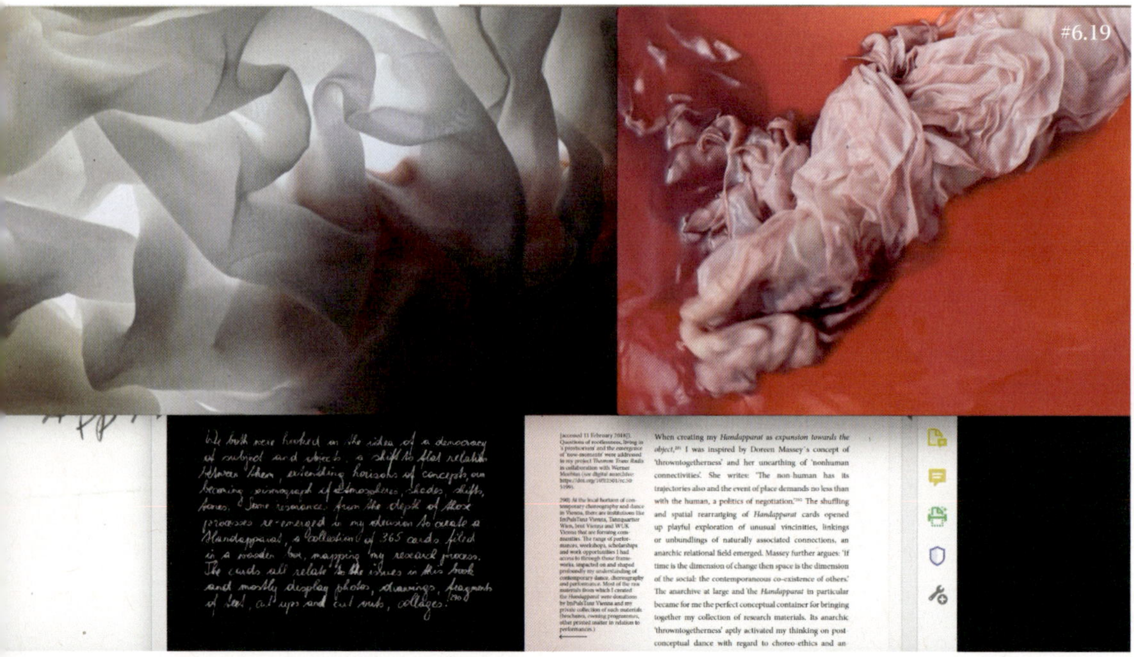

#6.19

#6.20

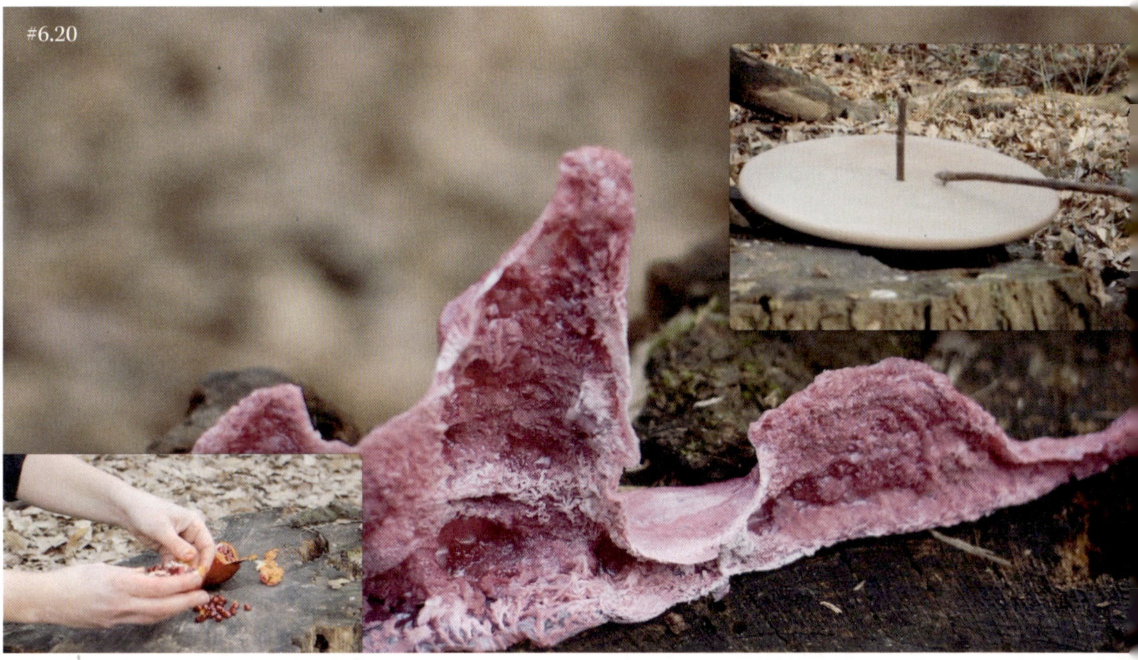

#6.21

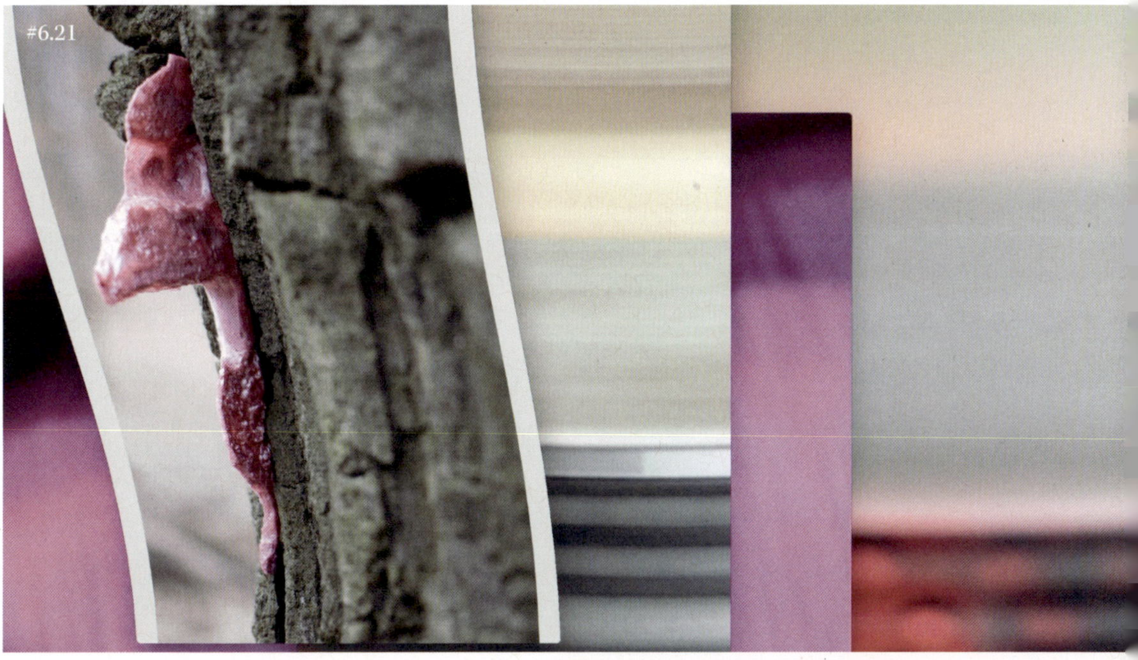

#6.22

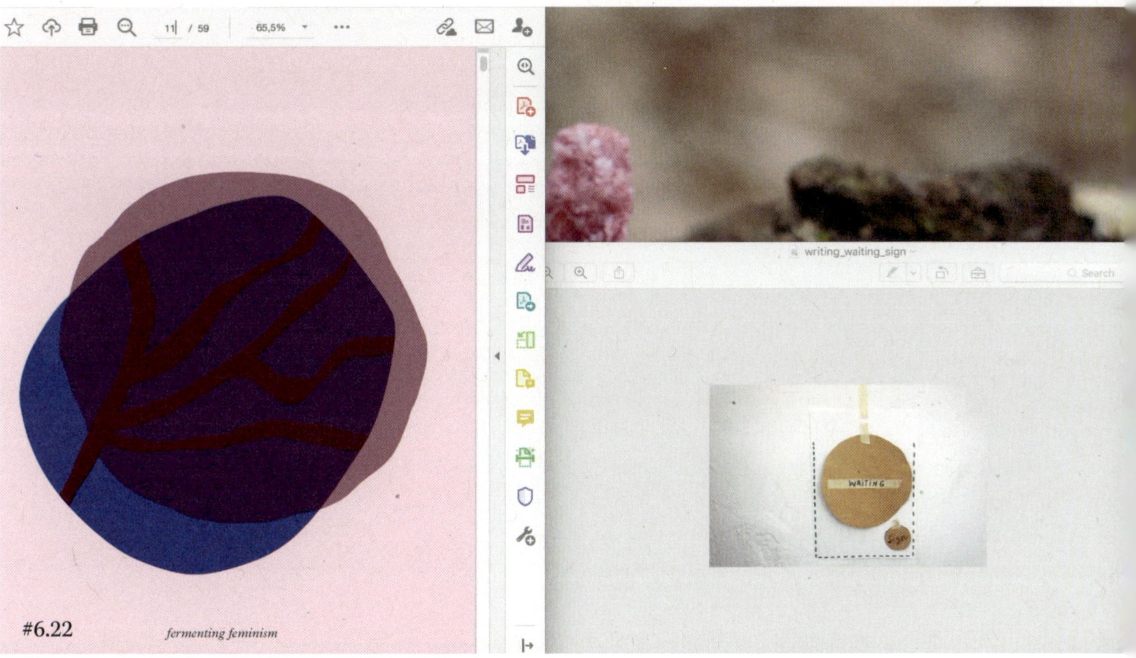
11 / 59
65,5%
fermenting feminism
writing_waiting_sign
Search
WAITING

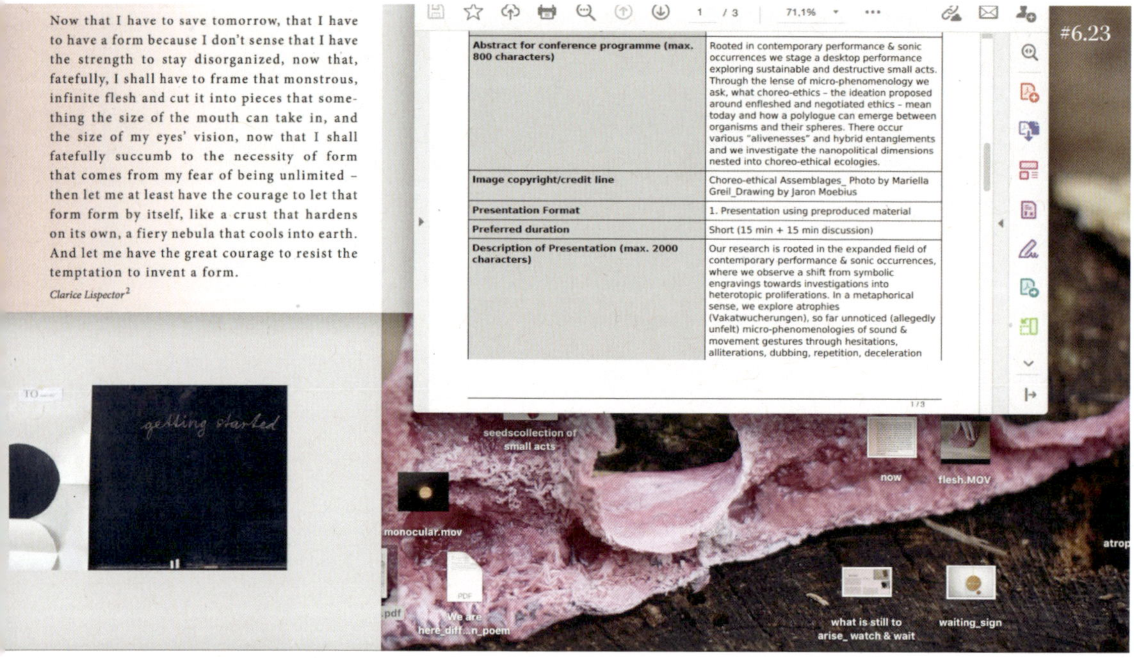
Now that I have to save tomorrow, that I have to have a form because I don't sense that I have the strength to stay disorganized, now that, fatefully, I shall have to frame that monstrous, infinite flesh and cut it into pieces that something the size of the mouth can take in, and the size of my eyes' vision, now that I shall fatefully succumb to the necessity of form that comes from my fear of being unlimited – then let me at least have the courage to let that form form by itself, like a crust that hardens on its own, a fiery nebula that cools into earth. And let me have the great courage to resist the temptation to invent a form.
Clarice Lispector[2]
getting started
1 / 3
71,1%
Abstract for conference programme (max. 800 characters)
Rooted in contemporary performance & sonic occurrences we stage a desktop performance exploring sustainable and destructive small acts. Through the lense of micro-phenomenology we ask, what choreo-ethics – the ideation proposed around enfleshed and negotiated ethics – mean today and how a polylogue can emerge between organisms and their spheres. There occur various "alivenesses" and hybrid entanglements and we investigate the nanopolitical dimensions nested into choreo-ethical ecologies.
Image copyright/credit line
Choreo-ethical Assemblages_ Photo by Mariella Greil_Drawing by Jaron Moebius
Presentation Format
1. Presentation using preproduced material
Preferred duration
Short (15 min + 15 min discussion)
Description of Presentation (max. 2000 characters)
Our research is rooted in the expanded field of contemporary performance & sonic occurrences, where we observe a shift from symbolic engravings towards investigations into heterotopic proliferations. In a metaphorical sense, we explore atrophies (Vakatwucherungen), so far unnoticed (allegedly unfelt) micro-phenomenologies of sound & movement gestures through hesitations, alliterations, dubbing, repetition, deceleration
1/3
seedscollection of small acts
now
flesh.MOV
monocular.mov
what is still to arise_ watch & wait
waiting_sign
#6.23

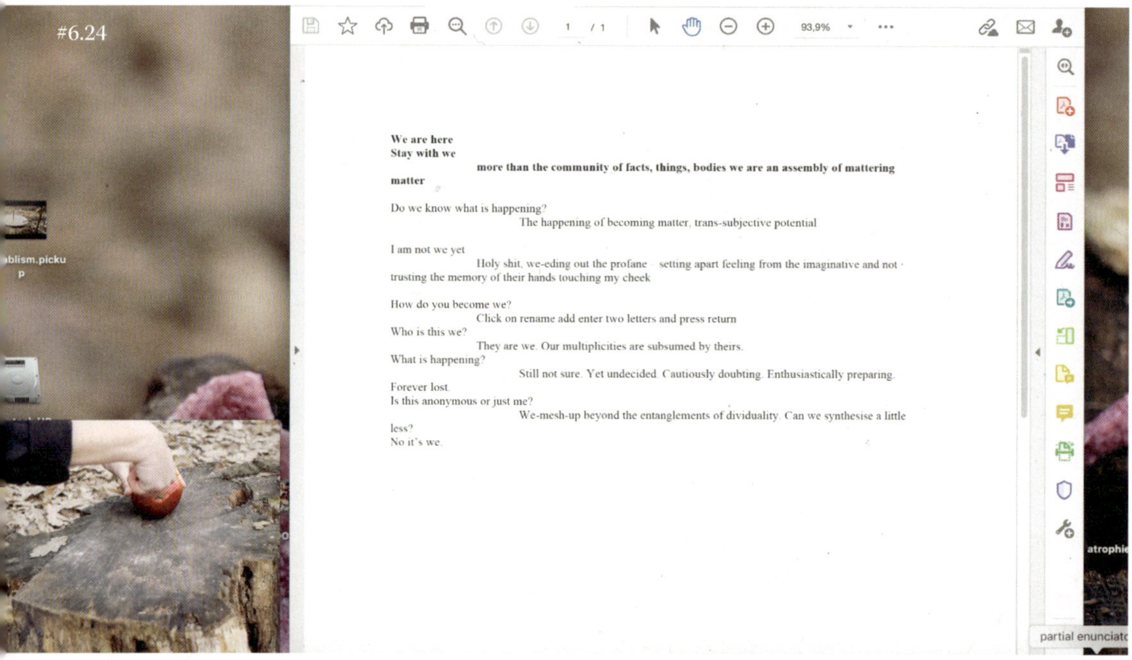
#6.24
1 / 1
93,9%
We are here
Stay with we
more than the community of facts, things, bodies we are an assembly of mattering matter
Do we know what is happening?
The happening of becoming matter, trans-subjective potential
I am not we yet
Holy shit, we-eding out the profane setting apart feeling from the imaginative and not trusting the memory of their hands touching my cheek
How do you become we?
Click on rename add enter two letters and press return
Who is this we?
They are we. Our multiplicities are subsumed by theirs.
What is happening?
Still not sure. Yet undecided. Cautiously doubting. Enthusiastically preparing.
Forever lost.
Is this anonymous or just me?
We-mesh-up beyond the entanglements of dividuality. Can we synthesise a little less?
No it's we.
partial enunciat

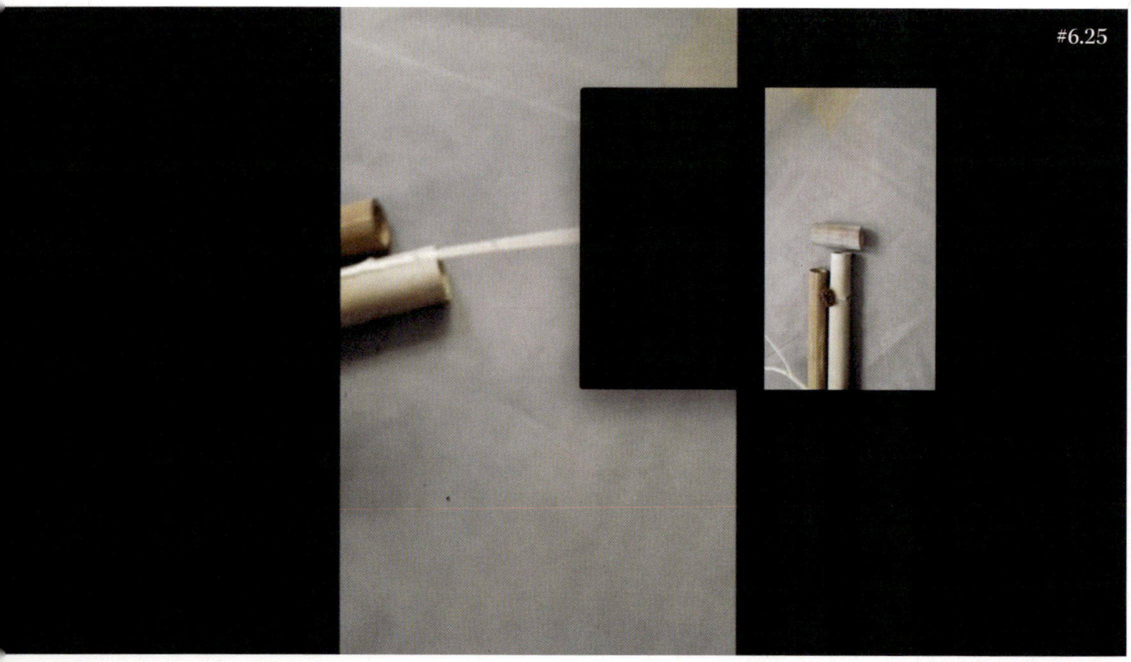
#6.25

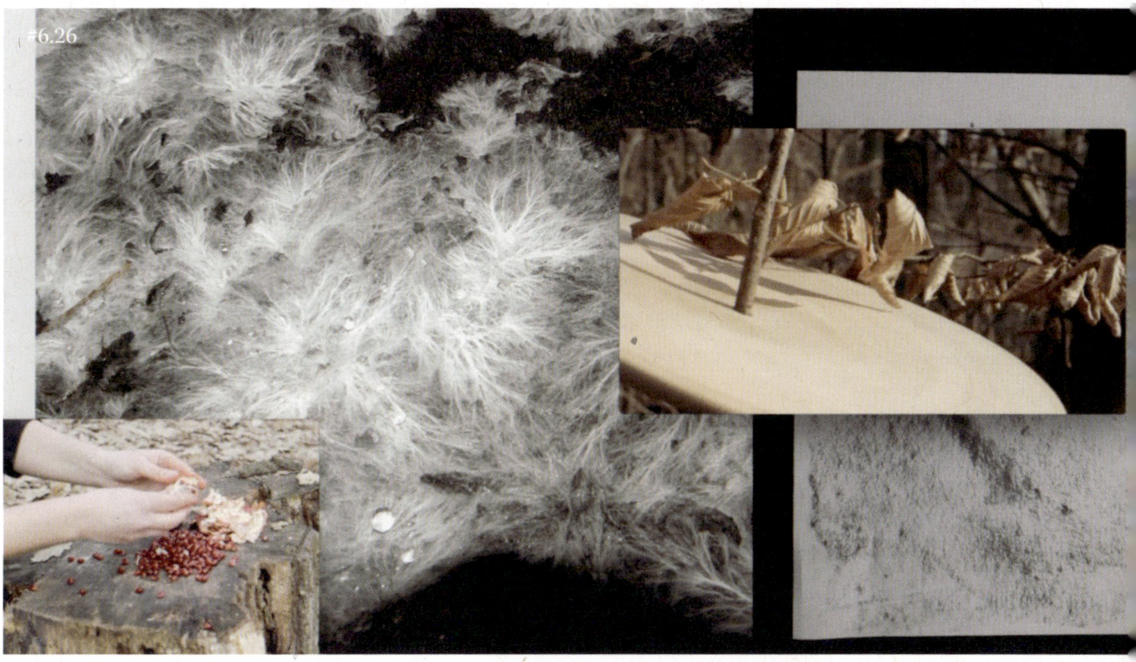
#6.26

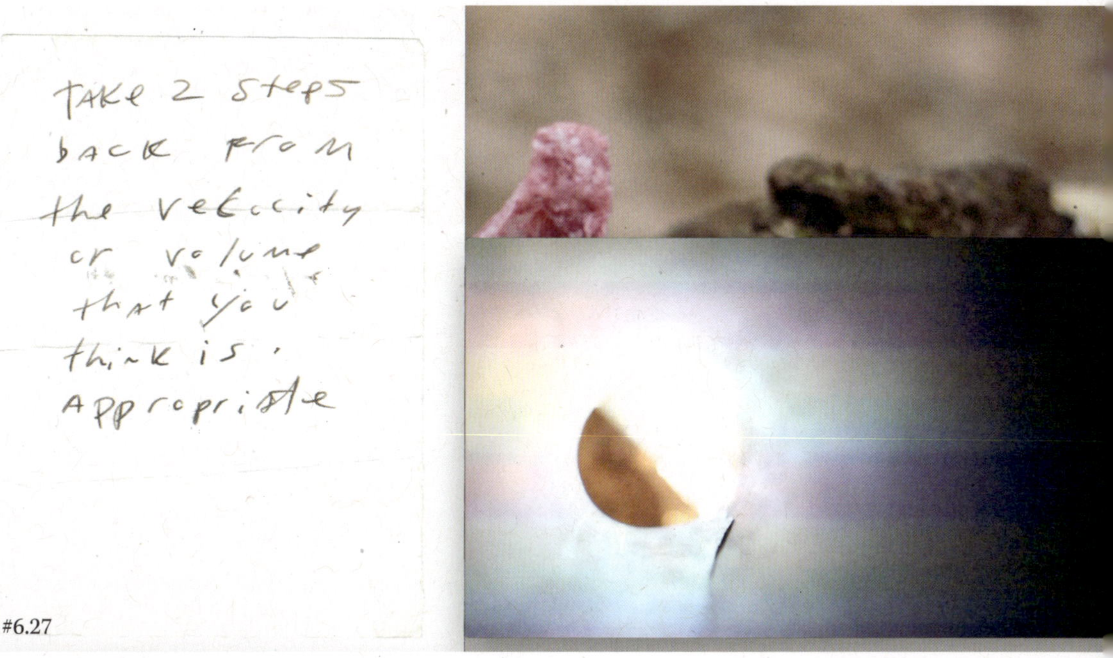
take 2 steps
back from
the velocity
or volume
that you
think is
appropriate
#6.27

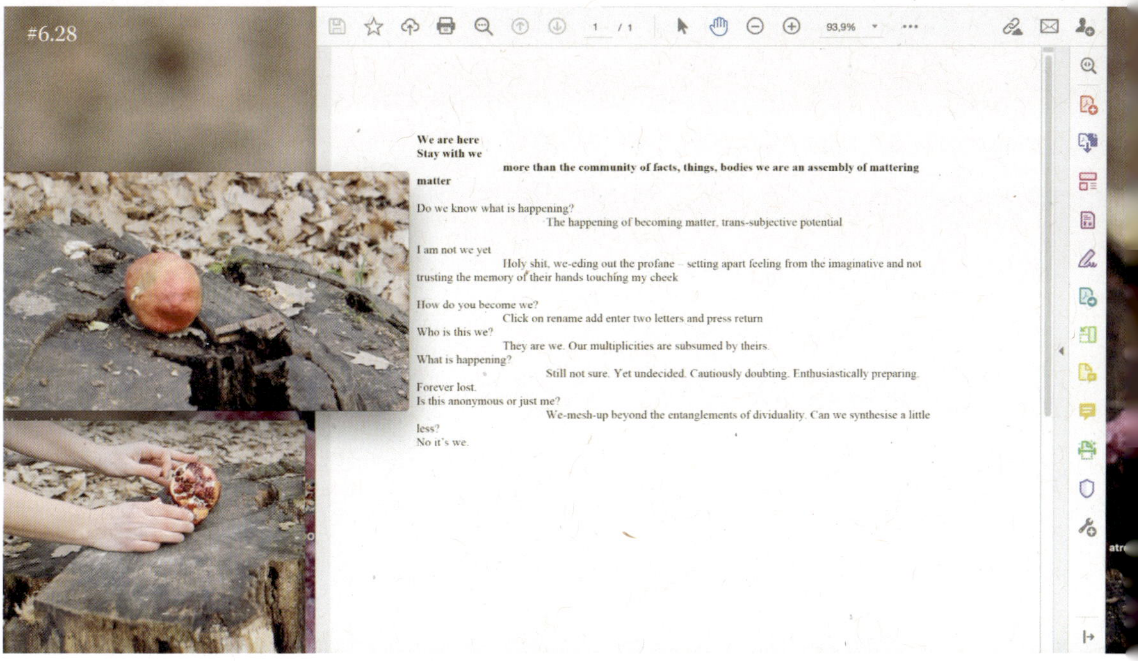
#6.28
1 / 1
93,9%
We are here
Stay with we
more than the community of facts, things, bodies we are an assembly of mattering matter
Do we know what is happening?
The happening of becoming matter, trans-subjective potential
I am not we yet
Holy shit, we-eding out the profane – setting apart feeling from the imaginative and not trusting the memory of their hands touching my cheek
How do you become we?
Click on rename add enter two letters and press return
Who is this we?
They are we. Our multiplicities are subsumed by theirs.
What is happening?
Still not sure. Yet undecided. Cautiously doubting. Enthusiastically preparing.
Forever lost.
Is this anonymous or just me?
We-mesh-up beyond the entanglements of dividuality. Can we synthesise a little less?
No it's we.

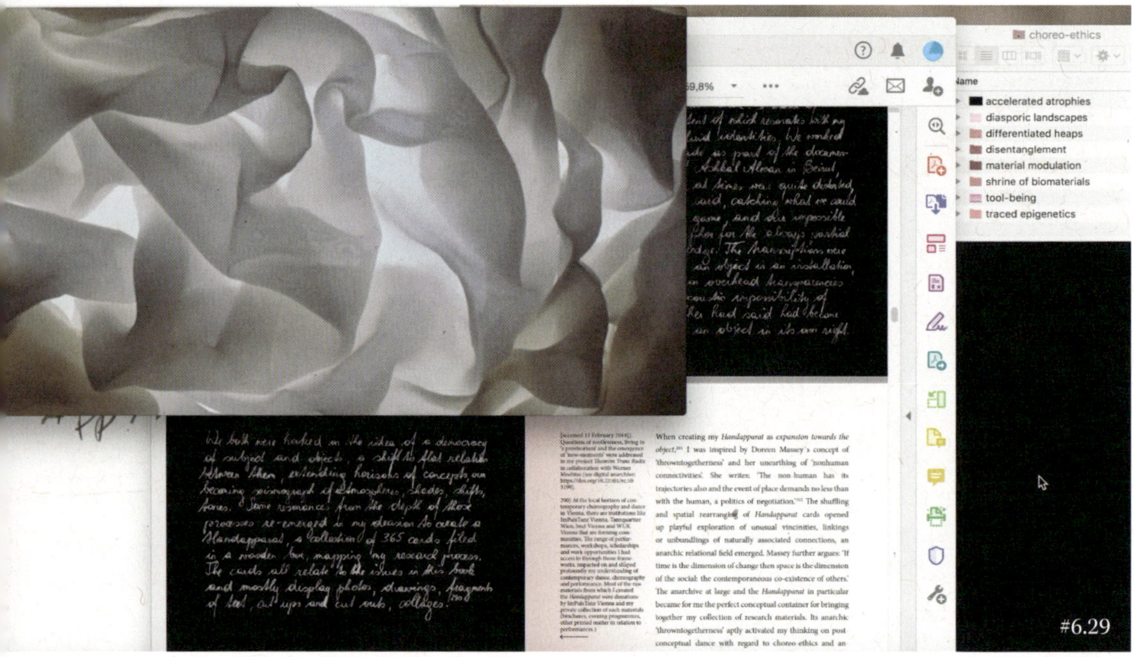
choreo-ethics
Name
accelerated atrophies
diasporic landscapes
differentiated heaps
disentanglement
material modulation
shrine of biomaterials
tool-being
traced epigenetics
We both were hooked on the idea of a democracy of subject and object, a shift to flat relations between them, extending horizons of concepts, our becoming seismograph of atmospheres, shades, shifts, forces. Some resonances from the depth of those processes re-emerged in my decision to create a Handapparat, a collection of 365 cards filed in a wooden box, mapping my research process. The cards all relate to the issues in this book and mostly display photos, drawings, fragments of text, cut-ups and cut outs, collages.
When creating my Handapparat as expansion towards the object, I was inspired by Doreen Massey's concept of 'throwntogetherness' and her unearthing of 'nonhuman connectivities'. She writes: 'The non-human has its trajectories also and the event of place demands no less than with the human, a politics of negotiation.' The shuffling and spatial rearranging of Handapparat cards opened up playful exploration of unusual vincinities, linkings or unbundlings of naturally associated connections, an anarchic relational field emerged. Massey further argues: 'If time is the dimension of change then space is the dimension of the social: the contemporaneous co-existence of others.' The anarchive at large and the Handapparat in particular became for me the perfect conceptual container for bringing together my collection of research materials. Its anarchic 'throwntogetherness' aptly activated my thinking on post conceptual dance with regard to choreo-ethics and an
#6.29

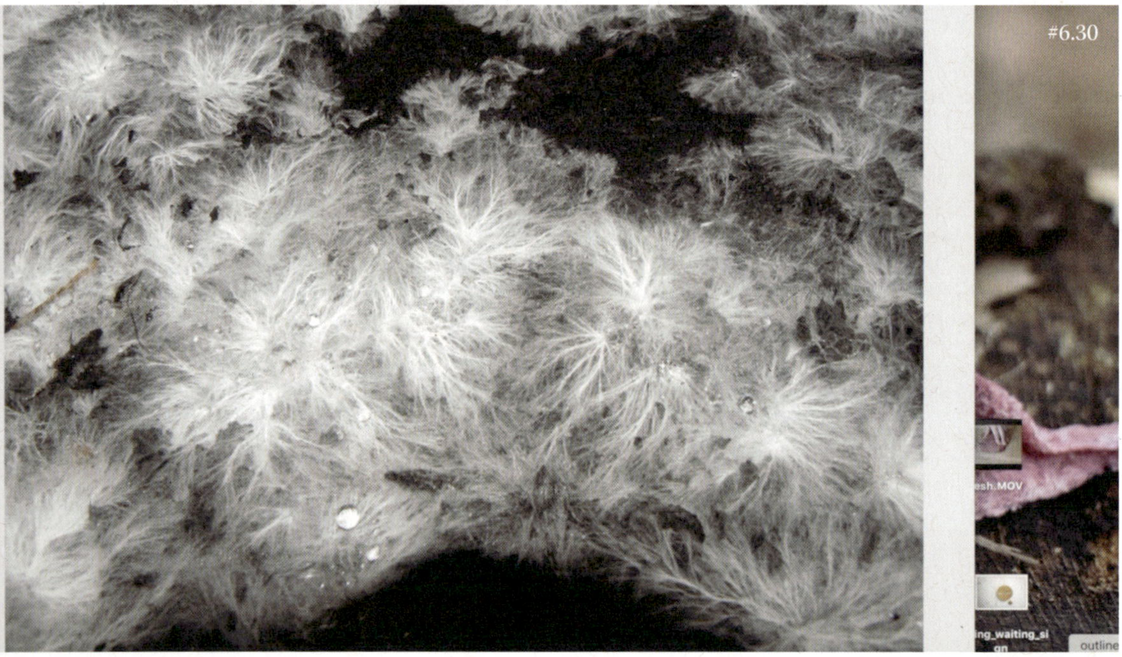
esh.MOV
outline
#6.30

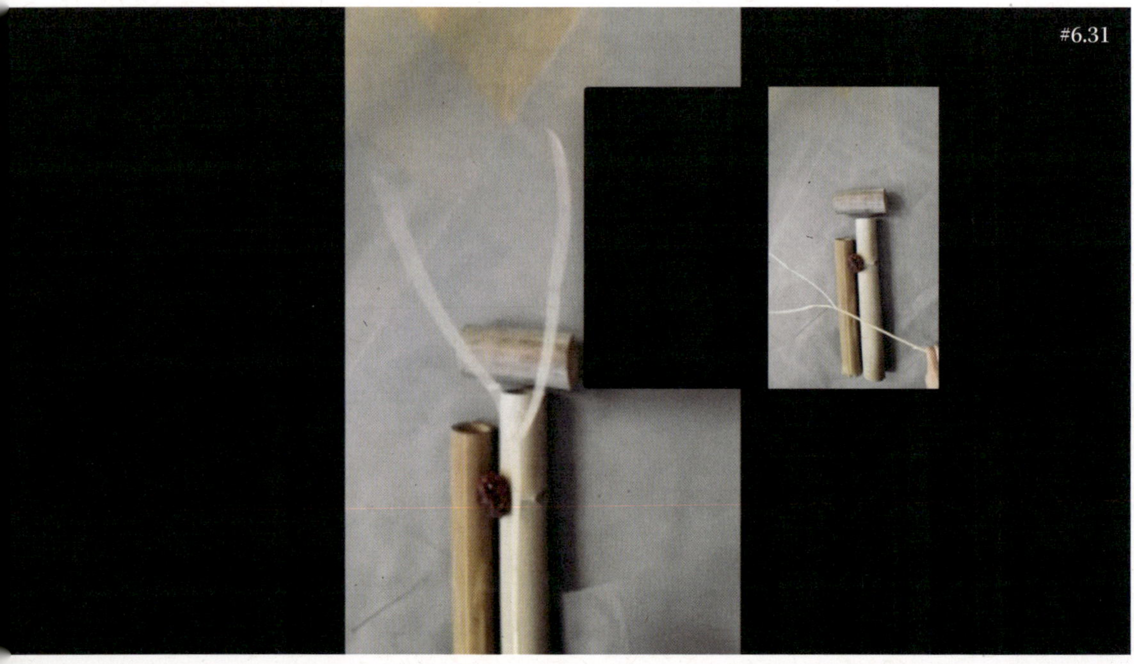
#6.31

#6.01: *Polylogic Organism – Performative Assemblages of Choreo-ethics (Gradually Slowing the BPM of the Pomegranate)*, desktop performance, 2021, © video stills and performance: Mariella Greil, Werner Moebius and Simona Koch.

#6.02–#6.04: *Polylogic Organism – Performative Assemblages of Choreo-ethics (Gradually Slowing the BPM of the Pomegranate)*, desktop performance, 2021, © video stills and performance: Mariella Greil and Werner Moebius.

#6.05: *Polylogic Organism – Performative Assemblages of Choreo-ethics (Gradually Slowing the BPM of the Pomegranate)*, desktop performance, 2021, © video stills and performance: Mariella Greil and Werner Moebius, with additional visual material from *Choreo-graphic Figures* (DOI:10.55776/AR283).

#6.06–#6.11: *Polylogic Organism – Performative Assemblages of Choreo-ethics (Gradually Slowing the BPM of the Pomegranate)*, desktop performance, 2021, © video stills and performance: Mariella Greil and Werner Moebius.

#6.12: *Polylogic Organism – Performative Assemblages of Choreo-ethics (Gradually Slowing the BPM of the Pomegranate)*, desktop performance, 2021, © video stills and performance: Mariella Greil and Werner Moebius, with additional visual material from Nikolaus Gansterer, Emma Cocker, and Mariella Greil, eds., *Choreo-graphic Figures: Deviations from the Line* (Edition Angewandte, De Gruyter, 2017).

#6.13–#6.21: *Polylogic Organism – Performative Assemblages of Choreo-ethics (Gradually Slowing the BPM of the Pomegranate)*, desktop performance, 2021, © video stills and performance: Mariella Greil and Werner Moebius.

#6.22: *Polylogic Organism – Performative Assemblages of Choreo-ethics (Gradually Slowing the BPM of the Pomegranate)*, desktop performance, 2021, © video stills and performance: Mariella Greil and Werner Moebius, with additional visual material from Nikolaus Gansterer and the book cover of Lauren Fournier, ed., *fermenting feminism* (Laboratory for Aesthetics & Ecology, 2017).

#6.23–#6.31: *Polylogic Organism – Performative Assemblages of Choreo-ethics (Gradually Slowing the BPM of the Pomegranate)*, desktop performance, 2021, © video stills and performance: Mariella Greil and Werner Moebius.

Desktop performances were a format explored in response to the Covid-19 pandemic, when live performances were cancelled. All desktop performances and video commentaries by Mariella Greil are available at https://choreoethicalassemblages.home.blog/publications.

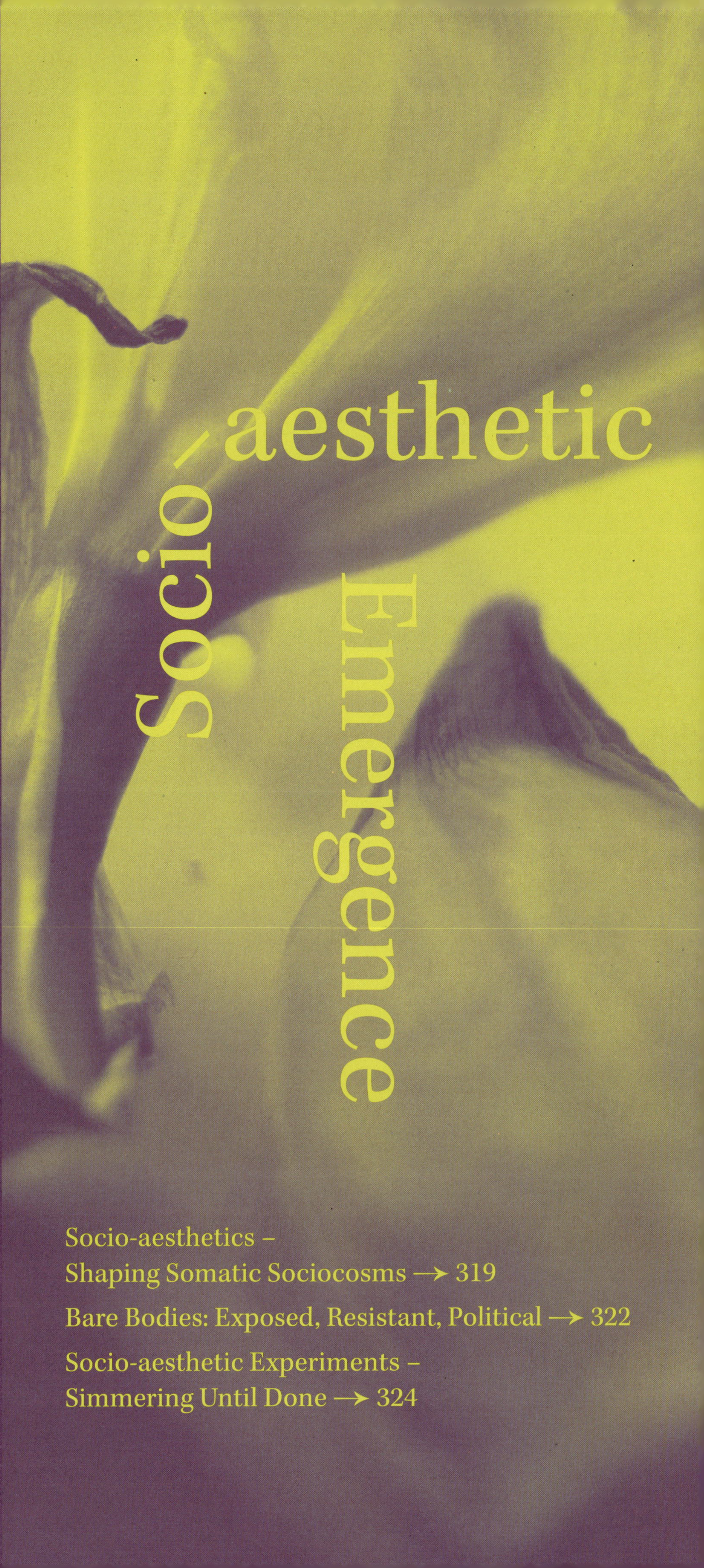

Socio-aesthetic Emergence

Socio-aesthetic emergence means the entanglement of two conceptual strands – *the social* and *the aesthetic* – within a process-oriented framework of emergence. In German, *Sozialästhetik* (socialaesthetics) is the term I use, which I have translated into English as *socio-aesthetics* for reasons of idiomatic coherence. My observation, however, is that the term *Sozialästhetik* has more to do with relational aesthetics, the affective or experiential qualities of being-together (that is, my field), whereas *socio-aesthetics* as it is usually used in the fields of philosophy, sociology, and cultural theory seems occupied with the social condition of aesthetic experience and production. As my research traverses both notions, and opting for readability, I have chosen to use *socio-aesthetics* while anchoring my line of argument in *Sozialästhetik*. In order to draw out the significance of this contraction, both of its components require a thorough exposition before their confluence can be addressed.

The category of *the social* in classical sociological thought has long been construed as the relational fabric that structures human life. From sociologist, ethnologist, and pedagogue Émile Durkheim's conception of 'social facts' ('faits sociaux')[320] as external constraints to economist, sociologist, and jurist Max Weber's interpretive focus on 'meaningful interaction',[321] the social has been seen as an all-encompassing field that organizes collective life. However, more recent discourse has destabilized the presumption of sociality as a given substrate. In philosopher, anthropologist, and sociologist Bruno Latour's actor-network theory,[322] for instance, the social is not a domain but an effect of heterogeneous associations – human and other-than-human, organic and technological. Similarly, in post-human and ecological perspectives, sociality cannot be restricted to human collectives but extends out towards multispecies entanglements, technological infrastructures, and environmental forces. This post-human-inspired understanding of sociality applies to my embodied research on the phenomenon of socio-aesthetics. Thus, *the social* appears less as a preordained field and more as a processual interweaving of relations that are continuously reconfiguring themselves. It is performative rather than ontological – it is not a fixed structure but a dynamic enactment. This creates space for moving-feeling-thinking about how the social is not merely lived but also shaped, sensed, and co-created through aesthetic modalities.

The aesthetic, historically tied to Alexander Gottlieb Baumgarten's (→ Generative Forces in Choreographic Environments, 99) mid-eighteenth century conception of 'scientia cognitionis sensitivae'[323] – the science of sensory knowledge – was initially formulated as a discipline that valorised sensory cognition alongside rational thought. Kant radicalized this field by assigning aesthetics a

320. Émile Durkheim, 'What Is a Social Fact?', chap. 1, in *The Rules of Sociological Method*, trans. W. D. Halls (Free Press, 1982).

321. Max Weber, 'Basic Sociological Terms', part I, chap. 1, in *Economy and Society: An Outline of Interpretive Sociology*, trans. Guenther Roth and Claus Wittich (University of California Press, 1978).

322. Bruno Latour, *Reassembling the Social: An Introduction to Actor-Network-Theory* (Oxford University Press, 2005).

323. Alexander Gottlieb Baumgarten, *Meditationes philosophicae de nonnullis ad poema pertinentibus* (Ioannis Henrici Grvnerti, 1735), 9, Münchner Digitalisierungezentrum Digitale Bibliothek, accessed 17 May 2025, https://mdz-nbn-resolving.de/details:bsb10820766 (my translation).

guiding function in *The Critique of Judgment*, where aesthetic judgment reveals a form of universality that is not necessarily conceptual and instead reflects experience, thereby shaping common understanding.[324] Aesthetics thus becomes both epistemological and ethical: a mode of attuning to polylogic appearances that negotiates both singularity and communality.

Contemporary aesthetic theory, as articulated, for instance, by Juliane Rebentisch (→ Generative Forces in Choreographic Environments, 99, and → Choreoethics as a Poetics of Being-in-the-Medium, 252), emphasizes aesthetics not as an autonomous sphere of beauty or taste but as an inquiry into forms of experience that are simultaneously individual and collective.[325] Aesthetic practices unfold as experiments in perception, reorienting habitual modes of relating to the self, the other, and the world. In my research, I have devoted myself to expanding the notion of choreography towards choreo-ethics and reflecting the tentacles of aesthetics as they stretch towards cosmopoietic practice, forming an œkology created from polymorphous narrations, polysensory encounters, and polyvalent performances (→ Polyvalent Performances, 170). Crucially, depth aesthetics becomes a field of

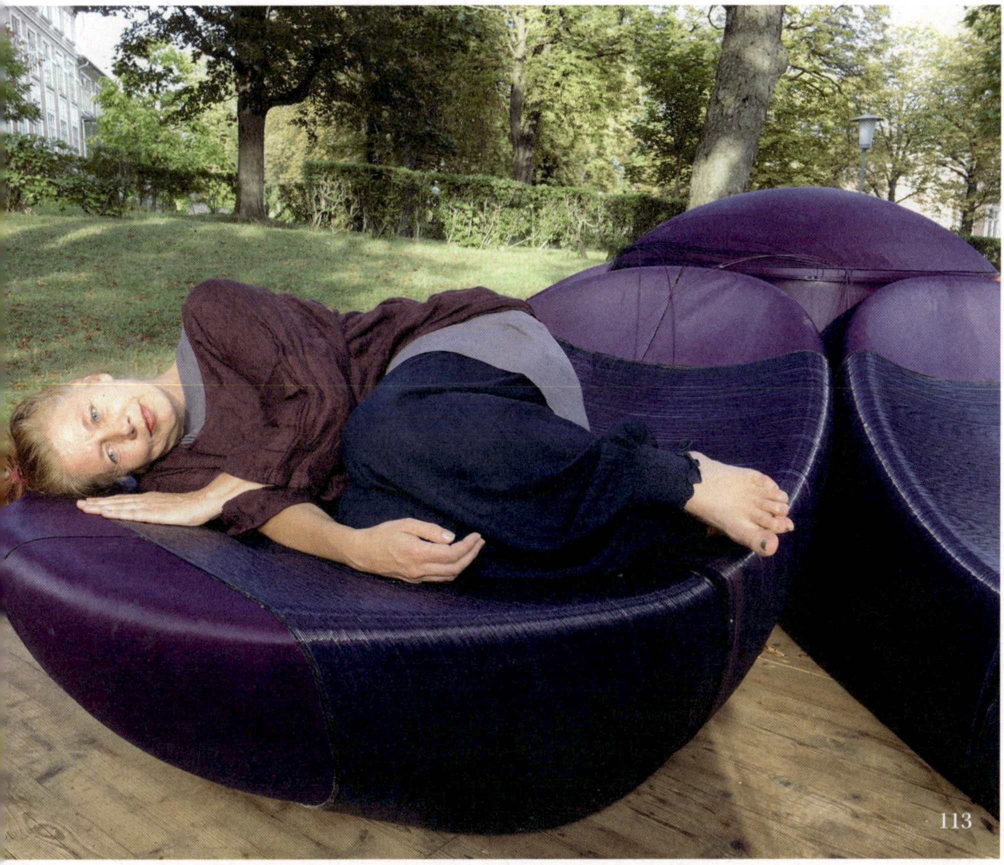
113

324. Immanuel Kant, *The Critique of Judgment*, trans. Werner S. Pluhar (Hackett Publishing, 1987 [1790]), in particular book 1, especially 53–63.

325. Juliane Rebentisch, *Aesthetics of Installation Art*, trans. Daniel Hendrickson with Gerrit Jackson (Sternberg, 2012).

Fig. 113: *Socio-aesthetic Resonance I to PAVILIOLA* by transparadiso, 2025, © photo: Werner Moebius, performance: Mariella Greil.

agency and relational negotiation, shaping how bare bodies and other agencies resonate with environments and each other.

If aesthetics cannot be reduced to representation but concerns the conditions of perception and the generativity (→ Generative Forces in Choreographic Environments, 99) of experience, then its force is inherently social. Aesthetic forms do not merely reflect but actively constitute modalities of being-together.[326]

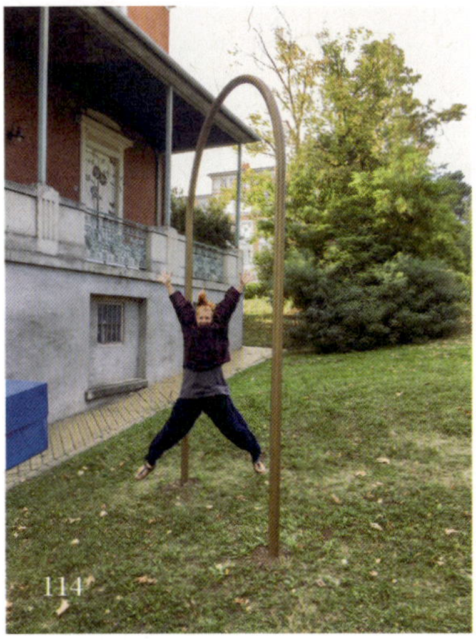

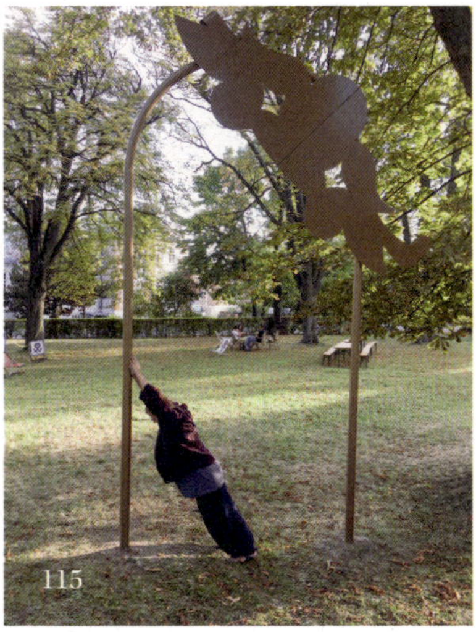

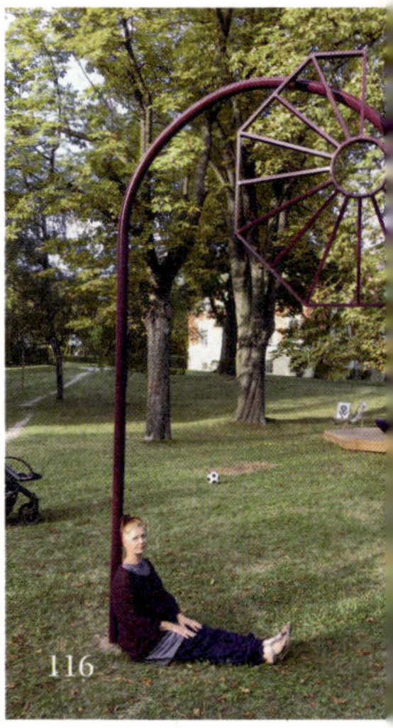

The concept of *emergence* draws on systems theory, complexity studies, and philosophies of process. Emergence designates the phenomenon of properties arising at a level of organization that cannot be predicted or reduced to the properties of individual components. In biological systems, consciousness, and collective behaviour, emergence signifies a self-organizing capacity that exceeds linear causality. Within social and aesthetic dimensions, *emergence* designates moments when relational constellations give rise to unforeseen forms of meaning, action, and value. It describes an open-ended temporal unfolding, where new modes of collectivity and perception materialize through processes of interaction and intra-action, reflection and projection. Emergence here is not merely descriptive but carries normative weight: it gestures toward a non-sovereign creativity rooted in interdependence.

To bring these terms together, I propose that *socio-aesthetic emergence* is the process through which sociality and aestheticity co-generate one another through performative and perceptual entanglements. It is neither a subsumption of the aesthetic under the social nor a reduction of the social to aesthetic play. Rather, the term signals their inextricability: the social is sensed and shaped aesthetically, while aesthetics is itself socially configured and transformative. In artistic research, socio-aesthetic emergence occurs when relational fabrics unfold through

326. *PAVILIOLA* is an example of how well-crafted aesthetic forms can materially support the idea of care as a common good accessible to everyone and create a place that invites people to linger, rest together in public, or begin a conversation with a stranger. transparadiso's work on the grounds of a former psychiatric hospital reminds visitors of the vital role that social interaction and inclusion in the community play for patients' recovery. See 'PAVILIOLA – Opening', accessed 7 September 2025, https://transparadiso.com/en/news/paviliola.

Figs. 114–116: *Socio-aesthetic Resonance II–IV to PAVILIOLA* by transparadiso, 2025, © photo: Werner Moebius, performance: Mariella Greil.

embodied perception, affective resonance, and sensorial negotiation. It points to moments when *aesthetic attunement* generates new forms of collective presence, and when social configurations acquire aesthetic force in the reorganization of perceptual fields. In the set-up of the choreographic environment, which was co-developed with architect and performer Walter Lauterer, this could range from the shared resonance in a performance situation (→ Micro-phenomenological Interview with Efva Lilja, 224) to the wilderness of rough performative provocation (→ Micro-phenomenological Interview with Kerstin Kussmaul, 272). The performed dynamics that emerged within the Polylogic Lab – movements, gestures, rhythms, and affects – created an emergent aesthetic form that reflected the related politics of communication. In this sense, socio-aesthetic emergence is a mode of co-creation that exposes itself to the unknown and therefore to uncertain outcomes. It affirms the generativity of relational processes, where the social and the aesthetic operate as mutually conditioning forces.

I first encountered the term socio-aesthetics in a book that I found in a second-hand bookshop – a tome published in 1913 by art historian, art critic, and diplomat Wilhelm Hausenstein, who fought against National Socialism and anti-semitism. The title of the book is *Der nackte Mensch in der Kunst aller Zeiten und Völker* (The Naked Human Being in the Art of All Times and Peoples). Hausenstein opens the first chapter of this more than one-hundred-year-old book with a print of Giovanni Battista Tiepolo's fresco *Chronos and Venus*, which depicts the Titan god of time and the goddess of erotic love and beauty in an embrace, giving the impression that they are looking down upon the world-in-progress. Psychologist James Hillman writes in his essay 'The Heart of Beauty', 'we must recover our lost aesthetic reactions, our sense of beauty'.[327] Somewhat daringly, we might say that, with artistic research, and within the project *Choreo-ethical Assemblages* in particular, we sensitize the 'thought of the heart as the aesthetic response'.[328] I will develop my train of thought in depth below (→ Socio-aesthetic Experiments – Simmering Until Done, 324).

Let me circle back to the huge book that I found in the second-hand bookshop. The title of Hausmann's first chapter is 'The Nature and Necessity of Socio-aesthetic Consideration' ('Wesen und Notwendigkeit sozialästhetischer Betrachtung'). In his first sentence, he lays the foundation for everything that will follow: 'Art is an expression of world history.'[329] From where the world and I stand today, I suggest swapping this around and conceptualising it the other way around, namely, in the proposition that the different worlds and their potentials are an expression of art, a form of making future worlds possible that starts by imagining and outlining future models through aesthetic, artistic research practice. In other words, I propose that we understand art and performance as cosmopoietic practices, the making of worlds by means of performance and art. My claim is that, just like scientific research,

327. James Hillman, *Thought of the Heart and the Soul of the World* (Spring Publications, 2021), 31.

328. Ibid.

329. Wilhelm Hausenstein, *Der nackte Mensch in der Kunst aller Zeiten und Völker* (R. Piper, 1913), 1.

aesthetic, embodied research radiates into and reflects the changing worlds. This embodiment of artistic research rehearses other worlds, sustainable worlds, worlds that differ from the versions in which we have lived so far. It is a potential outline for other modes of living together. Through imagination and alternative ways of organising, the various agencies can shift their values and envisage solutions that have not yet been. Ideally, *choreo-ethical assemblages* offer fertile ground for observing socio-aesthetic emergence. What I realized through my practice is that sociality is always aesthetic in its felt textures and temporal rhythms, and that aesthetics is irreducibly social in its capacity to generate new modes of relational existence. In this confluence, choreo-ethical assemblages attempt to reveal that *socio-aesthetic emergence* is not merely a conceptual category but a lived practice of co-constitution.

The etymological roots of the verb *to emerge* can be found in the Latin verb *emergere*, meaning to 'bring forth', 'to bring to light'. It therefore refers to a kind of rising from or out of anything that surrounds, covers, or conceals. Emergence implies a movement from concealment to manifestation, which makes it all the more intriguing that socio-aesthetics has not attained the visibility or resonance one might expect. Thus, we might ask, from which grounds can socio-aesthetics emerge? And maybe the more relevant question is, why has social aesthetics not gone viral today on so-called social media? Would this not be an appealing, powerful idea – especially today? Within the frame of my research, *socio-aesthetic emergence* can only be fully understood in its historical context. These concepts clearly have close ties to social-democratic ideas, and Hausenstein actively resisted the Nazis, which was certainly a risky form of embodied world-making. In Hausenstein's elucidations he is on-message for socio-aesthetics, which denotes an ardent social-democratic attitude in search of futures that bring about justice and equality across society. He writes, 'We seek the stirrings of the social', and speaks about the endeavour

> to expand the horizons of immediate existence; it should be an opportunity for the expansive feeling for life of a struggling generation to feel out to the outermost limits of humanity and to rediscover itself there.[330]

To me, this statement sounds rather contemporary, and, given that the world is in the midst of a crisis of major proportions, including the triple planetary crisis (global warming, loss of biodiversity, pollution), I wonder what 'stirring of the social' might mean. All the historical parallels are staggering: the political and social shift to the right, the erosion of liberal democracy, the rule of law and human rights, as well as (digital) threats.

330. Original: 'Wir suchen nach den Regungen des Sozialen'; '[...] die Horizonte des unmittelbaren Daseins zu dehnen; sie soll dem ausladenden Lebensgefühl eines kämpfenden Geschlechts Gelegenheit sein, bis zu den äußersten Grenzen des Menschlichen hinauszutasten und sich dort selber wiederzufinden.' Hausenstein, *Der nackte Mensch*, 1.

He continues, 'The social is the measure of our time and the rhythm of the foreseeable future.'[331] As I do not want to end this chapter on a discouraging note, let me rephrase this and affirmatively state that the social plays a significant role in constituting our present and future. It is therefore in our hands to navigate the space of what will come about tomorrow.

Socio-aesthetics – Shaping Somatic Sociocosms

If we want to radically illustrate the significance of the social for purely aesthetic problems, we need artistic occasions that are not overt political demonstrations. We need aesthetic motifs that are so general in nature that they cannot easily serve a social manifesto – nor should they be so specific that they complicate the discovery of the social dimension; finally, motifs that have been held in high regard throughout all periods of art-historical development and can therefore be considered classic motifs of all artistic cultures. These motifs are the forms of the naked human figure: the forms of the most elementary human existence.[332]

Wilhelm Hausenstein

The term *socio-aesthetics* is not to be mistaken for a mere amalgam of the social and the aesthetic but should be understood as a conceptual terrain that interrogates how aesthetic practices reflect social conditions as well as actively generate relational fabrics of existence. To bring socio-aesthetics into focus is to highlight the aesthetic, performative, sensory, and embodied forces through which social worlds are shaped, dismantled, and reconfigured. In my experience, embodied research

117
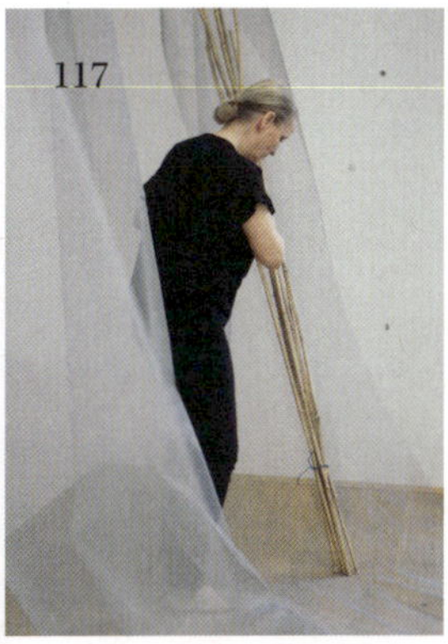
118
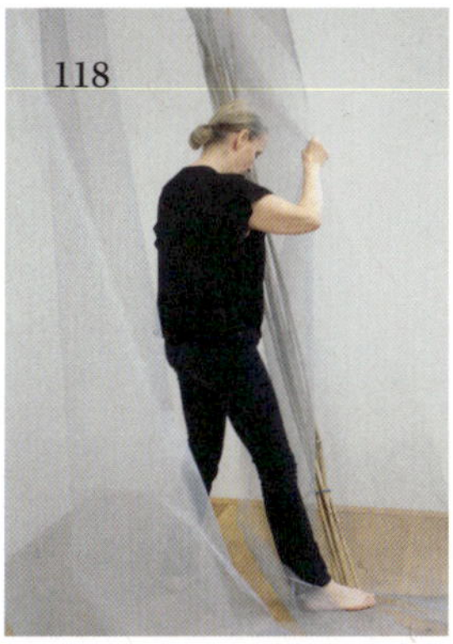
119
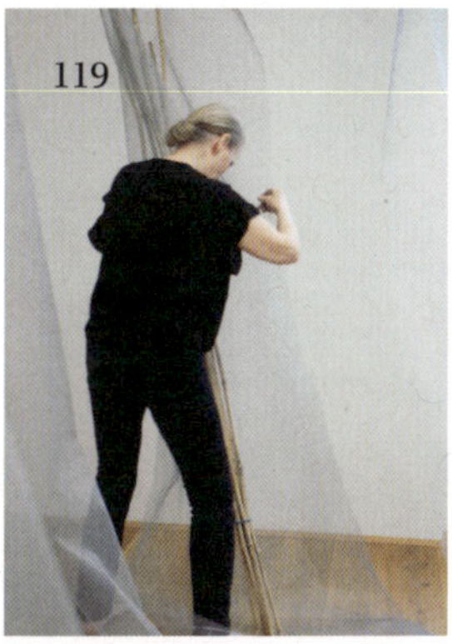
120
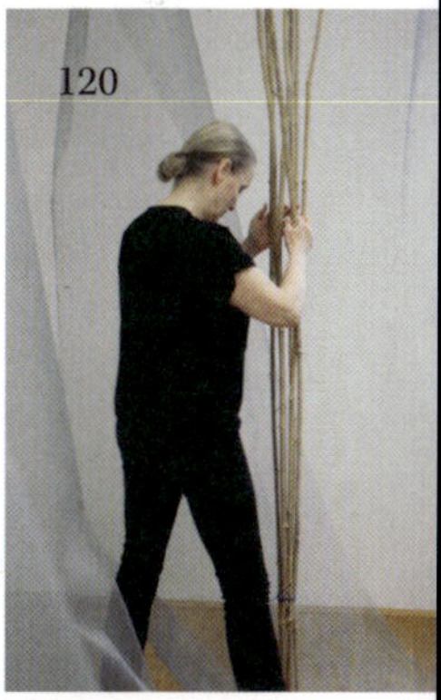

331. Original: 'Das Soziale ist das Maß unserer Zeit und der Rhythmus der absehbaren Zukunft'. Ibid., 2.

332. Original: 'Wollen wir die Bedeutung des Sozialen für rein ästhetische Probleme aber radikal dartun, so brauchen wir künstlerische Anlässe, bei denen es sich nicht um handgreifliche politische Kundgebungen handelt. Wir brauchen ästhetische Motive, die so allgemeiner Natur sind, dass sie sich zum sozialen Manifest nicht leicht eignen – auch nicht in einem entgegengesetzten Sinn so speziell sind, dass sie die Auffindung der sozialen Linie erschweren; Motive endlich, die in allen Zeiten kunstgeschichtlicher Entwicklung in Ansehen standen und darum als klassische Motive aller künstlerischen Kulturen gelten dürfen. Diese Motive sind die Formen der nackten menschlichen Gestalt: die Formen des elementarsten menschlichen Daseins.' Ibid., 12–13.

Figs. 117–120: *Choreo-ethical Assemblages – Un/bundling*, 2023, © photo: Mariella Greil, performance: Efva Lilja.

and, specifically, cosmopoietic practices oscillate back and forth between the Polylogic Lab and the world.

This embodied approach and the circulation between the broader and narrower contexts, the expanded and the intimate choreographies, insist that the aesthetic dimension of life cannot be isolated in an art-historical or philosophical enclave but pervades everyday encounters, infrastructures of attention, and dances of relation.

From this perspective, the aesthetic is not subordinated to representation but attends to processes of shaping perception, the distribution of the sensible,[333] and configurations of presence. Correspondingly, the social is not presupposed as a stable category but emerges through practices of co-presence, negotiation, and material-semiotic entanglements. *Socio-aesthetics*, in this context, designates a field of generativity, where perceptual, affective, and corporeal modalities shape collective experience. The emergence of relational intensities not only reveals but also configures modes of co-appearance – thereby preparing the ground for socio-aesthetics as the very practice of shaping sociocosms in their own contingent, yet embodied acts of world-making.

From a practice-as-research vantage point, socio-aesthetics must be approached through its performativity rather than through detached description. Embodied research emerges within and through practice – the 'Diffractive Dialogue Score', the 'Dark Bag Score', improvisational tasks, somatic exercises, collective rituals, and spatial or conversational experiments. The socio-aesthetic enquiry unfolds within, and is contained and framed by, choreographic environments where the sensorium is activated and relational dynamics are both tested and transformed.

This perspective draws on the understanding that practice produces forms of knowledge that cannot be reduced to discursive abstraction. In group sessions, the body's micro-perceptions, tactile attunements, and affective resonances generated epistemic fields in which the social became palpable not only as a structure but also as a texture, evidencing how social worlds are shaped through sensory micro-negotiations. Socio-aesthetics operates as a responsible mode of enquiry into how collective sensibilities arise, how environments choreograph sociality, and how bodies themselves function as dynamic sites of negotiation. Political scientist and women's studies scholar Joan C. Tronto states that 'responsibility is both central and problematic in an ethic of care; responsibility is among the handful of concepts that require constant evaluation'.[334] Practices of choreo-ethical assemblage cultivate precisely this awareness of checking-in with one's selves (yes, in the plural) and their inner micro-movements, tensions, and flows, recalibrating how bodies enter into resonance with other bodies and environments. These practices call for us to slow down, suspend habitual action, and cultivate receptivity – conditions that allow emergent social and aesthetic

333. See Mariella Greil, 'Of Golden Threads, Exploded Images and Magpies', *activate* 2, no. 1 (2013), accessed 13 September 2025, https://www.academia.edu/32529158/Activate_Vol_2_Issue_1_Figure_of_the_Sensible_Special_issue_Performing_relations; and, of course, Jacques Rancière, *The Politics of Aesthetics: The Distribution of the Sensible*, ed. and trans. Gabriel Rockhill (Bloomsbury, 2015).

334. Joan C. Tronto, *Moral Boundaries a Political Argument for an Ethic of Care* (Routledge, 2009 [1993]), 131.

patterns to become perceptible. The somatic emphasis on sensing and engaging with something renders agents porous to the sociocosmic field: the intricate mesh of human and other-than-human relations or mediations, and ecological interdependencies. The sociocosm becomes tangible as an aesthetic and ethical force field.

But let me introduce the term *sociocosm* in a bit more depth, as it brings into play a conceptual expansion: the *cosmos* as the ordered whole,[335] *social* as the domain of relationality. A sociocosm can be understood as a constellation of beings, (choreographic) environments, forces, things, and agents cohabiting and co-constituting shared worlds. It is an open, dynamic field in which individual and collective agencies are woven together. If we look at sociocosms, they manifest on multiple scales: from the intimate scale of two bodies attuning to one another in a duet to the expanded scale of public assemblies or multispecies habitats. What characterizes a sociocosm is not its size but the quality of relationality it embodies. The shaping of sociocosms is therefore a *socio-aesthetic practice* that reverberates into the broader fabric of social life. Of course, we must resist the temptation to romanticize collectivity and somatic relationality. Socio-aesthetic configurations are not inherently emancipatory, they can also reproduce hierarchies, exclusions, and power asymmetries. The cultivation of collective resonance can mask underlying inequalities of access, privilege, or authority, and for other others, there might also be differences in terms of visibility or mobility. The practice of *shaping somatic sociocosms* insists that the crafting of relational worlds is both methodological and ontological: it points to concrete bodily practices of sensing and to the recognition that the body itself is a site of cosmological entanglement, oriented toward the peripheries of perception, the lived relational atmospheres and collectivities. In this light, let me return to the theme of political responsibilities:

> The point that matters in all of this is that the nature of human action has changed in such a way that responsibility, in a previously inapplicable sense, with entirely new contents, and an unprecedented scope for the future, has entered the realm of political action and political morality.[336]

The sociocosmic perspective foregrounds that collective practices radiate into broader relational œkologies. The breath shared resonates with atmospheric

335. 'Cosmos', etymonline, accessed 21 August 2025, https://www.etymonline.com/word/cosmos.

336. Original: 'Der Punkt, auf den es bei allem ankommt, ist der, dass die Natur menschlichen Handelns, sich derart verändert hat, dass damit erst Verantwortung in einem bisher unanwendbaren Sinn, mit ganz neuen Inhalten und nie gekannter Zukunftsweite, in den Umkreis politischen Tuns und politischer Moral eingetreten ist.' Hans Jonas, *Das Prinzip Verantwortung: Versuch einer Ethik für die technologische Zivilisation* (Insel-Verlag, 1979), excerpt from Chapter 4, quoted in *Klimaethik: Ein Reader*, ed. Lukas Sparenborg and Darrel Moellendorf (Suhrkamp, 2025), 179.

conditions, the tactile encounter with another body reverberates with cultural histories of touch, and the rhythm of movement enters into dialogue with urban soundscapes. Shaping somatic sociocosms becomes both an artistic and an ethical project. It insists on the responsibility of practitioners and researchers to attend to the textures of relation they generate, to the atmospheres they cultivate, and to the sociocosmic resonances of their work. Obviously, critical thinking here is an integral component of practice, manifesting in reflective pauses, in an attentiveness to power asymmetries, and in a willingness to unlearn habitual modes of interaction. Often barely perceptible, both domination and commodification sneak in through gaps in attention or moments of unawareness, through rhythms of attention, patterns of exclusion, or economies of affect. Within the framework of *Choreo-ethical Assemblages*, the articulation of *socio-aesthetics* unfolds a practice of *shaping somatic sociocosms* that foregrounds creative practice as a mode of critical, ethico-political research.

Bare Bodies: Exposed, Resistant, Political

Hausenstein entitles the second part of his volume 'The Cultural Precondition of the Nude' and opens it with an epigraph by Julius Lange: 'Nudity, like death, is democratic.'[337]

In the early twenty-first century (as well as when I was finishing my PhD project in 2017), I purposefully crosschecked how AI-based translation systems translate the difference between *nude*, *naked*, and *bare* bodies into German. Back then, the translations I received were *nackt*, *nackt*, and *nackt* – collapsing any nuance. Today, in 2025, large language models (LLMs) have improved their neural machine-learning networks and can deal with this issue in the German language by differentiating between the word *nackt* (used by the LLMs to translate both *nude* and *naked*) and *bloß* for bare.

The notion of *bare bodies*[338] invites us to attend to corporeality in its most vulnerable and unadorned dimensions, while simultaneously recognising the resistant and political force that such exposure generates. Bare bodies are not simply naked in a physical sense but stripped of representational codes that conceal the somatic ground of presence. They are exposed to the gaze, to affect, to violence, and to care. They are resistant in their refusal to be subsumed under neat categories of

337. Original: 'Die Kulturelle Voraussetzung des Nackten'; 'Die Nacktheit ist wie der Tod demokratisch.' Hausenstein, *Der nackte Mensch*, 193.

338. In my first monograph, I differentiate between the trio of *nude, naked,* and *bare*, as I was not satisfied with the flat, shallow discourse in the performing arts that I had witnessed during the late 1990s and early 2000s. In particular, I discuss the resonances with and differences to Giorgio Agamben's term 'bare life'. Mariella Greil, *Being in Contact: Encountering a Bare Body* (Edition Angewandte, De Gruyter, 2021). Agamben points out the difference between *bios* (the form, quality, or manner in which life is lived) and *zoē* (the biological fact of life; *la vita nuda* or bare life). Giorgio Agamben, *Homo Sacer: Die Souveränität der Macht und das nackte Leben,* trans. Hubert Thüring (Suhrkamp, 2002 [1995]). He seems to mark with his term *bare life* a vacancy, a space of humility, where terminology stops being negotiable. My cross-reading of *the bare* and *the body in performance* manifests as a a differentiable, navigable, and existential actuality. I take up withdrawal as an ontological fact and conceive of bare bodies in terms of their dynamics relating to acts of concealing and revealing, always as part of concrete performative frames. Admittedly, the withdrawal of bare bodies in performance is a complex problem with ample scope for contradiction and unexpected interpretations.

representation or utility. And they are political in that their very exposure forces the recognition of structures of power, regimes of visibility, and conditions of precarity.

Exposure is a double-edged condition. On the one hand, bare bodies are exposed in their fragility: to others' gazes, to systems that render them precarious, and to the climate catastrophe – with the latter condition radically gaining in significance. This form of being-exposed is reminiscent of Giorgio Agamben's controversial figure of *bare life*,[339] a life reduced to biological existence outside political recognition. However, my concept of *bare bodies* insists on something different: not the de-politicisation of life but an aesthetic, ethical reclaiming of corporeal exposure as a site of generativity and creativity.[340]

In choreographic practice, exposure is cultivated through gestures of undressing, de-layering, or suspending theatricality, enabling the body to be encountered in its raw corporeality. This does not erase history or context; rather, it allows them to surface and heightens our awareness of history and context. In such settings, bare bodies become hypersensitised instruments, cultivating a subtle form of perception that exceeds the habitual sensorium. Exposure, then, is not passivity but an opening that enables new relational configurations. While exposure risks vulnerability, it simultaneously harbours resistance. The bare body resists objectification by refusing the trappings of symbolic reassurance. It insists on presence and undoes representation. In this sense, bare bodies resist being reduced to consumer objects. Resistance also emerges in the political sense: bare bodies placed in a public space confront dominant orders. Protest movements, from hunger strikes to die-ins, expose bare bodies as resistant sites of refusal. In these contexts, the body becomes both the medium and the message, articulating dissent through its visibility, fragility, and persistence. Resistance, however, can also be generative, and it sometimes takes on the form of cultivating shared vulnerability and reciprocity, enacting temporary micro-communities that foreground care. The power of resistance lies in creating conditions that resist commodification and instrumentalisation.

In her text 'Which Ethics for Democracy?', Chantal Mouffe writes, 'What to do with this violence, how to deal with this antagonism, those are the ethical questions to which a democratic politics will forever be confronted and for which there can never be a final solution.'[341]

Bare bodies are political because they draw attention to how power operates on and through the body. The political is inscribed into which bodies are allowed to be bare without consequence and which bodies are rendered abject, criminalised, or sacrificial when exposed. The maiming, starvation, and killing of civilians expose bare bodies to extreme violence while simultaneously erasing their

339. For a profound, nuanced philosophical discussion of the rather complex relationship between bare life, facticity, sovereignty, *Dasein, and the authentic self, see* Antonio Cimino, 'Bare Life, Facticity, and Biopolitics in Agamben and the Early Heidegger', *The Review of Politics* 85, no. 3 (2023): 354–74, https://doi.org/10.1017/S0034670523000098.

340. Some performance works that bear witness to artistic practices and address nude, naked, and bare bodies include: *Jérôme Bel* (1995) by Jérôme Bel, *low pieces* (2009) by Xavier Le Roy, *is maybe* (2011) by Angela Schubot and Jared Gradinger, and *The Red Pieces* (2014–17) by Mette Ingvartsen.

341. Chantal Mouffe, 'Which Ethics for Democracy?' in *The Turn to Ethics*, ed. Marjorie B. Garber, Beatrice Hanssen, and Rebecca L. Walkowitz (Routledge, 2000), 94.

political recognition. These bodies are rendered bare by systemic brutality – dispossessed, reduced to wounds, displaced, made expendable. They remind us that bare bodies, even when stripped of voice, generate political affects and ethical demands. The concept of bare bodies cannot remain confined to artistic or experimental spaces; it resonates powerfully with real-world politics. Images of exposed, wounded, or starved bodies circulate in the media, often reduced to symbols of suffering or political utility. The ethical challenge is to resist their instrumentalisation while recognising their political urgency. The atrocities taking place in many parts of the world exemplify this dilemma. The exposure of mutilated bodies in media coverage risks aestheticising horror, yet suppressing such images risks denial. Here, the notion of bare bodies compels us to consider how exposure can be both necessary for political recognition and dangerous in its potential to dehumanise.

Artistic practices engaging with bare bodies can intervene critically, offering modes of exposure, and can foster relational empathy instead of voyeurism, or open up spaces in which to feel-think-act differently, counteracting the desensitising circulation of images and restoring an ethics of encounter. My claim that *bare bodies are exposed, resistant, political* affirms their role as ethical agents in contemporary practice and politics. Exposure reveals vulnerability but also generates relational opening. Resistance confronts systems of domination while cultivating alternative collectivities. The political dimension underscores that bareness is never neutral but always situated within power relations, histories of violence, and the possibilities of solidarity. The concept of bare bodies foregrounds the aesthetic and ethical force of corporeal exposure, cultivates hypersensitive perception and creates spaces of encounter that are oriented towards ethically tuned worlding. Relating them to real-world atrocities sharpens the concept's critical edge; bare bodies in their sacrificial exposure demand recognition, resistance, and atonement. Bare bodies thus exceed both aesthetic formalism and political abstraction. They are sites of practice where subtle perception and worldly politics converge, reminding us that the most vulnerable exposures of corporeality are also the most powerful forces of resistance and political urgency.

Socio-aesthetic Experiments – Simmering Until Done

My research engages with the so far largely overlooked (and supposedly ineffable) micro-phenomenology of performative encounters and engages in explorations of *choreo-ethics* (→ Choreo-ethical Assemblages, 205). This concept has emerged from enfleshed and negotiated ethics shaped by the social and the choreographic. Staging microperformative narrations in their profundity opens up a polylogue between a range of agencies, humans, animals, things, plants – that is, organisms and their spheres. My artistic research project *Choreo-ethical Assemblages: Narrations of Bare Bodies* was rooted in the expanded field of contemporary choreographies, philosophy, and therapy and explored what forms of encounter arise from post-anthropocentric artistic methods. How do we engage with the microperformative entanglements and nanopolitical dimensions nested within choreo-ethical œkologies? Which criteria prove relevant for the ethics of the body? What are the wider implications of choreo-ethics, and how can we practice being an 'ethical subject'?[342] Intra-actions and diffractive dialogues modulate perceptions – which, in turn, are modulated by the environment – constituting micro-phenomena and entanglements between actualised and possible glocal worlds created through sustained life experimentation.

A touching more intimate than that of one hand taking hold of the other. A phenomenology of passage between interior and exterior.[343]

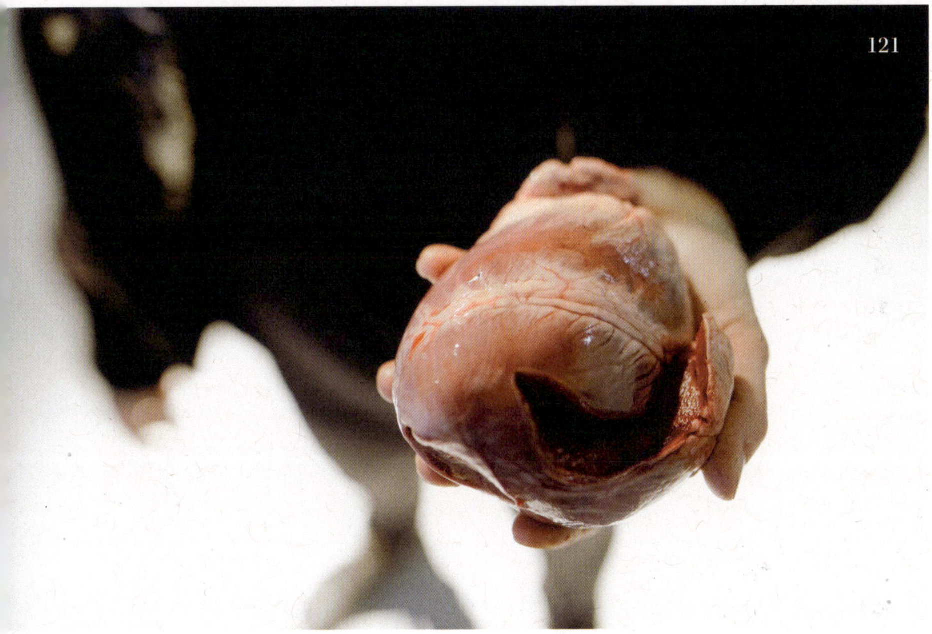
121

This is an excerpt from the performance monologue spoken live after the performer put her hand into the jacket and took out a heart. She spoke slowly:

Take the heart in your hand ...Unrest.
How to touch a beating heart?
How much tenderness, how much strength,
how much wholeheartedness does this need?
Touching the flesh.

Later she confessed, 'I'm intrigued by bare bodies, flesh and things that expose other things.'

342. Rosi Braidotti, 'Affirmation Versus Vulnerability: On Contemporary Ethical Debates', *Symposium: Canadian Journal of Continental Philosophy* 10, no. 1 (2006): 238.

343. Luce Irigaray, *An Ethics of Sexual Difference*, trans. Carolyn Burke and Gillian C. Gill (Cornell University Press, 1993 [1984]), 161.

Fig. 121: *Opening Up the Choreographic* at Angewandte Performance Laboratory (APL), Presence III, 2020, © photo: Mani Froh, concept and performance: Daniel Aschwanden, Mariella Greil, and Charlotta Ruth.

Sensing the weight of the flesh in my hand, feeling the texture, its smell, an intimate duet took place between hand and heart. The distance and proximity between us – the performer and wit(h)nesses – were measured and serious or staggered. Encouraging participants to engage with the complexities of the relationships between skin, touch, and species, the heart was passed on between the people in the room until it was returned to the collective cooking place in the centre of the space. It was then simmered until done.

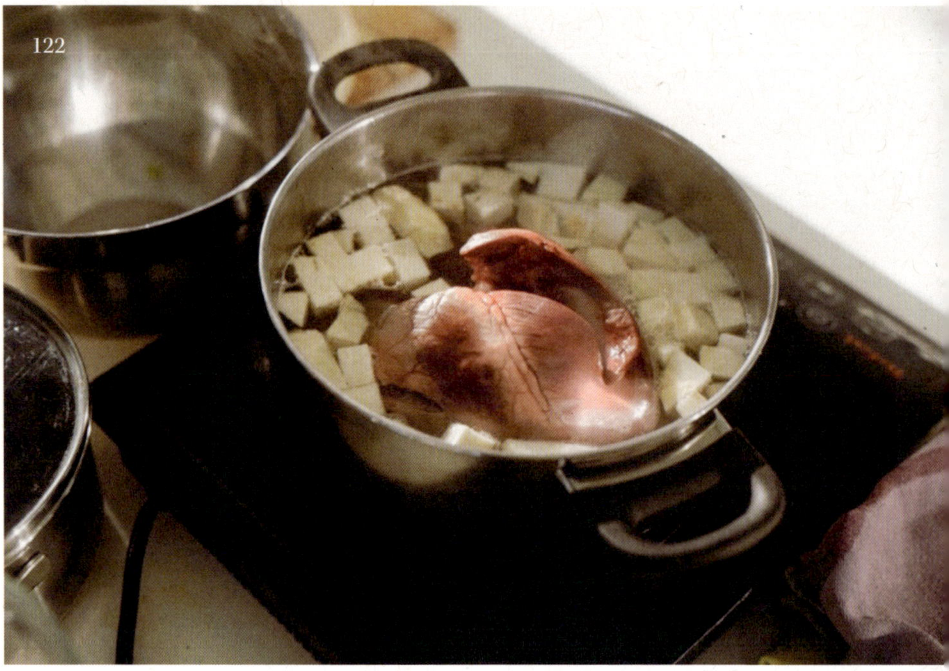

This real heart of a creature that was touched and ultimately prepared as food by so many hands was no longer beating, but it had once beaten. The question 'How to touch a beating heart?' did not just vivify our imagination but also deeply transformed the experience of touching – and chewing the heart's texture.

Together with my colleagues Daniel Aschwanden and Charlotta Ruth, I performed in the collaborative event with the title *Opening Up the Choreographic* at Angewandte Performance Laboratory (APL) in Vienna.[344] We each contributed our latest work and merged them together, co-creating a choreographed, looped lecture performance. We used time as something circular and layered instead of linear, and explored how our three choreographic methods became linked in three rounds. The performers and the audience participated in slow-cooking the heart before it was offered up for consumption – a visceral assimilation of the heart, not only as flesh, but in its socio-cultural significance, and ethical and conceptual weight.

344. *Presence 3: Opening Up the Choreographic* took place on 17 January 2020 at Flux 2, University of Applied Arts, Vienna. It was curated by the team at Angewandte Performance Laboratory (APL). The performance is documented here: Research Catalogue, accessed 4 October 2025, https://www.researchcatalogue.net/view/1250611/1250612.

Fig. 122: *Opening Up the Choreographic* at Angewandte Performance Laboratory (APL), Presence III, 2020, © photo: Mani Froh, concept and performance: Daniel Aschwanden, Mariella Greil, and Charlotta Ruth.

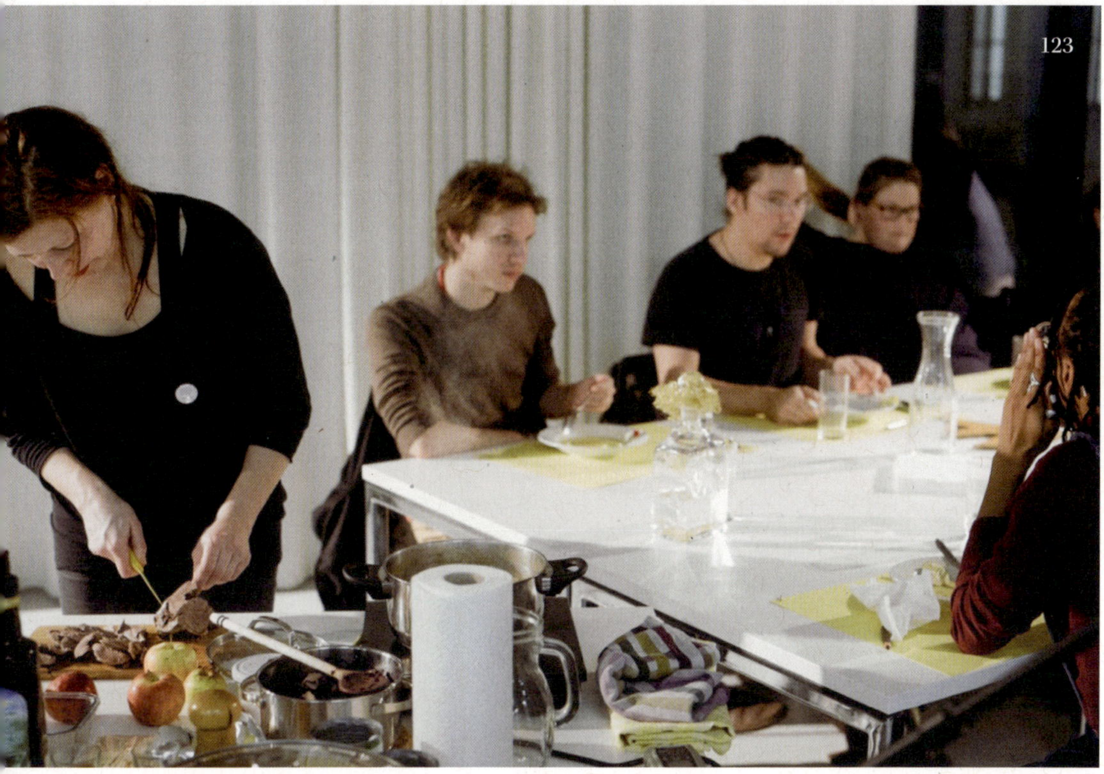

In times of crisis,[345] dystopia, and disorientation, it seems timely to investigate what choreo-ethics – the concept I have developed around enfleshed and negotiated ethics shaped by the social and the choreographic – can bring to the micro-phenomenologies inherent to glocal ethics and biospheric philosophy.[346] Jenn Joy discusses the 'choreographic as an atmospherics of encounter along its violent and erotic edge'.[347]

In this way, tuning into micro-phenomena, choreo-ethics attends to the dance of performing *presences* and reassesses contact, relation, and solidarity as an ethico-aesthetic project of current choreographic performances.[348] This proposition sets ethics in motion.[349]

345. This text was written during the Covid-19 lockdown in Austria but stems from an ongoing sense of urgency regarding alternatives to the still dominant capitalist forms of living together.

346. With *biospheric philosophy*, I propose an umbrella term – a combination of *biosphere* and *philosophy* – for a philosophy that includes ecologies (in the plural) in its thinking and practice, rooted in poststructuralist ethics. Instead of developing partial or hyphenated ethics that justify a particular morality, it has an eye on biospheric coherences and biotic community. Resonating with deep ecology, biospheric philosophy acknowledges the intricate interrelations between organisms and focuses on existing *socio-ethical relations* and their ecosphere.

347. Jenn Joy, *The Choreographic* (MIT Press, 2014), 7.

348. Mariella Greil, 'Being Human and Choreo-ethical Praxis', in *Being in Contact*, 269–90.

349. The desktop performance *Polylogic Organisms*, presented at the 2021 SAR Conference in Vienna (https://choreoethicalassemblages.home.blog/publications), is part of a series of works developed during the Covid-19 lockdowns. Emerging from conditions of physical isolation, these desktop performances set thinking in motion and radically expand the conventions and spatial imaginaries of contemporary choreographic practice.

Fig. 123: *Opening Up the Choreographic* at Angewandte Performance Laboratory (APL), Presence III, 2020, © photo: Mani Froh, performance: Mariella Greil, concept and performance: Daniel Aschwanden, Mariella Greil, and Charlotta Ruth.

Choreo-ethical practice works *with* and *through* the body, not as a subject, object, or artwork but as an instrument for diffracting the self through others – other humans, other species, other materials, other practices. In this sense, my concept of choreo-ethics foregrounds an ecology of immanence and openness in encounters, as well as the mobilising potential of transforming *othering*, into qualified ethical encounters between bodies. According to Daniel Birnbaum, 'Phenomenology's finite subject relates to objects in the world via others, and to itself only as another.'[350] I think that this is exactly where the potential of bringing phenomenological practice into contact with the performative lies. Such diffractive phenomenological processes can unfold for anyone ready to listen to the body and engage profoundly with the process of understanding. This readiness can be a mixture of conditions coming together, emerging from a choice and from the experiences that bodies bring with them, as well as from the practice itself. In my view, this is where the micro-phenomenological interview technique[351] has much to offer, as it unearths the situated, experiential, and emergent performative paradigm of artistic research,[352] which differs from qualitative and quantitative paradigms in scholarship.

In this context, and in my approach and work, I perceive a proximity between phenomenological practice, aesthetic experience, and artistic practice, all attending to the senses and the creation of meaning in its transformational and ephemeral potential. Lygia Clark saw herself as an 'initiator of processes'[353] that 'disclose us to ourselves', a conception of art that has proved useful in my own practice as an artist-researcher. I have conceptualised the choreographic as a complex field of revelatory experiences[354] built on ecologies of aesthetic perception, participation (*Teilhabe*), collaboration (*Zusammenarbeit*), and implication (*Einbeziehung*), as well as a matrix for realising ethico-political agency. Micro-phenomenology grounds ethico-political agency in the fine grain of lived experience.

Micro-phenomenology – understood in relation to the dimensions of time and space – shifts the choreographic as it is commonly understood towards minor gestures[355] and adds weight to minuscule performativity: the micro-phenomenology of diffractive dialogue and intra-action,[356] cellular processes, or tradable

350. Daniel Birnbaum, *The Hospitality of Presence* (Sternberg, 2008), IX.

351. Claire Petitmengin, Arnaud Remillieux, and Camila Valenzuela-Moguillansky, 'Discovering the Structures of Lived Experience: Towards a Micro-phenomenological Analysis Method', *Phenomenology and the Cognitive Sciences* 18, no. 4 (2018): 691–730.

352. Barbara Bolt, 'Artistic Research: A Performative Paradigm?', in *PARSE* 3 (2016): 129–42.

353. Lygia Clark, 'The Memory of the Body' (1973), accessed 10 October 2025, https://portal.lygiaclark.org.br/en/archive/4804/the-memory-of-the-body. In *The Memory of the Body*, Lygia Clark writes about '[d]isclosing us to ourselves'. In her text psychotherapy, art and philosophy become entangled.

354. Greil, *Being in Contact*, 269–90.

355. Erin Manning, *The Minor Gesture* (Duke University Press, 2016).

356. Karen Barad, 'Posthumanist Performativity: Toward an Understanding of How Matter Comes to Matter', *Signs* 28, no. 3 (2003): 801–31.

resources.[357] This zooming-in gesture unearths the previously overlooked (and supposedly unfelt) micro-phenomenology of the nanopolitics[358] that are at play in performative encounters. Conversely, focusing instead on the opening-up and expansion of speculative matter significantly redefines the means of performativity. The oscillation between these dimensions of perception aims at an extensive and intensive politics of articulation that ideally brings with it a *careful* politics of articulation.[359]

Micro-phenomenological Interview with Emma Cocker
Excerpt, edited transcript
26 September 2022

Mariella: If we go back to the very beginning, what was your very first impulse or – in your words – the first call?

Emma: The first call was just to lie down, which came before any interaction with the objects. And then I felt something related to moving in space. Maybe I wanted to get a sense of weight, or to just get an overview, before I realized that's not fully possible. I think those first calls were a kind of opening. And then came this immediate sense that certain objects belonged. *Belonging* ... I'm really captivated by that. I want to look at that word now, because it has *longing* inside it.
Be and *long*.
This idea of *being in longing*.
Or longing *to*.
There's a *long* in longing.
I've never looked at these words like this before.
After noticing this belonging in the space, hesitation came in. In general, I'm quite cautious about moving too fast. Maybe it was more a desire to go slow.

Mariella: Do you have a specific moment in mind concerning this hesitation?

Emma: Probably, if I had a whole day, I imagine maybe 80% of that day would be spent *not* making any interventions. I know I could have decided not to do anything. But in the end, I did quite a lot. *There's something about what happens when time is bound to certain frames and how I decide to use technology within those limits. I didn't take any photographs or make any recordings. I think I wanted to use my time to play with something unfamiliar.* Because I wouldn't normally work with objects like these.

---

357. My understanding of *microperformativity* embraces Bio Art, a term coined by Eduardo Kac in 1997. See Eduardo Kac, 'Bio Art: From Genesis to Natural History of the Enigma', in *Imagery in the 21st Century*, ed. Oliver Grau (MIT Press, 2011). This term gathers together art practices that work with live tissues, living organisms, and biological processes, expanding current understandings and practices of the term *performance*. Jens Hauser states that there is a structural kinship between Bio Art and performance. Jens Hauser, 'Bio Art – Taxonomy of an Etymological Monster', in Hybrid: Living in Paradox, ed. Gerfried Stocker and Christine Schöpf (Hatje Cantz, 2005). Together with the curators of the Symposium *Applied Microperformativity* (12–14 December 2019), Lucie Strecker and Klaus Spiess, Hauser opened up an expanded discussion that invited participants to 'encounter value as a critical experience, a force rather than a norm' (https://www.applied-microperformativity.net). Based on the practice of diffractive dialogue, I would like to expand this thought and revalue the *encounter* as a critical experience, as a force that holds the potential to transform norms. In her philosophical discussion of diffraction, Karen Barad refers to the optical phenomenon of light diffraction, which occurs right at the slit, where the light splits up into its spectral complexity. Similarly, an *embodied encounter* opens up the spectrum of sophisticated, entangled, and complex encountering.

358. The nanopolitics group gathered in 2010 in London around the question or how to think about politics with and through the body. The group published a handbook on embodied experience and the practice of nanopolitics, activating its interconnection with the major politics of our time. Their main argument is that it is vital for new modes of sensibility to intervene in order to enrich and support political engagement in the situated environment of urban collectivity. Paolo Plotegher, Manuela Zechner, and Bue Rübner Hansen, eds., *Nanopolitics Handbook* (Minor Composition, 2013).

359. With a sense of urgency, Eben Kirksey proposes that 'imaginative and intellectual work is needed – a careful politics of articulation' for addressing figures of hope and desire in entangled worlds. Eben Kirksey, 'Multiorgasmic Politics', conference paper, 14 December 2018, https://www.applied-microperformativity.net.

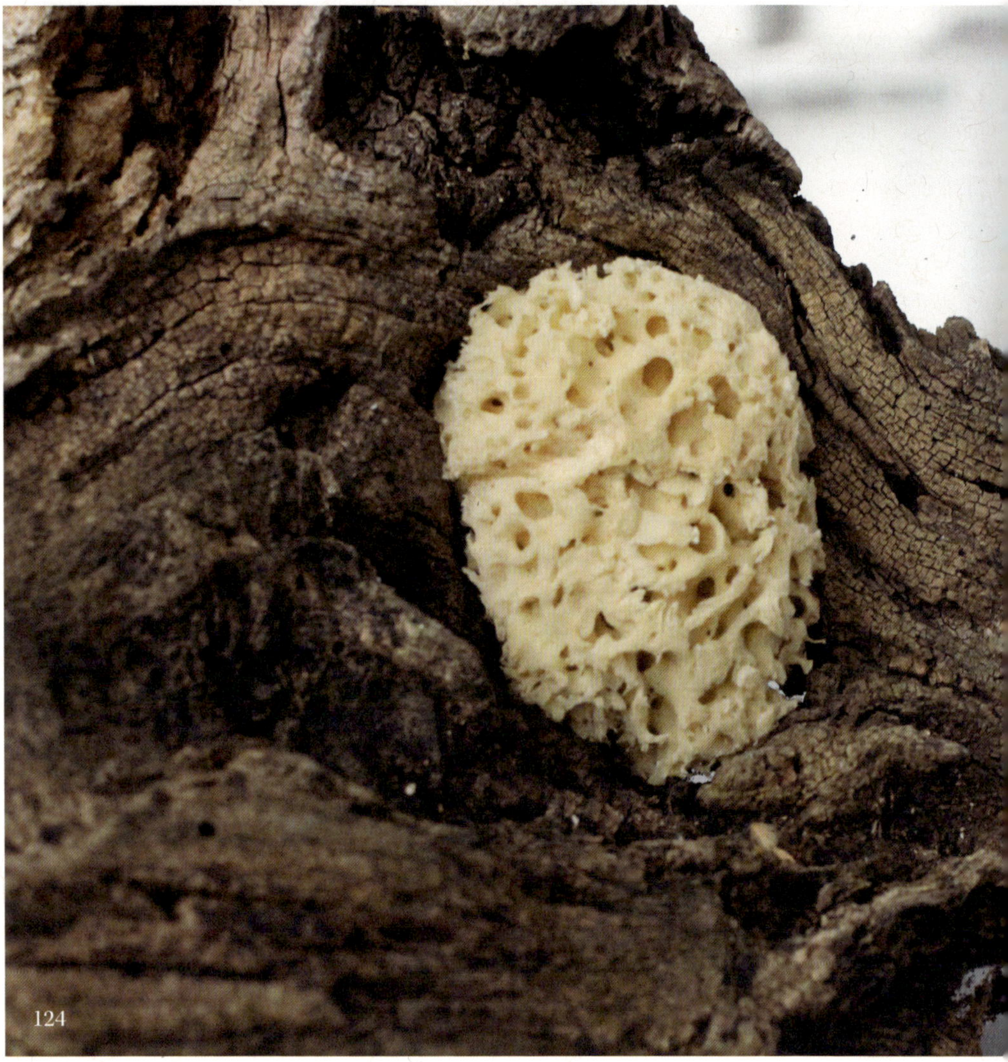

The interrelatedness of micro-phenomenology, choreo-ethics, and nanopolitics, with their hybrid entanglements, requires attentive negotiation, care, and for us to turn to a culture of ethical awareness. It is a mutual affection – like that between my hand, the beating heart in my body, and the heart that had stopped beating, which I held in my hand, allowing me to feel the materiality of another being's heart. Such redefinition uncovers a way to rethink the climate between us, minding the differences in political agencies and cultural performativities, and – even more generally – the conditions in which humankind lives on. Reversing the common cultural tendency to move from large to small, from rough to detailed, I propose a counterintuitive movement. It is an attempt to deepen our understanding of the flow of intensities and their transformations that we perceive on an ongoing basis. It is a movement from micro-phenomenology outwards towards the bigger picture that encompasses the other and the other other. I endeavour to reflect on the meaning of the smallest particles of encounter and the suspended solids of social choreographies.

Fig. 124: *Choreo-ethical Assemblages – Sponging*, 2022, © photo: Mariella Greil, performance: Efva Lilja.

In my research project *Choreo-ethical Assemblages: Narrations of Bare Bodies*,[360] such dialogic exchanges took place between interlocutors – people, but also other beings such as animals, plants, and things. These diffractive interlocutions could be fictive or real, opaque or perspicacious, and formed the very conditions for the artistic creations that decisively proliferated into practices of experimentation.

Writer, artist, and African American studies scholar Ashon Crawley states that 'breathing flesh makes apparent the importance of openness, of otherwise grammar, against borders'.[361] Here, I propose reading bare bodies[362] in relation to social-aesthetic flesh[363] and skin as its deep surface. The emergence of a bare body occupies these elemental and existential spaces that reveal and activate fragility, precarity, and vulnerability. Rosi Braidotti discusses 'exposure, availability, and vulnerability' as being key to 'ethical sustainability' in relation to a 'vision of the subject as a radically immanent, intensive body, that is, an assemblage of forces or flows.'[364] In the words of artist-philosopher Arno Böhler, 'sensitive zones [...] capture and make their surroundings perceptible in a lived-body by cross-linking them with all the fibres of flesh available to a body.'[365]

360. See https://choreoethicalassemblages.home.blog.

361. Ashon Crawley, *Blackpentecostal Breath: The Aesthetics of Possibility* (Fordham University Press, 2017), 59.

362. The chapter 'The Triplet Naked-Nude-Bare: Tones and Shades' in *Being in Contact* addresses how each term refers differently to the body and performativity. What might at first sight appear as semantic gimmick actually serves differentiation and nuance, and has the potential to assist in navigating the complex field between the artistic, the erotic, and the existential. I employ this trio to discuss the *embodiment of bareness* in contemporary choreographic performance. My proposition is to untangle and attend to the tones and shades where these paradigms meet, touch, and rub against each other. I exclusively employ the notion of the *bare* in this chapter.

363. *Flesh* is a core concept in Black studies. Hortense Spiller's differentiation between body and flesh is most useful. She writes, 'I would make a distinction in this case between "body" and "flesh" and impose that distinction as the central one between captive and liberated subject-positions. In that sense, before the "body" there is "flesh," that zero degree of social conceptualization that does not escape concealment under the brush of discourse, or the reflexes of iconography.' Hortense J. Spillers, 'Mama's Baby, Papa's Maybe: An American Grammar Book', *Diacritics* 17, no. 2 (1987): 67. Amber Jamilla Musser argues that flesh is the 'not quite human and not quite animal body, is a space of potentiality'. Amber Jamilla Musser, 'Habeas Viscus: Racializing Assemblages, Biopolitics, and Black Feminist Theories of the Human by Alexander G. Weheliye', *philoSOPHIA* 6, no. 1 (2016): 157. Weheliye argues that flesh could be read in connection with Agamben's bare life as its 'social (after) life'. Alexander G. Weheliye, *Habeas Viscus: Racializing Assemblages, Biopolitics, and Black Feminist Theories of the Human* (Duke University Press, 2014), 2.

364. Braidotti, 'Affirmation Versus Vulnerability', 237–38.

365. Arno Böhler, 'Sensorial Bodies, Forces – Bodies – Sensations', in Nikolaus Gansterer, Emma Cocker, and Mariella Greil, eds., *Choreo-graphic Figures: Deviations from the Line* (Edition Angewandte, De Gruyter, 2017), 210–11.

As part of my performance practice, which had to shift during the pandemic, I explored self-portraits, staging intra-actions with 'materials'. Bojana Cvejić points out that the 'term "material" has a peculiar status in choreographic and performance methodology [...]. They are materials in the sense that they operate in creation; they look back and give material resistance to actions.'[366] *Micro-phenomenology* implies a close reading of fragments or artefacts, acts and events that *do something*, that present and unfold *diffractive agency.* Stemming from my interest in 'instruments for the diffracting self', I used the re-growing material of hair and my pet-friend, a snail called Schmuck, for a process of staging other selves for the camera. Two series of self-portraits were created, one with the title *snailing snarl-up*, which came out of the sustained practice of spending time with a snail – which actually was my son's pet and had been living with us for a year. We fed it, cared for it during its hibernation, observed and played with this creature that moves in steady slowness through the world. The other series is called *Re-attachment Differs from Hair Extensions* and resulted from thinking about attachments and intersections, and processes of growing and pruning. The camera here became/was/acted as 'the other', an extended eye and an instrument used to reach towards a future wit(h)ness. *Doing something* stemmed from both an artistic desire and the pandemic rupture that was radically transforming my physical performance practice into a home-office setup. Since I had not worked with self-portraits, photo performance,[367] or desktop performances before, these were new formats to explore in response to the lockdown measures. The global shift rearticulated my artistic practice, foregrounding the dense entanglement between the world, the body, and futurity, in which intimate as well as extimate performance actions were threaded through modes of speculative imagination. Barbara Bolt writes, 'The performative act doesn't describe something, but rather it does something in the world. This "something" has the power to transform the world.'[368] It is a reciprocal, vital relationship; being sensitive and open to shifting my practice therefore became crucial to sustaining an artistic performance practice during the time of Covid-19, mediated through the camera and a 13-inch computer screen. Within the framework of of *Choreo-ethical Assemblages: Narrations of Bare Bodies*, it was a conscious decision to not focus on the training aspects of dance practice and to instead expose the creative process. Still, I want to acknowledge the continuous somatic work to keep the body supple and strong, the attention focused, and the mind serene, the daily practice of fine-tuning the body-mind connection, the corporeal instrument, as the basis for everything that comes after. These processes clearly form the backdrop to the *choreo-ethical practice* based on *performing with* the other. So, what happens when the other is not there in person? How can one still

366. Anne Teresa de Keersmaeker and Bojana Cvejić, *A Choreographer's Score: Fase, Rosas Danst Rosas, Elena's Aria, Bartók* (Yale University Press, 2020), 13.

367. Photo performance is an artistic practice where photography does not merely document performance but is integral to its conception, execution, and reception – making the photograph a site of performance, as in the work of Valie Export (*Body Configurations*, 1972–76), Ana Mendieta (*Silueta Series*, 1973–80), Cindy Sherman (*Untitled Film Stills*, 1977–80), Bruce Nauman (*Self-portrait as a Fountain*, 1966–70), and Gina Pane (*Actions Psychologiques*, 1970s), as well as in the photo performances of Guillermo Gómez-Peña, Gilbert & George, and Yoko Ono.

368. Bolt, 'Artistic Research', 137.

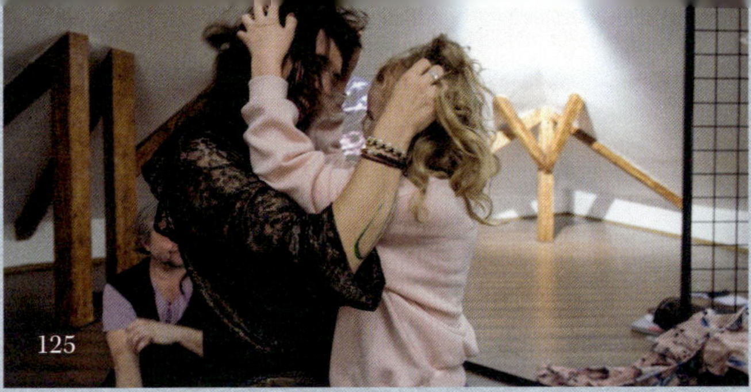

125

Wild Bonds

Intimate bonds form between mother and
daughter
weaving yesterday's crumbs into tomorrow's braid
with radiant joy.
Fingers move wildly and joyfully through
each other's shagginess
across generations and with the
emotional knowledge of
how to care for the young ones.

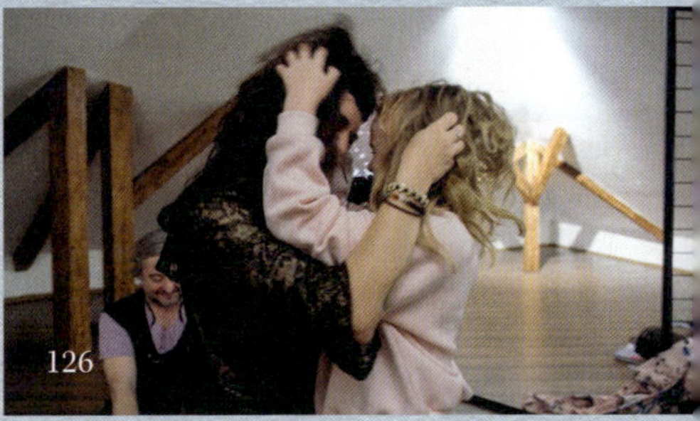

126

Entanglements emerge in plaited time,
intuitively higgledy-piggledy,
dash, mash, gather, breathe.
Each tug a quiet promise:
I am holding you
so you do not scatter.
We laugh together because hair remembers
what descendants keep secret:
the love, the discipline, the wildness.

Falling and crushing again,
the passing of touch,
from grandma's palm to mother's wrist to
grandchild's scalp,
generations practice
how not to let go.
Precise pressure that says
this is love, not control.
The gentle ache that means
someone loves you madly.

Past dancing with the future,
folded time sitting still
while fingers move quickly,
afraid that joy might slip away.
Repetition, familiar gravity,
her hair finer than mine,
a soft argument in my hands.
She squirms.
She laughs.
She tells me it pulls.
We both know: firm enough to hold,
gentle enough to stay.
A yes that travels skin to skin,
century to century,
small domestic choreography,
hands echoing feminine lineages.
We practice joy.

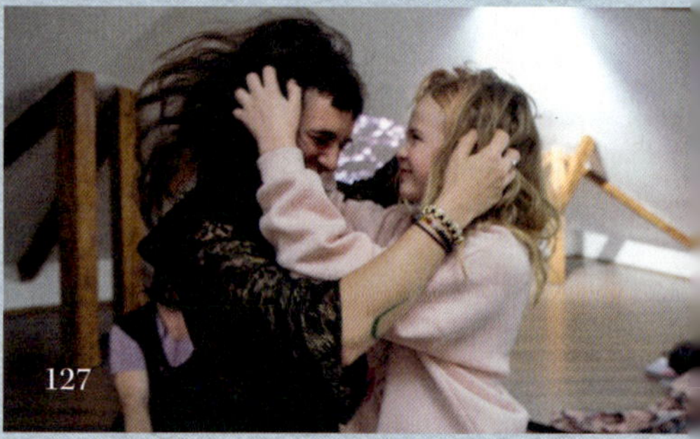
127

Joy lives in the midst of
the hairy mess.
the crossing point,
where we meet,
where difference agrees
to touch.
Looping, laughing,
loose hair gathers, we are entangled.
Across bodies, these lively gestures
belong only to the story of staying close.
Love remains after letting go.
Wisdom still warm
from heart to fingertips.

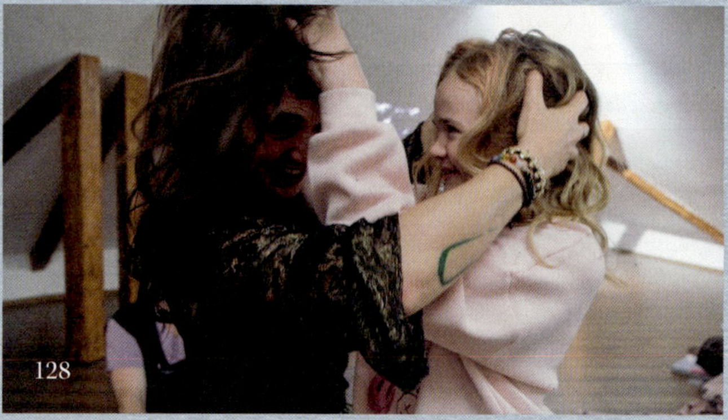
128

perform with the other, and what aspects of the practice need to be altered? Rather than allowing the restrictions of distancing to make a dialogical encounter impossible, I decided to work through mediated presence and explore its potential. This significant shift brought questions regarding the hospitality of presence into focus and foregrounded the phenomenon of embodied presence. How could I generate and stage the subtle layers of 'being there' as nuanced manifestations through micro-performativity – relentlessly emphasised by the unforgiving tool of the camera? The closeness, detail, and immediacy of the camera's 'gaze' were harsh, and underscored the mastery of actor Andrew Clement Serkis, who is known for his performance-capture work as computer-generated characters like Gollum in *The Lord of the Rings*. Decidedly staying away from postproduction, the focus of my performance for the camera became capturing a look in my own eyes, embodying a state.

However, I would like to return for a moment to the time before Covid-19, when performances with audiences were possible. During the event *Opening Up the Choreographic*, various openings took place, but I would like to focus on one specific act. Giving your heart to art is an act *in* and *of* itself. Then, it is up to the wit(h)nesses whether they eat the heart or not, giving weight to their choreo-ethical act. In the age of vegan food, I felt that offering the heart was a thought-provoking act, and only few wit(h)nesses chose to eat it. Some of us may have felt the vague but daunting echo of Aztec cultural heritage – a memory of the human sacrifices, the beating heart being ripped from the still-conscious victim. As we know, this was a strictly ritualised process of the highest spiritual significance and was considered a necessity

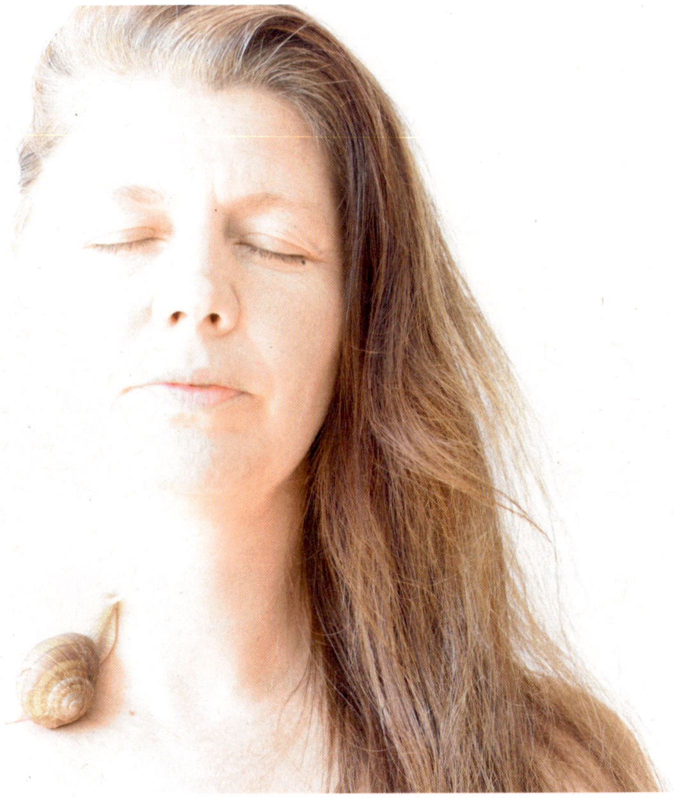

129

Fig. 129: *Self-portrait with Schŋuck* 2019, © photo: Werner Moebius, performance: Mariella Greil and Schŋuck.

for mankind's continued prosperity. The rationale for Aztec human sacrifice was, first and foremost, a matter of survival, argues John W. Verano, Professor Emeritus of Anthropology at Tulane University.[369] Reminiscent of these faint reverberations of another culture, we know that our contemporary life is full of ethical dilemmas. Today, we constantly need to be aware of violent acts of instrumentalisation and appropriation. As caring creatures, we need to reweigh each performative act. My share of this duty was to work with an awareness and a light touch though these faint reverberations, without claiming any cultural, intellectual, or ritual relevance, but while also acknowledging that these heritages of other times and cultures find me in my body and through my work. Ultimately, I aim to discuss a relational, biospheric perspective that invites involvement, civil courage, and ethico-political debate. With my artistic work, I take the heart into my hand and stand in for – as Judith Butler puts it – 'radical equality [...] affirming social and ecological interdependence'.[370]

As a choreographer and researcher, I am intrigued by embodied communication and feel drawn to its micro-phenomenological[371] density. Independent researcher Claire Petitmengin[372] developed micro-phenomenology as a new scientific discipline. She argues that this approach

> enables us to discover ordinary inaccessible dimensions of our lived experience and describe them very accurately and reliably. The development of this 'psychological microscope' opens vast fields of investigation in the educational, technological, clinical and therapeutic, as well as artistic and contemplative domains.[373]

Exploring the pre-reflective, transmodal, and gestural dimension of experience in relation to the emergence of meaning and understanding allows for a multi-layered,

369. John W. Verano, 'Where Do They Rest? The Treatment of Human Offerings and Trophies in Ancient Peru', in *Tombs for the Living: Andean Mortuary Practices*, ed. Thomas D. Dillehay (Dumbarton Oaks, 1995); see also Dave Roos, 'Did the Ancient Aztecs Really Perform Human Sacrifice?', History.com, 11 October 2018, https://www.history.com/articles/aztec-human-sacrifice-religion.

370. Judith Butler, *The Force of Nonviolence: An Ethico-political Bind* (Verso, 2020), 16.

371. See Masha Gessen, 'Judith Butler Wants Us to Reshape Our Rage', *The New Yorker*, 9 February 2020, https://www.newyorker.com/culture/the-new-yorker-interview/judith-butler-wants-us-to-reshape-our-rage. In her latest book, Judith Butler argues that 'interdependency [...] implies social equality'. At the same time, she values openness as well as ambivalence and critically draws out the difficult justification for violent self-defence in her sustainable argument for an ethic of non-violence. Butler, *The Force of Nonviolence*, 16.

372. Petitmengin is Professor Emerita at the Institut Mines-Télécom and a Member of the Archives Husserl at the École Normale Supérieure in Paris.

373. Claire Petitmengin, 'Exploring the Hidden Side of Lived Experience through Micro-phenomenology', xTalk seminar series, MIT, 2017, accessed 11 January 2020, https://openlearning.mit.edu/events/exploring-hidden-side-lived-experience-through-micro-phenomenology.

in-depth micro-phenomenological account of lived experience, focusing in particular on the fine-grained structure of experience as it unfolds in time and the moment-to-moment aspects of consciousness that are often pre-reflective or tacit. A glance, a shift in weight, a change in skin tone, a wrinkle, or a micro-gesture of the brow loom as sensate experiences, holding the irredeemable potential of bodies to generate presence – even an excess of it. In Hans Ulrich Gumbrecht's words, this is 'focused intensity', which allows us 'to really experience (*erleben*) the productive tension, the oscillation between meaning and presence'.[374] Practicing and reflecting on performativity – through the lens of micro-phenomenology as a method of artistic research, looking for tools to reveal and dismantle this notable performative dimension – feels like an exciting challenge and development that is profoundly grounded in the opening-up of the choreographic.[375] Issues of agency, contextualisation, social roles, and the distribution of power significantly constitute performativity and ultimately manifest in interdependent co-realities, which take shape through the radical immanence of embodiment, affective relationality, the potency of language, and the actualisation of the imagination. The above example, of taking the heart into the hand, was a set of performative instructions (an illocutionary and perlocutionary speech act) for a tactile interspecies encounter (or co-presence), but is also a German metaphor for being courageous. Courage wants to be experienced, and presence becomes co-corporeality. (→ Micro-phenomenological Interview with Kerstin Kussmaul, 272)

Jean-Luc Marion states, 'We can never stage an event; rather it stages us out of the initiative of its own *self* by *giving itself to us*.'[376] The gift of the moment, taking the heart into the hand, is given, handed over, passed on – it is transpassibility.

I love the passage in which philosopher Jean Luc-Nancy writes,

The heart is not an organ, and neither is it a faculty. It is: that I is broken and traversed by the other where its presence is most intimate and its life most open. The beating of the heart – rhythm of the partition of being, syncope of the

374. Hans Ulrich Gumbrecht, *Production of Presence: What Meaning Cannot Convey* (Stanford University Press, 2003), 107.

375. After developing my movement monochromes in the performance *Trilogy* (2005), I became hooked on creating micro-logics through movements and gestures, and scrutinizing their intrinsic coherences. Rooted in the ethical action of 'becoming minor' (Gilles Deleuze and Félix Guattari, *A Thousand Plateaus: Capitalism and Schizophrenia*, trans. Brian Massumi, reprint [Continuum, 2004 (1980)]) and revaluing the 'minor gesture' (Manning, *The Minor Gesture*), my interest in expanded choreography has revolved around microperformativity and nanopolitics, ultimately aiming at 'becoming revolutionary' in the sense of deterritorialising practices that stretch the imagination (through the medium of the body and movement), precisely when 'a group begins to imagine and feel things together'. Arjun Appadurai, *Modernity at Large: Cultural Dimensions of Globalization*, (University of Minnesota Press, 2005 [1996]), 8.

376. Jean-Luc Marion, 'The Event, the Phenomenon, and the Revealed', *Danish Yearbook of Philosophy* 40, no. 1 (2005): 61. (original emphasis).

sharing of singularity – cuts across presence, life, consciousness.[377]

Every heart-felt response evokes affects and causes diverse responses. On a quite different level, Jens Hauser discusses and 'switches back and forth between symbolic realm of art and the "real life" of the processes'. He proposes the term 'co-corporality' to describe the 'organic presence, with which the viewer comes into contact'.[378]

From a choreo-ethical perspective, bodily co-presence addresses the contiguous affordances of spaces and atmospheres, invites dialogue and the mutual mediation of sensory, relational engagement. In my example, all of this took place on the level of skin and texture (tactile and gustatory), but also as group dynamics (psychological), which emerged during a shared meal, with its metabolic, digestive, intellectual, and social processes. What if transmission, mediation, and processing are not restricted to biological and technical agencies, but return the question to human agency – calling for post-digital and post-human ethics, so to speak[379] – after an all-penetrating, ineradicable detour to technology and biology? What are the nanopolitical implications of such microperformative phenomena, diffractive dialogues, and negotiations – and ultimately, how will this change our being bodies? Artists – particularly body-based ones – are taking on the fundamental function and challenge of 'creating' presence – or better, of inviting in a different kind of presence, intimacy, freedom. We negotiate complex phenomenological relations with the world, which are mediated by the senses. How does the space between performativity in art and performativity in life communicate, and how do we nurture that vital zone as a relational space for experimentation? With *Choreo-ethical Assemblages*, I endeavoured to mine the deep surface and unearth narrations of bare bodies. My conception of *bare bodies*, as bodies that perform skin, attends to intensities and the choreography of the social, while interweaving imagination and materiality in a complex way. Philosopher and biologist Nicole C. Karafyllis considers skin in its mediality, regarding it 'not [as] a mere surface nor a physical container but instead as a hybrid of constantly rearranging natural and social orders'.[380] My interest is not so much in the rearranging of orders, nor am I modifying the materiality of the skin. Rather, I am modifying the materiality of how we think about skin and flesh in relation to their social meaning. Alongside the imaginary of the erotic evoked by touching skin or tasting texture, I recall Winfried Menninghaus' discussion of

377. Jean-Luc Nancy, *The Inoperative Community* (University of Minnesota Press, 1991 [1986]), 9.

378. Hauser, 'Bio Art', 89, 91.

379. Italian philosopher and author Giorgio Agamben states that new paradigms mean to think *with* and *through* rather than *about* things, arguing that 'to show a phenomenon in its original paradigmatic character means to exhibit it in the medium of its knowability'. Giorgio Agamben, 'What is a Paradigm?' August 2002, European Graduate School, transcript by Max van Manen, accessed 12 September 2019, http://www.maxvanmanen.com/files/2014/03/Agamben-What-is-a-paradigm1.pdf, 6. Therefore, post-digital means a thinking suffused with the digital, but goes beyond its confines. Similarly, my understanding of the post-human condition is rooted in an attempt to imagine other possibilities of being human.

380. Nicole C. Karafyllis, 'Endogenous Design and Biofacts: Tissues and Networks in Bio Art and Life Science', in *sk-interfaces*, ed. Jens Hauser (Liverpool University Press and FACT, 2008), 43.

'disgusting depths', where 'inner organs become visible'.[381] He later argues that 'the processing of what disgusts' constitutes 'the very "heart of the existence animating us"'.[382] In a double movement of thought, this relates to the above example of *taking the heart into the hand.* The materiality of thought (or, in other words, the material ties of thinking) manifests as something tactile and as the kinaesthetic body of the choreographic. In my work, I emphasise the ideokinetic paradigm as developed by Mabel E. Todd, a teacher of physio-mental processes, who articulated the empirical relationship between thought and movement, revealing the power that psychological and mental processes have on our physical movement and the embodiment of ideas. She writes, 'For every thought supported by feeling, there is a muscle change', and concludes, 'Through the imagination power is liberated [...]. When conditions are right, movement takes place.'[383]

For me as an artist-researcher and choreographer, the materialisation of thought is a physical, concrete *practice* that thrives on the mattering of metaphors, imagination, mindfulness, and, in general, the power of an embodied mind. In and through the project *Choreo-ethical Assemblages*, I explored the philosophical weight of choreo-ethical actions.

In the present context, I am focusing on the micro-phenomenological narration of the metabolic and metaphorical invitation that I extended to the audience during the lecture performance, proposing to imagine flesh, to touch, chew, and digest it, thereby activating the shift from spectators to *wit(h)nesses.* Based on ideas of co-poiesis and psychic trans*subjectivity, Bracha Ettinger, a visual artist, psychoanalyst, and feminist theorist of affect, has developed the concept of 'wit(h)nessing',[384] implying co-emergence in the space of the aesthetic encounter with the artwork:[385]

[T]he question of wit(h)nessing arises, where the I re-attunes itself in co-response-ability with the non- I's traces within a shared psychic space [...] where we can talk

381. Winfried Menninghaus, *Disgust: The Theory and History of a Strong Sensation* (State University of New York Press, 2003), 55.

382. Ibid., 343. Menninghaus quotes Georges Bataille, 'Attraction and Repulsion II: Social Structure', in *The College of Sociology, 1937–39*, ed. Denis Hollier, trans. Betsy Wing (University of Minnesota Press, 1988), 114.

383. Mabel Elsworth Todd and E. G. Brackett, *The Thinking Body: A Study of the Balancing Forces of Dynamic Man* (Princeton Book, 1937), 1.

384. Bracha Ettinger, *The Matrixial Borderspace* (University of Minnesota Press, 2006), 145; see also Bracha L. Ettinger 'Weaving a Woman Artist With-in the Matrixial Encounter-Event', *Theory, Culture & Society* 21, no. 1 (2004): 90.

385. Together with my colleagues Emma Cocker and Nikolaus Gansterer, I have conceptualised *practices of wit(h)nessing* that 'engage with the unfolding process [...] as a means of reconnection, the revitalising of one's engagement [...] as an enabling activity then, for re-activating heightened states of alertness, vigilance and receptivity'. Nikolaus Gansterer, Emma Cocker, and Mariella Greil, 'Practices of Wit(h)nessing', in *Choreo-graphic Figures*, 164. Drawing on Nancy's reflections on 'being-with' and the practices developed within the scope of *Choreo-graphic Figures*, I describe the impactful shift from spectator to wit(h)ness and elaborated on it in more detail in the chapter 'Between My Body and the Body of the Other' in *Being in Contact*, 87–99.

about co-response-ability and asymmetrical responsibility and coemergence-in-difference on a transsubjective level, as the time-space of encounter-event is shared by several borderlinking I(s) and non-I(s) […]. Here a copoietic jointness evolves, only inasmuch as it is transfused with compassion.[386]

The being-with in wit(h)nessing is an ethical, empathetic activity that entails thoughtfulness, curiosity about otherness, and dialogue. The metabolism[387] between ethical and choreographic agency was explored in practice through the collaborative lecture performance *Opening Up the Choreographic* and narrated with a specific focus on (micro-)performative phenomena. However, the digestion of metabolized, volatile matters of somatic perception, concrete contiguity, and affective sensations unleashes yet another level of taking the heart into the hand, on which becoming, the coming into existence of the courageous heart, turns out to be a sophisticated (maybe subtle or convoluted) process of assimilation. Let us once more take a closer look at the moments of contact with the heart – metaphorical, (corpo-)real, and metabolic. What makes it so challenging to contemplate this matter or – in the live situation of the lecture performance – to surrender to contact with the heart, opening up to becoming and touching flesh? Several phenomena come into play. First, confronting the dynamics of withdrawal inherent to bare bodies – whether in carnal lust or disgust, both evoking intimate intensities – requires courage and persistence, a willingness to remain rather than to turn away from the visceral experience of ingestion. Second, performance is a radically collaborative process, an intricate process of co-creation between performer and wit(h)ness. During the lecture performance, anonymity was not possible; instead, a shared space was actively sustained. To engage with a temporary community composed largely of strangers therefore demands trust. Finally, the metaphorical dimension of the flesh – unfolding between the concealed and the bare – emerges as a conceptual space of potentiality, situated between human and animal flesh. This dimension is laden with cultural and, indeed, ambiguous connotations – not least the metaphor of the heart. The common ground for experimentation ultimately relies on confidence in the framework of art as a potent, autonomous space for experiencing. All in all, the wit(h)ness invested in a relation to the choreographic work by *taking in* the experience of encountering the performance. This can be read as them entering into a commitment to the processuality of deeply

386. See Bracha L. Ettinger, 'Intimacy, Wit(h)nessing and Non-abandonment', Under Fire, accessed 14 March 2025, https://jordancrandall.net/main/+UNDERFIRE/site/files/q-node-562.html.

387. In the singular assemblage of participating hearts, qualitative transformations take place in both metabolic and metaphoric modality. In the above-mentioned lecture performance, it is not an either/or, but instead happens in intertwined synchronicity and ethical complexity.

The Pack

Straying towards an openness
while striving for different forms of kinship:
animalistic, animated, animistic,
anarchic beings
that stay together in a pack.
The interspace acts as connective tissue,
the exuviae of somatic ecstasy linger
on the grounds of entangled existence
and in the sharing of embodied practices.
Timefulness mothers us into
cosmopoietic œkology.

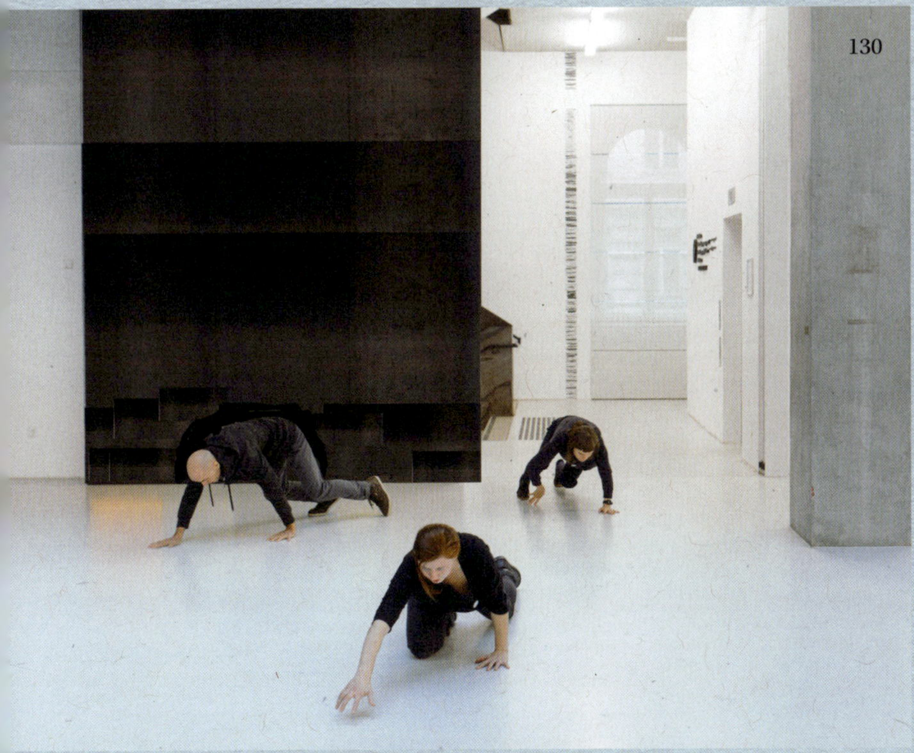

130

The pack of bodies thinks in slow lightning.
Between hot flashes and frozen shoulders,
there is trusting in our throwntogetherness.
Crawling, spawning, synchronizing,
weight shifting, spreading, happening at
the same time.
What manifests as a pride of people,
follows deep listening
to the dramaturgy of cranky bodies
and their anarchic responsibility.

empathetic meaning-making, and potentially as a willingness to embark on the qualitative transformation of sensations – the ground for exploring trans*subjectivites and trans*materialities.

Engaging with the profundity of micro-phenomenological narrations gives rise to a polylogue (→ Polylogic Labs, 178) between a range of agencies: humans, animals, organs, plants – in other words, organisms and their spheres. On a sliding scale from vitality to death, various 'alivenesses' emerge, while a shift from *biomimetic exploration* (i.e., becoming a heart) towards investigations into *heterotopic ecologies* (i.e., the courageous embodiment of cultural flesh) takes place. In the performance lecture – moving from touching the flesh to its visceral digestion – resonances of our glocal, cultural *anthropophagous practices*[388] manifested as anarchic, resilient, erotic, or symbiotic interspecies encounters. Exceeding language and sign systems altogether, the communicative abilities and intelligences of the wit(h)nesses activated vital survival forces and built on or towards organic 'ethical expertise'.[389] Microperformative entanglements and nanopolitical dimensions are nested within choreo-ethical ecologies, and the question remains of the wider implications and potential of choreo-ethics. How can we practice being an 'ethical subject'[390] – as entangled intra-actions? Actions and perceptions are always modulations of the environment, while enactive sensorimotor patterns[391] constitute the affordances of microperformatitivites. In conclusion, choreo-ethical practice might turn out to be the incessant problematising of our existence as

388. First, there were resonances with Aztec rituals, but there was also the metaphorical simmering and, ultimately, eating of the heart of the artist (metaphorically as a proxy for each of us), which was reminiscent of anthropophagy. In 2005, I collaborated with Mexican choreographer Montserrat Payro to co-create a cannibalistic fantasy that offended the director of the Catholic University in Guadalajara so much that he withdrew his sponsorship of the festival that had curated our performance (see http://www.mariellagreil.net/index.php?/project/pan-y-cebollas). Still, in a broad sense, cannibalism is a widespread ecological interplay of forces, especially in terms of cultural practices. I think of the acts of artists, curators, and cultural institutions, which consume each other as members of the same species, so to speak.

389. '[I]t is clear that an *ethical expert* is nothing more or less than a *full participant in a community*: we are all experts.' Francisco J. Varela et al. *The Embodied Mind: Cognitive Science and Human Experience* (MIT Press, 1999 [1992]), 24 (my emphasis).

390. Braidotti, 'Affirmation Versus Vulnerability', 238.

391. Sensomotoric is the biophysical and synaptic interplay between the body's sensory and motor systems. Alva Noë and J. Kevin O'Regan elaborate: 'A sensorimotor theory of perceptual experience "discussing" the idea that experience is not generated by brain processes themselves, but rather is constituted by the way these brain processes enable a particular form of "give-and-take" between the perceiver and the environment.' Alva Noë and J. Kevin O'Regan, 'What It Is Like to See: A Sensorimotor Theory of Perceptual Experience', *Synthese* 129 (2001): 79. In line with Maurice Merleau-Ponty's 'bodily subject' (*Phenomenology of Perception*, trans. Colin Smith [Routledge & Kegan Paul, 1962], 150) and what James Gibson calls 'affordances' (James J. Gibson, *The Ecological Approach to Visual Perception*, classic ed. [Psychology Press, 2015 (1979)], 119–36), Evan Thompson emphasises the enactive approach, arguing that 'autonomous agency and mode of coupling with the environment bear a constitutive relation, 'in the precise sense of that which is given to and experienced by the subject, is conditioned by the mental activity of the subject'. Evan Thompson, 'Sensorimotor Subjectivity and the Enactive Approach to Experience', *Phenomenology and the Cognitive Sciences* 4, no. 4 (2005): 407, 408. Let us recall Gibson's words: 'What we see now refers to the self, not the environment. The perspective appearance of the world at a given moment of time is simply what specifies to the observer where he at that moment.' Gibson, *The Ecological Approach to Visual Perception*, 243. In the example of the lecture performance, the wit(h)ness related the action of *taking the heart into the hand*, and *the perception of touching and chewing its texture* to the potential semantic space. The wit(h)nesses created relations between *sensing* the performative situation created by the artist – which involved a monologue, a repetitive movement sequence, and the slow cooking of the heart – and *sense-making*.

creative beings – beings fraught with pathos, passion, and passivity, as well as the wholehearted *possibilising*[392] *phenomenon* of the impossible 'ethical expertise'. It all boils down to radically and gently advocating for an assertive bodily presence and affirming interdependence – the artistic heart is already simmering.[393]

392. I prefer the verb *possibilising* as an active form, an activity, over than the noun possibilism – conveying an active occurrence! Possibilism is an area of study in cultural geography, and also a pillar of social geography today, dealing with the relations between space and society. The argument that the environment sets certain constraints, but culture is otherwise determined by social conditions, reverberates in my work of creating choreographic environments. In the framework of *Choreo-ethical Assemblages*, I collaborated with architect, sculptor, and performer Walter Lauterer. It is not a word game alone – possibilising constitutes my actual artistic practice.

393. This chapter is the edited and translated version of the text 'Choreo-ethische Assemblagen – Sozialästhetische Experimente', first published in *Heterotopien des Künstlerischen*, ed. Barbara Putz-Plecko (Edition Angewandte, De Gruyter, 2024.

In performance art, too, action is by no means to be understood as opposed to knowledge and technique. In the form of trained movements, habitualised habits or the execution of predetermined instructions (scores), it is part of a complex structure.
Action is produced by knowledge and techniques, just as new knowledge arises through experimentation and changes when techniques are interwoven.
Although the connection between knowledge and action is not a matter of course in art or everyday life, in recent years more and more artists have been addressing the question of how their art can contribute to creating new possibilities for action or new ways of linking knowledge and action.

Gerko Egert, *Performancekunst und die Politik des Handelns* (transcript, 2013), 28–29.

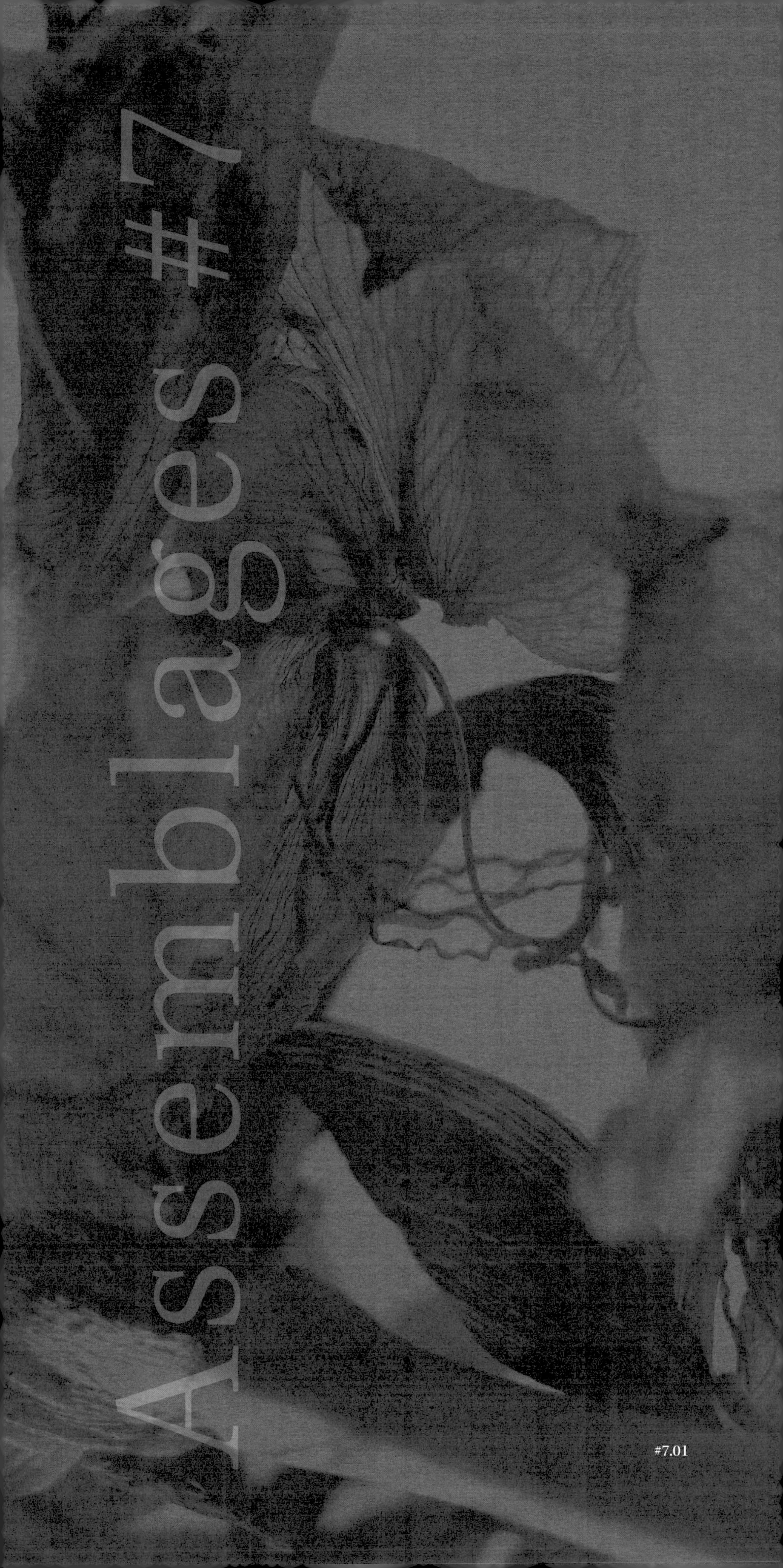
Assemblages #7
#7.01

#7.02

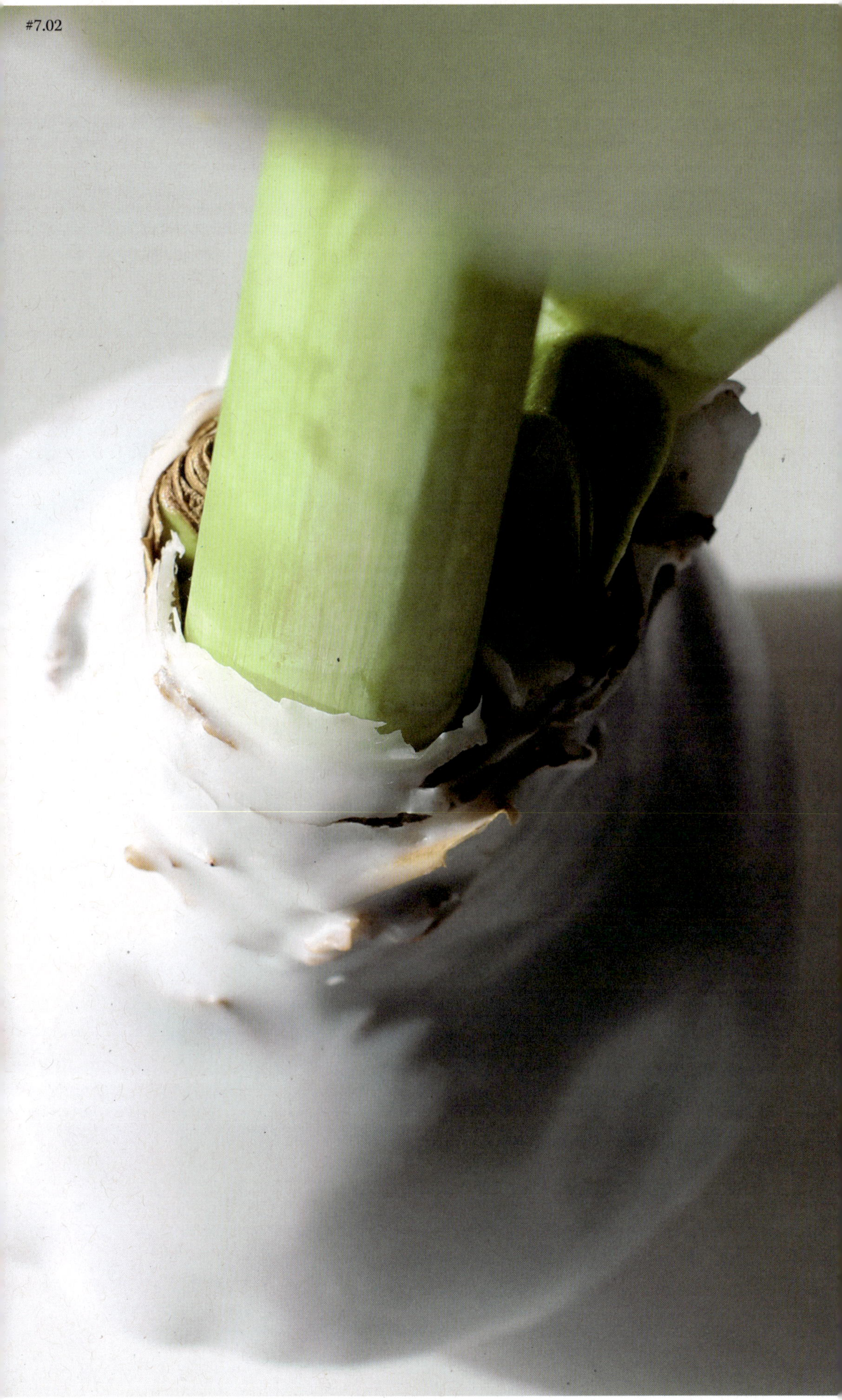

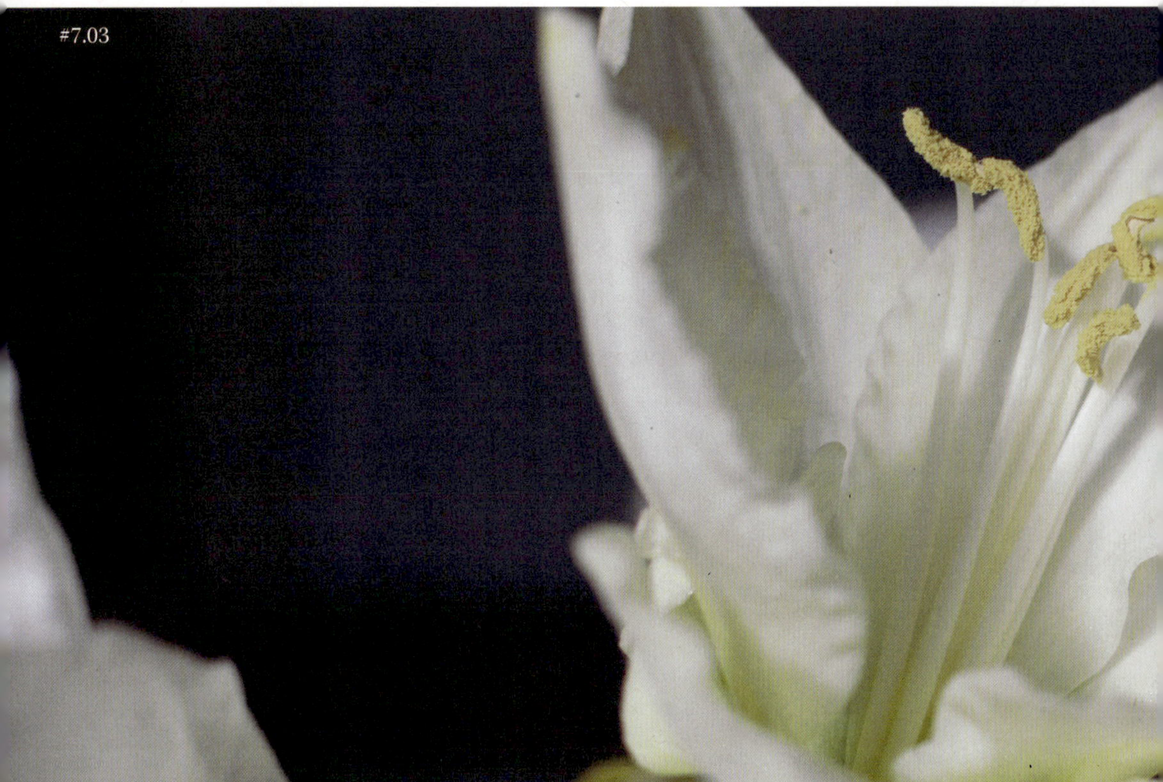
#7.03

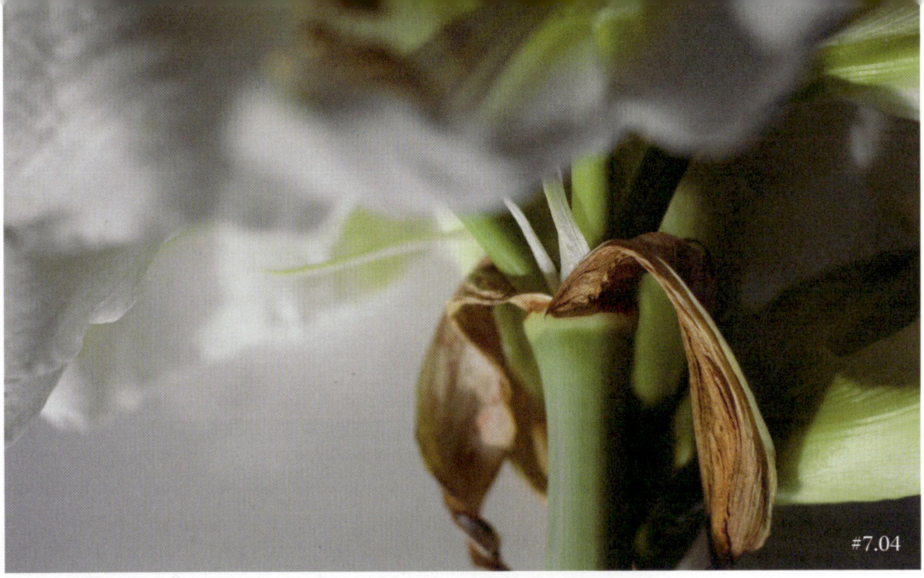

#7.04

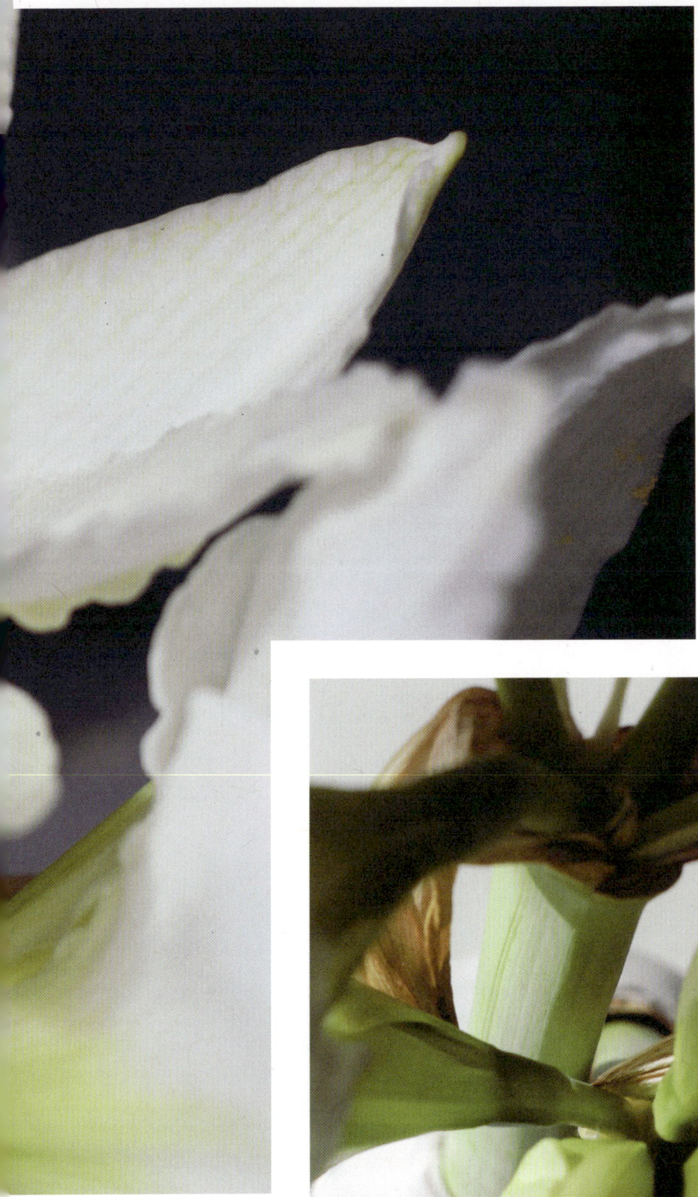

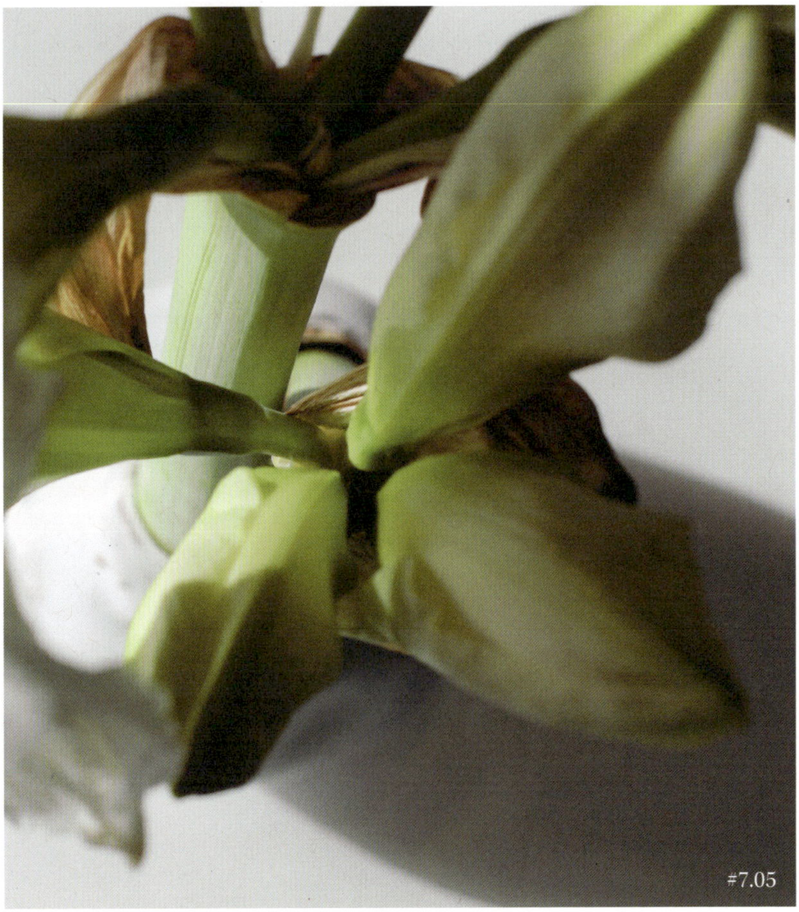

#7.05

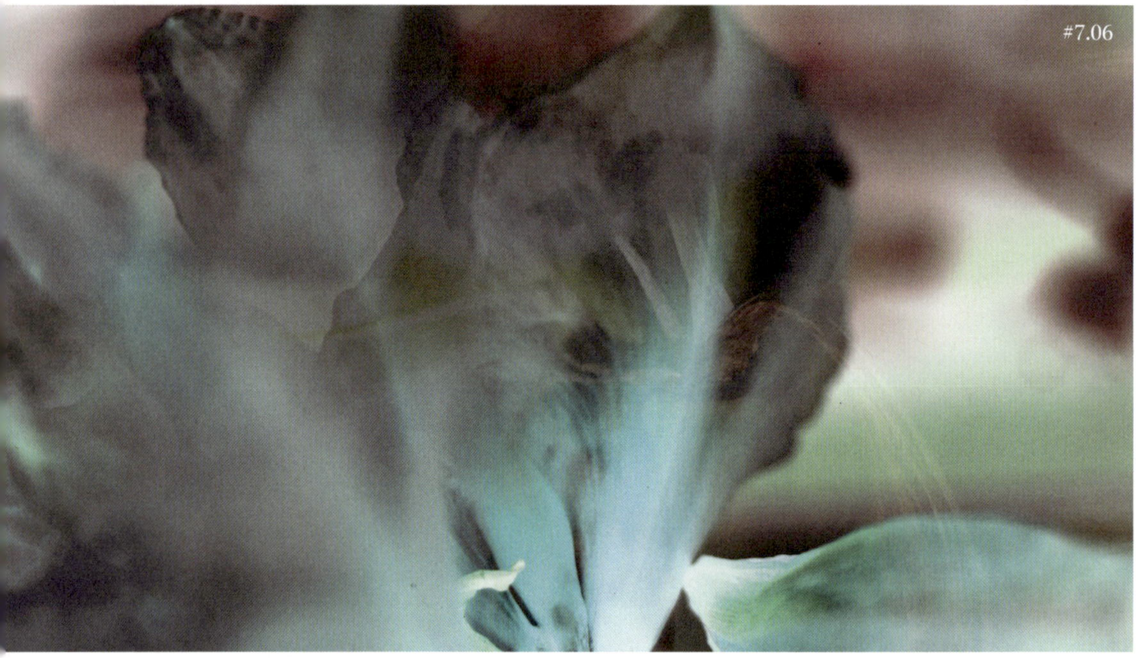
#7.06

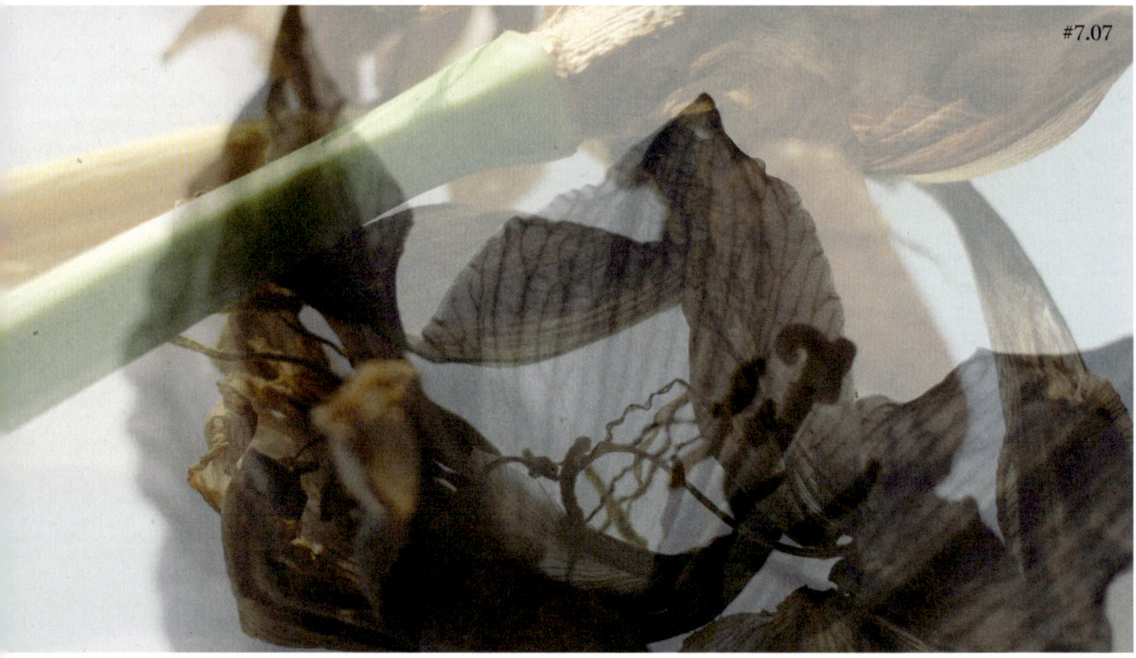
#7.07

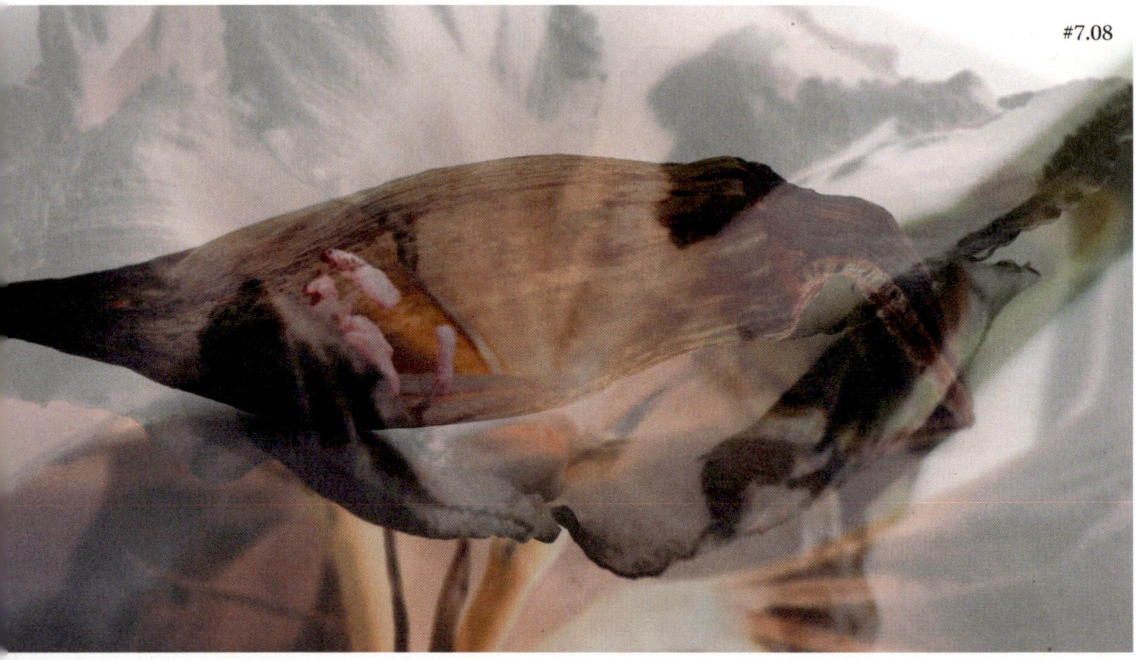
#7.08

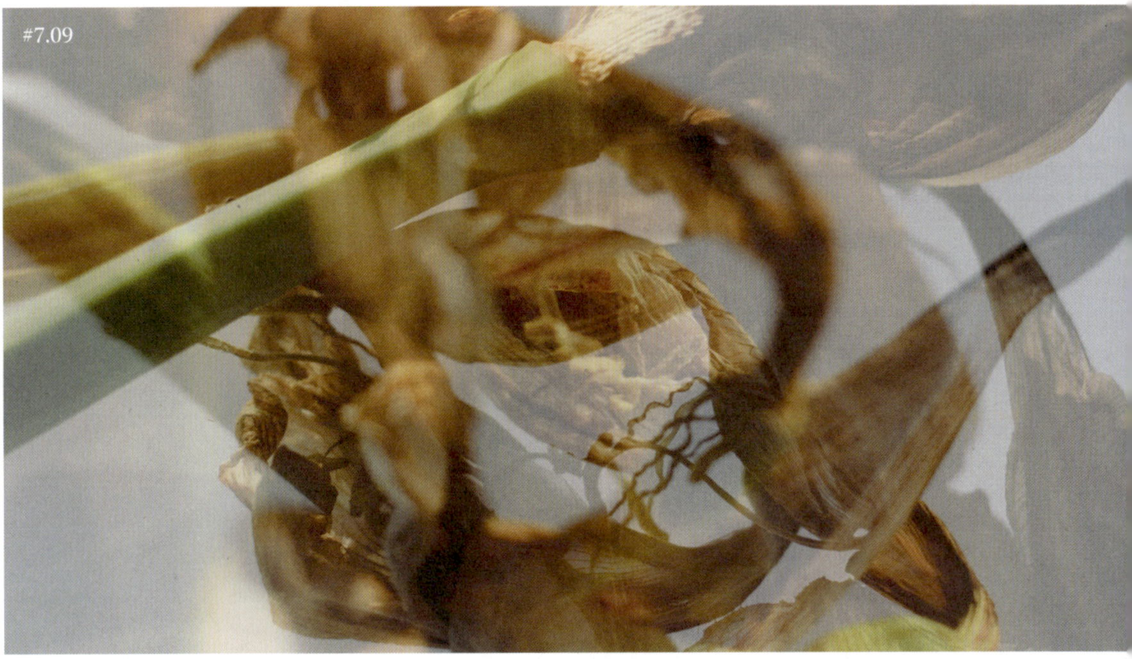
#7.09

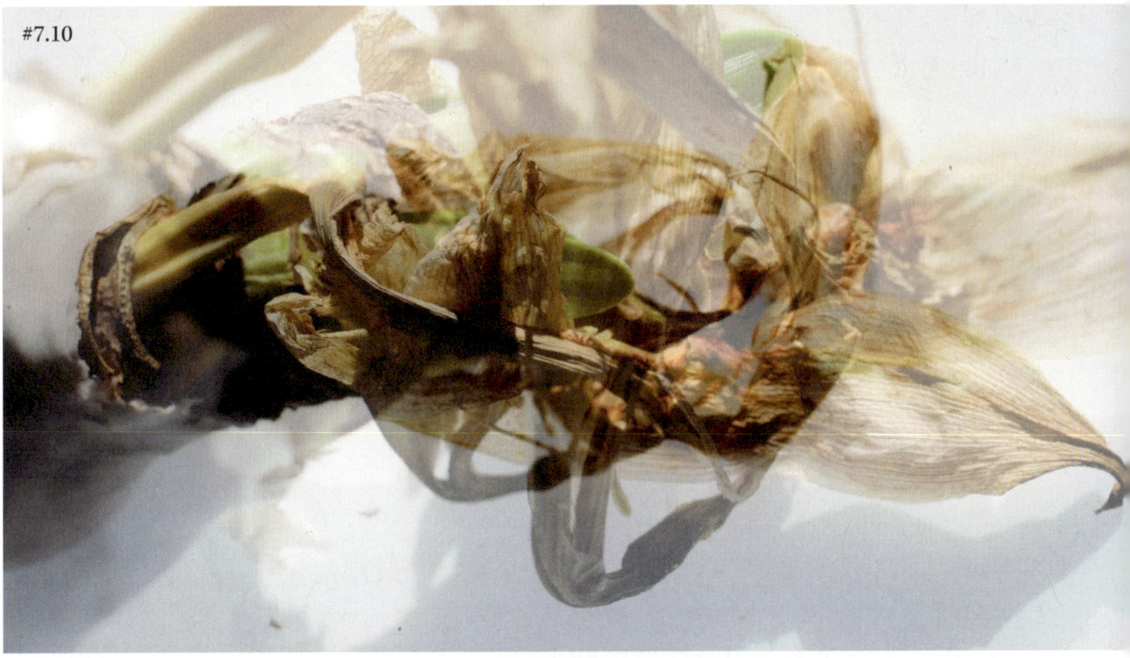
#7.10

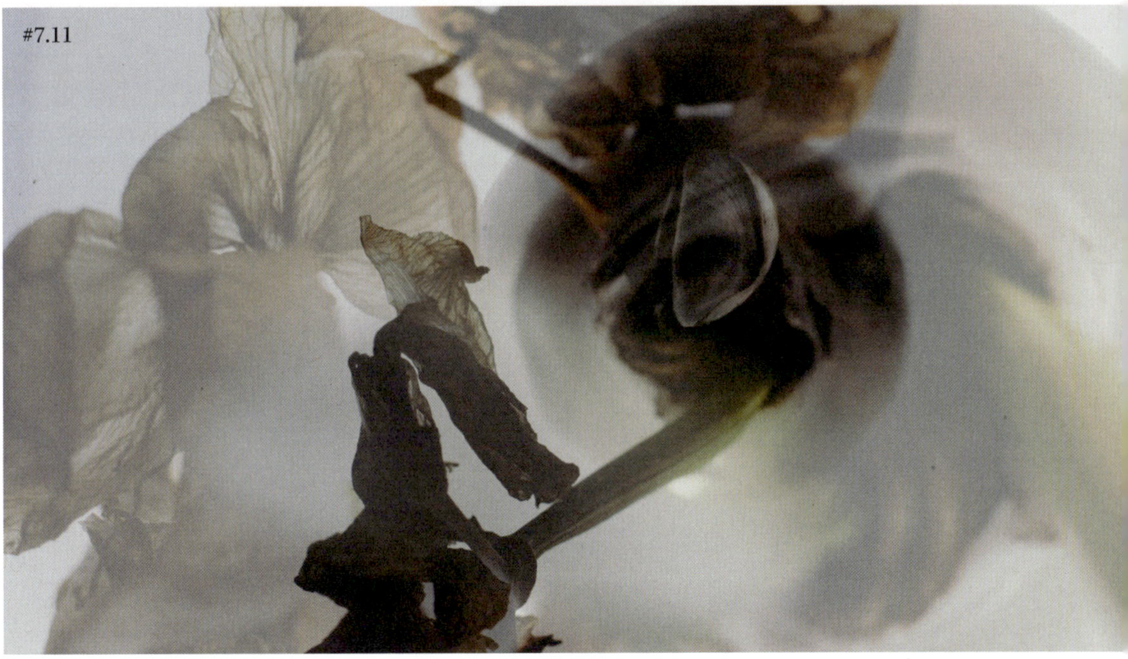
#7.11

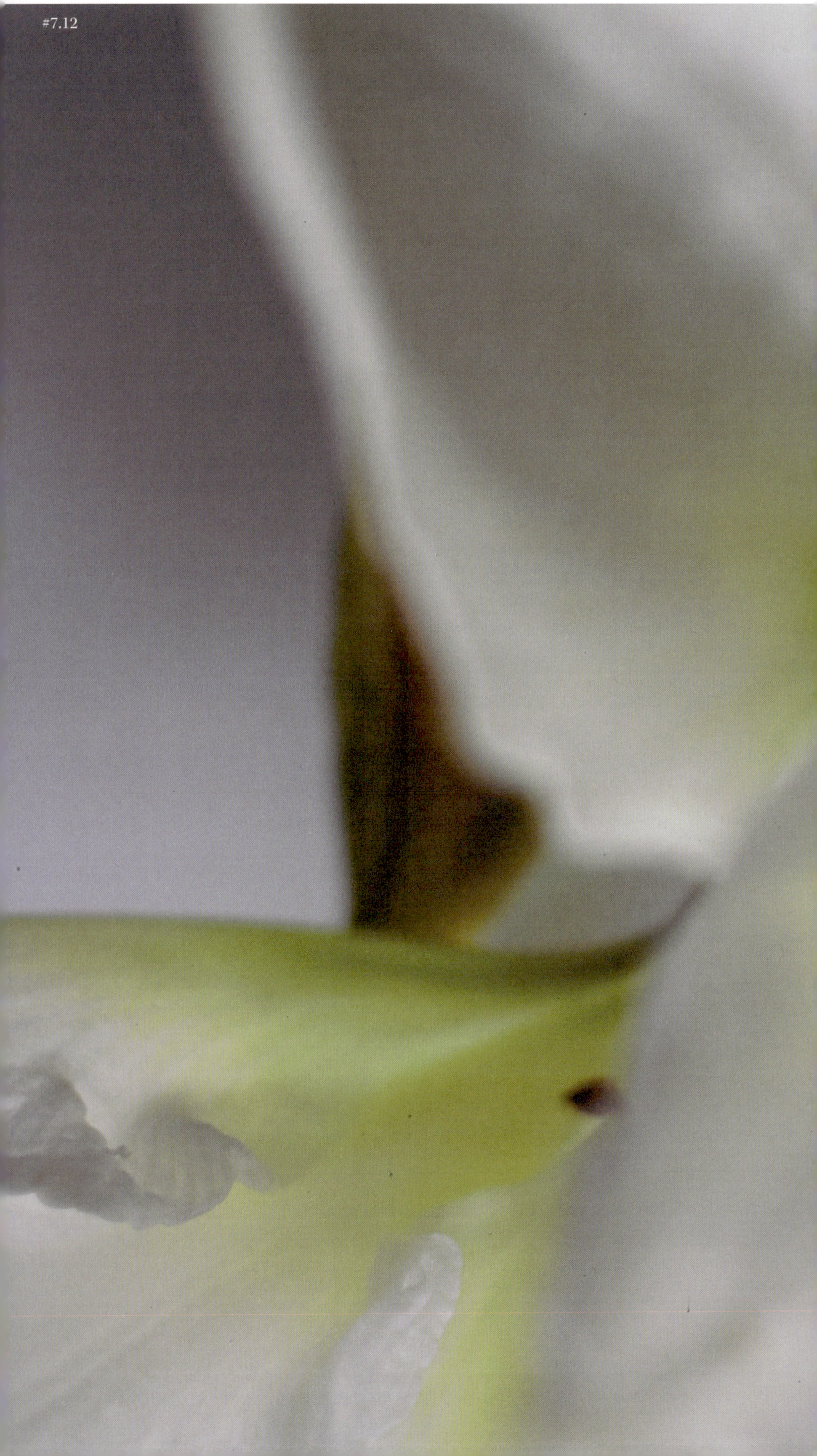
#7.12

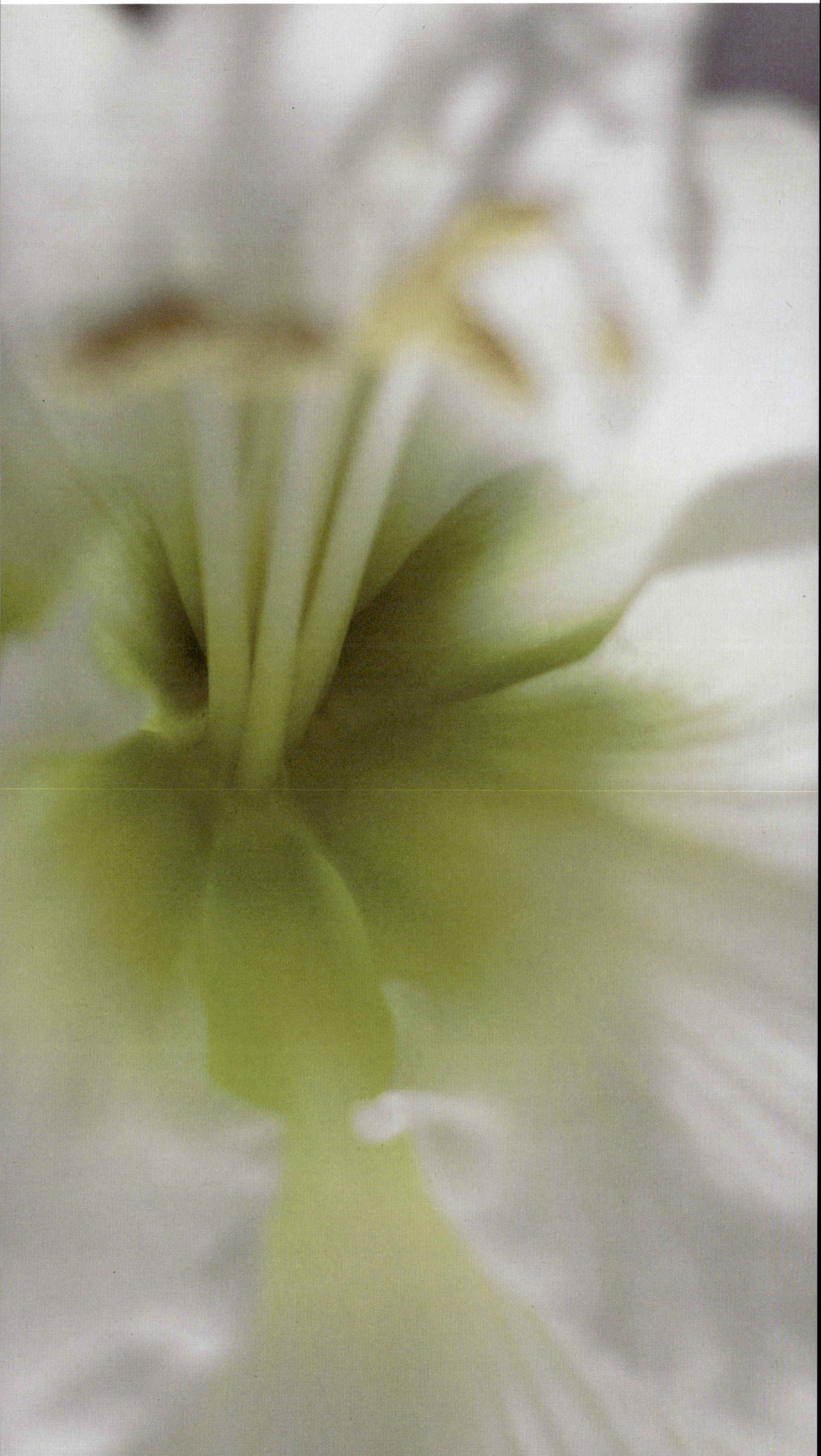

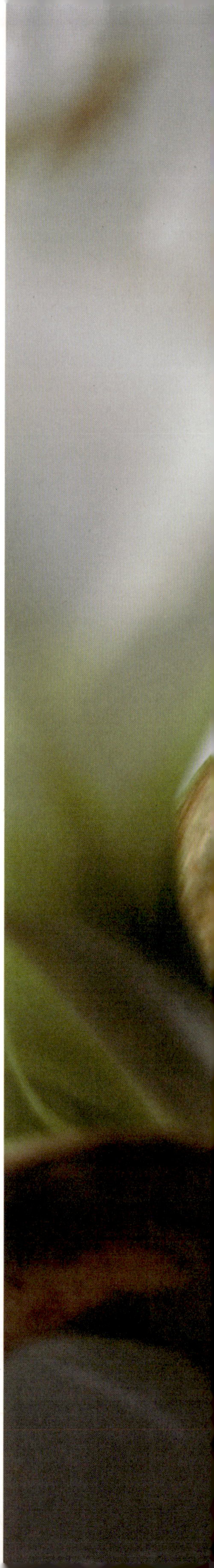

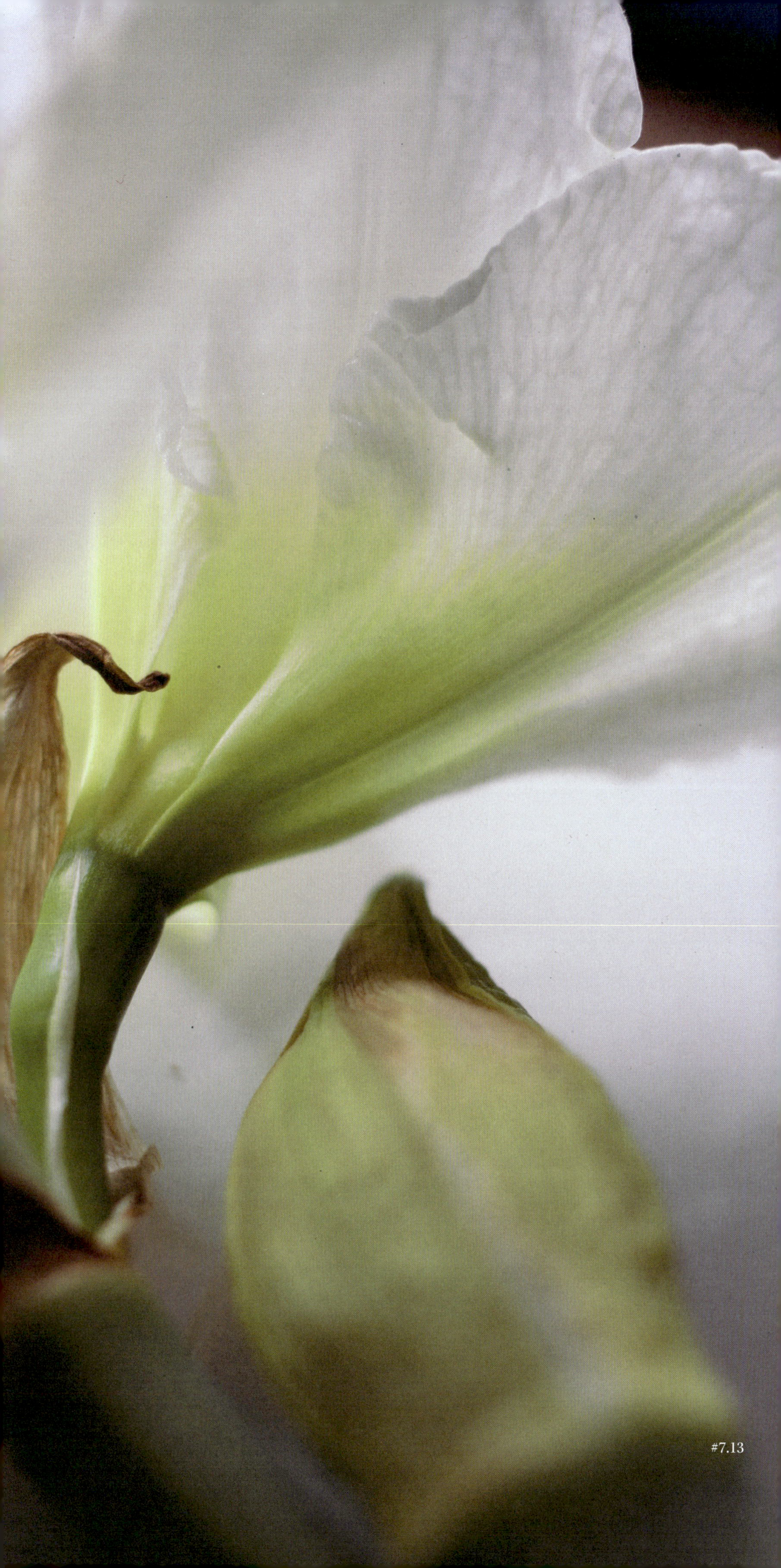

#7.13

#7.14

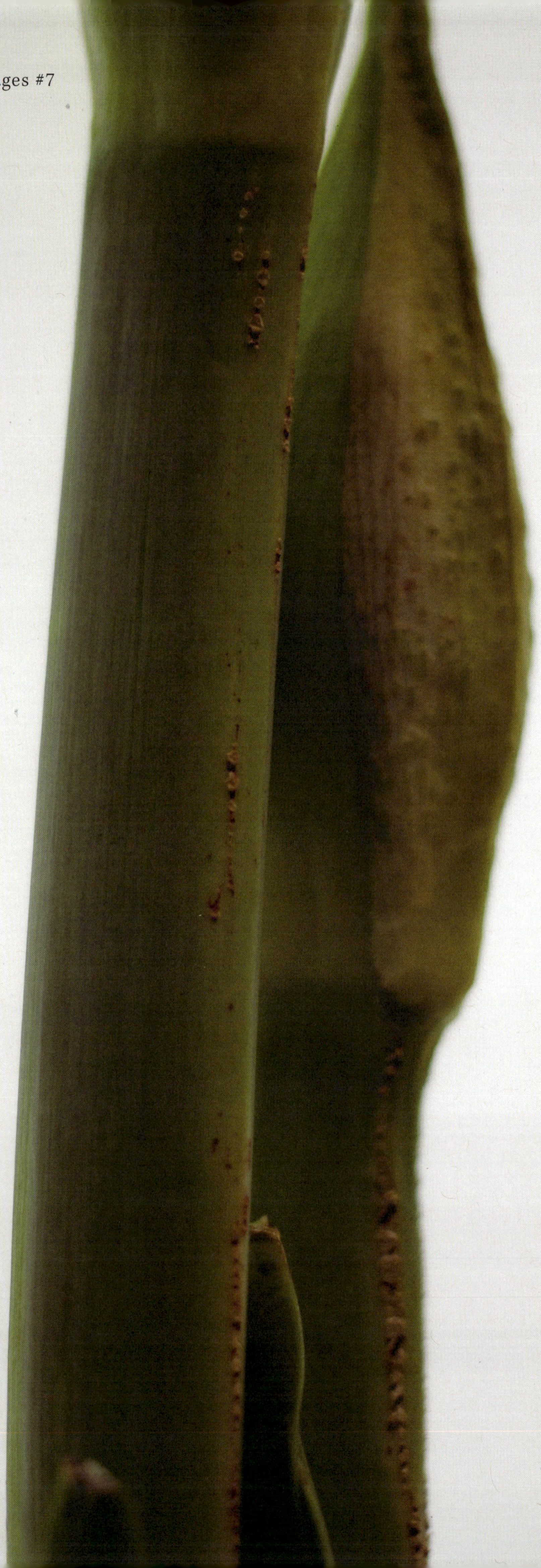

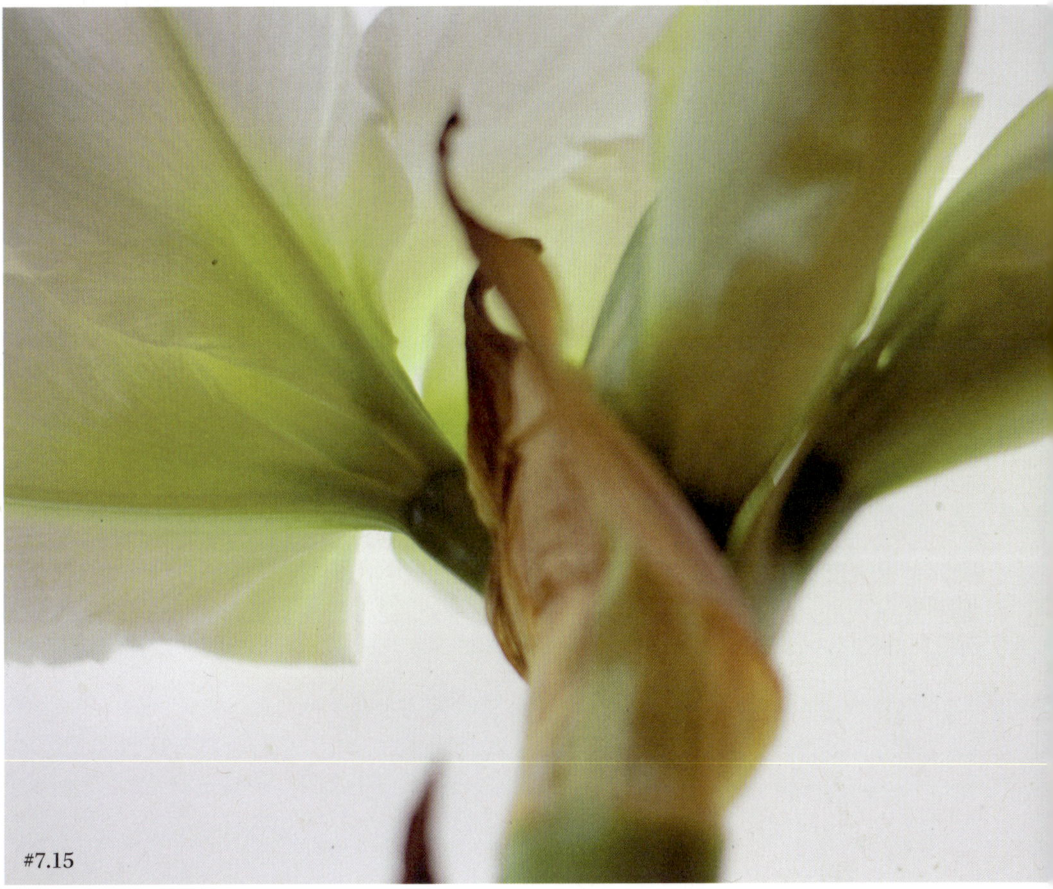

#7.15

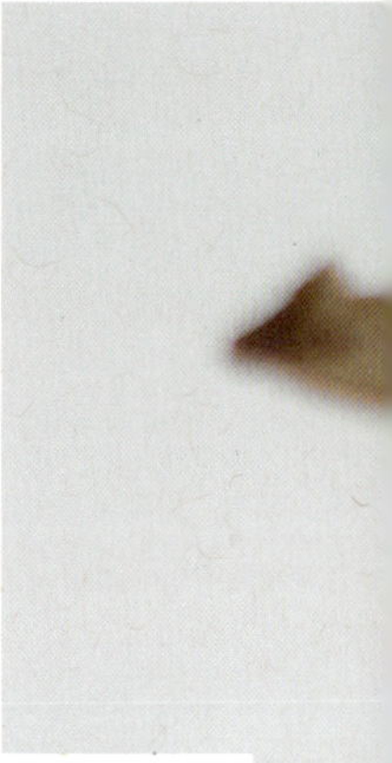

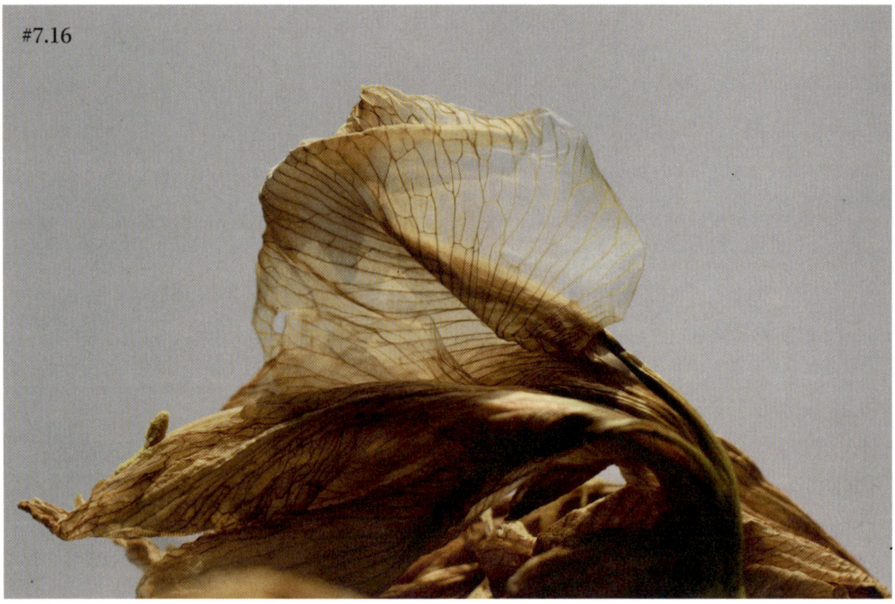
#7.16

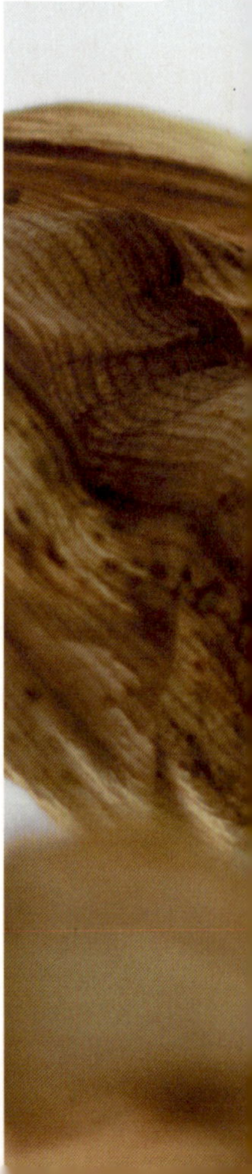

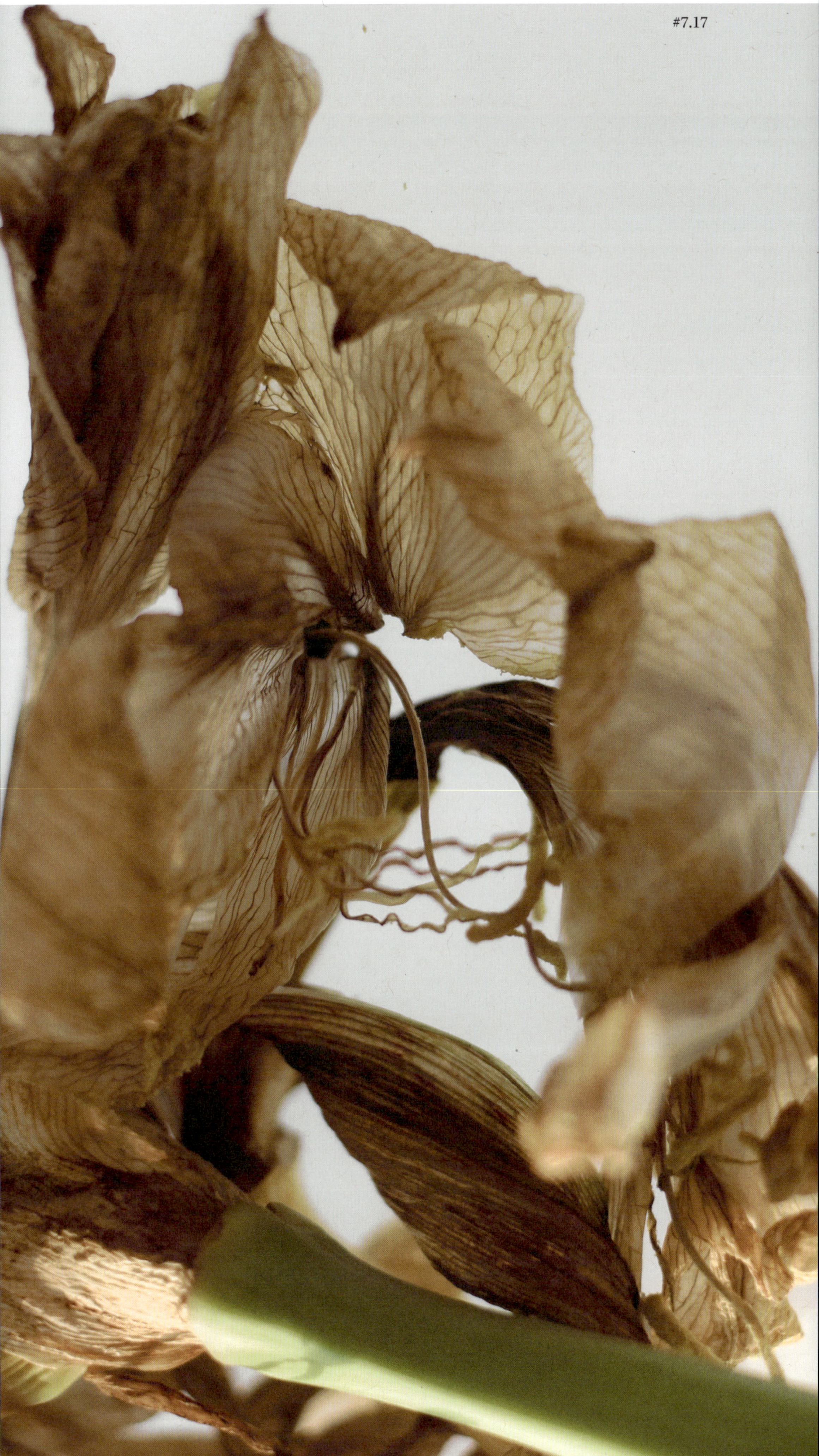
#7.17

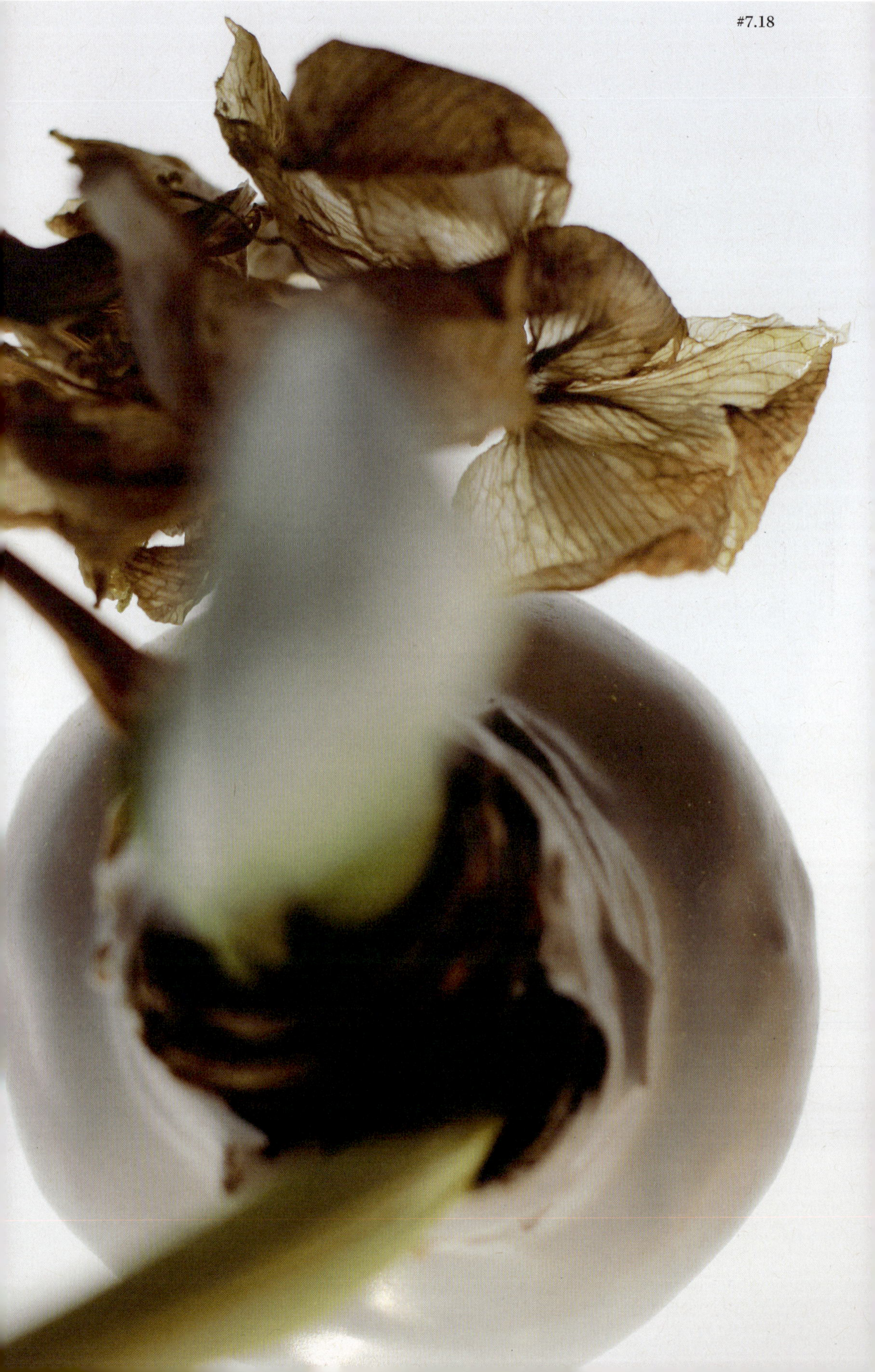

#7.18

#7.01: *Amaryllisation*, 2024, © photo: Mariella Greil and Simona Koch.

#7.02–#7.05: *Amaryllisation*, 2024, © photos: Mariella Greil.

#7.06: *Amaryllisation*, 2024, © video still: Mariella Greil and Simona Koch.

#7.07: *Amaryllisation*, 2024, © video still: Mariella Greil.

#7.08: *Amaryllisation*, 2024, © video still: Mariella Greil and Simona Koch.

#7.09–#7.18: *Amaryllisation*, 2024, © photos and video stills: Mariella Greil.

Choreo/ethical Relations and Diffractive Dialogues

Singularities are turning points and points of inflection; bottlenecks, knots, foyers, and centres; points of fusion, condensation and boiling; points of tears and joy, sickness and health, hope and anxiety, 'sensitive' points.[394]
Gilles Deleuze

We know that it is impossible to fully capture the *sensitive points* that have been touched or to make *embodied* experiences, encounters, and dialogues tangible in a book, and yet this book is a matter close to my heart. I feel the urgency and have the hope that, despite it all, it has been possible to describe and capture some of the processes and reflections in an accessible manner, though I remain fully aware of its partial nature. In this concluding chapter, I will make an attempt to summarise what this research process has meant for those engaged in it and how it might contribute to our future worldings. While there are probably not so many people who have encountered an artistic research lab set-up, embodied research in particular has an ephemeral quality and faces the challenge of how to process trans*subjective encounters. In micro-phenomenology, I have found an effective tool to make tangible the countless, infrathinly sliced fractals of experiences. The psychological magnifying glass of micro-phenomenological conversation techniques has proven to be a reliable instrument for expanding perception and clarifying the shifts that take place as we live and experience a moment.

So, *how* do choreo-ethical relations unfold through the practice of diffractive dialogue? Which methodologies really do go beyond arbitrary compilation or juxtaposition and instead become entangled with and refract practices, theories, and embodied agencies? In my research, the *in-between* of performance, philosophy, and therapy has been the site where such dialogues unleash their power: a polylogics of voices and bodies, and the time spent together echo in my collection of residues – the artefacts produced and epistemic objects.[395] It has been a collective effort across agents to prevent collapse into presumptions, sloppy consensus, or subsumption. In particular when the politics of touch came into play, the engagement with the degrees of human and other-than-human dignity emerged in all its complexity.

The prepared choreographic environment was a welcoming landing site for the various materials and bodies, which all came with their own idiosyncrasies and, of course, different modes of enquiry as well as diverse understandings of what defines a finding or insight. These findings ranged from hammering on a rotten pomegranate to becoming dangerously entangled with a screen while deep-dive dancing in the liquid void and source of all life forms – water. My artistic research practice involved feeding SCOBYs and providing palliative care for their collective bodies when they were facing desiccation as they transformed into artworks. In another

394. Gilles Deleuze, *The Logic of Sense*, trans. Mark Lester with Charles Divale (Columbia University Press, 1990), 52.

395. See → Assemblages #1–#5, 15, 81, 141, 189, 259.

Figs. 131–134: *Family Reunion*, co-created with Philipp J. Ehmann within the scope of the INTRA project *Withdrawing the Performer*, hosted by Jasmin Schaitl and Charlotta Ruth at Angewandte Performance Laboratory (APL), 2021, © photo: Mariella Greil, performance: Mariella Greil and Philipp J. Ehmann.

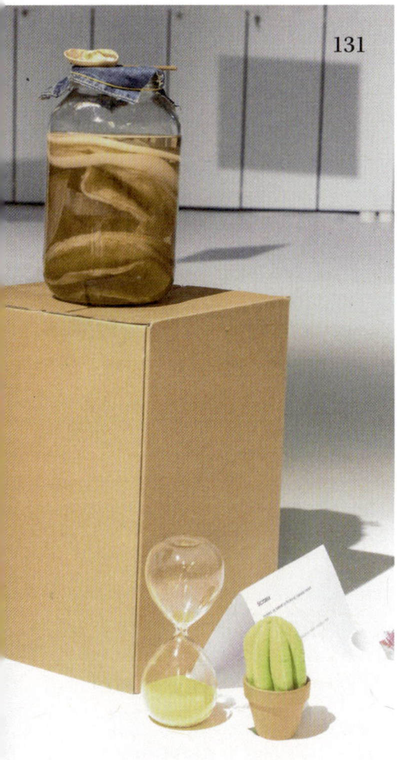

131

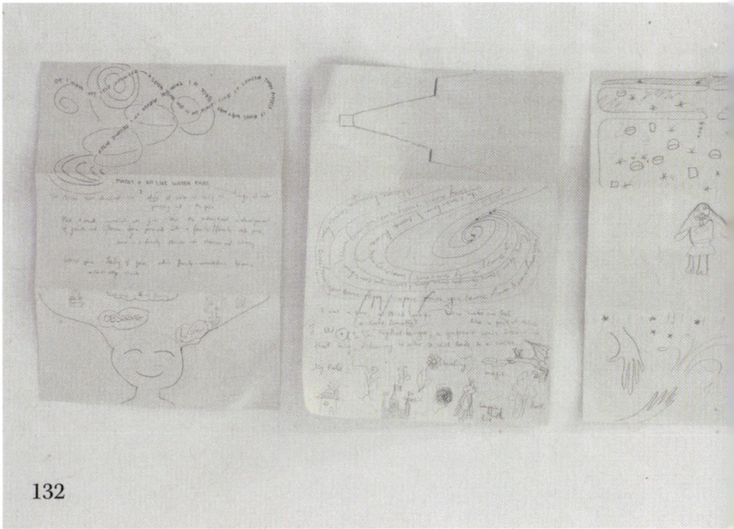

132

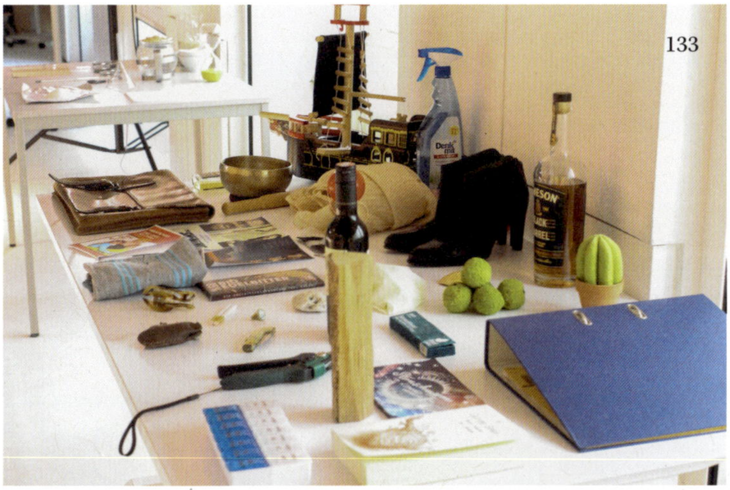

133

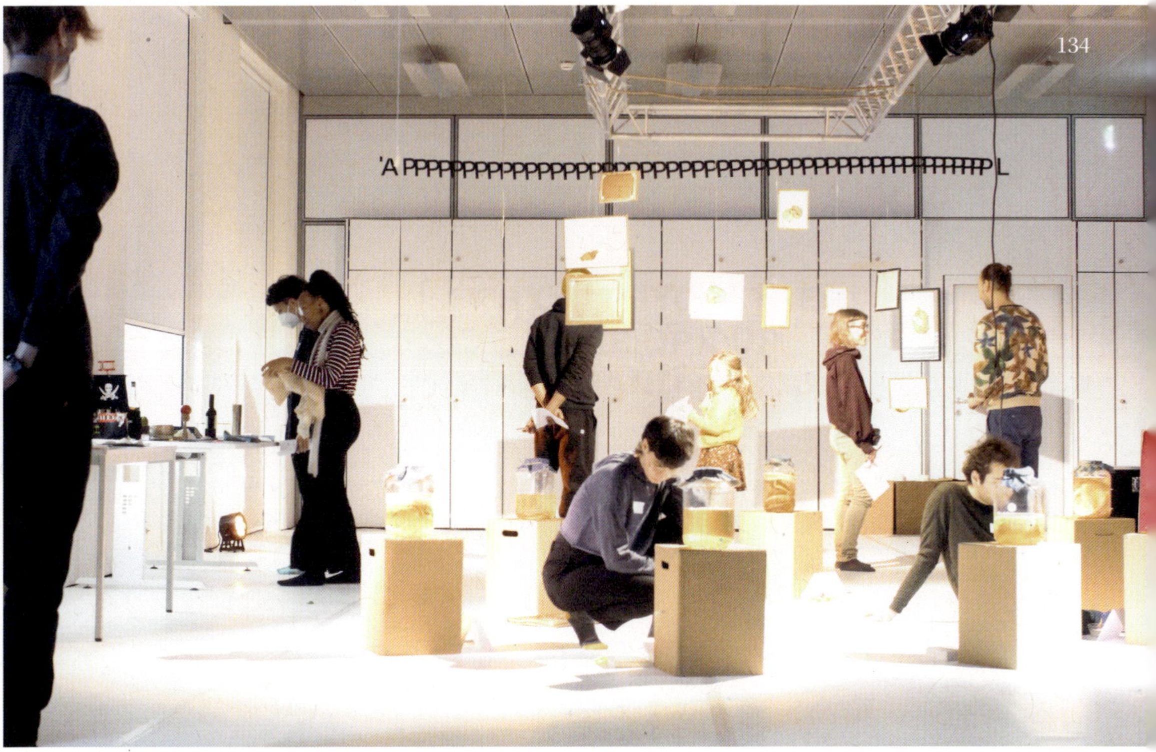

134

work step, I portrayed them, reprocessing and developing their stories. Through a mix of deep listening and fiction, I came up with names, attributions, multi-layered characters for the twelve SCOBYs. Some of these SCOBY portraits were also the protagonists of the participatory game performance, *family reunion.*[396]

I spent time with SCOBYs, drawing them and dancing for them. I also danced for and with the Naked Lady (as the Amaryllis is referred to in Great Britain). Through these contemplative practices, I refined my understanding of the differentiation between *nude*, *naked*, and *bare* bodies, learning from this plant and gaining profound and nuanced insights into life cycles. The findings of these research processes are documented in the collected volume that I edited, *Bare Bodies – Thresholding Life* (Edition Angewandte, De Gruyter, 2024).

Now, as I circle back through these methodological issues, I will highlight the singularities that became operative in this research project and will reflect on the modes of sense-making as well as meaning-making that have emerged across the choreo-ethical assemblages enacted throughout this enquiry. My guiding question was: Which *modes of singularity* operate within an artistic enquiry – based on diffractive dialogue practices and encounters in Polylogic Labs – between the lines of performance, philosophy, and therapy? Singularities, as they emerged in my research, were formed by collectively felt contingencies. They arose as *transversal intensities*, moments where embodied research found itself untethered from predetermined categories and instead generated unforeseen articulations in the in-between. They formed dances between disciplines; amid a range of material manifestations, in intervals, they appeared less as essences than as vectors – *points of inflection, where an assemblage revealed its heterogeneity without reducing itself to unity.* These presences resonate with what William Forsythe has said about dance as a living being: 'You can't force it, you can't bring it to you. You have to make yourself perceptible and then it will come.'[397] Here, Forsythe describes not the conventional understanding of dance techniques to be mastered but a mode of *becoming receptive*, of *attuning oneself to* what exceeds volition. The image he evokes here of dance as a creature one cannot command articulates the ethics of relationality that has guided my research. If you grip too hard, you will lose it, for this practice is required to cultivate levity, tenderness, and a soft focus. Likewise, diffractive dialogues cannot be summoned at will. They occur when attention is focused on relational field conditions, when one's own perceptual field is permeable enough to allow alterity to enter. Singularities thus mark those instances where the research process encounters its own strangeness, where something other than recognition takes place.

396. This work was co-created with Philipp J. Ehmann and presented in the futuristic '12th November 2102' scenario at the gallery of our ancestors in within the scope of the INTRA project *Withdrawing the Performer*, hosted by Jasmin Schaitl and Charlotta Ruth at Angewandte Performance Laboratory (APL; 2021/22).

397. Original: 'Du kannst es nicht zwingen, du kannst es nicht zu dir holen. Du musst dich selbst wahrnehmend machen, und es kommt.' Quoted in Peter Sinapius, 'Where You Are, There Is a Space for Me', in *Bildstörung: Künstlerische Projektarbeit in der Kinder- und Jugendpsychiatrie*, ed. Martin Böhm, Andreas Romberg, and Peter Sinapius (Claus Richter, 2012), 13–14.

The meaning-making that accompanies such singularities is not anchored in the individual subject; instead, it emerges through *polylogics*, which involve the interweaving of more than one discourse, more than one register of meaning.

They instantiate what could be referred to as excessive sensory research: an intuiting of iterative coherence as entanglements emerge and resonances reverberate. In *Choreo-ethical Assemblages*, residues from one encounter formed the beginning of another exchange. Polylogic exchanges in the lab, for me – as I was (together with the other presences in the choreographic environment) a constant agent in this field – challenged me to remain open to the various forms of contact with the prepared environment, to question the methods, to reflect on choreo-ethics. I practiced and analysed these exchanges through microphenomenological interviews, which allowed participants to experience themselves as complex sensing nodes in a multiplicity. What arose was less an articulation of identity than a performative practice of co-constitution: subjects emerged as trans*subjectivities, entangled across human and nonhuman agencies, materialities, and temporalities.

It is here that the question of selfhood becomes central. How can a sense of self beyond defined individual identity emerge through relational dynamics, diverse logics, and the co-constitution of trans*materialities? How does selfhood perform in the plural – and how do these selves relate to others, to other others, and also to each other? The diffractive dialogues provided a provisional answer: the selves appeared both as bound entities and as *relational remainders*. Recognizing and sensing the plural selves in the negotiation with others therefore began not with validation but through the disorientation of being immersed in polylogics. Indeed, much of the work during the diffractive dialogues consisted in *working one's way around difficulties* – misunderstandings, confusions, discomfort, at times ignorance, or the intimidating intensity of sudden proximity. Rather than smoothing over these frictions, the research framework valued them as generative moments. Instead of being clearly validated, the selves were stretched through opacity.

In this sense, philosopher and art historian Georges Didi-Huberman's notion of singularity as a complex, multiple generator of *strangeness*[398] becomes highly relevant. Singularities unfold through the intensities of divergence, functioning as sites of encounter with the strange and the irreducible other, beyond the logic of identity. This aligns with Deleuze's earlier theorization of singularities, especially in *Difference and Repetition*,[399] where he posits singularities not as objects or subjects but as differential events that structure the real without fixing it. For Deleuze, singularities are the topological points around which multiplicities organize themselves without closure. Translated into my research, singularities in choreoethical assemblages are the moments where embodied practices generate unexpected alignments or disjunctions, where difference itself becomes operative as the very precondition of relation.

398. Georges Didi-Huberman, quoted in André Lepecki, *Singularities: Dance in the Age of Performance* (Routledge, 2016), 6.

399. Gilles Deleuze, *Difference and Repetition, trans.* Paul Patton (Continuum, 2004 [1968]).

Didi-Huberman expands on this by emphasizing the *affective and aesthetic dimension of singularities*:[400] they confront us with strangeness, calling on us to inhabit rather than dissolve it. In this sense, the practice of diffractive dialogue is about more than consensus or mutual understanding – it is about cultivating the capacity to endure dissonance, to generate an ethics of togetherness without sameness. The relational difficulty – the intimidation we might feel when there is too much closeness, the bewilderment of not knowing how to understand the other – becomes the very fabric of the choreo-ethical field.

From here, the bridge to my own embodied practice emerges most clearly. Choreo-ethical assemblages are not blueprints but laboratories of singularity. They host and give shape to the polylogics of sense-making across artistic research and also expand into cosmopoietic œkologies – something that is of considerable importance to me – making worlds by understanding the *oikos,* the home or habitat, the living conditions or the grounds that host a space for our plural selves. In her monograph *Tausend Subjekte: Der radikal pluralistische Subjektbegriff im kritischen Posthumanismus und bei A. N. Whitehead* (A Thousand Subjects: The Radically Pluralist Concept of the Subject in Critical Posthumanism and A. N. Whitehead),[401] philosopher Isabella Schlehaider discusses the generative provocation of categories and concepts of agency, sociality, subjectivity, and objectivity. I feel affinities with her thinking, for the shift I propose towards trans*subjectivities and trans*materialities stems from similar grounds and observations. I find another kinship with Schlehaider in the fact that she also draws on posthumanist approaches to nature that go beyond simplifying dichotomies in order to reconceptualize what she calls 'political ecology beyond romanticisation or objectification'.[402] This resonates with how I conceptualise *cosmopoietic œkology.*

As far as I know, there has not yet been a model for embodied research as *cosmopoietic œkology*, so my quest into choreo-ethics served as a valid starting point. My embodied research is rooted in practice and theory in equal shares and draws on philosophy, performance, and psychotherapy. I began to experiment by merging practices from these three fields, in which I have a longstanding professional practice and from which I also source material as an artist researcher. Just like when a stone falls into water, the field expanded outwards in concentric circles through the use of the 'Diffractive Dialogue Score' with experts from these three fields. Together, the dialogue partners I invited to participate covered quite a range of expertise across these professional fields. This specific artistic enquiry thus operates less as a method of producing knowledge than as a method of cultivating modes of relation that manifest in both practices and reflections. Embodiment, for me, is more than just the medium – it is the precondition for such relations; it is

400. Didi-Huberman, quoted in Lepecki, *Singularities*, 6.

401. In 2024, I shared an evening with Isabella Schlehaider hosted by theatre studies scholar and performer Iris Julian at Depot marking the presentation of our three books. I found this, and a follow up exchange together with artist Kristoffer Stefan inspiring. Isabella Schlehaider, *Tausend Subjekte: Der radikal pluralistische Subjektbegriff im kritischen Posthumanismus und bei A. N. Whitehead* (Ibidem, 2021).

402. Ibid.

through the lived body, with all its vulnerabilities and intensities, that generative strangeness can be encountered, negotiated, and shared.

The research question also invites us to consider the generational continuity of these practices. The mode of singularity I have described – diffractive, polylogic, trans*material – does not remain bound to my research and is available to other artistic and research trajectories. This is evident in the work of Backpulver, a next-generation research collective whose project is to develop peer feedback frames[403] and that explicitly takes up the threads of diffractive dialogue. Their work is less focused on choreo-ethical assemblages; however, I see them as advocates for peer exchange and have been invited to contribute to, and witness how they engage in, community-building and collectivity on several occasions.

In closing this first part of the final chapter, I want to emphasize that the practice of choreo-ethical assemblages invites continued engagement with the difficulties and potentials of encountering the other, whether human or more-than-human. Choreo-ethical assemblages insist on the value of diffractive methodologies that embrace and cultivate tools for embodied research, such as movement research, attunement, and dialogic practice or micro-phenomenology. I am convinced, and this was confirmed in my exchange with dialogue partners, that through embodied research, choreo-ethical assemblages can pave the way for future forms of togetherness, where radical modes of singularity and encounters with strangeness continue to generate unforeseen articulations as choreo-ethical relations.

The Choreographic Environment as Cosmopoietic Œkology

Where in these fraught political moments are the tender and raw places between mere resistance and speculative futures; between the infra and the para; between a subversion that disrupts but does not change an established order, and a fugitivity that riskily composes new worlds in weird fidelities with the not-yet-legible; where new forms of care, new forms of belonging, and new cosmogonies are being born?[404]

Bayo Akomolafe

By shifting the focus from the choreographed body to the contained choreographic environment, the emphasis moves towards an 'ethics of materialization'.[405] The choreographic environment becomes a matrix[406] for cosmopoietic *œkology*. A matrix can mean a generative ground or medium – something that holds and gives form, like the womb. Both environments offered a form of *containment*. With the

403. See Backpulver, 'Unclear Definitions', Research Catalogue, accessed 4 October 2025, https://www.researchcatalogue.net/profile/show-exposition?exposition=2623760.

404. Bayo Akomolafe, LinkedIn, 23 February 2025, https://www.linkedin.com/posts/bayoakomolafe_where-in-these-fraught-political-moments-activity-7299070191009730561-MJLC.

405. Stephan Trinkaus, *Ökologien Des Prekären: Zu Einer Theorie Des Haltens* (transversal texts, 2022), 176.

406. 'Matrix', etymonline, accessed 13 September 2025, https://www.etymonline.com/word/matrix.

Greetings,
the family committee

PS:
As with all biological entities change is constant and your current form may diverge from previous forms.
Therefore we ask to give yourself a name and describe yourself:

Welcome to our family reunion!

Dear family members,

We wish to cordially invite you to our yearly family reunion. It will take place in the **gallery of our ancestors** at Georg-Coch-Platz on **12th November 2102**.

There will be drinks and refreshments. You will have the possibility to **recharge your symbiosis** in the kitchen, before you visit and commune with your ancestors. Attached you will find a short form of conduct, please consider it.

Greetings,
the family committee

PS:
As with all biological entities change is constant and your current form may diverge from previous forms.
Therefore we ask to give yourself a **name** and **describe yourself**:

135

light, suspended architectural structure and the layers of transparent fabric (designed and co-developed with Walter Lauterer), the layering of the fabric and the round structure created a warm, womb-like feeling. The other two habitats we explored were aquatic, which might indeed be an echo of or a longing for the prenatal ability to float freely in amniotic fluid. While the first choreographic environment functioned more like a *framing*, the second demanded full immersion in the *medium*.

Stefan Trinkaus writes, 'Framing is a radically relational event, part of the relational dimension of every practice, every appearance.'[407] The hyphenation of *being-in* as *being-in-the-medium* or *being-in-the-environment* already emphasizes the relational, bonding aspect of a being that leans towards the other. Let me first discuss the work of Hans Rainer Sepp and Jaco Kruger, before delving deeper into cosmopoietic œkology, the term I propose. Philosopher and German literary studies scholar Hans Rainer Sepp has developed the notion of *oikology* as an integrative from of knowledge. Interestingly, he clearly takes the body as the basis of experience

407. Original: 'Rahmung ist ein radikal relationales Geschehen, Teil der relationalen Dimension jeder Praxis, jedes Erscheinens.' Stephan Trinkaus, *Ökologien Des Prekären*, 75.

Fig. 135: *Welcome Play Score* for *Family Reunion*, co-created with Philipp J. Ehmann within the scope of the INTRA project *Withdrawing the Performer*, hosted by Jasmin Schaitl and Charlotta Ruth at Angewandte Performance Laboratory (APL), 2021, © design: Mariella Greil and Philipp J. Ehmann.

and, in his *prima philosophia*, searches for intercultural as well as interdisciplinary thought. Sepp discusses *being-in-the-house*, the body in its archic gravity. In another, later line of thought, the *in* is bent once again – this time as a prefix – into scrutinizing and reflecting on the concept of the *in-dividual*, which Gerald Raunig later picks up on in his work (→ Sympoiesis, 123, and → Purposeful Polysemy, 157).[408]

Sepp's exploration of oikology[409] presents it as a metatheoretical framework that examines the human capacity to transform life through knowledge. He posits that knowledge is not merely theoretical but encompasses pre-theoretical and extra-theoretical reflections. Sepp emphasizes that, while knowledge aims for objectivity, it often obscures the subjective experiences of those who acquire it. He draws upon the Greek notion of the οἶκος (*oikos*, household) to illustrate that dwelling is an existential disposition that shapes individual and collective life. Sepp's oikology reveals the genesis of social formations based on the in-dividual, highlighting the tension between bodily existence and social structures. He argues, 'The house, in its function of "being-in", transcends an existential disposition that forms its first "in" in the bodily act.'[410] This statement underscores the foundational role of the body in shaping our experience of dwelling. It aligns with the concept of œkology, which emphasizes the embodied nature of our interactions with the environment. However, Sepp's focus on the individual and the tension between bodily existence and social structures provoked me to further explore how choreographic practices can mediate these tensions, fostering environments that are both ethically attuned and ontologically aware.

Jaco Kruger's articulation of oikology enriches the discourse by integrating ecological considerations with a phenomenological analysis of the experience of the home. He critiques the mechanistic and materialist worldview that has dominated the natural sciences, asserting that it neglects the ethical and ontological dimensions of our relationship with the environment, the world that surrounds us. Kruger proposes a realist ontology of nature, one that is *oikos*-oriented, which connects to the speculative realist turn[411] in contemporary continental philosophy. He distinguishes his oikological approach from systems ecology by situating it within a broader worldview, characterizing the 'experience of home *(oikos*) [...] as the symbol for a very basic experience of self-awareness in relation to concern for a wider world'.[412]

These recent articulations of *oikology* propose that it is both an ethical and ontological investigation into dwelling, the home, and the environment. The perspectives of both Sepp and Kruger resonate with the concept of œkology (or,

408. Gerald Raunig, *Dividuum* (Semiotext(e), 2016).

409. Hans Rainer Sepp, 'Phänomenologie Als Oikologie', in *Die Lebendigkeit der Phänomenologie: Tradition und Erneuerung*, ed. Jan Giovanni Giubilato (Traugott Bautz, 2018), 276–94; Hans Rainer Sepp, 'Das maskierte Selbst: Zu einer oikologischen Phänomenologie der Person', *Phainomena* 19, nos. 74–75 (2010): 3–19, accessed 18 October 2025, https://www.dlib.si/details/URN:NBN:SI:doc-RFOXZIAZ.

410. Sepp, 'Phänomenologie als Oikologie'.

411. Quentin Meillassoux, *After Finitude: An Essay on the Necessity of Contingency*, trans. Ray Brassier (Continuum, 2008); Levi R. Bryant, Nick Srnicek, and Graham Harman, eds., *The Speculative Turn: Continental Materialism and Realism* (re.press, 2011).

412. Jaco Kruger, 'Ecology as Oikology – Reflections on Science and Worldview' in *South African Journal of Philosophy* 44, no. 2 (2025): 198.

conversely, œkology resonates with oikology), which seeks to cultivate environments that are ethically responsive and cosmopoietically generative. Kruger's emphasis on the experience of the home as a foundational form of self-awareness invites consideration of how practices of choreo-ethical assemblage can facilitate this experience, enabling individuals and communities to engage with their environments in meaningful, transformative ways.

This choreo-ethical engagement contests modern dichotomies – nature/culture, human/other-than-human – but also the disciplinary boundaries between performance, philosophy and psychotherapy. In my artistic practice, I highlight the foundational significance of the environment's infra-levels, from the soil to microbial life to the atmosphere. With the term *œkology*, where the ligature *œ* marks a confluence, a fusion, a literal joining of letters, I insist on amalgamation as something generative – that it is not merely environmentalism or ecological science but a reflexive ontogenesis. Dwelling is co-constitutive of the subject and the environment; how we dwell shapes us while simultaneously calling on us to take responsibility for what exceeds us. An ethical attention to care, maintenance, and responsiveness underpins the choreo-ethical framework, as do considerations of scale – temporal, spatial, and corporeal. While Sepp and Kruger provide invaluable insights into the concept of oikology, the notion of œkology introduces a distinct perspective. The merging of the *o* and *e* from *oikos* and *ecology* signifies an interwoven, even entangled approach to understanding the home and the environment. This fusion underscores the inseparability of dwelling and ecological systems, highlighting the performative and speculative dimensions of their interrelations. Unlike oikology, which often foregrounds dwelling, self-awareness, and worldview, œkology emphasizes performative and speculative ethical engagement through hands-on artistic practice. It is not only about inhabiting the world responsibly but about actively choreographing the conditions for co-appearance, transformation, and futurity. It is about exploring the possibilities of cosmopoietic œkology.

Another relevant key distinction emerges in the terms *polyvalent* and *ambivalent*. While *ambivalence* denotes a tension between opposing poles, *polyvalence* signals the coexistence of multiple meanings, forces, and trajectories without necessarily generating any contradiction. Œkology is polyvalent: the choreographic environment holds myriad potentialities, temporalities, and relational configurations at the same time. Human and nonhuman agencies, clarity and opacity, resistance and speculation – all coexist and interweave, generating a multiplicity of co-appearances and assemblages. This multiplicity is central to choreo-ethical practice, as it resists reduction to binaries and opens the environment up to cosmopoietic experimentation. Both Sepp and Kruger provide foundational insights that inform the concept of cosmopoietic œkology. Sepp's focus on the existential and subjective dimensions of dwelling complement the emphasis on the embodied and performative aspects of choreo-ethical assemblages. Kruger's integration of oikology into ecological and ontological considerations enriches our understanding of the choreographic environment as a site where ethical, ontological, and performative dimensions converge.

The concept of œkology, with its emphasis on the interweaving of crafted, choreo-graphic environments and the world, offers a framework for understanding how choreo-ethical practices can mediate collective contingencies in the macrocosm in order to – so the hypothesis goes – transfigure these experiences into the wider cosmos, making a contribution to an œkological culture. For me, this is acutely urgent as we are currently witnessing planetary destruction and spreading war. By focusing on understanding the performative and speculative dimensions of these relationships, growing transferable knowledge rooted in embodied experience, œkological culture will facilitate the creation of environments that are ethically attuned, ontologically aware, and cosmopoietically generative in the long run. The integration of Sepp's and Kruger's oikology into the concept of cosmopoietic œkology provides a comprehensive framework for understanding the choreographic environment as something crucial to the cultivation of cosmopoietic œkology. While oikology offers insights into the epistemological and ontological dimensions of dwelling, œkology expands this understanding by incorporating the performative, speculative, and ethical aspects of these relationships. In the bigger picture, this synthesis facilitates the creation of environments that are ethically responsive, choreographing new forms of care, belonging, and cosmogony into being and probing the possibilities of world-making.

Elastic Encounters – Experimental Forms of Being Together with Other Others

Subjects make decisions about objects, and those objects offer the greatest resistance to them.[413]
Stephan Trinkaus

My question here is: how do we become subjects and objects in the first place? The image with which Trinkaus confronts us – the resistance of the object – points towards the frictional quality of encounters, towards that elasticity that cannot be reduced to either pure subjectivity or pure objecthood. To take this resistance seriously means to engage with the elasticity of relation, with the experimental and durational qualities of co-presence that shape and reshape forms of being together with other others.[414] In this sense, the 'elastic encounter' is not a figure of consensus or transparency but of stretching, tension, reverberation, and unresolved becoming.

413. Original: 'Subjekte treffen Entscheidungen über Objekte, und diese setzen ihnen höchsten Widerstand entgegen.' Trinkaus, *Ökologien des Prekären*, 176.

414. *Other others* is a part of the title of the performance lecture *Thinking Matters Other Others – A Translecture*, a collaboration with Nikolaus Gansterer performed in 2014 at the Tanzquartier Wien within the framework of SCORES N°9 (No/Things). This work took an expanded view of choreography – beyond the body, towards the other-than-human. In the process of my choreographic mentoring of his solos, we discussed the following questions: How can we get matter to speak, and what organ can we use to listen to it? How do we reorganise perception? How do we assume responsibility for the surroundings that we ourselves shape? How do we focus on the ways in which things choreograph us? The work is documented here: Nikolaus Gansterer, 'Thinking Matters Other Others', accessed 29 September 2025, https://www.gansterer.org/thinking-matters-other-others.

Here are some thoughts on the full potential meaning of such a stretch in the *The Stanford Encyclopedia of Philosophy* entry on Henri Bergson:

> Bergson's third image is an elastic band being stretched. He tells us first to contract the band to a mathematical point, which represents 'the now' of our experience. Then, draw it out to make a line growing progressively longer. He warns us not to focus on the line but on the action which traces it. If we can focus on the action of tracing, then we can see that the movement – which is duration – is not only continuous and differentiating or heterogeneous, but also indivisible. We can always insert breaks into the spatial line that represents the motion, but the motion itself is indivisible. For Bergson, there is always a priority of movement over the things that move; the thing that moves is an abstraction from the movement. The elastic band being stretched is a more exact image of duration. But, the image of the elastic is still, according to Bergson, incomplete. Why? Because, for him, no image can represent duration. [...] Duration really consists in two characteristics: unity and multiplicity. This double characteristic brings us to Bergson's method of intuition.[415]

For me, this raises the question of how to articulate a choreo-ethical assemblage that accommodates such elasticities. The answer cannot be located in an anthropocentric ethics of decision-making, nor in a hermeneutic of stable meaning. Rather, it must be sought in the very texture of relationality, in an œkological poetics where the folds of encounter are continually being negotiated and renegotiated, performing elasticity. Philosopher and artist Erin Manning discusses 'the elasticity of the almost',[416] the title of a chapter that starts with the following epigraph by Gilles

415. Leonard Lawlor and Valentine Moulard-Leonard, 'Henri Bergson', 18 May 2004, *The Stanford Encyclopedia of Philosophy* (Winter 2022 Edition), ed. Edward N. Zalta and Uri Nodelman, accessed 17 July 2025, https://plato.stanford.edu/archives/win2022/entries/bergson.

416. Manning, 'Elasticity of the Almost', in *Relationscapes: Movement, Art, Philosophy* (MIT Press, 2009), 29–47.

Deleuze: 'Movement is not explained by sensation, but by the elasticity of sensation, its vis elastica.'[417]

The elasticity of sensation emerges as it translates into a sensory and sensate encounter with others and other others. These are felt encounters with the glass marble, dried apple, pins with black heads, the hand apparatus, the wig, the handpan and its sounds, and the delicate little plant next to the hardened lump of clay, as well as the scent of a human dialogue partner's perfume or a hair they might have left behind. Who knows what ethics are at play here? Karen Barad's insight resonates forcefully:

> Just as the human subject is not the locus of knowing, neither is it the locus of ethicality. We (but not only 'we humans') are always already responsible to the others with whom or which we are entangled, not through conscious intent but through the various ontological entanglement that materiality entails. What is on the other side of the agential cut is not separate from us – agential separability is not individuation. Ethics is therefore not about a right response to a radically externalized other, but about responsibility and accountability for the lively relationalities of becoming of which we are a part.[418]

Yes, the lively relationalities of becoming, they resonate. This ethical claim positions responsibility not as an act of volition but as an ontological condition: one does not choose to be responsible, one is already implicated.

Elastic encounters, then, are not primarily about mutual recognition or confirming one's identity; they are about sensing the stretch of responsibility in the interstices of interspecies cohabitation – just like I am living and sharing in the life cycle of the Amaryllis, or in other œkological entanglements that are neither steady nor free of friction. The encounter with other others – vegetal, animal, microbial, mineral, or machinic – cannot be reduced to the epistemological question of knowing them 'as they are'. Instead, these encounters are somatic and phantasmatic: embodied and imagined, vibrational and spectral, immanent to the very becoming of bodies.

417. Gilles Deleuze, *Logique de la sensation* (Éditions de la Différence, 1981), 45.

418. Karen Barad, *Meeting the Universe Halfway* (Duke University Press, 2007), 393.

It is here that the notion of *cohabitation* must be expanded beyond geographer Doreen Massey's influential concept of 'throwntogetherness'.[419] While Massey insists on the contingency of spatial co-presence, elastic encounters bring to the fore the durational and processual intensities of being-with. It is not only that we are thrown together – we are stretched together, extended beyond our own contours, engaged in resonant rhythms that exceed both subject and object. The somatic and phantasmatic cosmologies that emerge in this stretching invite us to think of togetherness as more than a juxtaposition, namely, as co-compositional elasticity. Moreover, this elasticity is not simply metaphorical. In interspecies sensing, one feels the tension between the perceptual apparatuses of different beings: the bat's echolocation, the slime mould's chemical trail, the dog's olfactory attunement, the human body's proprioceptive field. These are incommensurable perspectives, yet they touch upon one another, generating frictional zones of co-sensation. The cohabitation of worlds is here choreo-ethical in the deepest sense: the continuous negotiation of distance and proximity, timing and rhythm, elasticity and resistance.

The task of choreo-ethical assemblage, then, is to persist in this stretching. Bergson's image of the elastic band, while insufficient to fully capture duration, nonetheless provides a productive cue. Duration is indivisible, and so is the elasticity of the encounter. The tension between contracting to a point and extending into a line mirrors the simultaneity of unity and multiplicity in relational life. The elastic encounter thus foregrounds the action of stretching – the becoming-with that cannot be parsed into isolated instances or stable identities. This is why the micro-phenomenological tool for focusing on thc thin-slicing of a moment was such a valuable methodical instrument for zooming in further and further and further, until the movement itself came into focus.

As a method, elasticity resists closure: it is not about finding equilibrium but about sustaining disequilibrium, about learning to dwell in asymmetry and divergence. In this sense, choreo-ethical assemblages are cosmopoietic: of course, they do map and present a pre-existing cosmos; however, they also actively generate yet unknown worlds through the very acts of encounter and intra-action. These worlds are not bound wholes but porous, shifting constellations of relation. They are œkological insofar as they recognize the household (*oikos*) of existence as other-than-human, other-than-linguistic, other-than-individual.

What emerges from the consideration of elastic encounters is an ethics that does not depend on the sovereignty of the subject, one that instead becomes entangled – maybe even deliberately – with dynamics of becoming. Such an ethics is open to that which is yet to come and to the speculative, in the literal sense of *speculum* – 'mirror', 'reflection', 'diffraction'. Each encounter diffracts responsibility differently; each stretch calls forth a different figuration of togetherness. Let me amplify this: to think about and practice the elastic encounter is to recognize that resistance is generativity, that interspecies sensing is resonance, that œkological cohabitation is a durational choreo-ethical movement, and that somatic and phantasmatic cosmologies open up a horizon for rethinking what it means

419. Doreen Massey, *For Space* (Sage Publications, 2005), 160.

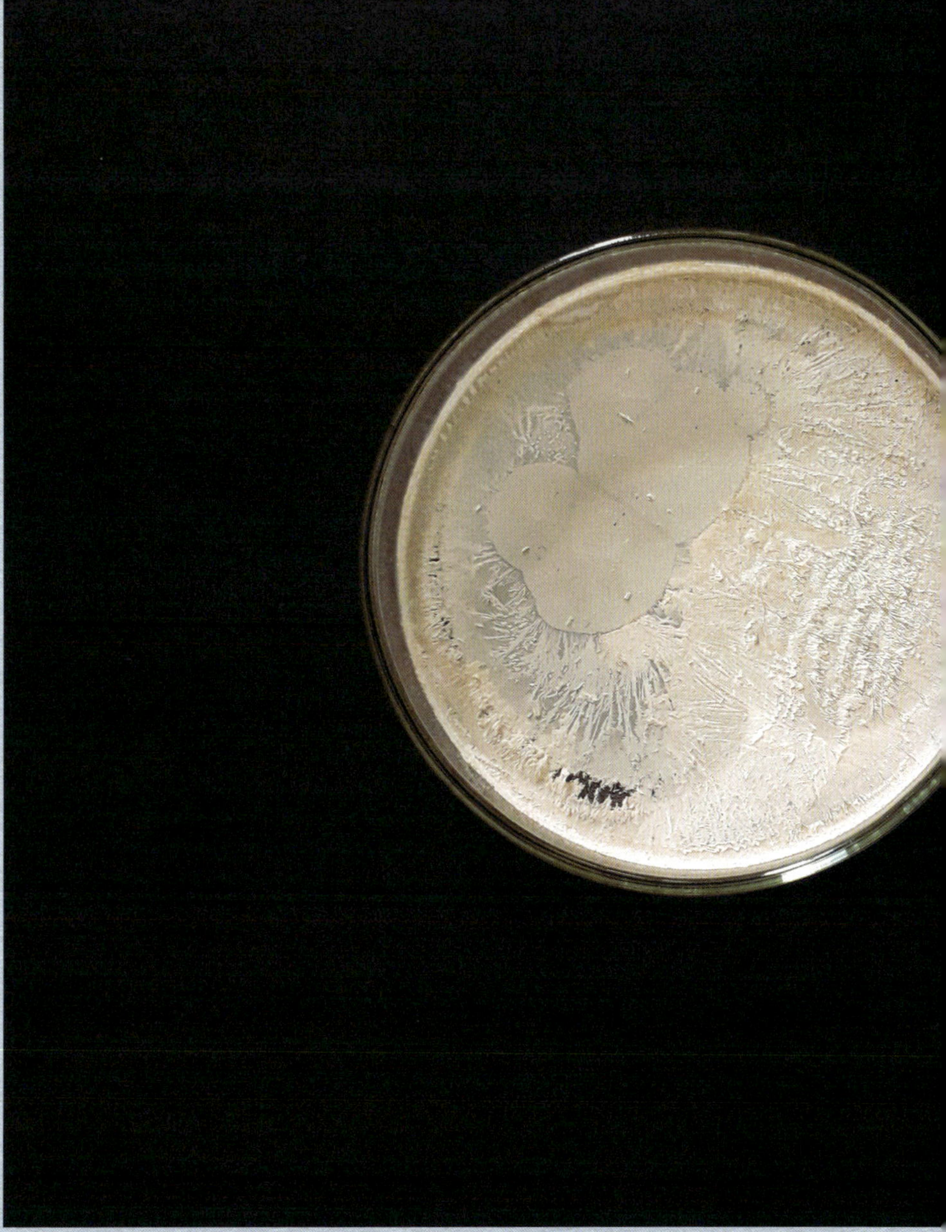

Experimental Forms

Resonances captured in the Petri dish
crystallize from within into fine sensory hairs.
Reaching for the white moon,
intuitive aesthetics accelerate the process
of poetic condensation.

In fact, the fissures that run through
the desiccating image
counter the idea that hearing rushes ahead
of seeing.
Their twilight state, between fluid
and withered,
clings to the surface of the glass.

Two bodies share the horizon,
nestled together
in silence and whiteness.
Do you see the dendrites of history?

In rounds of Chinese whispers they ask
how to hold another person's emotional
weight in equilibrium.
The gap finds the exact moment
when breath falters against the backdrop
of nothingness.
There, the curved shadow meets the
roundness of the planet.

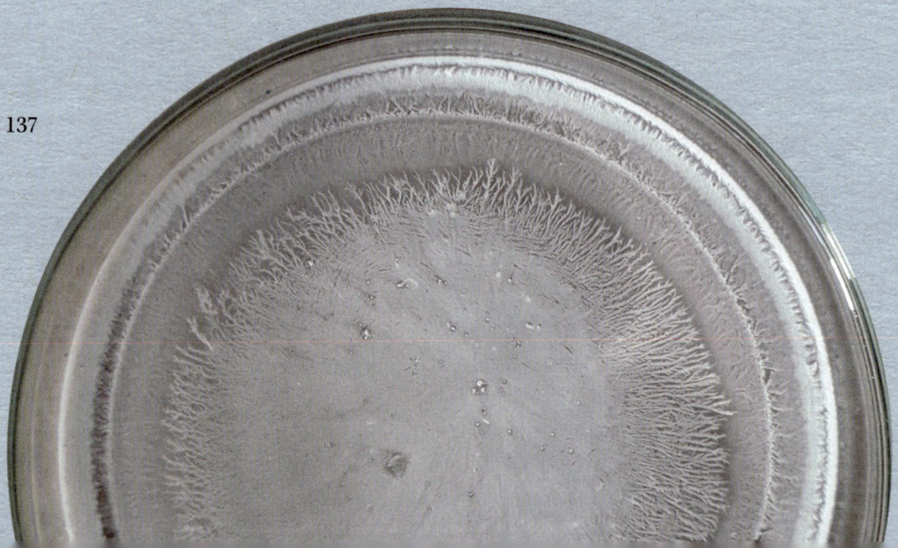

to be together with other others. If ethics is responsibility for the relationalities of becoming, then choreo-ethical assemblages are the laboratories of that responsibility, staging encounters that stretch and strain, that test and exceed the limits of the human. The elasticity of the encounter reminds us that we are neither autonomous decision-makers confronting resistant objects nor sovereign subjects parsing alterity from a safe distance. Rather, we are participants vibrationally entangled in an ongoing cosmopoietic œkology, where every relation is an experiment in world-making.

The Emergence of Choreo-ethics as Cosmopoietic Œkology

Imagination is work, it takes fortitude and commitment and courage, it takes courage, to live imagination as practice, as a way of life.[420]

Ashon Crawley

Indeed, it does take courage to imagine another world.

In retrospect, I can say that choreo-ethical assemblages became an imaginative tool for cosmopoiesis, a mode of world-making that cultivates civil courage as the ongoing negotiation, composition, and decomposition of relations, which it inevitably is and needs to be. Taking a stance through performative and artistic practices of assemblaging and a heightened sensitivity to socio-political developments aligns with 'silent activism', a term coined by Barbara Holub in 2015.[421] Furthermore, the practice of minor language lawlessness (MLL)[422] has led me to produce a collection of poems, of artistic condensations, as an outcome[423] of these years of research. They appear on the blue pages in this book.

I return to the question of imagination as a generative force for ethics as a practice and a way of life. Crawley's insistence that imagination requires courage reminds us that to envision something else, to embody cosmopoietic œkology, is neither naïve nor ornamental. Psychiatrist, psychotherapist, and Director of the Institute for Social Aesthetics and Mental Health Michael Musalek writes, 'As "homo faber", we are capable of creating worlds independently, of *autonomous cosmopoiesis*.'[424] For my research, the focus was on cosmopoietic practices emerging from collective contingencies across diverse agencies, including the other-than-

420. Ashon Crawley, 'It's Ok to be Afraid', *ashon crawley* (blog), 16 March 2020, https://ashoncrawley.com/its-ok-to-be-afraid/?srsltid=AfmBOoobKcmdpNBflwdQU-VHr5mrE_ROSGe2LKamKdA99LpjkHw4DLWp.

421. She writes, 'to be silently active is to persistently insist on engaging the public/audience not as the public in general, but as active individuals capable of taking the initiative and realizing a vision'. *Barbara Holub – Stiller Aktivismus / Silent Activism*, ed. Başak Şenova (Edition Angewandte, De Gruyter, 2023), 12.

422. MML is a humorous inversion (maybe also subversion) of large language models (LLMs).

423. Further outcomes of the research project *Choreo-ethical Assemblages – Narrations of Bare Bodies* are documented here: https://choreoethicalassemblages.home.blog.

424. Original: 'Als "homo faber" sind wir zur eigenständigen Weltenschöpfung, zur autonomen Kosmopoiesis fähig.' Michael Musalek, *Der Wille Zum Schönen*, vol. II, *Als Kulturgeschehen: Auf Dem Weg Zur Kosmopoesie* (Parodos, 2017), 130.

human. In *Der Wille zum Schönen I* and *II* (The Will to Beauty; 2017), Musalek proposes a shift from cosmopoiesis to *cosmopoetics*, which, for him, conveys a clear, neo-Romantic human orientation towards the beautiful. While I understand the desire for beauty, in my conception it is overwritten by a commitment to openness that values any form of expression. However, Musalek would probably agree that to *imagine* is the (at times strenuous) labour of reconfiguring the conditions of possibility. As we inhabit and cohabit in the fragile ecologies of a damaged planet, the cultivation of imagination requires commitment and volition. Imagination, in this sense, is not escape but endurance, a modality of living with others and other others that resists foreclosure and invests in the experimental capacities of encounter. Rosi Braidotti offers a necessary provocation:

> We need to find out by embracing an ethics of experiment with intensities. The ethical imagination is alive and well in posthuman subjects, in the form of ontological relationality. A sustainable ethics for non-unitary subjects rests on an enlarged sense of inter-connection between self and others, including the nonhuman or 'earth' others, by removing the obstacle of self-centred individualism on the one hand and the barriers of negativity on the other.[425]

What is at stake here is a shift from ethics as prescription to ethics as experimentation. Choreo-ethics is precisely such an experimental practice: it unfolds in movement, in the somatic and the phantasmatic, in the articulation of micro-worlds that are never isolated but always already enmeshed in larger scales of relation. James Hillman reminds us of the visceral stakes of such articulation: 'Every move we make, phrase we utter, is confession of our heart because it reveals our images.'[426] The simplicity of the direct link he makes between the heart and the imagination is striking, revealing a tool everyone can use. The emergence of choreo-ethics as cosmopoietic œkology therefore cannot remain an abstract theoretical exercise; it is embodied confession, lived through the rhythms of relation, exposed in gestures, utterances, pauses, silences. To practice choreo-ethical assemblages is to acknowledge the imaginal as a force of world-making, inseparable from the corporeal and the relational.

This leads us back to the story I shared in the introduction, where my friend insisted that 'everything has to pass through the heart'. The heart here is not a metaphor alone but a multidimensional organ of ethical attunement. Hillman elaborates:

425. Rosi Braidotti, *The Posthuman* (Polity, 2013), 190.

426. Hillman, *Thought of the Heart*, 24.

Mmmmmmagentic Listening

Deep magenta listening,
ear pressed to electric lavender rock
where obsidian is misread.
Affect slips into effect,
anarchic responsibility vibrating
through the pleasures we choose
when we have nothing to rely on
but each other and the sour taste left in our mouths
from an emotional hangover.

We discover spaces of togetherness
by transforming silence, staying gentle
when hooks of remembrance
try to catch us.
Lonely, layered accumulations loosen,
as we look into souls,
understanding the necessity of acting as a swarm
a radical sense of freedom
circling into concrete language
– direct address unshielded.

Openers of conversations run in parallel,
letting loose to unleash imagination
beyond expectation.
The stuff between us,
what makes us function,
forms a dissident space
that accommodates perspectives
rather than entangling with the other (Zapatista).
Time operates through rupture,
but infinity works easily
restoring balance,
caring where no one does.

Life to come will subvert modes of production.
This will be civil disobedience against a shrinking self,
– uncomfortability –
the refusal of fake utopias,
the dismantling of expectations,
delegating the frame.
Open fire: new sparks, radical immersion,
captaining the spaceship with radical trust.
Being together for real
means accepting the bumpiness
of belonging,
the flow of collective desire,
the portal for transformation:
we will be a chaotic mess.

Fall, suspend, let go!
Restlessness slows,
exceeds the human.
Hypersensitive touching,
painful listening beyond material boundaries,
and caring for the metabolism between us.
Practising the purest form of attention,
these urgencies need to be heard
inside loving communal bonds.
Justice becomes ethical know-how,
sensing beyond the skin.

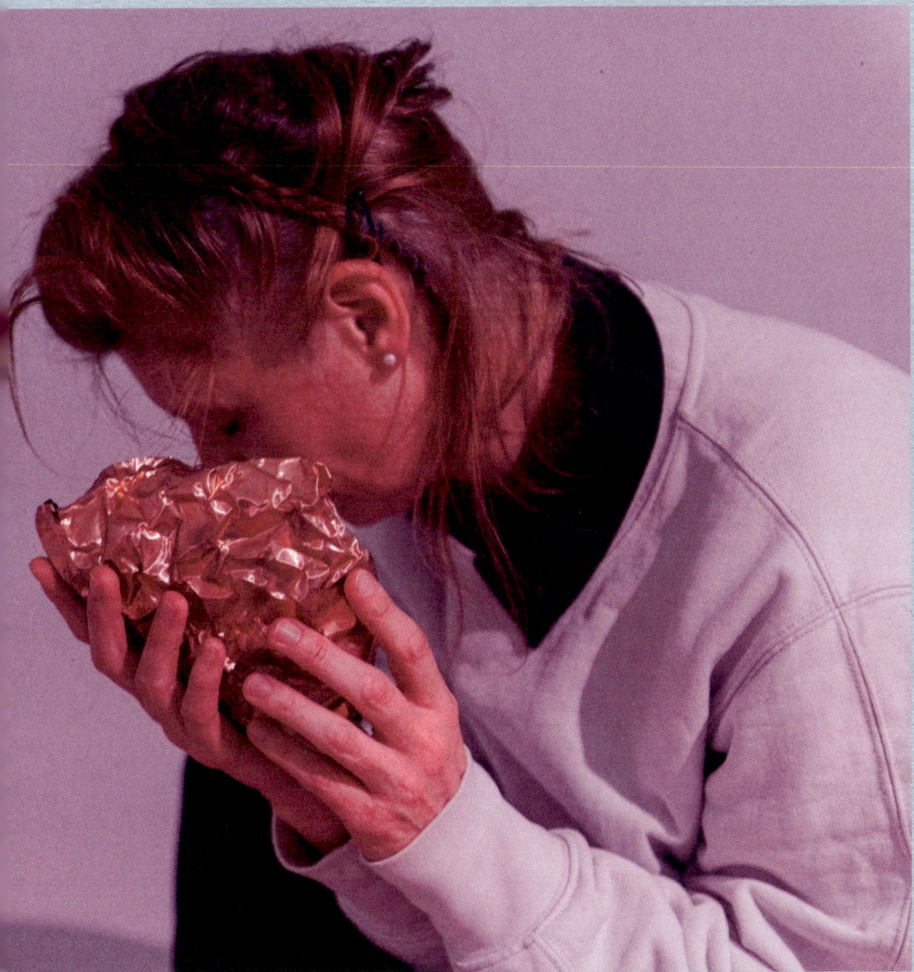

Gems of relation hang on our lips.
The tongue bends, radically open
to the violence of language and its shimmer.
Poetics, an extravagant sense:
resting only when covered by vowels.
Sounds never stand still;
they pulsate,
glow with meaning.

Dancedaydreaming, we sense with courage
reminding ourselves what is at stake.
We need poetry
to navigate the unspeakable of the heart.

> First: my heart is my humanity, my courage to live, my strength and fierce passion. By means of it nothing is foreign to me; all can be admitted to its kingdom of dignity. […] Second: my heart is an organ of the body. […] Third: my heart is my love, my feelings, the locus of my soul and sense of person. […] [T]he heart [is the] locus of the *sensus communis*, the place of natural law, connecting all individuals with each other and with the order of the world.[427]

Choreo-ethics as cosmopoietic œkology situates this heart at the centre of enquiry: the *sensus communis* is a pulsating site of connection between singular bodies, diverse agencies, trans*materialities in a shared cosmos, between intimate sensations and political urgencies.

The urgency of this ethical imagination cannot be divorced from the historical moment in which this book has been written. The genocides that the world is witnessing and that are being mediated through images, words, and silences are not a distant event but a rupture that tears through the very possibility of cosmopoiesis. To imagine a choreo-ethics that does not tend to this wound would be an abdication of responsibility. The question, then, is not only what happened in the Polylogic Labs – those spaces where choreo-ethical experiments were staged – but whether their micropolitics can radiate outward, inflecting real politics and world-making. The Polylogic Labs, as I have shown, were sites where we experimented with different forms of being-together: they cultivated attentiveness, elasticity in relation, and responsibility. Yet the challenge remains: How do we bridge the gap between these carefully tended micro-worlds and the brutality of geopolitical realities? How can we insist that the practices of listening, sensing, and stretching that unfold in these spaces matter not only for those immediately involved but for the broader ethical fabric of the world? The various struggles, wars, and climate catastrophes are forcing us to confront whether choreo-ethical practice is willing to claim its responsibility beyond the aesthetic field, whether it can pulse in resonance with hearts beating in grief, rage, and resistance. If imagination is work, then it is here that the courage Crawley speaks of must be enacted: to imagine that what is rehearsed in the Polylogic Lab has consequences beyond its walls, to insist that relational practices of care, attention, and elasticity are not ornamental but vital interventions. The cosmopoietic œkology of choreo-ethics thus includes a politics of resonance: the recognition that every gesture, every confession of the heart, participates in the larger world that we inhabit and co-create.

Thus, choreo-ethics is about more than somatic attunement or œkological cohabitation. It is about acknowledging that the body is never neutral, that

427. Ibid., 11.

the heart is never isolated, that every encounter contributes to the cosmopoietic unfolding of worlds. The performative power of choreo-ethical assemblages lies in their capacity to mobilize imagination as an ethical practice, one that embraces experimentation, intensities, and relationality across scales.

In this sense, the concluding gesture is also an opening: Laurie Anderson's invocation of (what was supposedly) Lenin's dictum – 'Ethics is the aesthetics of the future' [428] – during her violin concert *Songs for Lines/Songs for Waves*,[429] which she performed at the De Appel art gallery in Amsterdam in 1977, becomes a call to action. When we hear Anderson's bow draw sound into being, we witness the intertwining of aesthetic and ethical imagination, we sense in performance the ways in which the textures of future responsibility are rendered audible and visible. Ethics here becomes a performative unfolding, a tangible choreo-ethical experiment in the aesthetics of becoming. To say today, in 2026, that ethics are the aesthetics of the future is to align choreo-ethics with cosmopoietic œkology: both are oriented towards futures that are not yet given but must be enacted, performed, rehearsed. The future of ethics is not guaranteed, it requires the work of imagination, the courage of practice, the beating of hearts attuned to both the intimacy of encounter and the vastness of world-making.

Thus, choreo-ethics emerges as cosmopoietic œkology: a practice that confesses the heart, that stages elasticity or relations, that dares to experiment with intensities, and that insists that everything – every gesture, every silence, every vibration – is implicated in the making of worlds. It is in this insistence that its promise resides: to keep imagination alive as a way of life, to keep ethics vibrating as the aesthetics of the future.

428. My emphasis. Writer Jared Marcel Pollen points out that this quote that Laurie Anderson played on her tape-bow violin was falsely attributed to Lenin and that the writer and proponent of socialism Maxim Gorky was also misquoted. Gorky had written in relation to Anatoly France, 'Aesthetics was [his] ethics – the ethics of the future', Jared Marcel Pollen, 'Unsentimental Education: Peter Weiss's Aesthetics of Resistance', *Liberties*, July 2025, https://libertiesjournal.com/online-articles/unsentimental-education-peter-weisss-aesthetics-of-resistance.

429. Laurie Anderson, *Songs for Lines / Songs for Waves*, 1977, accessed 10 October 2025, https://www.youtube.com/watch?v=hXfMpZeiKtk&t=92s.

Dance scores, in general, do not aspire to this 'autonomy'. They are 'heteronomous' working tools, intended for use in a specific, local context, and most often as a supplement to oral instructions. The English word score is particularly useful from this perspective as it covers a much broader range than the French *partition*. French dance creator Mark Tompkins took this argument to its logical conclusion, defining a score, in his improvisational practice, as 'the determination of one or more parameters of decision-making in action'.

Myriam van Imschoot, 'Rests in pieces: Partitions, notation et trace dans la dans', *Multitudes* 21, no. 2 (2005): 107–16, trans. MG.

Scores

'Diffractive Dialogue Score' and 'Dark Bag Score': Tilling the Field

The 'Diffractive Dialogue Score' is a tool for negotiating choreo-ethics by preparing the field of action – the *choreographic environment* – and for making tangible the contingent potentials, inherent co-constitutive forces, and emergent potentials – *practices of polyvalence* – of all elements/agents/players involved in *Choreo-ethical Assemblages.*

A *diffractive* approach is practiced as exploration, as an unsettling of settled grounds and beliefs. The diffractive prism stretches beyond emotions, ideas, and states towards the luscious flavour of the present while accommodating various futures. The diffractive moment knows that there are fractions of manifold futures; it is a prism opening up a field of play between human and other-than-human bodies.

Heeding the Call of the Other-than-Human

There is a collection of objects with diverse stories – some have domestic functions, others perform aesthetic attraction(s), while others still were invented or created specifically for the *Choreo-ethical Assemblages* project collection. Some were gifts, one was stolen, none arrived without reason, though at times I might not have been aware of those reasons. These things brought a range of affects to the space that together formed an entangled field, a landscape of perceptual tones.

My interest was to scrutinize and understand in depth *how* artists, therapists, and philosophers engage with material, bodies, and environments in order to uncover the ethical issues associated with how we approach materials.

How does someone decide when to use certain materials, and why does a dancer turn to material materials rather than movement materials? What does this turn, this falling for an object, communicate, and how do we deal with the pitfalls of that object? More broadly, how can artistic research challenge practices of communication? How are practices of communication challenged by speculative materialist approaches? And how material are communication scores when we expand the dialogue out towards creative forms – going beyond simply taking turns to speak and listen, and instead immersing ourselves in creative and artistic practices?

As a dancer, I have spent most of my professional life working exclusively with the movements of my body, a quite ephemeral material. However, from a post-body[430] perspective, there is a current drive to extend beyond clear-cut categories of movement, matter, and aesthetics. When we observe the dynamics of the world, it becomes clear that it is predominantly affects, thoughts, and shapes that form human associations and narrations. However, there are further layers to be uncovered through the polylogics of intra-actions with the other-than-human.

430. In contemporary choreography and performance art the notion of the body as a fixed, autonomous, or purely human entity is increasingly scrutinized. Emphasizing the body as fluid, relational, and entangled with environments, non-human agents, and social or discursive structures as well as technologies, processes of emergence, transformation, distributed agency and material co-performances are in evidence.

Through the 'Diffractive Dialogue Score' practiced in the Polylogic Lab, a space emerged to practice motile ethics – or, more precisely, choreo-ethics. This terminology evolved and was refined within the scope of this project, designating an ethics constituted by a chorus of agencies comprising the living and non-living, matter and body, and entities and thresholds. The negotiation of these choreo-ethical assemblages was guided by a plurality of subjects and objects in dialogue with each other, all of them intentionally open to a practice of diffraction.

Even if the danger of hyper-complexity pervades the fields of art and communication – which sometimes seem like two expansive, endless areas of research – it was not just the project's institutional setting or affiliation that defined the specialized context in which my research was grounded. By all means, there was a clear sense of jouissance in affirming diffractive abundance and openness. It was not random openness, but a form of wild being[431] and assembling that I cultivated as an artistic and communicative practice, steadily aiming for the not-yet-known, digging deeper and weaving together a fabric of intuitions, visions, and speculations while simultaneously making concrete aesthetic and ethical decisions in each moment.

The practice of art and communication performed in the 'Diffractive Dialogue Score' and the 'Dark Bag Score' shifted known relationalities, temporalities, and hierarchies between things and no-things. It created alternative modes of interaction and critique, and formed constellations that were in ongoing dialogue with the prepared environment.

As expanded parameters of communication, artistic practice is simultaneously the mode (process) and work (product) of art. *Kunstpraxis als Werkform*[432]– literally art practice as a work form – means that practice itself becomes a recognized artistic form and is more than a preparatory stage. As something that involves bodies, materials, affects, temporalities, relations, and environments, art does not just *express* something, it operates communicatively. My claim is that the working method and the artwork itself are no longer separable; they are not sequential but coincidental.

In contemporary choreography and performance art, the notion of the body as a fixed, autonomous, or purely human entity is coming under increasing scrutiny. There is an emphasis on the body as something fluid, relational, and entangled with its environments, non-human agents, and social and discursive structures, as well as technologies, processes of emergence, transformation, distributed agency and material co-performances.

431. Esther Hutfless, 'Das wilde Sein – Akt – Ereignis – Schöpfung', in *Critica – Zeitschrift für Philosophie und Kunsttheorie*, vol. 1 (2012): 17–28.

432. See *Theorem Trans Radix* (2005), accessed 6 February 2026, https://mariellagreil.net/theorem-trans-radix.

Fig. 139: *In Blurry Layers* in the frame of The Polylogic Lab, 2025, © water colour: Mariella Greil.

Diffractive Dialogue Score

The Roles

The Host prepares the *choreographic environment*, which comprises a prepared environment. It is a crafted, still, open space that holds versatile potentials for dialogue. The diffractive quality emerges through relations between diverse agencies and generates unpredictable resonances, differences, and potentially shifts.

Diffraction[433] describes how waves bend, spread, and interfere when they encounter an obstacle or pass through an opening, producing overlapping patterns rather than sharp edges. In a broader sense (as in Barad's usage), *diffraction* emphasizes how differences emerge through entanglement, not separation, showing how phenomena emerge through relational interference rather than reflection.

In the context of my choreographic research, the 'Diffractive Dialogue Score' changes depending on the spatial as well as the performative set-up in which human and other-than-human agents co-compose. Through modulation and synthesis, bodies, materials, and affects perform specific patterns of difference that are brought about by *how* they encounter each other.

The Guest is an invited dialogue partner who will be introduced to the overall framework of the 'Diffractive Dialogue Score' by the Host. The roles start rolling, and as the Polylogic Lab unfolds its dynamics, shifts might occur between the activities of hosting and guesting, potentially blurring and complicating the roles. The score is intentionally articulated as an open task in order to establish an experimental system.

Preparatory Prompt

For the Guest. For the first encounter at the Polylogic Lab, please bring 1 to 5 objects with you that hold a 'choreo-ethical narration', meaning some sort of ethical issue that resonates with the *objectum.* It can be related to how the object came to you, what it stands for, who made it, etc.

Time Structure

There are three rounds of exploration, each lasting one hour.

In the **first round**, the Host is the 'keeper of the place' – a kind of guardian of the environment. The Host is responsible for preparing and maintaining the space, as well as marking the times for the diffractive practice, indicating when to move to the

433. Jesuit Priest, mathematician, and physicist Francesco Maria Grimaldi writes in the first proposition of his book *Physico-Mathesis de Lumine, Coloribus et Iride aliisque adnexis* (1665), 'Lumen propagatur seu diffunditur non solum Directe, Refracte, ac Reflexe, sed etiam alio quodam Quarto modo, DIFFRACTE' (Light is propagated or diffused not only directly, refractively, and reflectively, but also by another, fourth mode, DIFFRACTIVELY). Francesco Maria Grimaldi, *Physico-Mathesis de Lumine, Coloribus et Iride Aliisque Adnexis* (Johann Zieger,1665), 24, Biblioteca Europea Di Informatione e Cultura, accessed 15 December 2025, https://preserver.beic.it/delivery/DeliveryManagerServlet?dps_pid=IE7754640.

next round. During the first hour, the Host sits outside or at the edge of the prepared space, at the door, making sure that the Guest in the choreographic environment is not disturbed. It is the task of the host to safeguard the creative space and the exploration that is taking place within the choreographic environment. This act of holding space is a practice in and of itself. The host has the option to write, capturing this experience without censoring or sanitizing it.

During the first hour, the Guest is invited to think-move within the *choreographic environment* and to explore how to relate to it. It is a synthesis of *what* and *how* choreo-ethical assemblages emerge.

Then the roles are reversed. Now, in the **second round**, it is the Host who enters the room and the Guest must safeguard the space. The Host can read the traces of the Guest's presence, resonate with them, and respond to them in the form of a *diffractive dialogue* by reading the constellations of objects and responding creatively to the material traces and resonances that linger within the space. Some residues might have been left behind deliberately, others might be accidental, some may not be discovered and might stay secret – all of them inspiring further actions, interactions, or intra-actions emerging through relational processes. So far, the *diffractive dialogue* will have been mostly non-verbal and indirect.

In the **third round**, both dialogue partners explore the choreographic environment at the same time, with the roles of Host and Guest intermingling and entangling, and no longer remaining clear cut. The focus is on the polylogics that emerge between all agencies present in the space. Listening and performing, co-composing and de-composing, counteracting and activating take place.

Interpolation: Micro-phenomenological Interview

Between each of these three rounds, there is a 30-minute micro-phenomenological interview, which moves from the predominantly non-verbal space to the verbal space. In these interluding interviews, language and words come into play, led by the protocol of the micro-phenomenological interview technique, which is a guided form of conversation that zooms in on micro-perceptions. Diachronic analysis, the unfolding of experience moment by moment, traces the temporal micro-shifts of sensation, attention, affect, and meaning as they arise and transform within the lived experience.

Dark Bag Score

... creating a new thought for that object.[434]

To explore new relations *with* an object is to empathically engage with its presence, its capacities, and the network of relations in which it participates.

In the same way that one needs to be present in a situation in order to respond ethically to the circumstance, choreo-ethics are context-dependent and situated, with no exceptions. This is not relativism but a context-sensitive, practice-oriented ethics in which responsibility emerges through engagement with the situation itself. John Cage writes, 'Art comes from a kind of experimental condition in which one experiments with living.'[435] In my view, that can also be reversed. Both ethical action and artistic practice unfold as ongoing experiments in being-in-contact, where attentiveness to presence becomes the medium of engagement.

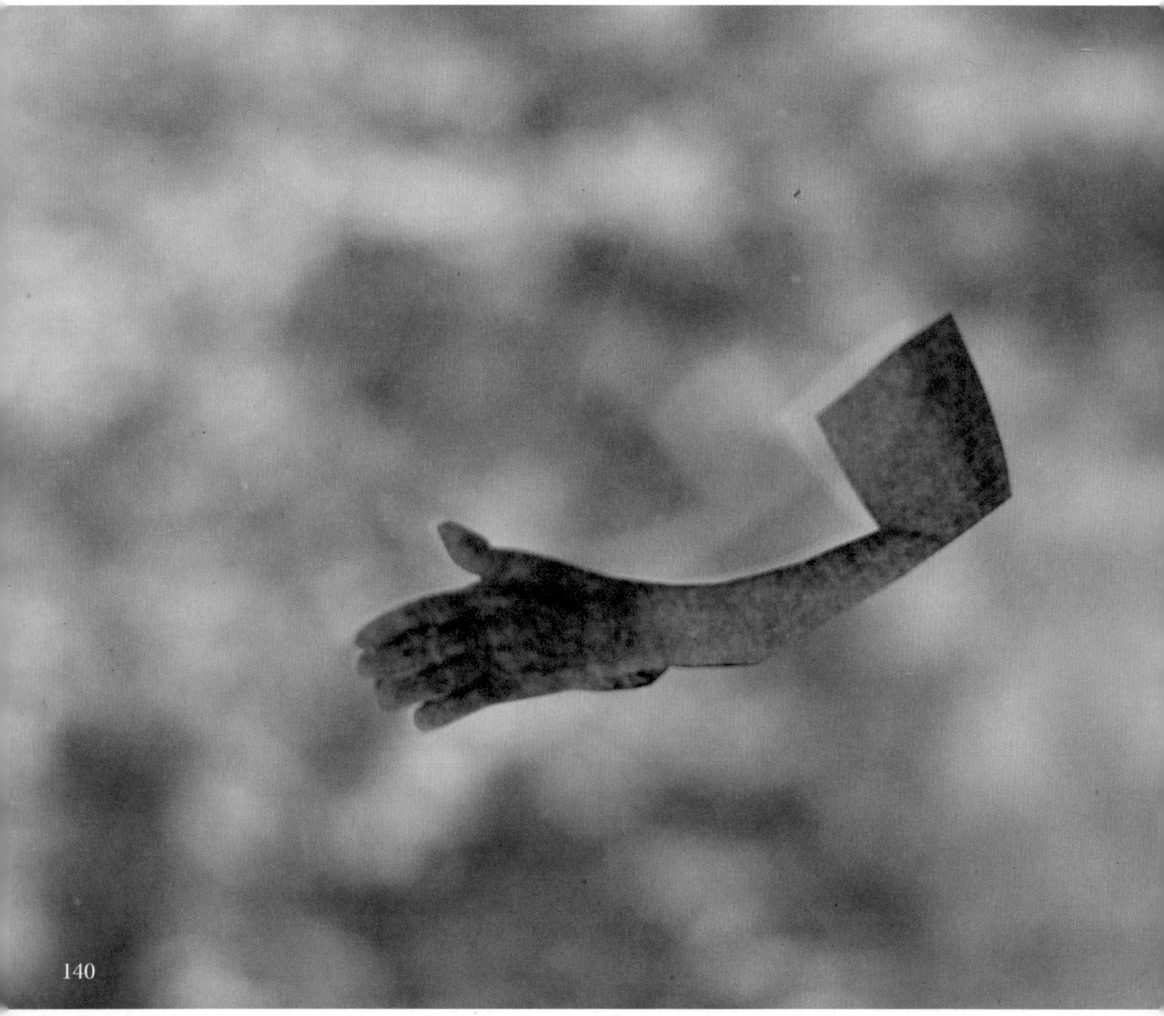

140

434. Marcel Duchamp, quoted in Leonard Koren, *What Artists Do* (Imperfect Publishing, 2018), 28.

435. John Cage, *Silence: Lectures and Writings* (Wesleyan University Press, 1961), 39.

Fig. 140: *in touch* in the frame of Passenger Diaries, 2022, © Photo: Mariella Greil.

The Roles

The Host provides a Dark Bag and introduces the Guest to the 'Dark Bag Score', placing the Dark Bag on the floor or table. While performing the score, the Host becomes the micro-phenomenological interviewer.

The Guest becomes the Contact Interactor / Toucher. In filmmaking, a dark bag (often called a changing bag) is a light-tight portable workspace used to handle light-sensitive film when a proper darkroom is not available. Similarly, the Dark Bag allows you to put your hands inside while keeping light out. The Host verbally guides the Guest through the 'Dark Bag Score'. It is an encounter that the Guest's hands have, in full darkness, with other-than-human agents by touch alone. After completing one encounter, the Guest pauses until another agent calls their attention and changes the temperature of the exploration. Finally, the Guest decides in favour of one object and stays with it during the micro-phenomenological interview.

Preparatory prompt

The 'Dark Bag Score' involves touch and haptics as its major sensory channel. While it plays on the adventurous atmospheres of lightless spaces – often clubs or bars – designed to enable anonymous, consensual erotic interactions mediated by touch rather than visual identification, in this context, it is a kind of safe micro-darkroom for hands alone. The Guest might encounter differing or similar textures or temperatures, hardness or softness, elasticity, weight, shape or contour, vibration or movement, moisture and surface irregularities, as well as more relational qualities like tension, relaxation, responsiveness, and rhythm.

Preparing the Setting: The Dark Bag

The first step for the Host is to prepare the Dark Bag with a selection of five objects that become the protagonists of the choreographic environment. The Host places the Dark Bag on the floor or table and instructs the Guest not to look inside and to assume that it contains weight.

Time structure

20 minutes.

Contact and Concurrent Micro-phenomenological Interview

The Contact Interactor / Toucher puts their hands inside the Dark Bag, ready to encounter what is in there. A point of contact is established. The touch is twofold: the touching hand is also touched. Often imagined as immediate, direct, and present, this contact is intensified by a concurrent Micro-phenomenological Interview that might have as its starting point a reflection on tactility, skin, surface, and proximity, but that will shift deeper into the details through the micro-phenomenological diachronic narration.

Concluding Statement

Rather than creating artefacts or materializations, the research project *Choreo-ethical Assemblages – Narrations of Bare Bodies* focused on the development of a methodological research outcome that can be described as a series of polyvalent practices.

In physics and chemistry, polyvalence refers to the ability of an atom or ion to form multiple chemical bonds with other atoms. More generally, polyvalence designates the capacity to engage in multiple simultaneous interactions, and to endure or function in multiple ways simultaneously. Practices of polyvalence resist a single fixed meaning, use, or interpretation, and are instead attuned to a polylogic that is attuned to generative forces in choreographic environments, and that trains purposeful polysemy and choreo-ethical assemblaging, cultivating an awareness of socio-aesthetic emergences through relational and diffractive dialogues.

Experimental forms of being together with *others and other others* highlight openness, relationality, and the co-existence of diverse effects or readings. The emergence of a cosmopoietic œkology is based on practices of polyvalence – consciously holding spaces open for experimentation and committing to the idea that there are polylogical possibilities beyond our own perspectives and that things could be other than they are. Practices of polyvalence maintain an attitude of openness and attentiveness, re-searching for perspectives, experiences, and knowledge systems other than our own, and allowing them to emerge and coexist. This soft approach fosters dialogue, relational understanding, and the possibility of encountering worlds that challenge or expand familiar frameworks of being-in-the-world.

Practices of polyvalence are process-oriented articulations in movement and were initiated through the 'Diffractive Dialogue Score' and the 'Dark Bag Score', both of which are based on epistemic gestures and situated knowledges. Experimental insights led to research findings related to performance and relationality, materiality and aesthetics, and reflection and discourse, as revealed in this monograph, which serves as a scholarly exposition, reflective documentation, and conceptual narration of evolved and evolving *Choreo-ethical Assemblages.*

Appendix

Bibliography

Abram, David. *The Spell of the Sensuous: Perception and Language in a More-than-Human World.* 20th anniversary ed. Vintage Books, 2017.

Adamatzky, Andrew, Giuseppe Tarabella, Neil Phillips, et al. 'Kombucha Electronics'. Preprint, Scientific Reports, 15 February 2023. https://doi.org/10.21203/rs.3.rs-2562074/v1.

Agamben, Giorgio. 'What is a Paradigm?' August 2002, European Graduate School. Transcript by Max van Manen. Accessed 12 September 2019. http://www.maxvanmanen.com/files/2014/03/Agamben-What-is-a-paradigm1.pdf.

Ahmed, Sara. *The Cultural Politics of Emotion.* 2nd ed. Edinburgh University Press, 2014 [2004].

Akomolafe, Bayo. LinkedIn, 23 February 2025. https://www.linkedin.com/posts/bayoakomolafe_where-in-these-fraught-political-moments-activity-7299070191009730561-MJLC.

Andersen, Lene Rachel. *Polymodernity: Meaning and Hope in a Complex World.* Nordic Bildung, 2023.

Appadurai, Arjun. *Modernity at Large: Cultural Dimensions of Globalization.* 7th ed. University of Minnesota Press, 2005 [1996].

Aristotle. *Metaphysics.* Translated by Joe Sachs. Green Lion Press, 1999.

Aristotle. *Poetics.* Translated by Stephen Halliwell. Harvard University Press, 1995.

Arteaga, Alex, and Nikolaus Gansterer, eds., *Contingent Agencies: Inquiring into the Emergence of Atmospheres.* Hatje Cantz, 2025.

Austin, John Langshaw. *How to Do Things with Words.* Harvard University Press, 1962.

Baldini, Irina. *Accountable Temporary Expedients.* Brave New Books, 2022.

Barad, Karen. 'Diffracting Diffraction: Cutting Together-Apart'. *Parallax* 20, no. 3 (2014): 168–87.

Barad, Karen *Meeting the Universe Halfway.* Duke University Press, 2007.

Barad, Karen. 'Posthumanist Performativity: Toward an Understanding of How Matter Comes to Matter'. *Signs* 28, no. 3 (2003): 801–31.

Basturk, Efe. 'Nancy and the Idea of "Being-in-common": An Alternative Existentiality for the Subjectivity'. *SATS* 21, no. 1 (2020): 61–80. https://doi.org/10.1515/sats-2019-0011.

Bataille, Georges. 'Attraction and Repulsion II: Social Structure'. In *The College of Sociology, 1937–39.* Edited by Denis Hollier. Translated by Betsy Wing. University of Minnesota Press, 1988.

Bateson, Mary Catherine. *Peripheral Visions: Learning Along the Way.* HarperCollins, 1995.

Bennett, Jane. *Vibrant Matter: A Political Ecology of Things.* Duke University Press, 2010.

Biller, Karlheinz, and Maria de Lourdes Stiegeler. *Wörterbuch der Logotherapie und Existenzanalyse von Viktor Emil Frankl.* Süddeutsches Institut für Logotherapie und Existenzanalyse, 2020.

Bishop, Claire. *Installation Art: A Critical History.* Tate Publishing, 2005.

Blanchot, Maurice. *The Space of Literature.* Translated by Ann Smock. University of Nebraska Press, 1989 [1955].

Böhler, Arno. 'Sensorial Bodies'. In *Choreo-graphic Figures: Deviations from the Line*, edited by Nikolaus Gansterer, Emma Cocker, and Mariella Greil. Edition Angewandte, De Gruyter, 2017.

Bolt, Barbara. 'Artistic Research: A Performative Paradigm?' *PARSE* 3 (2016): 129–42.

Borgdorff, Henk. 'Where Are We Today? The State of the Art in Artistic Research'. In *Art and Research*, edited by Janet Rittermann, Gerald Bast, and Jürgen Mittelstraß. Springer, 2011.

Braidotti, Rosi. 'Affirmation Versus Vulnerability: On Contemporary Ethical Debates'. *Symposium: Canadian Journal of Continental Philosophy* 10, no. 1 (2006): 235–54.

Braidotti, Rosi. *The Posthuman*. Polity, 2013.

Braidotti, Rosi. *Transpositions: On Nomadic Ethics*. Polity, 2006.

Brock, Bazon. *Ästhetik als Vermittlung: Arbeitsbiographie eines Generalisten*. DuMont, 1994.

Butler, Judith. *Precarious Life: The Powers of Mourning and Violence*. Verso, 2006.

Butler, Judith. *The Force of Nonviolence: An Ethico-Political Bind*. Verso, 2020.

Callicott, J. Baird. *Beyond the Land Ethic*. State University of New York Press, 2020.

Cimino, Antonio. 'Bare Life, Facticity, and Biopolitics in Agamben and the Early Heidegger'. *The Review of Politics* 85, no. 3 (2023): 354–74. https://doi.org/10.1017/S0034670523000098.

Clark, Lygia. 'Baba antropofágica'. Medien Kunst Netz – Media Art Net. Accessed 16 October 2025. http://www.medienkunstnetz.de/works/baba-antropofagica.

Clark, Lygia. 'The Memory of the Body'. 1973. Accessed 10 October 2025. https://portal.lygiaclark.org.br/en/archive/4804/the-memory-of-the-body.

Classen, Constance. *The Deepest Sense: A Cultural History of Touch*. University of Illinois Press, 2012.

Clough, Patricia Ticineto, ed. *The Affective Turn: Theorizing the Social*. Duke University Press, 2007.

Connolly, William E. *A World of Becoming*. Duke University Press, 2011.

Connolly, William E. *The Ethos of Pluralization*. University of Minnesota Press, 1995.

Connolly, William E. *The Fragility of Things: Self-Organizing Processes, Neoliberal Fantasies, and Democratic Activism*. Duke University Press, 2013.

Crawley, Ashon. *Blackpentecostal Breath – The Aesthetics of Possibility*. Fordham University Press, 2017.

Crawley, Ashon. 'It's Ok to be Afraid'. *ashon crawley* (blog), 16 March 2020. https://ashoncrawley.com/its-ok-to-be-afraid/?srsltid=AfmBOoobKcmdpNBflwd-QU-VHr5mrE_ROSGe2LKamKdA99LpjkHw4DLWp.

DeLanda, Manuel. *A New Philosophy of Society: Assemblage Theory and Social Complexity*. Continuum, 2006.

DeLanda, Manuel. *Assemblage Theory*. Edinburgh University Press, 2016.

DeLanda Manuel, *A Thousand Years of Nonlinear History*. Swerve, 2005.

Deleuze, Gilles. *Difference and Repetition*. Translated by Paul Patton. Continuum, 2004 [1968].

Deleuze, Gilles. *The Logic of Sense*. Edited by Constantin V. Boundas. Translated by Mark Lester with Charles Divale. Columbia University Press, 1990.

Deleuze, Gilles. *Logique de la sensation*. Éditions de la Différence, 1981.

Deleuze, Gilles, and Félix Guattari. *A Thousand Plateaus: Capitalism and Schizophrenia*. Translated by Brian Massumi. Reprint. Continuum, 2004 [1980].

Deleuze, Gilles, and Félix Guattari. *What Is Philosophy?* Translated by Graham Burchell and Hugh Tomlinson. Columbia University Press, 1994.

Dempster, M. Beth. *A Self-Organizing Systems Perspective on Planning for Sustainability*. Master's thesis, University of Waterloo, 1998.

Descola, Philippe. *Beyond Nature and Culture*. Translated by Janet Lloyd. University of Chicago Press, 2013.

Dodds, Joseph. *Psychoanalysis and Ecology at the Edge of Chaos*. Routledge, 2011.

Doubrovsky, Serge. *Fils*. Galilée, 1977.

Durkheim, Émile. *The Rules of Sociological Method*. Translated by W. D. Halls. Free Press, 1982.

Elo, Mika, and Miika Luoto, eds. *Figures of Touch: Sense, Technics, Body*. The Academy of Fine Arts at the University of the Arts Helsinki, 2018.

Ettinger, Bracha L. 'Intimacy, Wit(h)nessing and Non-Abandonment'. Under Fire. Accessed 14 March 2017. http://jordancrandall.com/main/+UNDERFIRE/site/les/q-node-562.html.

Ettinger, Bracha. *The Matrixial Borderspace*. University of Minnesota Press, 2006.

Ettinger, Bracha L. 'Weaving a Woman Artist with-in the Matrixial Encounter-Event'. *Theory, Culture & Society* 21, no. 1 (2004): 69–93.

Feld, Steven, and Keith H. Basso. *Senses of Place*. University of New Mexico Press, 1996.

Feld, Steven, and Katell Morand. 'Representing the Poetics of Place: A Conversation with Steven Feld'. *Éc(h)opoétiques* 87 (2020): 89–98.

Fellows, Andrew. *Gaia, Psyche and Deep Ecology: Navigating Climate Change in the Anthropocene*. Routledge, 2019.

Fischer-Lichte, Erika. *Ästhetik des Performativen*. Suhrkamp, 2004.

Fischer-Lichte, Erika. *The Transformative Power of Performance: A New Aesthetics*. Translated by Saskya Iris Jain. Routledge, 2008 [2004].

Fonagy, Peter, and Mary Target. 'Attachment and Reflective Function: Their Role in Self-Organization'. *Development and Psychopathology* 9, no. 4 (1997): 679–700.

Foucault, Michel. 'Maurice Blanchot: The Thought from Outside'. In *Foucault/Blanchot*. Translated by Brian Massumi. Zone Books, 1990.

Fournier, Lauren. *Autotheory as Feminist Practice in Art, Writing, and Criticism*. MIT Press, 2021.

Franke, Anselm, ed. *Animism*. Sternberg Press, 2010.

Frankl, Viktor. *Man's Search for Meaning: An Introduction to Logotherapy*. Beacon Press, 2005 [1959].

Gansterer, Nikolaus, Emma Cocker, and Mariella Greil, eds. *Choreo-graphic Figures: Deviations from the Line*. Edition Angewandte, De Gruyter, 2017.

Gansterer, Nikolaus. 'Thinking Matters Other Others'. Accessed 29 September 2025. https://www.gansterer.org/thinking-matters-other-others/.

Geller, Shari M., and Stephen W. Porges. 'Therapeutic Presence: Neurophysiological Mechanisms Mediating Feeling Safe in Therapeutic Relationships'. *Journal of Psychotherapy Integration* 24 (2014): 178–92.

Gendlin, Eugene T. *Experiencing and the Creation of Meaning: A Philosophical and Psychological Approach to the Subjective*. Free Press of Glencoe, 1962.

Gendlin, Eugene T. *Focusing*. Random House, 2003 [1978].

Gessen, Masha. 'Judith Butler Wants Us to Reshape Our Rage'. *The New Yorker*, 9 February 2020. https://www.newyorker.com/culture/the-new-yorker-interview/judith-butler-wants-us-to-reshape-our-rage.

Gherardi, Silvia. 'Sociomateriality in Posthuman Practice Theory'. In *The Nexus of Practices: Connections, Constellations, and Practitioners*, edited by Allison Hui, Theodore R. Schatzki, and Elizabeth Shove. Routledge, 2017.

Gibson, James J. *The Ecological Approach to Visual Perception*. Classic ed. Psychology Press, 2015.

Gilmore, Leigh. *The Limits of Autobiography: Trauma and Testimony*. Cornell University Press, 2001.

Gilmore, Leigh. 'The Mark of Autobiography: Postmodernism, Autobiography, and Genre'. In *Autobiography and Postmodernism*, edited by Kathleen Ashley, Leigh Gilmore, and Gerald Peters. University of Massachusetts Press, 1994.

Gilson, Erinn C. *The Ethics of Vulnerability: A Feminist Analysis of Social Life and Practice*. Routledge, 2014.

Gregg, Melissa, and Gregory J. Seigworth, eds. *The Affect Theory Reader*. Duke University Press, 2010.

Greil, Mariella, ed. *Bare Bodies – Thresholding Life*. Edition Angewandte, De Gruyter, 2024.

Greil, Mariella. *Being in Contact: Encountering a Bare Body*. Edition Angewandte, De Gruyter, 2021.

Greil, Mariella. *Choreo-ethical Assemblages: Narrations of Bare Bodies*. 7 June 2019. https://choreoethicalassemblages.home.blog.

Greil, Mariella. *Trilogy*. 7 September 2005. Documented in 'Digital Anarchive: Being in Contact – Encountering a Bare Body', Research Catalogue, 2019. Accessed 16 October 2025. https://www.researchcatalogue.net/view/505199/505200.

Gronau, Barbara. 'I Did Take the Role of the Shaman… The Artistic Rituals of Joseph Beuys'. *Documenta* 28, no. 1 (2010): 48–58. https://doi.org/10.21825/doc.v28i1.10529.

Guattari, Félix. *The Three Ecologies*. Translated by Ian Pindar and Paul Sutton. Continuum, 2000/1989.

Gumbrecht, Hans Ulrich. *Production of Presence: What Meaning Cannot Convey*. Stanford University Press, 2007.

Halberstam, Jack. *Trans*: A Quick and Quirky Account of Gender Variability*. University of California Press, 2018.

Haraway, Donna J. *Unruhig bleiben: Die Verwandtschaft der Arten im Chthuluzän*. Campus, 2018.

Haraway, Donna J. *Staying with the Trouble: Making Kin in the Chthulucene*. Duke University Press, 2016.

Haraway, Donna J. 'Situated Knowledges: The Science Question in Feminism and the Privilege of Partial Perspective'. *Feminist Studies* 14, no. 3 (1988): 575–99.

Haraway, Donna J. *When Species Meet*. University of Minnesota Press, 2008.

Hardt, Michael, and Antonio Negri. *Assembly*. Oxford University Press, 2017.

Hardt, Michael, and Antonio Negri. *Commonwealth*. Belknap Press, 2009.

Hauser, Jens. 'Bio Art – Taxonomy of an Etymological Monster'. In *Hybrid: Living in Paradox*, edited by Gerfried Stocker and Christine Schöpf. Hatje Cantz, 2005.

Hauser, Jens. 'Observations on an Art of Growing Interest: Toward a Phenomenological Approach to Art Involving Biotechnology'. In *Tactical Biopolitics: Art, Activism, and Technoscience*, edited by Beatriz da Costa and Kavita Philip. MIT Press, 2008.

Heidegger, Martin. *What is a Thing?* H. Regnery Co., 1967.

Hétier, Renaud, François Prouteau, Nathanaël Wallenhorst, and Michael Smith. 'From Resonance to Transformation of the World'. *Réseaux: Communication, Technologie, Société* 235 (2023): 169–91.

Hillman, James. *The Thought of the Heart and the Soul of the World.* Spring Publications, 2021 [1992].

Hobson, J. Allan, and Robert W. McCarley. 'The Brain as a Dream State Generator: An Activation-Synthesis Hypothesis of the Dream Process'. *American Journal of Psychiatry* 134, no. 12 (1977): 1335–48.

Howes, David, ed. *Empire of the Senses: The Sensual Culture Reader.* Berg, 2005.

Hui, Allison, Theodore R. Schatzki, and Elizabeth Shove, eds. *The Nexus of Practices: Connections, Constellations, and Practitioners.* Routledge, 2017.

Ingold, Tim. *Being Alive: Essays on Movement, Knowledge and Description.* New ed. Routledge, 2022 [2011].

Irigaray, Luce. *An Ethics of Sexual Difference.* Translated by Carolyn Burke and Gillian C. Gill. Cornell University Press, 1993 [1984].

Isar, Nicoletta. 'Environmental Humanities Glossary'. Arts and Cultural Studies, University of Copenhagen. Accessed July 10, 2025. https://artsandculturalstudies.ku.dk/research/art-and-earth/environmental-humanities-glossary/sympoiesis.

Jonas, Hans. *The Imperative of Responsibility in Search of an Ethics for the Technological Age.* University of Chicago Press, 1984.

Joy, Jenn. *The Choreographic.* MIT Press, 2014.

Julian, Iris. *Singular Plural Ways of Staging Together: Perspectives on Contemporary Dance, Art Performance and Visual Art.* transcript, 2024.

Juren, Anne. *Fantasmic Anatomies.* PhD diss., Stockholm University of the Arts, 2021. Accessed 7 October 2025. https://www.diva-portal.org/smash/get/diva2:1607139/FULLTEXT01.pdf

Kac, Eduardo. 'Bio Art: From Genesis to Natural History of the Enigma'. In *Imagery in the 21st Century*, edited by Oliver Grau. MIT Press, 2011.

Kant, Immanuel. *The Critique of Judgment.* Translated by Werner S. Pluhar. Hackett Publishing, 1987 [1790].

Kaplan-Solms, Karen, and Mark Solms. *Clinical Studies in Neuro-Psychoanalysis: Introduction to a Depth Neuropsychology.* Karnac, 2000.

Kaptchuk, Ted. *Chinese Medicine: The Web That Has No Weaver.* NTC Contemporary Publishing Group, 2000.

Karafyllis, Nicole C. 'Endogenous Design and Biofacts: Tissues and Networks in Bio Art and Life Science'. *sk-interfaces: Exploding Borders – Creating Membranes in Art, Technology and Society*, edited by Jens Hauser. FACT and Liverpool University Press, 2008.

Kimmerer, Robin Wall. *Braiding Sweetgrass.* Milkweed Editions, 2014.

Kirksey, Eben. 'Multiorgasmic Politics'. Conference Paper, 14 December 2018. https://www.applied-microperformativity.net.

Kruger, Jaco. 'Ecology as Oikology – Reflections on Science and Worldview'. *South African Journal of Philosophy* 44, no. 2 (2025): 198–209.

Kuiken, Don. 'Understanding the Depth Metaphor in Aesthetic Experience: Pressing the Limits of Psychological Inquiry'. In *Toward a Psychology of Persons*, edited by W. Smythe. Erlbaum, 1998.

Latour, Bruno. *Reassembling the Social: An Introduction to Actor-Network-Theory*. Oxford University Press, 2005.

Lawlor, Leonard, and Valentine Moulard-Leonard. 'Henri Bergson'. *The Stanford Encyclopedia of Philosophy: Winter 2022 Edition*, edited by Edward N. Zalta and Uri Nodelman. 18 May 2004. https://plato.stanford.edu/archives/win2022/entries/bergson.

Lepecki, André. *Singularities: Dance in the Age of Performance*. Routledge, 2016.

Levinas, Emmanuel. *Humanism of the Other*. Translated by Nidra Poller. University of Illinois Press, 2006.

Lilja, Efva. *Art, Research, Empowerment: On the Artist as Researcher*. Regierungskansliet, 2015. Accessed 24 September 2025. https://www.efvalilja.se/page.php?id=research&lang=eng.

Luhmann, Niklas. *Ecological Communication*. Translated by John Bednarz, Jr. University of Chicago Press, 1989 [1986].

Luhmann, Niklas. *Social Systems*. Translated by John Bednarz Jr. with Dirk Baecker. Stanford University Press, 1995.

Maldiney, Henri. *Art et Existence*. Klincksieck, 1987.

Maldiney, Henri. *Drei Beiträge zum Wahnsinn*. Translated by Till Grohmann und Samuel Thoma. Turia + Kant, 2018 [2007].

Mândruț, David-Augustin. 'Martin Buber and Henri Maldiney on the Notion of Event'. *META: Research in Hermeneutics, Phenomenology, and Practical Philosophy* 16, no. 2 (2024): 463–83.

Manning, Erin. *Always More Than One: Individuation's Dance*. Duke University Press, 2013.

Manning, Erin. 'Choreography as Reading Practice'. In *Thought in the Act: Passages in the Ecology of Experience*, edited by Erin Manning and Brian Massumi. University of Minnesota Press, 2014.

Manning, Erin. *For a Pragmatics of the Useless*. Duke University Press, 2020.

Manning, Erin. *Politics of Touch: Sense, Movement, Sovereignty*. University of Minnesota Press, 2007.

Manning, Erin. *Relationscapes: Movement, Art, Philosophy*. MIT Press, 2009.

Manning, Erin. *The Minor Gesture*. Duke University Press, 2016.

Margulis, Lynn. *Symbiotic Planet: A New Look at Evolution*. Basic Books, 1998.

Marion, Jean-Luc. 'The Event, the Phenomenon, and the Revealed'. *Danish Yearbook of Philosophy* 40, no. 1 (2005): 57–78.

Massey, Doreen. *For Space*. Sage Publications, 2005.

Massumi, Brian. 'Translator's Foreword: Pleasures of Philosophy'. In *A Thousand Plateaus: Capitalism and Schizophrenia,* by Gilles Deleuze and Félix Guattari. Translated by Brian Massumi. University of Minnesota Press, 1987.

Mazzotta, Giuseppe. *Cosmopoiesis: The Renaissance Experiment*. University of Toronto Press, 2001.

Menninghaus, Winfried. *Disgust: The Theory and History of a Strong Sensation*. State University of New York Press, 2003.

Merleau-Ponty, Maurice. *The Visible and the Invisible*. Edited by Claude Lefort. Translated by Alphonso Lingis. Northwestern University Press, 1968 [1964].

Moutoula, Antrianna. 'Unclogging the Ears: Nonstop Languaging as Autotheory in Art and Academia'. *Arts* 11, no. 6 (2022): 114. https://doi.org/10.3390/arts11060114.

Musalek, Michael. *Der Wille zum Schönen II – Als Kulturgeschehen auf dem Weg zur Kosmopoesie.* Parodos, 2017.

Musser, Amber Jamilla. 'Habeas Viscus: Racializing Assemblages, Biopolitics, and Black Feminist Theories of the Human by Alexander G. Weheliye'. *philoSOPHIA* 6, no. 1 (2016): 156–60.

Nancy, Jean-Luc. *Being Singular Plural.* Translated by Robert D. Richardson and Anne E. O'Byrne. Stanford University Press, 2000.

Nancy, Jean-Luc. 'Of Being-in-Common'. Translated by James Creech. In *Community at Loose Ends*, edited by The Miami Theory Collective. University of Minnesota Press, 1991.

Nancy, Jean-Luc, and Christopher Fynsk. *The Inoperative Community.* Edited by Peter Connor. Translated by Peter Connor et al. (University of Minnesota Press, 2008 [1986]).

National Human Genome Research Institute. 'Gene'. Talking Glossary of Genomic and Genetic Terms. Accessed July 12, 2025. https://www.genome.gov/genetics-glossary/Gene.

Neimanis Astrida. *Bodies of Water: Posthuman Feminist Phenomenology.* Bloomsbury Academic, 2019.

Nietzsche, Friedrich Wilhelm. *The Gay Science: With a Prelude in Rhymes and an Appendix of Songs.* Translated by Walter Kaufmann. Vintage Books, 1974 [1887].

Noë, Alva, and J. Kevin O'Regan. 'What It Is Like to See: A Sensorimotor Theory of Perceptual Experience'. *Synthese* 129 (2001): 79–103.

O'Doherty, Brian. *Inside the White Cube: The Ideology of the Gallery Space.* The Lapis Press, 1986 [1976].

Orange, Donna M. *Climate Crisis, Psychoanalysis, and Radical Ethics.* Routledge, 2017.

Parikka, Jussi. *A Geology of Media.* University of Minnesota Press, 2015.

Petitmengin, Claire, Anne Remillieux, and Camila Valenzuela-Moguillansky. 'Discovering the Structures of Lived Experience: Towards a Micro-Phenomenological Analysis Method'. *Phenomenology and the Cognitive Sciences* 18, no. 4 (2019): 691–730.

Petitmengin, Claire. 'Describing One's Subjective Experience in the Second Person: An Interview Method for the Science of Consciousness'. *Phenomenology and the Cognitive Sciences* 5, nos. 3–4 (2006): 229–69.

Pikler, Emmi. *Friedliche Babys – zufriedene Mütter.* Kösel, 1982.

Pirici, Alexandra, Sam Bardaouil, Till Fellrath, Catherine Nichols, and Hamburger Bahnhof – Museum für Gegenwart – Berlin. *Alexandra Pirici – Attune.* Silvana Editoriale, 2024.

Ploteghér, Paolo, Manuela Zechner, and Bue Rübner Hansen, eds. *Nanopolitics Handbook.* Minor Composition, 2013.

Pollen, Jared Marcel. 'Unsentimental Education: Peter Weiss's Aesthetics of Resistance'. *Liberties*, July 2025. https://libertiesjournal.com/online-articles/unsentimental-education-peter-weisss-aesthetics-of-resistance/.

Rapatahana, Vaughan. 'Obituary of Colin Wilson (1931–2013)'. *Philosophy Now* 101 (2014). Accessed September 5, 2025. https://philosophynow.org/issues/101/Colin_Wilson_1931-2013.

Raunig, Gerald. *Art and Revolution: Transversal Activism in the Long Twentieth Century*. Translated by Aileen Derieg. Semiotext(e), 2007.

Raunig, Gerald. *Dividuum: Machinic Capitalism and Molecular Revolution*. Translated by Aileen Derieg. Semiotext(e), 2016.

Raunig, Gerald. *Factories of Knowledge, Industries of Creativity*. Semiotext(e), 2013.

Rancière, Jacques. *The Politics of Aesthetics: The Distribution of the Sensible*. Edited and translated by Gabriel Rockhill. Translated by Gabriel Rockhill. Bloomsbury, 2013.

Rebentisch, Juliane. *Aesthetics of Installation Art*. Translated by Daniel Hendrickson with Gerrit Jackson. Sternberg, 2012.

Rebentisch, Juliane. *Ästhetik der Installation*. Suhrkamp, 2003.

Rebentisch, Juliane. 'Autonomie? Autonomie! Ästhetische Erfahrung heute'. In *Ästhetische Referring: Gegenstände, Konzepte, Geschichtlichkeit*, edited by Sonderforschungsbereich 626. 2006. https://www.geschkult.fu-berlin.de/e/sfb626/veroeffentlichungen/online/aesth_erfahrung/aufsaetze/rebentisch.pdf.

Rebentisch, Juliane. 'Singularität, Gattung, Form'. In *Generische Formen – Dynamische Konstellationen zwischen den Künsten*, edited by Kirsten Maar, Frank Ruda, and Jan Völker. August, 2017.

Robbe-Grillet, Alain. *Le Miroir qui revient*. Les Éditions de Minuit, 2010.

Rogoff, Irit. 'A Conversation with Irit Rogoff: Where Do We Sit Within All of This?', interview by Marina Vives and Sonia Fernández Pan, *A*Desk: Critical Thinking*, November 13, 2015. https://a-desk.org/en/magazine/a-conversation-with-irit-rogoff.

Roos, Dave. 'Did the Ancient Aztecs Really Perform Human Sacrifice?' History.com, October 11, 2018. https://www.history.com/articles/aztec-human-sacrifice-religion.

Rosa, Hartmut. *Resonance: A Sociology of Our Relationship to the World*. Translated by James Wagner. Polity Press, 2019.

Roszak, Theodore. 'Where Psyche Meets Gaia', in *Ecopsychology: Restoring the Earth, Healing the Mind*, edited by Theodore Roszak, Mary E. Gomes, and Allen D. Kanner. Sierra Club Books, 1995.

Schlehaider, Isabella. *Tausend Subjekte: Der radikal pluralistische Subjektbegriff im kritischen Posthumanismus und bei A. N. Whitehead*. Ibidem, 2021.

Schneede, Uwe. *Joseph Beuys: Die Aktionen*. Hatje Cantz, 1994.

Şenova, Başak, ed. *Barbara Holub – Stiller Aktivismus / Silent Activism*. Edition Angewandte, De Gruyter, 2023.

Sepp, Hans Rainer. 'Phänomenologie als Oikologie'. In *Die Lebendigkeit der Phänomenologie: Tradition und Erneuerung*, edited by Jan Giovanni Giubilato. Traugott Bautz, 2018.

Serres, Michel. *The Five Senses: A Philosophy of Mingled Bodies (I)*. Continuum, 1985.

Sinapius, Peter. 'Where You Are, There Is a Space for Me'. In *Bildstörung: Künstlerische Projektarbeit in der Kinder- und Jugendpsychiatrie*, edited by Martin Böhm, Andreas Romberg, and Peter Sinapius. Claus Richter, 2012.

Skantze, P. A. *Itinerant Spectator / Itinerant Spectacle*. Punctum Press, 2013.

Smit, Mo, and Els Leclercq. *Circular Communities the Circular Value Flower as a Design Method for Collectively Closing Resource Flows*. TU Delft Open, 2023.

Solms, Mark. *The Hidden Spring: A Journey to the Source of Consciousness*. W. W. Norton & Company, 2021.

Spillers, Hortense J. 'Mama's Baby, Papa's Maybe: An American Grammar Book'. *Diacritics* 17, no. 2 (1987): 64–68.

Spinoza, Benedict de. *Ethics,* edited and translated by Edwin Curley. Penguin Classics, 2005.

Stachelhaus, Heiner. *Joseph Beuys.* Heyne, 1989.

Stengers, Isabelle. *Cosmopolitics I.* Translated by Robert Bononno. Univocal / MIT Press, 2010 [1997].

Stengers, Isabelle. *Cosmopolitics II.* Translated by Robert Bononno. University of Minnesota Press, 2011.

Stengers, Isabelle. 'Introductory Notes on an Ecology of Practices'. *Cultural Studies Review* 11, no. 1 (2005): 183–96.

Temkin, Ann, and Bernice Rose. *Thinking Is Form: The Drawings of Joseph Beuys.* Thames and Hudson, 1993.

The Miami Collective, ed. *Community at Loose Ends.* University of Minnesota Press, 1991.

Todd, Mabel Elsworth, and E. G. Brackett. *The Thinking Body: A Study of the Balancing Forces of Dynamic Man.* Princeton Book, 1937.

Trinkaus, Stephan. *Ökologien des Prekären: Zu einer Theorie des Haltens.* Transversal Texts, 2022.

Tronto, Joan C. *Moral Boundaries: A Political Argument for an Ethic of Care.* Routledge, 1993.

Vandenabeele, Bart. 'Aesthetic Disinterestedness in Kant and Schopenhauer'. *Estetika: The Central European Journal of Aesthetics* 49, no. 1 (2012): 45–70.

Varela, Francisco J., Evan Thompson, and Eleanor Rosch. *The Embodied Mind: Cognitive Science and Human Experience.* MIT Press, 1999 [1992].

Verano, John W. 'Where Do They Rest? The Treatment of Human Offerings and Trophies in Ancient Peru'. In *Tombs for the Living: Andean Mortuary Practices,* edited by Thomas D. Dillehay. Dumbarton Oaks, 1995.

Viveiros de Castro, Eduardo. *Cannibal Metaphysics.* Edited and translated by Peter Skafish. Univocal, 2014.

Viveiros de Castro, Eduardo. 'Exchanging Perspectives: The Transformation of Objects into Subjects in Amerindian Ontologies' [2004]. *Common Knowledge* 25, nos. 1–3 (2019): 21–42.

Völker, Jan. *Ästhetik der Lebendigkeit.* Wilhelm Fink, 2011.

Wallace, Mark T., and Barry E. Stein. 'Development of Multisensory Neurons and Multisensory Integration in Cat Superior Colliculus'. *Journal of Neuroscience* 17, no. 7 (1997): 2429–44.

Weber, Max. *Economy and Society: An Outline of Interpretive Sociology.* Translated by Guenther Roth and Claus Wittich. University of California Press, 1978.

Weheliye, Alexander G. *Habeas Viscus: Racializing Assemblages, Biopolitics, and Black Feminist Theories of the Human.* Duke University Press, 2014.

Whitehead, Alfred North. *Process and Reality: An Essay in Cosmology.* Edited by David Ray Griffin and Donald W. Sherburne. Corrected ed. Free Press, 1978.

Winnicott, Donald Woods. *Playing and Reality.* Tavistock, 1971.

Yunkaporta, Tyson. *Sand Talk: How Indigenous Thinking Can Save the World.* The Text Publishing Company, 2023.

Zakravsky, Kath T. 'Passed Out – An Autobiographical Emergency'. In *Bare Bodies – Thresholding Life,* edited by Mariella Greil. Edition Angewandte, De Gruyter, 2024.

Human Index

Other-than-Human Index

Image Credits

Page 2:
Petridish I, experiment within the scope of *Passenger Diaries,* 2021, © photo: Mariella Greil and Simona Koch.

Assemblages #1

Pages 16–17:
#1.01: *Choreographic Environment,* 2022, © Mariella Greil, Walter Lauterer, and Simona Koch.
#1.02: *Choreo-ethical Assemblages,* 2023, © photo: Mariella Greil, performance: Efva Lilja.
#1.03: *Choreo-ethical Assemblages,* 2023, © photo: Evfa Lilja, performance: Mariella Greil.

Pages 18–19:
#1.04: *Choreographic Environment,* 2022, © Mariella Greil and Walter Lauterer.

Pages 20–21:
#1.05 and #1.06: *Choreo-ethical Assemblages,* 2023, © photo: Evfa Lilja, performance: Mariella Greil.
#1.07: *Choreo-ethical Assemblages,* 2023, © photo: Mariella Greil, performance: Efva Lilja.

Pages 22–23:
#1.08 and #1.09: *Choreographic Environment,* 2022, © Mariella Greil and Walter Lauterer.

Pages 24–25:
#1.10: *Choreo-ethical Assemblages,* 2023, © photo: Evfa Lilja, performance: Mariella Greil.
#1.11 and #1.12: *Choreo-ethical Assemblages,* 2023, © photo: Mariella Greil, performance: Efva Lilja.

Pages 26–27:
#1.13–#1.16: *Choreo-ethical Assemblages,* 2023, © photo: Mariella Greil, performance: Efva Lilja.

Pages 28–29:
#1.17–#1.20: *Choreo-ethical Assemblages,* 2023, © photo: Mariella Greil, performance: Efva Lilja.

Pages 30–31:
#1.21–#1.24: *Choreographic Environment,* 2023, © Mariella Greil and Walter Lauterer.

Pages 32–33:
#1.25–#1.26: *Choreo-ethical Assemblages,* 2023, © photo: Mariella Greil, performance: Werner Moebius.

Page 34:
#1.27: *Choreo-ethical Assemblages,* 2023, © photo: Mariella Greil, performance: Efva Lilja.

Ouverture in Two Acts: Introductions in the Plural

Page 37:
Chromatography, part of *Choreo-ethical Assemblages* in the exhibition *UNDERSTANDING – ART & RESEARCH,* MAK – Museum of Applied Arts, Vienna, 2019, © photo: Mariella Greil and Simona Koch.

Pages 45–47:
Figs. 1 and 2: *Choreo-ethical Assemblages* in the exhibition *UNDERSTANDING – ART & RESEARCH,* MAK, 2019, © photo: Mariella Greil.

Pages 51–52:
Figs. 3–6: *A Kiss Under Water,* TanzQuartierWien, 2025, © photo: Mariella Greil.

Pages 54–55:
Figs. 7–9: *Choreographic Environment,* 2020, © Mariella Greil and Walter Lauterer.

Pages 56–57:
Figs. 10–11: *Choreo-ethical Assemblages – Drowning in Depths,* 2025, © video still: Victor Jaschke, performance: Luisa Pisetta Ravanelli, concept: Mariella Greil.
Fig. 12: *Shaken Grounds – Sensory Deprivation Tank*, 2025, © video still: Victor Jaschke, performance: Lucie Strecker.
Fig. 13: *Shaken Grounds – Sensory Deprivation Tank*, 2025, © video still: Victor Jaschke, performance: Mariella Greil.

Page 59:
Fig. 14: *Choreo-ethical Assemblages,* 2022, © photo: Mariella Greil.

Page 65:
Fig. 14: *Shaken Grounds – Trembling Bodies*, 2025, © video still: Victor Jaschke, performance: Mariella Greil.

Pages 67–68:
Figs. 16 and 17: *Choreo-ethical Assemblages – Drowning in Depths*, 2025, © video still: Victor Jaschke, performance and concept: Mariella Greil.
Figs. 18 and 19: *Choreo-ethical Assemblages – Drowning in Depths*, 2025, © video still: Victor Jaschke, performance: Luisa Pisetta Ravanelli, concept: Mariella Greil.

Pages 74–75:
Figs. 20 and 21: *Choreo-ethical Assemblages* in the exhibition *UNDERSTANDING – ART & RESEARCH*, MAK, 2019, © photo: Mariella Greil.

Assemblages #2

Pages 82–96:
#2.01: *Choreo-ethical Assemblages* in the exhibition *UNDERSTANDING – ART & RESEARCH*, MAK, 2019, © photo: Mariella Greil and Simona Koch.
#2.02–#2.14: *Choreo-ethical Assemblages* in the exhibition *UNDERSTANDING – ART & RESEARCH*, MAK, 2019, © photo: Mariella Greil.
#2.15: *Chromatography* as part of *Choreo-ethical Assemblages* in the exhibition *UNDERSTANDING – ART & RESEARCH*, MAK, 2019, © photo: Mariella Greil.

Generative Forces in Choreographic Environments

Page 99:
Choreo-ethical Assemblages – Drowning in Depths, 2025, © video still: Victor Jaschke and Simona Koch, performance: fabric, concept: Mariella Greil.

Page 102:
Fig. 22: *Choreo-ethical Assemblages* in the exhibition *UNDERSTANDING – ART & RESEARCH*, MAK, 2019, © photo: Mariella Greil.

Pages 104–05:
Fig. 23: Screenshot, © Mariella Greil / text by Alexander Gottlieb Baumgarten (Alexander Gottlieb Baumgarten, *Meditationes philosophicae de nonnullis ad poema pertinentibus* [Ioannis Henrici Grvnerti, 1735], 39, Münchner Digitalisierungszentrum Digitale Bibliothek, accessed 17 May 2025, https://mdz-nbn-resolving.de/details:bsb10820766).
Fig. 24: Screenshot, © Mariella Greil / hand of anonymous archivist (Alexander Gottlieb Baumgarten, *Meditationes philosophicae de nonnullis ad poema pertinentibus* [Ioannis Henrici Grvnerti, 1735], 1 Münchner Digitalisierungszentrum Digitale Bibliothek, accessed 17 May 2025, https://mdz-nbn-resolving.de/details:bsb10820766).

Pages 108–09:
Fig. 25: *Choreographic Environment,* 2020, © Mariella Greil and Walter Lauterer.

Pages 111–12:
Figs. 26 and 27: *Choreo-ethical Assemblages,* 2022, © photo: Mariella Greil.

Page 117:
Fig. 28: *Choreo-ethical Assemblages – Drowning in Depths,* 2025, © video still: Victor Jaschke, performance: golden stone, slime, concept: Mariella Greil.

Page 118:
Fig. 29: *Choreo-ethical Assemblages – Drowning in Depths,* 2025, © video still: Victor Jaschke, performance: golden stone, slime, Mariella Greil and Luisa Pisetta Ravanelli, concept: Mariella Greil.
Fig. 30: *Choreo-ethical Assemblages – Drowning in Depths,* 2025, © video still: Victor Jaschke, performance: golden stone, slime, Mariella Greil, concept: Mariella Greil.
Fig. 31: *Choreo-ethical Assemblages – Drowning in Depths,* 2025, © video still: Victor Jaschke, performance: golden stone, slime, concept: Mariella Greil.

Pages 126–27:
Fig. 32: *Choreo-ethical Assemblages – Drowning in Depths,* 2025, © video still: Victor Jaschke, performance: Mariella Greil and Luisa Pisetta Ravanelli, concept: Mariella Greil.
Fig. 33: *Choreo-ethical Assemblages – Drowning in Depths,* 2025, © video still: Victor Jaschke, performance: SCOBYs, concept: Mariella Greil.

Pages 133–34:
Figs. 34–37: *under fields,* 2023, © video still: Victor Jaschke, concept and performance: Mariella Greil and Sylvia Scheidl, production: wine and lithium, Flechtwerk.

Pages 137–38:
Figs. 38–40: *Choreo-ethical Assemblages* in the exhibition *UNDERSTANDING – ART & RESEARCH,* MAK, 2019, © photo: Mariella Greil.

Assemblages #3

Page 142:
#3.01: *Choreo-ethical Assemblages – Drowning in Depths,* 2025, © video still: Victor Jaschke, performance: Mar Esteban Martin and magnets, concept: Mariella Greil.

Page 143:
#3.02–#3.04: *Choreo-ethical Assemblages – Drowning in Depths,* 2025, © video still: Victor Jaschke, performance: Mar Esteban Martin, Luisa Pisetta Ravanelli, stony corals, stones, somatic interface, and *Cypraea tigris,* concept: Mariella Greil.

Pages 144–45:
#3.05–#3.07: *Choreo-ethical Assemblages – Drowning in Depths,* 2025, © video still: Victor Jaschke, performance: Mar Esteban Martin, Luisa Pisetta Ravanelli, pomegranate, root, concept: Mariella Greil.

Pages 146–47:
#3.08–#3.09: *Choreo-ethical Assemblages – Drowning in Depths,* 2025, © video still: Victor Jaschke, performance: Mar Esteban Martin, Luisa Pisetta Ravanelli, singing bowl, golden stone, concept: Mariella Greil.
#3.10: *Choreo-ethical Assemblages – Drowning in Depths,* 2025, © video still: Victor Jaschke, performance: Mariella Greil and Luisa Pisetta Ravanelli, concept: Mariella Greil.

Pages 148–49:
#3.11: *Choreo-ethical Assemblages – Drowning in Depths,* 2025, © video still: Victor Jaschke, performance: Mariella Greil, kohlrabi, concept: Mariella Greil.
#3.12: *Choreo-ethical Assemblages – Drowning in Depths,* 2025, © video still: Victor Jaschke, performance: fabric, concept: Mariella Greil.

Pages 150–51:
#3.13–#3.16: *Choreo-ethical Assemblages – Drowning in Depths,* 2025, © video still: Victor Jaschke, performance: Luisa Pisetta Ravanelli and fabric, concept: Mariella Greil.

Pages 152–53:
#3.17–#3.19: *Choreo-ethical Assemblages – Drowning in Depths,* 2025, © video still: Victor Jaschke, performance: Mariella Greil, Luisa Pisetta Ravanelli, and fabric, concept: Mariella Greil.

Page 154:
#3.20–#3.23: *Choreo-ethical Assemblages – Drowning in Depths,* 2025, © video still: Victor Jaschke, performance: Mar Esteban Martin, Luisa Pisetta Ravanelli, and magnets, concept: Mariella Greil.

Purposeful Polysemy

Page 157:
Choreo-ethical Assemblages – Drowning in Depths, 2025, © video still: Victor Jaschke and Simona Koch, performance: golden stone, blood of trees, and SCOBY, concept: Mariella Greil.

Pages 162–63:
Fig. 41: *Goldring↔Schwartz* project, *Dialogue avec 'La Bête',* 2025, © video still: Laurent Goldring, performance: Wagner Miranda Schwartz and Alex Amann.
Fig. 42: *Goldring↔Schwartz* project, *Dialogue avec 'La Bête',* 2025, © video still: Laurent Goldring, performance: Wagner Miranda Schwartz and Alex Amann.

Pages 171–72:
Figs. 43 and 44: *Choreo-ethical Assemblages,* 2022, © photo: Mariella Greil.

Pages 175–76:
Figs. 45 and 46: *child taking the heart into its hands,* 2021, © photo: Mariella Greil, performance: Jaron Möbius.
Fig. 47: *bloody hands,* 2021, © photo: Mariella Greil, performance: Jaron Möbius.
Fig. 48: *heart,* 2021, © photo: Mariella Greil.

Page 178:
Fig. 49: *we aver,* 2025, © photo: Mariella Greil.

Pages 179–80:
Figs. 50 and 51: *Choreo-ethical Assemblages,* 2022, © photo: Mariella Greil.

Pages 183–84:
Figs. 52 and 53: *Choreo-ethical Assemblages* in the exhibition *UNDERSTANDING – ART & RESEARCH,* MAK, 2019, © photo: Mariella Greil.
Fig. 54: *Procedures,* 2022, © scan: Mariella Greil.

Pages 186–87:
Fig. 55: *Choreo-ethical Assemblages,* 2022, © photo: Mariella Greil.

Assemblages #4

Page 190:
#4.01: *SCOBY,* 2021, © scan: Mariella Greil and Simona Koch.

Pages 191–93:
#4.02 and #4.03: *SCOBY,* 2021, © scan: Mariella Greil.

#4.04: *Choreo-ethical Assemblages – Drowning in Depths,* 2025, © video still: Victor Jaschke, performance: SCOBYs, concept: Mariella Greil.
#4.05: *SCOBYs,* 2021, © scan: Mariella Greil.

Pages 194–95:
#4.06: *Choreo-ethical Assemblages – Drowning in Depths,* 2025, © video still: Victor Jaschke, performance: SCOBYs, concept: Mariella Greil.

Pages 196–97:
#4.07: *SCOBYs,* 2021, © scan: Mariella Greil.
Pages 198–99:
#4.08: *Choreo-ethical Assemblages – Drowning in Depths,* 2025, © video still: Victor Jaschke, performance: Mar Esteban Martin, Mariella Greil, Luisa Pisetta Ravanelli, and SCOBYs, concept: Mariella Greil.
#4.09: *Choreo-ethical Assemblages – Drowning in Depths,* 2025, © video still: Victor Jaschke, performance: SCOBYs, concept: Mariella Greil.

Pages 200–01:
#4.10–#4.13: *Choreo-ethical Assemblages – Drowning in Depths,* 2025, © video still: Victor Jaschke, performance: Mar Esteban Martin, Mariella Greil, Luisa Pisetta Ravanelli, and SCOBYs, concept: Mariella Greil.

Page 202:
#4.14: *Choreo-ethical Assemblages – Drowning in Depths,* 2025, © video still: Victor Jaschke, performance: golden stone, blood of trees, and SCOBY, concept: Mariella Greil.
#4.15: *SCOBY,* 2021, © scan: Mariella Greil.

Choreo-ethical Assemblages

Page 205:
heart print, 2021, © photo: Mariella Greil and Simona Koch.

Pages 206–07:
Fig. 56: *Shaken Grounds – Onomatopoetic Sound(e)scape: Slides and Slips Between Sonances and Symbiosis,* 2025, © video still: Victor Jaschke, performance: Mariella Greil, Lucie Strecker, and SCOBY.
Fig. 57: *Shaken Grounds – Onomatopoetic Sound(e)scape: Slides and Slips Between Sonances and Symbiosis,* 2025, © video still: Victor Jaschke, performance: Peter Kozek, Lucie Strecker, and SCOBY.
Fig. 58: *Shaken Grounds – Onomatopoetic Sound(e)scape: Slides and Slips Between Sonances and Symbiosis,* 2025, © video still: Victor Jaschke, performance: Mariella Greil and SCOBY.
Fig. 59: *Shaken Grounds – Onomatopoetic Sound(e)scape: Slides and Slips Between Sonances and Symbiosis,* 2025, © video still: Victor Jaschke, performance: Mariella Greil, Peter Kozek, Lucie Strecker, and SCOBY.

Page 209:
Fig. 60: *Self-portrait with Schŋuck,* 2019, © photo: Werner Moebius, performance: Mariella Greil and Schŋuck.
Fig. 61: *Eyes of Helix pomatia,* https://de.academic.ru/pictures/dewiki/72/Helix_pomatia_W.jpg.

Page 210:
Fig. 62: *Octopus,* 2026, © drawing: Mariella Greil.

Pages 214–15:
Figs. 63 and 64: *Choreo-ethical Assemblages – As/Dissembling,* 2022, © photo: Mariella Greil.

Pages 218–19:
Fig. 65: *Choreo-ethical Assemblages – Drowning in Depths,* 2025, © video still: Victor Jaschke, performance: Mar Esteban Martin, Luisa Pisetta Ravanelli, stony corals, and somatic interface, concept: Mariella Greil.
Figs. 66 and 67: *Choreo-ethical Assemblages – Drowning in Depths,* 2025, © video still: Victor Jaschke, performance: Mar Esteban Martin, Luisa Pisetta Ravanelli, singing bowl, and golden stone, concept: Mariella Greil.

Pages 221–22:
Figs. 68 and 69: *Choreo-ethical Assemblages,* 2022, © photo: Mariella Greil.

Page 223:
Fig. 70: *Russian Talisman,* guest object of Efva Lilja, 2023, © photo: Mariella Greil.

Pages 227–28:
Fig. 71: *Artistic Ancestral Tree,* 2020, © photo: Mariella Greil.

Page 230:
Figs. 72 and 73: *Agnus Dei,* 2012, © video still and performance: Victor Fuček.

Page 231:
Fig. 74: *BLEU REMIX,* 2008, © photo: Jakub Wittchen, performance: Yann Marussich.

Pages 233–34:
Fig. 75: Workshop with students at Angewandte Performance Laboratory (APL), 2021, © photo: Mariella Greil.
Fig. 76: Workshop with students from the master's course in Applied Human Rights, WUK (Werkstätten- und Kulturhaus), 2020, © photo: Mariella Greil.
Figs. 77 and 78: Workshop with students at Angewandte Performance Laboratory (APL), 2021, © photo: Mariella Greil.

Page 235:
Fig. 79: *Peeler,* guest object of Efva Lilja, 2023, © photo: Mariella Greil.

Page 237:
Fig. 80: *Choreo-ethical Assemblages* in the exhibition *UNDERSTANDING – ART & RESEARCH,* MAK, 2019, © photo: Mariella Greil.

Page 238:
Figs. 81–85: *Choreo-ethical Assemblages – Drowning in Depths,* 2025, © video still: Victor Jaschke, performance: SCOBYs, concept: Mariella Greil.

Pages 241–44:
Figs. 86–92: *Viscerā amaryllidis I–VII,* 2020, © scan: Mariella Greil.

Pages 245–46:
Figs. 93–96: *Withering Ovary,* Angewandte Performance Laboratory (APL), 2023, © photo: Mariella Greil.

Page 250:
Figs. 97 and 98: *Echoes of Light – Passing Sky,* 2023, © photo: Mariella Greil.

Assemblages #5

Page 260:
#5.01: *Simmering Until Done,* desktop performance, 2020, © video stills and performance: Mariella Greil and Simona Koch, with additional visual material by Boglárka Börcsök, Andreas Bolm, Paschalis Dougalis, Hugo Glenndinning, Anne Dufourmantelle, Mani Froh, Thomas Glavinic, Adrian Heathfield, Evá Kovács, Alphonso Lingis, Vivien Löschner, Carole Maurel, Annette Messager, and Peter Paul Rubens.

Pages 261–68:
#5.02–#5.25: *Simmering Until Done*, desktop performance, 2020, © video stills and performance: Mariella Greil, with additional visual material by Boglárka Börcsök, Andreas Bolm, Paschalis Dougalis, Hugo Glenndinning, Anne Dufourmantelle, Mani Froh, Thomas Glavinic, Adrian Heathfield, Evá Kovács, Alphonso Lingis, Vivien Löschner, Carole Maurel, Annette Messager, and Peter Paul Rubens.

Aesthetics and Ethics are Twins

Page 271:
SCOBYs, 2021, © scan: Mariella Greil and Simona Koch.

Pages 273–75:
Figs. 99 and 100: *Choreo-ethical Assemblages* in the exhibition *UNDERSTANDING – ART & RESEARCH*, MAK, 2019, © photo: Mariella Greil.

Page 284:
Figs. 101–02: *Choreo-ethical Assemblages – Drowning in Depths*, 2025, © video still: Victor Jaschke, performance: Mariella Greil and Luisa Pisetta Ravanelli, concept: Mariella Greil.
Figs. 103–04: *Choreo-ethical Assemblages – Drowning in Depths*, 2025, © video still: Victor Jaschke, performance: Luisa Pisetta Ravanelli, concept: Mariella Greil.

Page 285:
Figs. 105–08: *Polylogic Organism – Performative Assemblages of Choreo-ethics (Gradually Slowing the BPM of the Pomegranate)*, desktop performance, 2021, © video still: Werner Moebius, performance: Mariella Greil.

Page 286:
Fig. 109: *Shaken Grounds – Shifting Skies*, 2025, © video still: Victor Jaschke, performance: Mariella Greil.

Page 288:
Figs. 110 and 111: *Choreo-ethical Assemblages* in the exhibition *UNDERSTANDING – ART & RESEARCH*, MAK, 2019, © photo: Mariella Greil.

Pages 291–92:
Fig. 112: *Aria on Air*, student performance within the scope of an ecosexual ritual with Annie Sprinkle and Beth Stephens, Prague, 2024, © photo: Mariella Greil.

Assemblages #6

Page 300:
#6.01: *Polylogic Organism – Performative Assemblages of Choreo-ethics (Gradually Slowing the BPM of the Pomegranate)*, desktop performance, 2021, © video stills and performance: Mariella Greil, Werner Moebius and Simona Koch.

Page 301:
#6.02–#6.04: *Polylogic Organism – Performative Assemblages of Choreo-ethics (Gradually Slowing the BPM of the Pomegranate)*, desktop performance, 2021, © video stills and performance: Mariella Greil and Werner Moebius.

Page 302:
#6.05: *Polylogic Organism – Performative Assemblages of Choreo-ethics (Gradually Slowing the BPM of the Pomegranate)*, desktop performance, 2021, © video stills and performance: Mariella Greil and Werner Moebius, with additional visual material from *Choreo-graphic Figures* (DOI:10.55776/AR283).

Pages 302–04:
#6.06–#6.11: *Polylogic Organism – Performative Assemblages of Choreo-ethics (Gradually Slowing the BPM of the Pomegranate),* desktop performance, 2021, © video stills and performance: Mariella Greil and Werner Moebius.

Page 304:
#6.12: *Polylogic Organism – Performative Assemblages of Choreo-ethics (Gradually Slowing the BPM of the Pomegranate),* desktop performance, 2021, © video stills and performance: Mariella Greil and Werner Moebius, with additional visual material from Nikolaus Gansterer, Emma Cocker, and Mariella Greil, eds., *Choreo-graphic Figures: Deviations from the Line* (Edition Angewandte, De Gruyter, 2017).

Pages 304–07:
#6.13–#6.21: *Polylogic Organism – Performative Assemblages of Choreo-ethics (Gradually Slowing the BPM of the Pomegranate),* desktop performance, 2021, © video stills and performance: Mariella Greil and Werner Moebius.

Page 307:
#6.22: *Polylogic Organism – Performative Assemblages of Choreo-ethics (Gradually Slowing the BPM of the Pomegranate),* desktop performance, 2021, © video stills and performance: Mariella Greil and Werner Moebius, with additional visual material from Nikolaus Gansterer and the book cover of Lauren Fournier, ed., *fermenting feminism* (Laboratory for Aesthetics & Ecology, 2017).

Pages 308–10:
#6.23–#6.31: *Polylogic Organism – performative Assemblages of Choreo-ethics (Gradually Slowing the BPM of the Pomegranate),* desktop performance, 2021, © video stills and performance: Mariella Greil and Werner Moebius.

Socio-aesthetic Emergence

Page 313:
Amaryllisation, 2024, © photo: Mariella Greil and Simona Koch.

Pages 314–15:
Fig. 113: *Socio-aesthetic Resonance I* to *PAVILIOLA* by transparadiso, 2025, © photo: Werner Moebius, performance: Mariella Greil.

Pages 316–17:
Figs. 114–16: *Socio-aesthetic Resonance II–IV* to *PAVILIOLA* by transparadiso, 2025, © photo: Werner Moebius, performance: Mariella Greil.

Page 319:
Figs. 117–20: *Choreo-ethical Assemblages – Un/bundling,* 2023, © photo: Mariella Greil, performance: Efva Lilja.

Page 325:
Fig. 121: *Opening Up the Choreographic,* Angewandte Performance Laboratory (APL), Presence III, 2020, © photo: Mani Froh, performance: Mariella Greil, concept and performance: Daniel Aschwanden, Mariella Greil, and Charlotta Ruth.

Page 326:
Fig. 122: *Opening Up the Choreographic,* Angewandte Performance Laboratory (APL), Presence III, 2020, © photo: Mani Froh, concept and performance: Daniel Aschwanden, Mariella Greil, and Charlotta Ruth.

Page 327:
Fig. 123: *Opening Up the Choreographic,* Angewandte Performance Laboratory (APL), Presence III, 2020, © photo: Mani Froh, performance: Mariella Greil, concept and performance: Daniel Aschwanden, Mariella Greil, and Charlotta Ruth.

Pages 330–31:
Fig. 124: *Choreo-ethical Assemblages – Sponging,* 2022, © photo: Mariella Greil, performance: Efva Lilja.

Pages 333–34:
Figs. 125–28: *Wild Bonds*, 2024, © video still: Mariella Greil, performance: Darina and Sofia Alster.

Page 335:
Fig. 129: *Self-portrait with Schŋuck,* 2019, © photo: Werner Moebius, performance: Mariella Greil and Schŋuck.

Page 341:
Fig. 130: *Opening Up the Choreographic,* 2020, © video still: Mani Froh, concept and performance: Daniel Aschwanden, Mariella Greil, and Charlotta Ruth.

Assemblages #7

Page 346:
#7.01: *Amaryllisation*, 2024, © photo: Mariella Greil and Simona Koch.

Pages 347–49:
#7.02–#7.05: *Amaryllisation,* 2024, © photos: Mariella Greil.

Pages 350–51:
#7.06 and #7.08: *Amaryllisation,* 2024, © video stills: Mariella Greil and Simona Koch.
#7.07: *Amaryllisation,* 2024, © video still: Mariella Greil.
#7.09–#7.11: *Amaryllisation,* 2024, © photos and video stills: Mariella Greil.

Pages 352–60:
#7.12–#7.18: *Amaryllisation,* 2024, © photos and video stills: Mariella Greil.

Choreo-ethical Relations and Diffractive Dialogues

Page 363:
Choreo-ethical Assemblages – Drowning in Depths, 2025, © video still: Victor Jaschke, Mariella Greil and Simona Koch, performance: Mariella Greil and Luisa Pisetta Ravanelli, concept: Mariella Greil.

Pages 364–65:
Figs. 131–34: *Family Reunion*, co-created with Philipp J. Ehmann within the scope of the INTRA project *Withdrawing the Performer*, hosted by Jasmin Schaitl and Charlotta Ruth at Angewandte Performance Laboratory (APL), 2021, © photo: Mariella Greil, performance: Mariella Greil and Philipp J. Ehmann.

Page 370:
Fig. 135: *Welcome Play Score* for *Family Reunion*, co-created with Philipp J. Ehmann within the scope of the INTRA project *Withdrawing the Performer*, hosted by Jasmin Schaitl and Charlotta Ruth at Angewandte Performance Laboratory (APL), 2021, © design: Mariella Greil and Philipp J. Ehmann.

Pages 377–78:
Figs. 136 and 137: *Evaporation I&II,* experiment within the scope of *Passenger Diaries*, 2021, © photo: Mariella Greil.

Pages 382–83:
Fig. 138: *Magenta Listening,* performance within the scope of *Practice (!) Symposium – Tracing Presences*, Factory, Künstlerhaus, 2022, © photo: Suchart Wannaset, performance: Mariella Greil.

Scores
Page 391:
Fig. 139: *In Blurry Layers*, from the Polylogic Lab, 2025, © water colour: Mariella Greil.

Page 394:
Fig. 140: *in touch*, from *Passenger Diaries*, 2022, © photo: Mariella Greil.

Page 431:
Petridish I, experiment within the scope of *Passenger Diaries*, 2021, © photo: Mariella Greil and Simona Koch.

Biographies

Biographies of Dialogue Partners

Emma Cocker is a UK-based writer-artist whose research addresses the specificity of thinking-feeling-knowing within artistic process and practice while searching for language-based approaches capable of operating in fidelity to that embodied experience. Her practice involves diverse process-oriented, dialogic and collaborative, and poetic and performative approaches to working *with* and *through* language. Cocker is co-founder of the Society for Artistic Research Special Interest Group for Language-based Artistic Research and is Associate Professor in Fine Art at Nottingham Trent University (UK). https://not-yet-there.blogspot.com

Kerstin Kussmaul, PhD, is a movement researcher, educator, choreographer, and myoreflex therapist. She teaches somatic movement education focusing on the neuro-myo-fascial body. As an artist, her work focuses on site-responsive, transdisciplinary and participatory formats. www.fasciamatters.info; https://hdl.handle.net/2292/52574

Walter Lauterer works as a visual artist in the fields of sculpture, architecture, space, light and video installation, as well as performance and conceptual art.

Efva Lilija is an artist working globally with choreography as dance, visual arts, and text in works that take us through various layers of consciousness, erotic episodes, contemplative stillness, and playful moments with a political edge. She has received numerous awards, including the Gannevik Grant and the Stockholm City Honorary Award, and was named a cultural prize-winner by the Swedish Association of Cultural Directors. https://www.efvalilja.se

Werner Moebius works between visual art and music in the expanded field of sonic art and aesthetic practice. He addresses the plasticity of sounds in acoustic, intermedial, and performative contexts and facilitates dialogues between new music, electroacoustic improvisation, conceptual art, weird beats, and artistic research. For his work he has received awards such as the City of Vienna Prize and BMUKK scholarships for Chicago and Mexico City. http://www.wernermoebius.net

Rosa Wernecke is a media and performance artist. She combines a queer-feminist approach to content with a strong formal focus on the use of technical means from the fields of stage technology, light and video art, and new digital media. Her work has been shown at venues such as Moltkerei, Cologne; Synnika Art Space, Frankfurt; bauhaus reuse, Berlin; CLB, Berlin; Galerie Simone Menne, Kiel; and the Center for the Holographic Arts, New York. Her video and light settings have been part of various scenic arrangements, including shows at Radialsystem, Berlin; Elbphilharmonie, Hamburg; and Ruhrtriennale, Bochum. https://swooshlieu.com/en/about-us/rosa-wernecke

Biography of the Author

Mariella Greil, PhD, is an artist and researcher focusing on contemporary dance and performance, in particular its choreographic and ethical ramifications. She is a Senior Artist at the Angewandte Performance Laboratory (APL), University of Applied Arts Vienna, and performs and teaches internationally. She was a key researcher in the project *Choreo-graphic Figures: Deviations from the Line* and held an Elise Richter PEEK Fellowship (Austrian Science Fund, FWF) for *Choreo-ethical Assemblages – Narrations of Bare Bodies.*

Since 2023, she has been collaborating on the FWF-funded artistic research project *Shaken Grounds. Seismography of Precarious Presences*, which is currently being continued as an EU Creative Europe cooperation project.

She has co-edited *(per)forming feedback* (2016) with Vera Sander and *Choreo-graphic Figures: Deviations from the Line* (2017) with Emma Cocker and Nikolaus Gansterer. She has also published the monograph *Being in Contact – Encountering a Bare Body* (2021) and, more recently, the anthology *Bare Bodies – Thresholding Life* (2024). http://www.mariellagreil.net

Acknowledgements

I am immensely grateful to all those who have played a part in the realization of this tome, both human and other-than-human!

This book was made possible with financial support from the Austrian Science Fund (FWF; Elise Richter PEEK, Grant-DOI: 10.55776/V733, and Book Publications, Grant-DOI: 10.55776/PUB1302), Bildrecht (SKE Fonds), and the University of Applied Arts Vienna. My special thanks go to Ulrike Kuch, Rector of the University of Applied Arts Vienna, and Clemens Apprich, Vice-Rector for Research and Digitality, as well as Alexander Damianisch, Head of Support Art and Research, and Roswitha Janowski-Fritsch and Stefanie Schabhüttl in Publications for their encouragement and untiring support. I am grateful for the chance to carry out the artistic research project *Choreo-ethical Assemblages – Narrations of Bare Bodies*, which received the above mentioned Elise Richter PEEK grant from the FWF and was generously hosted by the Department for Arts and Communication Practices led by Sofia Bempeeza and Annette Krauss.

I am deeply indebted to artist and graphic designer Simona Koch, who is a dear friend and has been an inspiring sparring partner at all stages of this book's development. Thanks for your loving generosity, fine touch, and wisdom!

I would like to thank Lydia J. White for her dedicated and sensitive copy-editing to this project, Florian Regl for image editing, and Hannes Fauland at Gerin for his support. I also would like to acknowledge that parts of the writing process were supported by *DeepL* (DeepL SE) and *ChatGPT* (OpenAI, GPT-5) for translation or language refinement, and reference formatting was assisted by *Citation Machine*. As the author, I critically reviewed and edited all generated material. For their accompanying support throughout, I am also grateful to Katja Richter, Martina Kupiak, and Anja Haering at the publishing house De Gruyter. I extend my thanks to Walter Lauterer for co-developing the choreographic environment.

An important dialogue partner in the early stages of the project was Werner Moebius; later, Emma Cocker, Kerstin Kussmaul, Efva Lilja, and Rosa Wernecke joined me for micro-phenomenological interviews.

With gratitude I would like to acknowledge the care with which Luisa Pisetta Ravanelli, who was often the first to read newborn texts and particularly kept a both alert and tender eye on the readability of the texts 'Assemblages of Choreo-ethics – Simmering until Done', 'Ethics and Aesthetics are Twins', and 'Purposeful Polysemy' in their very early stages. Fondazione Cassa Rurale di Trento generously supported Luisa to participate in my artistic research project with a research scholarship. My heartfelt thanks also go to Mar Esteban Martin, who helped me to keep loose ends at bay and literally and metaphorically lent me her hands on the film *Drowning in Depths* together with Luisa and filmmaker Victor Jaschke. Victor, your artistic sensibility, vast knowledge of your art form, and crazy wisdom make it a joy to dream-work with you – diving into the deep with you is always full of surprises.

In particular, I would like to thank my colleagues at the Angewandte Performance Laboratory (APL), Peter Kozek and Nicole Janata, as well as the working group, comprising Stefano D'Alessio, Ricarda Denzer, Nikolaus Gansterer, Asher O'Gorman, Peter Kozek, Daria Lytvynenko, Timothy Nouzak, Charlotta Ruth, Jasmin Schaitl, and Lucie Strecker, for providing a critical artistic œkology. I am thankful to my colleagues at Home of Performance Practices, ArtEz (H.o.P.P.), who engaged in meaningful conversations with me about choreo-ethical assemblages, namely Andrea Pagnes, Anja Foerschner, Astarti Athanasiadou, Irina Österberg, Steef Kersbergen, Karina van Lenthe, Anushka Nair, Verena Stenke, Maria Pisiou, Malou Willemars, and many students. Furthermore, nourishing for my research were my exchanges with Rosanna Irvine, Jeroen Fabius, Jochem Naafs, and Falk Hübner in the Research Mentors Team, in collaboration with the Core Team of Michael O'Connor, Keith Randolph, Stephen Shropshire, Nikita Maheshwary, Honey Jones-Hughes, Denise Garcia Flores, and peers in the Co-Creation of Movement Masters programme, Codarts (COMMA). Conversations about human rights and arts with Walter Suntinger and Marilyn Volkman were especially meaningful.

From the bottom of my heart, I would like to express my gratitude to the Shaken Grounds Collective, comprising Nikolaus Gansterer, Peter Kozek, and Lucie Strecker, in collaboration with Victor Jaschke und Werner Moebius. Artist-researchers Pavlos Kountouriotis and Alex Arteaga keep inspiring and challenging me, and I would like to thank dancer and curator Linda Samaraweerova for the exchanges that were made possible through the opportunity of being invited to teach workshops as part of the TanzQuartier Wien programme.

Once again, I say thank you to the love of my life, Werner: your warm presence carries me through all life's challenging moments. And to my son Jaron: I would like to thank you for sharing your enthusiasm for things that I don't know about.

Imprint

Mariella Greil
University of Applied Arts Vienna
https://mariellagreil.net

This publication is the result of the Elise Richter PEEK project of the Austrian Science Fund (FWF) *Choreo-ethical Assemblages: Narrations of Bare Bodies* (2019–2026), led by Mariella Greil (Grant DOI: 10.55776/V733), and was additionally supported by FWF Book Publications (Grant DOI: 10.55776/PUB1302) and Bildrecht (SKE Fonds).

Project management 'Edition Angewandte' on behalf of the University of Applied Arts Vienna: Stefanie Schabhüttl, Vienna, Austria

Content editor on behalf of the publisher: Martina Kupiak, Munich, Germany
Production editor on behalf of the publisher: Anja Haering, Berlin, Germany

Concept:
Mariella Greil, Vienna, Austria

Copyediting and proofreading:
Lydia J. White, Wellington, New Zealand

Book design, layout, cover design, and typography:
Simona Koch, Vienna, Austria

Image editing:
Florian Regl, Vienna, Austria

Printing:
Holzhausen, die Buchmarke der Gerin Druck GmbH, Wolkersdorf, Austria

Paper:
Nautilus Classic 120 gsm

Typeface:
Kepler von Robert Slimbach, Adobe Originals

Library of Congress Control Number:
2026936940

Bibliographic information published by the German National Library. The German National Library lists this publication in the Deutsche Nationalbibliografie; detailed bibliographic data are available on the Internet at http://dnb.dnb.de.

ISSN 1866-248X
ISBN 978-3-68924-089-9
e-ISBN (PDF) 978-3-68924-090-5

Open Access
DOI: https://doi.org/10.1515/9783689240905

www.degruyterbrill.com
Questions about General Product Safety Regulation productsafety@degruyterbrill.com

The book is published open access at www.degruyterbrill.com.

FWF Österreichischer Wissenschaftsfonds

Bildrecht

MIX
Papier | Fördert gute Waldnutzung
FSC www.fsc.org FSC® C108696

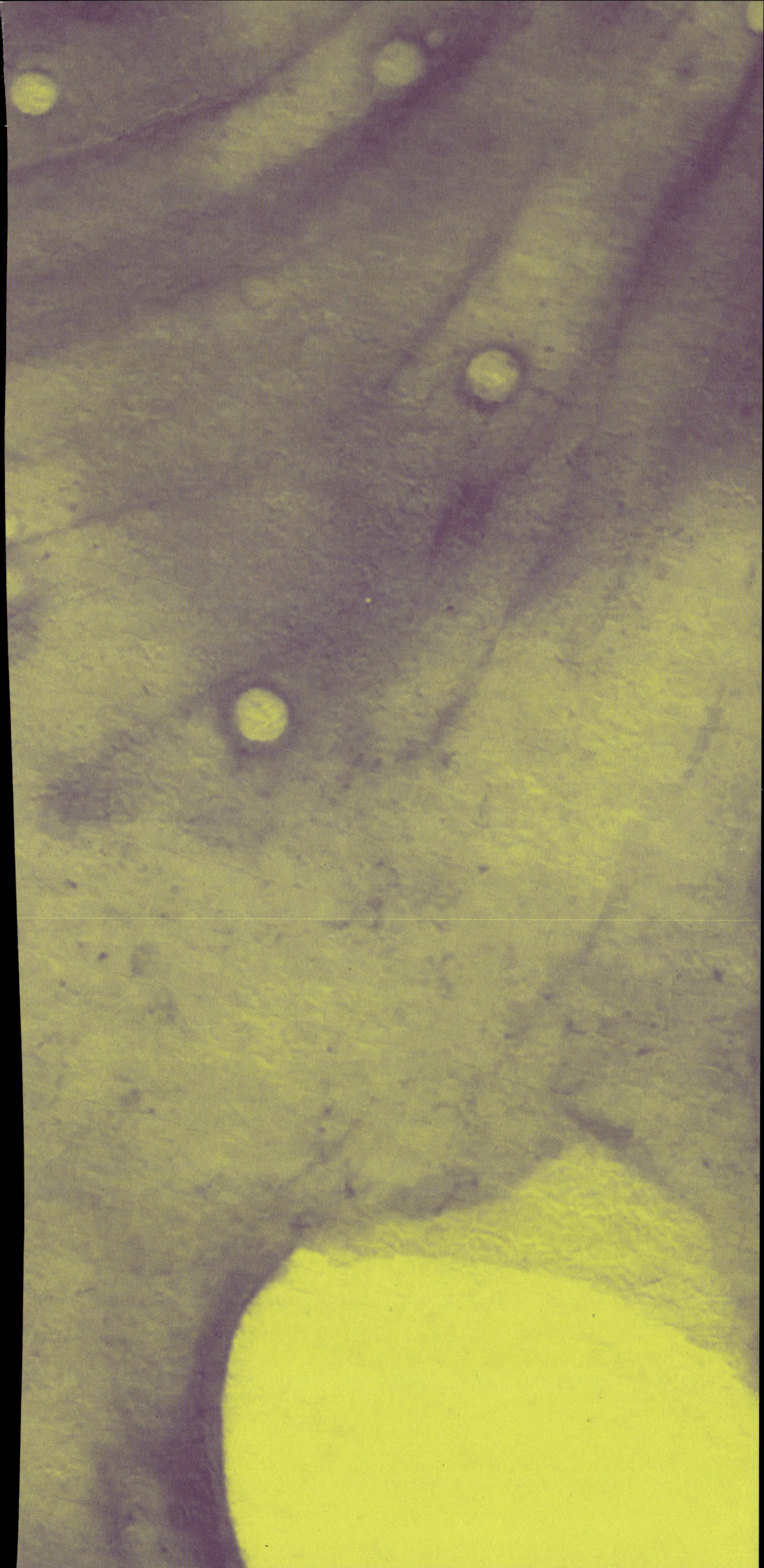

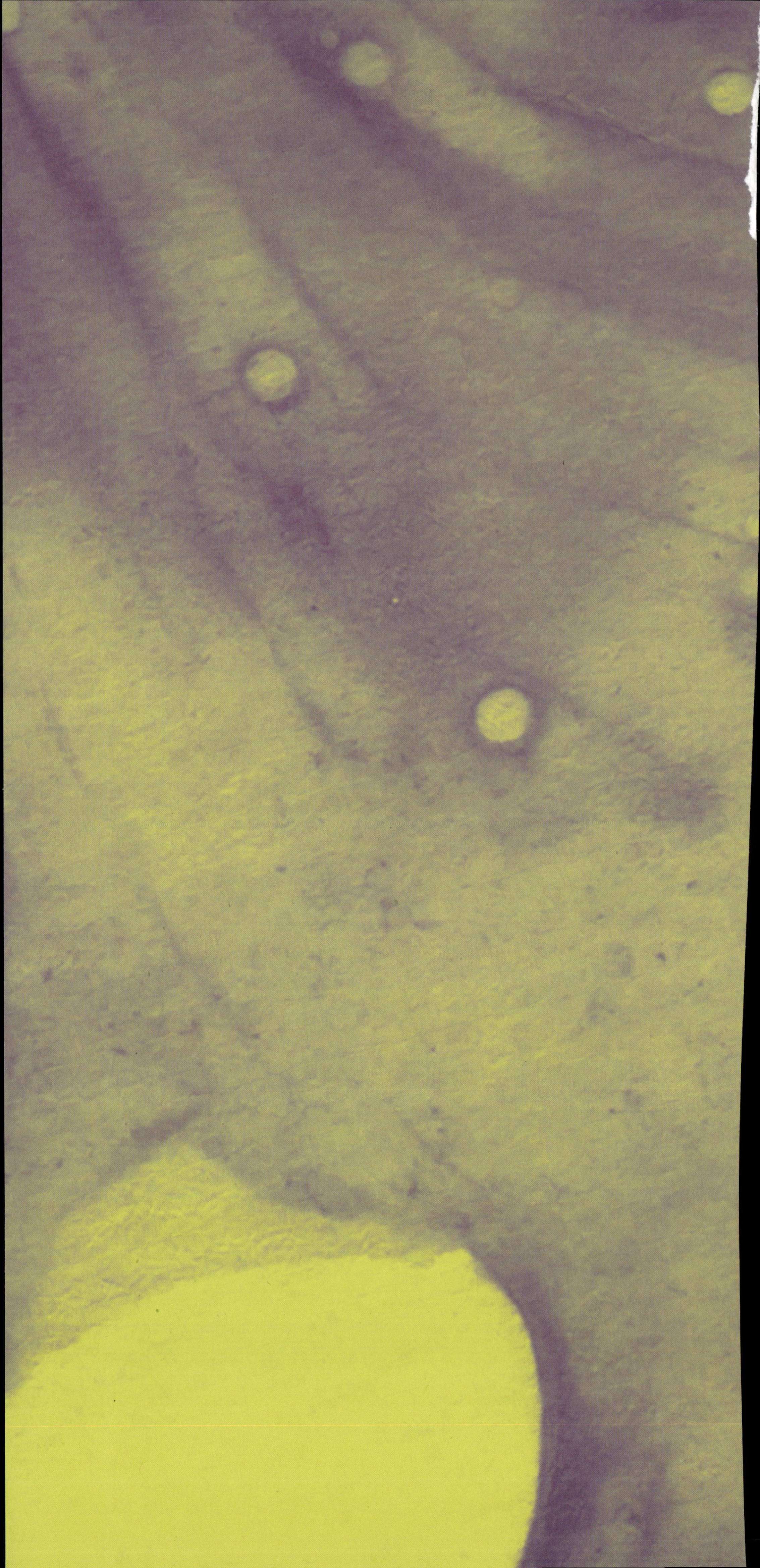